For Michele.
She is the best.

"Some are born great, some achieve greatness, and some have greatness thrust upon them."
-William Shakespeare

"The Jerk Store called. They're running out of you!"
-George Costanza

HEROES
AND
JERKS

The Best and Worst Who Ever Lived

ED DALY

Copyright © 2020 by Ed Daly

All rights reserved. No part of this publication may be reproduced, distributed or transmitted in any form or by any means, including photocopying, recording, or other electronic or mechanical methods, without the prior written permission of the author.

Edited by Meghan Stoll
Cover Art by Kazi Asif Ahmed
Timeline Art by Ed Daly
Book Designed by Owlebooks

CONTENTS

Introduction 1
Early Ancient History (Two million B.C. - 501 B.C.) 2
Late Ancient History (500 B.C. - 499 A.D.) 12
The Middle Ages (500 A.D. - 1499) 22
1500 - 1549 32
1550 - 1599 42
1600 - 1649 52
1650 - 1699 62
1700 - 1724 72
1725 - 1749 82
1750 - 1774 92
1775 - 1799 102
1800 - 1809 112
1810 - 1819 124
1820 - 1829 134
1830 - 1839 146
1840 - 1849 158
1850 - 1859 170
1860 - 1869 182
1870 - 1879 194
1880 - 1889 206
1890 - 1899 218
1900 - 1904 230
1905 - 1909 242
1910 - 1914 254
1915 - 1919 266

1920 – 1924	278
1925 – 1929	290
1930 – 1934	302
1935 – 1939	314
1940 – 1944	326
1945 – 1949	340
1950 – 1954	352
1955 – 1959	366
1960 – 1964	378
1965 – 1969	390
1970 – 1974	404
1975 – 1979	418
1980 – 1984	432
1985 – 1989	446
1990 – 1994	462
1995 – 1999	478
2000 – 2004	492
2005 – 2009	508
2010 – 2014	522
2015 – 2019	536
EPILOGUE	552
ACKNOWLEDGEMENTS	553
BIBLIOGRAPHY	554
INDEX	555

INTRODUCTION

In comparing our society's humble beginnings a few million years ago with what it has evolved into today, it's impossible not to be both impressed and terrified. We have cars, blue jeans, pizza, washing machines, and the internet! We also have racism, anti-Semitism, endless wars, pollution, and the musical *Cats*. In every era there have been transcendent individuals who have pushed the world to become a better place. Conversely, humanity has also had its fair share of individuals whose selfishness and malevolence have caused great pain.

This book identifies the ten best people from every period in human history and celebrates their great accomplishments. It also pinpoints the ten worst—those to blame for many bad times over the past two million years. And, since humans are complicated, some have landed on both lists. Since only ten can be selected for each list, some on the list are representative of similar accomplishments or failings of the day.

Of course, the argument of who is "best" and "worst" is somewhat subjective. As someone once said, "One man's terrorist is another man's freedom fighter." That's true… to a point. The passing of time does a pretty good job of clearing up the gray area for us to discern who was the oppressor or wrongdoer and who was the victim.

Another common objection to the judgment of history is that you can't hold people in the past to today's moral standards. For example, "Sure Thomas Jefferson owned slaves, but hey, everybody did back then." No. Plenty of people from Jefferson's era knew slavery was immoral and were very vocal about it. Jefferson and fellow slave owners just had too good a financial windfall by having free help so they did everything to keep it going. It's fair to give historical figures a pass for being less PC than what would be acceptable. But the big, ugly stuff like slavery? We absolutely can (and should) judge.

While there's no actual proof that Mark Twain actually said, "History doesn't repeat itself, but it does rhyme," there's a lot of truth to that statement. Things like fascism and war are reoccurring events in history. But so are ingenuity, kindness, and brilliance. We can learn from all these people. So here they are—the best and worst people who ever lived.

[Note: Lists are counted down 10 through 1 with #1 being the very best person (or the very worst person) and #10 being the tenth best (or worst). Honorable and Dishonorable Mentions are given in no particular order.]

| 1.8Million B.C. | 43000 B.C. | 5000 B.C. | 3500 B.C. |

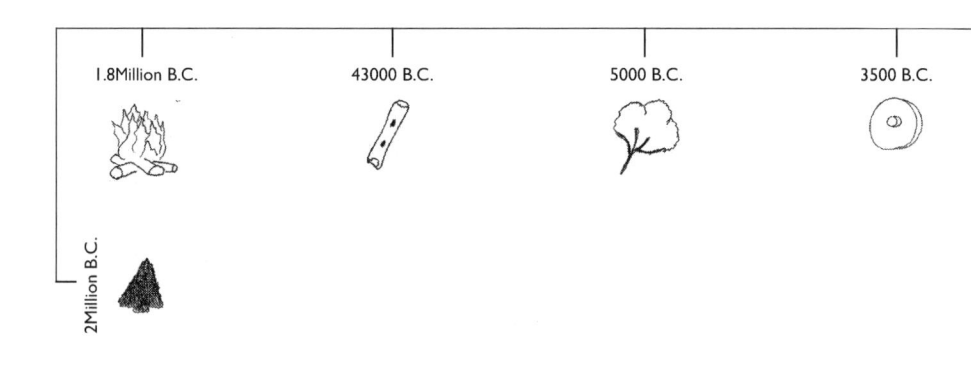

2Million B.C.

EARLY ANCIENT HISTORY
(TWO MILLION B.C. - 501 B.C.)

"Put more trust in nobility of character than in an oath."
-Solon

| 3500 BC | 2697 B.C. | 1550 B.C. | 820 B.C. |

560 B.C.

BEST

10. SUMERIANS
3500 B.C. - Zagros Mountains (Iran)

Just as we were taught rhymes and phrases to remember things like the order of the planets ("My Very Educated Mother Just Served Us Nine Pickles") in grade school, the Sumerians of the Zagros Mountains used a prayer to the goddess Ninkasi to remember and preserve their recipe for beer for future generations. What good was risking their lives every day without a little enjoyment? Plus, a little booze couldn't have hurt when they were trying to catch some z's on those uncomfortable dirt floors and rock beds.

9. TIEN-LCHEU
2697 B.C. - China

Until ink was invented for the purpose of recording significant information, people mostly relied on spoken word. As a result, most of what happened in humankind's first couple million years is either mysterious to us or, at the very least, inaccurate. About six thousand years ago, Sumerians started making drawings with rudimentary pencils, setting off an era of lots of writing tool creations which met with varying degrees of success. Around 2700 B.C., Chinese philosopher Tien-Lcheu created ink, the best and most permanent way of preserving drawings and information.

8. HOMO HABILIS
2 Million B.C. - Tarkana County, Kenya

As horrible as it is to imagine, we once had to do everything by hand. Just about every task ranked somewhere from tedious (picking plants out of the ground to eat) to difficult (separating animals' fur from their carcasses) to nearly impossible (stopping an attacking predator from eating you). Homo Habilis discovered tools and, probably, saved the human race. Tools make just about everything easier. Well, except for those crappy Ikea Allen wrenches.

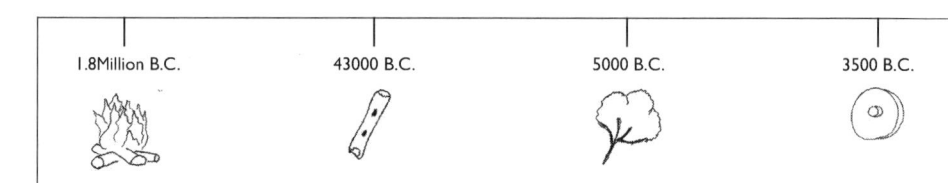

7. INDIAN WEAVER
5000 B.C. - Indus River Delta, India

Unless you're a 1970s rock star, it's tough to exist solely in a wardrobe made out of animal skins. Dealing with that oppressive Indian heat probably played a big role in the Indians finding a great use for the cotton plant: clothing. Cotton was woven and dyed, and the world was introduced to breathable garments.

6. SOLON
560 B.C. - Athens, Greece

In an era when poor people were essentially slaves, Solon reformed laws, created a more reasonable economic structure, and treated people more humanely (e.g., it was his idea that the answer to every crime didn't have to be the death penalty). Unsurprisingly, the rich ruling class was less than enthused about these changes. Maintaining the status quo is always the answer for the "haves," after all. But Solon stuck to his guns and is now credited with being the father of democracy.

5. SLOVENIAN FLUTE MAKER
43,000 B.C. - Cerkno, Slovenia

Considering hunters flirted with a high probability of getting mauled anytime they went out on the job, they sure as hell were going to use every part of the beasts they caught. Diverting from the usual utility of prey as food and clothing, one Slovenian hollowed out a cave bear's femur and fashioned the world's first musical instrument from it. Without that ingenious move, melody would never have been born. We'd have no Beethoven, Beatles, or Beastie Boys. No Mozart, Madonna, or Marvin Gaye. Music would've been one long drum solo.

4. HOMER
820 B.C. - Ionia, Greece

The blind Greek poet took Trojan War stories that had been passed down over centuries, sampled them, created twists and turns, and blended them into two epic stories. Essentially, Homer was a combination of Quentin Tarantino and Stevie Wonder. Homer's first story (*Iliad*) focused on the heroic exploits of the Trojan War. The sequel (*Odyssey*) focused on one hero's crazy journey as he returned home from the war. Many of us struggle to remember what we did a week ago, yet Homer's stories have endured nearly 3,000 years.

3. EBERS PAPYRUS AUTHOR
1550 B.C. - Thebes, Egypt

Given that the invention of electricity and the availability of clean, running water were still a good 3,500 years away, people had limited ways to stay cool and clean in the blistering 100°F Egyptian heat. Filth, disease, sweat, and body odor ruled the day. Luckily some unnamed proactive hero wrote what would become known as "Ebers Papyrus," a medical document that extolled the virtues of bathing regularly. The document detailed a soap-like substance made of oils and salts. While it wasn't a flawless text (e.g., it advised the consumption of half an onion and a beer to stave off death), it was an important first step in the field of hygiene.

2. HOMO ERECTUS
1.8 Million B.C. - Northern Africa

Before Homo Erectus discovered fire, mealtime was less a function of getting essential nutrients and more an exhausting exercise of tearing food apart with giant, pointy teeth. Not just meat. Try gnawing on a raw potato. If Homo Erectus had never started cooking their food over flames, we'd all still have enormous scary fangs like Pennywise the Dancing Clown.

1. MESOPOTAMIANS
3500 B.C. - Mesopotamia (Iraq)

The strangest thing about the greatest invention of all time (the wheel) is that it took nearly two million years for someone to realize that round objects roll and to utilize that knowledge to

| 1.8Million B.C. | 43000 B.C. | 5000 B.C. | 3500 B.C. |

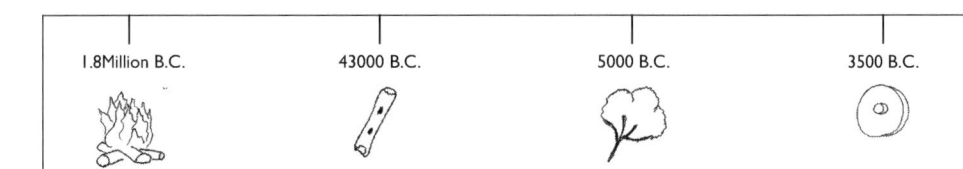

2Million B.C.

their advantage—i.e., to transport things. Before the wheel, home was wherever the food was. Finally, in 3500 B.C., some smart Mesopotamian invented the wheel. But even then, it was just used for sewing and pottery. It wasn't until the second century A.D. that an astute Chinese farmer looked at the wheel and recognized its potential in the form of a wheelbarrow.

| 3500 BC | 2697 B.C. | 1550 B.C. | 820 B.C. | 560 B.C.

Honorable Mentions: Siddhartha Guatama Buddha - 534 B.C. (kindness), Chinese - 3000 B.C. (noodles), Mayans - 1102 B.C. (chocolate), Coroebus - 776 B.C. (first Olympic champion)

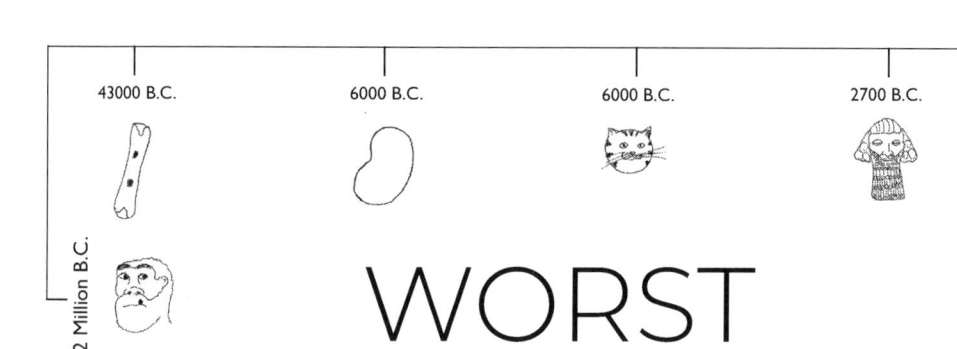

WORST

10. GILGAMESH
2700 B.C. - Uruk (Iraq)

Aside from being the subject of that awful book that everyone was forced to read in high school, Gilgamesh was a man who had people believing he lived for 126 years. He was the first documented case of a person insecure enough to lie about his age.

9. SLOVENIAN FLUTE MAKER
43,000 B.C. - Cerkno, Slovenia

As beautiful as music can be, it's not without its downside. Without musical instruments, the world would never have been subjected to "Macarena" and "Achy Breaky Heart."

8. PERUVIAN LIMA BEAN FARMER
6000 B.C. - Lima, Peru

If this Peruvian had turned a blind eye to that weirdly-shaped bean sprouting out of the ground, none of us would've ever been forced to eat this oddly textured, lacking-nutritional-value vegetable.

7. SEA PEOPLES
1180 B.C. - Aegean Sea, Egypt

For a century, the Sea Peoples appeared by ship and terrorized Egyptian coastal villages. Nobody seemed to know who they were working with or where they came from. They were to Egypt what Carnival Cruise travelers are to Caribbean islands.

6. NORTHEAST AFRICAN CAT OWNERS
6000 B.C. - Northeast Africa

On a good day, cats look disinterested in you. Most other times, they look like they're plotting to murder you. Well, about 8,000 years ago, some monster in Northeast Africa determined those frightening creatures belonged indoors. They can make alright housemates... just as long as you're feeding them. But what happens if you grow old with a cat, providing it a loving home through the years? The moment you die, it eats your face off.

5. DJOSER
2667 B.C. - Al Giza Desert, Egypt

Pharaoh Djoser was the first in a long line of self-absorbed assholes who were consumed with honoring themselves in death. In preparation for shuffling off this mortal coil, he had his chancellor Imhotep design the first ever pyramid for his residence in the afterlife. While the structures are iconic and striking, there was a catastrophic cost to those tasked with building them. Whether they were slaves or belonged to the next-lowest rung of society, they were the laborers who had no choice but to risk their lives daily so a corpse could rest in a cool pointy house.

4. AKHENATON
1350 B.C. - Amarna, Egypt

A few years after inheriting the throne from his father, King Amenhotep IV declared an end to the practice of any religious beliefs that conflicted with his own. He closed all the temples except for those dedicated to the worship of Aten, the Sun God. Since Amenhotep was the only person who could speak to this god, his new name would be Akhenaton and all of Egypt's priests would have to find a new line of work. After Akhenaton died, his son, King Tut, had to clean up this mess.

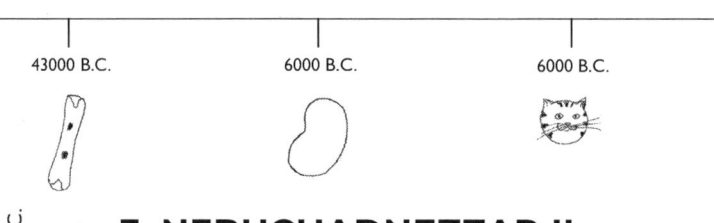

3. NEBUCHADNEZZAR II
597 B.C. - Babylon (Iraq)

For the strength of his rule and his strong international diplomacy, Nebuchadnezzar II was considered by many as the greatest Babylonian king. He was also a braggart who talked about how great he was at every turn. But not every turn was quite so great. Beyond that one stretch where he thought he was a werewolf, Nebuchadnezzar was a bully who expected everyone to give him their lunch money ("tribute," they called it). When Jehoiakim of Jerusalem stopped paying tribute, Nebuchadnezzar laid siege to the walled city and starved everybody inside, killing thousands.

2. DRACO
621 B.C. - Athens, Greece

From petty larceny to murder, the penalty given by Athenian lawgiver Draco was the same for all crimes: death. And so, for the past 2,600 or so years, anytime a rule seems severe or excessive, it's dubbed Draconian.

1. NUTCRACKER MAN
2 Million B.C. - Olduvai Gorge, Tanzania

Plio-Pleistocene hominin Paranthropus boisei had a jaw and teeth strong enough to crack nuts, earning him the moniker Nutcracker Man. He is also known for giving mankind genital herpes. A couple million years ago, Nutcracker Man was "scavenging ancestral chimp meat where savannah met forest." That chimp meat had genital herpes, so Nutcracker Man got it. Well, Nutcracker Man and Homo Erectus kind of hung around the same lakes and streams and, at some point, Homo Erectus either ate, had sex with, or did both with Nutcracker Man. It's been a blister on the genitals of unfortunate humans ever since.

2667 B.C.

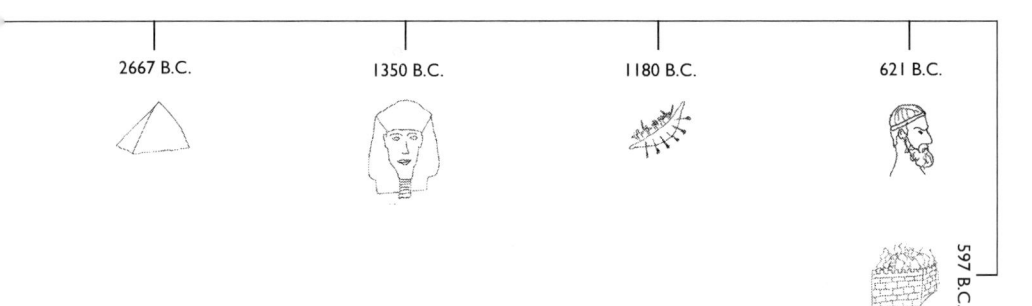

1350 B.C.

1180 B.C.

621 B.C.

597 B.C.

458 B.C.

423 B.C.

400 B.C.

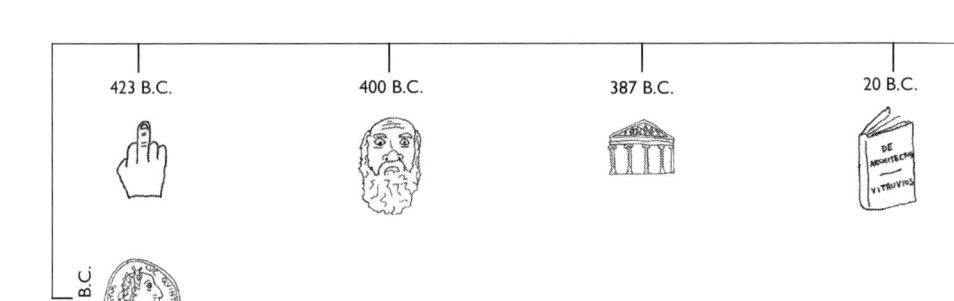

387 B.C.

20 B.C.

LATE ANCIENT HISTORY
(500 B.C. - 499 A.D.)

"Everybody has value; even if to serve as a bad example."
-Atilla the Hun

36 A.D.　　　50 A.D.　　　79 A.D.　　　105 A.D.

370 A.D.

BEST

10. HYPATIA
370 A.D. - Alexandria, Egypt

Alexandria was a city on the decline. Religious infighting was ripping the city apart. Meanwhile, Hypathia served as one of the only voices of reason. The influential scholar was not afraid to speak her mind when disagreeing with religious zealots, whether it was in regard to preserving the library or preaching the works of Plato and Aristotle. Sadly, the hostile dummies arranged her untimely demise.

9. PLINY THE ELDER
79 A.D. - Pompeii, Roman Empire (Italy)

Pliny was a jack of all trades (lawyer, military commander, philosopher, author) who wrote the first encyclopedia, *Natural History*. Unfortunately for Pliny, his skills didn't include clairvoyance. Within a few months of finishing the encyclopedia, he was killed by the eruption of Mount Vesuvius.

8. ARISTOPHANES
423 B.C. - Athens, Greece

When you get an infection, antibiotics are the great elixir. When you get cut off in traffic by some jerk driver, there is only one cure—flipping the bird. Comedic playwright and genius innovator Aristophanes created the simple dick-and-balls hand gesture in his comedy, *The Clouds*. That's right, he invented the middle finger.

7. HERON HO ALEXANDREUS
50 A.D. - Alexandria, Egypt

The Hero of Alexandria invented early versions of the steam engine, the vending machine, a syringe, wind-powered machines, power pumps, and lots of other powered devices.

6. TRUNG SISTERS
36 A.D. - Me Linh, Vietnam

After the Chinese Empire appointed an oppressive governor (To Dinh) to oversee Vietnam, a guy named Thi Sach and some other lords plotted a rebellion. The Chinese caught wind of it and executed the rebels. So Thi Sach's widow, Trung Trac, and her sister, Trung Nhi, responded by raising an army of eighty thousand, who pushed their oppressors all the way back to China. This bought Vietnam about five peaceful years until China came back in force. It was a good run, Trung Sisters.

5. LUCIUS QUINCTIUS CINCINNATUS
458 B.C. – Rome (Italy)

This aristocrat was forced to sacrifice most of his fortune to help out his son, so he became a humble farmer by trade. When Rome fell under attack, the people reached out to Cincinnatus to serve as their dictator. He defeated the rival tribes, solved his city's crisis, and promptly resigned to return to his farm. Future leaders like George Washington cited Cincinnatus as an example of great leadership and civic duty.

4. MARCUS VITRUVIUS POLLIO
20 B.C. – Rome, Roman Empire (Italy)

Vitruvius wrote *De architectura*, the most influential book on architecture of all time. The book stated that all architecture should be "sturdy, useful, and beautiful." Guess 1970s architects weren't big on reading the classics.

3. SOCRATES
400 B.C. - Athens, Greece

After returning from three brave campaigns in the Peloponnesian War, Socrates realized that ignorance was a real hindrance to

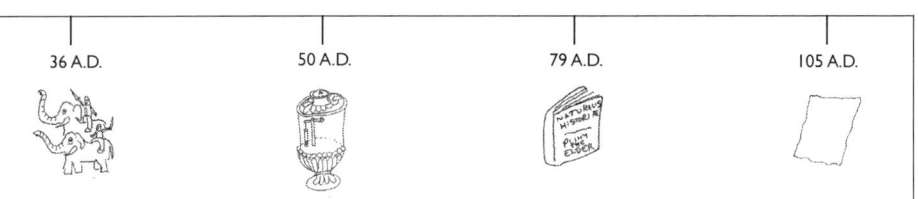

Greece. So he began asking questions to people around Athens His inquisitive process (dubbed the "Socratic method") led people to expand their minds and question their beliefs. Maybe more importance should be placed in improving one's government and living conditions rather than blind faith in the gods, he argued. Predictably, the powers-that-be had Socrates arrested and sentenced to death. While he had many opportunities to renounce his beliefs, he chose instead to drink his poisonous hemlock. Socrates stuck to his guns and showed the world that "an unexamined life is not worth living."

2. CAI LUN
105 A.D. - Luoyang, China

Ever wonder what life would be like if you had no genitals? No? Well, poor Cai Lun had plenty of time to think while serving as the palace eunuch for Emperor Hedi. All that free time led to one of the great inventions of all time—paper. Congrats, Cai Lun. Sorry about your nether regions.

1. PLATO
387 B.C. - Athens, Greece

People would never know about Socrates, the "father of Western philosophy," if it weren't for his star pupil, Plato. Socrates never wrote anything down. When he was forced to commit suicide, it would've been a good idea for Plato to move to a safer line of work. Instead, Plato doubled down and put all of Socrates' lessons into a book (Republic). The remainder of his life was dedicated to improving government and teaching philosophy. Plato's institute for higher learning in Athens laid out the blueprint for Western thinking.

423 B.C.

400 B.C.

387 B.C.

20 B.C.

458 B.C.

Honorable Mentions: Zhang Heng - 138 A.D. (seismometer), Slavic farmers - 400 A.D. (heavy plow), Hippocrates - 430 B.C. ("father of Western medicine"), St. Nicholas - 340 A.D. (Turkish bishop), Pericles - 561 B.C. (patron of the arts), Euclid 300 B.C. (mathematician), Archimedes - 212 B.C. (scientist), Asclepiades - 75 B.C. (physician), Aristotle - 350 B.C. ("father of logic")

36 A.D.　　　　　50 A.D.　　　　　79 A.D.　　　　　105 A.D.

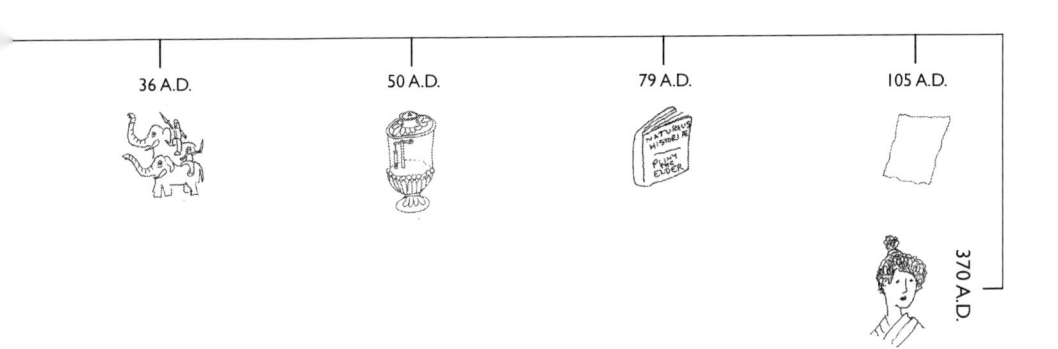

370 A.D.

| 37 A.D. | 64 A.D. | 160 A.D. | 180 A.D. |

399 A.D.

WORST

10. AVIDIUS CASSIUS
160 A.D. - Parthia (Iran)

Some villains are intentional and, in this Roman general's case, some are accidental. After marching into Parthia, Cassius' army contracted smallpox (or perhaps it was measles) and had to retreat. The troops returned to Rome and brought the Antonine Plague with them. By the year 180, 30 percent of the Roman population had been wiped out.

9. ATHENIAN JURY
399 B.C. - Athens, Greece

Despite being one of history's greatest thinkers, Socrates was persona non grata in Athens in 399 B.C. because he dared to challenge the government. After a sham trial, the majority of this mouth-breathing jury convicted a man for questioning some of the gods. Rather than fight or escape Athens, the brilliant Socrates opted for a hemlock death cocktail.

8. ZHU GE LIANG
230 A.D. - Jingzhou, China

Some inventors make life easier or more enjoyable. Zhou Ge Liang invented the land mine and the automatic weapon—two things that have been responsible for killing unimaginable numbers of innocent people.

7. CARACALLA
211 A.D. – Rome, Roman Empire (Italy)

At fourteen, Caracalla married a girl and had her father killed. He later grew tired of his wife and had her exiled and killed. At twenty-three, he was named co-emperor with his brother, whom he then had killed. After that, he killed all of his brother's friends. When he grew tired of killing everyone around him, Caracalla attacked and destroyed his allied German forces. To cap it off, he massacred the citizens of Alexandria. After six bloodthirsty years, the game of murderous spin-the-bottle landed on Caracalla himself, and he got what was coming.

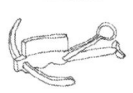

6. EMPEROR THEODOSIS
390 A.D. - Thesalonica, Greece

In 390, a popular charioteer was arrested for homosexual activity and thrown in a dungeon on the eve of chariot games. Crowds of people rioted in protest. The emperor indicated the charioteer would be allowed to ride. When the fans entered the stadium the next day, Theodosius had his goons murder every one of them—seven thousand—in retaliation. Plus, this clown banned the Olympics because it wasn't Christian enough. Clearly, discus and javelin = the devil.

5. LUCIUS AELIUS AURELIUS COMMODUS
180 A.D. - Rome, Roman Empire (Italy)

Rome had been humming along nicely for nearly a century when Commodus assumed power. Then the wheels quickly fell off. Within two years, Commodus' sister and some senators plotted to kill him. Starting to lose his mind, Commodus grew increasingly violent, renamed Rome Colonia Commodiana ("Colony of Commodus"), and sicced lions and people on each other in rigged gladiator fights. In his twelfth year as emperor, a wrestler choked him to death, but the damage was already done. Rome was in disarray and slipped into a civil war.

4. QIN SHI HUANG
220 B.C. - Julu Commandery, China

While he does get credit for unifying China, it must also be noted that Qin Shi Huang was hot garbage. A believer in legalism (basically, "everyone is evil and need lots of rules"), he didn't tolerate the slightest dissent. He burned books and beheaded scholars who were perceived threats. He jacked taxes so that many people became forced laborers. He executed family members (even his daughter). And, in his quest to live forever, he brought in hundreds of wizards and scientists to come up with a cure for mortality. When they proved to be useless, he buried them alive.

3. GAIUS JULIUS CAESAR AUGUSTUS GERMANICA ("CALIGULA")
37 A.D. – Rome, Roman Empire (Italy)

Caligula (meaning "little soldier's boot") weaseled his way into Emperor Tiberius' good graces, was made heir to the throne, and then turned into a full-blown monster. He abused power like it was his job—slept with allies' wives, made high-ranking senators run themselves to exhaustion, prohibited anyone from mentioning goats (because he looked like a goat), blew money in every way possible, and forced soldiers to collect shells in their helmets. Predictably, the emperor's guards eventually got sick of his antics and stabbed him.

2. ATTILA THE HUN
433 A.D. - Pannonia (Transdanubia, Hungary)

Attila and his brother ruled the Huns together... until Attila got tired of sharing duties and murdered him. From there, his bloodlust only intensified. Attila destroyed or seized most of the Eastern Roman Empire. Even when rulers would pay him protection money, he broke his promises and spilled blood and terror in their lands anyway. There are no accurate records of Attila's death count, but pretty much everywhere he went (present-day Germany, Russia, Ukraine, and the Balkans), tens of thousands of deaths piled up.

211 A.D.   220 A.D.   230 A.D.   390 A.D.

433 A.D.

1. LUCIUS DOMITIUS AHENOBARBUS ("NERO")
64 A.D. - Rome, Roman Empire (Italy)

Well, what can you say about a mullet-coiffed emperor who poisoned his step-brother, had his mom executed, spent every cent of public money on personal whims, burned more than half of Rome to make room for his new villa, blamed the fire on the hot new religion (Christianity), and killed anyone who he perceived to be a threat? Yep, he was awful.

Dishonorable Mention: Pope Damasus - 384 A.D. (sex slavery)

568   724   822   1100

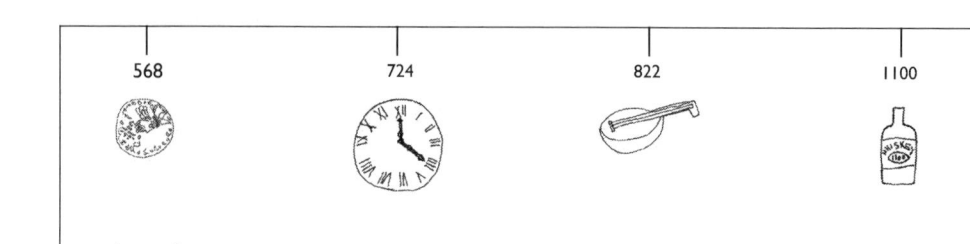

540

MIDDLE AGES
(500 A.D. - 1499)

"He who does not punish evil, commands it to be done."
-Leonardo da Vinci

BEST

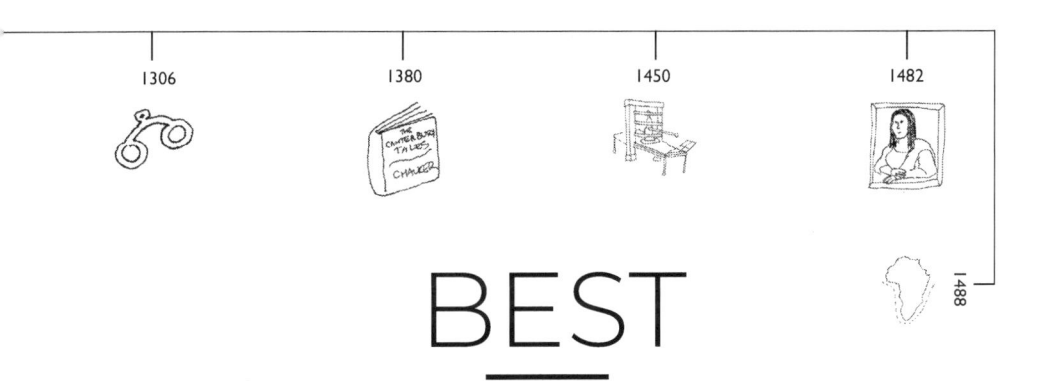

10. KING KHOUSRAU
568 - Persia (Iran)

Khousrau took over a declining Sāsānian empire full of religious and social unrest. He had two options: rule with an iron fist and try to ride this life of privilege out, or try to make his world a better place. He chose the latter. Right away, he decentralized the government and reduced the power of the monarch. He overhauled the tax laws, vastly improved the infrastructure, and built canals. After a steady decline in conditions under previous emperors, the common worker was given relief and hope. Khousrau championed the arts and welcomed new ideas. Greek philosophers migrated to his empire and initiated a cultural evolution. Architecture improved. Sadly, nothing lasts forever. After Khousrau died, his son took over, turned into a typical tyrant, and ruled the empire into the ground.

9. ABDUL-HASSAN ALI ("ZIRYAB")
822 - Baghdad, Mesopotamia (Iraq)

The Baghdad musician was a mixture of David Bowie and Martha Stewart. Before Ziryab, Iraq was full of people who looked like extras from *The Last Temptation of Christ*. After his meteoric rise to stardom, men started cutting their hair short, women wore scarves with his lyrics embroidered on them, people changed styles with the seasons, grooming became a focus, and some admirers even began decorating their homes differently. Ziryab was the original baller and shot-caller.

8. IRISH MONKS
1100 - Dublin, Ireland

Tasked with creating alcoholic beverages but having limited access to grapes and other resources, some Irish monks used their abundance of barley to create the gold standard of all libations—whiskey. On behalf of everyone who has needed a little help listening to the boss drone on about his kids at the holiday party or every person stuck on the end of the table at a group dinner, we raise our glasses to you.

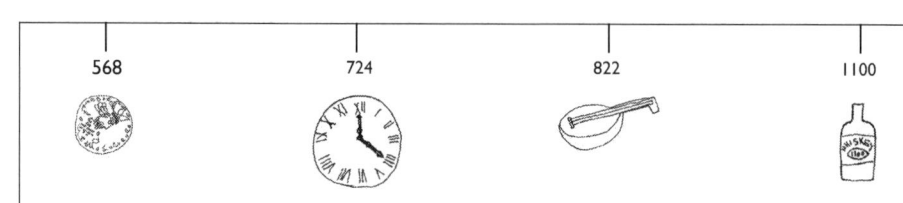

7. CASSIODORUS
540 - Vivarium, Roman Empire (Italy)

As the Roman Empire began to crumble and barbarianism took over, this retired statesman founded Vivarium, a monastery designed to preserve the culture of Rome. While not a great writer or scholar himself, Cassiodorus was instrumental in preserving the great works of art and manuscripts produced in Rome's heyday. He was like a one-man Library of Congress.

6. BARTOLOMEU DE NOVAES DIAS
1488 - Lisbon (Portugal)

Bartolomeu Dias was the Rodney Dangerfield of explorers. Though he was the first to make the monumental journey around Africa which opened up trade routes between Europe and Asia (via India), people only seem to recall Columbus' trip to a bunch of small islands four years later. And, unlike the enslaving and mutilating Columbus, Dias made stops en route to provide natives with gifts in order to spread goodwill. When Dias returned to Portugal, the king gave him a terrible welcome. Sometimes it takes five centuries for true greatness to be recognized.

5. ALESSANDRO DELLA SPINA
1306 - Pisa, Roman Empire (Italy)

While he never claimed to have invented corrective eyeglasses, this Italian friar was the first person to share the invention with the general public. If not for Alessandro della Spina's generosity, the last eight hundred years would have played out like one of those Velma-gets-her-glasses-knocked-off scenes in *Scooby-Doo*.

4. YI XING
724 - Chang'an, China

Buddhist monk and mathematician Yi Xing designed the first

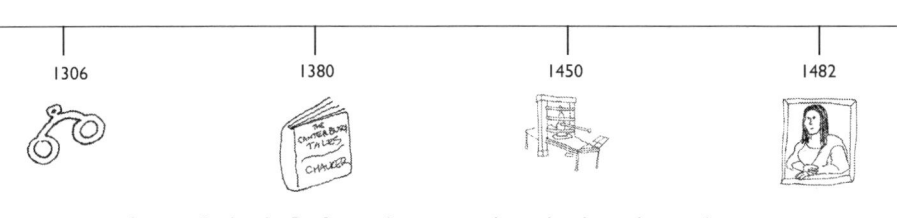

ever mechanical clock. Before that, people relied on hourglasses and, even worse, sundials. Pretty much every meeting had to be scheduled with a wide window of time, like the cable company still does for technician home visits.

3. GEOFFREY CHAUCER
1380 - Canterbury, England

Before *The Canterbury Tales*, books were rarely written for or about the common person. First off, they were generally written in Latin and, in the off chance they were in English, they didn't read remotely like the vernacular. In the various short stories in *The Canterbury Tales*, Chaucer wrote about interesting, relatable (for the time) people that connected with a wide-ranging audience and inspired a new style of writing for centuries to come. Granted, if you tried reading it today, you'd probably find more joy and humor in chewing glass, but its legacy is unparalleled.

2. LEONARDO DA VINCI
1482 - Milan (Italy)

There was very little Leonardo da Vinci couldn't do. As an artist, he produced two of the most famous paintings ever made (*The Last Supper, Mona Lisa*). He also became an engineering advisor, an influential urban planner, and an inventor (canal locks and an early version of the helicopter). In the field of medicine, da Vinci's observations formed the basis for human anatomy study. He was like the Swiss army knife of human beings, only wayyy more useful.

1. JOHANNES GUTENBERG
1450 - Strasbourg, France

Before Gutenberg invented movable type, knowledge was pretty much confined to super rich people. Everyone else relied on sloppy storytelling for their information. Thanks to Gutenberg's printing press, books became available for the masses. People became enlightened. As knowledge increased, so did curiosity. The engaged, interconnected world as we know it started with this amazing innovation, the printing press.

540

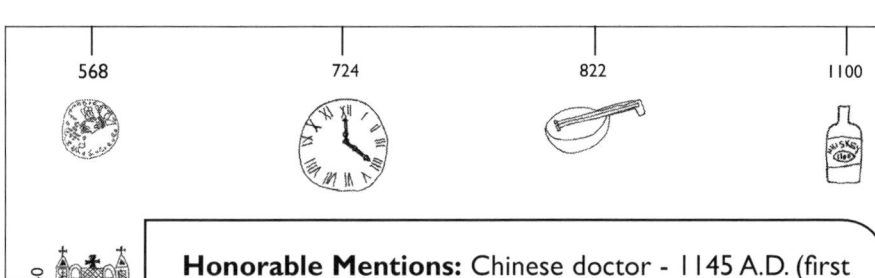

568

724

822

1100

Honorable Mentions: Chinese doctor - 1145 A.D. (first autopsy), Joan of Arc - 1430 (Hundred Years' War hero), Dutch farmer - 1180 A.D. (windmill)

1306

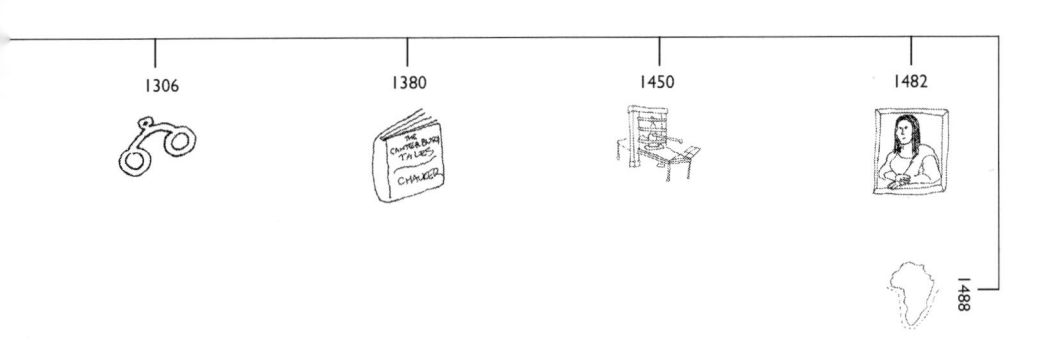

1380

1450

1482

1488

WORST

10. CHARLEMAGNE
782 – Verden, Saxony (Germany)

Charlemagne's goal was to unite all Germanic people into one kingdom. And by "unite," he meant, "kill everyone who refuses to convert to Christianity." At the Massacre at Verden, Charlemagne ordered the slaughter of 4,500 Saxons to help set the Christian-or-dead tone.

9. POPES STEPHEN VI, JOHN XII, AND SERGIUS III
897-1127 – Perugia, Roman Empire (Italy)

When Marcellus Wallace says the line, "Imma get medieval on your ass," to Zed in *Pulp Fiction*, the subtext read that things were about to get ugly. The Medieval Period was a brutal time full of brutal leaders with ugly, self-serving agendas. Perhaps the epicenter of medieval ugliness was at Lateran Palace in Rome, home of the pope. Many popes in those days were morally bankrupt pieces of garbage. There was Stephen VI, the grudge-holding pope. He had a previous pope exhumed and propped him up *Weekend at Bernie's*-style so he could stand trial. There was Pope John XII, the have-sex-with-as-many-men-and-women-and-children-and-family-members-as-possible-and-castrate-your-enemies pope. There was also Sergius III, the execution-ordering pope. He had the rare distinction of not only taking one pope out of the world (by having Antipope Christopher killed) but also bringing a new pope into it (by getting frisky with the daughter of one of his friends, who gave birth to the future Pope John XI).

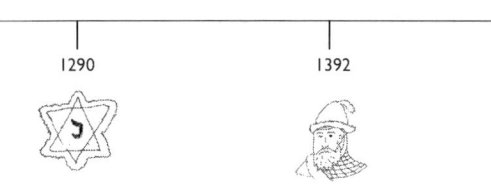

8. KING JOHN
1215 - Windsor, England

John was bad at everything. Firstly, he was a bad brother. As soon as his brother, King Richard, was out of the country, he tried to seize the throne. Secondly, he was a bad leader. His idea of leadership was to extort the hell out of the people (this is the Robin Hood king) and lose nearly every strategic battle. He gets credit for putting his name on the *Magna Carta*, but that was because it was forced onto him. Finally, John was an abhorrent uncle for murdering his nephew, Arthur of Brittany.

7. RICHARD I
1189 - London, England

When he was only sixteen, Richard the Lionheart tried desperately to overthrow his dad. The plan didn't work but Henry II eventually died anyway, leaving Richard in charge. On day one of his reign, Richard's first order was to ban Jews. When some Jewish dignitaries brought gifts to honor him (and, hopefully, change his mind a little), the new king had them stripped of their gifts, beaten, and banished. This move prompted widespread violence towards Jews across the country. After that, Dick the Lionheart moved on to bigger and better things—i.e., murdering tons of people across Europe in the name of Christ.

6. EDWARD I
1290 - London, England

Even if you look past his depiction in the somewhat-historically-inaccurate *Braveheart*, "Longshanks" was a terrible, terrible guy. When he wasn't busy fathering his sixteen kids, the king was attacking people and carrying out grudges. To finance his military takeover of Wales, Edward taxed the Jewish moneylenders. When they ran out of money, he labeled the Jews disloyal and made them wear gold star patches (which inspired a certain awful guy in Germany 650 years later). Eventually, the Jews in England were banished, brought to the Tower to be executed, or killed in their homes.

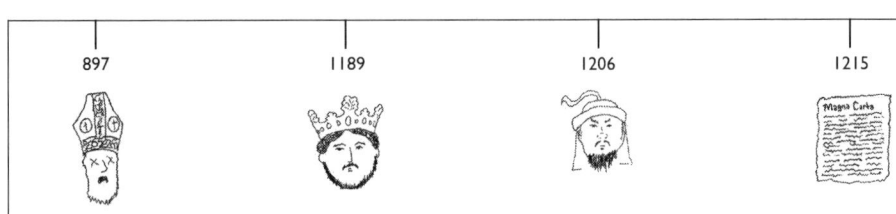

5. TIMUR ("TAMERLANE")
1392 - Hakkari, Mesopotamia (Kurdistan)

Tamerlane's life's ambition was to recreate the empire of Genghis Khan. That meant death—lots and lots of death. His armies were responsible for killing seventeen million people (about 5 percent of the world's population). At first, the sole focus seemed to be expanding his territory. By the end, he was just slaughtering people for fun. He annihilated Indian and Pakistani people so he could conquer the Hindu religion. In Baghdad in 1399, he required each of his soldiers to produce two severed heads before him. Probably should've picked a better role model.

4. GILLES DE RAIS
1432 - Orléans, France

Joan of Arc's brave lieutenant in the Hundred Years' War had a horrible dark side. The war hero by day was a sadistic child predator by night. He was hanged in 1440 after being condemned for raping, torturing, and murdering anywhere between 150 and 800 children across France.

3. GENGHIS KHAN
1206 – Ulaanbaatar, Mongolia

The Mongol leader was very progressive. He believed in religious freedom, created the first international postal system, and established a meritocracy-based system that enabled former enemies to become trusted generals. But there's one more important detail about Genghis Khan's time ruling twelve million square miles of territory—he is responsible for about forty million deaths (or about 11 percent of the earth's population at the time).

2. VLAD DRACULA
1456 - Transylvania (Romania)

When one of the all-time most repulsive horror villains is named after you, chances are you probably aren't a good dude. Everything about Vlad Dracula was about exerting power and instilling fear. He truly took pleasure in the suffering of others. He earned the nickname "Vlad the Impaler" because of his affinity for, well, impaling people. He murdered elderly people. He murdered children. He drank their blood. He hung their corpses up for all to see. Vlad Dracula was pure evil.

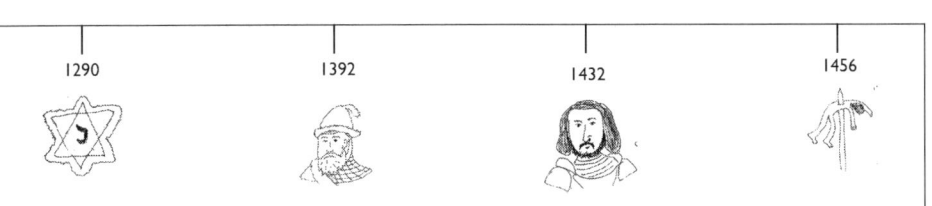

1. TOMAS DE TORQUEMADA
1482 - Segovia, Spain

Torquemada was a garbage human who convinced King Ferdinand and Queen Isabella that all non-Christians were a threat to Spain. Their edict given on March 31, 1492 led to 40,000 Jews fleeing Spain for their lives. As for those who remained—Grand Inquisitor Torquemada tortured and killed thousands of innocent people, all in the name of God. More than 2,000 people were burned at the stake on his watch. Must've missed that part of the Bible.

> **Dishonorable Mentions:** Godfrey of Bouillon - 1099 (massacred Jews and Muslims), Phalaris - 570 (tyrant), Basil II - 1015 ("Basil the Bulgar slayer," gouged out eyes of 14,000 Bulgarian soldiers), Eric the Red - 985 (lied and convinced a bunch of people to move to Greenland, most of whom died), Christopher Columbus - 1492 (didn't discover America, enslaved natives in Caribbean and South America)

| 1508 | 1521 | 1521 | 1527 |

1508

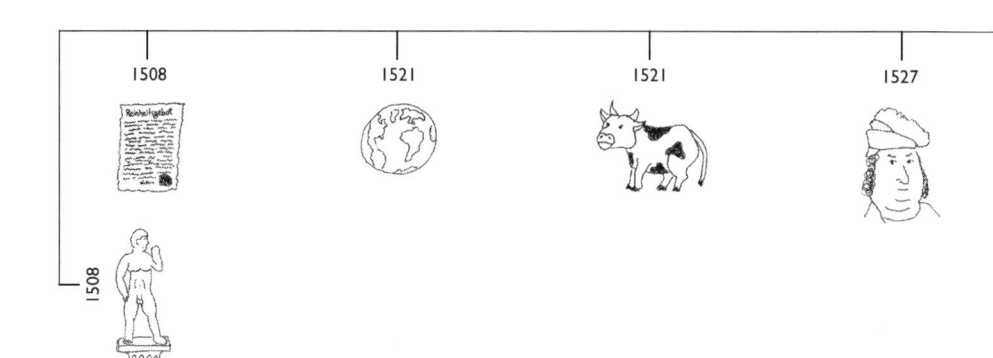

1500-1549

"To know that we know what we know, and to know that we do not know what we do not know, that is true knowledge."

-Nicolaus Copernicus

BEST

10. MARTIN LUTHER
1537 - Eisleben, Saxony (Germany)

Martin Luther was a pretty terrible dude but he does deserve credit for establishing the most iconic Christmas tradition of all—a decorated tree. To replicate the appearance of twinkling stars on evergreen trees, the strict Protestant leader put candles in trees. So, at least, he merits a bit of praise. Then again, he has indirectly caused tons of deadly house fires.

9. WILHELM IV
1516 - Ingolstadt, Bavaria (Germany)

Since long before Germany was called Germany, its people have been drinking a lot of beer. Although beer was one of the safer beverages on the market because the brewing process killed germs, brewery conditions were still abysmal. Wood shavings and fungi sometimes found their way into the product, causing many to get sick. So, in 1516, Duke Wilhelm IV proclaimed the *Reinheitsgebot*, a mandate that beer could only contain four ingredients: barley, hops, wheat, and water. The Bavarian Beer Purity Law combined two of Germany's great loves (rules and beer) and became the world's first consumer protection law.

8. PARACELSUS
1527 - Basel, Switzerland

Around the time Paracelsus graduated from school, the prevailing view in the medical community was that the stars and planets controlled the human body. Wounds were dressed with weird stuff like moss. Paracelsus rejected all these teachings and sought out the wisdom of old wives rather than that of stuffy university professors in his research of most effective medical treatments. He championed the role of chemistry in medicine. He emphasized the need for cleanliness. Most importantly, he placed great emphasis on proper training to increase the skills of surgeons (who, at the time, barely had any). Not every one of his solutions was perfect (he seemed to dole out mercury a little too liberally), but people like Paracelsus were crucial to the development of the study of medicine.

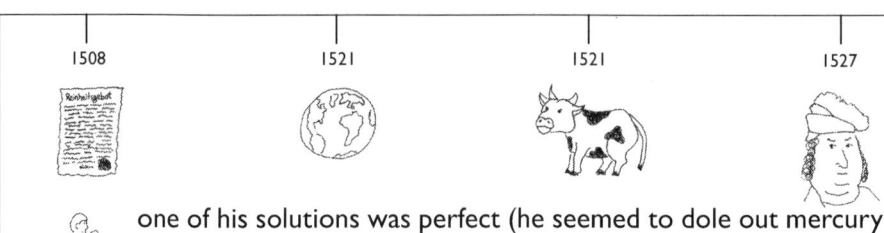

7. GREGORIO DE VILLALOBOS
1521 - New Spain (Mexico)

Some rules are made to be broken—especially ones barring deliciousness. The Spanish sea captain ignored the law prohibiting cattle trading in Mexico and shipped six cows and a bull over to Veracruz, Mexico. The rest was North American food history.

6. FRANCOIS RABELAIS
1534 - Centre-Val de Loire, France

People who are little too into anything (football, religion, wine, yoga, politics, food…) are terrible. Always. Through his five satirical novels (*The Life of Gargantua and of Pantagruel* series), Rabelais was able to point out the ridiculousness of medieval and Renaissance extremists. Plus, there were lots of dick jokes. Rabelais was basically the sixteenth-century *South Park*.

5. ENRIQUE OF MALACCA
1521 - Cebu, Phillippines

Magellan's slave Enrique was forced to accompany him on his attempted journey around the world. When Magellan was killed in the Philippines, his will stated Enrique was to be freed. But the next man in charge refused to free Enrique, who could now speak the local language and could be used as a translator. So, Enrique instead tipped off the Filipinos on how to kill his enslaving crew. Finally, he was a free man. He made his way back to his native Malaysia, thus making him the first person to truly circumnavigate the earth. Take a bow, Enrique.

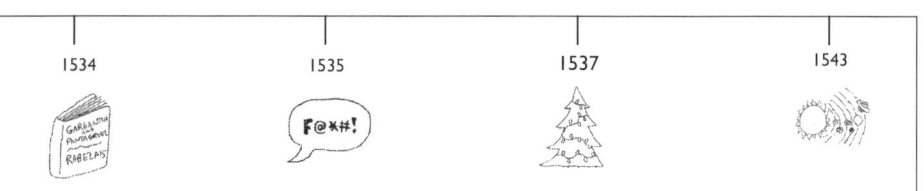

4. DAVID LYNDESAY
1535 - St. Andrews, Scotland

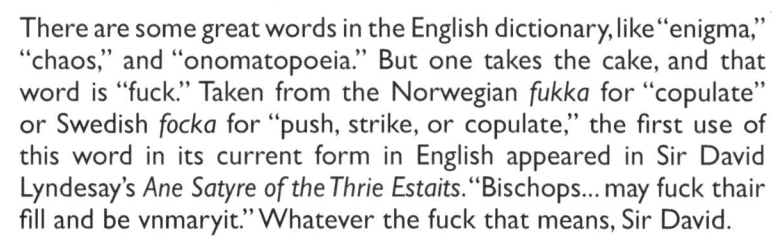

There are some great words in the English dictionary, like "enigma," "chaos," and "onomatopoeia." But one takes the cake, and that word is "fuck." Taken from the Norwegian *fukka* for "copulate" or Swedish *focka* for "push, strike, or copulate," the first use of this word in its current form in English appeared in Sir David Lyndesay's *Ane Satyre of the Thrie Estaits*. "Bischops... may fuck thair fill and be vnmaryit." Whatever the fuck that means, Sir David.

3. MICHELANGELO
1508 - Rome, Roman Empire (Italy)

Michelangelo had the Midas touch. As a sculptor, he became the greatest of all time with projects like *Virgin Mary* and *David*. When asked to take his talents to architecture, he created some of Italy's greatest, most famous structures. As for his painting chops, well, ever heard of the *Sistine Chapel*? Michelangelo was the world's first superstar artist.

2. GABRIELE FALLOPPIO
1548 - Ferrara (Italy)

This anatomist's cadaver study led to breakthroughs in understanding the ear and the female reproductive organs. Falloppio named the vagina, placenta, and clitoris. He discovered the tubes (hence "fallopian") that connect the ovaries to the uterus. But his most important contribution was his treatise on condom use to help prevent syphilis. Smartly, he fought hard to not have his name attached to the penis sheath. That unfortunate honor fell on the Earl of Condom 150 years later.

1. NICOLAUS COPERNICUS
1543 - Frombork, Poland

Since the dawn of time, humans have been rather self-centered but up until the mid-sixteenth century, people were rather literal about it. They believed Earth was the center of the universe

| 1508 | 1521 | 1521 | 1527 |

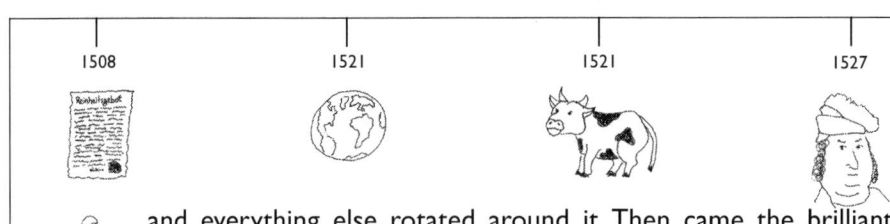

and everything else rotated around it. Then came the brilliant Copernicus who realized that Earth, just like every other planet, revolved around the sun. Sadly, Copernicus died only a few months after publishing his findings and never got his due accolades. In that sense, he was kind of like Otis Redding.

1534 1535 1537 1543 1548

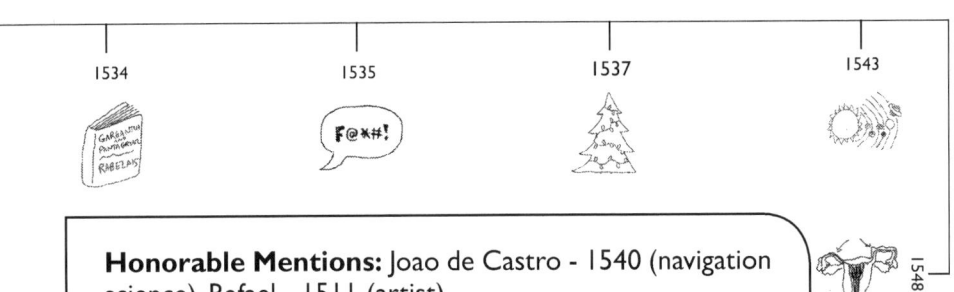

Honorable Mentions: Joao de Castro - 1540 (navigation science), Rafael - 1511 (artist)

WORST

10. JACQUES CARTIER
1534 - Brittany, France

Cartier made three voyages to North America, each less successful than the last. On the first trip, he landed on Newfoundland and kidnapped a couple of natives. He returned and pissed off the Iroquois. The third time, he failed to set up a sustainable settlement and stole a bunch of worthless minerals to make up for it.

9. RICHARD RICH
1535 - London, England

The man with the unimaginative name was one of the all-time most spineless henchmen. Aligning himself with every one of King Henry VIII's whims, Rich was perfectly content to switch up his personal beliefs as necessary. When Henry was evangelical, Rich tortured and killed conservatives. When the portly king felt conservative, evangelicals were in harm's way. When the protestant Edward VI became king, take a wild guess what religion Richie Rich adopted? The only constants for Rich were his lies and desire to maintain power and influence. Thank goodness we no longer have politicians who behave that way.

8. WILLIAM SHARINGTON
1546 - Bristol, England

William Sharington was the Bernie Madoff of sixteenth-century England. As head of the only mint in England located outside of London, Sharington used his position to line his own pockets. He overproduced coins and made the gold coins lighter than standard. When he felt the walls were caving in on him, he cut a deal with the powerful Lord Seymour—he agreed to bankroll Seymour's attempt to overthrow the king if Seymour would ensure him protection. When the plot was foiled, Sharington rolled over on Seymour to save his own ass. I guess when you're a traitor and a thief, adding "backstabber" to the list is no big deal.

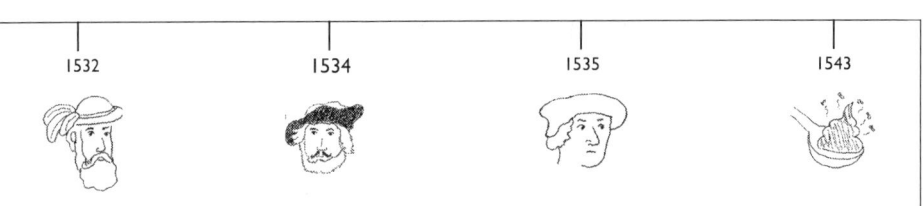

7. POPES JULIUS II, PAUL III, AND ALEXANDER VI
1501 – Rome, Roman Empire (Italy)

By the end of the Middle Ages, it was well established that most popes were bad guys. In the sixteenth century, the bar was lowered even further. When Julius II wasn't hiring Michelangelo to paint the Sistine Chapel, he was focusing most of his efforts on driving non-Catholics out of Italy and starting wars. Also, his interpretation of the whole "love thy neighbor" message of the Bible manifested in the form of male prostitutes. Julius II had the honor of being the first pope to contract syphilis. Paul III's love of money, specifically his quest to inherit his family fortune, drove him to murder his mother and his niece. While he did seem to have an open mind about prostitution, Paul's main motivation was to take a cut of the profits of Rome's 45,000 hookers. It doesn't appear that too many people opposed him, though. Those who did, he was known to strangle or set on fire. Pope Alexander VI was another "love thy neighbor" pope, fathering an Antonio Cromartie-like seven-kid brood with various mistresses while preaching abstinence. Plus, the dude's favorite activities were watching horses have sex and demeaning prostitutes in an event called "Joust of the Whores." Guess he was going with the "do as I say, not as I do" approach to Catholicism.

6. HENRY VIII
1509 - London, England

We all know about the wives and the beheadings. Henry also was an egomaniac who chased glory and trapped England in costly wars (from both a human and financial standpoint). But where Henry should be most criticized is his contribution to the practice of eavesdropping. He promoted a culture of people spying on others and reporting back to him. He even put wooden figures along the eaves of Hampton Court to remind everyone that they were being watched. Hence the term "eavesdropping."

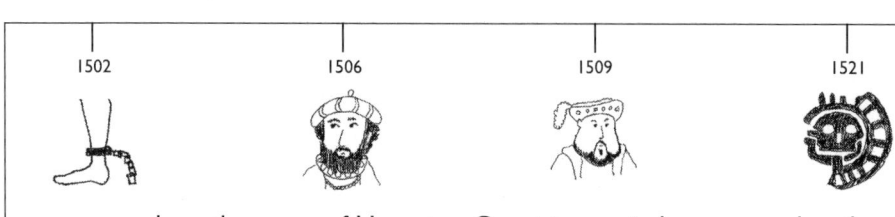

5. KING MANUEL I
1506 - Lisbon, Portugal

In 1496, King Manuel I forced all Portuguese Jews to either convert to Christianity or evacuate the country. One night, a bunch of Christians insisted that the glowing crucifix on a church was a divine sign. When one of the "new Christians" pointed out that the light was probably just a reflection, a Dominican priest went nuts and instigated the massacre of around two thousand Jews.

4. HERNAN CORTES
1521 - Tenochtitlan (Mexico City, Mexico)

There are two reasons to dislike Cortes. One, he slaughtered thousands of Aztecs and destroyed a highly developed society and entire city. Two, he conquered Montezuma and now everyone who goes to Mexico is cursed with diarrhea.

3. FRANCISCO PIZARRO
1532 - Lima, (Birú) Peru

After getting the thumbs-up (and the funds) from the King Charles V of Spain, Pizarro marched into Peru. He approached Incan King Atahualpa and proposed to hold a feast in his honor. Atahualpa agreed. While at the feast, Pizarro kidnapped Atahualpa and had his men slaughter the present company of five thousand unarmed Incans in less than an hour. Atahualpa offered a room full of gold for his release. Pizarro agreed on the condition that the king would pacify his remaining soldiers. After taking the gold, Pizarro killed everyone in sight, effectively ending the Incan civilization.

2. MARTIN LUTHER
1543 - Eisleben, Saxony (Germany)

Many claim the Protestant reformer was one of the great figures of the sixteenth century. He challenged the pope, he translated

| 1532 | 1534 | 1535 | 1543 |

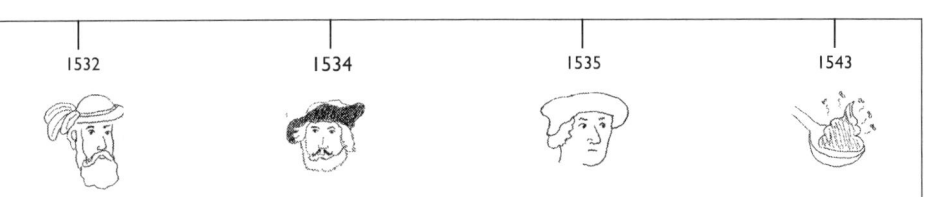

the Bible to German, and he rejected indulgences. You know what else this great man did? Wrote the book *The Jews and Their Lies*, in which he accused the Jews of being "full of the devil's feces" and advocated burning down schools and synagogues. Thanks for fanning the flames of anti-Semitism in Europe, dickhead. Besides, if anyone was full of feces, it was Martin Luther. The guy ate a spoonful of his own excrement every day (because he thought it warded off diseases). The only thing more vile than Martin Luther's breath (keep in mind toothpaste was nearly three hundred years away) was his soul.

1546

1. JUAN DE CORDOBA
1502 - Hispaniola (Dominican Republic)

History is full of meaningful pioneers. But being first at something isn't always a good thing. For example, in 1502, Juan de Cordoba decided to send several of his slaves in Spain to work on his Caribbean plantation, therefore introducing North America to slave trading. Congrats on being a trailblazing monster, Juan.

| 1558 | 1565 | 1568 | 1570 | 1581 |

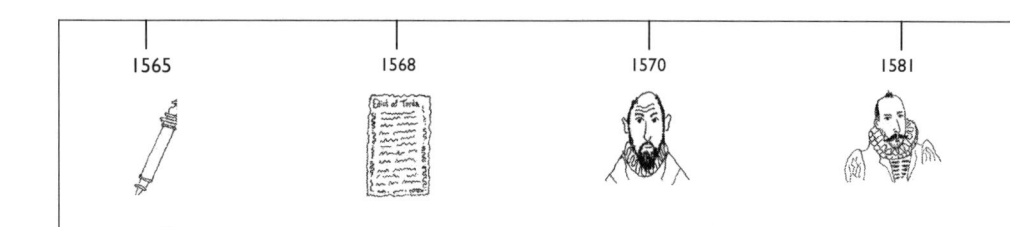

1500-1599

"All the evils of the world are lukewarm Catholics."
-Pope Pius V (Inquisition revivalist)

BEST

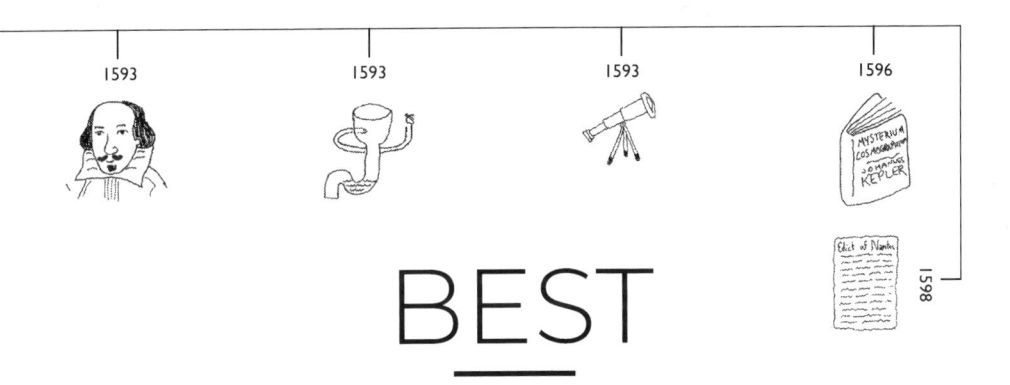

10. CONRAD GESSNER
1565 - Zurich, Switzerland

The father of modern zoology and botany is probably best known for inventing the pencil. Graphite left a dark mark yet was extremely brittle, so Conrad Gessner put it in a wooden tube to prevent it breaking. The Gessner pencil wasn't just any pencil; it was the preferred writing utensil of William Shakespeare. Without this pencil, Shakespeare would have been stuck with laborious quills and maybe, just maybe, would have settled for writing just the sonnets instead of the greatest plays of all time.

9. JOHN SIGISMUND ZÁPOLYA
1568 - Transylvania (Romania)

If there was one constant in the sixteenth century, it was that most people in power were intolerant assholes. Each religion in Transylvania (Catholics, Lutherans, Calvinists, and anti-Trinitarians) wanted theirs to be the only game in town. So King John Zápolya set up a series of debates. After hearing them out, he issued the Edict of Torda, the first religious freedom act in a Christian state.

8. MICHEL DE MONTAIGNE
1581 - Bordeaux, France

Michel de Montaigne was a refreshing blend of skepticism and optimism. On one hand, the Renaissance philosopher believed academics were often full of shit, whereas most ordinary people didn't give themselves enough credit. He believed in the great capabilities of the human mind, regardless of social standing or level of education. In his series of philosophical essays produced throughout the final few decades of his life, Montaigne expounded on everything from impotence to cultural relativism, all while avoiding the boring fifty-cent words that populated other academic works of his era. Beyond seeming pretty cool and open-minded, he was a major influence on future eighteenth-century greats Voltaire and Rousseau.

7. DOMENIKOS THEOTOKOPOULOS ("EL GRECO")
1570 - Toledo, Spain

Before El Greco, every portrait was pretty boring, usually featuring grim-looking rich or religious people posing uncomfortably. While El Greco painted his fair share of religious figures, his versions were much more distorted than realistic. The paintings told a story. They were unusual and cool. Over time, his work inspired other artists, which led to the rise of expressionism and cubism. Without El Greco, there probably wouldn't have been a Picasso.

6. ELIZABETH I
1558 - London, England

When dad kills mom because the newborn wasn't a boy, it tends to put pressure on a girl. After dad (Henry VIII) died, Elizabeth's older sister, Mary, ruled… and threw Elizabeth in the slammer for an attempted rebellion. Eventually, Mary died too and Elizabeth took over a country mired in a costly war with France and a real Catholic-Protestant problem domestically. Thanks to her chaotic upbringing, Elizabeth was well-suited to tackle whatever challenges life gave her. She quickly settled things domestically. When her cousin, Mary Queen of Scots, tried to have her assassinated, Liz took care of business (farewell, Mary). When the Spanish Armada tried attacking, Elizabeth's soldiers sent them right back where they came from. She was a badass. Under her reign, England was more tolerant of religion, a champion of the arts, and a supporter of scientific exploration.

5. HENRY IV
1598 - Aquitaine, France

"Good King Henry" accomplished a ton during his time as king: he made peace both domestically and abroad, lowered taxes, and had tons of sex (earning himself the nickname "*Le Vert Gallant*"—"the Gay Old Spark"). But the high water mark for Hank was his Edict of Nantes, which promoted religious tolerance. Considering religious intolerance is responsible for approximately 95 percent of the world's problems over the past two thousand years, this was a solid move.

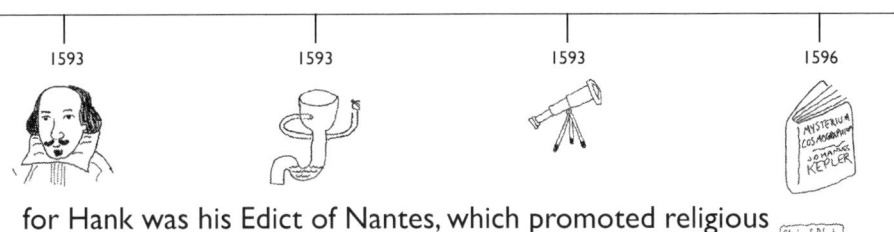

4. JOHANNES KEPLER
1596 - Graz, Austria

Four hundred years ago, religious nuts distrusted science. Well, maybe not that much has changed. But Kepler didn't let simpletons dampen his intellectual curiosity. His book, *Mystery of the Cosmos*, helped us better understand the solar system and the ocean tides and laid the scientific foundation for the work of others (like Isaac Newton).

3. GALILEO GALILEI
1593 - Tuscany (Italy)

No matter where he was, Galileo was always the smartest guy in the room. For more than twelve hundred years, people blindly accepted and applied Aristotle's explanation of logic to just about everything. But, after studying Aristotle's theories on physics at the University of Pisa, Galileo challenged those old conclusions with the scientific method. He continued that approach when he moved on to astronomy. He took a basic telescope invention and made it more than 650 percent stronger. With his souped-up 'scope he was able to confirm Copernicus' theory that the Earth wasn't the center of the universe. Unfortunately for Galileo, the bullies in the Catholic Church thought his findings might undermine their teachings, so they gave him strict guidelines on how he could present them. Galileo responded by giving them the intellectual middle finger and publishing *Dialogue Concerning the Two Chief World Systems*. In it, he acknowledged the pope's point of view, then ridiculed it. The move landed him a lifetime of house arrest but the championship belt for badassery.

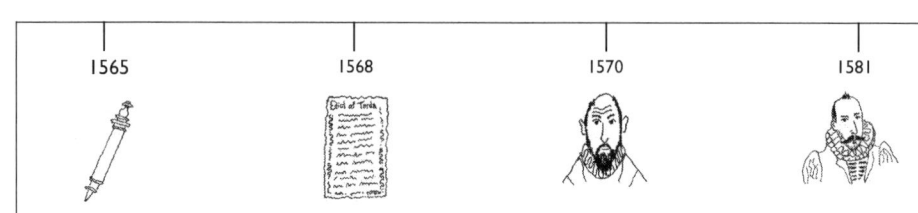

2. JOHN HARRINGTON
1596 - London, England

In his masterpiece, *The Metamorphosis of Ajax*, the potty-mouthed favorite of Queen Elizabeth I published the design for the first flushable toilet. Before that, it was a bucket or the woods for most people. The queen herself was only using a glorified stool with a bedpan. Even rich people's homes in that era must have smelled like a drifter's corpse.

1. WILLIAM SHAKESPEARE
1593 - London, England

Not a whole lot is known about William Shakespeare except for his staggering oeuvre. By the time he was thirty-six, Shakespeare had already written *Taming of the Shrew* (1593), *Romeo and Juliet* (1594), *Midsummer Night's Dream* (1595), *Merchant of Venice* (1596), *Much Ado About Nothing* (1598), and *Julius Caesar* (1599). In 1599, he was successful enough to open his own theater (The Globe) along the Thames River in London. Shakespeare then kicked off the seventeenth century with *Hamlet* (1600), *Othello* (1604), *King Lear* (1605), *Macbeth* (1605), and *The Tempest* (1611). Four centuries later, his stories are still being told and retold in a variety of ways and his contributions to the English language (e.g. the phrases "foregone conclusion," "wild goose chase," "good riddance," "in my heart of hearts," "full circle," etc.) are unparalleled. Methinks the gent was the greatest writer of all time.

| 1593 | 1593 | 1593 | 1596 | 1598 |

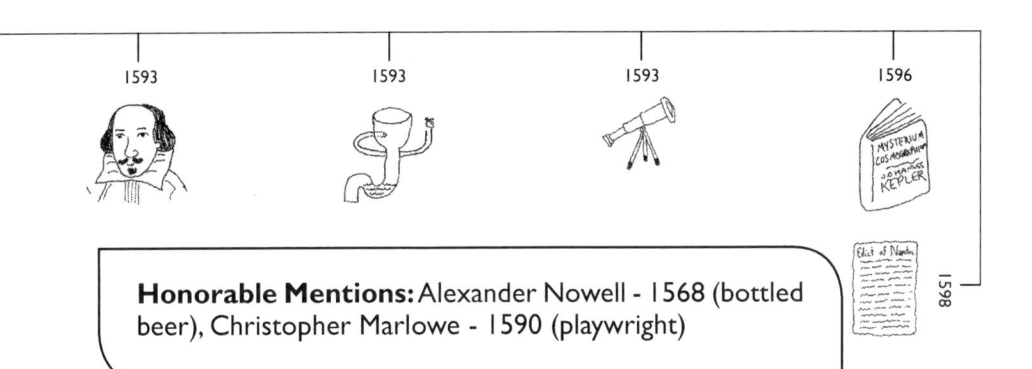

Honorable Mentions: Alexander Nowell - 1568 (bottled beer), Christopher Marlowe - 1590 (playwright)

WORST

10. ROBERT GREENE
1592 - London, England

In late sixteenth-century London, the rising star was William Shakespeare. Literary elite member Robert Greene was jealous. So the accomplished scholar wrote a pamphlet trashing his rival, calling him an "upstart crow." Essentially, Greene didn't want an actor stepping into his profession and tried to derail his career. Greene died later that year and his publisher issued an apology for the pamphlet. Shakespeare went on to have a (moderately) successful career.

9. JAMES VI
1597 - Edinburgh, Scotland

King James VI was one of those guys who needed a scapegoat for everything. When he had a rough trip home from Denmark, he blamed the bad weather on witches. Suddenly, everyone who had an issue with a woman could accuse her of witchcraft. Thanks to a bad mixture of sea-sickness and misogyny, hundreds were killed in the following year.

8. FRANCIS DRAKE
1565 - Hispañola (Dominican Republic)

Francis Drake was a quick learner as a sea merchant apprentice and, by his early twenties, was the captain of his own ship. Sadly, Drake used his powers for evil instead of good. Francis and his cousin went straight to Africa and become prominent illegal slave traders. Years later, he became a war hero for England against the Spanish Armada, so the narrative of his life shifted drastically. But being one of the most famous slave traders of all time earns him a place in the villain column of historical characters.

7. JUAN DE OÑATE
1598 - New Spain (New Mexico)

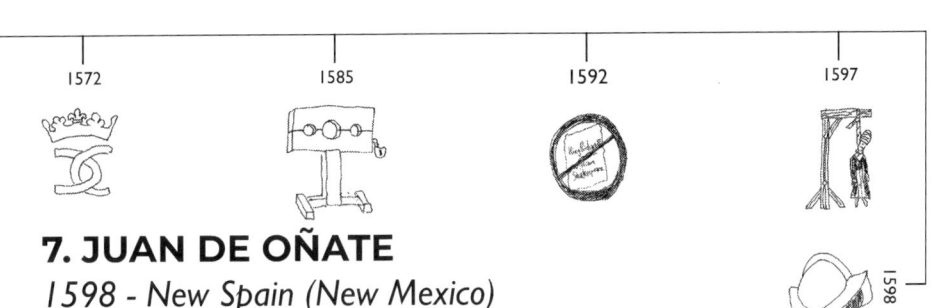

This conquistador is revered for discovering the territory that is now known as New Mexico on behalf of Spain. Statues of Oñate have been erected across the state in his honor. In reality, he was a soulless monster who caused carnage in his empty quest for gold. Juan de Oñate and his men rolled into the Acoma Pueblo and decimated the people living in the area. He enslaved many and cut off the feet of twenty-four men to instill fear. Let's put it this way: putting an Oñate statue up in New Mexico is akin to placing a Bin Laden statue in downtown New York.

6. POPE JULIUS III
1550 - Rome, Italy

Unlike most of his predecessors, Pope Julius III was elected to be the pope. Not unlike most of his predecessors, Julius III had lots of bad appetites—abusing finances and pedophilia, to name a couple. One day, he fell so hard for a fifteen-year-old homeless boy that he had his brother adopt him. Then, to increase their time together, Julius III promoted the teenager to the position of cardinal. Good thing popes are infallible according to the Catholic Church. Otherwise, that would've looked pretty weird.

5. MARY I
1553 - London, England

Mary I, a castoff of her atrocious dad's (Henry VIII) first marriage, managed to ascend to the throne after a few people in the way died. When she became queen, she was determined to produce a Catholic heir. So she married Philip II of Spain and delivered a bunch of religious edicts, which pissed off the Protestants. Mary didn't like the dissension, so she had about 280 people burned at the stake, earning herself the nickname "Bloody Mary."

4. POPE PIUS V
1566 - Rome, Italy

In order to be declared a saint by the Catholic Church, a person must: serve God, show "heroic virtue," and have two miracles attributed to him or her. As Antonio Ghislieri became Pope Pius V, he could check number one off his list. As for the heroic virtue part? Well, that's a bit iffy. In his quest to reform the church, he essentially revived the Inquisition and made life hell for all Jews, Protestants, and Muslims across Europe during the sixteenth century. Humiliation, exile, and death were pretty much his only responses to heretics (non-believers). He did express one big regret, though—that he wasn't tyrannical enough. As for miracles, he definitely had one: getting anyone to view him favorably.

3. ELIZABETH BATHORY
1585 - Sárvár, Hungary

Sometimes relatives can be valuable mentors—they can promote a love of reading, they can teach you how to play basketball, they can be trusted advisors, and so on. Elizabeth Bathory's aunt and uncle taught her about S&M. When she grew up to be a countess living in a castle, she took her interest in bondage to the next level by having her husband build a torture chamber. At first, she did things like jamming pins under the fingernails of servants. Over time, she turned it up a notch by kidnapping peasant girls and making them eat their own flesh. This escalated for twenty-five years until she was caught murdering the children of fellow nobles.

2. IVAN IV
1550 - Moscow, Russia

Considering he was the grandson of a guy named Ivan the Great, much was expected of Ivan IV. And he did make a name for himself. Unfortunately for the people of Russia, that name was Ivan the Terrible. Ivan suppressed the poor, had his thugs confiscate the property of rivals, and ruled by fear. When St. Basil's Cathedral was built in 1561, Ivan had the architects murdered so the beauty of that structure could not be duplicated. In 1582, after suffering a defeat in the Livonian War, Ivan killed his own son. Guess we can add "sore loser" to his list of faults.

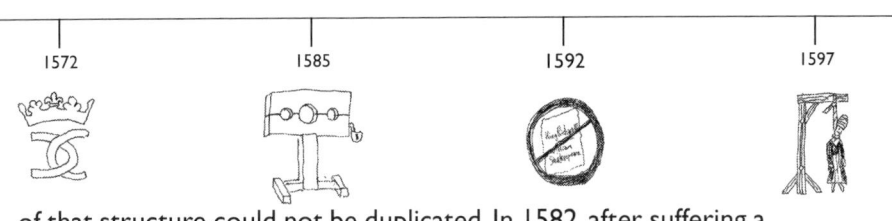

1. CATHERINE DE' MEDICI
1572 - Paris, France

The mother of King Charles IX had an issue with a Huguenot (French Protestant) leader, so she ordered his assassination. When that plot failed, Catherine convinced her son that all the Huguenots were planning a rebellion. Charles listened to Mom and had a bunch of Huguenot leaders murdered the next morning. This set off a chain reaction which led to the murder of 70,000 Huguenots across France. A civil war followed. Mother of the year!

Dishonorable Mentions: Oda Nobunga - 1582 (backstabbing warlord), Diederik Sonoy - 1568 (rat torture enthusiast)

1611

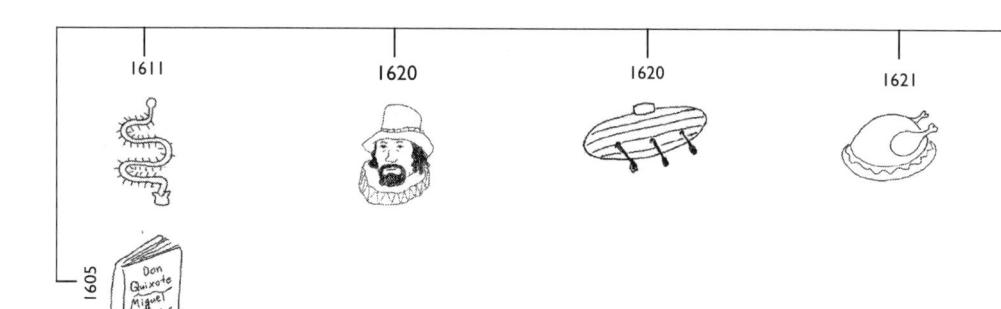

1620

1620

1621

1605

Don Quixote Miguel Cervantes

1600-1649

"The greatest minds are capable of the greatest vices as well as of the greatest virtues."

- René Descartes

BEST

10. CORNELIS DREBBEL
1620 - London, England

Four hundred years ago, this Dutch inventor created a submarine for King James I that was made out of leather-coated wood. And it actually worked! In 1620s London, the streets were covered in horse manure, automobiles were still a few hundred years away, but Debbel miraculously found a way to create a vehicle that allowed people to stay underwater for three hours.

9. SAMUEL COLE
1634 - Boston, Massachusetts

The life of early settlers was not fun. Every day was a game of eat, sleep, and try not to die. There were breweries that produced beer but there still weren't establishments to drink it. Then, the Samuel Cole created America's first-ever bar and named it The Three Mariners. Before Sam "Mayday" Malone, there was Samuel "let's party and forget this miserable life" Cole.

8. EVANGELISTA TORRICELLI
1643 - Tuscany, Italy

Evangelista Torricelli's mentor was one of the smartest men of all time, Galileo. In order to prove Galileo's theory that air was weightless (and disprove Aristotle), Torricelli created a vacuum, which led to the invention of the mercury barometer. Nowadays, barometric pressure is used to predict weather on the evening news by orange guys with over-whitened teeth.

7. FRANCIS BACON
1620 - London, England

Before this scientist with the delicious last name, the world thought Plato and Aristotle had discovered all that needed to be discovered in the field of science. Bacon went further, though. He believed in separating church and science. His scientific method was about getting proof, not just relying on logic. Unfortunately, he was also the shadiest scientist of all time. The dude admitted to bribery and corruption when he served office. And chew on this: he married a thirteen-year-old when he was forty-five. That makes the plot of the movie *Manhattan* look downright wholesome.

6. TISQUANTUM ("SQUANTO")
1621 - Plymouth, Massachusetts

The origin story of greatest holiday in America is equal parts inspiring and sad. Squanto, a member of the Wampanoag tribe, saw a bunch of religious English settlers struggling desperately to survive in the New World, so he decided to help them. The former slave knew some English and was able to teach the Pilgrims how to live off their new land. By November 1621, the surviving Pilgrims had learned enough from Squanto that they decided to have a three-day party to celebrate. Captain Miles Standish invited Squanto and some of his tribe to the feast. When ninety of the Wampanoag showed up, the Pilgrims realized they didn't have enough food. So Massasoit, the leader of the tribe, had to send out his men to bring the food. They finally had a peaceful feast that marked the start of friendly relations between the two groups. Well, it was friendly until the arrival of new settlers who didn't have any use for the Massasoit. By 1637, the settlers had slaughtered more than five hundred of the Wampanoag. But, over time, that awful story has been retold and cherry-picked to form an ongoing American tradition where loved ones gather and reflect on what they are thankful for… well, until Uncle Carl ruins it by mouthing off about politics.

5. MIGUEL DE CERVANTES
1605 - Madrid, Spain

Before Tolstoy, Dickens, or Hemingway, there was Cervantes, author of the first great modern novel. Prior to *Don Quixote*, the only long works of fiction were written in verse. You know how tough it is to sit through a poetry reading? Well, think about a poem lasting four hundred pages. That was the standard in literature back then.

4. SANTORIO SANTORIO
1611 - Padua, Italy

Though he probably spent the first ten minutes of every conversation convincing people he should be taken seriously despite the dumb name, Santorio was a brilliant physician. Besides making significant contributions to the study of weight and metabolism, Santorio invented the early version of the body temperature thermometer. No longer was the hand-to-forehead method the best way to gauge a fever.

3. WILLIAM HARVEY
1628 - London, England

Some might question a man who dissected live animals, but it's a fact that Harvey was the first person to figure out how the human circulatory system works. Before Harvey, doctors were going off 1,400-year-old theories and believed that bloodletting was the best way to kill off disease.

2. REMBRANDT HARMENSZOON VAN RIJN
1642 - Amsterdam, The Netherlands

One of the great painters in history reached his apex in 1642 with his masterpiece, *The Night Watch*. Rembrandt was influential for his use of shadows and expressions on the faces of his subjects. The Dutch painter's artwork came alive and set the tone for the art world. Unfortunately, much like so many other famous painters throughout history, Rembrandt was never able to properly monetize his genius and died penniless.

1. RENÉ DESCARTES
1637 - Indre-et-Loire, France

If you can get past his pervy facial hair, Descartes is one of the most important figures in history. Mr. "I-think-therefore-I-am"

1611   1620   1620   1621

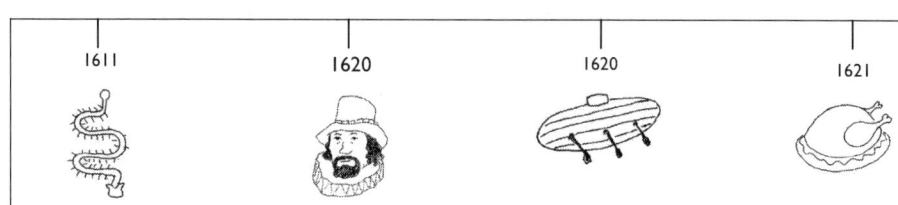

1605 — Don Quixote Miguel Cervantes

set the tone for Western philosophy as we know it. He believed people were rational and rejected authoritarian rule—which had a major influence on John Locke, which had a major influence on Thomas Jefferson, which had a major influence on the United States, which has had a major influence on democracies around the world.

1628

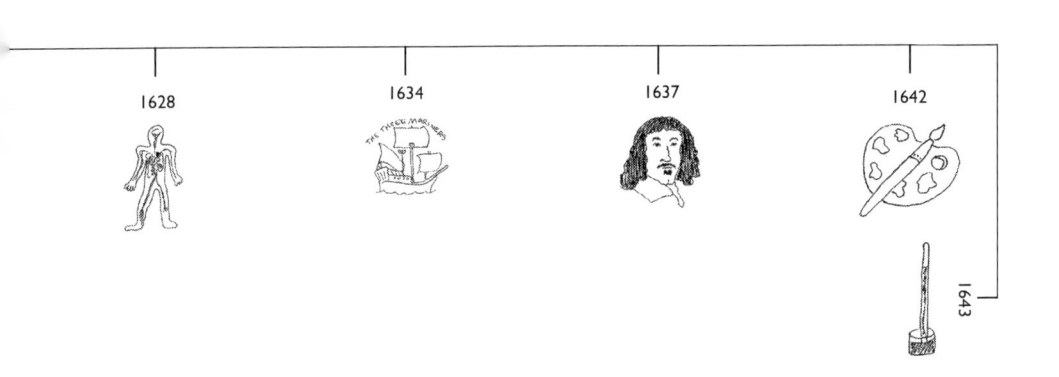

1634

1637

1642

1643

WORST

10. DUTCH TRADERS
1637 - Amsterdam, The Netherlands

Over a few years in the 1630s, tulips went from being a nice-looking flower to an insanely valuable commodity. Speculative traders drove the price up of single bulbs to insane levels—more than some people made in a year. Bulbs were changing hands five to ten times a day. Then, one day, someone realized that a flower wasn't worth the same price as a mansion and the market instantly crumbled. Lots of money was lost and everyone learned a valuable lesson: Speculative trading is a bad idea and would never ever happen again in human history.

9. JOHN ROLFE
1612 - Jamestown, Virginia

This settler was attracted to a seventeen-year-old captive named Pocahontas but didn't want to be with a non-Christian. So he had her convert to Christianity and change her name to Rebecca, and then he married her. He brought her to England, where she caught a disease and died. Oh, he also was the father of the U.S. tobacco industry.

8. CHARLES I
1642 - London, England

Charles I believed he didn't have to answer to anyone but God. When Parliament members disagreed with him, he had them dismissed. In fact, for eleven years, he dissolved Parliament altogether. Finally, when he wanted to go to war with Scotland, Charles was forced to bring back Parliament. They responded by giving him 204 reasons why he sucked. In response, he tried to have five MPs arrested. This led to all-out civil war. Maybe God wanted him to be a horrendous leader.

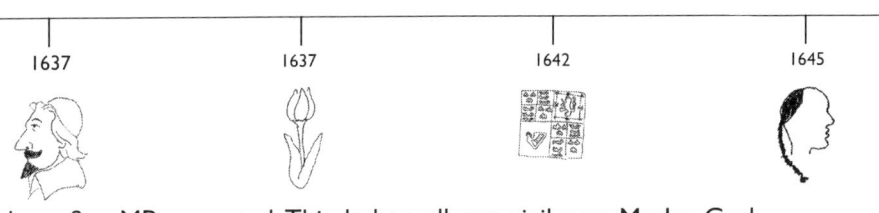

7. POPE URBAN VIII
1633 – Rome (Italy)

Infuriated that someone would have the gall to suggest that the Earth wasn't the center of the universe, the pope summoned Galileo to Rome and demanded he recant his work. The Church banned Galileo's fact and logic books suggesting the sun was the center of the universe and placed the astronomer under house arrest. In the Church's defense, they eventually admitted they were wrong… 359 years later.

6. CATALINA DE LOS RÍOS Y LISPERGUER ("LA QUINTRALA")
1630 - Santiago, Chile

La Quintrala was beautiful, rich, and a spoiled brat. Despite being waited on hand and foot and given large plots of land, she still was not satisfied. So, to scratch her psychopathic itch, she enjoyed whipping and knifing her servants. Sometimes, she tortured them to death. Once she got bored with that, she poisoned her own father, the guy who paid the bills. After years of killing, La Quintralla got caught… but died of old age before having to serve any time in the slammer.

5. ALBRECHT VON WALLENSTEIN
1632 - Bohemia (Czech Republic)

This Holy Roman Empire general lived by one motto: "The war will feed itself." In other words, he felt it was up to the individual soldiers, during wartime, to invade and take whatever they desire. Thus, the army paid for itself (through looting). This merciless strategy financially ruined Germany for decades. And here's another factor of the guy's shitheadedness—as the Thirty Years' War progressed, Wallenstein grew increasingly sensitive to noise and demanded his troops kill every dog, cat, and chicken in every town they passed through.

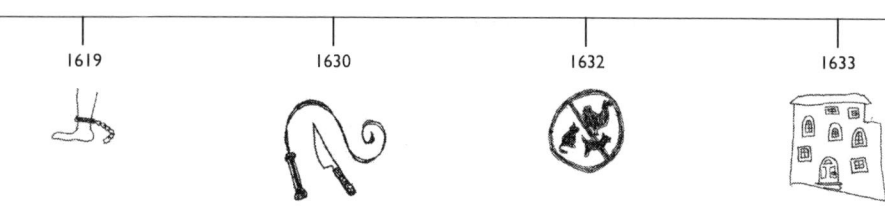

4. DORGON
1645 - Beijing, China

In an effort to unify China, the Qing dynasty ruler mandated that every man must shave his forehead and braid the rest of his hair like the Manchus. The alternative was death. And this wasn't some empty threat. Over 100,000 men were murdered for not complying with the stupid "keep your hair and lose your head, or keep your head and cut your hair" mandate. In the history of man, there have only been two men who could successfully pull off braids: Willie Nelson and Snoop Dogg.

3. JOHN JOPE
1619 - Jamestown, Virginia

Jope's vessel "The Flying Dutchman" robbed a Spanish ship of its cargo. In this case, the cargo was twenty African slaves. He took these slaves and sold them to the colonists at Jamestown for some corn, thus kicking off a disgraceful 250-year era of American history.

2. OLIVER CROMWELL
1649 - Drogheda, Ireland

On one hand, the guy who helped England revolt against the monarchy and install a more democratic system should be celebrated. On the other, when you consider Oliver Cromwell became famous for murdering every Irish person in sight (even after they surrendered) at the Siege of Drogheda, you kind of have remind yourself that he was awful. Plus, the man hated Christmas! So, essentially, he was the Grinch (if the Grinch executed all the Whos in Whoville, set up a sham parliament with a bunch of his buddies, and tried to enforce tons of crazy anti-blasphemy laws).

1. CARDINAL RICHELIEU
1637 - Paris, France

Throughout his time as Louis XIII's chief minister, the head bad guy from *The Three Musketeers* did everything he could to suppress any

| 1637 | 1637 | 1642 | 1645 |

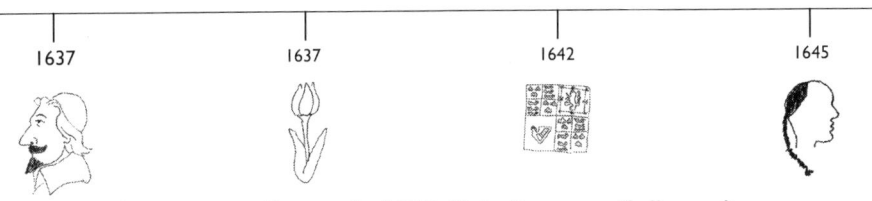

1649

possible dissension in France. In 1628, Richelieu cut off all supplies to the Huguenots and eventually starved a group of 25,000 down to about 5,000. Whenever he encountered a potential threat to his role as minister, he found a way to have the person involved executed. Pretty much everyone hated him, and he knew it. So, in anticipation of getting stabbed whenever he sat down at dinner, Richelieu ordered the points on every knife at the table to be shaved down. Creating the dinner knife was the only silver lining to that bastard's life.

Dishonorable Mentions: Thomas Granger - 1644 (Pilgrim teenager who had sex with a turkey, a cow, a mare, two goats, five sheep, and two calves)

1655 — electricity noun a form of energy resulting from the existence of charged particles

1656 — [compass/clock]

1666 — [apple]

1667 — Paradise Lost, John Milton

1650 — Two Treatises of Civil Government, John Locke

1650-1699

"It is legal because I wish it."
-Louis XIV

BEST

10. CHRISTIAAN HUYGENS
1656 - The Hague, The Netherlands

Through a telescope which Huygens himself had upgraded, he became the first to discover the moon and rings of Saturn. From there he moved on to the study of light and invented the first pendulum clock, which was much more effective than previous versions. But probably his most important invention was the pocket watch. Before the pocket watch, keeping good time wasn't an option. Life before Christiaan Huygens featured an inordinate amount of waiting around.

9. THOMAS BROWNE
1655 - Norwich, England

This physician and philosopher was a weirdo recluse who believed in witches, but he was also responsible for creating hundreds of great English words, including: "electricity," "hallucination," "medical," and "ferocious." If only the monster who came up with the words "moist" and "gurgle" could've taken a lesson from Browne.

8. FRANCIS DAVID PASTORIUS
1688 - Philadelphia, Pennsylvania

Pastorius, a German Quaker, was unhappy that many of his fellow Quakers (including William Penn) had slaves, so much so that he wrote a formal protest. It pointed out the hypocrisy of people who came to Pennsylvania to escape religious persecution and were then enslaving others because of the color of their skin. This document, which was signed by three other German Quakers, was the first step in the fight against slavery in America.

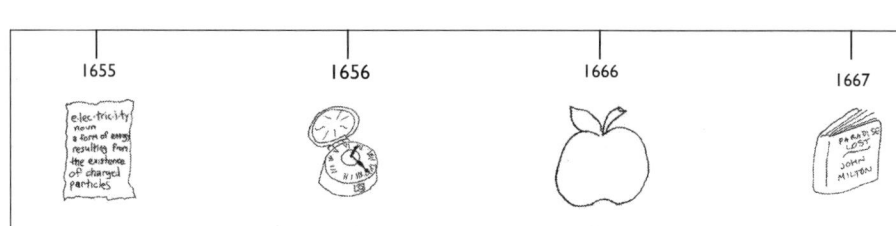

7. ANTONIE VAN LEEUWENHOEK
1674 - Delft, The Netherlands

As a general rule, people who actively collect samples from teeth scrapings, raindrops, and their own feces should be avoided at all costs. In Van Leeuwenhoek's case, maybe we'll give him a pass. He studied these samples with his homemade microscopes and found what he called "animalcules" (single-celled animals and plants). He later discovered bacteria and spermatozoa. He is considered the father of microbiology.

6. JEWISH BAKER
1683 - Krakow, Poland

The legend is that some Jewish baker made a roll in the shape of the King Jan Sobieski's stirrup to honor him for saving Austria from a Turkish invasion. The baker called it a *beugel* (the Austrian word for "stirrup"). He boiled the bread so it wouldn't get stale. The result? Today's bagel. (Documentation for this incident is sketchy at best, but we do know that bagels first appeared in Poland in this era and somebody deserves to be honored for this fantastic food. And, to quote Mark Twain, "Never let the truth stand in the way of a good story.")

5. JOHN MILTON
1667 - Chalfont St. Giles, England

John Milton was blind. His second wife had just died. England was turning back into a monarchy (after five years of Oliver Cromwell's rule). He was bummed out and grasping for meaning in life. Then, for the next several years, he dictated a blank-verse (i.e., non-rhyming) poem to his daughters—*Paradise Lost*. The epic poem, broken up into twelve sections, was a fictional retelling of the beginning of the Old Testament (the angels, devil, Adam and Eve stuff). *Paradise Lost* covered rebellion, some kick-ass monologues from the devil, redemption, and took some political jabs at Charles II. Milton challenged censorship and broke the mold for writers who were constrained by the need to rhyme all the time in their poems. *Paradise Lost* inspired everything from

| 1674 | 1675 | 1683 | 1688 |

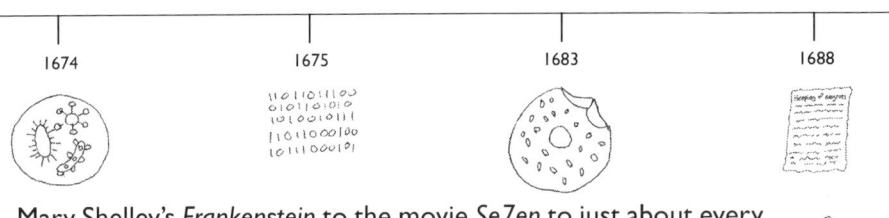

Mary Shelley's *Frankenstein* to the movie *Se7en* to just about every heavy metal lyric from the 1980s.

4. SOR JUANA INÉS DE LA CRUZ
1691 - Mexico City, Mexico

In just about every era, women have been treated like second-class citizens. Education and career opportunities were extremely limited. Juana chose to become a nun at an early age so she would be able to have the freedom to study and have access to literature. From there, she became a famous poet. Her poems featured strong women, so much so that the Church wrote her a scathing review. Instead of shutting up and taking it, Juana fired back a thoughtful response defending women's rights and, as a result, became a pioneer of the feminist movement.

3. GOTTFRIED WILHELM LEIBNIZ
1675 - Paris, France

Leibniz grew up in a Germany that had been ravaged by the Thirty Years' War. The self-taught boy genius believed that language, in general, was too unclear, and arguments and wars arose from simple misunderstandings. So, he sought out to create a universal language (like math) that would eliminate conflict. By mapping out the foundations of human thought through symbols, he set an early blueprint for those who developed artificial intelligence a few hundred years later. He also created the first calculator, invented calculus (independent of Newton), and refined the binary system used in every computer today.

2. ISAAC NEWTON
1666 - Lincolnshire, England

When Cambridge University shut down in 1665 due to the plague, Newton returned to his family's farm and studied on his own. As it turned out, he was smarter than all his professors. During this time, Newton invented a new type of math (infinitesimal calculus) and laid the foundation for the studies of light, color, and planetary motion. Oh, and he saw an apple fall and started thinking about gravity. Over the years, he invented the reflective telescope, wrote some of the most significant scientific papers on physics and astronomy, and got into a whole bunch of fights with other scientists. Considering he barely got along with anyone and is the father of some of the most miserable classes you had to take in school, he was probably a real bummer to hang out with. But, in terms of importance, he's probably one of the greatest men who ever lived.

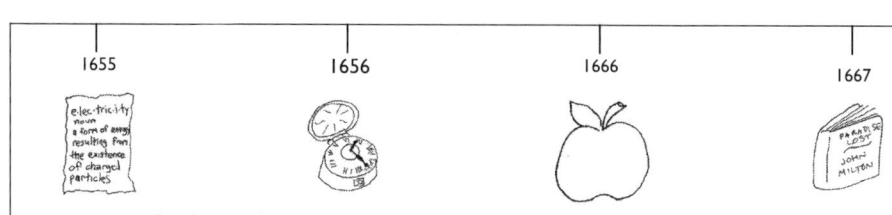

1. JOHN LOCKE
1688 - London, England

The U.S. Founding Fathers are lauded for their foresight in creating democracy. Their views on individual rights, self-determination, separation of church and state, and education were ahead of their time. You know who wrote about those things nearly a century earlier? John Locke. His *Two Treatises of Civil Government* was pretty much the blueprint for Jefferson, Madison, and Hamilton. In an era when kings and queens were considered superior humans at birth, John Locke wrote about how everyone is born with a clean slate. He saw the whole "divine rights of kings" thing for what it was—crap.

1674   1675   1683   1688

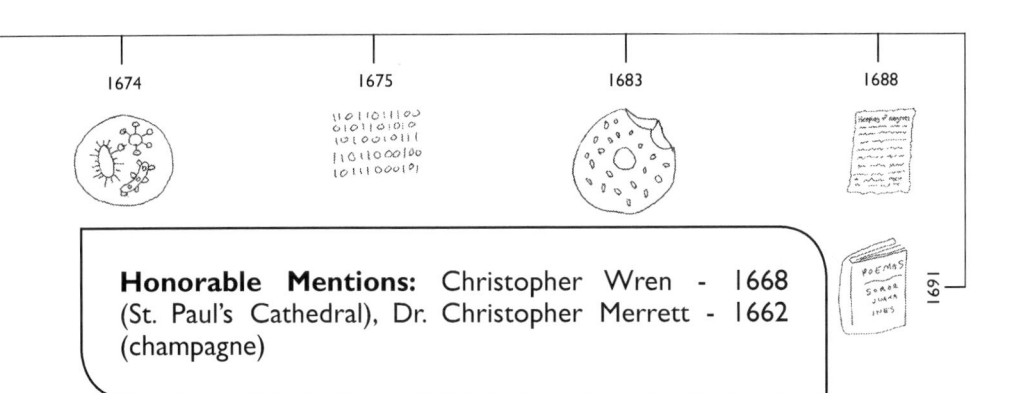

Honorable Mentions: Christopher Wren - 1668 (St. Paul's Cathedral), Dr. Christopher Merrett - 1662 (champagne)

1691

WORST

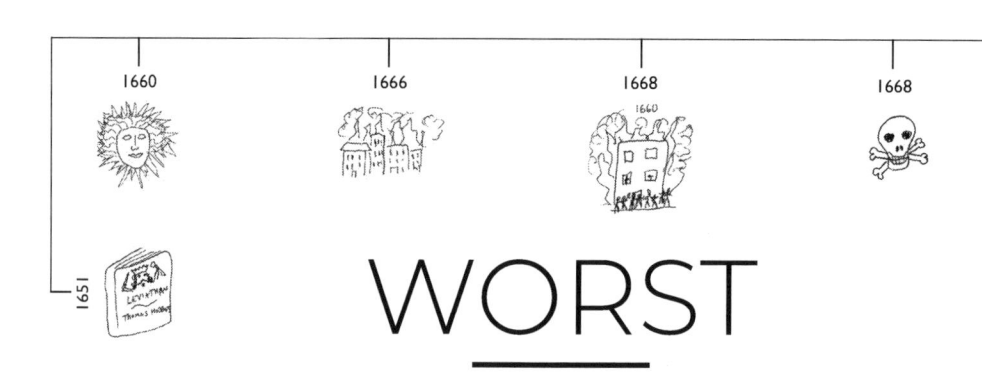

10. CHARLES PERRAULT
1697 - Paris, France

The "father of fairy tales" became famous for being the first person to write down old tales for children. Except Perrault's creepy stories needed a ton of watering down before being remotely appropriate for kids. Bluebeard was a guy who murdered all his wives. Puss in Boots stole a boy's clothes and threatened to cut people into mincemeat if they didn't go along with his plans. And Little Red Riding Hood took off her clothes before getting into bed with the wolf who murdered her. Sleep tight, kids!

9. THOMAS FARRINOR
1666 - London, England

To get through life, we have to blindly trust others. We trust that our airline pilots are competent and sober. We trust that our builders didn't forget to add a necessary support beam. In the seventeenth century, Londoners needed to trust that the baker on Pudding Lane would remember to extinguish his oven. He didn't. And the town full of people living on top of each other in dry timber houses went up in flames. Farrinor's fire burned 80 percent of the city. Shockingly, only sixteen people died.

8. THOMAS HOBBES
1651 - Paris, France

A few years after the English Civil War, the famous philosopher wrote *Leviathan*, a book that examined the social contract between a government and its citizens. He abhorred fighting and made the case that civil wars are counterproductive. But, to avoid conflict, he argued that we all need to follow rules from a powerful leader. People are inherently evil and will mess everything up unless they are given lots of rules. As long as the ruler doesn't actually murder us, we should put up with whatever oppression they're strapping us with because... well... at least we're alive. The book is a dictator's dream.

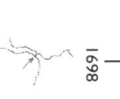

7. FRANCESCO MOROSINI
1683 - Athens, Greece

Pissed off that he lost Crete to the Ottomans, Francesco Morosini became obsessed with taking back part of Greece. When the Turks spotted the old Venetian general and his men moving on the Acropolis, they hid their gunpowder in the Parthenon (figuring it would be safe there because, well, who in their right mind would attack maybe the most famous building in history). Well, the Turks did and Parthenon was badly damaged. C'mon Morosini, you dummy! That was like trying to stop an attack at the Louvre by setting the *Mona Lisa* on fire.

6. PETER MESSENGER
1668 - London, England

Just a year and a half after most of the city burned down, Messenger and a group of four to five hundred apprentices wanted to make a statement against King Charles II. So what did they do? They attacked brothels ("bawdy houses," as they were called) around the city and literally razed them to the ground, leaving many homeless. To make a statement about some insanely rich guy, you need to attack a group of hardworking women actually putting smiles on people's faces? Great plan, jerk.

5. FRANCOIS L'OLLINAISE
1668 - Caribbean Sea

L'Ollinaise was an angry ex-indentured servant who became a buccaneer in the Caribbean. Like other pirates, he plundered, raped, and pillaged whenever possible. But what made him stand out was his exceptional cruelty. And all of his focus was on the Spanish. He enjoyed skinning them alive, removing their tongues, cutting off their feet, beheading them, and on one particular occasion, he cut out one of their hearts and ate it. In a fitting end, L'Ollinaise was ripped to shreds by some natives in Panama.

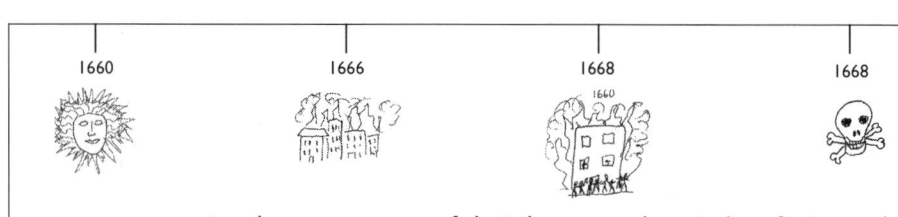

4. JOHN HATHORNE, SAMUEL SEWALL, AND WILLIAM STOUGHTON
1692 - Salem, Massachusetts

These three dopes were the Salem Witch Trial judges who sentenced nineteen innocent people to death on the count of witchcraft. Their main evidence? The testimony of a group of ridiculous young girls. If you want to identify terrible music, rely on the testimony of young girls. If you're deciding someone's fate, you're probably going to want to rely on facts.

3. WILLIAM PATERSON
1698 - Edinburgh, Scotland

A sailor told William Paterson about Darien, a wonderful region in Panama filled with friendly Indians. Paterson became convinced that if Scotland colonized the area, it would control access from the Atlantic to the Pacific (without having to deal with going around the dangerous Cape Horn below South America) and thus become a world power. So he raised £400,000 and embarked on the colonizing mission. When his five ships arrived, it was clear that Paterson's sailor buddy had lied. There were huge mountains separating the Atlantic and Pacific coasts, the Indians weren't pleased to see them, and the Spanish were already in control of Panama. About 2,000 of the 2,500 settlers died, Scotland lost 20 percent of its money, and the kingdom went into a downward spiral. This led to them having to join Great Britain. Probably best to do a little due diligence first, sport.

2. WILLIAM BERKLEY
1676 - Jamestown, Virginia

The governor of Virginia and his rich plantation-owning friends relied on the labor of indentured servants. Unfortunately for them, once these servants gained their freedom, they became citizens who needed actual help—either with better land access or protection from natives. However, the governor already had a fur-trading side deal with the local natives, so he just ignored the freedmen. This led to a civil war called Bacon's Rebellion. The rebellion didn't last but it did enough damage to remind the aristocrats they needed to find cheaper labor that would never be freed. That is when slavery went from being just kind of a thing to the backbone of America's southern states.

1. LOUIS XIV
1660 - Versailles, France

Anytime a toddler is put in charge of nineteen million people, it's safe to say there will be ego problems. As a Catholic, Louis XIV (the self-proclaimed "Sun King") persecuted the Protestant population of France and destroyed their churches and schools. Since he had married a Spanish woman, he believed it was his right to control Spain. So he attacked (and lost). When that didn't work, he attacked the Dutch (and won). Fed up with him, the Dutch, Spanish, and British cozied up to each other and attacked France in the Nine Years' War, decimating France both militarily and financially.

> **Dishonorable Mention:** Icelandic children's author - 1650 (invented Grýla, the most terrifying holiday tradition of all-time)

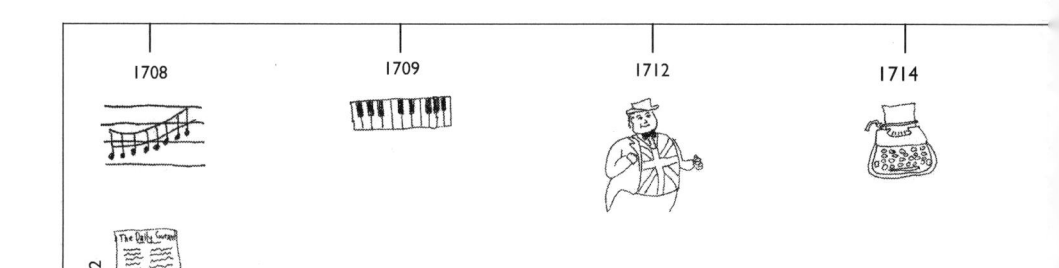

1700-1724

"All political parties die at last of swallowing their own lies."
-John Arbuthnot

BEST

10. HENRY MILL
1714 - London, England

In the beginning of every child's education, painstaking efforts are taken to make sure proper handwriting is mastered. Then we spend the rest of our lives disowning that skill. Most people's handwriting is an abomination. Luckily, in 1714, English engineer Henry Mill saved his fellow human from a lifetime of confusion by creating the first typewriter. Too bad Mill didn't appear to be much of a businessman. He never cashed in on his creation and most history books credit some Italian guy for inventing the typewriter more than a century later.

9. ANTONIO VIVALDI
1723 - Mantua, Italy

Vivaldi was an ordained priest with chronic respiratory problems and a passion for music. So, he abandoned the priesthood and mastered the violin. His violin concerto "The Four Seasons" made him a favorite of European royal families… until they died or fell out of favor. Then he was back to being a broke guy with a violin. His great work was rediscovered a couple hundred years later and is now revered alongside that of Bach and Beethoven.

8. DANIEL FAHRENHEIT
1724 - Amsterdam, The Netherlands

Despite having no formal scientific training, Fahrenheit was able to develop the first accurate thermometer. Previous thermometers had no standard temperature gauge; one man's seventeen was another man's thirty. Water and alcohol would stick to the sides of the thermometer's interior or be affected by fluctuations in air pressure. Fahrenheit used mercury, and the standard was set.

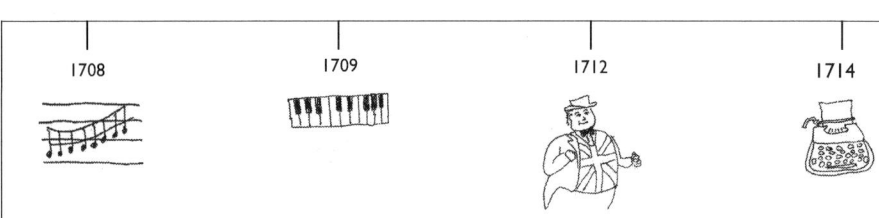

7. JOHN ARBUTHNOT
1712 - London, England

In the early eighteenth century, it was nearly impossible to question authority. So John Arbuthnot created a series of satirical pamphlets about a character named John Bull that showed how the ruling-class Whigs were benefitting from England's involvement in the War of Spanish Succession. Over time, the character John Bull became England's version of Uncle Sam but, three hundred years ago, he was England's version of *The Daily Show* crossed with *South Park*.

6. BARTOLOMEO CRISTOFORI
1709 - Florence, Tuscany (Italy)

An early eighteenth-century Italian harpsichord maker made some tweaks to his instrument (replacing the plucking mechanism with little hammers) and created the piano. Just like that, music took a shift from creepy to beautiful. Just think, without Cristofori's invention, John Lennon's *Imagine* would sound like it belongs on some spooky Halloween playlist.

5. DANIEL DEFOE
1719 - London, England

Kind of like the Coen Brothers claiming *Fargo* was based on a true story, Defoe originally released his narrative adventure *Robinson Crusoe* as if it was written by the title character himself. The reality is that Defoe based the story on the life of Scottish castaway Alexander Selkirk, who was marooned off the coast of Chile for four years. The book was an instant hit and kicked off a new genre in literature—realistic fiction. When it was clear people were digging it, Defoe made sure his name was attached to later editions of the book.

4. FRENCH HOPFFER
1722 - London, England

Before 1722, if a fire broke out in your home or office, you'd better have a big bucket of water within reach or you were in bad shape. Building materials back then ranged from flammable to quite flammable, so if you didn't put the fire out quickly, you were toast. British chemist French Hopffer determined that a cask filled with a certain solution and, of all things, gunpowder could do an even better job than buckets of water. Hopffer created the first fire extinguisher.

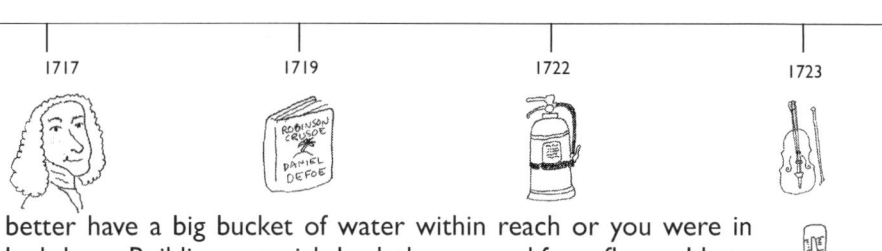

3. FRANCOIS-MARIE AROUET
1717 - Paris, France

The French writer better known as Voltaire wasn't afraid to question or be critical of authority. Each time he wrote an essay or play that criticized government or religion, he was jailed or exiled. And every time he returned, he fired right back at the French government and religion, which got him right back in hot water. But he never backed down and today is regarded as one of the greatest Enlightenment writers. He is also famous for some of the greatest quotes of all time, but he probably wouldn't care much about that because, as he said, "a witty saying proves nothing."

2. JOHANN SEBASTIAN BACH
1708 - Weimar, Germany

Young Johann had a voice of an angel, earning him a scholarship to a prestigious school. Then puberty hit and Bach was encouraged to pick up an instrument. He proved to be a quick learner at both violin and organ and, before long, was composing music for churches around Germany. By the time he reached thirty, he was performing for royalty. Three hundred years later, it is impossible to watch a study montage or an exterior shot of a prep school in any movie or TV show without hearing Bach's famous compositions.

1. ELIZABETH MALLETT
1702 - London, England

Before the advent of newspapers, most people got their news from word of mouth. It was like some bad game of telephone—mangled details, biased opinions, clouded stories, and so on. Then

1708   1709   1712   1714

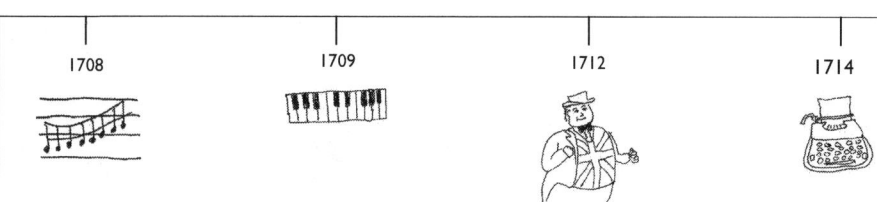

1702 journalist Elizabeth Mallett produced *The Daily Courant*, the first regularly issued English-language newspaper. The one-page paper was strictly facts and let the readers draw their own conclusions about its content. Of course, it was published under the gender-neutral abbreviated "E." Mallett because men back then (and, if we're being honest, plenty of men today) were chauvinist pigs.

1717 1719 1722 1723

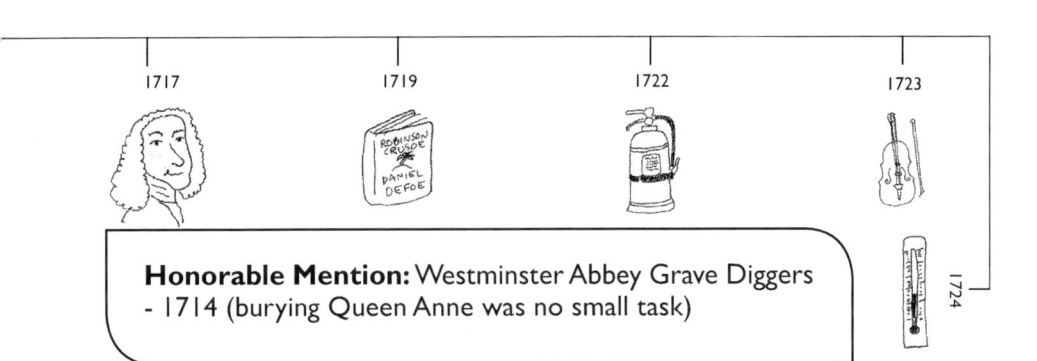

1724

Honorable Mention: Westminster Abbey Grave Diggers - 1714 (burying Queen Anne was no small task)

WORST

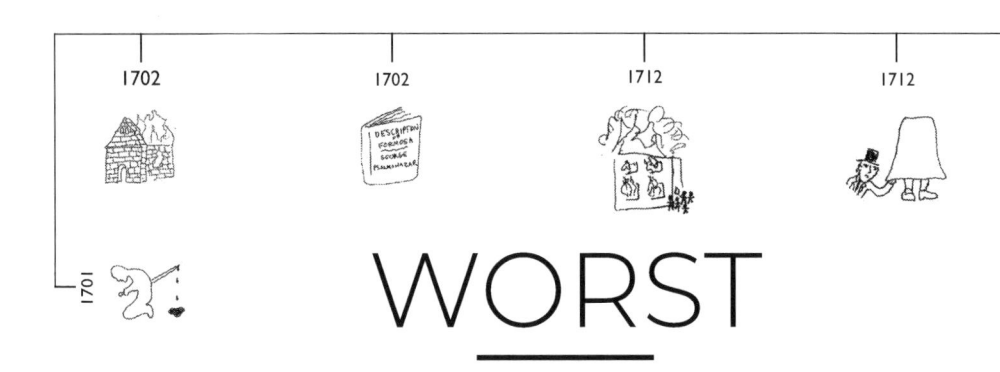

10. GEORGE PSALMANAZAR
1702 - London, England

George Psalmanazar was kind of like Leo DiCaprio in *Catch Me If You Can*, except without the Spielberg direction and Hollywood score. The French-born Psalmanazar was one of history's most famous imposters. He must've been good at it because, despite having blonde hair and blue eyes, he convinced everyone he was Taiwanese. He even charmed famous man of letters and dictionary author Samuel Johnson. Eventually Psalmanazar ran out of people to hoodwink and got a job writing encyclopedia entries for twelve hours a day while on opium. Hey, real life usually doesn't have Hollywood endings.

9. KIRA YOSHINAKA
1701 - Edo, Japan

Egomaniac Kira Yoshinaka didn't like the size of the gift he received from one of his pupils (Asano Naganori), so he relentlessly harassed him. Eventually reaching his boiling point, Asano drew his sword. Though he didn't finish the job, Asano was still sentenced to *seppuku* (forced suicide by disembowelment). Forty-seven of Asano's followers then exacted their revenge—first by killing sixteen guards, then beheading Kira. These forty-seven *Ronin* (masterless samurai) were then sentenced to *seppuku* as well. So that's sixty-five dead bodies, all because some jerk didn't like the size of his present.

8. JONATHAN WILD
1724 - London, England

In early eighteenth-century England, there really wasn't a formal police force to effectively patrol the streets. So, they relied on "thief takers" (private citizens who would prevent or stop crimes for a reward). In reality, most thief takers were criminals themselves. The most successful thief taker in London was Jonathan Wild. Wild would recruit criminals then blackmail them so he could never be implicated. At the same time, he would tip off authorities about crimes so he could get paid from the other side as well. He was both a rat and a thief.

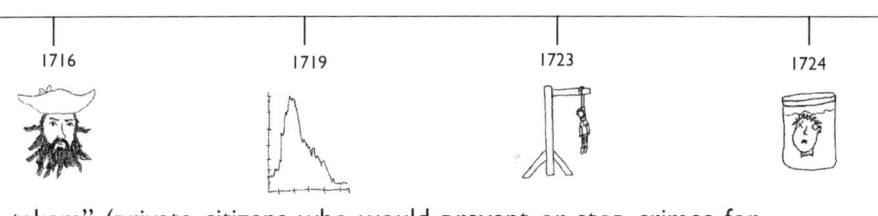

7. JOHN HOSKINSON
1712 - London, England

John Hoskinson patrolled London at night, posing as a thief taker. He approached women and, if they didn't have a good reason for being alone after dark, he'd threaten to turn them in for being "night walkers." The only way he'd let them go is if they performed sexual favors for him. Luckily, this jabroni was eventually caught by the guy he was impersonating with his hand under a woman's skirt.

6. PYOTR "THE GREAT" ROMANOV
1724 - St. Petersburg, Russia

The primary thing Pyotr "the Great" was really great at was cheating on his wife. When we say he had a lot of mistresses, we're talking might've-had-a-hundred-illegitimate-kids a lot. But, when he found out his wife Catherine, happened to have a lover of her own (Wilhelm Mons), he didn't react well. Pyotr had Mons convicted on some trumped-up charges, forced Catherine to watch his beheading, then put Mons' head in a jar by her bedside. And, despite actually changing the law to make it so that the tsar can name his own successor, "the Great" failed to name one before dying. This led to fifteen years of chaos (including an infant being named "Tsar"). Maybe "the Great" was a nickname for Pyotr the same way some big guys are called "Tiny."

5. EDWARD "BLACKBEARD" TEACH
1716 - New Providence (Bahamas)

Blackbeard, along with most other pirates during the "Golden Age of Piracy," was a real boil on the skin of society. Regardless of their cute nicknames, pirates were thieving assholes. For about a five-decade stretch, nobody traveling by sea felt safe from the threat of getting robbed or murdered.

4. ROBERT WALPOLE
1723 - London, England

Food was scarce for people of Britain. Some resorted to poaching livestock to put food on their tables. Prime Minister Robert Walpole finally addressed the issue by punishing the poor even further. Walpole's "Black Act" added fifty capital offenses to the body of law. Essentially, if you killed a rabbit for dinner in a royal forest, you'd be executed, same as if you'd killed King George. If you were caught in the forest in disguise of any kind, you'd be executed. The reality is, Walpole saw the "Blacks" as Jacobites (Catholics who didn't believe Protestant George had claim to the throne), so he had them killed.

3. JOHN AISLABIE
1719 - London, England

This crooked politician pushed for a bill in the House of Commons that allowed the South Sea Company to assume all government debt in exchange for exclusive trading rights to supply the Spanish colonies with slaves. For this, Aislabie was given £20,000 (over £2.8 million today) in shares of the company. Then he and others fueled rumors that the Spanish colonies were lined with gold, causing his South Sea Company shares to soar. The bubble eventually burst and Aislabie was sent to the pokey.

2. ROBERT HUNTER
1712 - New York, New York

In the early 1700s, New York City had a population of six thousand, and about one sixth of them were slaves. Since NYC isn't all that spread out, slaves were able to communicate with each other. In 1712, a bunch of those slaves organized a rebellion. New York Governor Robert Hunter ordered his militia to forcefully

| 1716 | 1719 | 1723 | 1724 |

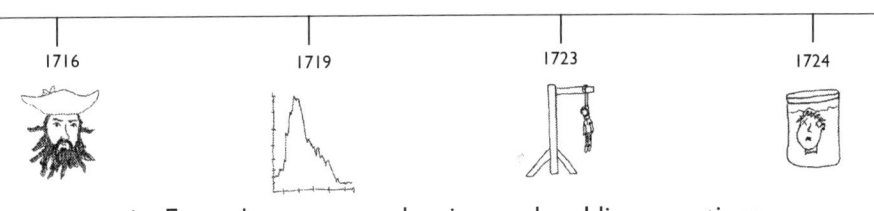

suppress it. Examples were made via cruel public executions (four slaves were set on fire, one was crushed by a wheel, one was chained and starved to death, many were hanged). In 1727, Hunter's slave-suppression talents were called upon by the British government in Jamaica where Maroons (escaped Spanish slaves) were fighting back and upsetting plantation owners. For the next seven years, he did his best to trample the rights of brown people in the Caribbean. Thankfully, a guerrilla warrior relieved him of his earthly duties in 1734.

1. FRANCOIS DE LANGLADE DU CHAYLA

1702 - Le Pont-de-Montvert, France

François de Langlade du Chayla liked working from home. Unfortunately, his work mostly involved torturing Protestants. The Catholic abbé, who was fond of burning fingers and plucking beard hairs, was killed when Protestants trapped him inside and set his house on fire.

Dishonorable Mentions: Johann Dippel - 1700 (grave robber, *Frankenstein* inspiration)

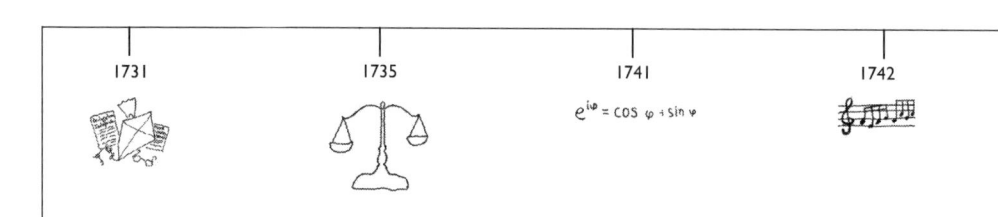

1725-1749

"If all printers were determined not to print anything till they were sure it would offend nobody, there would be very little printed."

-Benjamin Franklin

BEST

10. ADAM SMITH
1748 - London, England

Adam Smith, the father of laissez-faire capitalism, is often derided for creating Gordon Gekko-like assholes who think the goal of life is to amass wealth and pretend trickle-down economics helps out the less fortunate. But Smith didn't advocate that at all. Smith's main goal in his famous 1776 book *The Wealth of Nations* was stating that the measure of a country's wealth is in its GDP, not its vaults full of gold and silver. While he did believe a free market economy was best for the overall well-being of a country, he also showed deep concern for poverty and disdain for corruption of the rich. Smith believed societies were stronger when everyone's basic needs (food, clothing, and lodging) were met.

9. JOHN HARRISON
1749 - London, England

British sailors had a pretty crummy grasp of longitude (east and west). Their ships frequently got lost and wrecked. While, in theory, people could approximate longitude degrees based on time traveled and speed, the clocks in those days were pendulum clocks, and thus were rendered useless on rocky seas. So the government challenged the public to come up with a solution. Harrison, a clockmaker and carpenter, figured it out and earned a £20,000 reward. He used that funding to tackle an even more ambitious project—creating the most accurate clock in history. His competitors laughed at his arrogance, but his theories were eventually proven right. Too bad for him "eventually" meant the year 2015.

8. GEORGE FRIDERIC HANDEL
1742 - London, England

Handel's dad wanted him to be a lawyer, so he had to practice music secretly in his attic. Eventually he became one of the premier opera composers in the world. When public interest in Italian operas began to wane, he mixed it up and wrote *The Messiah*, a cantata that used extracts of the King James Bible. Crowds went nuts and Handel was once again the hottest ticket in town. *The Messiah* is most famous for "Hallelujah," the song featured in seemingly every movie that has a eureka moment.

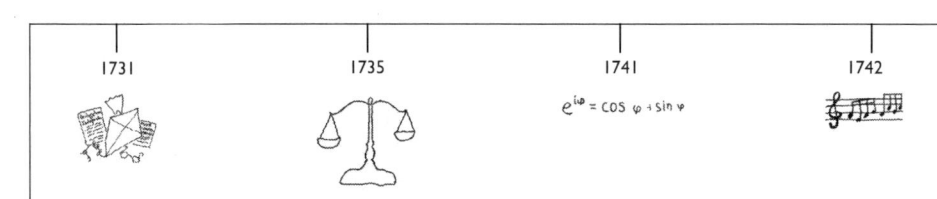

7. JONATHAN SWIFT
1726 - Dublin, Ireland

Like his good friend John Arbuthnot, Jonathan Swift used satire and comedy to point out people's ridiculousness. In his book *Gulliver's Travels*, Swift told the tale of a traveler who wandered into wacky places which had eerie similarities to parts of Western Europe. Gulliver—and the reader—were forced to confront the worst aspects of human nature that were often ignored: tyranny, pomposity, weakness, and more. Even cranky old people took a beating. *Gulliver's Travels* was an eighteenth-century version of *The Onion*.

6. LEOHNARD EULER
1741 - Berlin, Germany

You know those weird buttons at the top of the calculator that don't make any sense? Leohnard Euler was responsible for a lot of them. From geometry to trigonometry to calculus, Euler was a pioneer of mathematics. He solved problems others deemed impossible. Even when he went blind later in life, the guy was able to do staggering amounts of calculations in his head. Euler was the greatest mathematician of all time.

5. JAMES LIND
1747 - Plymouth, England

James Lind was a physician's assistant on a ship full of sailors suffering from bleeding gums in the West Indies. So he tested out different remedies like seawater, horseradish, garlic, lemons, and oranges on ten of the scurvy-infected men and observed the results. Those who ate citrus improved while the others just had worse breath to complement their bleeding gums. Sea travel remained a pretty disgusting endeavor but, thanks to Lind, scurvy was no longer a problem.

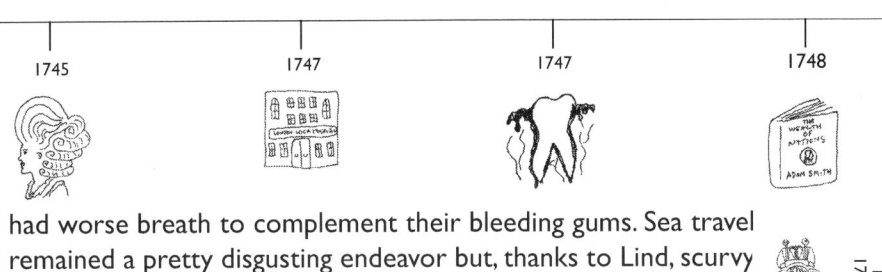

4. MADAME POMPADOUR
1745 - Paris, France

Pompadour was an ambitious woman in a time when women weren't really allowed to do much of anything. Luckily for her, Louis XV's mistress had just died and he was in the market for a new side piece. Pompadour pounced on the opportunity and became one of the most influential people in France. With her love of architecture and paintings, she encouraged the king to become a patron of the arts. At her urging, Louis XV hired her friend Voltaire as the royal historiographer. Even when their physical relationship waned, Louis XV kept Pompadour around as a confidant. Plus, her hair inspired Elvis, Conan O'Brien, and Silvio from *The Sopranos*.

3. LONDON LOCK HOSPITAL DOCTORS
1747 - London, England

Syphilis was ravaging Europe, yet no one would address it. Depending on the patient's place in the societal hierarchy, certain hospitals might've treated the "secret malady" but if some street walker came down with the ailment, she was most likely shunned. Finally, in 1747, the first ever hospital opened with the sole purpose of treating the victims of "wages of sin."

2. ANDREW HAMILTON
1735 - New York, New York

Famous Philadelphia lawyer Andrew Hamilton stepped up and defended John Peter Zenger for publishing a less than flattering portrait of royal governor William S. Cosby in a time when it was illegal to even criticize government. Zenger was locked up and sued for libel. Hamilton argued that the burden was on Cosby to prove the accusations were false before finding Zenger guilty—

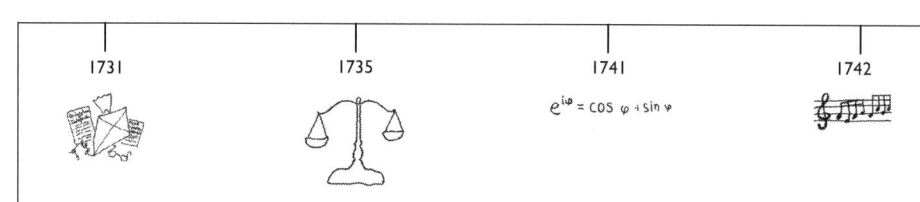

the old "prove you're not awful" libel defense. The prosecution couldn't, and the jury sided with Zenger. The not-guilty verdict was the first step in establishing the First Amendment.

1. BENJAMIN FRANKLIN
1731 - Philadelphia, Pennsylvania

There are great men, and then there's Ben Franklin. For the bulk of the eighteenth century, the brilliant once-printing apprentice was a dominant force in the world. In his twenties, he established the first lending library and created *Poor Richard's Almanack*, a publication of weather, puzzles, and sayings like, "Fish and visitors stink after three days," and "Three may keep a secret, if two of them are dead." In his thirties, he started the first ever volunteer fire department, invented a more heat-efficient stove, and made major contributions in the field of meteorology. In his forties, Franklin co-founded Philadelphia's first hospital, established its first property insurance company, invented the lightning rod, and discovered the properties of electricity. In his fifties, he wanted to improve the speed by which mail traveled by sea, so he charted the Gulf Stream and shaved two weeks off the average postal journey. He also moved to London and advocated for Americans in front of Parliament. In his sixties, he invented flippers for swimmers and the iconic pro and con list. In his seventies, he focused his efforts on American independence (helped draft the Declaration of Independence, convinced the French to provide military and financial aid, and negotiated the peace treaty with the British). In his spare time he wrote a popular humorous essay called "Fart Proudly." In his final decade, he invented bifocals and worked to end slavery. In his eighty-four years on Earth, Benjamin Franklin lived twenty lives.

1745　　　1747　　　1747　　　1748

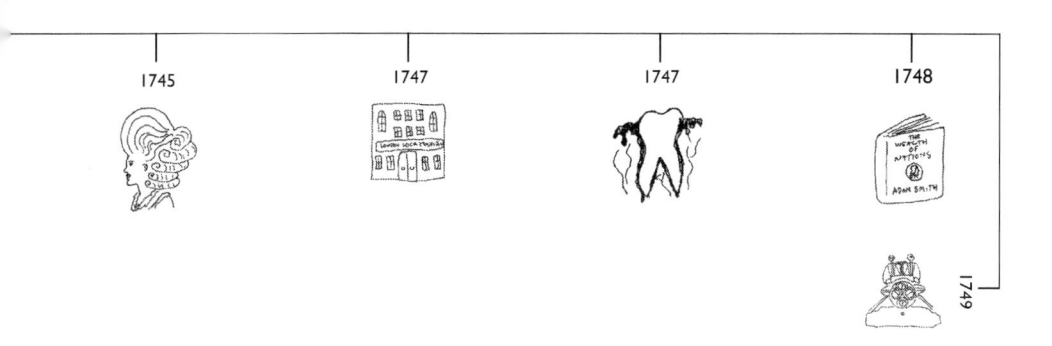

1749

WORST

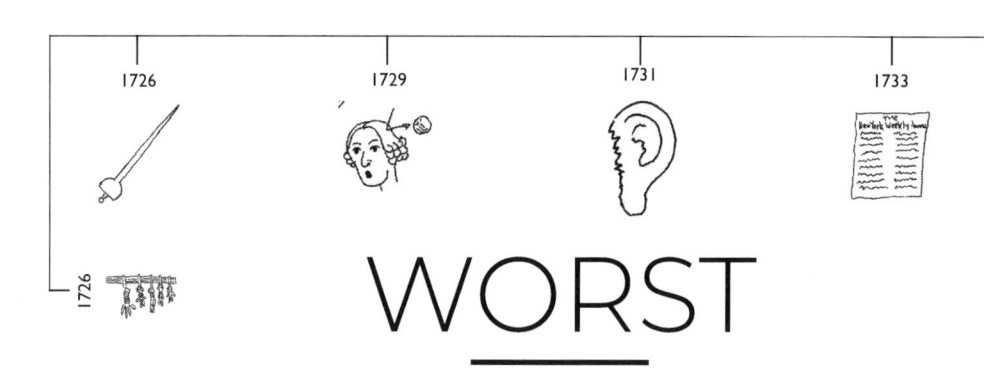

10. DICK TURPIN
1739 - York, England

There are many ways a guy can be a loser. He can constantly steal livestock. He can rob and kill travelers on the highway. He can fight with his landlord and shoot his rooster, thus landing himself in jail. He can reach out to his brother for help but get no response because the brother doesn't bother to pay the postage. Or he can feel compelled to pay for five people to attend his execution just to have some warm bodies present. Dick Turpin was all those guys.

9. WILLIAM COSBY
1733 - New York, New York

William S. Cosby was pretty much the epitome of political corruption. From the minute this prick arrived in New York, he was a disaster. He rigged elections, he fired judges that didn't rule in his favor, and he granted favors to the detriment of his constituents. *New York Weekly Journal* editor John Peter Zenger publicly challenged him and was promptly thrown in jail. After a high-profile trial (the future United States of America's first case involving freedom of the press), Zenger was found not guilty. What are the odds a guy named Bill Cosby would turn out to be a bad dude?

8. FREDERICK, PRINCE OF WALES
1729 - London, England

"Poor Fred" was an insufferable rich kid who nobody seemed to like. When he was dissatisfied with his allowance from his father (King George II), Frederick pressured members of the House of Commons to pass a law requiring the king to increase the amount. Some people just can't help but give off that only-a-mom-could-love-them vibe. The problem for Frederick was that his mom detested him. In fact, as she was getting ready to throw in the towel, she remarked, "At least I shall have one comfort in having my eyes eternally closed—I shall never see that monster again." Even your mom knew you were a turd, Fred. The world caught a break in 1751 when Frederick was killed by a cricket ball.

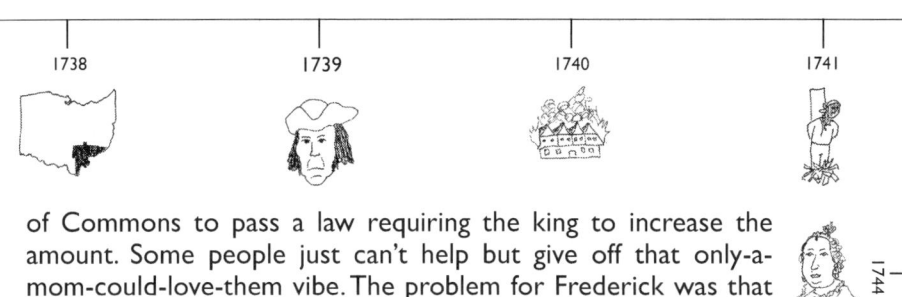

7. CHEVALIER DE ROHAN
1726 - Paris, France

This nobleman got into a war of words with Voltaire. Unsurprisingly, Voltaire got the upper hand with the best insult. Then, like a rich villain in a cheesy movie, Chevalier had his goons beat up Voltaire as he looked on. To retaliate (in the most eighteenth-century French way possible), Voltaire took fencing lessons and challenged Chevalier to a duel. The rich snob wanted no part of mixing it up with someone from the middle class, so he had Louis XV lock Voltaire up in the Bastille. Luckily Voltaire talked his way into being exiled to Great Britain instead.

6. SAMUEL STEVENS
1726 - London, England

In 1533, England passed the Buggery Act, which made homosexual activities a capital offense for the next few centuries. The draconian law didn't turn everyone straight (amazingly); it just forced gay people to find underground clubs to frequent, like Mother Clap's Molly House in London. For two years, Margaret Clap ran her popular club until a scorned lover tipped off the Society for the Reformation of Manners. The Society sent in their undercover snake of an informant, Samuel Stevens, who ratted them out and provided testimony that led to the arrests of Clap and forty men. Within a couple months five men were hanged for their "crimes."

5. MARY BURTON
1741 - New York, New York

A sixteen-year-old Irish indentured servant named Mary Burton worked at a tavern where a robbery was being investigated. After interrogating her, police gave Mary a choice: tell what she knew and be set free or give the cops nothing and stay a servant. You'll never believe what option she chose: to drop a dime and go free! She implicated her employers, then blamed the one group of people that she was higher than on the food chain—slaves. Her bosses, along with thirty slaves, were executed and another seventy slaves were deported. The power-drunk Burton then embellished her story, prompting more arrests. Eventually she started accusing prominent white people as well. Suddenly, the police felt they had all the information they needed, handed Mary a hundred bucks, and sent the lass on her way.

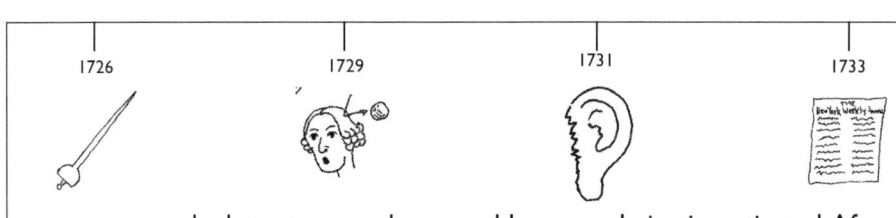

4. ROBERT DINWIDDIE
1738 - Richmond, Virginia

The British government wanted someone to oversee trade and enforce tax collection in the colonies, so they appointed the Scottish-born Dinwiddie to the post of surveyor-general. Unfortunately, he was a shady opportunist who took advantage of pretty much everyone but his rich friends. After being promoted to lieutenant governor of Virginia, Dinwiddie (who happened to also have a large financial interest in the Ohio Company) made decisions (like trying to drive the French out of Ohio) that directly led to the French and Indian War.

3. JUAN DE LEON FANDINO
1731 - Havana, Cuba

Tensions were high between England and Spain in 1731. So when Spanish Captain Fandino caught a British ship with contraband, it was advisable to act with diplomacy. Instead, Fandino turned into Mr. Blonde from *Reservoir Dogs*, cut off British Captain Robert Jenkins' ear, and said if the King of England were present, he'd be cutting off *his* ear. Unsurprisingly, this led to a war between England and Spain that lasted for three years.

2. MARIA THERESA
1744 - Prague, Czech Republic

Maria Theresa was groomed to be a princess, not a ruler. But, since there were no male heirs to take over once her dad died, Maria was forced to lead the Habsburg Empire. The only thing she seemed to do well was have kids—sixteen of them (one of them being Marie Antoinette). Her cabinet lacked capable people; she suffered major defeats to the Prussian army; and she struggled to maintain allies internationally. Her domestic agenda was largely driven by her devout Catholicism. In short, she hated non-Catholics, especially Jews. "I know no greater plague than this race," she stated. In 1741 she banished all Jews from Prague. In the ensuing months she expanded her decree and expelled all of them from Bohemia. The ones who stayed were subjected to a life of misery.

1. ADRIAAN VALCKENIER
1740 - Batavia (Jakarta, Indonesia)

For years, the Dutch East India Company made its profits in Southeast Asia off the backs of cheap Chinese labor. Dutch Governor-General Adriaan Valckenier pushed Chinese workers to their breaking point in Batavia in 1740. So the Chinese confronted their Dutch tormentors, killing several of them in the process. Valckenier responded by ordering an attack on just about all Chinese people living in the city. Over the next two weeks, ten thousand Chinese men, women, elderly, and children were slaughtered in what became known as the 1740 Batavia Massacre. When the dust settled, Valckenier was arrested for his actions. He died in prison a decade later.

Dishonorable Mentions: George Cheyne - 1740 (overzealous health nut), White New Hampshire volunteers - 1725 (scalped ten sleeping Indians).

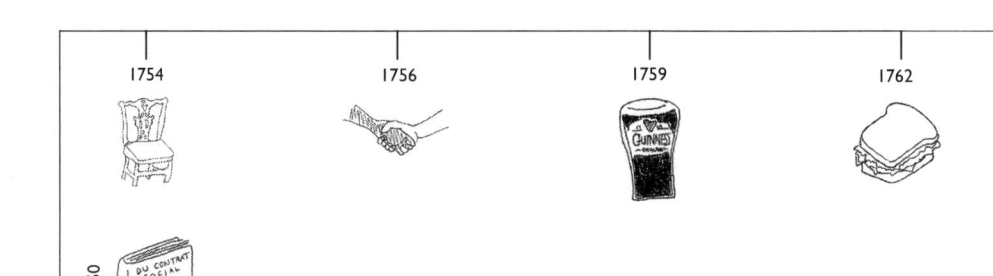

1750-1774

"To be good, and to do good, is all we have to do."
-John Adams

BEST

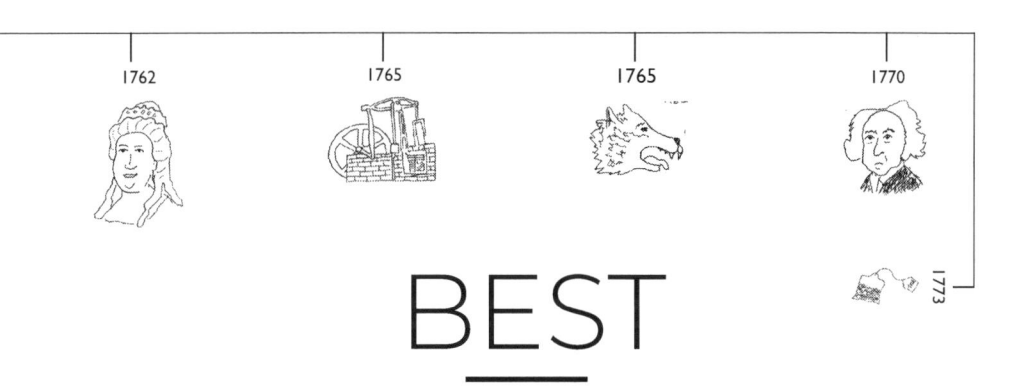

10. ANTOINE DE BEAUTERNE
1765 - Gevaudan, France

Being a woman or child in Gevaudan, France in 1765 was about as safe as being a soldier for Louis XV's army. For a few years, a giant wolf absolutely terrorized this region of France, killing between 80 and 113 women and children. The so-called "Beast of Gevaudan" would strike while they were alone in the fields tending to crops or animals, then retreat to the woods. Many efforts were made by local search groups but the killings continued. Eventually, beast-hunter Antoine de Beauterne showed up and killed the double-sized wolf, its mate, and its offspring. Then he sent proof of his heroic deed to Versailles. Unfortunately the carcass had already begun to rot upon its arrival, so Louis XV was subjected to a pretty awful stench. Then again, Louis XV was kind of a dick so let's give Antoine another high-five!

9. JEAN-JACQUES ROUSSEAU
1750 - Paris, France

In direct contrast to Thomas Hobbes, Rousseau believed that man is inherently good. Empathy and morals do a better job governing people than the arbitrary rules of some incompetent clown who inherits the royal throne. France, at the time, was full of narcissists who were more concerned with keeping up with the Joneses than being good to each other. Rousseau yearned for the days of the "noble savage." He also extolled the virtues of child-centered education and breastfeeding. It was the job of the parents to protect their kids from corruption and not expose them to it, he stated. It was tremendous parenting advice… from a guy who gave all five of his wife's babies to an orphanage.

8. WILLIAM JOHNSON
1756 - Mohawk Valley, New York

In a time when just about every powerful person in the American colonies was a complete asshole toward natives, William Johnson was the exception.

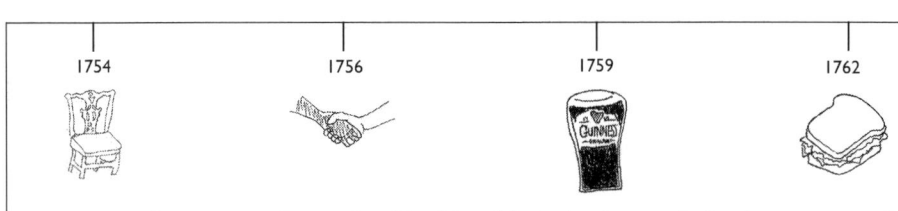

As soon as he arrived in New York, he learned the language and customs of the nearby Iroquois. Thanks to his ability to grasp the saying, "you get more flies with honey than vinegar," Johnson befriended the nearby tribes, promoted trade, and helped lead them to victory in the Seven Years' War (a.k.a. the French and Indian War). He even married an Iroquois woman after his first wife died. While it's sad to commend a rich white guy just for not being awful, history has proven Johnson to be a rarity. His example inspired others in the local region to keep the peace for the next couple decades.

7. SAMUEL ADAMS
1773 - Boston, Massachusetts

Samuel Adams was a brewer. A terrible one. When the beer-making thing didn't work out, he turned to politics. His first big foray into public affairs was protesting the Tea Act (where Parliament required the colonists to only purchase British tea, which came with an excessive tax). Since complaining about the British government was going nowhere, Adams organized people and planned the Boston Tea Party. Within fifteen months, the colonists were fighting for their independence in the Revolutionary War.

6. CATHERINE THE GREAT
1762 - St. Petersburg, Russia

The German Catherine was stuck in a loveless arranged marriage to a king who was about to have her killed. So she made a power play and sexed up some guys who could help her overthrow him. Once in charge, Catherine quickly turned Russia into a world power. She eliminated the use of torture, reformed the military, improved education, and invested heavily in the arts.

5. THOMAS CHIPPENDALE
1754 - London, England

Life in the eighteenth century was painfully boring. The only options for recreation were getting drunk or reading by candlelight. And, unless you were filthy rich, even your household furnishing was

| 1762 | 1765 | 1765 | 1770 |

boring. Then Thomas Chippendale, a British cabinet maker, wrote the most influential book on furniture and cabinet-making of all time. The book inspired many to create interesting designs for more affordable and accessible furniture for the masses. Just how influential was this furniture maker, you ask? His name inspired male strip clubs! You don't see shirtless dudes in bowties at the Raymour & Flanigan lounge.

1773

4. JOHN MONTAGU
1762 - Sandwich, Kent, England

The Earl of Sandwich loved to gamble, so much so that he avoided pretty much any activity that took away his time from it, even sitting down for dinner. One night, during a marathon poker game, Montagu instructed a servant to just bring him some meat between two pieces of toast. And, with that, the sandwich was born. One man's debauchery was the world's gift. He also was really into all things pornographic (including X-rated shrubbery) but considering his contribution to gastronomic culture, let's not focus on that.

3. ARTHUR GUINNESS
1759 - Dublin, Ireland

Mid-eighteenth century Ireland's drinking water was disgusting. Thanks to garbage- and sewage-polluted water causing widespread illnesses, people avoided it as much as possible and turned to gin. This led to drunkenness, which led to increased crime and a downward spiral for the lower class. Some, like brewer Arthur Guinness, turned to beer as a healthier alternative. Guinness signed his nine thousand-year-lease at £45 per month and began making one of the greatest beers on Earth at an affordable price for anyone to drink. When the venture proved to be extremely profitable, Guinness felt a social responsibility to help his fellow citizens. He donated to charities, helped the poor get health care, was a patron of the arts, and fought to improve working class conditions across Ireland. So the next time you drink a pint of the famous stout, give yourself a cheers. You're honoring a hero.

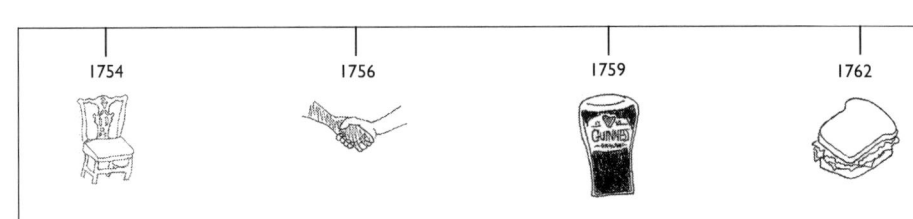

2. JOHN ADAMS
1770 - Boston, Massachusetts

The most underappreciated Founding Father co-authored the Declaration of Independence, represented America at the Treaty of Paris, and, as president, helped the new nation patch up its alliance with France in the wake of the 1800 XYZ affair. But maybe John Adams' greatest achievement was representing the British soldiers after the Boston Massacre. While the rest of Boston was out for blood, Adams still believed the soldiers deserved a fair trial (even if it meant risking his own career). If America wanted to build a new nation on strong principles, they needed to stick to them. John Adams kept a wannabe nation's eyes on the prize.

1. JAMES WATT
1765 - Glasgow, Scotland

Sometimes a good walk is needed to clear the head and regain focus. In Watt's case, a good walk helped him change the world. Before Watt's famous walk on Glasgow Green, productivity was limited to inefficient steam pumps, horse power, human power, and flowing water. After Watt came up with his revelatory idea to more than triple the efficiency of the steam engine, the world transformed from an agricultural one to an industrial one. Of course Watt couldn't start right away, because that walk he took happened on a Sunday and Scottish Sabbath rules were in place. The Industrial Revolution had to wait until Monday.

1762 1765 1765 1770

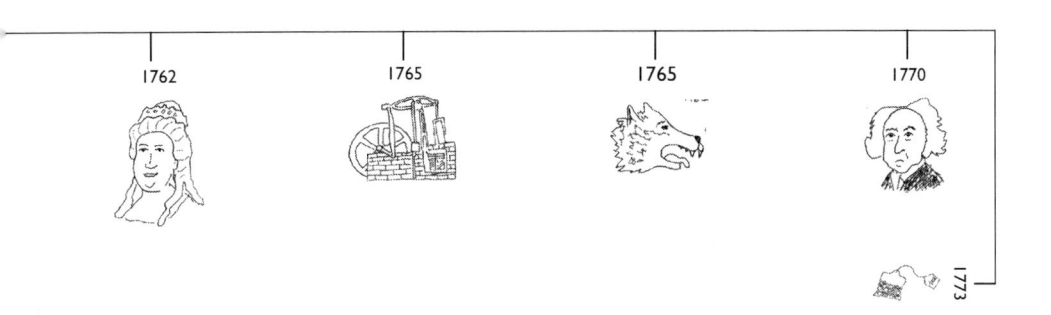

1773

WORST

10. THOMAS PACKER
1768 - Portsmouth, New Hampshire

Twenty-five-year-old Ruth Blay was unjustly charged with the murder of her baby, who was stillborn. While waiting to be hanged, she argued her case to the governor, who gave her four different reprieves. On the fifth scheduled execution date, many rushed to her defense, insisting on her innocence. Selfish Sheriff Thomas Packer ignored the pleas and hanged Blay that afternoon. His reason? He didn't want to be late to dinner.

9. THOMAS DAY
1769 - London, England

Despite being rich, generous to the poor, kind to animals, and a seemingly magnanimous humanitarian, Thomas Day was hideous-looking and a poor conversationalist. Whatever he was selling, eligible women weren't buying. So, twenty-four-year-old Day set out to create the perfect wife. He went to the local orphanage and picked up a couple girls (aged eleven and twelve), changed their names, and moved them to France. This way, the girls couldn't be tracked and they wouldn't understand anybody outside their new house. He then put them through a year of vigorous training to become the perfect wife (which involved everything from teaching them to read to pouring wax on their backs to build toughness). Not surprisingly, Day's misogynistic fantasy never came to fruition. He sent one of them back to the orphanage and focused his efforts on the other, who never fell in love with him and eventually married one of his creepy buddies instead.

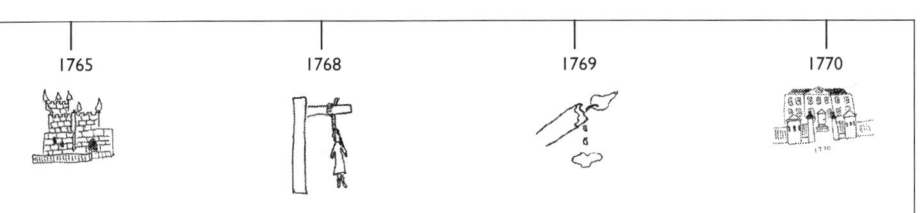

8. JAMES ABERCROMBIE
1756 - Ft. Carillon, New York

This British general from the French and Indian War was one of the most incompetent military leaders in history. Instead of employing basic strategies like flanking the French troops or waiting for his own troops to be ready, Abercrombie rushed into the Battle of Carillon and got a thousand of his men killed (even though he had almost a two-to-one advantage). He was never asked to lead soldiers into battle again. Nice effort, sport.

7. WILLIAM TRYON
1770 - Raleigh, North Carolina

Even though excessive British taxation of colonists was already a contentious issue, the royal governor thought it would be a good idea to build a giant palace in his own honor and have the taxpayers foot the bill. The already-stretched-thin North Carolinians reached their boiling point and rioted, which led to the Battle of Alamance, where fifteen hundred British forces subdued the poorly armed Regulators. Incidents like these were catalysts for the Revolutionary War.

6. GEORGE GRENVILLE
1764 - London, England

After the Seven Years' War, England was in bad financial shape. So, new Prime Minister Grenville had the ingenious plan of excessively taxing those guys in the New World through the Sugar (1764), Stamp (1764), and Quartering (1765) Acts. If they didn't like these new rules, it didn't matter. It's not like they had a say in the government. But, instead of producing additional revenue, these Acts cost the British government increased headaches and expenses simply trying to enforce them. Grenville was quickly dismissed from his post and the wheels of the American Revolution were put in motion.

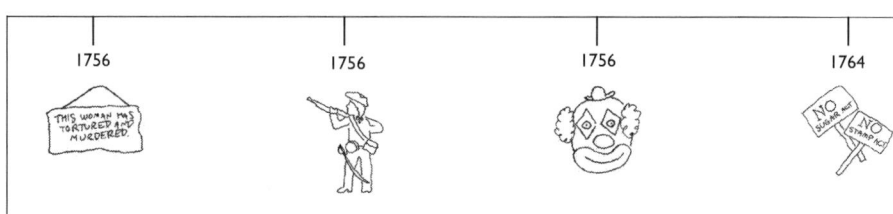

5. PHILIP ASTLEY
1768 - London, England

The former cavalry sergeant major realized that if he kept his horse running in tight circles, he could do a bunch of tricks from her back. He later added some clowns and music to the fray and called it Astley's Amphitheater. It was essentially the first modern circus. Two hundred fifty years later, his legacy of tortured animals and terrifying clowns still looms large.

4. CROWN PRINCE SADO
1752 - Changgyeong Palace, Seoul, Korea

Unless you're a burial box wholesaler, it's probably not good to be known as "the Coffin King." Since he was born to one of the king's concubines and not the queen, Sado grew up in a palace far away from his father—a place without any discipline. The spoiled Sado quickly grew into a sadistic monster. He regularly raped and killed palace staffers to relieve stress. Several bodies were carried out of the Palace of the Crown Prince every day. Eventually, he turned to harassing and terrorizing his own sister. At that point, the king had to step in. Since he was not permitted to murder his son outright, he instead opted to put him in a small box with no ventilation or food. Game over.

3. LEWIS HUTCHINSON
1765 - Edinburgh Castle, Jamaica

Immediately after Lewis Hutchinson moved to Jamaica in the 1760s, people started disappearing. The ginger Scotsman indiscriminately killed dozens of people and had his slaves toss them in a sinkhole on his property (known as Hutchinson's Hole). The Mad Master of Edinburgh Castle's exploits were so well-known that people were afraid to actually arrest him. For good reason, too; when a British soldier finally came to get him, Hutchinson shot him. Thankfully for the rest of the British Navy, Hutchinson's red hair gave him away as he tried to escape. During his trial, prosecutors discovered Hutchinson had received help from some sadistic friends, who also were given the death penalty.

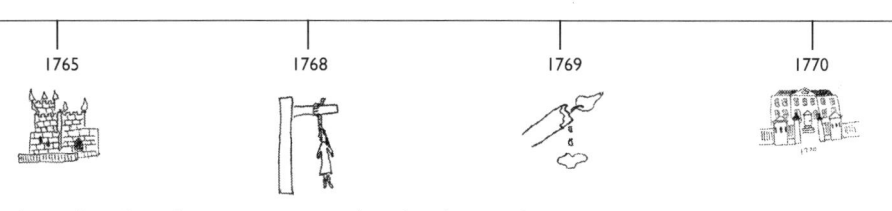

2. DARYA SALTYKOVA
1756 - Moscow, Russia

Darya Saltykova was a rich widow who despised young women. So she tortured and killed over a hundred of them. She broke their bones, gouged out their eyes, cut off their limbs, and maybe even ate some of them. Since the victims were usually her servants, she got away with it for years. After years of investigation, they finally caught her, made her wear a sign around her neck that read THIS WOMAN HAS TORTURED AND MURDERED, and sent her to prison for the rest of her miserable life.

1. LUISA DE JESUS
1772 - Coimbra, Portugal

Coimbra, Portugal's Casa da Roda was a place that took in abandoned babies. When a family was willing to adopt, a local girl named Luisa de Jesus would deliver the baby, along with some clothing and money, to the new parents. Then, one day, a Roda worker discovered a sloppily-buried baby with strangulation marks on its body. An investigation found a total of thirty-three corpses buried in similar fashion. Luisa da Jesus, the "Baby Farmer," had been making up adoptive parent names, killing the babies, and collecting the money. She was arrested and admitted to killing twenty-eight babies. She was whipped, hanged, and set on fire in the town square.

Dishonorable Mentions: Christian VII - 1766 (crazy Danish king, chronic masturbator), Jacob Frank - 1750 (cult/religious leader who molested people), Lord North - 1773 (proposed Parliament's tea tax, which led to the Boston Tea Party)

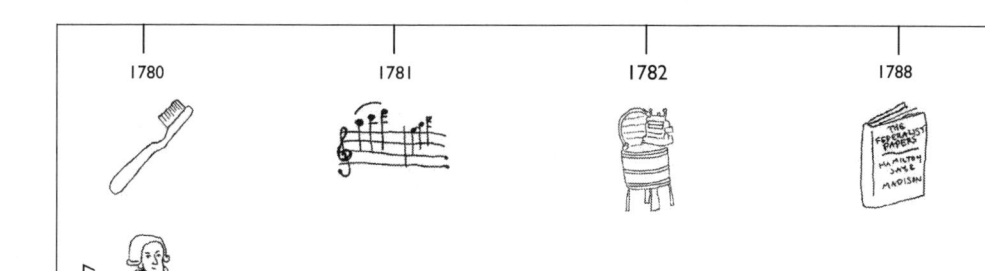

1775-1799

"Perseverance and spirit have done wonders in all ages."
                -George Washington

BEST

10. H. SIDGIER
1782 - London, England

Before 1782, cleaning clothes was labor intensive, tedious, and inefficient. So you know what people most likely did? They rarely did laundry. Yep, they smelled like outhouses. Then Sidgier designed the first ever washing machine. The rotating drum design made cleaning clothes much easier and could do the work of several washerwomen at once. Sidgier's design was quickly copied by many and is still the basis for most modern washing machines.

9. FRANCESCO LEONARDI
1790 - Rome, Italy

Before 1790, there was pasta and there was tomato sauce. But Francesco Leonardi was the first to suggest the two should be served together, in his cookbook *L'Apicio moderno*. Ever since, the two products have been making sweet love in our mouths. That sounds a little gross. But it was a great gastronomic innovation.

8. BENJAMIN BANNEKER
1793 - Baltimore, Maryland

From the moment they were shipped to a new continent against their will, blacks in America have had to claw for acceptance and respectability in a way that whites have not. Even freedmen like Benjamin Banneker were never given access to proper education and, therefore, were expected to be laborers for their whole lives. But, through sheer will, Banneker taught himself to be one of the great intellectuals of his day. At just twenty years old, he built an accurate clock and created an irrigation system for his family farm. After America was formed, Banneker was a key member of a team that surveyed the land that would eventually become Washington, D.C. Later in life, he published *Banneker's Almanacs*, which featured everything from astronomy to tide tables to political essays. Banneker was so well respected that he was even able to correspond with Secretary of State Thomas Jefferson in 1793. He called out the slaveholding Jefferson for his hypocrisy and treatment of blacks (and also mailed him a copy of his almanac). Jefferson quickly responded and publicly praised Banneker for being a credit to his race (then went back to his slave-cooked dinner).

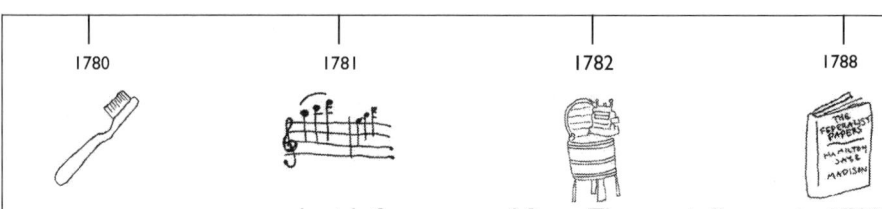

7. ALEXANDER HAMILTON
1788 - New York, New York

After achieving success as George Washington's advisor during the Revolutionary War and a law practitioner in New York, Hamilton took aim at the Articles of Confederation, which he thought were pretty weak. Essentially, without a strong federal government, the newly formed United States wouldn't be united all that long. So, he (along with James Madison and John Jay) wrote the *Federalist Papers*. These were pivotal in the ratification of the Constitution. And when Washington became president, he named Hamilton the first Secretary of the Treasury, where he turned around an economy mired in post-war debt. Pretty much the only thing Hamilton wasn't able to accomplish was a lasting friendship with Aaron Burr.

6. MARQUIS DE LAFAYETTE
1777 - Bunker Hill, Charlestown, Massachusetts

One of the most beloved American Founding Fathers was a Frenchman. At the age of nineteen, Lafayette sailed to America with a stockpile of cognac and a willingness to assist the colonists in their fight against the British. Obviously, it didn't take him long to make friends and he quickly proved he was more than just talk. He served as a brilliant military tactician for the colonists, a trusted advisor to General Washington, and a liaison to France during the American Revolution. Inspired by the birth of the United States, Lafayette returned to Paris and focused his efforts on establishing a government that represented everyone (not just the rich). With help from Thomas Jefferson, Lafayette wrote *Declaration of Rights of Man and the Citizen*. This document, which stated that all men should be afforded basic equal rights, was adopted by the National

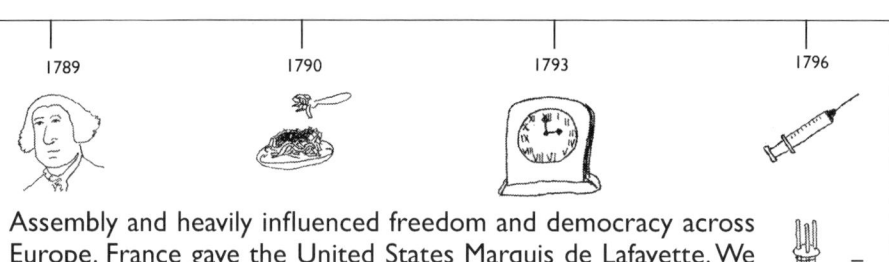

Assembly and heavily influenced freedom and democracy across Europe. France gave the United States Marquis de Lafayette. We returned the favor with Jerry Lewis.

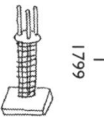

5. GEORGE WASHINGTON
1789 - New York, New York

The first president of the United States might have been the least intellectual president the country has ever known but, at the same time, was probably its greatest leader. While the guy with the bad teeth rose to fame leading the U.S. to victory in the Revolutionary War, his greatest accomplishment was teaching the modern world how to run a democracy. At the time of GW, there was no blueprint. People worshipped him for his success leading the infant nation. And yet he pumped the brakes. He could have been president for life—America would have become just another monarchy—but Washington limited himself to two four-year terms. As a rich landowner, he could have looked out solely for his own self-interests, yet he actually cared about the common good. Since he wasn't confident in his ability to be president, he surrounded himself with men whom he considered much more intelligent. Because of these actions, he laid a solid foundation for a sustainable democracy going forward.

4. ALESSANDRO VOLTA
1799 - Como, Italy

News spread that Luigi Galvani, an Italian biologist, was poking dead frog legs with different metals until the muscles twitched. His conclusion was that animals contained electricity. But Alessandro Volta, a science professor, believed it wasn't the animal but rather the liquid in the leg which caused the twitching. After experimenting with brine and various metals, he eventually figured out the positive/negative properties of copper and zinc and created the first battery. The dude created a way to harness electricity, and all we gave him was the word "volt"?

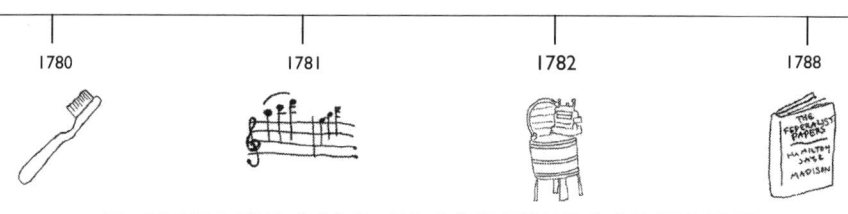

3. WOLFGANG AMADEUS MOZART
1781 - Vienna, Austria

Mozart was a perfect storm of musical genius and financial stupidity. As a result, the world was treated to a staggering number of masterpieces. The child prodigy was able to succeed at any style of music he wanted. And he was forced to keep composing because he kept running out of money. Whether it was piano concertos (like No. 20 in 1785), operas (like *Marriage of Figaro* in 1786 or *The Magic Flute* in 1791), or symphonies (like No. 40 in 1788), Mozart was transcendent. Plus, his songs are still relevant hundreds of years later, in the context of cultural showpieces like *Looney Tunes* and *Trading Places*.

2. WILLIAM ADDIS
1780 - London, England

People had been (sort of) brushing their teeth for years. The Chinese tried to clean their teeth with bamboo. Europeans used twigs and bird feathers. In 1780 a rag trader sitting in a London prison invented the modern toothbrush. Not much is known about William Addis, but suffice it to say he felt that bird feathers, twigs, and bamboo weren't getting the job done. Essentially, mankind had morning breath for two million years until some random guy reached his boiling point. It's not entirely clear why Addis was in prison but, unless it was for genocide, that man was the greatest humanitarian the world has ever known.

1. EDWARD JENNER
1796 - Gloucestershire, England

For thousands of years, mankind's greatest nemesis was smallpox. Smallpox killed millions when the world didn't have many people to begin with. Then one day, Edward Jenner, a medical student, noticed that milkmaids who were infected with cowpox (a nasty scabby condition) never contracted smallpox. So he took an extraction of fluid from a cowpox blister and scratched it into an eight-year-old boy's skin. He then injected the boy with smallpox and observed that nothing happened. If you can get past the fact

| 1789 | 1790 | 1793 | 1796 |

1799

that this is one of the grossest stories ever, you have to give Jenner a standing ovation. He created the first vaccine.

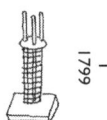

> **Honorable Mentions:** Immanuel Kant - 1781 (*Critique of Pure Reason*), Louis Sebastien - 1783 (invented the parachute), Bernardo de Galvez - 1778 (helped the Americans in rebelling against the British)

WORST

10. WILLIAM BARTON
1782 - Philadelphia, Pennsylvania

Founding a new country means creating a whole new identity. You need some common values. You need a flag. And you need a cool mascot. And what did this Philadelphia artist come up with for America? A terrible bird. C'mon, pal. England has a lion. India has a Bengal tiger. Even Moldova has some cool-looking bull thing. And Barton picked what Ben Franklin called "a bird of bad moral character." As impressive as it looks, an eagle is just a dumb bully who steals its food from others. I'm pretty embarrassed on your behalf, William.

9. THOMAS CONWAY
1777 - Philadelphia, Pennsylvania

This Irishman sucked. After fighting in the French Army for several years, Conway left and joined the Continental Army as a major general, where he was an immediate pain in the ass. The narcissistic Conway was jealous of George Washington's status so he tried to start up a movement to have him removed (so that he himself could be the hero). When that plan failed, the man whom Alexander Hamilton called a "villainous calumniator" threatened to quit. To his surprise, Congress took him up on his offer. Hit the bricks, pal.

8. CARDINAL DE ROHAN
1785 - Paris, France

Desperate for attention from royal society, Rohan was duped by a couple of scam artists into thinking that a certain hooker was actually Marie Antoinette. After an encounter with this woman,

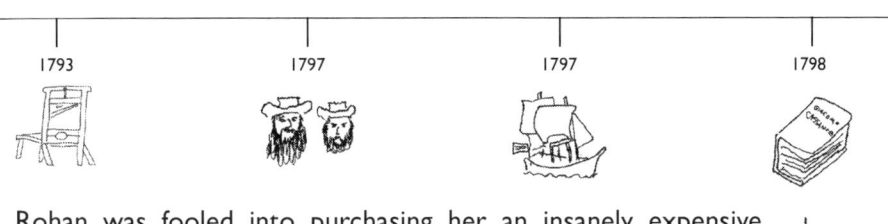

Rohan was fooled into purchasing her an insanely expensive diamond necklace (valued at around 100 million Euro in today's market). The con artists took the gaudy necklace and sold it in individual pieces. Rohan was disgraced and, since many believed she actually had been part of the scam, Antoinette's already shaky reputation was destroyed. The Diamond Necklace Affair was the last straw before the French Revolution.

7. GIOVANI GIACAMO CASANOVA
1798 - Bohemia (Czech Republic)

If a seventy-three-year-old man told you he wanted you to read a three thousand-page memoir bragging about all the women he had banged (possibly including his own daughter), you would run the other way. Yet, somehow, Casanova has become some sort of romanticized cocksman. In large parts of his life, he was just a sleazy conman who bilked rich women out of their money and was responsible for introducing the lottery to Paris. Hard pass on your memoir, Casanova.

6. HE SHEN
1799 - Beijing, China

It is awfully difficult for one man to bring down an entire dynasty, but this guy did his best. By the age of thirty, He Shen had worked his way into the role of Qing Dynasty Emperor Qianlong's most trusted official. In no time, he was shaking down pretty much anyone in China. By the time he died at age forty-nine, his total assets were around a hundred million taels (an old unit of gold weight). To put that in perspective, China's average annual fiscal revenue was about forty million taels. People weren't happy with He bleeding their country dry. When Emperor Qianglong died, He Shen was sentenced to death faster than a fat kid chasing an ice cream truck.

5. CHARLES MAURICE TALLEYRAND
1797 - Paris, France

After the French Revolution, France was strapped for cash and facing threats across Europe. French Foreign Minister Talleyrand's solution? Extort money from the new United States. France would seize American merchant ships and hold them until demands were met—up to and including bribes. Understandably, the U.S. balked and the two countries nearly went to war (called the "XYZ affair").

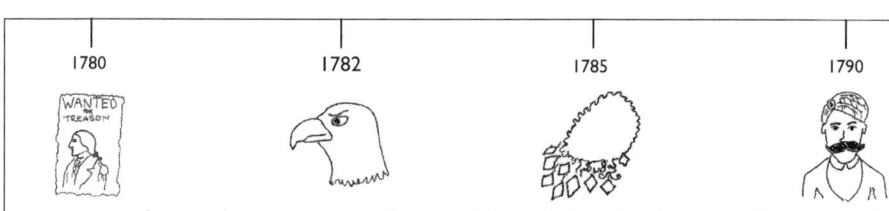

4. MICAJAH AND WILEY HARPE
1797 - Knoxville, Tennessee

Big and Little Harpe were a couple of bad dudes—and not in a bad-meaning-cool kind of way. After the North Carolina-born brothers fought for the British in the Revolutionary War, they fled to the mountains, bitter about the family property they had to leave behind. They focused their anger toward the settlers and committed to a life of crime at their expense. First it was robbery, but it soon escalated to murder. The Harpes killed for the smallest of reasons (food, fun, because someone was snoring too loudly, etc.) and terrorized the region for a few years. They were eventually caught, hanged, and beheaded.

3. BENEDICT ARNOLD
1780 - West Point, New York

Arnold was a general in the U.S. Army who had a habit of not getting along with superior officers. So, when it was time for promotions, Benedict continually found himself getting passed over. Peggy Shippen, his much younger wife (who happened to be a loyalist to George III), convinced him to talk to the British. Before long, Arnold was giving Brits key secrets from West Point. When he was caught, he switched sides to the British army, where he was continually passed over for promotions.

2. THUG BEHRAM
1790 - Oudh, India

The most famous thug in history was the leader of the Thugee Cult, a group responsible for between fifty thousand and two million deaths over a forty-year span. (Behram admitted to killing more than nine thousand by his own hand). The crew would befriend travelers before robbing and murdering them. Behram convinced his followers that their killing was the will of the goddess Kali. When he finally was caught, Thug Behram doubled down on his notoriety by snitching on his cult members to avoid execution.

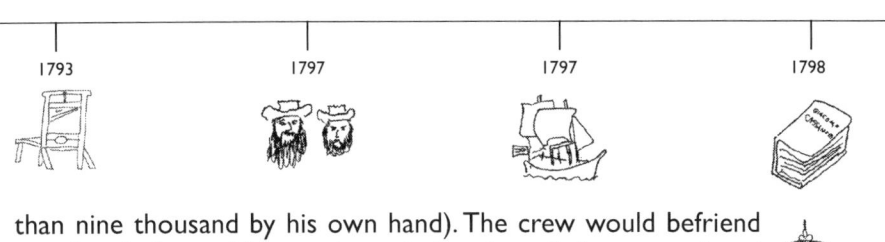

1. MAXIMILLIAN DE ROBESPIERRE
1793 - Paris, France

Due to his virtuous convictions and strong objections to the tyrannical King Louis XVI, Robespierre quickly rose to power in the Jacobin faction of the French Revolution. Once in power, the wheels came off. Robespierre's strategy was to eliminate any potential dissenting voice, even when facts were inconclusive. Over the next eleven months, over three hundred thousand people were arrested and denied a fair trial during the "Reign of Terror." More than seventeen thousand were executed, mostly by guillotine. By the summer of 1794, everyone had grown weary of the power-mad Robespierre and showed him the exit, also by way of the guillotine. The Reign of Terror's craziness weakened the ideals of the French Revolution and France fell back into its old ways. This opened the door for a Napoleon takeover just a few years later.

Dishonorable Mention: Catherine the Great - 1791 (restricted where Jews could live)

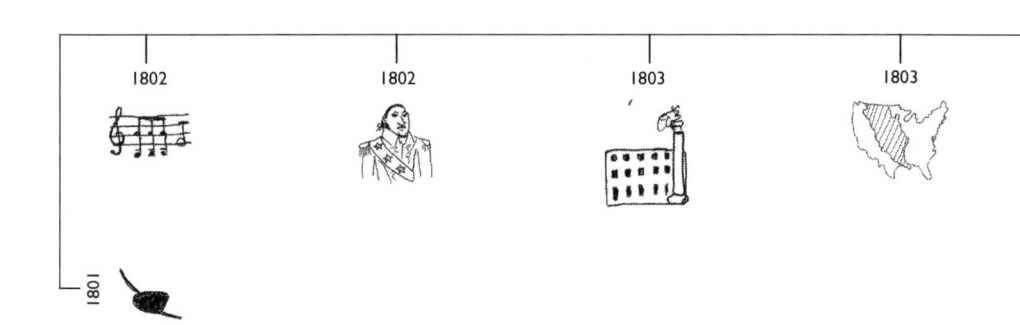

1800-1809

"The most dangerous worldviews are the worldviews of those who have never viewed the world."

-Alexander von Humboldt

BEST

10. SACAGAWEA
1805 - Hidatsa-Mandan Settlement (South Dakota)

Thomas Jefferson bought 828,000 acres of land from the French but didn't know a whole lot about what lay beyond the Port of New Orleans. So he sent his old secretary, Meriwether Lewis, to go explore it with his friend William Clark. Sure, they were brave. But they had no chance of surviving their journey to the Northwest without help. Enter a seventeen-year-old Shoshone woman who had just given birth two months earlier. Sacagawea enabled the expedition to the Pacific and back—all while toting her newborn. Thanks to her knowledge of the territory, quick thinking, an ability to pick out which plants and berries were edible, and, most importantly, her translation skills (which protected the crew from getting attacked by other native tribes), the American government was able to learn about its new territory.

9. ROBERT OWEN
1802 - Montgomeryshire, Wales

Factory owners in early nineteenth-century England had a pretty good racket: they employed poor children to do backbreaking work at dirt-cheap wages. Textile mill owner Robert Owen, however, was disgusted by the process and lobbied to change it. Eventually, Owen persuaded another factory owner (Robert Peel, who happened to be a member of Parliament and father of the prime minister) to push through new regulations. The Health and Morals of Apprentices Act led to a reduction of work hours, cleaner conditions, and improved education for all children.

8. WILLIAM WILBERFORCE
1807 - London, England

Unlike many politicians who used their platform to assuage their ego and revel in power, William Wilberforce worked tirelessly to improve the world around him. As a member of Parliament, Wilberforce was instrumental in improving the educational system and factory conditions, as well as banning cruelty to animals. But Wilberforce's biggest contribution was his eighteen-year fight to abolish slavery throughout Britain. In 1807, Parliament agreed to stop trading, though they didn't free those who were already enslaved. Wilberforce continued his fight for total freedom, which was achieved in 1833.

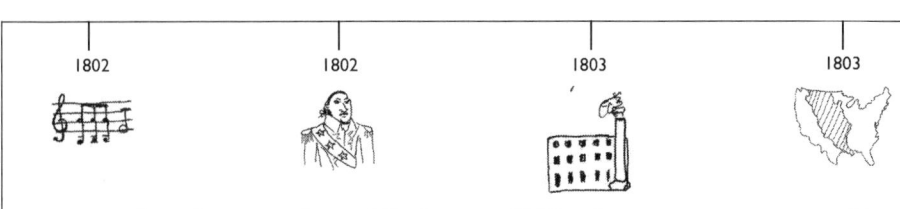

7. GEORGE CAYLEY
1804 - Yorkshire, England

For centuries, man had been trying to fly like the birds. Nearly every design was a variation of the same concept—some contraption with giant, flapping wings. Then George Cayley changed the game with a low-in-the-center and higher-at-the-ends fixed-wing glider. For the next fifty years, Cayley tweaked his design and laid the foundation for Wilbur and Orville Wright to make their historic flight in 1903.

6. TOUSSAINT L'OUVERTURE
1803 – Saint-Domingue (Haiti)

In 1801, a self-educated slave with no military experience led a revolt against sugar plantation owners which culminated in Haiti's independence. The following year, L'Ouverture clashed with Napoleon's army, who had been ordered to reinstate slavery in the French portion of the island. Once again, L'Ouverture and his men fought until the tiny tyrant agreed to a peace treaty. In evil Napoleon fashion, when L'Ouverture showed up to negotiate, he was arrested and thrown on a ship bound for France. The move only inspired L'Ouverture's men to keep fighting until their eventual victory.

5. ALEXANDER VON HUMBOLDT
1804 - Paris, France

More places on Earth have been named after Alexander von Humboldt than any other human being in history. Why haven't you heard of him, then? Because he was an early nineteenth-century scientist. Humboldt believed that to learn all you could about the world, you had to travel it. When he received a massive inheritance, he used it to study the largely unknown continent of South America. On his journey, he discovered more new plants and species than anyone in history. The data he collected contributed to just about every area of scientific study going forward. Without Humboldt, there would never have been a Charles Darwin.

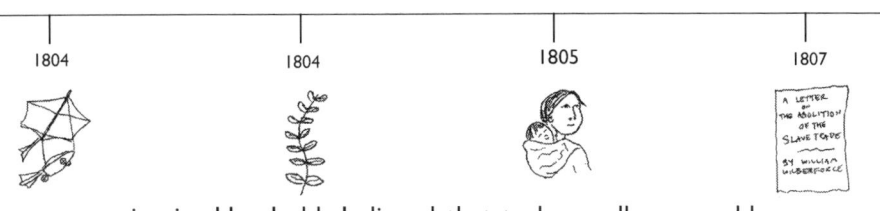

4. HORATIO NELSON
1801 - Copenhagen, Denmark

The one-eyed, one-armed British naval commander was one of the key figures responsible for slowing down Napoleon's complete takeover of Europe. In the Battle of Copenhagen (a battle instigated to ensure Denmark wouldn't side with Napoleon), Nelson's indecisive commander (Admiral Sir Hyde Stewart) gave the signal for Nelson to retreat. Nelson famously told his captain that since he was blind in one eye, he couldn't see that retreat signal. Within a few hours, the British had won the battle and the phrase "turn a blind eye" was born. Nelson's badassery at sea continued for several more years until he gave his life in the Battle of Trafalgar. He went out like the boss he always was. They preserved his body in brandy until he was brought back to London.

3. THOMAS JEFFERSON
1803 - Washington, D.C.

By the time he was named the United States' third president, Jefferson had already accomplished a ton (e.g., wrote the Declaration of Independence, served as ambassador to France, Secretary of State, Vice President, and so on). Once he took office, he set his sights on acquiring the port of New Orleans. He approached its owner, France, and made a low-ball offer of $2 million. They balked, but Jefferson knew Napoleon's aggressive military agenda had the country strapped for cash. So he waited a bit, then bumped up the offer to $12 million—for New Orleans *and* all the land between the Mississippi River and the Rockies. This time, France jumped on Jefferson's proposal and sold these 828,000 acres to the United States. The Louisiana Purchase worked out to cost three cents per acre. In today's money, that's less than fifty cents per acre! Nice work, Tommy.

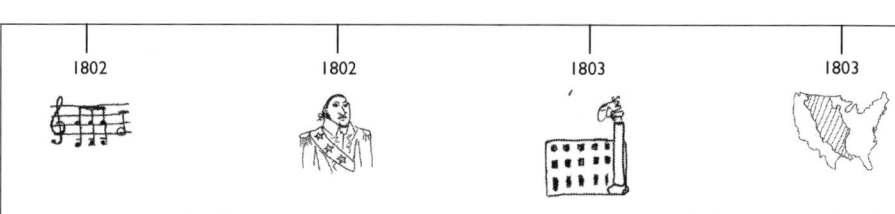

2. ROBERT FULTON
1807 - New York, New York

Robert Fulton, a successful portrait artist, became fascinated with steamship travel and set out to improve this new mode of transportation. When John Fitch built the first steamboat in 1787, the idea never really took off, for a variety of depressing reasons. Fulton relentlessly raised capital, tweaked Fitch's design, used a British steam engine, and achieved his dream. Fulton's quest, first deemed "folly," had a swift and dramatic effect on the Industrial Revolution, since steamships allowed manufacturers to obtain raw materials and deliver finished goods much easier. The steamship's impact on the world was similar to the affect gamma rays had on the Incredible Hulk.

1. LUDWIG VON BEETHOVEN
1802 - Vienna, Austria

Ludwig von Beethoven's abusive, alcoholic father obsessed over creating a music prodigy. While the fear-inspiring approach didn't immediately turn him into the superstar his dad had hoped, Ludwig did become an incredible piano player. Once his dad was out of the picture, he was sent to Vienna, the music capital of the world, where he learned from superstars like Bach, Salieri, and Haydn, and created some of the most memorable music in history. Unfortunately, his success coincided with his loss of hearing. He continued to write at a blistering pace throughout his life despite the ironically cruel fate of no longer being able to enjoy the sound of his own music. And we still enjoy the fruits of his labor (via weddings, car commercials, the movie *Die Hard*) two centuries later.

1804   1804   1805   1807

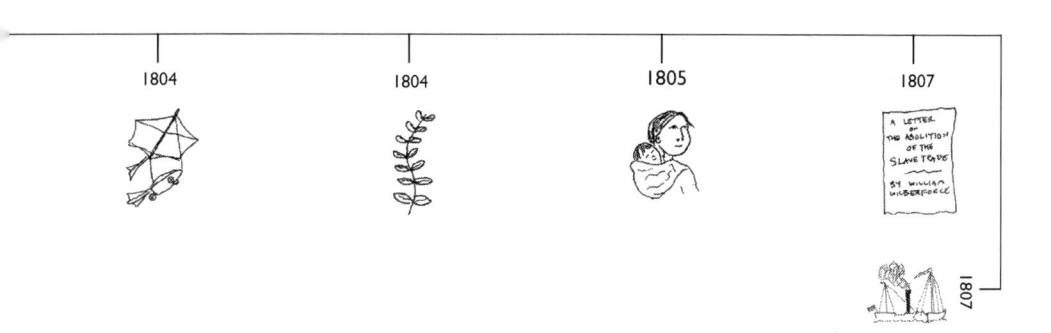

WORST

10. CARL AUGUST WEINHOLD
1809 - Halle-Wittenberg, Germany

Carl Weinhold was a mad scientist. Inspired by Giovanni Aldini and galvanism, Weinhold believed he could bring dead tissue back to life by replacing the nervous system with metals and wires. He'd take decapitated cats, rip out their spinal cords, replace them with zinc and silver batteries, and mistake their twitching for actual success. His madness served as the inspiration for Mary Shelley's *Frankenstein*. Then he got really crazy. In 1827, he proposed that fourteen-year-old boys should have their genitals mutilated in order to fix the overpopulation problem. That's when people stopped listening to Carl.

9. TSAR PAUL I
1801 - St. Petersburg, Russia

After having his shady father killed, Catherine the Great really didn't pay much attention to their son, Paul. Left alone, Paul acted like a twelve-year-old for the next thirty years. He dressed in uniform, played with soldiers, and had them perform lots of meaningless military parades for his delight. When Catherine died, the now forty-two-year-old became Tsar of Russia. What did Paul do with this newfound power? He played with soldiers and had them perform meaningless parades. He also changed the military uniforms to be fancier, changed a lot of his mom's successful policies, prevented all foreign travel, and banned all foreign books and newspapers. All of these things went over like a turd in a punchbowl. Unsurprisingly, the guards who were forced to march in sham parades were a little lax with the security and soon a group of conspirators sent Paul to the big parade in the sky.

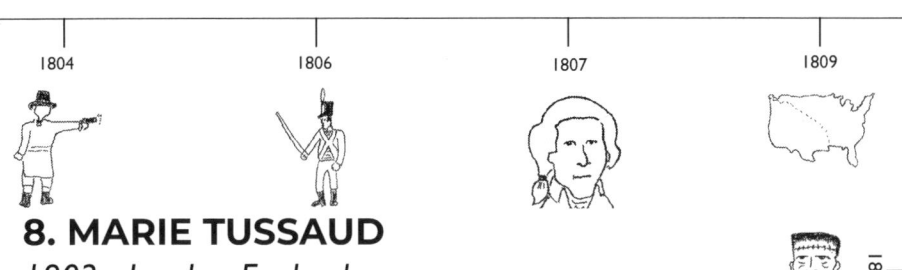

8. MARIE TUSSAUD
1802 - London, England

After learning how to mold wax from her uncle (which definitely qualifies him as the creepy uncle), Marie Tussaud became a favorite of powerful French families. During the Reign of Terror, Tussaud was commissioned to make molds of guillotined heads (like that of Marie Antoinette and Louis XVI). Hey, it was a scary time. She did what she had to do. But, after the Terror ended, she took those heads and started touring England, Ireland, and Scotland with them. It became a big hit and eventually turned into this whole creepy wax museum empire. Thanks for the nightmare fuel, Madame.

7. WILLIAM BLIGH
1806 - New South Wales (Australia)

The famous captain of the *Bounty* (of *Mutiny on the Bounty* fame) was known to have a short temper but was never charged with mistreatment of his crew during the 1797 incident. In fact, after the mutiny, he was promoted several times. In 1806, Bligh was made governor of New South Wales, where he treated even more people terribly. While the colony (which was mostly populated with minor criminals) had started to evolve into a productive society, Bligh wanted to continue to run it like a prison. When he discovered some officers were trading rum on the side, he shut it down. Bligh's typical lack of tact led to a much bigger confrontation—in this case, a military coup called the Rum Rebellion. Less than eighteen months into the job, he was again reassigned, but this time to a position where he wasn't the guy in charge.

6. THOMAS JEFFERSON
1807 - Washington, D.C.

While Jefferson's successes—the Louisiana Purchase, Lewis and Clark's expedition, and great economic plans—were all revered, they also represented political one-eightys. Jefferson's embargoes, ordered in an attempt to stay neutral in the war between Britain and France, managed to piss everyone off. But, way worse than being a hypocrite and a subpar foreign policy guy, Thomas Jefferson was a despicable slave owner. While slave owners are often explained away by being a product of a different time, Thomas "all men are created equal" Jefferson went above and beyond in his deplorable treatment of non-whites. In his lifetime, he owned more than six hundred slaves. He ripped apart families and had children whipped. The only slaves he freed were the ones he fathered. In retirement, he had a real opportunity to help right some of those wrongs, but instead he doubled down. He was chock full of fallacious ideas that essentially went like this: "let's teach black people to print but not write (because they'll turn to forgery)," or, "we can't give blacks their deserved emancipation because unleashing black people on the white population would be disastrous." When he had issues with the Missouri Compromise, he fired off a strongly worded letter that bemoaned the fact that we couldn't just ignore slavery instead of drawing a specific line of demarcation. In 1824, the slave-owning-and-sexing Jefferson finally came up with a solution to end slavery: ship all the slaves born in America down to Santo Domingo (Haiti). Bravo, Tommy. Let's tear families apart and dump our "problems" on a small island a couple thousand miles away!

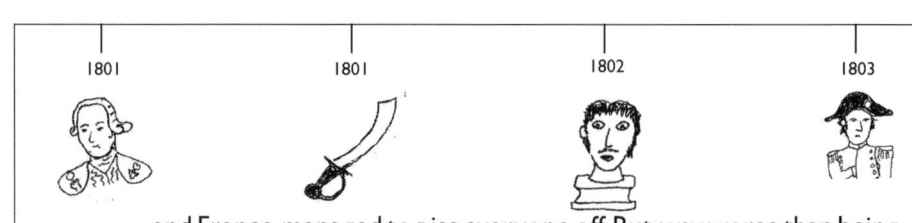

5. AARON BURR
1804 - Weehawken, New Jersey

In many ways, Aaron Burr was a man ahead of his time. The commendable Revolutionary War hero worked hard at making government more transparent and elections more democratic. He also improved the infrastructure and the financial stability of the lower classes and treated women as intellectual equals. Alexander Hamilton was also a principled man who happened to disagree with and personally dislike Burr. When the 1800 election came down to Jefferson and Burr (two guys whom Hamilton greatly opposed), Hamilton publicly backed the one he thought would make the better president—Jefferson. A few years later, the scorned Burr challenged Hamilton to a duel, won the duel, and killed a great American (who, by the way, shot into the air rather than at Burr). After that, the disgraced Burr's plan B was an attempt to take away the southwestern part of the Louisiana Territory and Mexico and create an independent country (where he could be leader). The plan failed. Sorry, bro. Nobody wanted you in charge.

4. BARBARY PIRATES
1801 - Tripoli, Libya

The newly formed United States relied heavily on exports to keep itself afloat. But every time American merchant ships tried to carry goods through the Mediterranean, pirates from Tripoli attacked them. While the pirates claimed it was their duty to kill non-believers (non-Muslims, that is), they really were just shaking the U.S. down for money. Over time, the bribe money grew to be 20 percent of the national budget. Finally, America had enough, built up the navy and marines, and attacked the pirates. After two wars with the pirates over a fifteen-year span, American ships were done being harassed by the Tripoli pirates. And that is why the first line of the Marine Hymn features "the shores of Tripoli."

3. JAMES WILKINSON
1809 - New Orleans, Louisiana

Former Revolutionary War general James Wilkinson's quest to be rich and powerful took him down some dark paths. After Jefferson bought the Louisiana Territory, Wilkinson tried to get paid by America's neighbor to the south (Spain) by giving them coordinates on how to thwart Lewis and Clark's expedition. Wilkinson then aligned himself with Aaron Burr (who was planning a traitorous plot to take over the southwestern part of the territory). When that plan didn't work out, he ratted out Burr. Oh, and he may have murdered Meriwether Lewis.

2. PHILIP GIDLEY KING
1801 - New South Wales (Australia)

When you show up in someone else's home uninvited, you're probably going meet a little resistance. And that's the response the British got from the Aborigines when they landed in what's now Australia. The new Governor Philip King needed to step up and provide a solution that would restore peace in the region. His grand plan? Give the colonists free rein to shoot any Aborigine in sight.

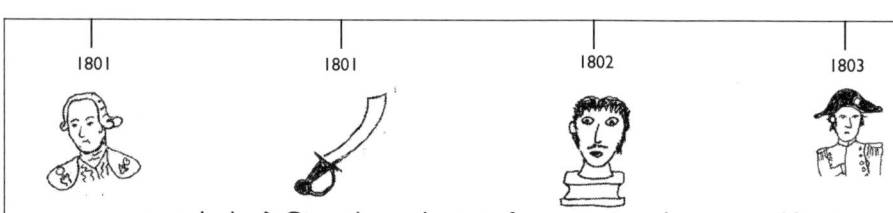

1. NAPOLEON BONAPARTE
1803 - Paris, France

Usually, when parents send their kids off to military school, they're hoping for a little more focus and discipline to be instilled. The Bonapartes sent their five-foot-six son to military school and he graduated as one of the most notorious monsters the world has ever known. After the revolution, France was vulnerable to a powerful leader with a clear vision. Napoleon pandered to his weary fellow citizens and seized the role. Once in charge of the French military, Napoleon attacked every major neighboring country—Austria, Holland, Spain, Italy, and others. All that combat led to two massive problems: one, the country went broke (which forced him into one of the worst real estate deals of all time—the Louisiana Purchase); and two, success made Napoleon even more bloodthirsty and careless. Napoleon invaded Russia in the middle of winter (which is about as smart as, well, invading Russia in winter), got his ass kicked, and spent a year in exile. After twelve months, he gave it another shot and arrogantly invaded Waterloo, a small town in Belgium, where British and Prussian forces were well-positioned to destroy French troops. His final mission was being exiled by his countrymen... this time, for good.

1804　　　　　1806　　　　　1807　　　　　1809

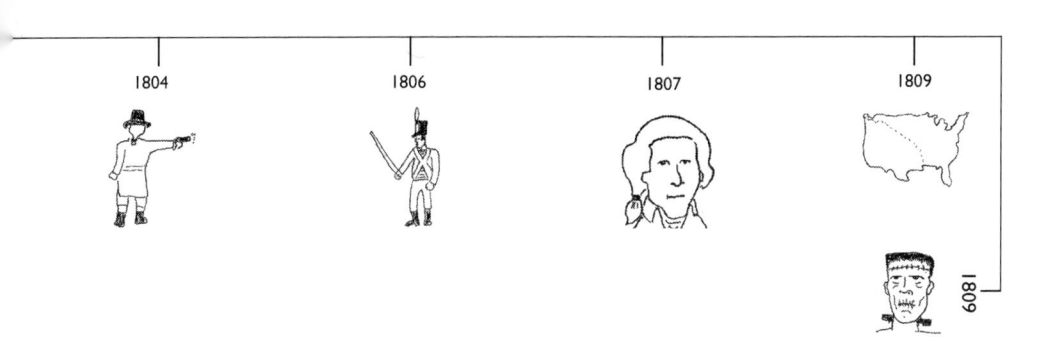

1809

| 1810 | 1811 | 1811 | 1812 | 1813 |

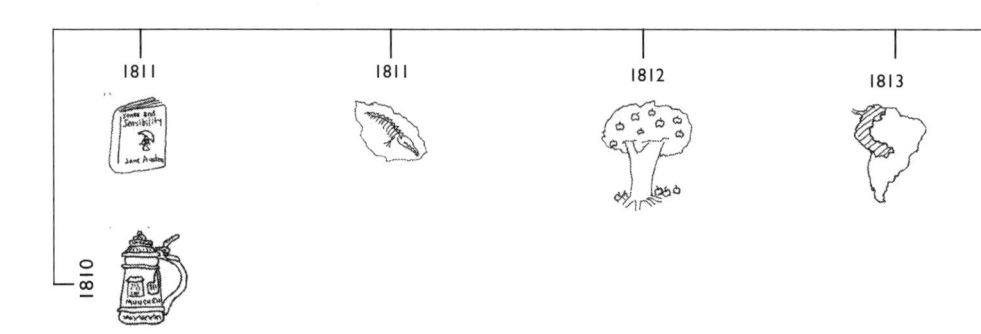

1810-1819

"An ignorant people is the blind instrument of its own destruction."
-Simon Bolivar

1814	1816	1817	1817

1819

BEST

10. CROWN PRINCE LUDWIG
1810 - Munich, Bavaria (Germany)

Normally, going to a wedding where you barely know the couple getting married is about as fun as getting a colonoscopy. But in the case of the marriage of the Crown Prince of Bavaria and Princess Therese, everyone in Munich was invited to the party, *and* it was fun. They had music. They had horse races. And they had lots and lots of beer. The following year, the prince (who would later be king) threw another celebration. And, with that, Oktoberfest was born. The annual celebration (where more than a million gallons of beer is consumed each year) is still enjoyed today.

9. JOHN CHAPMAN
1812 - Mansfield, Ohio

Normally when you cross paths with a barefoot nomad in a flour bag spouting off about religion and vegetarianism, you try to avoid him. John Chapman was that guy but he was also the American folk hero known as Johnny Appleseed. In the early 1800s, drinking water was a dangerous proposition. Only poor people drank it (and risked death due to contaminants). If they had the means, people drank cider. So Chapman purchased land throughout New York, Pennsylvania, and Ohio, planted apple seeds, gave the land to people less fortunate, and moved on. Also, during the War of 1812, Chapman saved even more lives by making a thirty-mile journey (some say on his bare feet) to warn settlers of an impending attack by the British and natives.

8. DOLLEY MADISON
1814 - Washington, D.C.

During James Madison's term as president of the United States, America was still struggling to find its way. And the uncharismatic five-foot-four bookworm was hardly the guy to put everyone at ease. But he married well. His wife,

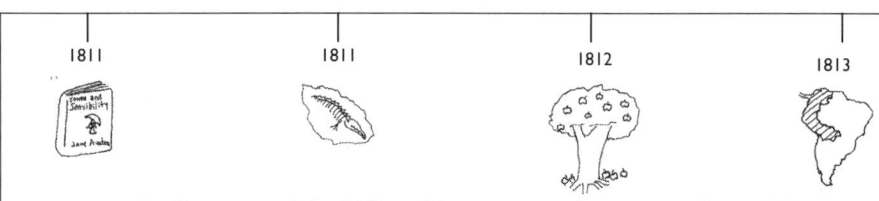

Dolley, turned the White House into a big party where differences were ironed out and ordinary Americans felt welcome. Not only was the First Lady a tremendous ambassador, but also she was pretty cool. During the War of 1812, the British burned down most of Washington. Everyone from guards to staffers got the hell out of town. Dolley was urged to take off as well but refused to go without first packing valuable presidential artifacts (including a famous portrait of George Washington).

7. MARY ANNING
1811 - Lyme Regis, England

Eleven-year-old Mary Anning used to stroll the seashore in her southern England town to look for shells to sell. One day in 1811, Mary spotted a skull sticking out of some rock. She carefully chipped away at it and uncovered the first ever complete fossil of several dinosaur species. It turned out that the area was flush with them. Soon thereafter, scientists from all over flocked to Lyme Regis to speak with Anning. Despite her lack of a formal education and any sort of financial backing, Mary was described as "the most important fossilist the world ever knew." Not bad for a kid in her awkward years.

6. RENE LAENNEC
1816 - Paris, France

Before 1816, when a doctor wanted to examine a heartbeat, he just jammed his head against the patient's chest and listened. This was problematic for several reasons: one, it was inexact; two, it was 1816 and most people smelled terrible; and three, patients (especially women) were subjected to random guys rubbing their heads against their chests. Enter Rene Laennec, a shy physician who didn't feel particularly comfortable pushing his head against a plump woman's large chest one day. So he rolled up twenty-four sheets of paper and put it over her heart. Over the next few years he fine-tuned it and called it the "stethoscope" (a combination of the Greek words for "chest" and "examination").

1814　　　　　　1816　　　　　　　1817　　　　　　　　1817

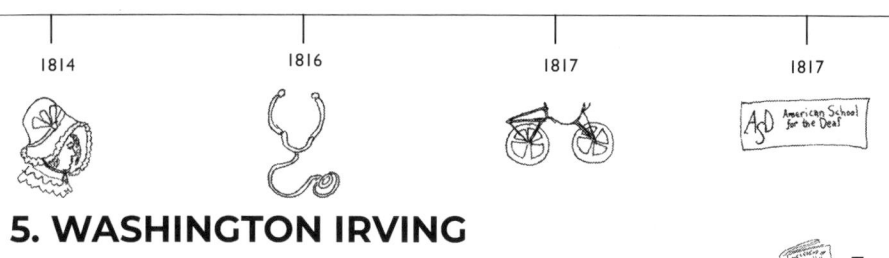

5. WASHINGTON IRVING
1819 - New York, New York

Washington Irving was America's first star. The writer of *The Legend of Sleepy Hollow* and *Rip Van Winkle* was successful both in the U.S. and abroad. What set Irving apart from writers before him was his ability to work across genres—from biography to comedy to horror. No matter what he wrote, Irving's storytelling abilities connected with a vast audience. Before America had Scorsese, it had Washington Irving.

4. THOMAS GALLAUDET
1817 - Hartford, Connecticut

Thomas Gallaudet was a brilliant guy (he graduated first in his class at Yale when he was only seventeen) who was determined to become a preacher. Then he met his neighbor's deaf nine-year-old daughter and felt compelled to study methods for teaching students who couldn't hear. First he went to England and tried to learn from the Braidwood family, but they were kind of selfish pricks about sharing their methods. Then he met with Abbe Sicard, who invited Gallaudet to visit his school for the deaf in Paris. Sicard and his colleagues generously shared their techniques using the manual method of communication. Gallaudet then returned to America and worked tirelessly to raise the funds for the American School for the Deaf. Once it opened, his first student to be admitted was his neighbor's daughter. The school is still in operation today.

3. KARL DRAIS
1817 - Mannheim, Germany

After a volcanic eruption on an Indonesian island in 1815, dust settled all over the globe. Because of this, 1816 didn't really have a summer—which was catastrophic for farming. The crop shortage was disastrous for many horses, which were weakened by or died of starvation. Along came Karl Drais, Mannheim's chief forest ranger, who had a lot of ground to cover at his job yet no horses to help him. Drais invented the velocipede, a two-wheeled vehicle with no pedals. Yep, the prototype of a bicycle. Drais continued to invent things like a meat grinder, a typewriter, and a contraption that recorded piano music on punch paper.

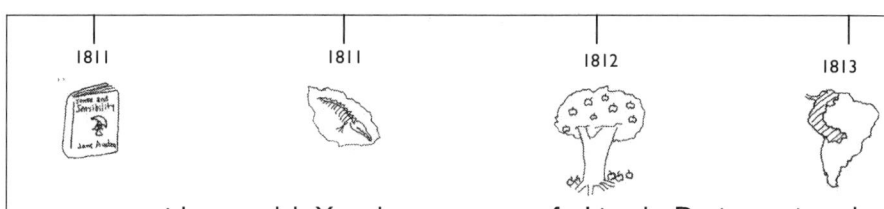

2. JANE AUSTEN
1811 - Hampshire, England

At age thirty-six, Jane Austen published her first novel, Sense and Sensibility, anonymously (identified only as "a lady"). Over the next few years, she also wrote *Pride and Prejudice* (1813), *Mansfield Park* (1814), and *Emma* (1816). While her novels achieved modest success during her lifetime, it wasn't until about a century later that people truly recognized her greatness. Thanks to still relatable subject matter (and the fact that Hollywood struggles to come up with new ideas), her work is as influential today as it ever was. Whether it's *Clueless* (the Beverly Hills version of *Emma*) or *Bridget Jones* (the modern London version of *Pride and Prejudice*), Austen's humorous tales of love and social status are never going away.

1. SIMON BOLIVAR
1813 - Caracas, Venezuela

In the early nineteenth century, Spain pretty much had South America all to itself. Then, when Napoleon named his brother head of Spain and all its colonies, a guy with some serious muttonchops named Simon Bolivar took a stand. The Venezuelan-born Bolivar led various campaigns which eventually led to freedom from Spanish rule for the territory that would become Venezuela, Colombia, Peru, and Ecuador. El Libatador ("the Liberator") was so revered, they even named Bolivia after him. Sure, he tried to name himself president for life (which didn't go over quite as well) but you can't blame a boy for trying.

| 1814 | 1816 | 1817 | 1817 | 1819 |

Honorable Mentions: Laura Secord - 1813 (badass who took over for fallen husband in the War of 1812), Mary Shelley - 1818 (*Frankenstein*)

WORST

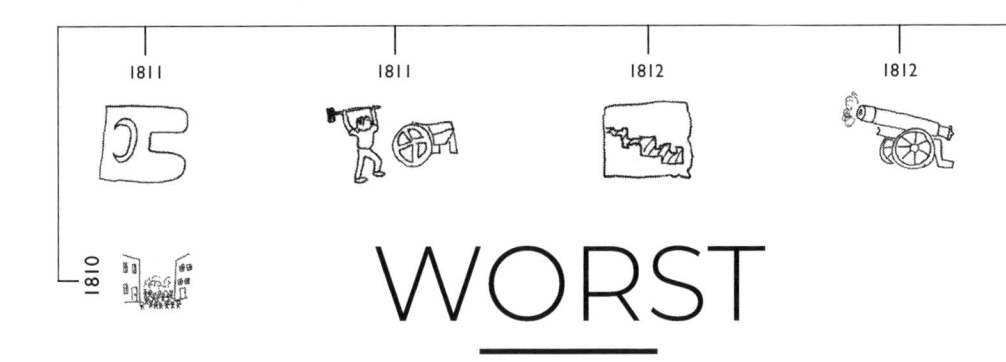

10. THEODORE HOOK
1810 - London, England

When someone is known as a practical joker, chances are that person is just an asshole. Thomas Hook was one of those assholes. For no apparent reason, the well-to-do Hook hired a ton of random tradespeople (barbers, wine merchants, painters, grocers, and so on) and sent them to the home of some rich lady for a supposed job. Hook's famous prank led to chaos, a horrible traffic jam, and a wasted day for many hardworking people around London. The big takeaway from the day: pranks are for jerk-offs.

9. LUDDITES
1811 - Nottingham, England

While today's usage of the term "Luddite" doesn't exactly match up to what the Luddites of two hundred years ago stood for, they were still the dingbats of the workplace. Thanks to the Napoleonic Wars, England was plagued with widespread poverty. In addition to that problem, the Industrial Revolution led to an influx of machines that made many jobs redundant. So the Luddites went to factories with sledgehammers and smashed as many of those job-stealing machines as they could. The hope was that if they smashed the machines, the factory owners would see the error of their ways and hire back the twenty guys needed to do the work of one machine. The movement died down when the Luddites realized you can't fight change (and property damage leads to arrest).

8. GEORGE CRICK'S BOSS
1814 - London, England

When you hear the phrase "beer flood," you might imagine a

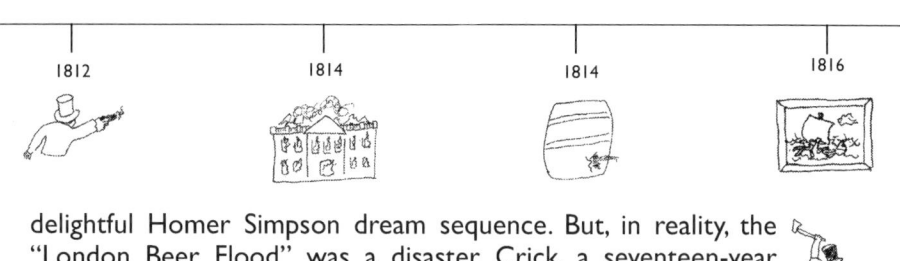

delightful Homer Simpson dream sequence. But, in reality, the "London Beer Flood" was a disaster. Crick, a seventeen-year employee of the Meux and Co. Brewery, noticed that one of the seven hundred-pound iron hoops holding a vat together was broken. He reported it, but his boss just told him to write it down in a letter. Within a few hours, the vat burst, which caused another vat to burst… and 8,500 barrels of beer flooded the nearby neighborhood, causing eight women and children to drown. D'oh!

7. WILLIAM WINDER
1814 - Bladensburg, Maryland

Good military leaders have several qualities in common: they're inspirational, they're great tacticians, and they're unrelenting. None of those words would describe William Winder. The Potomac District general had massive advantages in both number of troops and position against the advancing British in the War of 1812, yet somehow he failed. British Major General Robert Ross landed ashore and easily overmatched Winder's shoddy troops en route to Washington. Within a few hours, Winder had folded. By evening, the White House was set on fire. You had one job, Winder!

6. JOHN BELLINGHAM
1812 - London, England

British Prime Minister Spencer Perceval was a garbage politician. Under his watch the country was broke, and in true holier-than-thou fashion, he persecuted people who didn't completely agree with him. He needed to go. And he did… but not for those reasons. Crummy businessman John Bellingham got into a bad deal in Russia and ended up in jail for five years. Upon his release, he went to Parliament and expected to be compensated for his losses. Parliament wasn't on board. So he killed the prime minister. That is what you call an overreaction.

5. HENRY ADDINGTON
1819 - London, England

After the Napoleonic Wars, England was a hot mess. People were poor, hungry, and disenchanted with their government. So, in 1819, a large group rose up in Manchester in a peaceful protest calling for Parliament reform. Soldiers swooped in, the situation turned ugly, and dozens were killed. The mood after that didn't exactly improve. Nobleman Henry Addington, in all his wisdom, used the situation to propose harsher laws to Parliament—namely, the Six Acts. Essentially, any meeting calling for any sort of reform would be considered an act of treason with harsh penalties. Shockingly, the Six Acts didn't prove to be effective.

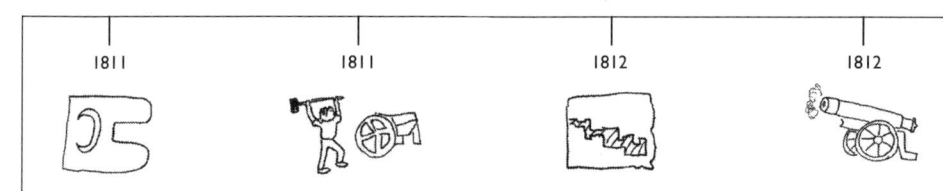

4. MOHAMED ALI
1811 - Cairo, Egypt

Mohamed Ali strengthened and modernized Egypt and is considered one of its greatest leaders. He was also a crummy guy. Ali shrewdly worked his way up through the military and political ranks but still struggled with controlling the Mamluks (descendants of the slave-warrior class). So, one evening in 1811, he invited the Mamluks over to the citadel for a feast. The five hundred or so Mamluks were treated to a pleasant discussion, then were led down a narrow, closed-off hallway. Ali's soldiers opened fire from above on the trapped group. Next, they stormed Cairo and killed a few thousand more Mamluks. That's how Ali achieved total control. Plus, the guy fathered ninety-five kids. Can you imagine the insecurities a good ninety-three of them must've grown up with?

3. HUGUES DUROY DE CHAUMEREYS
1816 - Senegal

The subject of a famous Louvre painting, *The Raft of the Medusa*, was based on a very real and terrible event, thanks to de Chaumereys. In 1816, while leading his ship, the *Medusa*, on an expedition to repossess the West African colony of Senegal, de Chaumereys ran into a sandbank. There weren't enough lifeboats so the captain proposed they take apart some of the *Medusa* and fashion a raft to be towed by the ship. That didn't work, so de Chaumereys cut the tow rope and left the men onboard the raft to fend for themselves with only some wine and a few biscuits.

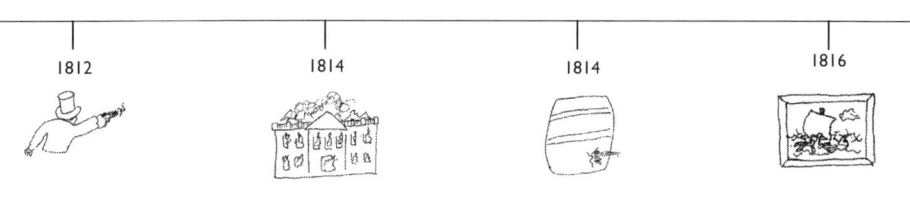

The 147 quickly turned to suicide, murder, and cannibalism. By the time the raft was rescued, only fifteen men were alive (and five of those men died shortly after).

2. HENRY DEARBORN
1812 - Washington, D.C.

During the American Revolution, Henry Dearborn valiantly fought in the Battle of Bunker Hill and others. After the war he served in the House of Representatives and several other decorated posts for the new nation. He did some bad stuff too, though. As Secretary of War, Dearborn helped plan mass Indian removals west of the Mississippi River. His belief that Canada was ripe for the picking was a major contributor to the War of 1812 (a dumb war where both sides claimed success but neither actually achieved it). The Canada invasion was a costly waste of time and resources. Dearborn was eventually removed from his post and sent out to pasture.

1. ELBRIDGE GERRY
1812 - Cambridge, Massachusetts

The Massachusetts governor signed into law a plan to divide electoral districts in a way that benefitted his political party greatly. *The Boston Gazette* called him out on it and combined his last name with the gibe "salamander" to form the word "gerrymander." More than two centuries later (from the division of the Dakotas to pick up two Republican-leaning states instead of one, to the marginalization of minorities in the Deep South in the 1960s), Gerry's appalling legacy continues.

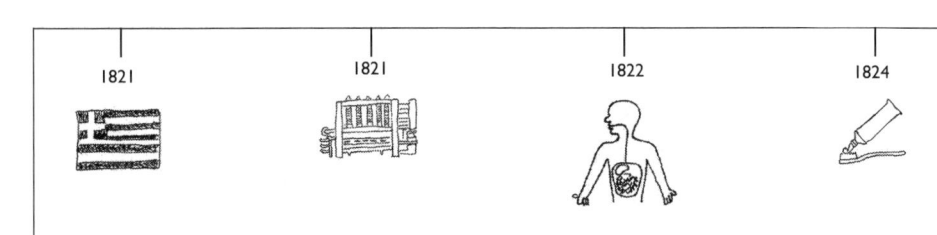

1820-1829

"...to the victor belong the spoils."
-New York Senator William L. Marcy (after Andrew Jackson's 1828 presidential victory)

BEST

10. THE WORKIES
1827 - Philadelphia, Pennsylvania

Life sucked for the Philadelphia working class. Men were expected to work twelve hours a day, six days a week, and in terrible conditions. Then, in June of 1827, a group of carpenters finally walked out on the job. They were soon followed by bricklayers, painters, and many other craftsmen, all demanding a ten-hour workday. By October, the group of laborers made it official and became the first ever union across craft lines—the Mechanics Union of Trade Association (or "the Workies"). The city of Philadelphia conceded, and more than fifty professions had their daily work hours reduced from twelve to ten.

9. MANTO MAVROGENOUS AND LASKARINA BOUBOULINA
1821 - Spetses, Ottoman Empire (Greece)

The old saying "behind every great man is a great woman" is unbelievably condescending. It's basically an approving pat on the head. Well, during the Greek War of Independence, it was abundantly clear that two particular women were great on their own. For hundreds of years, Greece was mostly ruled by the Ottoman Empire. Any attempt made by the Greeks to break free quickly fizzled out, mostly due to a lack of financial backing. But Mavrogenous and Bouboulina changed that in 1821. Instead of enjoying a cushy, conflict-free life, the two rich women spent all their money bankrolling the Greek nationalists' successful fight for independence.

8. WILLIAM BEAUMONT
1822 - Mackinack Island, Michigan

When life gave Alexis St. Martin lemons, William Beaumont turned it into lemonade for just about everyone but Alexis St. Martin. The twenty-year-old St. Martin was accidentally shot in the side while hunting and Beaumont, an army doctor, treated him. While he was able to save St. Martin's life, Beaumont was unable to completely close the wound. As Beaumont fed St. Martin and nursed him back to good health, the open hole in his side allowed Beaumont to observe the digestive process. Beaumont continued to experiment with and study St. Martin for another decade. His findings laid the foundation for how the medical community understands the digestive process today. And despite the disgusting gaping hole in his abdomen, St. Martin lived a long, healthy life.

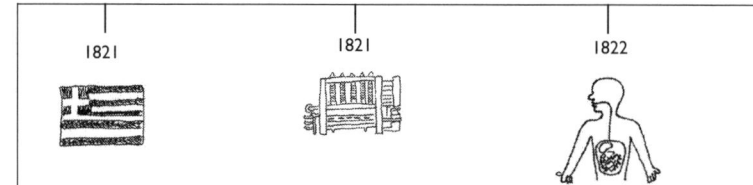

7. LOUIS BRAILLE
1824 - Paris, France

A twelve-year-old student at the National Institute for Blind Youth listened to Captain Charles Barbier of French Army explain how the troops tried to communicate silently in the dark using raised dots on paper to represent sounds. The method never really panned out for the soldiers, but Louis Braille thought it might work for blind kids. For the next few years, Braille worked to create a simple system that would allow the average blind student to read and communicate. By the age of fifteen, he had perfected the six-dot Braille system. Nearly two hundred years later, this basic system is still used around the world in hundreds of languages.

6. THOMAS HANCOCK
1820 - London, England

Thomas Hancock lived in a world where people had to button all their undergarments. Bras had no support. Socks were baggy pieces of cloth around people's ankles. A world with baggy socks and poorly-fitted bras is a world with no hope. Then Hancock developed a way to turn rubber strips into elastic. So the next time you go to the gym or have an IDGAF day where you just want to wear sweats, thank Thomas Hancock.

5. SAMUEL MORSE
1825 - New Haven, Connecticut

In 1825, if you were delivering urgent news, it was a good idea to be within speaking distance to the person receiving it. Otherwise, you could expect a major delay. Unfortunately for portrait artist Samuel Morse, learning of his wife's complications from childbirth and subsequent death took far too long. While working in Washington, D.C., he received news of his wife's condition. By the time he got back to New Haven to see her, she had already been buried. From that point on, the heartbroken Morse set out to invent a way to communicate instantly. Several years later, Morse met an inventor, Charles Thomas Jackson, and the two began working on his idea. The telegraph was finally finished in 1837.

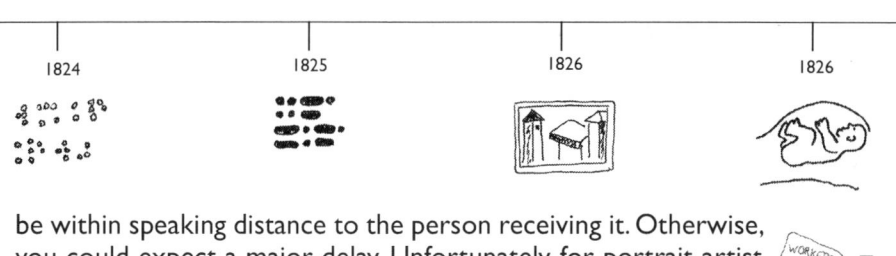

4. JAMES BARRY
1826 - Capetown, South Africa

Two hundred years ago, Caesarean sections were a brutal, last-resort option that resulted in the mother's death. But, in 1826, British Army surgeon James Barry performed the first ever successful C-section in which both the mother and baby lived. Barry had a checkered four-plus-decade military career full of promotions, demotions, admirers, and enemies. He was lauded for improving hygiene standards at medical facilities and making great strides in the treatment for cholera. Oh… and he also happened to be a woman. Turns out that Margaret Ann Bulkley had posed as a man in order to be admitted into medical school. From there, the *Mrs. Doubtfire*-like charade lasted for forty-six years in the British Army. Her true sex wasn't known by the army until her autopsy in 1865.

3. JOSEPH-NICEPHORE NIEPCE
1826 - Chalon-sur-Saône, France

After inventing the Pyréolophore (a combination of the Greek words for "fire," "wind," and "I produce") in 1807, Joseph and his brother Claude spent the better part of two decades perfecting their internal-combustion engine. When Claude took their invention to London to promote it, Joseph turned his attention to the French fad of lithography. He just had to overcome two problems: he was a subpar artist, and he didn't have proper lithographic stones. So he set out to make pictures automatically.

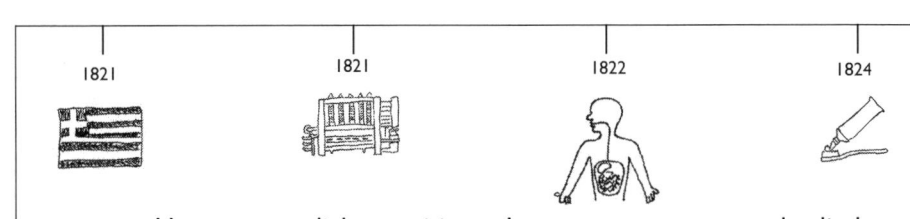

He put some light-sensitive substances on pewter and relied on the sun to expose an image. The end result? The first photograph. Thanks to a smart guy who couldn't draw, people of the future were able to document images of objects as they actually were, not just as they appeared through an artist's interpretation.

2. DR. PEABODY
1824 - USA

Not a whole lot is known about Dr. Peabody, not even his first name. But it is widely accepted that this American dentist was the first person to use soap in toothpaste to, you know, actually get teeth clean. Before Peabody's cleaning paste, people were using burnt toast, egg shells, and salt to try to clean their mouths. So, if ever given the chance to climb in a time machine, it's probably best to choose a destination after the year 1824.

1. CHARLES BABBAGE
1821 - London, England

Babbage, a brilliant mathematician and inventor of such things as the metal guard in front of a train that clears its path (the cowcatcher), had grown frustrated with the shoddy work he found on astronomical tables. Human calculation errors had a frequent negative impact on society, from financial mistakes which damaged businesses to navigational errors which wrecked ships. So he set out to create an automatized method of making these computations. Over the next decade, Babbage worked on what he called the "Difference Engine." This calculator-like machine eventually morphed into the "Analytical Engine," which is now considered the first ever computer.

1824   1825   1826   1826

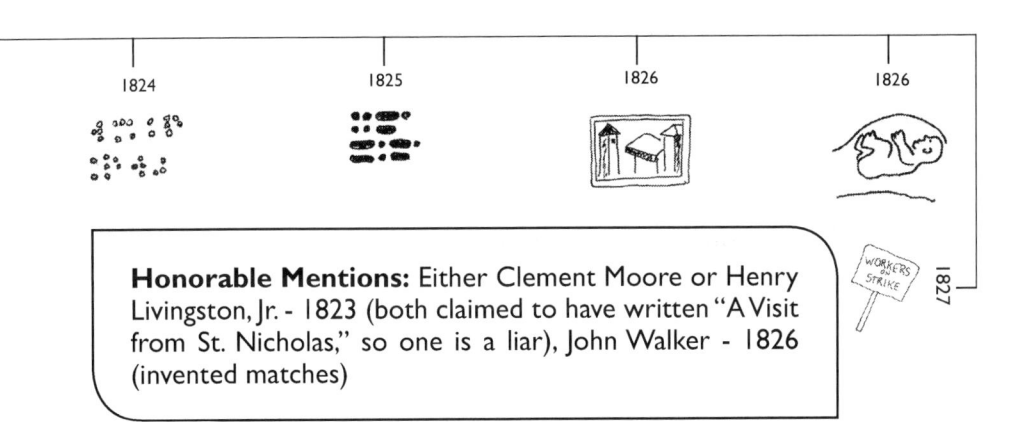

1827

Honorable Mentions: Either Clement Moore or Henry Livingston, Jr. - 1823 (both claimed to have written "A Visit from St. Nicholas," so one is a liar), John Walker - 1826 (invented matches)

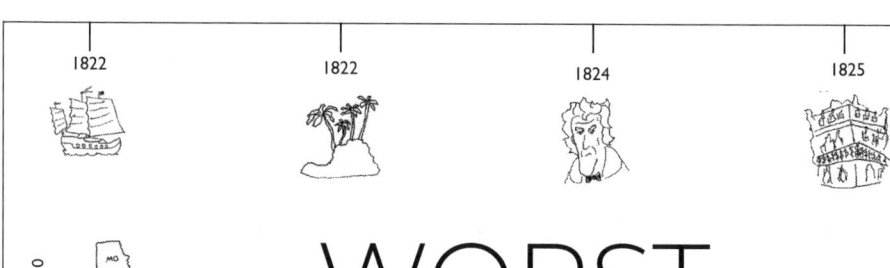

WORST

10. CYRILL DEMIAN
1829 - Vienna, Austria

Demian, an Austrian organ builder, created a free-reed instrument with buttons and called it the *"akkordeon"* (from the Italian word *accordare* for "sound together"). The instrument's buttons allowed the player to produce multiple harmonies, thus eliminating the need for a multi-instrument band. The other thing accordions eliminate? Fun.

9. ETHAN ALLEN HITCHCOCK
1826 - West Point, New York

West Point used to be kind of a joke. Anyone was accepted for attendance and there were only three teachers. Then, after the U.S. military's shaky performance in the War of 1812, more emphasis was placed on improving the academy. Enter Colonel Sylvanus Thayer, a hard-ass who whipped the institution into the well-oiled machine that you see today. One of his rules was no alcohol. This was a problem for the students, especially those looking to blow off some end-of-the-year steam. On Christmas Eve 1826, Captain Hitchcock served as the hall monitor for the cadets. Sometime after midnight, Hitchcock was woken up by some guys who had snuck in a few gallons of whiskey to add to their eggnog. Instead of looking the other way and letting the cadets enjoy some Christmas Eve cheer, Hitchcock stormed the dorms and became the fun police. Hitchcock's angry confrontation led to the so-called "Eggnog Riot." Nearly a third of the campus was reprimanded (including Jefferson Davis) and nineteen cadets were expelled.

8. EDWARD GIBBON WAKEFIELD
1827 - Liverpool, England

Edward Wakefield desperately wanted to become rich and powerful but wasn't a fan of hard work. So he married rich, but then she died. Since he didn't feel like going through the whole courtship thing for a second time, he thought he'd just coerce another rich heiress into marriage. In 1827, Wakefield showed up at a boarding school with his brother and kidnapped fifteen-year-old heiress Ellen Turner. His plan was thwarted shortly thereafter and he was thrown in jail. While in prison and unable to procure any more rich girls, Wakefield was bored enough to start using his brain. He came up with ways to utilize the British colonies of Australia and New Zealand for greater economic profit. His influential essays dramatically changed his nation's approach to colonization. Ed Wakefield—kid toucher, colonial reformer.

7. IO TAUKO
1822 - Gaspar Straits (Indonesia)

Thanks to a crippling nationwide addiction to opium, China's economy was on the fade. Any trading vessel was pivotal to keep the struggling country afloat. So, Io Tauko loaded down his ship (*Tek Sing*) with porcelain, silk, and spices, destined for Jakarta. On top of that, sixteen hundred emigrants boarded in hopes of finding a better life working on sugar plantations. Besides dangerously overloading the ship, Captain Io Tauko carelessly took shortcuts which led the ship into a nasty storm. They hit a reef and capsized, everyone died, and the remains weren't found for a couple hundred years.

6. HENRY VALANCE
1826 - Batavia, New York

In 1826, William Morgan learned the hard way that snitches get stitches. The ex-freemason Morgan wanted to expose the shady, secretive world of the Masons in a book but, before it was published, Henry Valance took Morgan to the Niagara River and dumped him in the falls. The Masons already had a bad reputation.

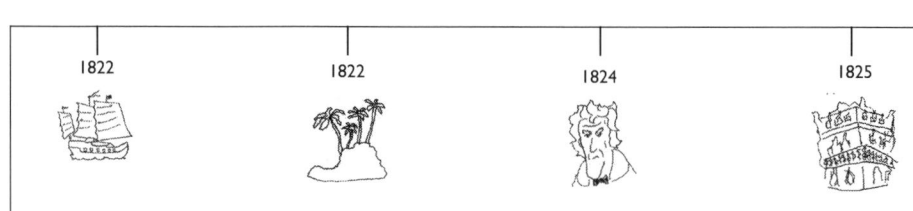

Morgan's murder didn't help. On his deathbed, Valance later confessed to the murder—which, in a sense, made him a snitch too.

5. GREGOR MCGREGOR
1822 - London, England

In 1820, a guy with a ridiculous name (Gregor McGregor) met with investors and showed them a document signed by King Frederic Augustus anointing him the title of prince of Poyais (located along the Bay of Honduras). Since most Britons at the time didn't know a whole lot about Central America, they believed him. After hearing of Poyais' thriving community with a central banking system, an army, and willing native workers, they invested £200,000 (over $20 million today) in Poyais bonds. The reality is, a drunken King Augustus signed a document giving McGregor access to a small area of infertile land with four rundown buildings. By the time the investors learned it was a scam, McGregor was out of the country.

4. MARK JEFFRIES
1826 - Hobart, Australia

Bushrangers were criminals in the British colony of Australia who escaped imprisonment and went out in the bush to evade law enforcement. They were, for the most part, bad dudes. And then there was Mark Jefferies. Unlike other more colorful bushrangers who have since been immortalized in Australian lore, Jefferies was just an animal. After initial time served, Jeffries got a seemingly perfect job for his sadistic nature: flagellator (the guy who flogged people) at the Launceston Gaol. It didn't last long. Soon enough he was back to his violent life of crime (robbing, raping, murdering, eating people). Finally, in 1826 a guy named Batman (John Batman) caught the murderous cannibal and hanged him.

3. HENRY CLAY
1820 - Washington, D.C.

Missouri wanted to enter the country. Southerners wanted the "Show Me" State to join as a slave state. The North disagreed.

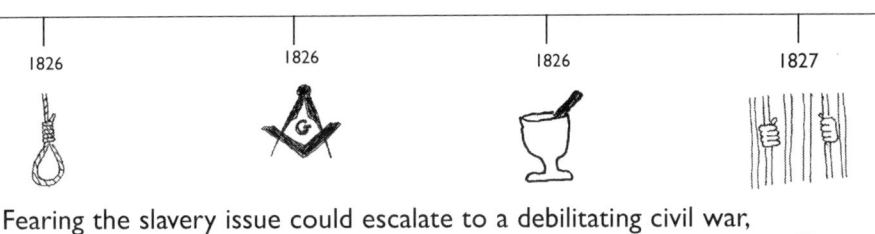

Fearing the slavery issue could escalate to a debilitating civil war, Henry Clay came up with the Missouri Compromise—Missouri enters as a slave state, Massachusetts gets carved into two, the new state that is formed is called Maine and kept a free state, and no more slavery is allowed north of some arbitrary line (the Mason-Dixon Line) going forward. The two sides agreed. Instead of treating slavery like an unconscionable human rights issue, the Kentucky slave owner Clay's proposal just turned it into a political bargaining chip, adding a new slave state in the process.

2. DELFINE LALAURIE
1825 - New Orleans, Louisiana

By 1825, Delphine LaLaurie was on her third husband in New Orleans and living a life of leisure (i.e., slaves waited on her hand and foot). It was well known she treated her servants poorly but, in those days, slaves weren't even considered people. If one of her children showed a modicum of decency towards one of them, LaLaurie would beat them. In 1833, a teenaged slave jumped out of a second-story window to her death rather than face LaLaurie's wrath. But it wasn't until the following year that New Orleans would learn the true depths of LaLaurie's depravity. When a fire broke out in her French Quarter home, people spotted LaLaurie frantically trying to salvage her valuables without any help. When a fire brigade finally arrived to put out the blaze, they discovered a seventy-year-old woman chained to the stove and a torture chamber full of slaves in the attic. Slaves or not, the people of New Orleans had seen enough. Four thousand people looted her home as the fire blazed and LaLaurie fled to Paris.

1. ANDREW JACKSON
1824 - Washington, D.C.

The first six American presidents were wealthy landowners from Virginia or the Adams family. Then came Andrew Jackson, hero of the War of 1812 and the first "common man" to be elected president. And that's pretty much where the cool facts end for the wildly-popular-at-the-time Jackson. The man was a monster. Even if we look past the fact that he actually killed a rival horse breeder for insulting him (duels were an accepted thing back then), we cannot look past the fact that the man was a complete dick. As president, the angry Jackson was an egomaniac who thrived on absolute power. He abused the ability to veto more than all the previous presidents combined. The phrase "...to the victor belong the spoils" was said about Jackson's lack of desire to appease anyone but himself after winning the election. After the Supreme Court found his Indian Removal Act of 1830 unconstitutional, Jackson essentially flipped them the bird and carried it out anyway. He had his troops hold the Georgia Cherokee at gunpoint and forced them to vacate all land east of the Mississippi. More than a quarter of them died on the Trail of Tears. He decided the Bank of the United States was bad for ordinary citizens, so he shut it down (in spite of that move also being deemed unconstitutional). This led to a financial crisis in Martin Van Buren's subsequent presidency. And he enjoyed being the heel. When his rivals called him a jackass, he owned it and turned the donkey into the symbol for the Democratic Party.

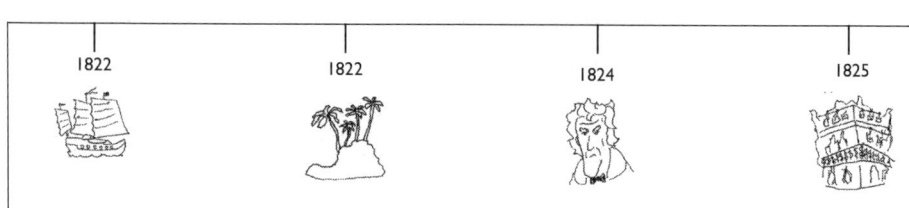

1826　　　1826　　　1826　　　1827

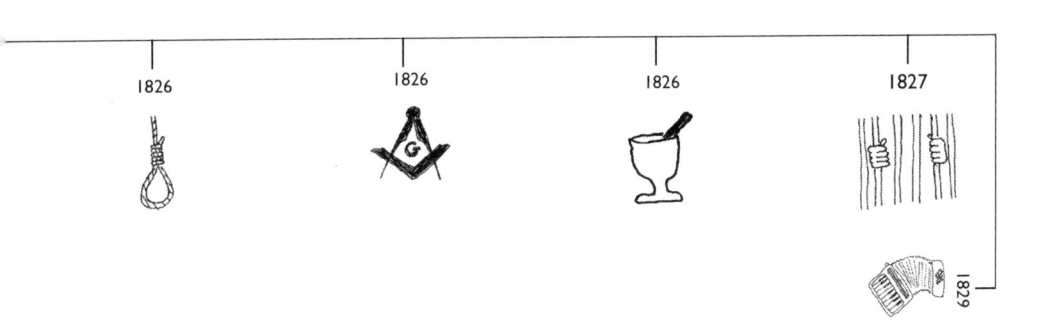

1829

| 1830 | 1830 | 1831 | 1835 |

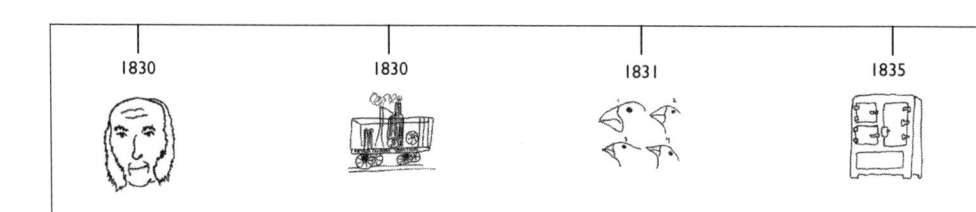

1830

1830-1839

"Have a heart that never hardens, and a temper that never tires, and a touch that never hurts."

-Charles Dickens

BEST

10. ROWLAND HILL
1837 - London, England

In the mid-1830s, the British postage system was a mess. The cost was skyrocketing and, since the burden of payment for mail was the responsibility of the recipient, many letters went unclaimed. So Rowland Hill completely overhauled the postal system. Every letter had a standard charge (one penny), which would be paid up front. Proof of payment would be on a small, black piece of paper with a picture of Queen Victoria affixed to the outside of each letter. The "Penny Black" was an instant success. Within a decade of implementing the first stamp, the number of sent letters quintupled.

9. PETER COOPER
1830 - Ellicott Mills, Maryland

In 1830, Baltimore's fledgling B&O Railroad was struggling to get any real traction with businesses or the general public, who still shipped their cargo via wagon road or canals. Engineer Peter Cooper built a small locomotive and set up a competitive race between his engine, *Tom Thumb*, and a horse-drawn carriage to draw interest. Even though his engine broke during the competition, Cooper accomplished his goal. The horse was clearly giving all it had, but the locomotive was just scratching the surface of its potential. B&O stopped using horse-drawn carriages and, within a couple years, the locomotive was pulling cargo for hundreds of miles. Later in life, Cooper founded the Cooper Union, a tuition-free university for people too poor to afford higher education.

8. JOHN QUINCY ADAMS
1830 - Washington, D.C.

The most productive thing John Quincy Adams did during his unsuccessful presidency was swim naked in the Potomac. But, after his one term was over, Adams returned to Massachusetts and ran for Congress. During his nine post-presidential terms in Congress, Adams did what he thought was right, not what would curry favor with voters or powerful benefactors. Most importantly, he thumbed his nose at the House's ridiculous "gag rule," which prevented members from even bringing up the issue of slavery. Adams brought it up at every turn, regardless of the consequences. Thanks to his persistence, they eventually dropped their dumb gag order.

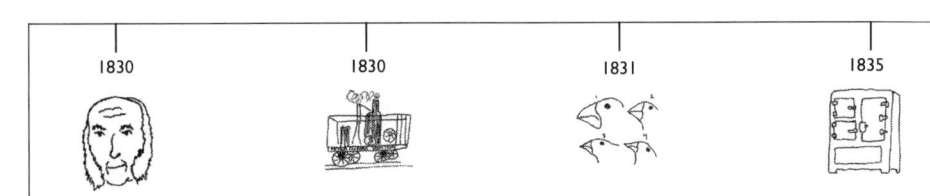

7. DAVID CROCKETT
1830 - Washington, D.C.

The legendary Davy Crockett wasn't exactly the guy that Disney cinematized, but he was definitely a badass. By the time he was thirteen, Crockett was already a skilled hunter and the income provider for his destitute East Tennessee family. He hunted for troops in the Creek War (a war to keep Creek Indians from helping the British in the War of 1812 but, in reality, an excuse for Andrew Jackson to kill natives). Crockett's front row seat to Jackson's despicable treatment of the Creek Indians left a lasting impression. So, after his popularity (and legend) grew in the years following the war, Crockett tried his hand at politics and became a thorn in the side of fellow Southern Democrat Jackson. Crockett called Jackson out on everything from his bumbling of the economy to his disgraceful Indian Removal Act. Jackson's cronies helped defeat Crockett in a reelection bid in 1833. When Jackson's lackey, Martin Van Buren, became the next president, Crockett did what so many disillusioned people threaten to do but never actually do—he left the country. Crockett went to Texas in an attempt to start a new life. Unfortunately, his new life in Texas was located near the Alamo, and Crockett was killed in the battle to defend it.

6. JOHN DEERE
1837 - Grand Detour, Illinois

Deere, a blacksmith, found himself making the same repairs to cast-iron plows over and over again. Clearly these plows struggled with the rough soil of the Midwest. So, one day, he decided to make his own plow out of discarded steel. His curved design was a huge success—the soil just rolled off, making the actual work much less back-breaking. Within a few years, he was making thousands of them and had revolutionized the farming industry.

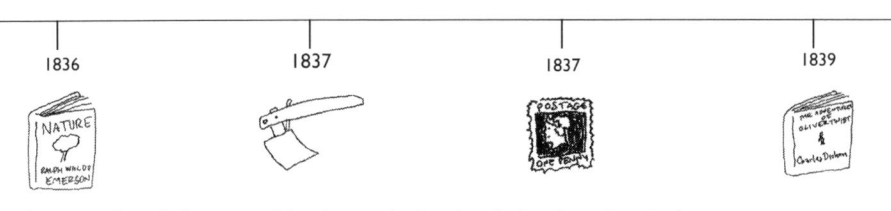

5. CHARLES DARWIN
1831 - Plymouth, England

Twenty-two-year-old Charles Darwin got a job as a naturalist on Captain Robert FitzRoy's five-year survey voyage around the world on the HMS *Beagle*. When the *Beagle* reached the Galapagos Islands a few hundred miles west of South America, Darwin noticed how finches' beaks were different on each island. These observations formed the backbone for his theories on natural selection and evolution. If a species were to survive, it needed to adapt—humans too. Darwin's theories were a slap in the face to the Church back home in England, which staunchly taught that God creates everything exactly in its current form. Despite the backlash, Darwin persevered with his research over the next two decades and, by 1859, his theory of evolution had changed the world.

4. CHARLES GOODYEAR
1839 - Woburn, Massachusetts

Rubber had potential in the field of manufacturing in the Industrial Age, but it wasn't too practical considering it melted in summer's heat and turned brittle in winter. For five years Charles Goodyear took it upon himself to address the latter issue. Eventually all of his investors backed away and Goodyear ended up in debtors' prison. But, in 1839, he mixed sulphur and latex to create a rubber that was resistant to extreme temperatures. He called the process "vulcanization" after Vulcan, the Roman god of fire. Since everyone considered him the kook from debtor's prison, it took him five years to get a patent. By that time, a British raincoat manufacturer had snuck in and stole the idea, leaving Goodyear forever broke. Nearly fifty years later, some other guys started a tire company and named it in Charles' honor.

3. RALPH WALDO EMERSON
1836 - Concord, Massachusetts

After his wife died, Unitarian minister Ralph Waldo Emerson

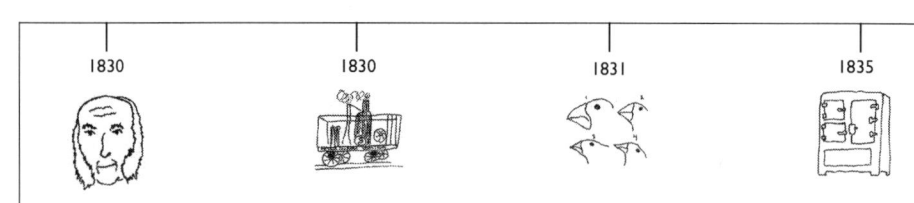

left the church and did some soul searching. He went to Europe, studied Buddhist and Hindu scriptures, met with prominent writers, and returned to America a changed man. But the New England that he returned to seemed like a place bogged down in a believe-whatever-the-church-tells-us-to-believe mindset. When he started writing about his newfound perspective, he became hugely successful. His 1836 essay *Nature* established him as the transcendentalist movement's first major voice. Emerson's writing and guidance greatly influenced Henry David Thoreau, who in turn greatly influenced people like Gandhi and Martin Luther King, Jr.

2. CHARLES DICKENS
1839 - London, England

When Charles Dickens was eleven, he was forced to drop out of school and work at a blacking factory for eleven hours a day. After a few years, Dickens was able to leave the brutal factory work and return to school, but those rough years stayed with him forever. He worked in journalism and wrote fiction on the side. His 1839 novel, *Oliver Twist,* was a massive success for two reasons: one, it was full of great characters who illustrated the social injustices of the Victorian era; two, it was cheap enough to be accessible to the masses. Since only rich people could afford leather-bound books during that time, Dickens' novels were sold in serialized form. His stories built buzz, and soon he was the most popular writer around. A few years later, he wrote *A Christmas Carol*, the greatest holiday story ever told. Despite being over 170 years old, this tale of self-examination and redemption has been adapted hundreds of times (from the Muppets to *The Six Million Dollar Man*). He came out with many other titles which are beloved and widely read to this day.

1. JACOB PERKINS
1835 - London, England

Before Jacob Perkins, people had to do the sniff-and-see-if-it's-still-good test with food every day. Everything was tepid. People ended up pickling and salting much of their meats and produce. Food, like most of early nineteenth-century life, was gross. Then

| 1836 | 1837 | 1837 | 1839 |

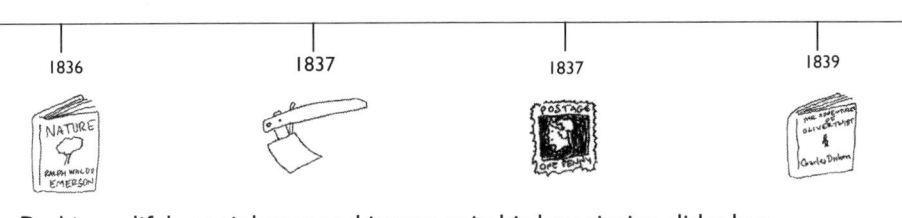

1839

Perkins, a lifelong tinkerer and inventor in his late sixties, did what Benjamin Franklin and Oliver Evans could never complete: the first working refrigerator. Unfortunately, since Freon was ninety-four years away from being discovered, he had to rely on dangerous chemicals like ammonia and ether to cool the food. But it sure beat having meal after meal of pickled meats.

Honorable Mention: Hans Christian Anderson - 1835 (book of fairy tales)

WORST

10. GIACOMO LEOPARDI
1837 - Naples (Italy)

There are downers, and then there was Giacomo Leopardi. The brilliant Italian poet had a rough life and, without question, needed some psychological help. But, while dying from cholera, Leopardi is responsible for writing probably the most depressing set of final thoughts that have ever been published. He wrote thousands of pages saying, essentially, that mankind is doomed. People are incapable of getting better. Society will never improve. We are all doomed to be unhappy. There is no such thing as pleasure. Sorry about the cholera, Giacomo, but you're really bumming us out.

9. DOM PEDRO I
1831 - Rio de Janeiro, Brazil

When Dom Pedro declared Brazil's independence from Portugal in 1822, it was less about gaining independence and more about creating an empire for himself. In 1831, after failed wars with Argentina and Uruguay and a disastrous attempt at dismissing his cabinet, people were fed up with the Brazilian ruler. So Dom Pedro decided to abdicate and bounce back to Portugal. His successor was… his five-year-old son Pedro II. "Hope you don't mind, Brazilians, but you now have to follow orders from someone who regularly falls for the 'Got your nose!' trick."

8. MARTIN VAN BUREN
1830 - Washington, D.C.

The fancily dressed, short-statured New Yorker had two nicknames: one, the "Little Magician" (for his political maneuvering skills); and two, "Blue Whiskey Van" (for his love of booze). As a president, he was somewhere between forgettable and terrible (economic panic of 1837, Trail of Tears, Amistad). But his main legacy is building the horrific monstrosity known as the two-party system in America. In an attempt to break away from regional voting, Van Buren strongly advocated for national parties that represented people across the map. He was staunchly in favor of sticking to the party line, no matter the issue at hand. This led to the dumpster fire we have today in Washington, D.C.: extremists dictating party lines, people compromising themselves socially because of their economic desires, and, most importantly, the stifling of any third-party candidate who might have a realistic shot at winning. Finally, Van Buren is responsible for the birth of the phrase "O.K." during his campaign. He was from Old Kinderhook, New York and said "O.K." to mean things were all good. Sure, we're okay with O.K. these days, but it was the nineteenth-century equivalent of LOL. Problematic.

7. JOSEPH SMITH
1830 - Palmyra, New York

Let's say you meet a guy in upstate New York who claims to be a "seer" (a cooler name for a psychic). And that guy claims that when he was seventeen, some angel named Moroni came to him and told him he buried some gold plates containing ancient texts written in Egyptian characters. He saw the plates, but then they disappeared. But the angel gave him another chance to see the gold plates a year later. In order to decipher the text, the guy would have to stare at magic rock that he hid in his hat. So he buried his head in his hat, stared at the magic rock, and the words came flowing out of him. And he wrote feverishly until the translation was completed. He wanted to publish it immediately, but he was out of cash. As fate would have it, the man told his neighbor that God told him that his neighbor was supposed to pick up the $3,000 publishing tab! And, luckily, he was able to transcribe that entire 588-page text before the gold plates disappeared forever. Would you take his word for all this? That's pretty much the story behind *The Book of Mormon*.

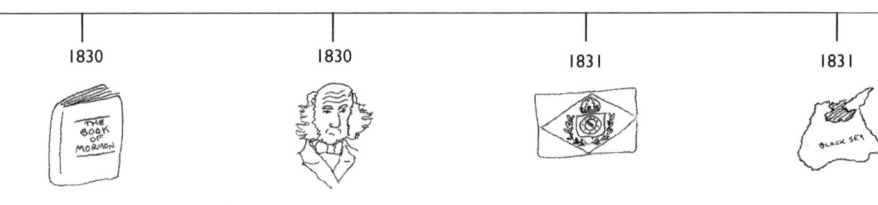

6. PHINEAS TAYLOR BARNUM
1835 - New York, New York

When hustler P.T. Barnum was twenty-five, he heard about a slave from Kentucky, Joice Heth, who claimed to be 161 years old and George Washington's former nurse. So he purchased her and put her on display. The curiosity proved to be a huge hit. And, with that, Barnum kicked off a long career of exploiting people and animals for profit. After touring with his storytelling slave, he set up a freak show museum featuring various curiosities like child dwarf Tom Thumb, Siamese twins Chang and Eng, and the Feejee Mermaid (which was a monkey with a fish tail sewn onto it). When his museum burned down, Barnum took his show on the road and created the three-ring circus, featuring dozens of creepy clowns and tortured animals like Jumbo the elephant. The self-proclaimed "Prince of Humbug" loved the spotlight. Too bad he didn't care how he got it.

5. JANE AND GEORGE BERKSHIRE
1835 - London, England

Jane and George Berkshire were like the evil Ropers from *Three's Company*. The snooping landlords believed one of their tenants (William Bonill) was gay, so they spied on him through his keyhole. They claimed to have witnessed two of his male friends (James Pratt and John Smith) having sex and called the police. Pratt and Smith were charged with "buggery" and hanged. Bonill was deported to Australia for being an accomplice.

4. THE GUY WHO SHOT ELIJAH LOVEJOY
1837 - Alton, Illinois

Elijah Lovejoy had a clear vision of right and wrong and a steel set of balls. The Presbyterian minister moved from Maine (a free state) to Missouri (a slave state) to publish *The St. Louis Observer*, a weekly paper that denounced slavery. The slave-owning locals weren't big fans of his and, one day, they destroyed the *Observer's* printing press. So Lovejoy moved his operation over to Alton, Illinois (a free state) to start the *Alton Observer*. Unfortunately, just because Illinois was a free state didn't mean it was devoid of violent cretins. Shortly after the new printing press arrived, an angry, drunken mob attacked his place and shot Lovejoy. Lovejoy's murder galvanized the abolitionist movement and is considered one of the key moments that led to the Civil War.

3. THOMAS DARTMOUTH "DADDY" RICE
1830 - New York, New York

Thomas Rice was a working stage actor in New York City. His big break came when he started playing Jim Crow in blackface—a new character that mocked southern slaves. Over time, the shabbily dressed character's clumsiness and stupidity got more cartoonish. And white audiences loved it. Even in communities that no longer kept slaves, Rice's Jim Crow did incredible damage to widespread perception of the black community. Over time, "Jim Crow" became a blanket term for racist laws. Daddy Rice's legacy is atrocious.

2. NICHOLAS I
1831 - St. Petersburg, Russia

Nicholas I was the classic bully. As a way to combat his insecurities, the tsar surrounded himself with military men and lashed out at any perceived threat. When the Polish tried to break free from the autocratic tsar, his Russian troops repressed the revolution, which kicked off the Great Emigration. For the next forty years, millions of Polish people left home to find a better life (including Frederic Chopin, one of the great composers of all time). The paranoid Nicholas continued to make shaky isolationist decisions that set Russia back decades. He was such a turd that he got Russia into the disastrous Crimean War—a war in which the Brits and French chose to fight on the same side! It takes a special kind of jerk to make that happen.

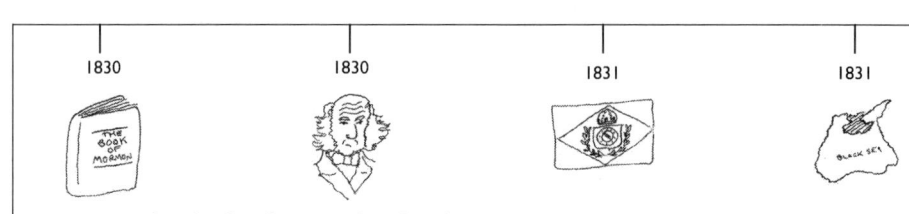

1. EDWARD COVEY
1833 - Talbot County, Maryland

When a local slave was giving their owner too much trouble, they were sent to Edward "the Slave-Breaker" Covey's farm. Covey would work and beat the slave until they lost their will to rebel. One day, he was given fifteen-year-old Frederick Douglass to whip into shape. It took six months for Covey to push Douglass to the breaking point. When he reached it, Douglass fought back and won. If word spread, this would have been devastating for Covey. So, Douglass' next six months on the farm were whip-free.

1833   1835   1835   1837

Dishonorable Mention: Queen Victoria - 1839 (Lady Hastings scandal)

1837

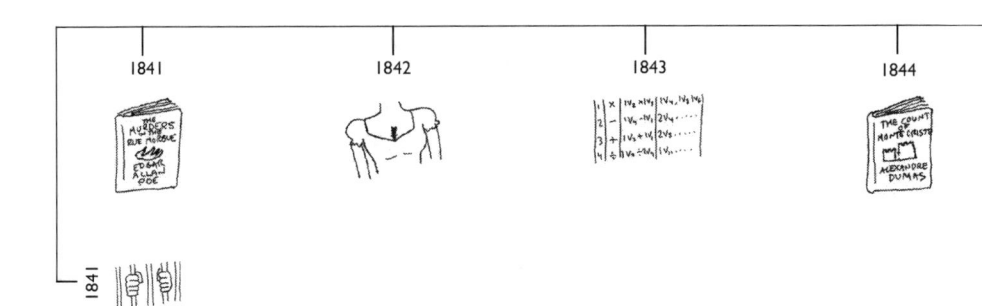

1840-1849

"The history of the past is but one long struggle upward to equality."
-Elizabeth Cady Stanton

BEST

10. ALEXANDER CARTRIGHT
1846 - Hoboken, New Jersey

A few years before heading west for the California Gold Rush, New York bank teller Alexander Cartwright got some buddies together and created the game of baseball. Various versions of the game (which clearly drew inspiration from games like cricket and rounders) sprouted up in the mid-nineteenth century, but the first time a game lasted nine innings and had foul territory, bases ninety feet apart, and nine players on each team was in a 1846 game between the New York Baseball Club and the Knickerbockers. Cartwright umpired the first game, which was won by the New York Baseball Club 23-1. Guess he didn't explain the gameplay too well to the Knickerbockers.

9. HANSON GREGORY
1847 - New England, USA

Fried pastries have been around for centuries in many cultures, but the best of all is the doughnut. Hands down. The inventor of the circular-with-the-middle-cut-out fried pastry was a sixteen-year-old guy on a lime-trading schooner. Hanson Gregory noticed that the outsides of the fried dough would cook thoroughly but the insides would still be raw and covered in grease. And this gave his shipmates lots of digestion issues. So he took the circular lid off the ship's pepper box and used it to cut a hole out of the center of the dough before frying. The result? Mmm, doughnuts.

8. FRANZ LISZT
1842 - Hamburg, Germany

Child-prodigy-turned-teacher-turned-concert-pianist Franz Liszt was the world's first rock star. Instead of the standard recital format, Lizst turned the piano so the audience could see his face and the emotion he put into his performance. Also, he played from memory, which was taboo at that time. Lisztomania caused women to lose their minds. They threw clothing on stage, they scavenged for his old cigar butts to tuck into their cleavage, they wore lockets containing his picture, and they would start fights over locks of his hair. Liszt capitalized on his soaring popularity by raising money for Hamburg, Germany after half the city burned down in 1842. In his later years, Liszt was a game-changing orchestra conductor and composer.

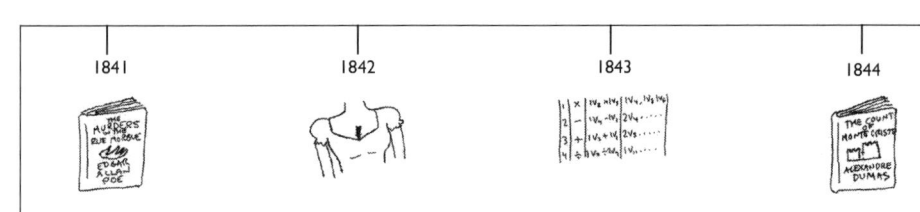

7. WALTER HUNT
1849 - New York, New York

The prolific inventor Walter Hunt was struggling financially in 1849. He owed a buddy $15 and wasn't sure how he was going to pay it back. So he sat in his workshop and nervously twirled an eight-inch-long brass wire around his finger. He noticed that he could clasp and unclasp the ends of the wire while the coil retained its spring. He wrote up an explanation, filed the patent for the safety pin, and sold it to W.R. Grace and Company for $400. First thing he did with his payoff was to pay back his friend. W.R. Grace made millions off the simple invention (which is still used today) but, hey, at least you could never call Walter Hunt a deadbeat.

6. ELIZABETH BLACKWELL
1849 - Geneva, New York

When Elizabeth Blackwell was growing up in Ohio, women had two choices: become a teacher or find a husband. Then, after a terminally ill friend complained about having to rely solely on male doctors, Elizabeth decided to apply to medical school. Every school turned her down except Geneva College in upstate New York (because they thought it was a joke). Well, it wasn't a joke. Elizabeth ended up graduating at the top of her class, the first woman in history to get a medical degree. Sexism continued to be a major blockade for Blackwell after school, so she opened her own clinic that specialized in treating poor women. After her clinic proved to be successful, she moved to England and became a professor at the London School of Medicine for Women.

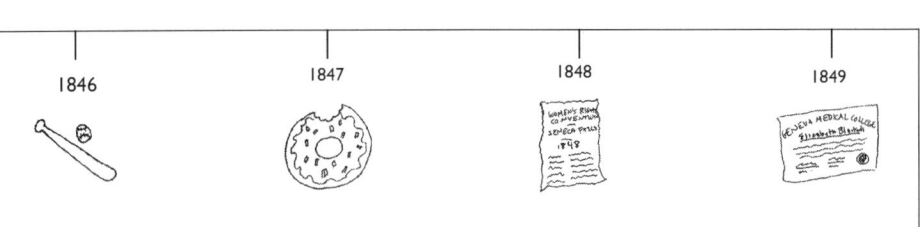

5. ALEXANDRE DUMAS
1844 - Paris, France

Dumas, the bastard son of a former Haitian slave, had a simple yet unique writing style that is still emulated today. Rather than going for the more formal style of his era, Dumas' sole motivation was to entertain. And, in 1844, he published his masterpiece, *The Count of Monte Cristo*, one of the greatest stories of all time. It's a tale of injustice and well-plotted revenge. The book is still entertaining and easy to read nearly two centuries later. All hail Alexandre Dumas, king of the beach books. (We'll look past the fact that he spent most of adulthood fathering dozens of kids and avoiding creditors.)

4. EDGAR ALLAN POE
1841 - Baltimore, Maryland

Edgar Allan Poe was often broke, he married his thirteen-year-old cousin, and he was not well respected by many of his peers. But in other ways, he was terrific. His 1841 detective story, *The Murders in the Rue Morgue*, paved the way for Arthur Conan Doyle and Agatha Christie. *The Pit and the Pendulum*, his creepy, suspenseful 1843 short story about torture during the Inquisition, inspired a genre for writers like Steven King. But Poe's career highlight (albeit without much financial reward) was his 1845 poem *The Raven*. Poe wasn't the first horror and suspense writer, but his use of intense psychological anguish helped elevate the genre. While he probably wasn't looking for this type of career boost, Poe's mysterious death at just forty made him more popular in death than in life.

3. DOROTHEA DIX
1841 - East Cambridge, Massachusetts

While teaching Sunday school in a women's prison, Dorothea Dix was deeply affected by the appalling conditions she saw—hardened criminals grouped together with mentally ill women (who had committed minor crimes) in barren, dark, dirty, smelly, unheated jail cells. From that point forward, she devoted the rest of her life to being the "voice for the mad." After successfully lobbying for expanded mental health treatment in her home state of Massachusetts, Dix moved on to fourteen neighboring states. Eventually, she turned her focus to Europe and presented her findings to the pope. After hearing her report, Pope Pius IX personally ordered the construction of a mental health hospital. Dorothea Dix gave a voice to a group that was never able to speak for themselves.

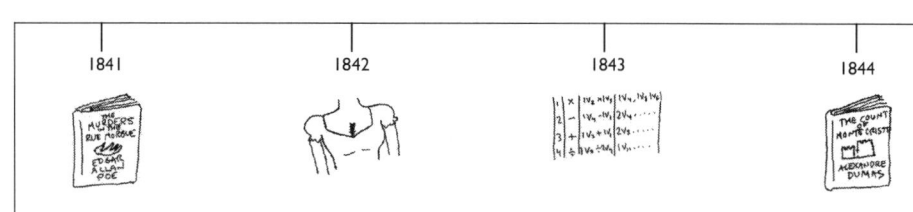

2. ADA LOVELACE
1843 - London, England

Anne Byron's famous, flighty husband (Lord Byron) had just left her to raise an infant by herself. In an effort to ensure their daughter Ada didn't go down that same mercurial, artistic path, Anne raised her to be a self-sufficient intellectual. No expense was spared to educate young Ada by London's best tutors. At seventeen, Ada met and became friends with Charles Babbage, the father of computers. When studying Babbage's Analytical Engine, Ada made her own observations and improvements to the functionality of the machine: codes could be created so the engine could process both numbers and symbols, instructions could be repeated, and so forth. These findings, which were published in an English journal in 1843, were well ahead of her time. Ada Lovelace is considered the first computer programmer.

1. ELIZABETH CADY STANTON
1848 - Seneca Falls, New York

After being separated from the men at the World Anti-Slavery Convention in 1840, activists Elizabeth Cady Stanton and Lucretia Mott felt compelled to get more aggressive in pushing for women's rights. The two organized the Seneca Falls Convention, which was attended by three hundred women. Stanton's "Declaration of Sentiments" was a landmark women's rights document that demanded, among other things, the right to vote. A few years after that, Stanton began what would be a half-century-long partnership with Susan B. Anthony advancing the rights of women in America. Stanton wrote the speeches and letters, and Anthony

| 1846 | 1847 | 1848 | 1849 |

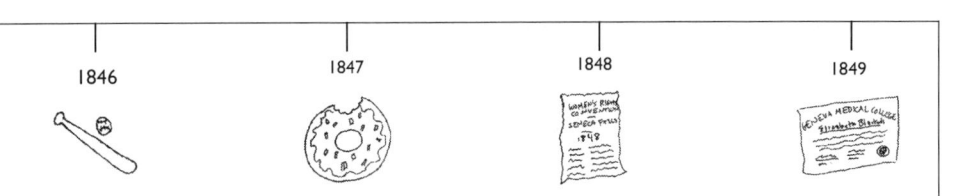

beat the streets. Although it was Anthony who eventually got on the dollar coin, it was Stanton who provided the words and got the ball rolling.

1849

Honorable Mentions: George Sand - 1848 (female nineteenth-century French novelist, also ran a newspaper), Antoine-Joseph "Adolphe" Sax (saxophone)

WORST

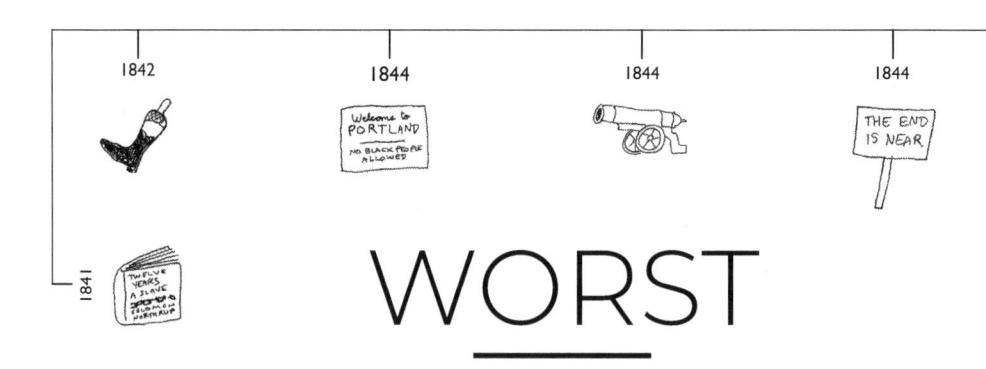

10. WILLIAM MILLER
1844 - Burlington, Vermont

In the 1830s, Baptist preacher William Miller spoke of Jesus' impending return. His dimwitted followers (Millerites) believed that on March 21, 1843, the good would be sucked up into heaven and the bad and non-believers would be stuck on an Earth that would be engulfed in flames. When March 21 came and went, Miller just moved the target. Again Millerites sold their possessions and waited. And they still remained on Earth. The sham was pulled off twice more before people gave up and newspapers called it the "Great Disappointment."

9. ROBERT STOCKTON
1844 - Mt. Vernon, Virginia

President John Tyler and four hundred others were invited aboard the USS *Princeton* to cruise the Potomac River. It was a good opportunity for the fifty-four-year-old recent widower Tyler to hit on twenty-year-old Julia Gardiner, and it was a good opportunity for Captain Robert Stockton of the *Princeton* to show off its brand-new 27,000-pound cannon, the Peacemaker. The Peacemaker's designer advised against firing the cannon on the cruise, since it had not yet been properly tested. Stockton ignored him and fired it a few times. The third time caused the cannon to explode, killing two of Tyler's cabinet members and several others, including Julia Gardiner's father, David. Guessing Tyler didn't close the deal that night.

8. ANTONIO LOPEZ DE SANTA ANNA
1842 - Mexico City, Mexico

General Santa Anna, famous for his victory in the battle at the

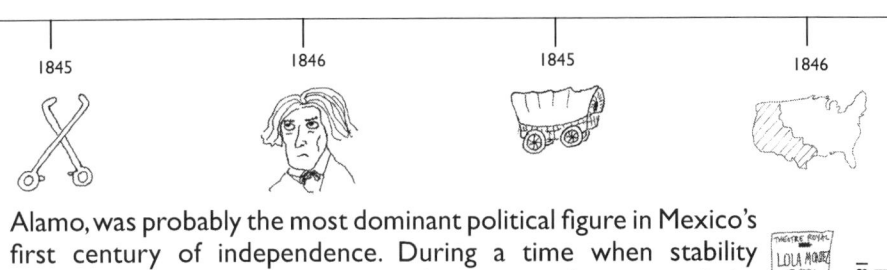

Alamo, was probably the most dominant political figure in Mexico's first century of independence. During a time when stability was needed, the eleven-time president erratically governed the place into further chaos. In 1842, President Santa Anna, the self-proclaimed "Napoleon of the West," was so proud of himself that he gave his amputated leg a full state parade and burial. Just two years later, after Santa Anna failed to keep the country together and was forced to surrender millions of acres to the United States, the people grew tired of his routine. So they dug up his shriveled leg from its grave, dragged it through the streets, and shouted, "Death to the cripple!"

7. LOLA MONTEZ
1848 - Munich, Bavaria (Germany)

Irish-born Marie Gilbert, under the name Lola Montez, danced onstage in London and other European capitals, gaining the attention of rich and famous benefactors (Franz Liszt, Alexandre Dumas). When she got to Munich in 1843, "Lola Montez, the Spanish Dancer" caught the eye of fifty-seven-year-old King Ludwig I of Bavaria, who immediately offered to build her a castle. Wow, sounds like the sex well had run dry for the king. She accepted his offer and became the Countess of Lansfeld. Once she had the king by the balls (both literally and figuratively), she ruled his Bavarian regime into the ground. By 1848, he was forced to abdicate the throne and Lola went back to London.

6. JOSEPH RUSSELL AND ALEXANDER MERRILL
1841 - Saratoga Springs, New York

Solomon Northup was a free black man living in New York until these two monsters came into his life. Russell and Merrill heard about Northup's proficiency at the violin and asked him to play for their circus in Washington, D.C. While on the trip, Northup was drugged and sold into slavery. For the next dozen years, Northrup lived in brutal captivity on Louisiana plantations. In 1853, Solomon regained his freedom and wrote *Twelve Years a Slave*. Russell and Merrill were arrested and charged with kidnapping but, since they were white guys in the 1850s who were accused by a black man, the charges were eventually dropped.

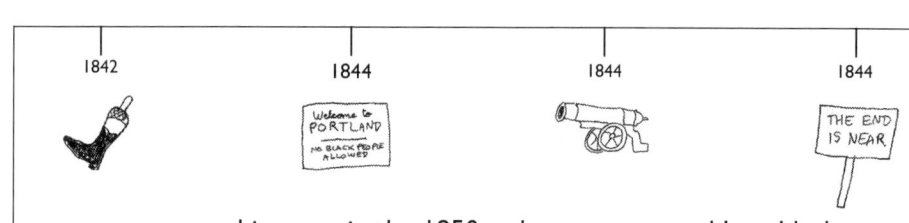

5. LANSFORD HASTINGS
1845 - Alta, California

Lansford Hastings was a young lawyer with a big idea: if he were able to convince a bunch of people to come to Northern California and then convince Northern California to break away from Mexico, he could be the leader of that independent territory. He knew he needed to get people to California quick, so he wrote a guidebook in 1845 pointing out the westward trails to take. It also included a shortcut that he had never actually seen with his own eyes. So when the Donner party, a group of eighty-nine people emigrating from Illinois, followed that "shortcut," it cost them an extra eighteen days on the road, which depleted their resources and left them stranded in the Sierra Nevada Mountains for the winter. They ran out of food and turned to cannibalism, and only forty-five survived. Thanks for the tip, Lansford!

4. JAMES K. POLK
1846 - Washington, D.C.

At a brief glance, James Polk accomplished quite a bit in his one-term presidency. America expanded its borders to encompass what are now Texas, California, Arizona, Nevada, Utah, New Mexico, Colorado, Wyoming, Oregon, Idaho, and Washington. But, look a little closer and you see the guy was the lying politician we all detest. Thanks to a botched childhood surgery, Polk was impotent. Ironically enough, the man became a walking hard-on for Manifest Destiny aggression. When Congress wouldn't let Polk attack Mexico, he manufactured a war by provoking the first battle. At Polk's urging, half of the United States' troops were sent to disputed territory (which everyone but Texans viewed as Mexico). Of course a fight broke out, and sixteen soldiers were killed. This provoked a nearly two-year war which cost another thirteen thousand Americans and countless innocent Mexicans their lives.

3. J. MARION SIMS
1845 - Montgomery, Alabama

J. Marion Sims was the first American surgeon to have a statue erected in his honor and has been called the "father of gynecology." The man was responsible for solving the condition of fistula, a complication from childbirth that can be devastating. And he made these breakthroughs while heartlessly operating on helpless slaves. Sims never even bothered to use anesthesia on his black patients (one of whom was operated on forty times before success was reached). White women, on the other hand, were somehow always deemed worthy of ether to numb the pain during surgery. Without question, Sims was an important pioneer in gynecology. But at what cost?

2. PETER BURNETT
1844 - Portland, Oregon

You know how, despite how progressive the state is perceived as, pretty much the only black people in Oregon happen to be on the Portland Trailblazers? That's not a coincidence. In 1844, in an effort to create a "racist utopia" in the new Oregon territory, government leader Peter Burnett declared that black men had two years to get out of the territory. Women had three. If any failed to comply, they'd be publicly lashed up to thirty-nine times. The "Peter Burnett Lash Law" was eventually repealed, but new blatantly racist laws were enacted in its place. When Oregon officially became a U.S. state, blacks weren't allowed to own property or reside there. The state didn't even ratify the Fourteenth Amendment (the post-Civil War one) until 1973!

1. JOHN CALHOUN
1846 - Washington, D.C.

South Carolina Senator John Calhoun was a massive political figure for the relatively new nation. He helped establish the Second Bank of the United States and worked hard to improve America's infrastructure. And that's where the good times screech to a halt. Early in his career, the "War Hawk" aggressively pushed the

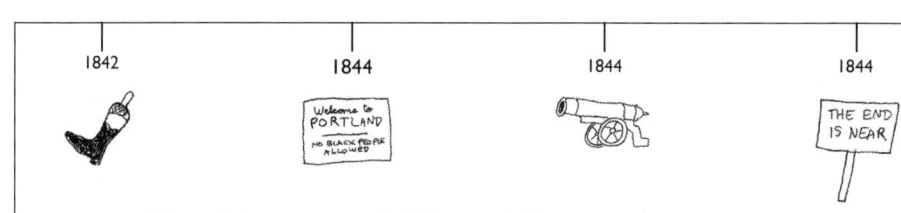

United States into the War of 1812, a war that America's military wasn't fully prepared to fight. Calhoun was also fiercely protective of the "Southern way of life." In other words, he was a racist. As California was entering the union, David Wilmot, a Congressman from Pennsylvania, proposed that no new territory be admitted as slave states. Calhoun considered it a slap in the face and helped rally the senate to shoot the Wilmot Proviso down, escalating tensions between the South and North.

| 1845 | 1846 | 1845 | 1846 |

1846

Dishonorable Mention: William Henry Harrison (got famous for setting Shawnee territory on fire, gave a two-hour inaugural address)

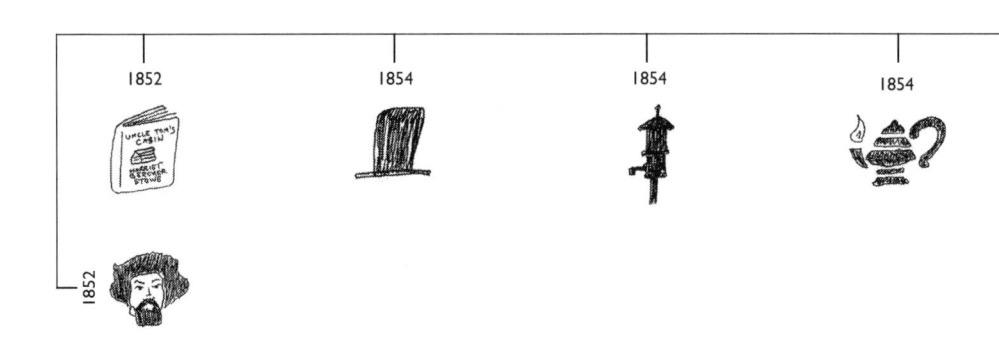

1850-1859

"Man's greatness consists in his ability to do and the proper application of his powers to things needed to be done."

-Frederick Douglass

BEST

10. ELISHA GRAVES OTIS
1857 - New York, New York

Elevators of some form or other had already been around for many years. Louis XV used a "flying chair" to transport his mistress to the third floor at Versailles. The Industrial Revolution introduced motorized pulleys to the contraption, but the ropes often wore out and broke. Most people preferred the stairs. Then, in 1852, Elisha Otis invented a pulley with a safety brake. Otis sold a few but his business didn't explode until 1857, when he installed the first commercial elevator in a five-story New York City department store. Suddenly, a higher-floor location was no longer a burden but a privilege. Thousands of elevator-operator jobs were created. People could rise hundreds of feet in the air without exerting any energy... well, except for the brutal, forced waiting-for-your-floor chit-chat.

9. WALT WHITMAN
1855 - Brooklyn, New York

In 1843, Ralph Waldo Emerson wrote "The Poet," an essay throwing down the gauntlet for American poets. Someone needed to emerge as the country's voice. In 1855, Walt Whitman answered the call with his twelve-poem collection, *Leaves of Grass*. Unlike anything previously written (in both format and content), Whitman's free-verse poems openly discussed everything from race to democracy to sex. Much like America, *Leaves of Grass* continued to evolve over the years. For the rest of his life, Whitman tinkered with his masterpiece, expanding it to nearly three hundred poems.

8. HARRIET BEECHER STOWE
1852 - Brunswick, Maine

Harriet Beecher Stowe supported the Underground Railroad and, on multiple occasions, took in runaway slaves. After the Fugitive Slave Law was passed in 1950, Stowe felt compelled to write about the evils of slavery. So she drew upon some of the horrifying stories she had heard and penned *Uncle Tom's Cabin*. Stowe's story portrayed black people as humans, showed how the slave trade was ripping loving families apart, and exposed just how awful slaves were treated. *Uncle Tom's Cabin* sold hundreds of thousands of copies in the North and built resentment in the South. It sold even more copies in Great Britain than in America. At the time, the British Parliament was enjoying America ripping itself apart. Hey, maybe soon they'd have a vulnerable half-country to reclaim. After the success of *Uncle Tom's Cabin*, public pressure made it impossible for Parliament to support the Confederacy in their fight. "Uncle Tom" may now be considered a pejorative term, but Harriet Beecher Stowe's novel was one of the most important books ever written.

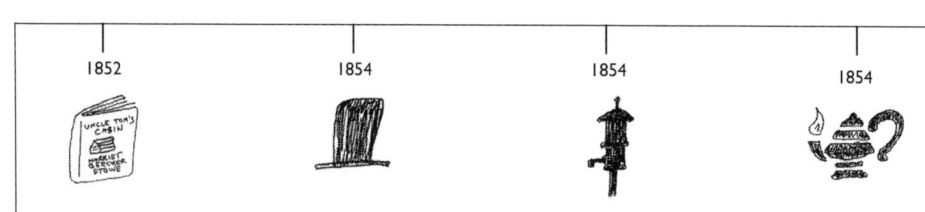

7. JOSEPH GAYETTY
1867 - New York, New York

Before toilet paper, people used leaves, newspaper, and sponges on a stick to clean themselves. It was horrible. Then Joseph Gayetty came up with an alternative: hemp paper sheets with a touch of aloe. Unfortunately, Gayetty never made money on it but, considering it's a six-billion-dollar-a-year business in the United States alone, it's safe to say it was a monumental invention. If you don't believe it, try wiping your ass with newspaper.

6. FREDERICK DOUGLASS
1852 - Rochester, New York

By the age of twenty, Frederick Douglass had taught himself to read and write, became a leader of fellow slaves, and escaped on a ship headed to Massachusetts. Instead of laying low once he was free, Douglass spent the rest of his life crusading for anti-slavery and basic human rights. In 1852, he was asked to appear at a Rochester event commemorating the signing of the Declaration of Independence. It was there he gave his famous speech: "This Fourth of July is *yours*, not *mine*. *You* may rejoice, I must mourn." The eloquent Douglass went on to point out the hypocrisy of a country that preached about all men being created equal yet

| 1855 | 1857 | 1857 | 1859 |

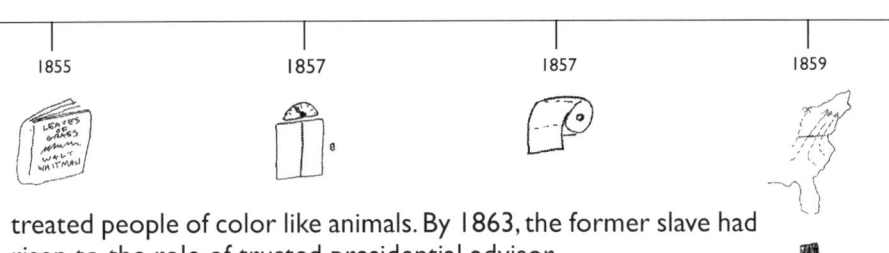

treated people of color like animals. By 1863, the former slave had risen to the role of trusted presidential advisor.

5. FLORENCE NIGHTINGALE
1854 - Constantinople (Istanbul, Turkey)

Florence Nightingale, a highly respected young nurse from London, was tasked with assembling a group to tend to sick and wounded soldiers in the Crimean War. When she arrived at the British hospital base, she was met with a horrendous situation. More men were dying from infection and sickness than war wounds. The place was dirty, the water was contaminated, and patients were wallowing in their own filth. Nightingale swiftly changed conditions. She opened windows, cleaned linens, served healthy meals, and brought in books to stimulate the patients' minds. Deaths were quickly cut down by two-thirds and Nightingale earned the nickname "Angel of Crimea." Florence Nightingale transformed the role of the nurse from lowly assistantship to an honorable profession.

4. HARRIET TUBMAN
1859 - Auburn, New York

After her Maryland plantation owner died in 1849, slave Harriet Tubman feared she and her family would be split up and sent to the Deep South. So she escaped to Pennsylvania, made a little money working odd jobs, and then went back down below the Mason-Dixon line to help her siblings. What started as a small rescue mission became an effort to help all enslaved. Using the North Star as guide, the brilliant and tough Tubman spent the next decade leading over three hundred escaped slaves along the Underground Railroad, staying at safe houses by night. At first the destination was just Pennsylvania. Then, after the Fugitive Slave Law of 1850 passed, Tubman had to stretch the Railroad all the way to Canada to ensure their freedom. Despite a huge price tag on her head, Harriet Tubman always completed her missions and never lost a life.

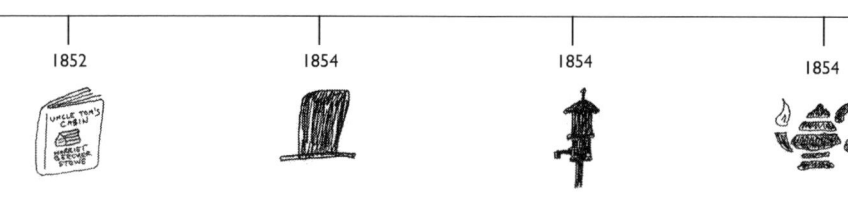

3. ABRAHAM LINCOLN
1854 - Peoria, Illinois

The greatest president in American history launched his second act in politics with a speech denouncing the indefensible Kansas-Nebraska Act. This act, which allowed racists to move slavery north of the previously-agreed-upon Missouri Compromise line, combined with the disastrous Dred Scott Supreme Court decision (the one that told a slave living in a free state that he must remain a slave) were attempts to appease slave states. For the next decade, Lincoln railed against America's agree-to-disagree stance on slavery ("A house divided against itself cannot stand!") while raising his political profile in the process. By 1860, the pro-Union, anti-slavery Lincoln was elected president. Despite inheriting a shitstorm, in just four years, Lincoln was able to rescue a nation circling the drain and put it on the road to recovery. He accomplished it by being savvy (the Emancipation Proclamation tied the Civil War to slavery and led to 200,000 much-needed black soldiers joining the Union army) and inspirational (his two-minute-long Gettysburg Address reminded everyone what they were fighting for), and by showing tremendous character (won reelection without backpedaling on his emancipation stance). And to top it all off, the man established the greatest American holiday—Thanksgiving!

2. HENRI DUNANT
1859 - Solferino (Italy)

A day after the Battle of Solferino (a battle so brutal it essentially ended the Second Italian War of Independence), Swiss businessman Henri Dunant had an appointment with Napoleon III. When he got to Solferino, he toured the battlefield and saw the bloody, mangled bodies strewn about. Unable to shake what he had witnessed, Dunant returned home to Switzerland and wrote about the experience. Dunant believed nations should band together and provide care for the sick and wounded, regardless of what side they were on. He spent the next few years setting up the International Committee of the Red Cross and later the Geneva Convention. While Dunant's dedication to charity afforded him only a life of poverty, in 1901 he was awarded the first ever Nobel Prize.

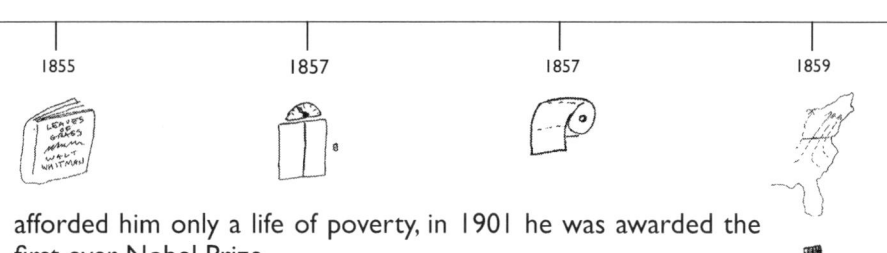

1. JOHN SNOW
1854 - London, England

For more than two decades, doctors in London were baffled by cholera. Despite countless hours of lab study, their only (and incorrect) guess was that it was airborne. Six cholera pandemics had killed millions around the world in the nineteenth century. After five hundred people died from it in the city's SoHo neighborhood in just ten days, Dr. John Snow tried a different approach—he mapped out its progress. Snow found the cholera cases were heavily concentrated around the Broad Street water pump. He also noticed that for some reason, those who worked at the local brewery never got sick. Since the brewery gave all its employees free beer, they never bothered to drink water. Snow concluded that cholera was waterborne and soon discovered that Broad Street pump's water supply was contaminated with runoff from a nearby cesspool. Shortly thereafter, contributions by Italian physician Filippo Pacini and Spanish bacteriologist Jaume Ferran i Clua helped the world come up with a cure.

Honorable Mentions: Lakshmi Bai - 1857 (India's Joan of Arc), Herman Melville - 1851 (*Moby Dick*), George Crum - 1853 (potato chips), Edmund Beckett Denison - 1859 (Big Ben), John Stuart Mill - 1850 (fought slavery, proponent of women's rights, labor unions), Ida Lewis - 1854 (lighthouse hero), Hymen Lipman - 1858 (first pencil with an eraser), Lucy Stone - 1850 (abolitionist, women's rights advocate), Felix Mendelssohn - 1858 ("Wedding March"), Ellis Chesbrough - 1856 (Chicago sewer system), Henri Giffard - 1852 (flight pioneer), Joseph Bazalgette - 1858 (London sewer system), nine Jewish guys - 1852 (Mount Sinai Hospital), Etienne Lenoir - 1859 (automotive pioneer)

WORST

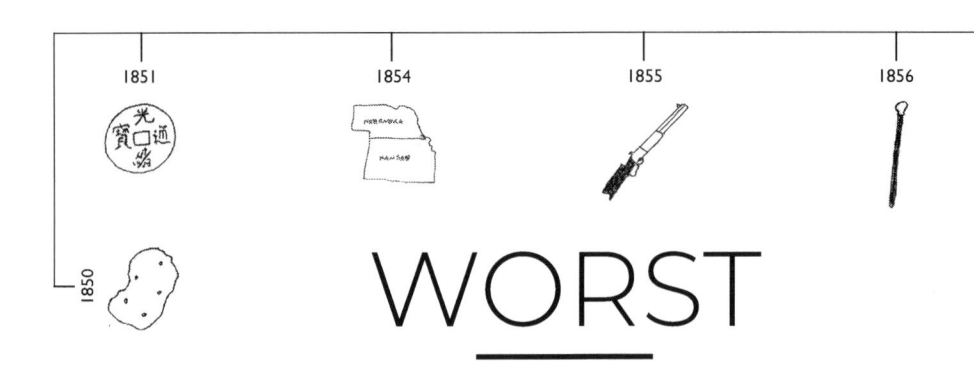

10. THOMAS AUSTIN
1859 - Victoria, Australia

Rabbits have those cute, perky ears, adorable little tails, and a delightful little hop. Another fun fact about them? They're complete nightmares. Unchecked, they eat everything in sight. Unfortunately for Australia, Thomas Austin liked hunting rabbits, so he imported twenty-four of them from England. But, since he didn't hunt all two dozen before they "fucked like rabbits," they quickly became an epidemic. Millions of acres of Victoria's flora and fauna were destroyed. By 1920, the rabbit population had reached ten billion. Those little buck-toothed jerks were destroying the land. For the past century, the nation has struggled to lower that number and protect their crops.

9. CHARLES LUTTWIDGE DODGSON
1856 - Oxford, England

Let's say a "confirmed bachelor" shows great interest in taking children's photographs, some of them nude or semi-nude. And let's say that guy spends an inordinate amount of time hanging out with the very young daughter of a neighboring family until they abruptly cut off all ties with him. A few years after that, the guy presents the girl with the gift of a novel bearing her name. In the story, the girl consumes lots of unknown foods, pills, and liquids and goes on a psychedelic adventure. He eventually publishes the novel under a fake name so nobody knows who wrote it. Would you be okay with that guy? Well, that guy was Charles Dodgson, pen name Lewis Carroll. His book was *Alice's Adventures Under Ground*.

8. JAMES BUCHANAN
1856 - Washington, D.C.

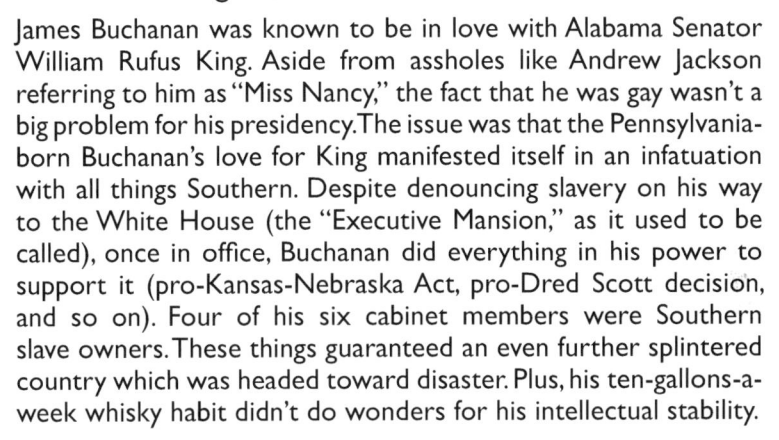

James Buchanan was known to be in love with Alabama Senator William Rufus King. Aside from assholes like Andrew Jackson referring to him as "Miss Nancy," the fact that he was gay wasn't a big problem for his presidency. The issue was that the Pennsylvania-born Buchanan's love for King manifested itself in an infatuation with all things Southern. Despite denouncing slavery on his way to the White House (the "Executive Mansion," as it used to be called), once in office, Buchanan did everything in his power to support it (pro-Kansas-Nebraska Act, pro-Dred Scott decision, and so on). Four of his six cabinet members were Southern slave owners. These things guaranteed an even further splintered country which was headed toward disaster. Plus, his ten-gallons-a-week whisky habit didn't do wonders for his intellectual stability.

7. PRESTON BROOKS
1856 - Washington, D.C.

Massachusetts Senator Charles Sumner thought the South's attempt to spread slavery into Kansas was disgraceful, so he made an impassioned "Crime Against Kansas" speech to the Senate. In his speech, Sumner said Illinois Democrat Stephen Douglas was "not a proper model for an American senator" and accused the absent South Carolina Democrat Andrew Butler of "taking an ugly mistress named slavery." A few days later, South Carolina Representative Preston Brooks approached a defenseless Sumner while he was sitting at his desk and nearly beat him to death with his metal-tipped cane. It took Sumner three years to recover from the beating. There was a feel-good ending to the story, however. The caning galvanized the abolitionist movement and Brooks died of the croup eight months later.

6. PIERCE BUTLER
1857 - Savannah, Georgia

Pierce Butler inherited his family's plantation and then spent the next two decades pissing away his inheritance. Not only did he lose his estimated $700,000 (keep in mind mansions cost $30 grand back then), but also he fell deeply in debt. So he looked to sell whatever he could to climb out of the hole. He decided to sell his slaves—436 of them—over a two-day period. This largest ever slave auction was known as the "Weeping Time." Husbands and wives were sold away from each other. Children were separated from their parents. Siblings were forever parted. All because some inheritance baby couldn't maintain a fortune that had been handed to him on a silver platter.

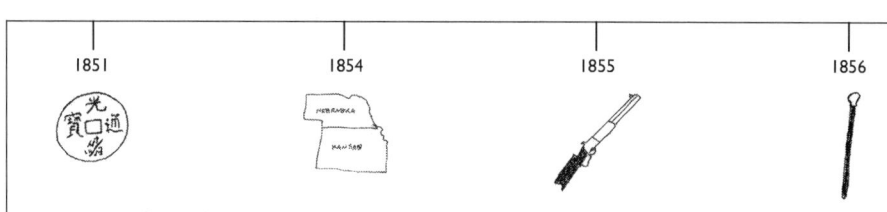

5. ROGER TANEY
1857 - Washington, D.C.

In 1857 the Supreme Court heard the case of slave Dred Scott (living in Illinois, a free state) who had sued for his freedom before he was sent to Missouri (a slave state). Unfortunately for Scott, seven of the justices had been appointed by Southern pro-slavery presidents. And of those seven, five owned slaves themselves. Predictably, the court denied Scott his freedom. Of the majority opinion, Supreme Court Chief Justice Roger Taney provided the reason: Dred Scott wasn't a citizen. Blacks may have been free in some states, but they were never actually citizens... so the Constitution didn't apply to them. "Sorry, Dred. We rich racists have to look out for number one."

4. STEPHEN DOUGLAS
1854 - Washington, D.C.

Nebraska and Kansas wanted to join the union but, once again, slavery was the major sticking point between the North and South. So Illinois senator Stephen Douglas proposed the Kansas-Nebraska Act, which basically allowed both states in and had their citizens vote to be slave or free. For Douglas, gaining both of those states in the union meant that the Transcontinental Railroad would be able to add a northern route to California (which would make his Chicago real estate worth a fortune). He pushed for—and got—both of them into the United States. And the small detail about leaving the slave-or-free issue up to a vote instead of sorting it out first meant that extremists from both sides rushed the area, leading to years of brutal violence. The Civil War was inevitable.

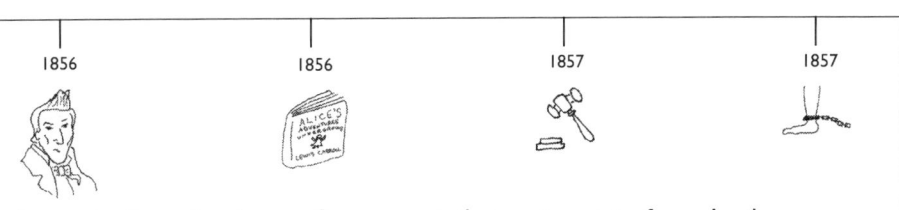

3. FRANKLIN COLEMAN
1855 - Lawrence, Kansas

As Northern abolitionists and pro-slavery Southerners flooded the Sunflower State in an attempt to sway upcoming votes their way, pro-slavery Franklin Coleman shot and killed free-state settler Charles Dow. From there, Kansas turned into the Thunderdome. Missouri senator David Aitchison implored Missourians to "kill every God-damned abolitionist in the district." Fuel to the fire, abolitionist John Brown and his crew dragged pro-slavery men out of their homes and hacked them to death. The era was known as Bleeding Kansas. Maybe violence was inevitable, but the one who got the murder ball rolling was Franklin Coleman.

2. HONG XIUQUAN
1851 - Nanjing, China

The Qing Dynasty was in trouble. Peasants were miserable and much of the country's resources had been bogged down in the Opium Wars with the British. Then Hong Xiuquan, a guy claiming to be Jesus' younger brother, proclaimed it was time for a new dynasty—the Taiping Tianguo ("Heavenly Kingdom of Great Peace"). One slight problem: Xiuquan, the Heavenly King, was just some dipshit who had failed the civil service exam three times. While sulking, he claimed he had had a vision, a bunch of people believed him, and the Taiping Revolution broke out. At first, Hong's troops succeeded against the inept, corrupt, and strung-out-on-opium Qing army. European countries stepped in and helped the Qing fight back. Between ten and twenty million lost their lives during the failed fourteen-year rebellion, all because Jesus' kid brother couldn't pass a test.

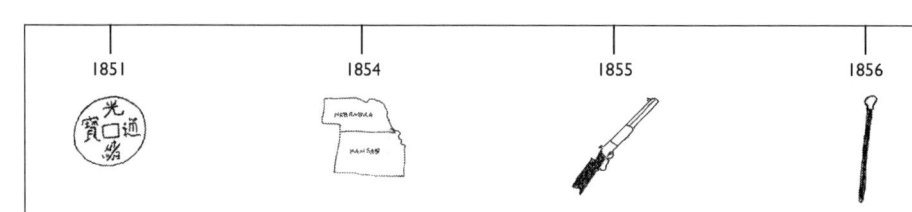

1. CHARLES TREVELYAN
1850 - London, England

From about 1845 to 1852, a deadly fungus ravaged potato crops across Ireland. Considering potatoes were pretty much the only thing poor people could afford to grow, thousands and thousands of people starved. Instead of lending a hand, British Secretary of the Treasury Charles Trevelyan believed the potato blight represented "the judgment of God" and that disease and famine were an "effective mechanism for reducing surplus population." So Trevelyan refused to help the Irish; he denounced members of the coast guard who tried to assist them and turned away ships with food donations from America. In the end, about a million people died and another million moved away. Ireland's population is still smaller than it was before the famine, thanks to Trevelyan.

1856   1856   1857   1857

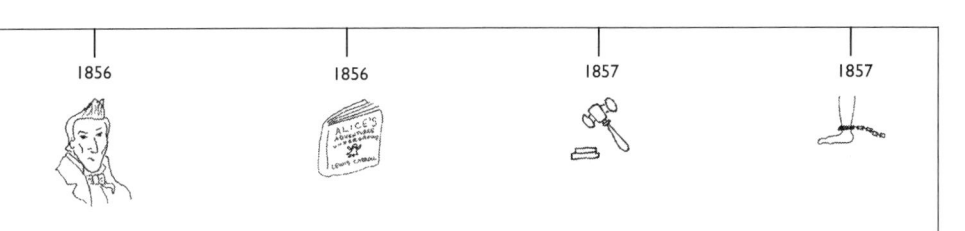

1859

Dishonorable Mentions: Joshua Ward - 1850 (massive slave owner), Jan Schenkman - 1850 ("Zwarte Piet"), Neil Dow - 1851 (Napoleon of Temperance), William Pierce - 1856 (Great Gold Robbery), Franklin Pierce - 1854 (pro-slavery puppet), William Walker - 1855 ("king of the filibusters"), Pope Pius IX - 1858 (kidnapping pope), Joaquin Murrieta - 1853 (*Zorro* inspiration, murderer), Louis Bonaparte - 1851 (crappy nephew)

| 1862 | 1862 | 1862 | 1864 |

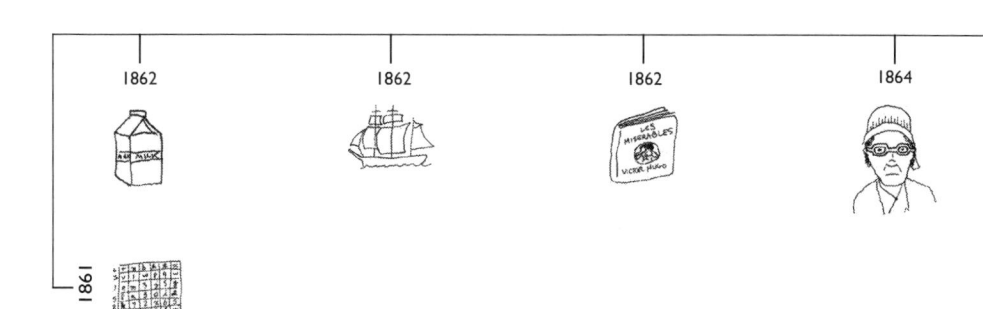

1861

1860-1869

"I distrust those people who know so well what God wants them to do, because I notice it always coincides with their own desires."

-Susan B. Anthony

BEST

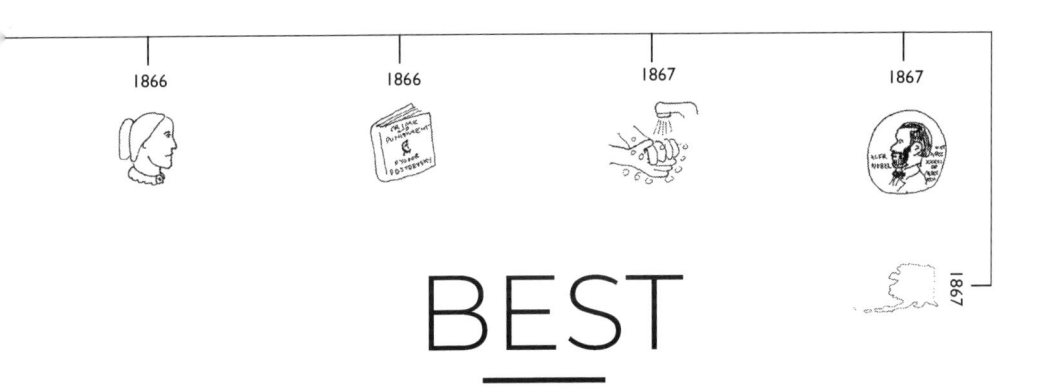

10. ELIZABETH VAN LEW
1861 - Richmond, Virginia

Despite being a rich white woman living in the capital of the Confederacy, Elizabeth Van Lew did everything in her power to help the North win the Civil War. Following the Battle of Manassas, Elizabeth donated supplies and volunteered as a nurse for captured Union soldiers. Locals tried to bully her but that only strengthened her resolve. Over the next few years, Van Lew led a spy network around Richmond. This network included Mary Bowser, a slave at Confederate President Jefferson Davis' house. Soon General Grant was getting Confederate army plans even before some of its high-ranking officers. This information helped Grant take Richmond and, soon thereafter, win the Civil War.

9. WILLIAM SEWARD
1867 - Washington, D.C.

After getting the Republican presidential nomination over William Seward in 1860, Abraham Lincoln added the New York senator to his cabinet as secretary of state. Seward's foreign policy maneuvers to isolate the Confederacy during the Civil War proved to be monumental. Without outside help, the South was doomed. In 1867, Seward arranged the purchase of Alaska from Russia, the lone bright spot in the sad presidency of Andrew Johnson. The two-cents-per-acre purchase, originally derided by the *New York Tribune* as "Seward's Folly" and "Walrussia," turned out to be a tremendous boon for America. It tightened the screws on Britain to let Canada be independent; the U.S. could expand its borders without conflict; and, within a short period of time, Alaska turned out be a great source of oil and gold.

8. VICTOR HUGO
1862 - Guernsey, United Kingdom

Thanks to the massive success of his poetry, plays, and *The Hunchback of Notre*

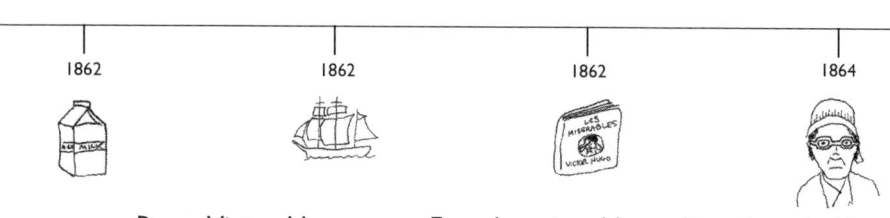

Dame, Victor Hugo was a French national hero. But, after clashing with Napoleon III in 1851, he became persona non grata, fled to Brussels, and eventually moved to the UK. It was on the isle of Guernsey where he completed his work on one of the great novels in history, *Les Misérables*. The story about redemption, set during the French Revolution, was translated into other languages and became a huge global success. By 1870, Hugo returned to a hero's welcome in Paris and Napoleon III was the one in exile in England.

7. ALFRED NOBEL
1867 - Stockholm, Sweden

After Alfred Nobel's brother died in a nitroglycerin factory explosion, he set out to make a safer alternative to the current, extremely combustible options, gunpowder and nitroglycerin. His invention of dynamite (named after the Greek word for "power") made him extremely rich. Unfortunately, it also earned him the nickname "the Merchant of Death." Determined to change his legacy, Nobel left a huge sum of money in his will (worth more than a quarter billion dollars today) to be awarded as prizes for achievements in the disciplines of medicine, physics, chemistry, and literature. Today, the name Nobel is synonymous with greatness.

6. FYODOR DOSTOYEVSKY
1866 - St. Petersburg, Russia

In 1849, a young Fyodor Dostoyevsky and some fellow intellectuals met regularly to discuss the problems with serfdom. One day, the group was arrested for dissension and given a penalty of death by firing squad. At the eleventh hour, his life was spared. Instead, he was sentenced to a work camp in Siberia for four years. It was there that he found his focus as a writer. He was drawn to explore the depths of humanity through his stories; in short, the guy loved to examine human misery. Thanks to a growing gambling problem, Dostoyevsky was highly motivated to publish prolifically to cover his debts. As he was getting his finances in order, he wrote *Crime and Punishment*, one of the greatest novels of all time.

| 1866 | 1866 | 1867 | 1867 |

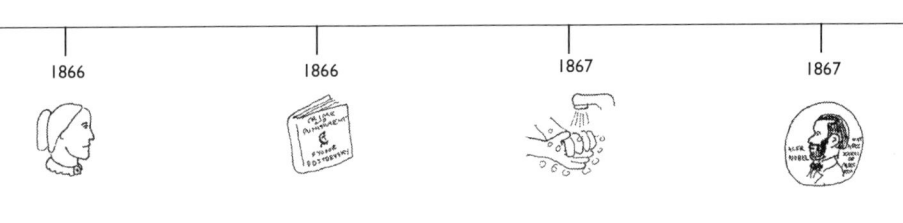

5. ROBERT SMALLS
1862 - Charleston, South Carolina

A Confederate steamer had docked for the night with eight slaves aboard. One of those slaves was very familiar with the Charleston harbor—twenty-two-year-old Robert Smalls. Smalls had learned how to navigate while serving as a wheelman on many previous ships. So, at 2:00 a.m., Smalls put on the captain's hat, raised the flags, honked the horns, flashed the right signals, and folded his arms like the captain did. He set off with his small crew. Along the way, he picked up his wife and kids. After passing enemy lines, Smalls swapped the Confederate flag for a white bed sheet and headed straight for a Union blockade. Once free, he recruited five hundred black soldiers to fight for the Union army and used that same steamer to attack the Confederacy. After the war, Smalls returned to South Carolina and served five terms in the U.S. House of Representatives. Robert was the original Biggie Smalls.

4. LOUIS PASTEUR
1862 - Lille, France

In 1856, an alcohol manufacturer hired Louis Pasteur to figure out what was causing its booze to go bad. In his investigation Pasteur noticed the appearance of a microbe that was different than yeast. One possible answer would be to boil the liquid to kill these germs; the problem was, that process would kill the taste as well. So Pasteur came up with a way to heat the liquid to the precise temperature needed to kill the bacteria and then quickly cool it, which would preserve the taste. Pasteurization was used for wine, beer, and eventually milk. After making this discovery, the "father of microbiology" turned his attention to humans and saved countless lives by developing cures for cholera, anthrax, and rabies.

3. SOJOURNER TRUTH
1864 - New York, New York

Shortly after gaining her freedom in 1826, Sojourner Truth sued a white guy in Alabama who had recently bought her five-year-old son. And she won! Truth then spent the rest of her life fighting for the abolitionist and women's suffrage movements. During the Civil War, she advocated for and recruited blacks to join the Union Army and fight for their freedom. In 1864, she advised Abraham Lincoln on the slave experience. She even pulled a Rosa Parks one hundred years before Rosa Parks did, by boarding white streetcars and challenging the law. Sojourner Truth was a titan in the civil and women's rights movements.

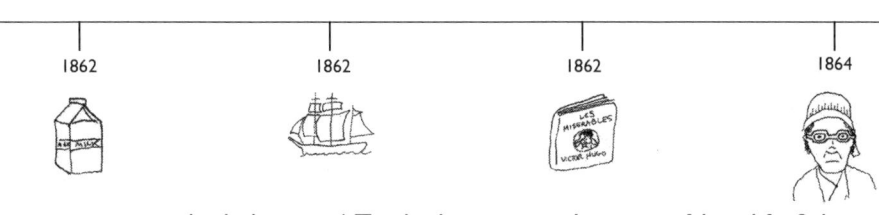

2. JOSEPH LISTER
1867 - Glasgow, Scotland

When a patient goes into surgery, they should hope their surgeon is well-trained, not inebriated, and washed hands first. Prior to the 1860s, number three was not a given. Doctors frequently walked into the operation room with little to no prep. As a result, nearly half of amputation patients died from sepsis. After reading Louis Pasteur's theory on microorganisms, Dr. Joseph Lister decided to use phenol as an antiseptic whenever performing surgery. Within four years, the mortality rate had dropped to 15 percent. Dr. Lister was probably responsible for saving more lives than any other surgeon in history.

1. SUSAN B. ANTHONY
1868 - New York, New York

In the years following the Civil War, the fight for women's rights was put on the back burner. Susan B. Anthony and Elizabeth Cady Stanton refused to let it stay there. Starting in 1868, the two published a women's rights newsletter that encouraged women to strive for more. Although the paper was commercially unsuccessful, it introduced crucial ideas (suffrage, women in the workforce, divorce, reproductive rights, and so forth) to a grossly underrepresented group in America. For the rest of her life (and even against doctor's orders), Susan B. Anthony fought like hell for women's rights. In her final speech in 1906 at age eighty-six, Anthony reminded women that, in their fight for suffrage, "failure is impossible." Fourteen years after her death, the Nineteenth Amendment finally passed.

| 1866 | 1866 | 1867 | 1867 |

Honorable Mentions: Thomas Morris Chester - 1865 (war correspondent), Ignacio Zaragoza - 1862 (Cinco de Mayo hero), Allan Pinkerton - 1861 (super detective), William Leggett and William Gunmere - 1869 (invented college football), Charles Pearson - 1863 (London Underground, humanitarian), Alfred Ely Beach - 1869 (NYC subway), Mary Ann Bickerdyke - 1862 (Civil War hospital hero), Giuseppe Fiorelli - 1860 (discovered Pompeii), Edmund McIlhenny - 1868 (Tabasco), Frederick Walton - 1860 (linoleum), George Francis Train - 1860 (first British street railway), Andrew Ranking - 1866 (urinal), Christopher Sholes - 1868 (QWERTY)

WORST

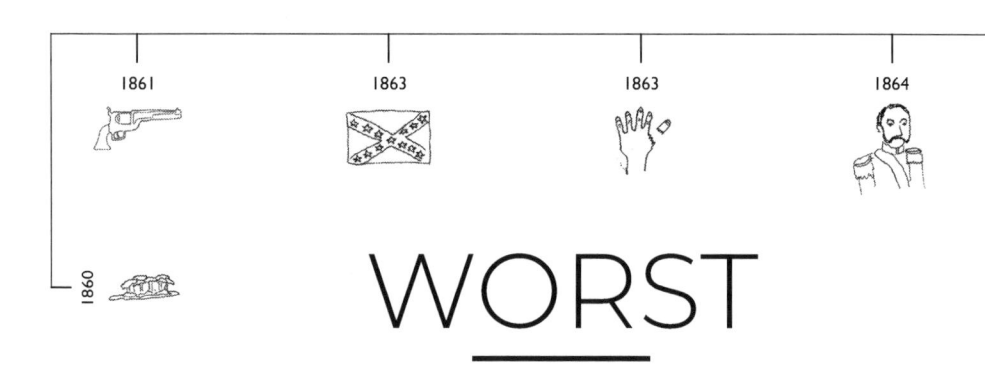

10. ANDREW JOHNSON
1865 - Washington, D.C.

Andrew Johnson was the only Southern senator to not abandon his post after secession. For that, Abe Lincoln asked him to be his VP during his second term. One month into that second term, Lincoln was shot, and the unqualified, ill-equipped Johnson became America's commander-in-chief. Before being sworn in, Johnson slugged back three belts of whiskey and gave an incoherent "hello" to the shaken American public. It was all downhill from there. Instead of a strong leader to shape post-war America, we got a weakling who allowed the South to revert back to its ugly ways. There was no redistribution of land and no assistance to recently freed slaves. Johnson's entire presidency could be summed up in one of his quotes from 1866: "This is a country for white men, and by God, as long as I am president, it shall be a government for white men." Thanks, Andy. Now go fuck yourself.

9. EDWARD JOHN EYRE
1865 - Morant Bay, Jamaica

Even though slavery had been abolished in Jamaica more than a half-century earlier, life for black people was still rough. After a black man was thrown in jail for trespassing on an abandoned plantation, tempers boiled over. Former-slave-turned-politician William Gordon marched upon the capital to demand change, and Colonial Governor Edward Eyre responded by declaring martial law. Over a thousand homes belonging to former slaves were burned down and four hundred former slaves were executed, including Gordon. The ugly incident didn't go over well back at the mother ship (England) and Eyre was removed from his post.

8. JEFFERSON DAVIS
1863 - Richmond, Virginia

While Abe Lincoln surrounded himself with a great team, Confederate President Jefferson Davis ignored potential assets (like Joseph E. Johnston) because he didn't like them and placed incompetent boobs (like Braxton Bragg) in key posts. While Bragg was running the army, he gave himself two positions—general and quartermaster—and then, torn between the two sets of duties, proceeded to get into a lengthy argument with himself. Davis' domestic policies were disastrous as well. During the war, food prices soared while wages remained stagnant. People were hungry and angry. Davis' solution was to ask everyone to pray and fast for the cause. That rah-rah suggestion only led to the Richmond Bread Riots. After four blunder-filled years and a failed escape, Jefferson Davis was jailed for treason.

7. SAMUEL COLT
1861 - Hartford, Connecticut

After raising enough money selling hits of nitrous oxide, Samuel Colt designed a pistol that didn't need to be reloaded after each shot. His business took off during the 1840s and 1850s when America looked to expand its borders. As tensions rose between the North and South, Colt took full advantage and sold tons of weapons to the soon-to-be-Confederate states. In fact, Colt was still shipping guns to Richmond three days after the Civil War had started. Only when this trade became forbidden did he stop. At best, he was a ruthless capitalist that treated his workers like trash. At worst, he was a traitor who helped kill lots of Americans and prolong slavery.

6. J. PIERPONT MORGAN
1863 - New York, New York

J.P. Morgan was like the cartoonish evil rich guy in an old-timey movie. During the Civil War he took advantage of the pay-$300-to-let-an-Irish-immigrant-fight-in-your-place rule to get out of the draft. He then spent the war getting richer, buying thousands of rifles for dirt cheap ($3.50 each), then selling them at a 600 percent markup ($22) to the military. The reason those rifles were so cheap was that they were defective—the shooter could lose his thumb upon firing. But what did J.P. Morgan care? He wasn't the one shooting. He was gettin' paid! Later in life, Morgan got into a pissing match with a robber baron named E.H. Harriman while trying to corner the railroad market and caused a stock market plunge (the Panic of 1901). The panic did everything from destroying many people's life savings to severely delaying the invention of the radio (Nicola Tesla's project had to be scrapped when the market collapsed).

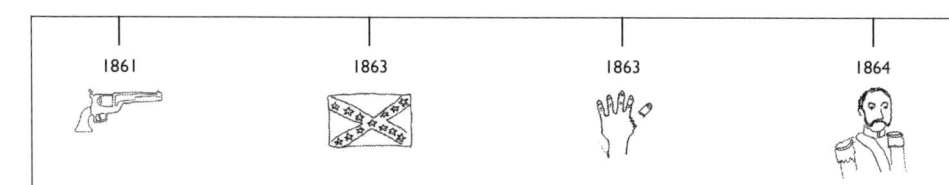

5. SEMAN WRIGHT
1860 - Eureka, California

After the Gold Rush, settlers struggled to coexist with local native tribes. One day, Seman Wright figured that if he could just wipe out the nearby tribe, it would make life a lot easier for him and his buddies. So he waited until the men of the tribe were out collecting supplies, then led a group of six who called themselves the Humboldt Volunteers to the tribe's small island home and slaughtered with axes and knives between 80 and 250 women, children, and elders. The attack nearly wiped out the entire Wiyot community.

4. JOHN WILKES BOOTH
1865 - Washington, D.C.

Despite being a Southern white supremacist, actor John Wilkes Booth was profoundly inspired by militant abolitionist John Brown's crimes in 1859. While volunteering with the Virginia state militia to oversee Brown's execution, Booth saw a man who was so committed to his cause that he was willing to give his life to it. In the following years, Booth dedicated his life to preventing a corrupt (in his mind) politician from eradicating slavery. So, in 1865, when President Lincoln visited Ford's Theatre (a place Booth had unfettered access to), Booth snuck into Lincoln's box and shot him in the ear. Lincoln died and, instead of the South being avenged (as Booth shouted while fleeing), one of the worst presidents in history took over and presided for a term which proved disastrous for the South.

3. JOHN MANNERS-SUTTON
1869 - Victoria, Australia

Inspired by some of the great reforms going on in England, the Australian parliament wanted to enact some of their own change to grant all men the ability to vote, provide free education for all, and protect Australia's indigenous people. Except... the Aboriginal Protection Act of 1869 (signed into law by Governor John Manners-Sutton) wasn't really about protecting them at all. The act gave an administrative board complete control over where Aborigines could live, what jobs they could have, and who they could marry. It eventually led to the removal of mixed-race children from their families so they could become wards of state. In the hundred-plus years after the act, between twenty-five and thirty-five thousand children were taken from their families.

2. NATHAN BEDFORD FORREST
1865 - Pulaski, Tennessee

Christmas Eve is a day when lots of people spend quality time with their families or spread good cheer to others. But for a group of butt-hurt former Confederate soldiers in 1865, Christmas Eve was the day to form the worst hate group in American history. In the post-Civil War South, white men no longer had total authority (just *almost* total authority), so Forrest and his goon friends formed the Ku Klux Klan to try to change things. They used violence and intimidation against blacks and Republicans in an effort to influence the 1868 election. What the hateful dummies failed to consider was that their violent actions would make Northerners realize that these racists hadn't learned their lesson. That led to harsher restrictions in the South and the passing of the Fifteenth Amendment (allowing every black man to vote). And Republican Ulysses S. Grant still won the election easily. Rather than realize there was no returning to the antebellum way of life and give up, Forrest's club of pathetic, bedsheet-wearing losers has endured, accomplishing nothing but perpetuating racist stereotypes about the South.

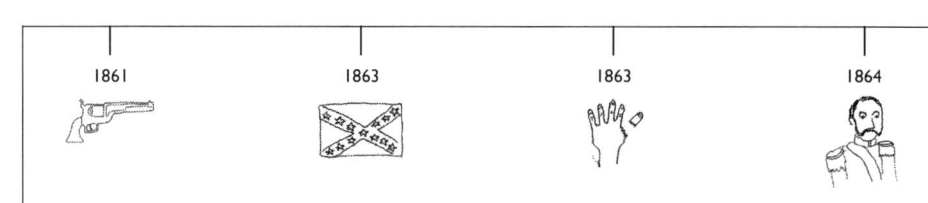

1. ALEXANDER II
1864 - St. Petersburg, Russia

After Russia got its ass handed to it in the Crimean War, Alexander II needed to make major changes to rebuild his demoralized nation. The first thing he did was get rid of the serf system. Like American slaveholders in the South, Russia was still clinging to the past while the rest of the world had moved on to the Industrial Age. Freeing the serfs, in theory, was a good thing. Unfortunately, Alexander did a lousy job quarterbacking the transition, so rich landowners ended up seizing all the good land while peasants took on insane debt to purchase insufficient scraps of property. The second thing he did was pick a scapegoat for everyone to rally around in hate: the Circassians. In 1864, he had his army burn down villages and murder between 650,000 to 1.5 million of northwest Russian ethnicity. The rest were deported to Turkey. "Ethnic cleansing" is never the answer, Alex.

1865

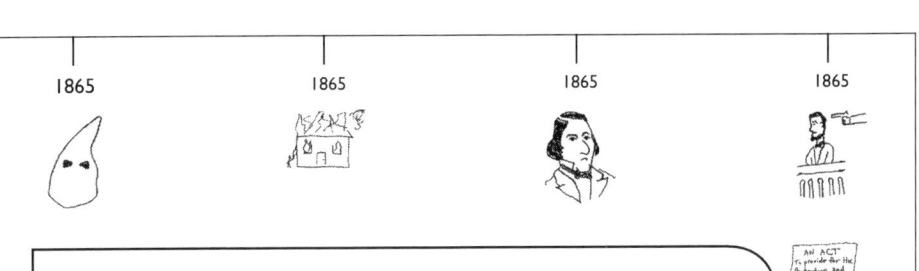

1865

1865

1865

1869

Dishonorable Mentions: Hippolyte Mege-Mouries - 1869 (margarine), Alexander Stephens - 1861 (cornerstone speech), Jeremiah Curtis and Benjamin Perkins - 1860 (Mrs. Winslow's Soothing Syrup), Darius Malott - 1860 (Lady Elgin disaster), Salon jury - 1863 (Manet outrage), Thomas Clark Durant - 1869 (robber baron), John Manning - 1860 (racist South Carolina governor), Fredric Speed - 1865 (SS Sultana disaster), Jesse James - 1869 (outlaw)

1870-1879

"Patriotism is supporting your country all the time, and your government when it deserves it."

-Mark Twain

BEST

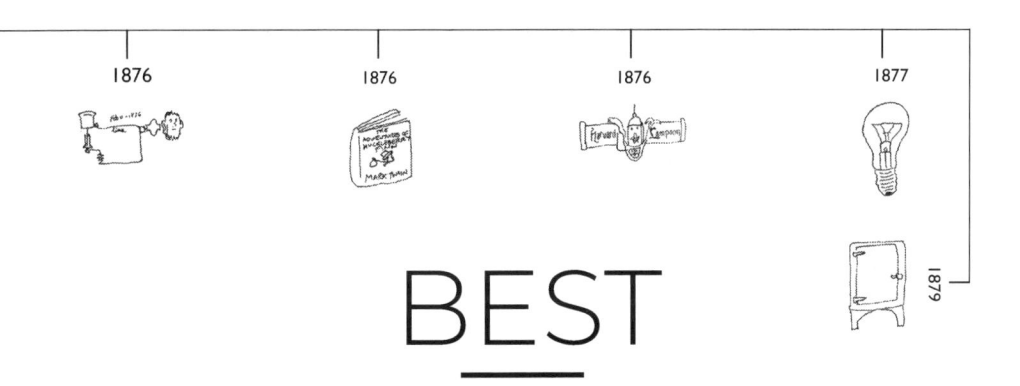

10. JOHN TYLER WHEELWRIGHT
1876 - Cambridge, Massachusetts

Sometimes, the best way to point out injustice or ridiculousness in the world is to make fun of it. So, Wheelwright and six of his Harvard classmates started a publication modeled after *Punch*, the British humor magazine. Over the years, *Harvard Lampoon* satirized everything. It also served as a boot camp for some of the big names in comedy and literature over the past century: John Updike, George Plimpton, Conan O'Brien, and writers of *The Simpsons, Seinfeld, The Office*, among others. Eventually it spun off into *National Lampoon*, which is responsible for producing a lot of the first cast of *Saturday Night Live*, the *Vacation* movies, *Animal House*, writers for *Late Night with David Letterman*, and many more. *Harvard Lampoon* is the top branch of the American comedy family tree.

9. THOMAS NAST
1871 - New York, New York

One of the most influential Americans of the nineteenth century was a cartoonist originally from Germany. At just eighteen, Thomas Nast drew wildly popular political cartoons for *Harper's Weekly*. For his work portraying the evils of slavery, Abe Lincoln called Nast "our best recruiting sergeant." After the war, Nast set his sights on corruption in New York City, which was being run into the ground by Boss Tweed and his Tammany Hall political machine. Despite Tweed's power and influence, Nast took repeated shots at the man who had pilfered between $30 and $200 million from the people. Many of his immigrant supporters couldn't read the papers, but Nast's drawings were accessible to all. By November, the Tammany Hall members were swept in the election and later sent to prison. Nast is also responsible for the most prominent drawing of Santa with his "naughty and nice" list as well as popularizing the signature Democrat donkey and Republican elephant.

8. THOMAS ELKINS
1879 - Albany, New York

There are lots of great ideas that lose something in execution and turn out to be not so great. Thomas Elkins, a black pharmacist and highly respected member of the Albany community, was the guy who improved those not so great things. In between assisting escaped slaves, Elkins filed for several key patents (like the ironing board and the toilet) throughout the 1870s. In 1879, Elkins came up with an improvement to the refrigerator. While his patent seemed to focus more on the utility of keeping corpses cool, it provided the framework for the modern fridge—coils which provided a more even cooling, rather than relying on a single cold area to reduce the interior temperature of an entire unit.

7. CHARLOTTE RAY
1872 - Washington, D.C.

After finishing school at age nineteen, Charlotte Ray got the best (and just about only) job an educated black woman could—teaching. But her heart wasn't in it. So she applied to Howard's law school under the initials C.E. Ray and was accepted. At Howard Law, Charlotte excelled and, in 1872, became the first black woman in America (and the third woman of any color) to receive a law degree and pass the bar. Despite being the first woman to ever try a case in front of the Supreme Court, she wasn't able to get enough work to make a decent living. So Charlotte moved up north, resumed teaching in New York, and focused her efforts on the suffrage movement.

6. MARK TWAIN
1876 - Elmira, New York

Missouri steamboat captain-turned-reporter Sam Clemens started writing editorials under the pen name Mark Twain (steamboat slang for a depth of twelve feet of water). After gaining national acclaim and a reputation for his humor and ability to point out nonsense in the world, he followed up by writing two of the great American novels, *The Adventures of Tom Sawyer* and *Adventures of*

| 1876 | 1876 | 1876 | 1877 |

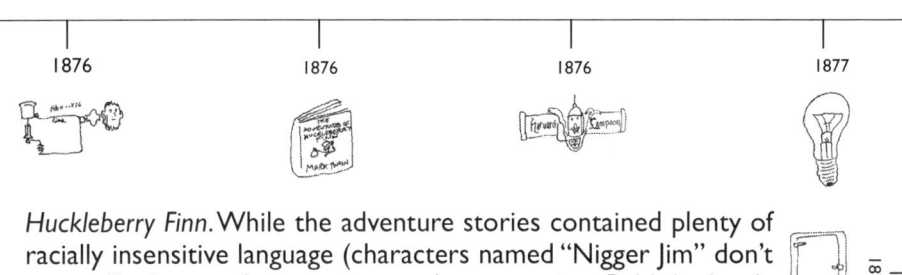

1879

Huckleberry Finn. While the adventure stories contained plenty of racially insensitive language (characters named "Nigger Jim" don't age well), the novels were extremely progressive. Published only a couple decades after the Civil War, *Tom Sawyer* and *Huck Finn* thumbed their noses at racism and slavery. To quote the great Ernest Hemingway: "All modern American literature comes from one book by Mark Twain called *Huckleberry Finn*."

5. FERDINAND HAYDEN
1871 - Yellowstone National Park, Wyoming

In the late 1860s, the land in the United States was getting swallowed up by railroad companies and factories. Ferdinand Hayden, the head of the U.S. Geological Survey of the Territories, heard about a majestic region in the Wyoming Territory and decided to check it out. When he returned to Washington, D.C. to share photographs of this amazing place, Hayden warned against the dangers of letting private development overtake and ruin it. A.B. Nettleton, a lobbyist working for Northern Pacific, urged Hayden to go to Congress and have them pass a bill forever protecting this land. Otherwise, the Wyoming Territory would soon be a thing of the past. He did. It passed. And Yellowstone became the first national park in the world.

4. LEO TOLSTOY
1875 - Yasnaya Polyana, Russia

After fighting in the Crimean War, Tolstoy returned to Russia, grew a crazy big beard, and wrote some of the greatest novels of all time (*War and Peace*, *Anna Karenina*). He created the most nuanced characters to ever exist in literature and wasn't afraid to take a thousand pages to examine them. While his novels focused on love, fate, class, unhappiness, and revenge, the main overall theme to Tolstoy's writing could probably be boiled down to "don't judge a book by its cover." Considering the man looked like he lived under a bridge, that's a pretty good motto to live by.

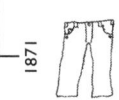

3. ELISHA GRAY
1876 - Highland Park, Illinois

Who invented the telephone? WRONG. It was Elisha Gray, the head of Western Electric (the technical advisors for Western Union). The natural progression of the telegraph (remote written communication) became reality when Gray's liquid transmitter design produced results. He submitted his invention to the patent office on Valentine's Day, 1876. Miraculously, Alexander Graham Bell, a guy who had never previously talked about or worked on any liquid transmitters, submitted the exact same design to the patent office on the same day. After about a month, Bell was the one who was granted the patent, became insanely wealthy, and now is one of the most famous men who ever lived. The bewildered and embittered Gray became a college professor in Ohio.

2. JACOB DAVIS
1871 - Reno, Nevada

Jacob Davis, a tailor, couldn't make pants strong enough to withstand the working conditions for miners—the pockets and button flies would constantly rip. Then he started making riveted trousers using duck cloth, a type of canvas. Lacking the money for a patent, Davis partnered up with Levi Strauss, a German immigrant who was running a dry goods store in San Francisco. Strauss ran the business and Davis was the production manager. Soon they replaced the duck cloth with blue denim, a more flexible material, and the business exploded. Jeans went from blue collar attire, to casual wear, to now being a wardrobe staple for most. Considering there are maybe three occasions in the average life where it's not appropriate to wear jeans, it's safe to call Davis's invention the greatest moment in the history of fashion design.

1. THOMAS EDISON
1877 - Menlo Park, New Jersey

"The Wizard of Menlo Park" didn't invent nearly as many things as you believe he did, but he did have two monumental achievements.

1876	1876	1876	1877

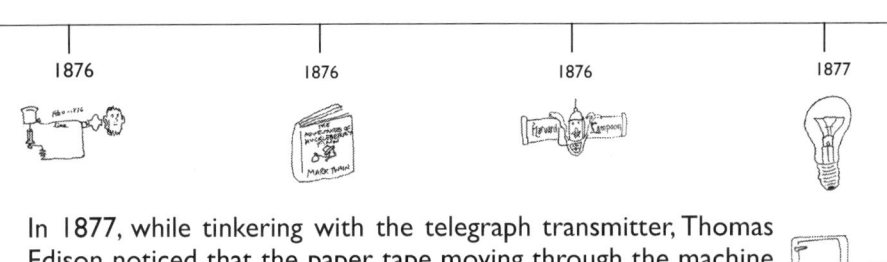

In 1877, while tinkering with the telegraph transmitter, Thomas Edison noticed that the paper tape moving through the machine sounded like voices talking. He switched from paper to a tinfoil-covered cylinder and invented the first record player. A few years later, Edison tackled the light bulb. There were others who tried but, for one reason or another, the didn't work. For example, Humphrey Davy's bulb was too bright, Warren de la Rue's cost too much, Joseph Swan's burned out quickly, and Henry Woodward and Matthew Evans' was powered by explosive nitrogen. But, in the late 1870s, Edison and his team came up with an affordable carbonized bamboo filament that could last over twelve hundred hours. By 1880, the Edison Electric Light Company manufactured light bulbs that very much resembled the ones used today.

1879

Honorable Mentions: Jules Verne - 1870 ("father of science fiction"), Elijah McCoy - 1872 ("the real McCoy"), Gerhard Hansen - 1873 (cured leprosy), Henrik Ibsen - 1879 (*A Doll's House*), Frank Woolworth - 1879 (five-and-dime stores), Eadweard Muybridge - 1878 (motion picture pioneer), Standing Bear - 1879 (Native American activist), Albert Spalding - 1874 (sporting goods), Dr. Joseph Bell - 1877 (Scottish doctor, inspiration for Sherlock Holmes), Edward L. Youmans - 1872 (*Popular Science*), Fred Goldsmith - 1870 (curveball), James Ritty - 1879 (cash register), Cajun/Creole/African people - 1872 (jambalaya), Victoria Woodhull - 1872 (first female presidential candidate)

WORST

10. MARY ANN COTTON
1873 - West Aukland, England

Some people are creatures of habit. Unfortunately for about twenty-one people in nineteenth century England, Mary Ann Cotton's habit was murder by arsenic. Her pattern was nearly the same each time: meet a man, marry him, have some kids, then poison all of them. She'd then use the insurance money to get out of Dodge. In each new town, Mary quickly identified her next mark and convinced him to put her in his will. Once the ink dried, the husband was soon to go. After killing a couple of her third husband's kids, forensics caught up to her. A suspicious doctor was able to test for arsenic and it came back positive. Mary Ann was hanged.

9. JOHN HARVEY KELLOGG
1876 - Battle Creek, Michigan

The "father of breakfast cereal" was a full-on weirdo. At the age of twenty-four, he took over the Seventh-day Adventist Western Health Reform Institute (which was renamed the Battle Creek Sanitarium). From there, he tried to improve wellness by promoting healthier diets while incorporating an anti-sex agenda. At the "San," Kellogg tried to curb masturbation and libido through bland food and sticking yogurt up guys' asses. He was even opposed to marital sex: he kept a separate bedroom from his wife and adopted all of his kids. Even his cereal ideas were flaccid. His famous invention, which he called "granola," was a complete rip-off of James Caleb Jackson's "granula."

8. RICHARD WAGNER
1870 - Munich, Germany

The man responsible for composing the song that appeared in the greatest Bugs Bunny short ("What's Opera, Doc?") was a flaming pile of dogshit. During the Revolutions of 1848, Wagner fled from his home in Germany to Zurich, Switzerland. He spent the next eleven years screwing some other guy's wife and writing the anti-Semitic screed, "Jewishness of Music." In his philosophical musings about the Jews, Wagner blamed them for pretty much everything wrong in art and society. But he composed a few popular operas and returned to Germany a hero. In 1870, his greatest work, *Ride of the Valkyries* (a.k.a. "Kill the Wabbit"), cemented his status as one of the most influential composers of all time. Guess who was a particularly big fan of both his music and philosophies? Adolph Hitler.

7. BOSS TWEED
1876 - New York, New York

Boss Tweed was the definition of crooked politician. Throughout the 1860s, Tweed controlled just about every facet of the New York Democratic Party while pocketing incredible sums of cash in the process. If someone wanted to become governor, state senator, or mayor of New York City, they had to come to Tweed. For well over a decade, the Tweed's Tammany Hall bled the city dry through fraudulent contracts and misdirection of funds. The party came crashing down for Tweed and his cronies in the 1870s. In 1873, Tweed was thrown in jail but managed to escape to Cuba and then Spain. In 1876, someone recognized him from a Thomas Nast cartoon and he was arrested again.

6. ANTHONY COMSTOCK
1872 - New York, New York

After serving in the Union Army during the Civil War, Anthony Comstock moved to New York City and made himself leader of the fun police. In 1872, the deeply religious man with giant, connecting muttonchops kicked off a four-decade crusade against what he deemed inappropriate behavior (i.e., sexual activity of any kind). Comstock's crew raided stationary stores and made arrests for pornography. After that, he went down to Washington and lobbied for what would be known as the Comstock Law, which banned contraceptives. Comstock then was given a special post at the U.S. Postal Service, where he inspected packages for dildos and birth control.

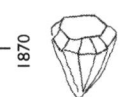

5. MARSHAL FRANCIS BAKER
1871 - Los Angeles, California

One fall night in Los Angeles, gunfire broke out in a rough part of town, leaving saloon owner Robert Thompson dead. LA's top cop Marshal Francis Baker showed up, deputized a group of men to assist him in apprehending the killer, then called it a night. The angry mob used their "authorized" status as their opportunity to take all their aggressions out on the Chinese people of the area. The mob grew to about five hundred people (about a tenth of the city's population at the time). When the dust settled, seventeen Chinese men and boys were lynched, including a well-respected doctor. The incident, which bumped the Great Chicago Fire from the front page of *The New York Times*, produced few arrests and, thanks to a bumbling district attorney, even fewer convictions.

4. GEORGE CUSTER
1876 - Little Bighorn River, Montana

People can argue about whether or not General George Custer was a racist or merely a product of his time. But there is no arguing he was a moron. After finishing last in his class at West Point, Custer entered the Civil War and made his name surviving battles he never should've entered in the first place. His leadership skills were nonexistent. He carelessly endangered the lives of his subordinates on numerous occasions. Finally, in 1876, Custer's hubris got the best of him when he led an attack into Lakota and Cheyenne territory, despite the native leader (Crazy Horse) seeking a peaceful negotiation. The general and about five hundred of his men were slaughtered at the Battle of Little Bighorn.

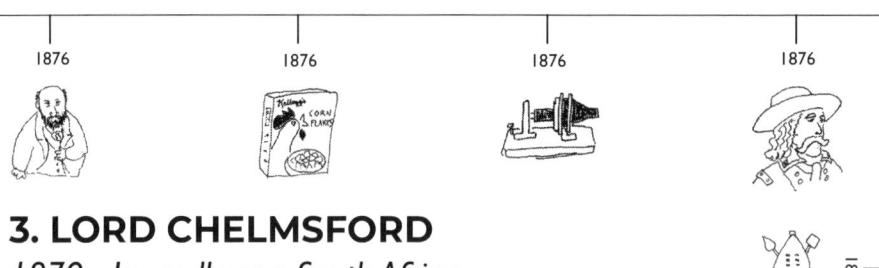

3. LORD CHELMSFORD
1879 - Iswandlwana, South Africa

Zulus were viewed as a threat to the British domination of southern Africa. So Lord Chelmsford, Britain's ambitious, arrogant wanker of a general, decided he'd wipe them out. But he didn't even bother to come up with a good plan; he figured they'd roll up on the guys with the spears and slaughter them easily. Instead, at the Battle of Islandlwana, it was the Brits who got hammered. Of their 1,750 officers, 1,350 were killed. In the aftermath, Chelmsford blamed the loss on a lack of sufficient weapons and got away with it by stifling potential witnesses and by pinning the whole scheme on Colonel Dunford, a poor sonuvabitch who was killed in the battle.

2. ALEXANDER GRAHAM BELL
1876 - Washington, D.C.

Aleck Bell knew Elisha Gray was working on the harmonic telegraph (i.e., the telephone). As luck would have it, Zenas Fisk Wilber, a guy at the patent office, was an old Civil War buddy of Bell's lawyer. On top of that, he was a drunk saddled with gambling debts. Bell's lawyer had Wilber tip him off if Gray tried to file a patent. So when Gray did so, Bell gave Wilber $100 to let him take a look at it. Bell made some modifications to his own design and filed his own patent with the same filing date. Shockingly, the boozy patent clerk with a connection to Bell's lawyer and a tremendous need for quick cash granted the patent to Alexander Graham Bell. Using Gray's design, Bell got famous and rich for his "Watson— come here—I want to see you" origin story. Ten years later, Wilber admitted to the fraud, but it was too late. The Bell Telephone Company was too big to be challenged. Aleck Bell knew Elisha Gray was working on the harmonic telegraph (i.e., the telephone). As luck would have it, Zenas Fisk Wilber, a guy at the patent office, was an old Civil War buddy of Bell's lawyer. On top of that, he was a drunk saddled with gambling debts. Bell's lawyer had Wilber tip him off if Gray tried to file a patent. So when Gray did so, Bell gave Wilber $100 to let him take a look at it. Bell made some modifications to his own design and filed his own patent with the same filing date. Shockingly, the boozy patent clerk with a connection to Bell's lawyer and a tremendous need for quick cash granted the patent to Alexander Graham Bell. Using Gray's design, Bell got famous and rich for his "Watson— come here—I want to see you" origin story. Ten years later, Wilber admitted to the fraud, but it was too late. The Bell Telephone Company was too big to be challenged.

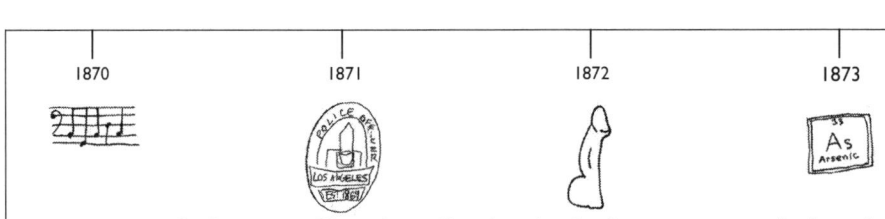

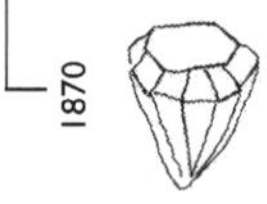

1. CECIL RHODES
1870 - Kimberley, South Africa

In 1870, seventeen-year-old Cecil Rhodes arrived in South Africa with £3000 from his aunt. He invested the money in diamond mining and, within a few years, was running the De Beers diamond cartel. As with just about every other super rich person, once he achieved a supreme level of wealth, he confused that with being super enlightened. Rhodes dreamed of an Africa full of Anglo-Saxons saving the world from itself. He devoted efforts to building a railway that stretched from Cape Town to Cairo. When he wasn't getting help from the British government, he stoked fears that the Germans, Dutch, and French had designs on moving into their African territory. Suddenly, he had the British army at his disposal to displace African people from their homes by any means necessary. Before long, Rhodes had successfully conquered vast territories that were eventually named after the racist prick—Northern Rhodesia (which became Zambia in 1964) and South Rhodesia (which was re-named Zimbabwe in 1980). He never built that railroad but is considered the architect of apartheid in South Africa.

1876

1876

1876

1876

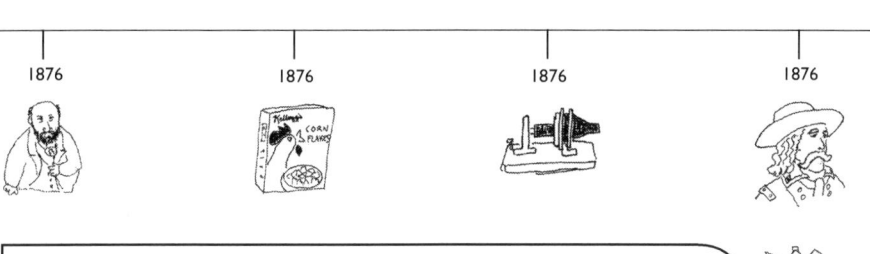

1879

Dishonorable Mentions: Adam Worth - 1876 (the Napoleon of the criminal world), Vatican Council I - 1870 ("the pope is infallible"), George Hull - 1870 (Cardiff Giant), Harrison Weir - 1871 (Cat Fancy), Michael Ahern, John English, James Haynie - 1871 (blamed Great Chicago Fire on immigrant), Richard Crowley - 1872 (opposed women's suffrage), Charles Annan - 1871 (stole paper bag idea), Jack McCall - 1876 (murdered Wild Bill Hickok), Rudolph Virchow - 1877 (anti-evolution), Giovanni Passannante - 1878 (anarchist)

| 1881 | 1883 | 1883 | 1885 |

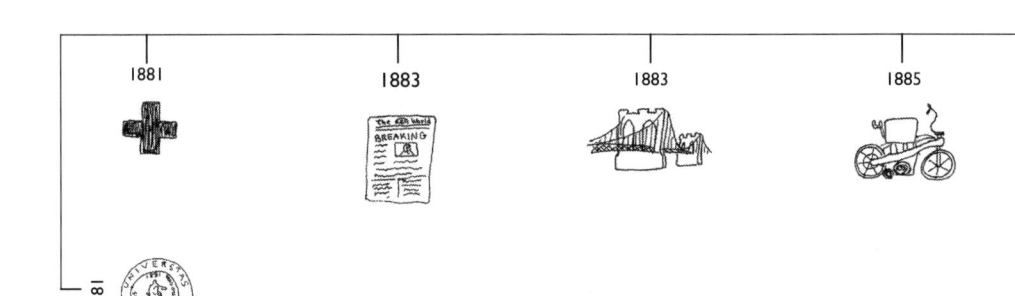

1881

1880-1889

"Character, not circumstances, makes the man."

-Booker T. Washington

BEST

10. (TIE) EMILY ROEBLING
1883 - Brooklyn, New York

Right before construction was set to begin on the world's largest suspension bridge between Brooklyn and Manhattan, the architect, John Roebling, got his toes smashed by another boat. Within a few weeks, he died of tetanus. So his son, Washington, took over the project. For the next fourteen years, six hundred workers worked on the monster project. But then Washington Roebling was crippled on the job and Emily took over. In an era when women were only expected to make sandwiches for their working husbands, Emily Roebling led the biggest construction project in the world. Finally, in 1883, the Brooklyn Bridge opened. For many years, the "eighth wonder of the world" was the tallest structure in the Western hemisphere. More than 130 years later, the iconic bridge is still highly functional, supporting 150,000 pedestrians and vehicles per day.

10. (TIE) HELEN KELLER AND ANNE SULLIVAN
1887 - Tuscumbia, Alabama

Helen Keller was only nineteen months old when a childhood illness left her deaf and blind. When she was eight, her mother brought her to the Perkins Institute for the Blind to work with Alexander Graham Bell (who was focusing his efforts on charity since he was rich and also possibly feeling a little guilty about being an invention-stealing louse). Bell suggested the child meet with a recent graduate from Perkins, twenty-year-old Anne Sullivan. Sullivan and Keller instantly bonded. Through the use of physical objects, Sullivan taught Keller about communication and the world, beyond anyone's wildest expectations of her potential. Keller learned to speak, lip-read, and eventually graduate from college. Her success gained her admirers like Mark Twain and Frank Sinatra. Keller and Sullivan showed the world that people with physical disabilities not only shouldn't be discarded but also can be productive, inspirational members of society.

| 1881 | 1883 | 1883 | 1885 |

1881

9. MARCELLUS GILMORE EDSON
1884 - Montreal, Canada

In 1884, lots of people had terrible teeth, which made chewing food a tough endeavor. Then, a pharmacist from Montreal invented a delicious paste made of peanuts. Suddenly, old people and people with terrible oral hygiene were easily able to ingest protein. Others refined the process over the next couple decades, so Edson himself never got the fame or fortune. Peter Pan, Skippy, and Reese's all owe their fortunes to the Canadian pharmacist.

8. GEORGE EASTMAN
1888 - Rochester, New York

In the late 1870s George Eastman was planning a trip to Santo Domingo when a coworker advised him to document the journey with photographs. Given the fact that he would've had to spend most of his time lugging heavy equipment, Eastman scrapped his travel plans and instead focused his efforts on creating a more user-friendly camera. By 1888, he launched the Kodak camera with the slogan, "You press the button, we do the rest." Soon, Eastman became one of the richest men in America. Instead of hoarding it, though, he was extremely generous with his money. He donated to Rochester Institute of Technology, the Tuskegee Institute, Hampton, and MIT; he set up one of the first ever stock-option plans for his employees; and he helped improve military equipment. Even his final words were tremendous: "My work is done. Why wait?"

7. JOSEPH PULITZER
1883 - New York, New York

Joseph Pulitzer, a Jewish Hungarian immigrant, went from being a poor, gangly kid who barely spoke English to being the most powerful voice in the history of journalism. After working his way up the ranks in St. Louis, Pulitzer left the *St. Louis Post Dispatch* and took over the struggling *New York World* newspaper. Before Joseph Pulitzer, newspapers were just lots of small words. Nothing but the paper's name stood out. To draw people to his paper, he invented the headline. He built the *New York World* into a dominant force by fighting against inequalities and crusading for working class people. Later in life, Pulitzer founded the Columbia University School of Journalism. Today, his name is synonymous with excellence in his beloved field.

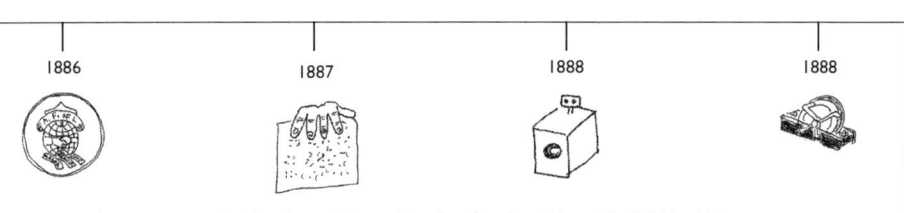

6. SAMUEL GOMPERS
1886 - New York, New York

Samuel Gompers was an active member of the Cigar Makers' International Union, but there was only so much influence he could exert in that role. Unsatisfied with the secretive and not-quite-effective-enough Knights of Labor, Gompers helped form what would eventually be known as the American Federation of Labor. Gompers kept the mission simple: to make life better for all workers whereas the KofL excluded bankers, doctors, liquor-manufacturers, and Chinese workers. The AFL fought for things like the eight-hour workday, stricter child labor rules, and the six-day workweek. Over the next forty years as head of the AFL, Gompers had a major impact on sweeping changes for workers. In effect, Samuel Gompers created the middle class in America.

5. RAFFAELE ESPOSITO
1889 - Naples, Italy

There was a dish called "pizza" way before 1889, but it was just flatbread with any random trash thrown on it. It wasn't until the late nineteenth century that Rafaela Esposito created the mozzarella/red sauce thing that everyone knows and loves and orders in for every party night. King Umberto I's wife, Queen Margherita, was visiting Naples and wanted the best pizza maker in town to come up with something special in her honor. Esposito put mozzarella, marinara, and basil leaves on top of flatbread to represent the three colors of the Italian flag (white, red, and green) and named it after her. The Queen sent him a letter of praise and, in true pizza-shop-owner fashion, Esposito proudly displayed it on his wall.

| 1881 | 1883 | 1883 | 1885 |

4. GOTTLIEB DAIMLER
1885 - Stuttgart, Germany

Gottlieb Daimler was an engine nerd. When he wasn't fixing engines for work, he was tinkering with them in his free time. Together with his collaborator Wilhelm Maybach, Daimler came up with a fuel-powered engine with a carburetor that was more than five times more efficient than its predecessors. They attached it to a bike and created the first ever motorcycle. Granted, the thing only went seven miles per hour, but it was a start. The obvious next step for Daimler and Maybach was the first four-wheeled automobile, but they got derailed by money woes. That honor went to Karl Benz in 1886.

3. CLARA BARTON
1881 - Washington, D.C.

During the Civil War, Clara Barton earned the nickname "Angel of the Battlefield" for her ubiquity as a combat nurse. Once the fighting was over, Barton focused her efforts on reuniting missing soldiers with their families. Finally, her doctor told her to take a break from tending to others so Clara went to Europe, where she quickly joined the International Red Cross to assist with the victims of the Franco-Prussian War. When Barton returned to the United States, she fiercely lobbied for her country to adopt an American branch of this organization, which they did in 1881.

2. BOOKER T. WASHINGTON
1881 - Tuskegee, Alabama

After the Civil War, it's not like confetti dropped from every ceiling and black people were given high-fives and well-paying jobs. Black people had "freedom," and that's about it. It was up to them to figure out how to make it in a white-dominated world. Black Americans needed a superstar, and they got him: Booker T. Washington. The educated former Virginia slave believed that the best way to combat the economic inequalities in America was through education. As head of the Tuskegee Institute, he designed the curriculum to focus heavily on vocational skills, from

| 1886 | 1887 | 1888 | 1888 |

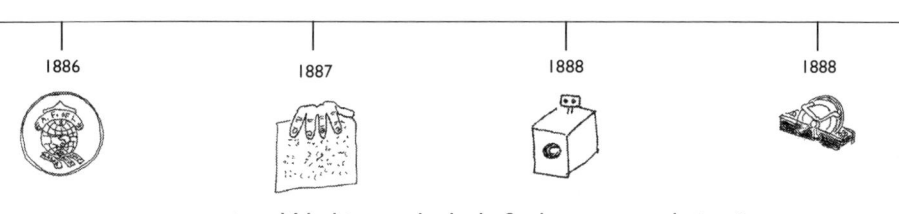

carpentry to sewing. Washington's let's-find-a-way-to-thrive-in-the-white-man's-world approach eventually brought the praise of white leaders like Teddy Roosevelt and the scorn of black leaders like W.E.B. DuBois. Nevertheless, in 1881, the struggling American South needed a visionary like Booker T. Washington, and he delivered.

1. NIKOLA TESLA
1888 - New York, New York

While working to improve Thomas Edison's direct current (DC) power plant, Croatian-born Nikola Tesla had an even better idea: alternating current (AC). It was much more practical and could reach farther distances. Then the two had a falling out, so Tesla teamed up with George Westinghouse to expand his exploration of AC. Within five years, they were tasked with lighting up the World's Fair in Chicago. Tesla invented electricity as we know it today. But, rather than bask in the literal glow of his monumental achievement, he moved on to the next thing: wireless communications. The "Tesla oscillator" made it possible to communicate from great distances, whether with people or remote-controlled vehicles. A few years later, with the backing of Thomas Edison and seventeen of Nikola Tesla's patents, Guglielmo Marconi "invented" the radio. It wasn't until two years after Tesla's death that the patent office ruled that Marconi was pretty much just piggybacking off of Tesla's invention. Nikola Tesla was one of the great minds in world history.

> **Honorable Mentions:** Maurice Koechlin - 1889 (Eiffel Tower), Kate Shelley - 1881 (railroad heroine), Josephine Cochrane - 1886 (dishwasher), Frédéric Auguste Bartholdi - 1886 (Statue of Liberty), Dan Rylands - 1889 (screw-cap bottles), Nellie Bly - 1888 (pioneering journalist), William Le Baron Jenney - 1884 (first skyscraper), Auguste Rodin - 1880 (The Thinker), Emmeline Pankhurst - 1888 (UK suffragist), "Mum" - 1888 (deodorant), Adolph Fick - 1887 (contact lenses), Julia Sand - 1881 (great citizen), Calixa Lavallée - 1880 ("O Canada"), Edward Berner - 1881 (ice cream sundae)

WORST

10. (TIE) GEORGE RENNINGER
1880 - Philadelphia, Pennsylvania

While working at the Wunderlee Candy Company, George Renninger invented a confection made of sugar and corn syrup. After being heated in a large kettle, the gooey mixture was poured into corn kernel-shaped molds. And for over a century now, the resulting candy corn has tortured the masses. This tricolored sugar nightmare has the terrible distinction of making the consumer feel like they're chewing on some monstrous cross between a candle and a piece of sidewalk chalk.

10. (TIE) KLARA POLZL
1889 - Braunau am Inn, Austria-Hungary

Gave birth to Adolph Hitler.

9. THOMAS EDISON
1885 - New York, New York

History has given the "Wizard of Menlo Park" a pass on being an incredible asshole. In 1885, Edison promised Serbian immigrant Nikola Tesla that if he were able to dramatically improve his direct current (DC) generator, Edison would give him $50,000. It took Tesla a few months but when he came to collect, Edison claimed he'd been joking. The pissed-off Tesla left to work on his alternating current (AC) electricity research with the backing of George Westinghouse. So, rather than adapt to the times and work on the more efficient form of electricity, Edison doubled down on DC development and went on an AC smear campaign. Edison held exhibitions where he killed animals with AC to show it was unsafe. He started with dogs, then used a horse and its calves, then Topsy the elephant on Coney Island. To further prove his point, Edison invented the AC-powered electric chair so the state of New York could fry convicted murderer William Kemler. Thomas Edison's sadistic smear campaign never worked. Alternating current won.

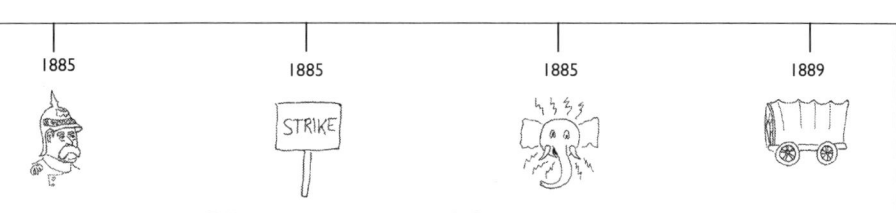

8. JOHN D. ROCKEFELLER
1882 - Cleveland, Ohio

The richest businessman who ever lived (he would be worth about $340 billion today) amassed his fortune through relentless bullying. His plan was always the same: one, buy an oil company; two, grow and grow it; three, bully the most competitive oil company into selling; four, if that oil company doesn't sell, strike an under-the-table deal with the local railroad that will make life miserable for this competitor; and five, swoop in and buy the company once wounded. Rockefeller also figured that if he set up Standard Oil as a trust instead of a corporation, he wouldn't be bound by all of the U.S. monopoly regulations. By the time Rockefeller's oil cartel was finally broken up by the U.S. government in 1911, it was divided into thirty-four different companies. And these companies weren't mom-and-pops. The thirty-four companies owned by Standard Oil turned into behemoths like Exxon, Amoco, Mobil, Chevron, Esso, and more.

7. JAY GOULD
1885 - New York, New York

During the Civil War, railroad developer Jay Gould colluded with fellow robber barons Jim Fisk and Daniel Drew and shady politician Boss Tweed to prevent Cornelius Vanderbilt from growing his railroad empire. While lining his pockets, as well as those of his greasy inner circle, Gould also managed to cause the financial panic in 1869. He continued to buy large chunks of Union Pacific Railroad and took over Western Union Telegraph Company. When his workers went on strike over their abysmal wages, Gould brought in Chinese scabs which caused a spike in hate crimes against the Chinese. Gould couldn't care less. His response to a railroad strike in 1886: "I can hire one half of the working class to kill the other half."

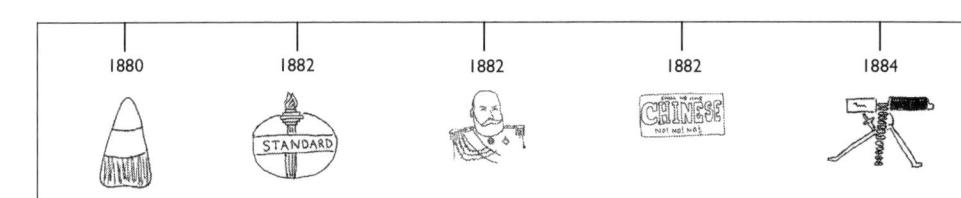

6. HENRY BLAIR
1882 - Washington, D.C.

Conditions for American workers were eroding and people were fed up. Looking for a scapegoat for their problems, they blamed Chinese laborers. Instead of addressing the labor conditions of his constituents, New Hampshire Senator Henry Blair pandered to their ignorance and pushed for a ban on Chinese people entering the country. Chinese represented 0.002 percent of the U.S. population and were given the worst jobs (like building the railroads) at even worse wages. The Chinese weren't the problem. Nonetheless, Blair's legislation (the Chinese Exclusion Act of 1882) was passed. The act stood until 1943, when China became our World War II ally. When you wonder why U.S.-Chinese relations have never been all that great, think about scourges like Henry Blair.

5. HIRAM MAXIM
1884 - London, England

Hiram Maxim was a prolific inventor. But despite creating everything from the hair-curling iron to mousetraps to locomotive headlights to amusement park rides, he didn't think he wasn't making enough money. So the Maine-born Maxim moved across the pond to England (leaving his two wives and four kids behind). When he got to England, someone told him if he really wanted to make a "pile of money," he had to invent a way for Europeans to slaughter each other easier. So, drawing on his own experience with weapons and the recoil phenomenon, Maxim invented the machine gun. Thirty years later, Maxim's invention was responsible for killing millions in World War I. He did make that pile of money he wanted… but the exposure to constant gunfire caused him to go deaf.

4. BENJAMIN HARRISON
1889 - Washington, D.C.

On March 3, 1889, President Benjamin Harrison declared that, in April, the state of Oklahoma would essentially turn into a

| 1885 | 1885 | 1885 | 1889 |

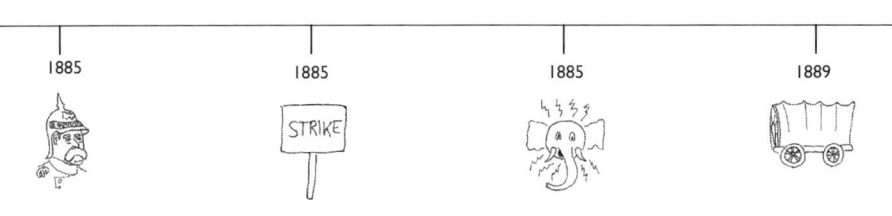

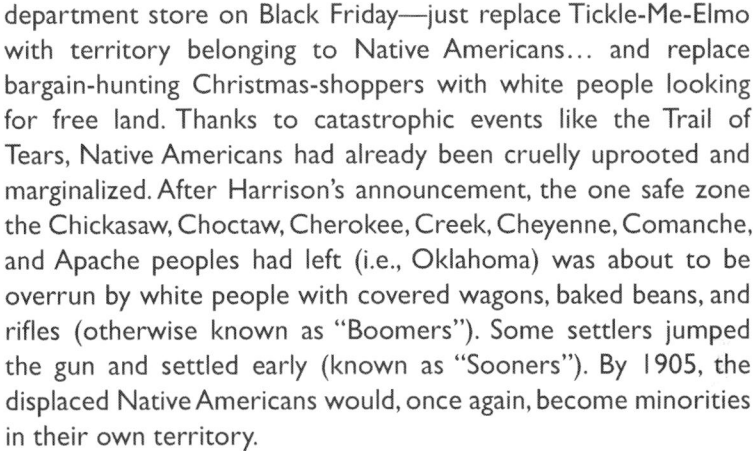

department store on Black Friday—just replace Tickle-Me-Elmo with territory belonging to Native Americans... and replace bargain-hunting Christmas-shoppers with white people looking for free land. Thanks to catastrophic events like the Trail of Tears, Native Americans had already been cruelly uprooted and marginalized. After Harrison's announcement, the one safe zone the Chickasaw, Choctaw, Cherokee, Creek, Cheyenne, Comanche, and Apache peoples had left (i.e., Oklahoma) was about to be overrun by white people with covered wagons, baked beans, and rifles (otherwise known as "Boomers"). Some settlers jumped the gun and settled early (known as "Sooners"). By 1905, the displaced Native Americans would, once again, become minorities in their own territory.

3. ALEXANDER III
1882 - Saint Petersburg, Russia

In the months following Alexander II's death, an increasing number of violent pogroms (attacks on an ethnic group) were directed at Russia's Jewish communities. Murders, rapes, and looting became the norm throughout southern Russia. When the new tsar, Alexander III, investigated the pogroms, he concluded the Jews must have brought it upon themselves. So, with Alexander III's backing, a commission determined the best way to increase the peace would be to confine Jews to a small substandard geographical area. This prompted a mass exodus to the United States in the ensuing years.

2. OTTO VON BISMARK
1885 - Berlin, Prussia (Germany)

The man credited by many for unifying Germany used one of history's sad-yet-all-too-frequent methods for rallying his people together: blaming immigrants. When the economy stalled, people complained of Polish workers taking all the good jobs. Despite that being false (most of the jobs the Polish held were cheap, migrant worker gigs), the Notorious O.V.B. made the decree that all foreign-born Poles (a third of which were Jewish) had to leave. Over the next five years, thirty thousand Poles were bounced forcefully and the "Aryan superiority" seed was planted in Germany.

1. KING LEOPOLD
1880 - Brussels, Belgium

In the nineteenth century, European powers carved up the continent of Africa. Belgian King Leopold went after the big rainforest region in the middle—the Congo. Under the guise of educating and assisting the natives from evils like the Arabs from the North, Leopold sent troops in to absolutely decimate the region. The "Congo Free State" was essentially Leopold's free rubber work camp. Locals either busted their asses to make Leopold rich or had their limbs chopped off. Basically, it was resist and be decapitated. Between 1880 and 1920, Leopold's regime cut the population from about twenty million in half. That's right. That motherfucker was responsible for a population drop of *ten million* people! Shamefully, besides Joseph Conrad's famous novel *Heart of Darkness*, the rape of the Congo has been largely forgotten.

| 1885 | 1885 | 1885 | 1889 |

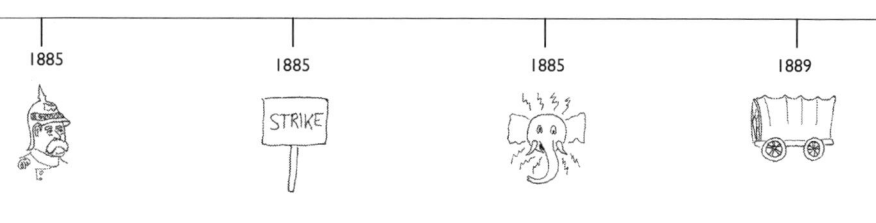

Dishonorable Mentions: Ned Kelly - 1880 (Australian bushranger, murderous thief), Ike Clanton and Tom McClaury - 1881 (O.K. Corral bad guys), Roderick MacLean and Charles J. Guiteau - 1881-1882 (political assassins), Doctor Willard Bliss - 1881 (never washed hands, killed Garfield), Ferdinand Ward - 1884 (Ponzi schemer), Josiah Leeds - 1887 (uptight censor), Jack the Ripper - 1888 (killer), Rebecca Felton - 1886 (banned booze in Atlanta, lynching enthusiast)

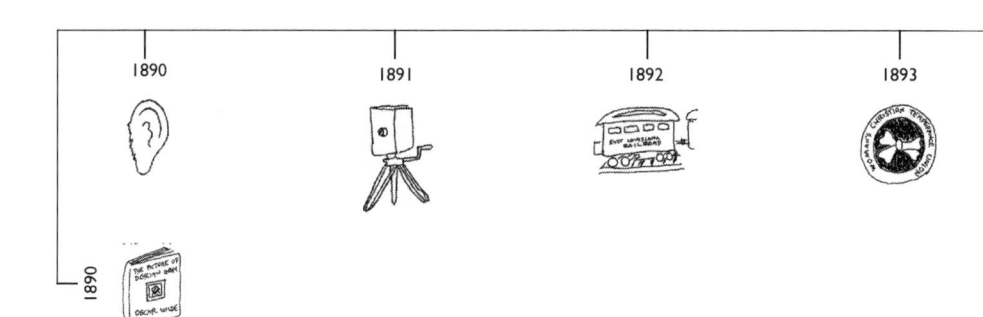

1890-1899

"Some cause happiness wherever they go; others whenever they go."
-Oscar Wilde

BEST

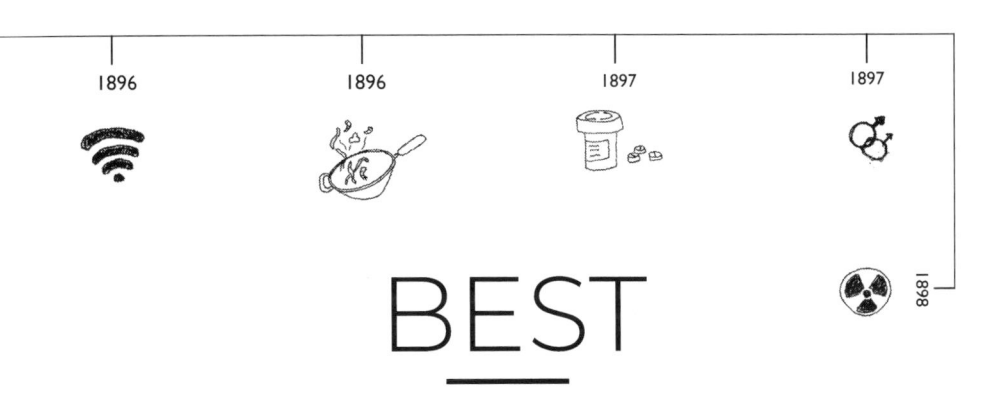

10. LI HUNG-CHANG
1896 - New York, New York

Chinese statesman Li Hung-Chang went on a goodwill trip to the United States with the mission to gain support from the Americans against the Japanese. In some ways, the trip was a flop. Grover Cleveland never lent China a hand and, when Li returned home, he received a cool reception from fellow statesmen. In other ways, though, the trip to New York was a huge success. The curiosity about the exotic visitor and the personal chefs who accompanied him inspired many local restaurants to adopt a Chinese-like meal on their menu—chop suey. Chinese cuisine became a big hit. Chinese-Americans, who had been brought over to work on railroads then discarded soon thereafter, found work in the restaurant industry and social acceptance in their new country. Racial progress sometimes starts with a wok.

9. MAGNUS HIRSCHFELD
1897 - Berlin, Germany

After being subjected to a "sexual degeneracy" lecture where a naked gay man was treated like a lab rat, Magnus Hirschfeld dedicated his life to changing perceptions. Through literature and scientific research, Hirschfeld provided the German parliament with evidence that homosexuality was a natural thing. He was so persistent that they put the law up for a debate. While it was defeated in the end, the doctor was able to sway many in power to not enforce it so harshly. As Hirschfeld's pro-gay reputation grew, his office became a safe haven for the community. He also strongly advocated for birth control, treatment of STDs, and transgender rights (and even performed one of the first-ever gender reassignment surgeries). Hirschfeld fled Nazi Germany in 1932.

8. OSCAR WILDE
1890 - London, England

In the 1890s, Oscar Wilde started a prolific run where he kicked out famous novels like *The Picture of Dorian Gray* and plays like *The Importance of Being Earnest*. Unfortunately for him, uptight Victorian England was a difficult place to live as a gay man. While it was kind of an open secret that Wilde liked the company of men, the father of his boyfriend (the Marquess of Queensbury) wasn't all that progressive. Queensbury ran a smear campaign against Wilde, who in turn took him to court. Wilde lost and was thrown in jail. From there, he went on a downward health spiral and died a few years later.

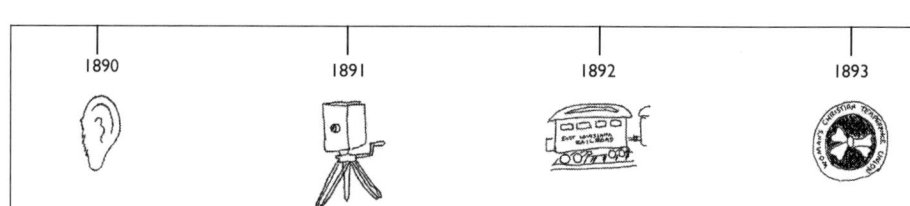

7. JAGADISH CHANDRA BOSE
1895 - Calcutta, India

Since he was a colonized Indian, Jagadish Bose was never given access to proper laboratory conditions and was forced to work in a twenty-four-square-foot room. But racism was never going to stop one of the great scientists in history. Besides his exceptional contributions to plant science, Bose is considered a pioneer of wireless communication. In 1895, he was the first to publicly demonstrate it by sending electromagnetic waves through several walls and a distance of seventy-five feet to ring a bell. He never patented it and Marconi eventually used Bose's Mercury Coherer receiver to become famous for inventing the two-way radio.

6. ARTHUR EICHENGRUN
1897 - Berlin, Germany

In 1934, Felix Hoffman told a nice story about how he invented aspirin so he could treat his rheumatism-inflicted dad. Too bad it was a myth. In reality, Arthur Eichengrun, the head of experimental pharmacology at Bayer, invented it in 1897. Felix Hoffman had been his lab assistant. But, in the 1930s, the Germans rewrote history books so Jews like Eichengrun wouldn't get any credit. Eichengrun eventually left Bayer to start his own successful lab while Bayer mass-marketed his pain-reducing, stroke-preventing drug. Once the Nazis took over, Eichengrun was forced to sell his business and got thrown in a concentration camp. When he reached out to Bayer for assistance, they were nowhere to be found.

| 1896 | 1896 | 1897 | 1897 |

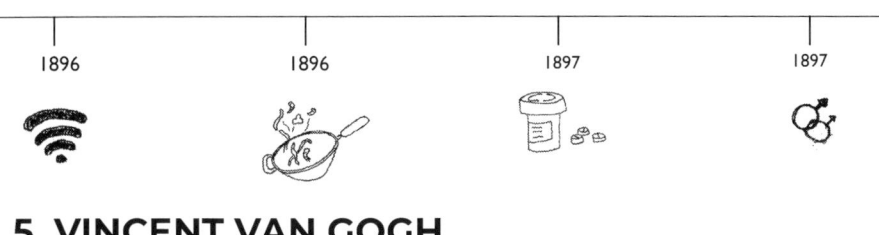

5. VINCENT VAN GOGH
1890 - Auvers, France

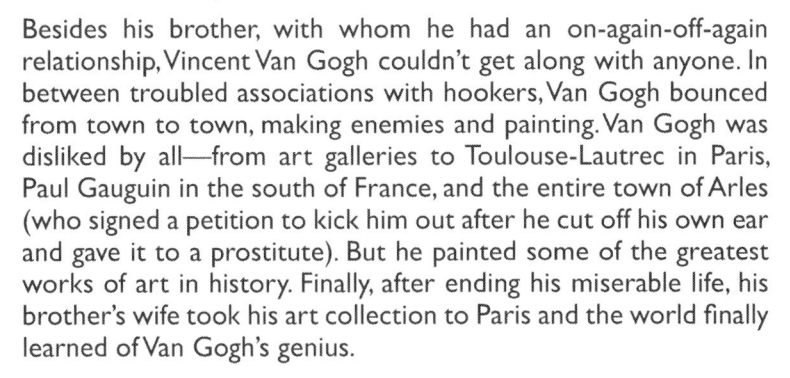

Besides his brother, with whom he had an on-again-off-again relationship, Vincent Van Gogh couldn't get along with anyone. In between troubled associations with hookers, Van Gogh bounced from town to town, making enemies and painting. Van Gogh was disliked by all—from art galleries to Toulouse-Lautrec in Paris, Paul Gauguin in the south of France, and the entire town of Arles (who signed a petition to kick him out after he cut off his own ear and gave it to a prostitute). But he painted some of the greatest works of art in history. Finally, after ending his miserable life, his brother's wife took his art collection to Paris and the world finally learned of Van Gogh's genius.

4. W. K. L. DICKSON
1891 - West Orange, New Jersey

In 1887, Thomas Edison assigned a talented young guy working at his lab, William Dickson, the task of figuring out how to make motion picture. Following Edison's instruction that the camera should work like a phonograph, Dickson unsuccessfully tried various ways of projecting pictures in a cylinder. Then, in the summer of 1889, while Edison was in Europe, Dickson tried a camera-roll strategy and it worked. He filmed some coworkers clowning around for the camera and created the first motion picture. Edison swooped in and recruited major vaudeville acts and stars like Annie Oakley to appear in the earliest films. Being the swell guy that he is, Edison took sole credit for the "kinetoscope." Dickson, justifiably pissed, went to a competitor.

3. HOMER PLESSY
1892 - New Orleans, Louisiana

Homer Plessy was only one-eighth black, so most people just figured he was white. While life would've been a lot easier letting people think that, Plessy never shied from revealing his identity. So, on a random Tuesday in 1892, the shoemaker bought a first-class ticket on an all-white carriage from New Orleans. When the conductor made the rounds, Plessy let the man know he was black, he was an American citizen, he had paid full price, and he had no intention of giving up his seat. Sixty-three years before Rosa Parks had her famous bus protest, Homer Plessy made this major civil rights stand. The ensuing legal battle (*Plessy v. Ferguson*) led to the terrible "separate but equal" Supreme Court ruling and marked an important, early step in the civil rights movement.

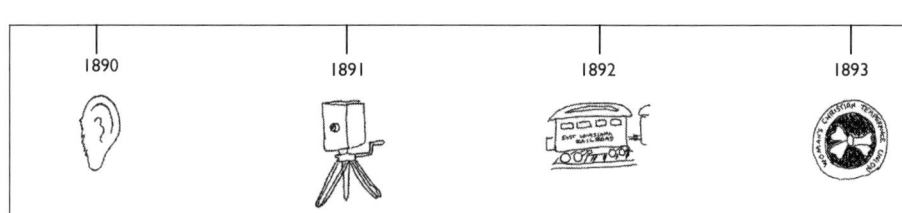

2. KATE SHEPPARD
1893 - Christchurch, New Zealand

While trying to get liquor prohibition passed for the New Zealand Women's Christian Temperance Union, Kate Sheppard was reminded that nothing would ever change (temperance, contraception, divorce, and so forth) unless women were able to vote. If she wanted to make a difference, Sheppard would have to lead the nation's suffrage movement. So for the next eight years, she was a tireless advocate for women. Finally, in 1893, Sheppard showed up at Parliament with a thirty thousand-signature petition. Considering New Zealand was less than a million people, Kate's petition was impossible to ignore. A few months later, New Zealand's governor signed a bill allowing its women to be the first in the world to vote.

1. MARIE CURIE
1898 - Paris, France

French physicist Henri Becquerel discovered that uranium emitted radiation without any help from the sun. A couple years later, a Polish-born woman living in France took Becquerel's work and ran with it. Within a few days, Marie Curie discovered that the element thorium also gave out rays. It was then that she coined the word "radiation." Her July 1898 paper about the power of radiation earned Curie (and her husband) a Nobel Prize for physics and inspired scientists to harness the power of radiation for projects like cancer treatment and nuclear power. That wasn't the only Nobel Prize in the family. Eight years later, Marie landed another for chemistry and, in 1935, her daughter earned one as well.

1896　　　　　1896　　　　　1897　　　　　1897

1898

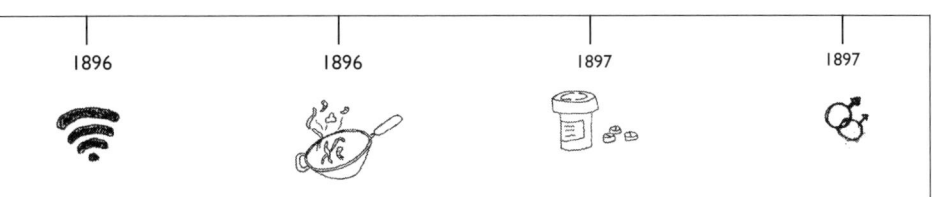

Honorable Mentions: James Naismith - 1892 (basketball), Pyotr Ilyich Tchaikovsky - 1892 (composer), Paul Cezanne - 1893 (cubism), Auguste and Louis Lumiere - 1895 (film pioneers), Arthur Conan Doyle - 1891 (Sherlock Holmes creator), Charles Weaver - 1892 (escalator), Martha Hughes Cannon - 1896 (first female U.S. Senator), Francis Pharcellus Church - 1897 ("Yes Virginia, there is a Santa Claus"), Filippo Milone - 1898 (pizza evangelist), John Burr - 1899 (rotary blade lawnmower), Louis Glass - 1890 (jukebox), Pierre, Baron de Coubertin - 1896 (modern Olympics), Amos Alonzo Stagg - 1899 (sports innovator), John Dewey - 1897 (educational reform), John Muir - 1890 (naturalist), John Phillip Holland - 1897 (gas-powered submarine), Bram Stoker - 1897 (*Dracula*), Henri Toulouse-Lautrec - 1895 (artist), Giacomo Pucini - 1896 (*La Boheme*), Henri Becquerel - 1896 (discovered radioactivity), Wong Kim Ark - 1898 (Asian-American activist), Stephen Crane - 1894 (*Red Badge of Courage*), Richard Canfield - 1894 (club sandwich), George Washington Ferris - 1893 (ferris wheel), Daniel Williams - 1893 (first open-heart surgery), Victor Horta - 1891 (art deco architect), Kid Blink - 1899 (newsboy union leader), Lemuel Benedict - 1894 (eggs Benedict), Herman Hollerith - 1890 (tabulating machine), Wilhelm Conrad Roentgen - 1890 (x-ray)

WORST

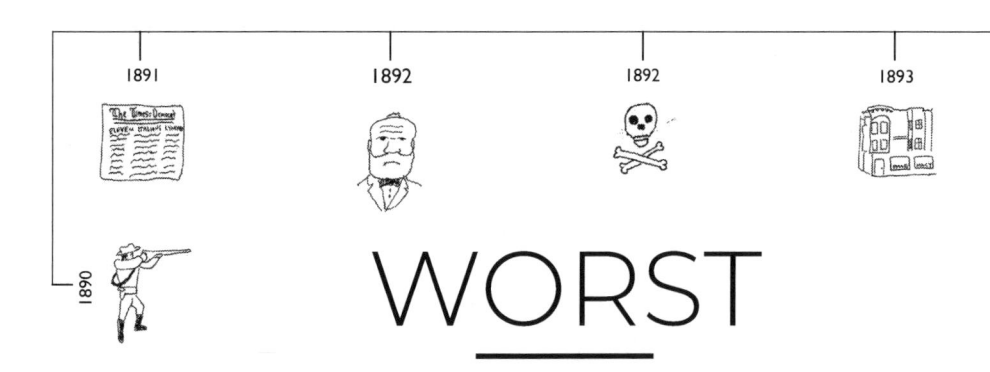

10. THOMAS NEILL CREAM
1892 - London, England

Wherever the Scottish-born Cream went, death followed. After killing his pregnant wife in a failed abortion, the doctor moved from Canada to England. When his pregnant mistress was found dead in the alley behind Cream's practice, he moved to Chicago. While performing illegal abortions for prostitutes, he killed one but got away with it. But then he got caught poisoning his mistress' husband and was sent to prison for life. Somehow he got out and moved back to London. Once again, prostitutes in the area started dying from poisoning. Cream was arrested and put on trial. While on the stand, the doctor accidentally did himself in by revealing the type of poison that killed the women even before that evidence had been produced. Game over.

9. WILLIAM RANDOLPH HEARST
1898 - New York, New York

William Randolph Hearst was in a battle with Joseph Pulitzer (and nearly fifty other daily newspaper publishers) for supremacy of the New York market. Over time, the competition turned into a contest of who could be more sensational and inflammatory (a.k.a. "yellow journalism"). During the Cuban Revolution of 1895, Hearst's slanted stories about oppressive Spanish overlords pandered to working class Americans. He sent photographers down to Cuba with the mandate, "You furnish the pictures. I'll furnish the war." And that's exactly what he did. Hearst whipped the public into a hawkish frenzy thinking the Spanish had sunk a U.S. battleship (which was really an accident). The public panic led to a war in which three thousand Americans were killed. But at least the rich guy sold his papers.

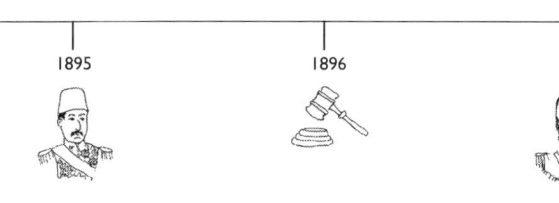

8. VALERIANO WEYLER
1897 - Havana, Cuba

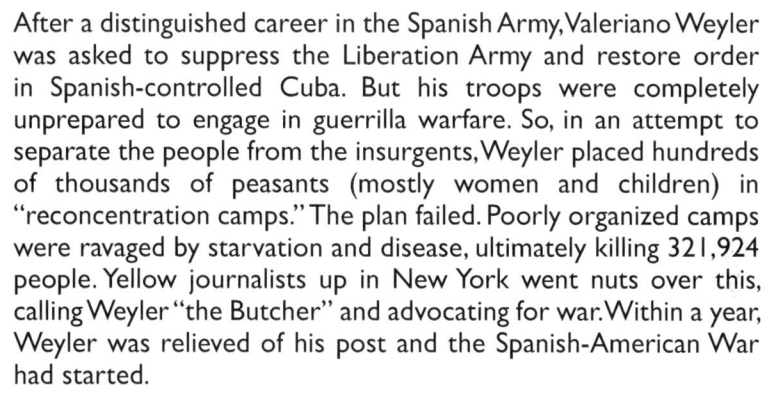

After a distinguished career in the Spanish Army, Valeriano Weyler was asked to suppress the Liberation Army and restore order in Spanish-controlled Cuba. But his troops were completely unprepared to engage in guerrilla warfare. So, in an attempt to separate the people from the insurgents, Weyler placed hundreds of thousands of peasants (mostly women and children) in "reconcentration camps." The plan failed. Poorly organized camps were ravaged by starvation and disease, ultimately killing 321,924 people. Yellow journalists up in New York went nuts over this, calling Weyler "the Butcher" and advocating for war. Within a year, Weyler was relieved of his post and the Spanish-American War had started.

7. ANDREW CARNEGIE AND HENRY FRICK
1892 - Homestead, Pennsylvania

Andrew Carnegie's three-year contract with the steelworkers' union was just about up, and Carnegie wanted to break the union. So, right before he left for his summer vacation in Scotland, he instructed his henchman Henry Frick to crush them in his absence. Frick slashed wages, locked the workers out of the plant, hired scabs, and brought armed guards to protect the facilities. Things turned violent. Seven striking workers and nine Pinkerton guards were killed in the chaos, and poor Andrew Carnegie's reputation was forever tarnished. "Nothing... in all my life, before or since, wounded me so deeply." Boo-hoo, Andrew. Hope the solace of being one of the richest guys in world history (with about four times the net worth of Bill Gates) helped you through those sleepless nights.

6. HENRY BILLINGS BROWN
1896 - Washington, D.C.

The worst decision in U.S. Supreme Court history was written by this jerkoff. After Homer Plessy refused to surrender his seat on a whites-only train carriage, he was arrested and the *Plessy v. Ferguson* case made it all the way to the Supreme Court. In writing the eight-to-one majority decision, which ruled that separate-but-equal facilities were totally constitutional, Henry Billings Brown said that mixing races wasn't the answer to racial harmony. In his esteemed legal opinion, wearing blinders and ignoring the Thirteenth and Fourteenth Amendments were the best course of action. The one dissenting justice, John Marshall Harlan, warned that the decision would eventually look as bad as the Dred Scott case. He was right. Henry Billings Brown was a big, fat idiot.

5. JOHN PARKER
1891 - New Orleans, Louisiana

Throughout American history, each new wave of immigrants has faced awful discrimination. In the late nineteenth century, Italians were taking the hit. A corrupt New Orleans police chief was ambushed by gunmen outside his home one morning. With his dying breaths, he blamed it on "the dagoes." So, dozens of Italians were arrested on little to no proof. When the jury trial ended with acquittals and mistrials, John Parker (the future governor of Louisiana) formed a mob and stormed the county prison. Nine of the defendants, along with two other Italians awaiting trial for unrelated charges, were lynched. The mass violence was met with extreme indifference by everyone from future President Teddy Roosevelt ("a rather good thing") to *The New York Times* ("sneaking and cowardly Sicilians").

4. JAMES MCLAUGHLIN
1890 - Standing Rock Reservation, South Dakota

After Little Bighorn, Sitting Bull and the Sioux were people without a home. They bounced around a bit before reluctantly accepting the United States' proposal to settle on a reservation. Some of the Sioux felt that, by doing so, they were abandoning their culture. So they performed the Ghost Dance, which would force the gods to allow society to start over. James McLaughlin, head of the reservation police, misinterpreted the dance as the signal of an uprising, so he sent some guys to arrest Sitting Bull.

The naked fifty-nine-year-old chief, who had nothing to do with the Ghost Dance, didn't go quietly. Shots were fired and Sitting Bull and twelve other Sioux were killed. A couple weeks later, the reservation police brutally massacred a bunch more Sioux at the "Battle" of Wounded Knee.

3. H. H. HOLMES
1893 - Chicago, Illinois

After a questionable past (fraud, polygamy), H. H. Holmes moved to Chicago and became a full-blown monster. In 1886, he "purchased" (the owners were never seen again) a pharmacy and settled into the community. While building a massive three-story building across the street, Holmes scammed contractors into building parts of the house without asking questions, then drove them to quit before they realized what they were doing. When the place was finally built, it was full of gas chambers, chutes to an incinerator, secret passageways, and dead ends for Holmes' future victims. The 1893 World's Fair brought people to Chicago in droves. Many young women looking for work or excitement took up residence in Holmes' "murder castle." Holmes killed them, stripped their flesh, and sold the skeletons for medical examination. He eventually got caught in one of his many insurance fraud schemes, but not before killing more—possibly hundreds.

2. SULTAN ABDULHAMID II
1895 - Constantinople, Ottoman Empire (Istanbul, Turkey)

Things were looking good for the Ottoman Empire. Murad V had taken over from his autocratic father (Abdulaziz) and was creating positive changes for his people. Unfortunately Murad had a mental breakdown so his tyrannical brother, Abdulhamid, took over. When many complained about his ascent to power, Abdulhamid sent a message. In bully-like fashion, he decided to cripple the most vulnerable part of his population—the Armenians. When the Armenians didn't pay his excessive taxes, Ottoman troops burned down their villages and killed thousands. When the Armenians retreated to their one place of refuge, the cathedral of Urfa, he burned that down, killing another three thousand. Protests and deaths continued for the next dozen years until Abdulhamid was forced out in 1908.

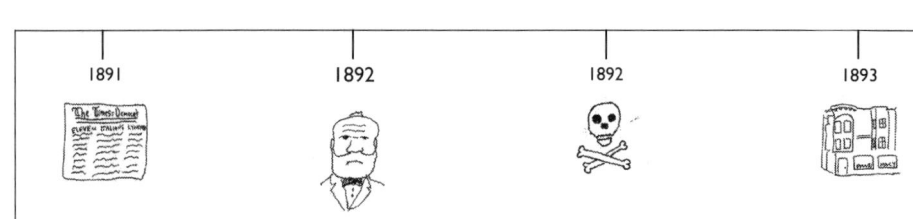

1. NICHOLAS II
1896 - Moscow, Russia

Almost fourteen hundred people were trampled to death and thousands more were injured Nicholas II's coronation ceremony. And it only got worse from there. His disastrous two-decade run (Russo-Japanese War, Bloody Sunday, food shortages, widespread poverty) as the final tsar in Russian history finally came to an end in 1917. Ninety thousand people in Petrograd were fed up with his mismanagement and yet another war (World War I), so they took to the streets. Nicholas' response was to turn his already stretched-thin army on them. It didn't go well. The army sided with the protesters, and Nicholas and his family fled to the mountains. The next year, the Bolsheviks hunted them down and executed his entire Romanov inner circle, even the maid.

1895　　　　　1896　　　　　1896　　　　　1897

　　　　　　　　　　　　　　　　　　　　　　　　　1898

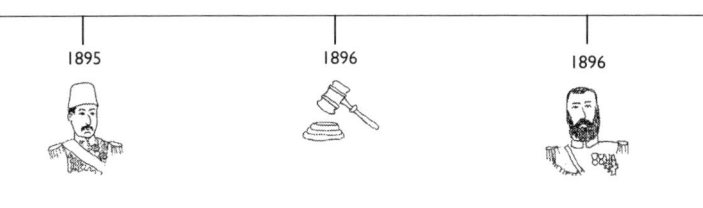

Dishonorable Mentions: Howard Hyde Russell - 1893 (Anti-Saloon League), Hermann Ahlwardt - 1892 (anti-Semite), William Owen Smith - 1893 (overthrew Hawaiian monarchy), Joseph Vacher - 1894 (French serial killer), Lizzie Borden? - 1892 (murderer?), Rudyard Kipling - 1899 ("white man's burden"), Soapy Smith - 1898 (swindler), Cordelia Botkin - 1898 (murderer via poisoned chocolates), Jane Toppan - 1895 (murderous nursemaid), Martial Bourdin - 1894 (anarchist), Tsuda Sanzo - 1891 (Ōtsu incident), Joseph Pulitzer - 1899 (teamed with Hearst to cheat the newsies), Emmett Dalton - 1892 (violent thief), Martin Ward, W.A. Webster, Ezra McKnight, Henry Stokes, Henry Godwin, Moultrie Epps, Charles D. Jayner, Oscar Kelly, Marion Clark, Alonzo Rogers, Edwin M. Rogers, Joseph P. Newham, and Early P. Lee - 1898 (racist murderers), James Martin - 1897 (head of xenophobic Coal and Iron Police)

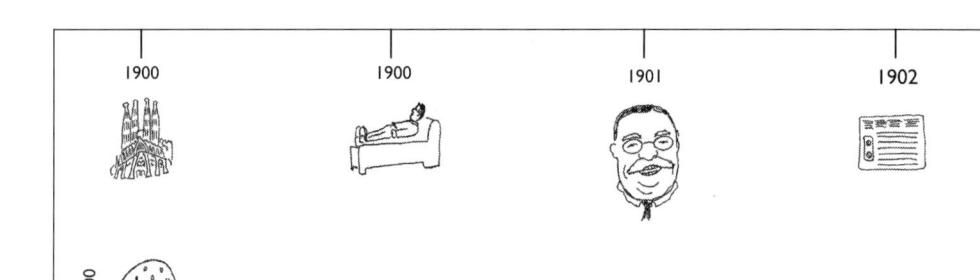

TWENTIETH CENTURY
1900-1904

"The cost of liberty is less than the price of repression."
-W.E.B. DuBois

BEST

10. ENRICO CARUSO
1902 - Milan, Italy

In the late 1890s, the only way people could listen to music of their choosing would be to put a nickel in a gramophone machine on the street and listen to a song with an ad interrupting it midway through. But the Berliner Company wanted to expand their gramophone business to the home market. So they sent out Fred Gaisberg to find the best talent in the world and give people a reason to buy. For just a hundred pounds sterling, Gaisberg got twenty-nine-year-old star tenor Enrico Caruso to record ten songs. People heard that booming Italian voice singing things like "O Sole Mio" and "Santa Lucia" and lost their collective mind. After that, they couldn't produce records and gramophones fast enough. Caruso's stardom at the time was bigger than Elvis, the Beatles, Michael Jackson, and Madonna wrapped in one.

9. SIGMUND FREUD
1900 - Vienna, Austria

Sigmund Freud was mostly wrong, not to mention a weirdo. Every theory he had seemed to come back to either boys wanting to bang their moms or women wanting to have a penis. He viewed childhood as a series of sexual stages (oral, anal, phallic). There's no real evidence of the id, ego, or superego being real things. His thoughts on homosexuality were flat-out incorrect. But his positive impact on the world was massive. Before Freud, therapy wasn't much of a thing. Freud was the first to really explore the subconscious mind and the impact of childhood experiences on adulthood. The mind is a powerful engine. Freud was one of the first to realize that engine sometimes needs serious maintenance.

8. ANTONI GAUDI
1900 - Barcelona, Spain

Before Antoni Gaudi, architecture was very structured—columns, walls, and windows had their established places. Then came an eclectic Catalan architect who broke the mold. Instead of working from drawings, Gaudi used small 3D models. This tactic made his creations feel more like sculptures than buildings. For over fifty years, Gaudi created some of the most unique buildings and structures around Barcelona—everything from residences to parks. For the final sixteen years of his life, the deeply religious Gaudi focused entirely on a cathedral called Basilica i Temple Expiatori de la Sagrada Familia. He even lived there. The incredible-yet-slowly progressing project, which started in 1882, features an impressive eighteen towers and is set to be completed in 2026, an even hundred years after the architect's death.

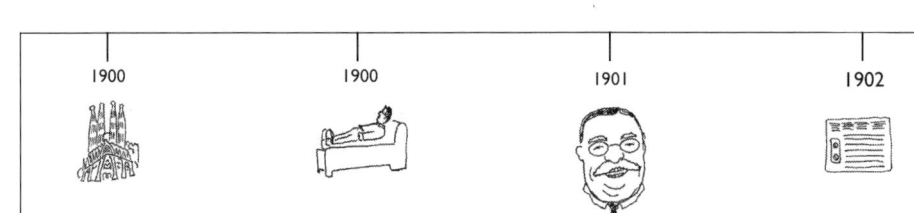

7. CHARLES FOLLIS
1904 - Wooster, Ohio

Four decades before Jackie Robinson's monumental breakthrough in baseball, Charles Follis did it in football. While becoming the first black professional football player, the "Black Cyclone from Wooster" faced ugly resistance through cheap shots and racist threats. But Follis never lost his cool and earned the deep respect of his teammates. One of those teammates was an Ohio Wesleyan student named Branch Rickey, the future owner of the Brooklyn Dodgers. In 1945, Rickey signed Jackie Robinson.

6. MARY ANDERSON
1903 - Birmingham, Alabama

On a cold, wet winter day, Mary Anderson's trolley driver had the window down and wiped the windshield by hand. For the passengers in the front, this sucked because they were getting pelted with freezing rain. For the rest, it was dangerous and terrifying. Inspired by the uncomfortable experience, Anderson came up with a spring-loaded arm made of wood and rubber that would wipe the windshield when a lever was pulled from the dashboard. In November of 1903, she received the patent for the windshield wiper. Unfortunately for Mary, barely anyone outside the big cities owned cars in 1903. By the time faster cars were being mass-manufactured, Mary's patent had run out and her design was copied.

| 1902 | 1903 | 1903 | 1903 |

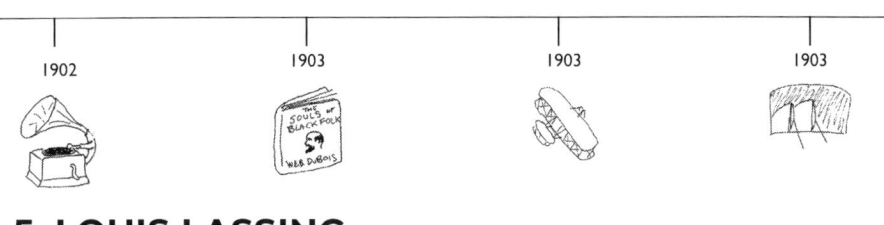

5. LOUIS LASSING
1900 - New Haven, Connecticut

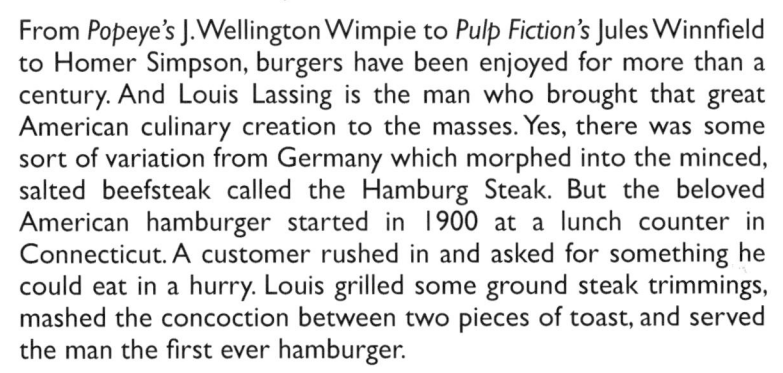

1904

From *Popeye's* J. Wellington Wimpie to *Pulp Fiction's* Jules Winnfield to Homer Simpson, burgers have been enjoyed for more than a century. And Louis Lassing is the man who brought that great American culinary creation to the masses. Yes, there was some sort of variation from Germany which morphed into the minced, salted beefsteak called the Hamburg Steak. But the beloved American hamburger started in 1900 at a lunch counter in Connecticut. A customer rushed in and asked for something he could eat in a hurry. Louis grilled some ground steak trimmings, mashed the concoction between two pieces of toast, and served the man the first ever hamburger.

4. THEODORE ROOSEVELT
1901 - Buffalo, New York

Teddy Roosevelt was hawkish, he had troubling views on race, and he was an egomaniac. But, from the moment he was sworn into office, he got things done. His progressive ideas terrified his fellow Republicans, so they tried to bury him in the office of the vice president. But after President William McKinley was assassinated, Teddy was in the driver's seat going a hundred miles per hour. He slashed railroad rebates, broke up monopolies, established restrictions for the food industry, set aside hundreds of acres of wildlife for protection, built the Panama Canal, helped end the Russo-Japanese War, and added the forward pass to the game of football. Maybe it was the gallon of coffee he drank every day.

3. WILLIS CARRIER
1902 - Brooklyn, New York

The "King of Cool" actually got his start in the heating business. While working for the Buffalo Forge Heating Company, Willis Carrier realized their heaters were inefficient. Within a few months, Carrier had studied the designs, made some structural changes, and saved the company tons of money. After being promoted to head of experimental engineering, Carrier was tasked with reducing the humidity in a Brooklyn printing shop. The twenty-six-year-old designed a system that closely resembles the air conditioner that we use today—filtered air was forced through a compressor and pumped over cold coils, then blown out with a fan. Word spread and soon many businesses (and eventually homes) wanted air conditioning.

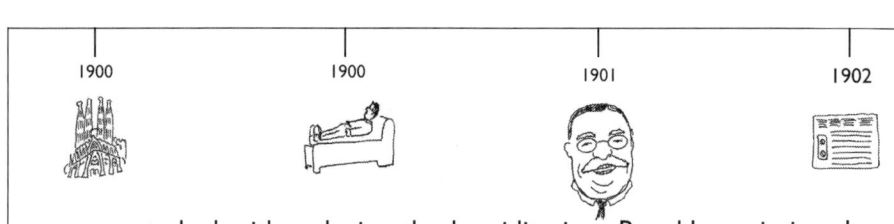

2. ORVILLE WRIGHT, WILBUR WRIGHT, AND CHARLES TAYLOR
1903 - Kitty Hawk, North Carolina

After George Cayley and Otto Lilienthal made huge strides in the field of aviation in the nineteenth century, Ohio bicycle shop owners Orville and Wilbur Wright threw their hats in the ring. Wilbur tweaked Lilienthal's basic glider model with rotating flaps (which resembled the way birds tilt their wings in action) and tested it on a five-foot kite. When that worked, the brothers (along with their mechanic Charlie Taylor) built a bigger version. Taylor built the engine out of light aluminum, and the boys took their plane to a town in North Carolina that had pretty consistent, flying-friendly weather. After some dangerous mishaps, Wilbur finally made his famous nearly nine hundred-foot flight, staying in the air for a minute. Manned flight was possible.

1. W. E. B. DU BOIS
1903 - Atlanta, Georgia

William Edward Burghardt "W. E. B." Du Bois felt black people in America should aim higher than just carving out a meager existence while white men ruled over their heads. Every aspect of life in America, according to the Fourteenth Amendment, should be equal. No more compromising. Du Bois, the first ever black graduate of Harvard University, burst on the scene in 1903 with his book *Souls of Black Folk*, a collection of essays that detailed what it was to be black over the past century in America. By 1909 he co-founded the N.A.A.C.P. and published their monthly magazine. W.E.B Du Bois carried the baton for the black rights movement for the first half of the twentieth century. He died a day before Martin Luther King's "I Have a Dream" speech.

1902   1903   1903   1903

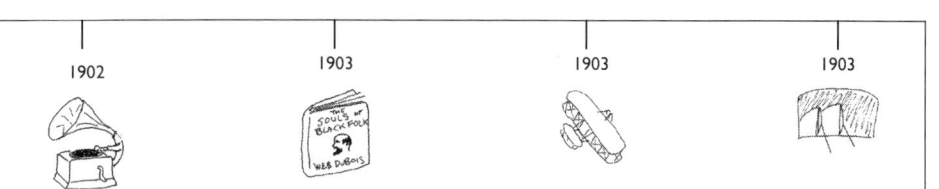

1904

Honorable Mentions: Henri Matisse - 1900 (artist, started Fauvist movement), Maggie Walker - 1901 (first woman to start a bank), Christian Hulsmeyer - 1904 (RADAR), Frederick Kipping - 1901 (silicone), Willem Einthoven - 1903 (EKG), Guglielmo Marconi - 1901 (radio), George Bang - 1904 (ice cream cone), Emily Hobhouse - 1900 (Boer War protester), Walter Reed - 1900 (Spanish-American War doctor), L. Frank Baum - 1901 (*The Wonderful Wizard of Oz*), Herbert Cecil Booth - 1901 (electric vacuum cleaner), Beatrix Potter - 1902 (*The Tale of Peter Rabbit*), Scott Joplin - 1902 ("The Entertainer"), Ida Tarbell - 1904 (investigative journalist)

WORST

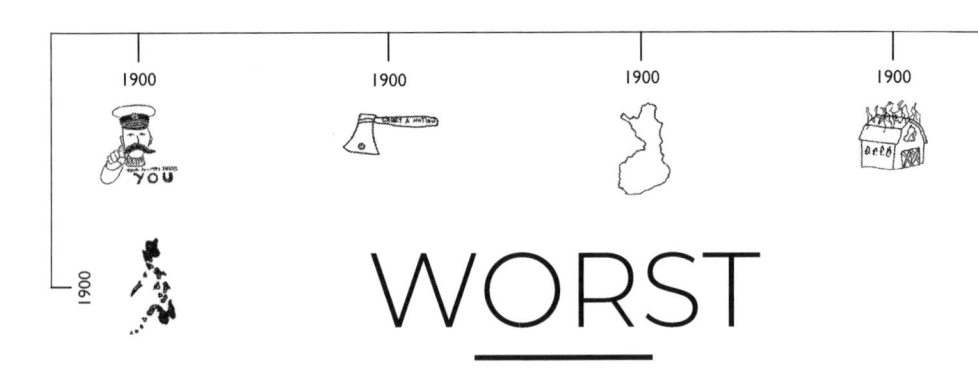

10. LEON CZOLGOSZ
1901 - Buffalo, New York

Leon Czolgosz had no job and had no friends. When he tried to join anarchist groups, they wouldn't take him. Then, after reading about Italian King Umberto's assassination by an anarchist, Czolgosz decided to take matters into his own hands. In August of 1901, Czolgosz moved to Buffalo, the city hosting the Pan-American Exposition. When President McKinley visited the expo, Czolgosz waited in a receiving line to meet him. Instead of shaking McKinley's hand, he pulled out a revolver, shot, and killed him. In his confession, he mentioned it was unfair the president had a job and he didn't.

9. NIKOLAI IVANOVICH BOBRIKOV
1900 - Helsinki, Finland

In 1898, Russian military chief Nikolai Bobrikov was appointed governor general of the Grand Duchy of Finland. As soon as he stepped into the role, Bobrikov dissolved the Finnish military and tried to turn everything (financial institutions, schools, language) into Russia. Any pushback was met with extreme censorship—newspapers were shredded, protesters were beaten. Things looked bleak. So a carefully planned assassination plot was hatched. While the group was ironing out the details, some twenty-nine-year-old clerk walked into the stairway of the senate and shot Bobrikov three times in the head and himself twice in the chest. All's well that ends well.

8. CAO FUTIAN
1901 - Peking, China (Beijing)

After centuries of isolationism, the Sino-Japanese War in 1895 was a wake-up call to China that the rest of the world had had passed them by. To the dismay of nationalists in the Guangdong Province, the country began working with the outside world. So the Cao Futian-led group (Society of Righteous and Harmonious Fists) started attacking all foreigners. When the hundred thousand-man army, who believed their martial arts expertise would make them impervious to bullets, made its way to Peking, foreigners were given twenty-four hours to pack up and get out of China. Instead, British, Russian, American, Japanese, French, and German troops banded together and crushed the Boxer Rebellion. As it turned out, those martial arts moves couldn't stop bullets. The centuries-old Qing Dynasty was toast by 1912.

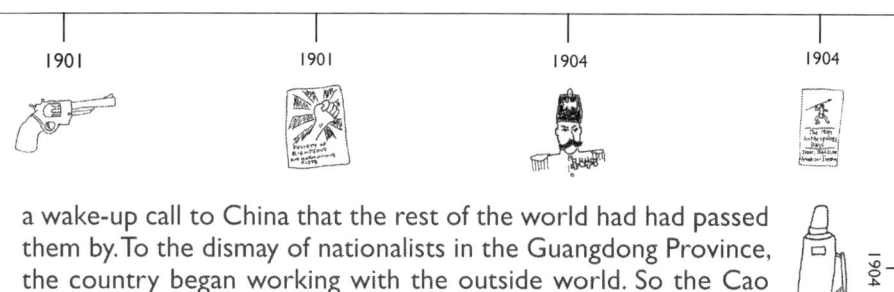

7. REINHOLD BURGER AND ALBERT ASCHENBRENNER
1904 - Munich, Germany

On January 20, 1892, Englishman James Dewar (yes, related to the booze company) invented a flask that contained a bottle inside of it and vacuumed the air between the two containers. Then he wrapped the inner bottle in foil. The foil reflected the infrared radiation and the liquid inside would maintain its original temperature for hours. Hot stayed hot and cold stayed cold. Unfortunately, before Dewer patented the "Dewar Flask," some German glassblowing jackals swooped in and stole his invention. Burger and Aschenbrenner held a contest which named the vacuum flask "Thermos" (after the Greek word *therme* meaning "hot"). Dewar sued, but it was too late. The Thermos company rakes in a couple hundred million per year for Dewar's invention.

6. CARRY NATION
1900 - Wichita, Kansas

Carry Moore's first husband drank himself to death, so she spent the rest of her life fighting alcohol consumption. She married a preacher, became Carry A. Nation, and moved to Kansas. As a leader in the Women's Christian Temperance Union, she lobbied to ban booze in the Sunflower State. When bar owners ignored the dumb rule, Nation went from being a nuisance to a criminal menace. At first she tried blocking the doors of saloons and bumming everyone out by publicly praying for their lost souls. Later, she got destructive by smashing up places with a hatchet. Digging the celebrity status it brought her, Nation traveled to free-drinking states and smashed up their saloons with her hatchet and bricks.

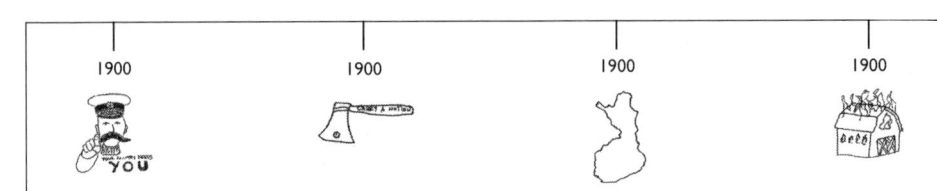

5. JAMES EDWARD SULLIVAN
1904 - St. Louis, Missouri

In an attempt to show off the greatness of American athleticism in the third Olympic games, James Sullivan set up a sideshow of minorities and foreigners ("primatives," as he called them) to compete in what he called the "Special Olympics." Sullivan had Indians, Pygmies, Argentinians, Turks, and other "savages" compete in events like javelin and sprints so people could compare them to the white Olympians. When nobody seemed interested in Sullivan's Anthropology Games, he took a different tack: he put the non-whites in a zoo-like setting and had them compete at tree-climbing and mud-flinging. Even in racist times, Sullivan's racist Olympics stood out for its ugliness.

4. BELLE GUNNESS
1900 - Chicago, Illinois

In 1881, Belle Gunness immigrated to the "Land of Opportunity" for a chance at the life she couldn't have back home in Norway. She met a man, opened a candy store with him, and waited for those greenbacks to start pouring in. When business got off to a slow start, she went in a different direction and burned it down for the insurance money. Then she turned her insurance scam on people—first her two young children, then her husband, then back to a burned-down farm. Despite looking like Paul Bunyan's twin sister, Belle kept snaring new rich guys and they kept dying. Finally, after suspicions grew, Belle's bank account was emptied and her barn burned down (with four bodies inside). Nobody knows what happened to her.

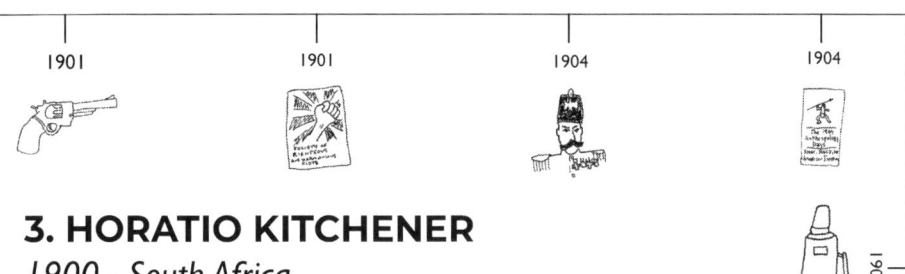

3. HORATIO KITCHENER
1900 - South Africa

As chief-of-staff to the British commander during the second Anglo-Boer War (a war about British imperialism and diamonds), Lord Kitchener was given the task of suppressing the locals. And suppress he did. He threw women and children in disease-infested concentration camps. Of the 115,000 Boers in camps between June 1901 and May 1902, about twenty-eight thousand died (twenty-two thousand of whom were children). Another twenty thousand or so black people in the region died in other camps. This all might've been swept under the rug had British pacifist Emily Hobhouse not visited the camps and written about the atrocities. Kitchener moved on to different government posts before meeting his death in World War I.

2. ALBERT BEVERIDGE
1900 - Washington, D.C.

America saw European powers taking over territories across the globe and wanted in on the white-guys-should-rule-the-Earth action. After defeating Spain in the Spanish-American War, Indiana Senator Albert Beveridge declared, "The Philippines are ours forever!" One slight problem: a few months before the end of the Spanish-American War, the Philippines had already proclaimed its independence from Spain. Beveridge doubted if the people there were "capable of self-government in the Anglo-Saxon sense" and declared it was America's duty to fight for it. The result was the brutal Philippine-American War, which relied on concentration camps and resulted in twenty thousand Filipino soldiers, another two hundred thousand Filipino civilians, and forty-three hundred Americans dead from combat and disease.

1. LOTHAR VON TROTHA
1904 - German South West Africa (Namibia)

Unfortunately, World War II wasn't Germany's only dive into genocide in the twentieth century. Like all the other European powers, Germany had carved up a piece of Africa (the southwest

| 1900 | 1900 | 1900 | 1900 |

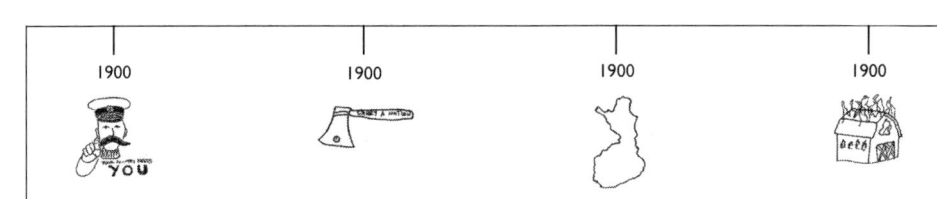

portion) and, in the process, overwhelmed the locals. When the Herero and Nama tribes pushed back in 1904, Germany sent in Lothar von Trotha, the nastiest sonuvabitch in the German military. Von Trotha declared, "Only following this cleansing can something new emerge," then had his ten thousand troops try to wipe them off the map. The locals could either choose to die in battle or flee into the Kalahari Desert (and die a slow death there). By 1907, the Herero population had dropped from eighty thousand to fifteen thousand. The Nama tribe went from around twenty thousand to nine thousand.

Dishonorable Mention: Gaetano Bresci - *1900* (assassinated Umberto I)

1901　1901　1904　1904

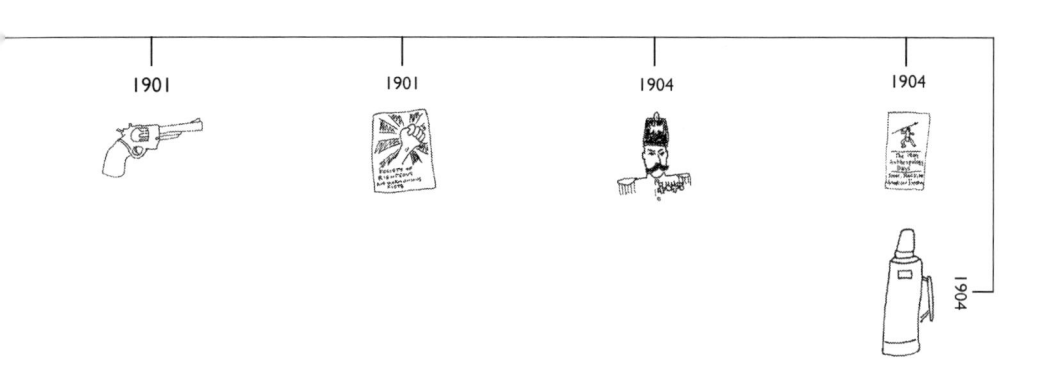

1904

| 1905 | 1905 | 1905 | 1906 |

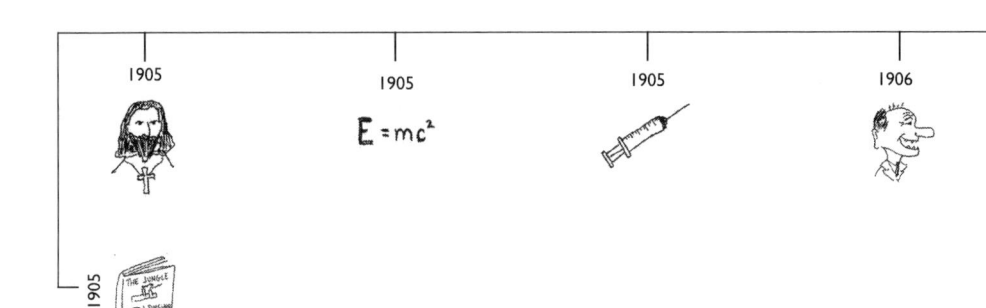

E = mc²

1905 — THE JUNGLE / UPTON SINCLAIR

1905-1909

"Two things are infinite: the universe and human stupidity; and I'm not sure about the universe."

-Albert Einstein

BEST

10. MILTON HERSHEY
1907 - Hershey, Pennsylvania

Since the age of fourteen, Milton Hershey wanted to make a living in the candy business. Success eluded him until his thirties, when he returned to his native Lancaster, started a successful caramel company, and sold it for one million dollars. With that money he established the Hershey Chocolate Company. After creations like the Hershey Kiss in 1907, the business exploded. For the rest of his life, Hershey invested greatly in improving the community around him (schools, parks, and other institutions). In 1909, he opened the Hershey Industrial School for orphans, which he would fund for the rest of his life. When he died, he gave away all of his Hershey shares to the school's trust. To this day, the school provides a quality boarding school education for nearly two thousand children from troubled backgrounds.

9. J. STUART BLACKTON
1906 - New York, New York

In 1896, the Edison Company hired British-born vaudeville cartoonist J. Stuart Blackton to make three films drawing various figures. That was enough for Blackton to catch the film bug. Over the next few years, he experimented with film and drawing. In 1906, he released *Humorous Phases of Funny Faces*, the first ever animated film. The film, which was stop-motion chalkboard drawings of a creepy clown and a guy growing hair and blowing smoke into a woman's face, wasn't exactly *Toy Story*. But it was a start. Blackton's misogynistic hairy guy begat Mickey Mouse, which led to Bugs Bunny, Fred Flintstone, Homer Simpson, and SpongeBob SquarePants.

8. ALFRED EINHORN AND MENDEL NEVIN
1905 - Munich, Germany

When someone needed a local anesthetic in the early 1900s, the popular choice was cocaine. It was all well and good from a numbing perspective, but the side effects (heart palpitations, bad withdrawals, getting a little too excited by dance music) were problematic. So German chemist Alfred Einhorn created Procaine, which mimicked the numbing from booger sugar but lacked the dangerous side effects. A couple years later, a visiting dentist named Dr. Mendel Nevin happened to be lecturing through Europe at the time and learned about Einhorn's local anesthetic, now known as novocaine. Nevin returned to North America and applied it to dental procedures, making trips to the dentist a lot less painful.

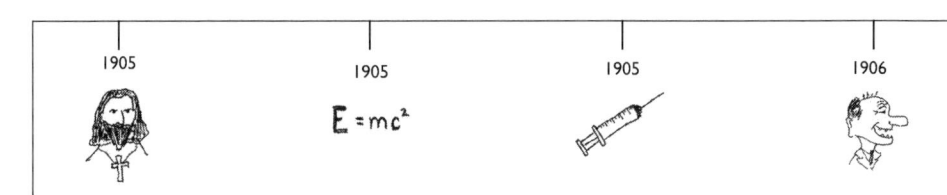

7. ARTHUR SCOTT
1907 - Old Chester, Pennsylvania

Arthur Scott had a huge problem. His entire railroad car full of toilet paper was rolled too thick and therefore rendered useless to consumers. Then Scott remembered a story he read in the newspaper about a schoolteacher who gave her runny-nosed students a soft piece of paper instead of a shared towel, which spread germs. So Scott perforated his discarded paper and marketed it as disposable towels to hotels and restaurants to use in their restrooms. "Sani-Towels" (i.e., paper towels) were an instant hit.

6. UPTON SINCLAIR
1905 - Chicago, Illinois

Since there wasn't any competition, monopolies like Armour (a meatpacking company) felt no motivation to provide quality working conditions for its employees. So socialist newspaper *Appeal to Reason* sent New York City writer Upton Sinclair to Chicago to do an exposé. Over time, Sinclair's exposé turned it into an entire book, titled *The Jungle*. What started as an examination of working conditions grew into an indictment of the food processing business. Even the walking Republican hard-on, Teddy Roosevelt, who detested socialism and "crackpots" like Sinclair, could not deny the hard truths *The Jungle* raised. "There is filth on the floor, and it must be scraped up with the muckrake," said the president. Hence, the nickname "muckrakers" for investigative reporters. By the end of 1906, the Pure Food and Drug Act and the Meat Inspection Act were both passed.

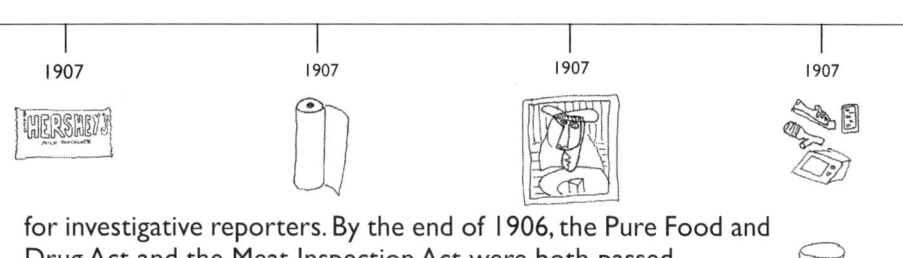

5. GEORGY GAPON
1905 - St. Petersburg, Russia

Tone-deaf Tsar Nicholas II was running Russia into the ground, and it took heroes like Father George Gapon to take him down. Unlike the sham trade union leaders put in place to make disillusioned workers think they were being represented, Gapon actually took his job seriously. The Orthodox priest listened to concerns and complaints and helped the workers unite for a peaceful protest. In 1905, Gapon led a march to Nicholas' Winter Palace to hand-deliver their demands to the tsar. Before they could get there, armed goons told them to turn around. Gapon kept marching, so the chief of police, who happened to be the tsar's uncle, opened fire, killing between two hundred and a thousand people. The revolution soon followed.

4. LEO BAEKELAND
1907 - Yonkers, New York

In 1899, Leo Baekeland sold his photographic paper company to George Eastman for a million dollars (nearly $30 million in today's money). Instead of enjoying the fact that he was set for life at the age of thirty-six, Baekeland poured his money into a laboratory in Yonkers and worked on creating Bakelite, a synthetic substitute for the shellac used in electronic insulation. This insulation substitute proved to be incredibly durable and could withstand high temperatures. By 1907, Baekeland had created the first practical plastic. It was immediate hit. By the time he died in 1944, the plastic industry had created 175 thousand tons of Bakelite. Today, plastic is in absolutely everything—cars, houses, shoes, toys, televisions, laptops, phones, medical devices, and, unfortunately, oceans.

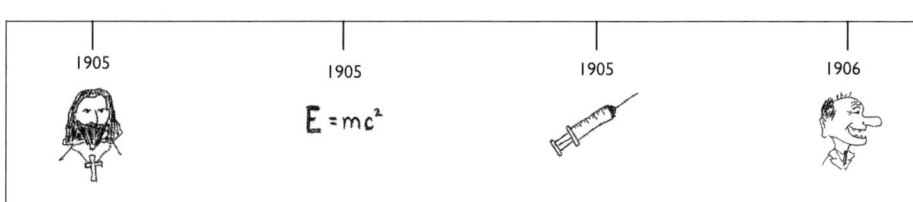

3. PABLO PICASSO
1907 - Paris, France

Spanish child prodigy Pablo Picasso excelled at art at an early age—standard portraits, landscapes, sculptures, ceramics, and even poetry. But none of those things are the reason he's considered one the greatest artists in history. After moving to Paris and becoming part of the eclectic art community, Picasso took the art world in wildly different directions and achieved unparalleled success. Whether it was his blue period, his rose period, or his co-founding the cubist movement, Picasso kept breaking the mold. His 1907 masterpiece, *Les Demoiselles d'Avignon* (a painting with five naked hookers with mask-like faces) sprayed lighter fluid on the modern art movement. In 1937, Picasso was asked to create an anti-Generalissimo Francisco Franco painting for the Spanish pavilion at the upcoming World's Fair. After about a month, he delivered *Guernica*, an 11.5 by 25.5-foot black-and-white, anti-war "fuck you" to fascism and the horrors of war, putting an exclamation point on a career full of them.

2. JOHN LEAL
1908 - Boonton, New Jersey

A Paterson, New Jersey physician, John Leal was surrounded by cholera and typhoid outbreaks. Since he already used chlorine to kill disease anytime he went to infected homes, Leal figured maybe he could save everyone a lot of time and death by putting a little chlorine directly into the water supply. In 1908, Leal got a chance to test his theory on Jersey City Water Supply Company's new seven-billion-gallon reservoir. Immediately, illnesses plummeted. Within a decade, infant mortality rates had dropped and typhoid cases were about a third of what they had been in 1900. Let's raise our glasses of water and toast John Leal.

| 1907 | 1907 | 1907 | 1907 |

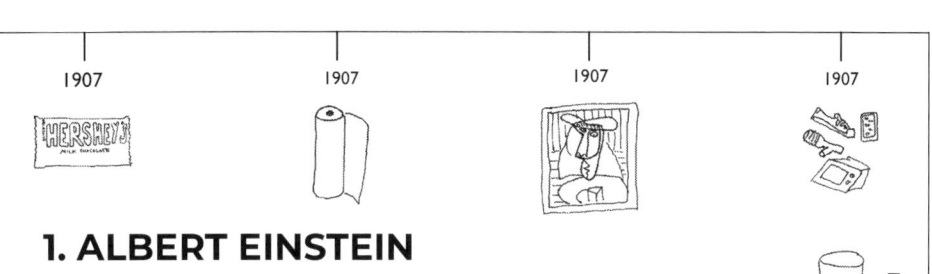

1. ALBERT EINSTEIN
1905 - Bern, Switzerland

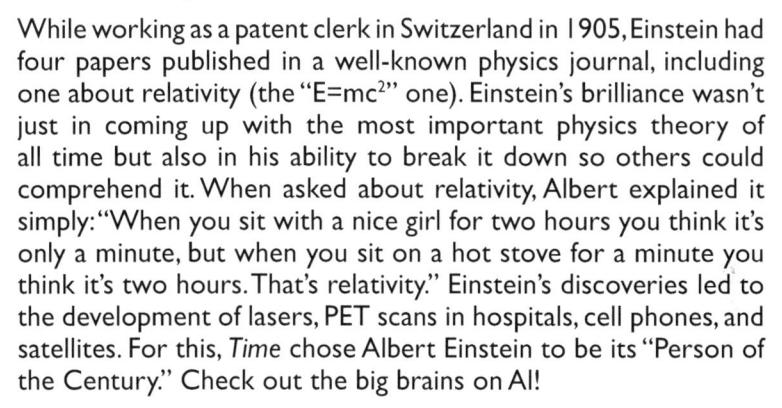

While working as a patent clerk in Switzerland in 1905, Einstein had four papers published in a well-known physics journal, including one about relativity (the "$E=mc^2$" one). Einstein's brilliance wasn't just in coming up with the most important physics theory of all time but also in his ability to break it down so others could comprehend it. When asked about relativity, Albert explained it simply: "When you sit with a nice girl for two hours you think it's only a minute, but when you sit on a hot stove for a minute you think it's two hours. That's relativity." Einstein's discoveries led to the development of lasers, PET scans in hospitals, cell phones, and satellites. For this, *Time* chose Albert Einstein to be its "Person of the Century." Check out the big brains on Al!

Honorable Mentions: Leonardo Torres Quevedo - 1906 (remote control), Albert Marsh - 1906 (toaster), Gennaro Lombardi - 1905 (first NYC pizzeria), Frank Epperson - 1905 (popsicle), Frederick Cook - 1908 (discovered North Pole), O. Henry - 1905 (*Gift of the Magi*), Ole Evinrude - 1907 (outboard motor), Charles Curtis - 1907 (first Native American senator), Billy Murray - 1908 ("Take Me Out to the Ballgame"), Jack Johnson - 1908 (boxer), Lee de Forest - 1906 (transistor radio)

WORST

10. LEOPOLD MARKBREIT
1908 - Cincinnati, Ohio

Cincinnati Mayor Leopold Markbreit wasn't exactly open-minded when it came to the fairer sex. In 1908—the infant days of the car—Mayor Markbreit declared that "women are not physically fit to operate automobiles" and asked his city council to pass laws that would prevent them from driving. Luckily for women, Markbreit's kidneys took a turn for the worse before the law could get any real traction. But, as long as women couldn't vote, there would be many more Leopold Markbreits standing in their way for any sort of progress.

9. MRS. WILLIAM FORCE SCOTT
1909 - New York, New York

Without voting rights, there was a limit on how conditions for women could improve in America. It's not surprising that men opposed women's suffrage (since that would mean they wouldn't be the only ones calling the shots any longer). But you'd think, even if they weren't actively protesting, women wouldn't oppose the suffrage movement. Unfortunately, monsters like Mrs. William Force Scott existed. In her anti-suffragist rant in front of the Woman's University Club in 1909, Scott argued that women voting against men would be "more dangerous than labor against capital." Self-loathing women like Scott were why it took another eleven years for women to get the chance to participate in an election.

8. WILLIAM HAYWOOD
1905 - Caldwell, Idaho

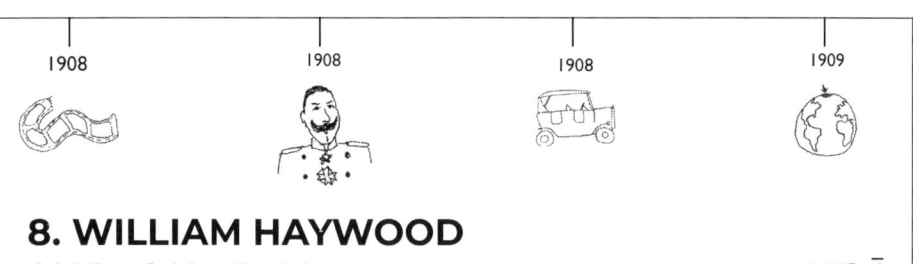

In Idaho, labor union-friendly Governor Frank Steunenberg was in a tough spot. During one dispute, the Western Federation of Miners, led by William "Big Bill" Haywood, responded to management by blowing up an entire mine with dynamite. As much as Steunenberg was a fan of the little guy, he had to prevent this type of anarchy in his state. So he called for federal troops to enforce peace. Haywood felt betrayed by Steunenberg's decision to suppress the union's actions. A few years later, the then-former governor was killed by a bomb rigged to his front gate. The man responsible for the bomb was a professional hitman who admitted he'd been hired by Big Bill Haywood. Sadly, violent actions by men like Big Bill Haywood have continually destroyed the trust and undermined the message of unions in America.

7. ROBERT PEARY
1909 - New York, New York

Despite zero proof, Robert Peary wanted to be known as the guy who got to the North Pole first. But word spread that Dr. Frederick Cook was on his way to New York to announce he discovered it a year earlier (on April 21, 1908). Despite Cook's meticulous notes of the experience, a *National Geographic* committee (made up of three of Peary's friends) examined the dispute and determined Peary was the guy. It wasn't until 1988 that a *National Geographic* writer revisited the case and concluded that Peary was a fraud. In addition to being a liar, the man was a psychopath. He dug up Greenland graves to sell the remains to a museum of natural history and kidnapped natives to be studied like artifacts.

6. ABE RUEF
1906 - San Francisco, California

Abraham Ruef graduated with highest honors from the University of California, got a law degree, learned eight languages, and was determined to make a difference in the shady San Francisco political scene. And he did. He made it worse. After finding out how hard it would be to change things, Ruef bribed and extorted his way into city hall and, in 1902, he even got a puppet (Eugene Schmitz) elected mayor. For four years, Schmitz did whatever Boss Abe told him, and kickback money poured in. Then the massive 1906 earthquake hit, which magnified the office's shortcomings—untested fire hydrants didn't work, unqualified men had been given pivotal posts, and so on. Abe Ruef's grift was over. He was sentenced to San Quentin for fourteen years.

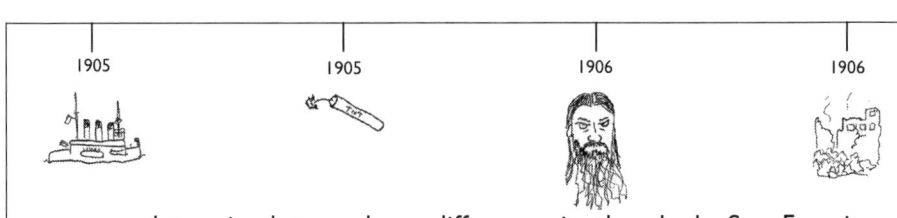

5. YVGENY GOLIKOV
1905 - Sevastopol, Russian Empire (Ukraine)

Life aboard Russian battleship *Potemkin* was miserable. In the wake of a demoralizing loss in the Russo-Japanese War, the crew's borscht lunch was crawling with maggots. When they complained, officers told them to eat it anyway. When the crew refused, Captain Yvgeny Golikov lined them up on deck and called in the firing squad. The sailors revolted and a full-on mutiny broke out. Golikov was killed in the process but that was not the end of the bloodshed. The post-mutiny crew then took the *Potemkin* to Odessa, where they were warmly received by thousands of protesting workers. Knowing this could be the start of something bad, Nicholas II sent his military to the harbor and mowed down everyone in sight, killing a thousand.

4. THOMAS EDISON
1908 - Menlo Park, New Jersey

In 1908, Thomas Edison told all major silent film manufacturers that he owned the patent for the camera and, by extension, the entire movie industry. His draconian rules (no stars' names on screen, no movie longer than twenty minutes, no nickelodeon screenings) kept him in charge and severely limited creativity. Finally, a guy named Carl Laemmle broke away, lured a big-name star, gave her top billing, and undercut Edison's pricing at all the nickelodeons. Edison sued him 289 times. Laemmle (later joined by Adolph Zuckor and William Fox) countersued Edison for antitrust violations. A district court eventually ruled in their favor. The three dissenters ended up doing pretty okay in Hollywood (Laemmle—Universal Studios, Zuckor—Paramount, Fox—Twentieth Century Fox).

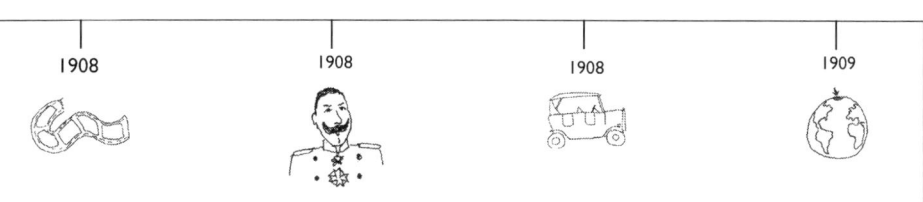

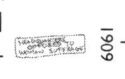

3. GRIGORI RASPUTIN
1906 - St. Petersburg, Russia

Russian doctors had no idea what to do with Tsar Nicholas II's hemophiliac son. In stepped this calm, confident "mystic" with a long beard, questionable hygiene, and creepy eyes who declared he could keep the boy alive. So Nicholas' wife, Alexandra, kept him around as a trusted advisor. Rasputin's closeness to the royal family deeply concerned everyone from the general public to the prime minister. But whenever someone tried to get rid of him, they were killed. By World War I, the smelly weirdo was essentially co-running the country. So Prince Yusupov and friends decided to end his life. Rasputin was poisoned, shot several times, and beaten with a club, but he just wouldn't die. So they stuffed him in a sack and dumped him in the Neva River.

2. KAISER WILHELM II
1908 - Berlin, Germany

Queen Victoria's eldest grandson was jealous of Britain's navy so he rapidly expanded Germany's. Understandably, the rest of the world was alarmed. To assuage everyone's fears, he gave an interview to Britain's *Daily Telegraph*. It went poorly. The obnoxious and unfiltered Wilhelm managed to offend Brits by saying Germans didn't like them and calling them "mad, mad, mad as March hares." Then he sold out the French and Russians for trying to get Germany to join them in defeating the British in the Boer War. Last but not least, he said the ramped-up navy was more intended for taking on the Japanese rather than the Brits. So, in one interview, Kaiser Wilhelm II managed to piss off Great Britain, Russia, France, and Japan. Within six years, Germany was embroiled in World War I.

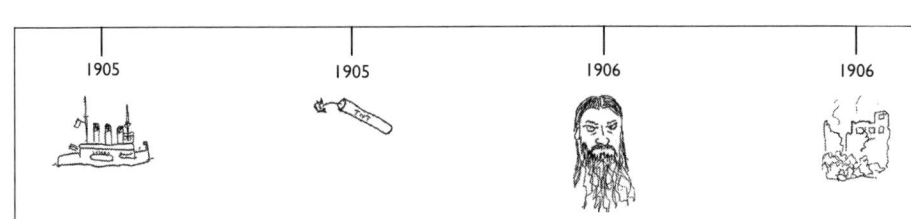

1. THOMAS DIXON
1905 - Greensboro, North Carolina

As a boy during the Reconstruction Era, Thomas Dixon was taught that blacks were an inferior race. To Dixon, the Ku Klux Klan lynchings were justice being carried out. After stints in politics and ministry, Dixon committed his life to writing hateful novels about reconstruction and glorifying the KKK. Guys like Dixon contributed to the rebirth of the KKK, a group of chickenshit guys dressed in bedsheets who pine for the good ol' days (when life was only good for privileged white guys). Besides his screeds on racial purity and justifying hate, Dixon also had a close relationship with Woodrow Wilson, who used his time in office to set race relations back sixty years. Dixon's trash brain finally had a cerebral hemorrhage in 1946. Good riddance.

1908　　　　　1908　　　　　1908　　　　　1909

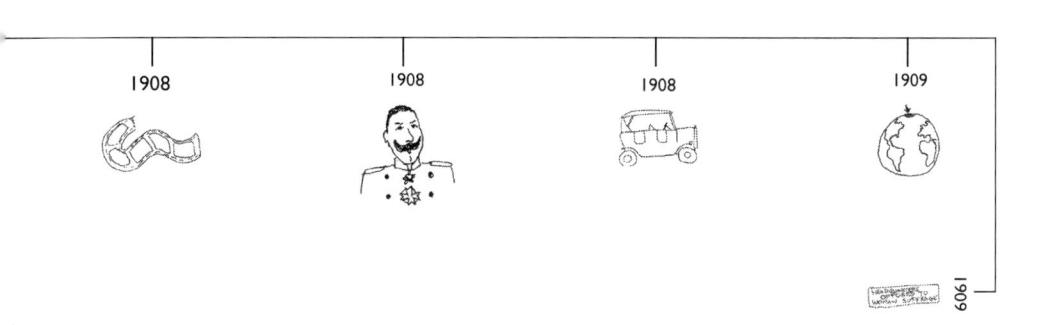

1909

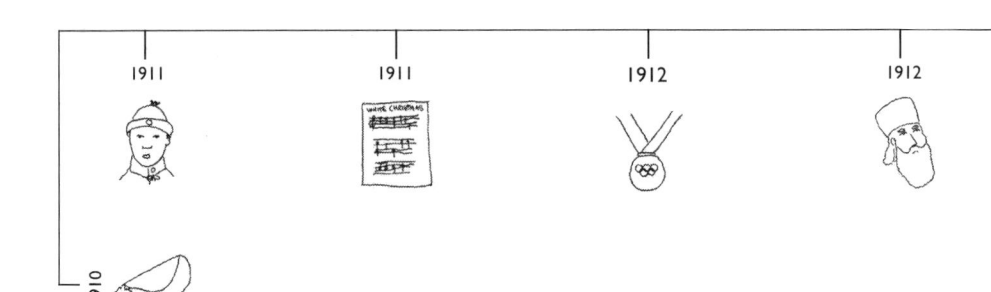

1910-1914

"I can't say that the brassiere will ever take as great a place in history as the steamboat, but I did invent it."

-Caresse Crosby

BEST

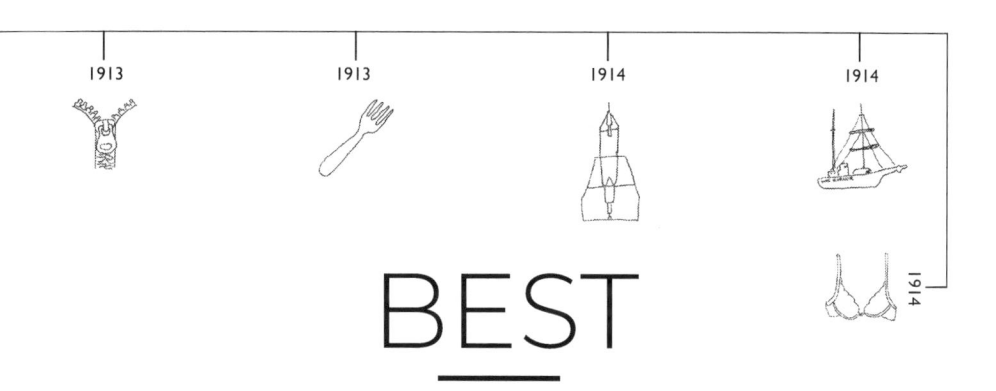

10. ABDU'L BAHA
1912 - New York, New York

Growing up in Persia, Abdu'l Baha closely followed the teachings of his father, Bahá'u'lláh, the founder of the Bahá'í Faith. When his dad passed away in 1892, there was a power struggle which left Baha thrown in jail for sham charges. Instead of a bitter Count of Monte Cristo-style counterattack after his 1908 release, Abdu'l Baha spent the rest of his life traveling the Earth, preaching and writing about a few things that are in short supply among humanity: peace, love, and understanding. For his well-publicized trip to New York, many donated so he could travel in style on a luxury liner. Instead he took a cheaper route and donated the rest of the money to charity. Good call. That luxury liner turned out to be the *Titanic*.

9. HARRY BREARLEY
1913 - Sheffield, England

Because of its strength, steel (which is just iron with carbon added to it) has been used for thousands of years—from construction to vehicles to salad forks. But because it has iron in it, steel eventually rusts and erodes. Even the strongest beams turn to dust. Scientists worked on ways to combat that problem but were unsuccessful until 1912, when Harry Brearley was hired by a small arms manufacturer to try to extend the life of their guns. The gun maker didn't like Brearley's "rustless steel," but no worries, he found a buyer in his buddy's cutlery company. Now it's tough to imagine life without stainless steel. From the top of the Chrysler building to the fork you used for last night's dinner, Brearley's creation is everywhere.

8. IRVING BERLIN
1911 - New York, New York

Israel Beline and his family fled anti-Semitic Russia and moved to New York City. Despite mastering only the black keys on the piano, Beline was able to carve out a living in music instead of having to resort to manual labor. By 1907, nineteen-year-old Beline had published his first song—but the sheet music had his name listed incorrectly as "I. Berlin." For the next half century, he used the Americanized name Irving Berlin and established himself as the premier songwriter in America. Berlin created iconic standards, musicals, and the entire genre of pop Christmas music ("White Christmas" jump-started the whole thing). Despite humble beginnings, Irving Berlin lived the American Dream. Maybe that's why he wrote "God Bless America."

7. ROBERT GODDARD
1914 - Princeton, New Jersey

While Robert Goddard wasn't alone in trying gunpowder for rocket propulsion, it was he who first opined that the lack of oxygen would eliminate combustion in space. So, in 1914, Goddard filed the patent for a rocket using liquid fuel. When the Smithsonian published his proposal to send rockets to the upper atmosphere, he was mocked by the press, especially *The New York Times*. He died in 1945 with 214 patents to his name. Thirty-five years to the day after Goddard launched his first liquid-fueled rocket, NASA named the Goddard Space Flight Center. Eight years after that, man landed on the moon, Goddard had a crater named after him, and *The New York Times* issued a correction.

6. BOB BARTLETT AND KATAKTOVIK
1914 - Arctic Ocean

In the summer of 1913, ten scientists, thirteen crew members, four Inuit hunters, a seamstress and her two kids, and some random passenger were on a Western Arctic exploratory journey aboard the *Karluk* when they got stuck. Considering he was surrounded by a bunch of nerds and people with no Arctic experience, the ship's Captain Bob Bartlett needed to step up and rescue them. He built igloos for the people, then Bartlett and Inuit hunter Kataktovik went for help. The two embarked on a seven hundred-mile, forty-eight-day sledge journey to Alaska via Siberia and the Bering Strait. Once the twelve remaining survivors were rescued, Bartlett received loads of accolades. But it wouldn't have happened without Kataktovik as well.

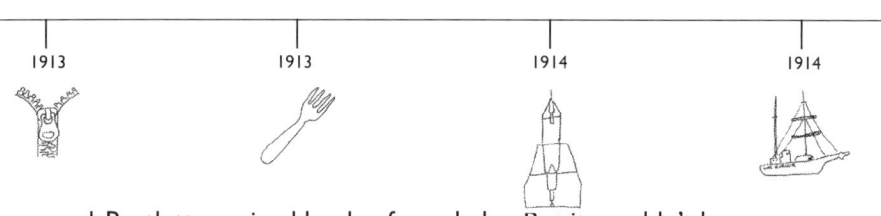

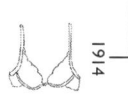

5. JUAN MENDEZ
1910 - Juarez, Mexico

While the word "burrito" appeared in the *Diccionario de Mexicanismos* way back in 1895 ("A rolled tortilla with meat or other ingredients inside…"), the food really didn't gain widespread popularity outside of Northern Mexico until the 1910 Mexican Revolution. Juan Mendez, a taco vendor from Chihuahua, loaded up his donkey with food and made his way across the Rio Bravo to sell it in the United States. Since the taco meat would have gotten cold by the time he crossed the border, he opted for burritos, which kept the meat warm wrapped inside of tortillas. It eventually made its way north to LA and San Francisco and morphed into the Mission-style burrito we know today.

4. SUN YAT-SEN
1911 - Wuchang, China

China was in a bad place towards the end of the Qing Dynasty's 250-year reign—they had just been buzz-sawed in the Sino-Japanese War, foreign nations were shaking them down (like the Brits fleecing them out of Hong Kong), all the men had to have dopey haircuts (the queue), and their new leader was a two-year-old (Emperor Puyi). Luckily for the people of China, Sun Yat-sen was fighting for change. After his failed Guangzhou rebellion, Sun was exiled for sixteen years but continued to plan attacks from afar. His 1911 attack on a state-run newspaper group, however, successfully caused the Qing dominoes to fall and the child emperor was forced to abdicate. While the early stages were messy, Sun Yat-sen gave China a chance to finally succeed.

3. GIDEON SUNDBACK
1913 - Hoboken, New Jersey

Swedish immigrant Gideon Sundback fell in love, quit a good job at Westinghouse in Pittsburgh, and went to work for a struggling company in Hoboken, New Jersey. When his wife died just two years later, Sundback overcame his grief by throwing himself into his work for a shoe fastener manufacturer. Rejecting the complicated series of hooks and eyes, Sundback designed a fastener made up of rows of teeth that would mesh and clamp together by pulling a fastener. About ten years later, B.F. Goodrich began selling galoshes that were fastened with Sundback's "Hookless Fastener" and called them Zipper Boots—hence, the name "zipper."

2. JIM THORPE
1912 - Carlisle, Pennsylvania

When he was sixteen, Sac and Fox tribe member Jim Thorpe went to a Pennsylvania boarding school for Native Americans. When the track coach (Pop Warner) saw the overalls-clad Thorpe mess around and break the school record for high jump, he knew he had something special. No matter what sport Thorpe competed in (track, football, hockey, tennis, boxing, baseball), he was the best. His domination in both the pentathlon and decathlon at the 1912 Olympics in Stockholm, Sweden was unprecedented. People like to praise Michael Jordan as the gold standard of sports, but it was Jim Thorpe. Michael Jordan was just the Jim Thorpe of basketball.

1. MARY PHELPS ("POLLY") JACOB
1914 - New York, New York

Twenty-one-year-old New York socialite Polly Jacob was fed up with the support rods sticking out from under her dress so she took two silk handkerchiefs, pink ribbon, and a cord and had her housekeeper sew it all together. She got a patent for the Backless Brassiere (from an old French word for "upper arm") and was soon selling bras to all her friends under the name "Caresse Crosby." As a second act in life, Polly got into the book business, publishing the early works of Ernest Hemingway, D.H. Lawrence, and James Joyce.

| 1913 | 1913 | 1914 | 1914 | 1914 |

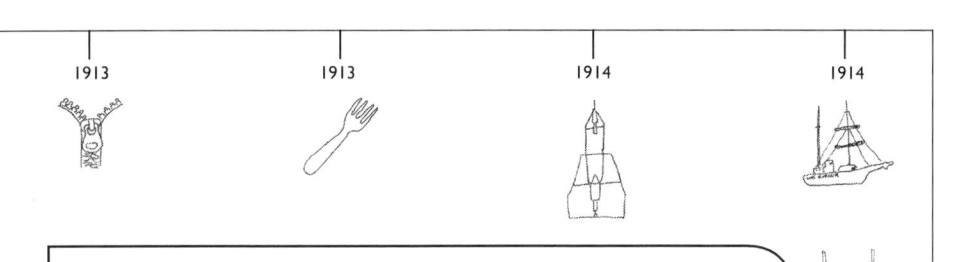

Honorable Mentions: George Bernard Shaw - 1912 (Pygmalion), Madam C.J. Walker - 1913 (philanthropist), Annie Murray - 1913 (Clorox bleach), Ernest Rutherford - 1911 (structure of the atom), Emily Davison - 1913 (suffragist), Roald Amundson - 1910 (reached South Pole), George Claude - 1910 (neon light)

WORST

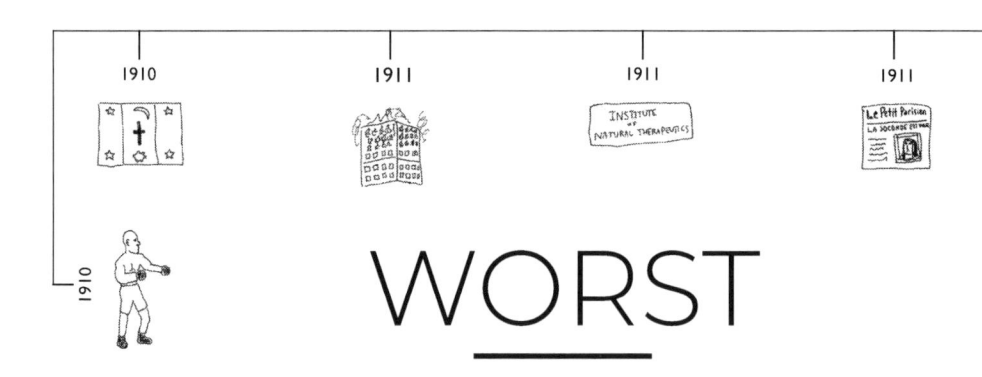

10. VINCENZO PERUGGIA
1911 - Paris, France

The greatest art heist of all time was pulled off by a nincompoop without a thorough plan. Failed artist Vincenzo Peruggia was working a job at the Louvre when he realized they had pretty lax security. Since it was pretty clear his work was never going to hang in the Louvre, he went with the "if you can't beat 'em, steal 'em" strategy. He put on a workman's smock, slipped the *Mona Lisa* off the wall, and took it home. Without contacts in the stolen art underground, the *Mona Lisa* sat in his closet for two years. Finally, in December of 1913, he tried selling it to a gallery in Italy. The buyer turned him in and Peruggia went to the pokey for six months.

9. PARISIAN SNOBS
1913 - Paris, France

On May 29, 1913, a bunch of upper-class people jammed the newly opened Théâtre des Champs-Élysées in Paris to see a ballet featuring the music of up-and-coming Russian composer Igor Stravinsky and choreography by the legendary Vaslav Nijinsky. Unlike traditional ballets, *Rite of Spring* featured unique, complex music and violent dance steps that depicted fertility rites. The audience "awash with diamonds and furs" lost their minds. First they fought each other, then they pelted the orchestra with vegetables. Nijinsky and Stravinsky took their bows to irate theater-goers. The big question remains: Why the hell did rich people bring vegetables to the ballet?

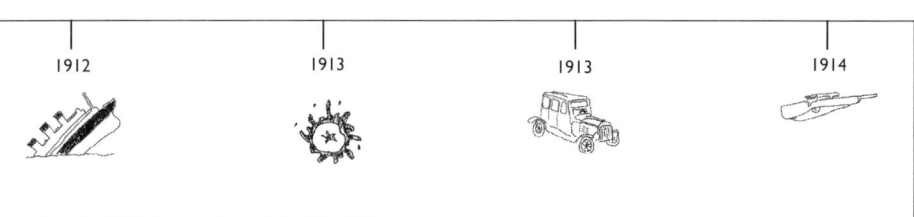

8. GERMAN SNIPER
1914 - Festubert, France

World War I was infinitely more brutal than anyone expected. Technological advances led to significantly more lethal firepower. Gone were the drummer boys leading men with muskets. Enter high-powered rifles, machine guns, tanks, mustard gas, barbed wire, and aircraft attacks. Tens of thousands of young men were killed every day. In December of 1914, Pope Benedict XV called for a temporary hiatus of war for Christmas. The German and British soldiers actually adhered to it. They men left their trenches, sang Christmas carols, exchanged food, booze, and cigarettes, and even played soccer with their enemies. Then a German sniper ended all the fun when he took out two British soldiers on Christmas morning. Truce over.

7. LINDA HAZZARD
1911 - Ollala, Washington

Despite no formal training, the state of Washington inexplicably granted Linda Hazzard a medical license. Hazzard put ads in the Seattle papers for her "Institute of Natural Therapeutics" extolling the virtues of resting the digestion system, which gave the body time to cleanse and fight off ailments and disease. The treatment was simple: two cups of canned tomato broth per day, along with hour-long enemas. That's right, she starved her patients. By 1911, more than a dozen patients were dead and Linda had helped herself to their clothing and jewelry. She eventually got caught and sent to jail but, by 1920, Hazzard was out and back in the starvation game. She killed several more people. Fittingly, in 1935, Hazzard starved herself to death.

6. EDWARD SMITH
1912 - North Atlantic Ocean

The RMS *Titanic* received a warning about ice in its path from a fellow ship traversing the North Atlantic. Captain Edward Smith ignored it. Later that day, Smith cancelled a planned lifeboat drill. Smith then received a more dire warning but opted to attend a private party in the ship's restaurant with the ship's fat cats (including a man with the glorious name Major Archibald Butt). After the party, Smith ignored a third ominous warning because he was tired. At 11:40 p.m., the crew of the *Titanic* spotted an iceberg but it was too late to avoid collision. Since everyone was so ill prepared, lifeboats were sloppily loaded and only about seven hundred out of fifteen hundred people survived. And, to twist the knife even deeper, Captain Smith's incompetence inspired James Cameron to make that awful movie.

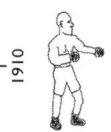

5. JAMES ROBERT MANN
1910 - Chicago, Illinois

After the Industrial Revolution, many women were moved to the city, got jobs, and felt it was within their rights to <gasp> be sexually active. This was a crushing blow for white guys in power. So, Congressman James Mann drafted a poorly-worded bill that would stop this crisis of immorality. The Mann Act gave prosecutors carte blanche to prevent people having sex. It also gave racists another weapon at their disposal. The heavyweight boxing champion at the time (Jack Johnson) happened to be black. Since nobody could beat him in the ring, they caught him with a white woman and ended his career with James Mann's ambiguous, garbage "White-Slave Traffic Act."

4. ISAAC HARRIS AND MAX BLANCK
1911 - New York, New York

"Shirtwaist Kings" Isaac Harris and Max Blanck were ruthless sweatshop overlords. Almost all of their employees at the Triangle Shirtwaist Company were young immigrant women working twelve-hour days every day for only $15 per week. When the women tried to strike, Harris and Blanck paid off politicians to have them arrested. In 1911, a fire broke out on the eighth floor. Harris and Blanck climbed to neighboring rooftops. The workers inside weren't so lucky. Since one stairwell was locked (to prevent theft), two hundred women had to try to escape via one staircase and one barely-functioning elevator. Within eighteen minutes, the entire building was engulfed in flames and 145 women died. After avoiding manslaughter convictions, Harris and Blanck actually profited $60,000 from insurance payouts.

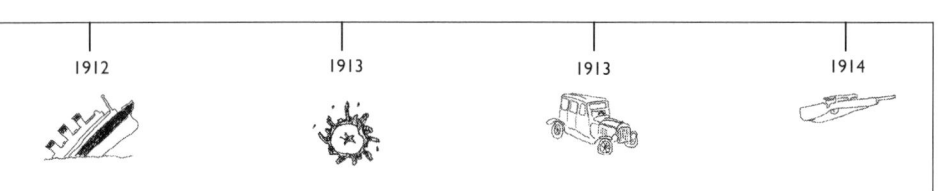

3. PORFIRIO DIAZ
1910 - Chihuahua, Mexico

During his thirty-five-year reign as Mexican dictator, Porfirio Diaz modernized and stabilized Mexico. Too bad he trampled on most of his countrymen on his path to success. Only about two percent of Mexicans were allowed to own land; the rest were homeless or essentially slaves. To deal with natives like the Yaqui Indians (who held rich mining and agricultural territory), Porfirio Diaz provoked them into rebellion so his troops had an excuse to mow them down and take their land directly. Then he gave the land to his rich friends, who exported the crops for even more profits while the natives starved. By 1910, the life expectancy in Mexico was thirty years (compared to fifty years in the United States). Finally, a 1911 peasant uprising (organized by Pancho Villa and Pascual Orozco) forced Diaz into exile.

2. HENRY FORD
1913 - Dearborn, Michigan

It's common misconception that Henry Ford invented the automobile and the assembly line. Ford's genius was simply in marketing. His Model T made him the richest guy in the world. And he was an awful person. As an employer, he was disgraceful. To maintain a workforce of fourteen thousand at any given time, Ford had to hire fifty-two thousand people in 1913. Ford employees made a higher hourly wage than the standard, but the trade-off was letting the corporation micromanage their lives—from spending habits to sex lives. Foreign-born workers were subjected to Americanization classes where the "impurities of foreignness were burnt off as slag to be tossed away leaving a new 100% American." And if any of those workers wanted to strike, the Ford Service Department, a private army full of ex-cops and ex-cons, were sent in to break up those protests. But, worst of all, Ford was a nasty anti-Semite. His personal newspaper, the *Dearborn Independent*, published a story entitled, "The International Jew:

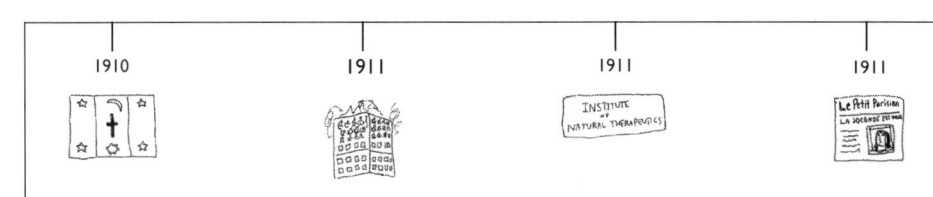

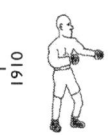

The World's Foremost Problem." From claiming that Lincoln's assassination was the work of a Jew, that Jews created jazz as a way to corrupt and ruin America, and that Jews ran Hollywood so they could control the public's mind, Henry Ford constantly tried to turn the world against Jews. For his fine work, he was honored with the Grand Cross of the German Eagle from Hitler's Nazi government in July, 1938.

1. DRAGUTIN DIMITRIJEVIĆ
1914 - Belgrade, Serbia

Dragutin Dimitrijevic (known as "Apis") was a Serbian nationalist who wanted to end Austria-Hungary's rule in the Balkans. So, in 1914, Apis sent a few nineteen-year-old guys to Sarajevo to kill Hungarian Archduke Franz Ferdinand. The fact that Ferdinand's exact tour route was published and he rode in a convertible with limited security didn't help his case. One of the assassins threw a bomb at Ferdinand's car but missed. While trying to escape, Ferdinand's driver made a wrong turn and pulled up right next to assassin Gavrilo Princip. The assassin shot the archduke in the neck at point-blank range and, a month later, the world was at war. Thirty-seven million people died in "the Great War." At the conclusion of this "war to end all wars," seeds were planted for a second world war, which killed another sixty million.

1912 1913 1913 1914

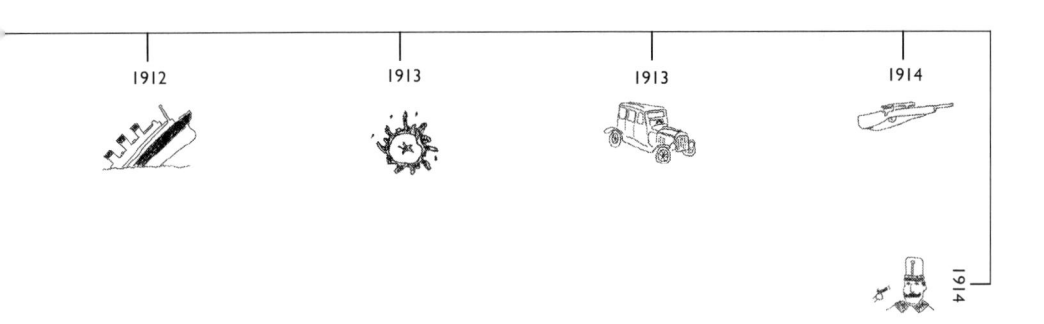

1914

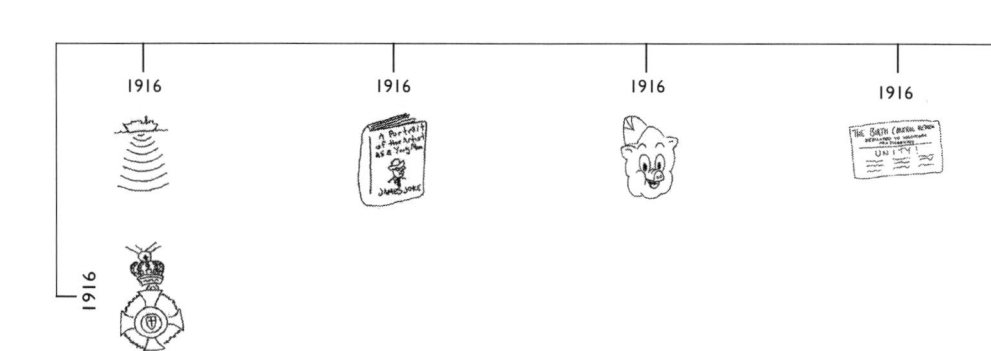

1915-1919

"We can have democracy in this country, or we can have great wealth concentrated in the hands of a few, but we can't have both."

-Louis Brandeis

BEST

10. CLARENCE SAUNDERS
1916 - Memphis, Tennessee

Before Clarence Saunders, buying groceries was a tedious process of waiting for the clerk to find your requested items. Then the Memphis-area businessman had the idea to open up a self-service grocery store. Without all the excess workers needed for picking out food items, Saunders' Piggly Wiggly stores were able to lower prices during World War I. Unfortunately for Clarence, he got caught trying to corner the stock market in 1922 and was forced to sell. He never achieved that lofty success he sought, but the blueprint for grocery markets was established.

9. JAMES JOYCE
1916 - Zurich, Switzerland

Despite a hardscrabble childhood in Dublin, James Joyce was fiercely dedicated to giving himself a good education. He was such a motivated student that he learned Norwegian just to be able to read the works of Henrik Ibsen. But Dublin was controlled by the Catholic Church, which Joyce wanted nothing to do with. So he left Ireland and spent his life writing about it. Joyce's *Portrait of an Artist as a Young Man* in 1916 and *Ulysses* in 1918 were two of the most influential books of the twentieth century. Through his stream-of-consciousness writing style, Joyce reminded readers that people don't have to live high-profile lives to be interesting and he represented the fact that people don't think in complete paragraphs but rather in disconnected thoughts.

8. M. CONSTANTIN CHILOWSKY AND PAUL LANGEVIN
1916 - Paris, France

Starting the day after the *Titanic* sunk, there was a rush to develop technology that would help sea vessels avoid collisions. Russian inventor M. Constantin

Chilowsky suggested to the French government that they use the same kind of high-frequency waves that are used in wireless communications. Professor Paul Langevin liked the idea and invited Chilowsky to join him in Paris to work on the project. By early 1916, the device could detect a sheet of metal two hundred meters away. The Russian inventor's vision and Langevin's execution had created the first sonar. Countless lives have been saved by advance detection of icebergs, unexpected reefs, and submarines. Later on, the high-frequency technology was developed to assist doctors monitor the progress of unborn babies via ultrasound.

7. FLORENCE LAWRENCE
1917 - Hollywood, California

Florence Lawrence was the rare child star who maintained a successful career into adulthood. From her days as a three-year-old vaudevillian ("Baby Flo, the Child Wonder Whistler") to being the first person ever to get their name on a movie billing, Florence Lawrence was the first movie star. Because of that success, Lawrence was also one of the few women of her time to own a car. As a driver, Lawrence noticed some potential dangers on the road and set out to correct them. She threw her efforts into creating the very first mechanical turn and brake signals.

6. ALICE CATHERINE EVANS
1918 - Washington, D.C.

Agricultural whiz Alice Evans was working at the U.S. Department of Agriculture when she identified that a certain bacterial infection in cows caused sickness in humans. Whether it was due to sexism or the fact that the study was coming from someone without a doctorate, veterinarians and the dairy industry didn't listen to her. But, after another decade of people continually getting sick from milk, skeptics gave Alice's recommendation for milk pasteurization a shot. It worked. Alice got some long-overdue praise and was elected the first ever female president of the American Society of Bacteriologists.

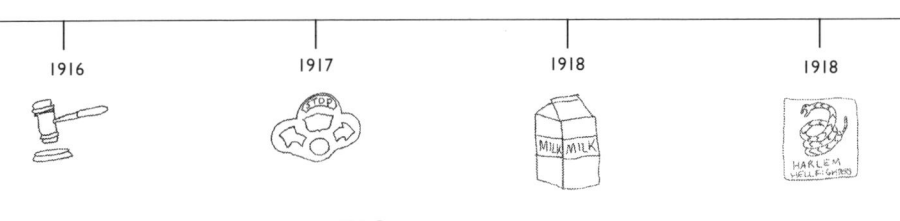

5. LOUIS BRANDEIS
1916 - Washington, D.C.

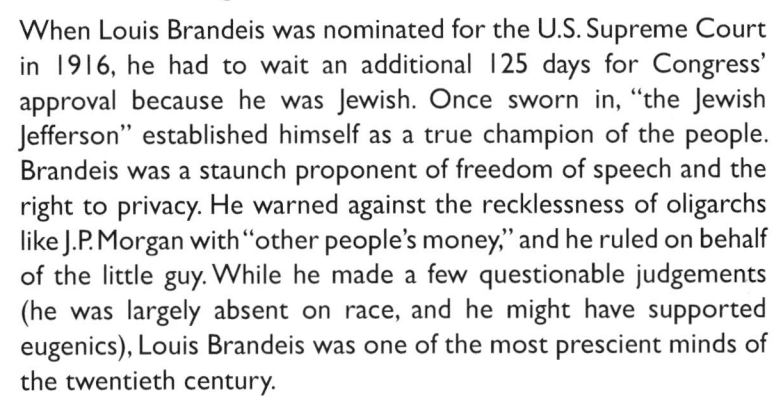

When Louis Brandeis was nominated for the U.S. Supreme Court in 1916, he had to wait an additional 125 days for Congress' approval because he was Jewish. Once sworn in, "the Jewish Jefferson" established himself as a true champion of the people. Brandeis was a staunch proponent of freedom of speech and the right to privacy. He warned against the recklessness of oligarchs like J.P. Morgan with "other people's money," and he ruled on behalf of the little guy. While he made a few questionable judgements (he was largely absent on race, and he might have supported eugenics), Louis Brandeis was one of the most prescient minds of the twentieth century.

4. MILUNKA SAVIĆ
1916 - Crna Bend, Macedonia

In 1913, Milunka Savić's brother was called to duty by the Serbian army to fight in the Balkan War. Instead, the 24-year-old Savić cut off her hair, dressed in men's clothing, and took his place. She quickly proved to be a beast on the front lines and was promoted to corporal. By the time they figured out she was a woman, she had become too valuable to dismiss. During World War I, Savić singlehandedly captured 20 German soldiers in the Battle of Kolubara, another 23 Bulgarians in the Battle of Crna Bend, and received two Karađorđe Stars (Serbia's highest military commendation). The French awarded her the Légion d'Honneur twice as well as making her the only female recipient of their war cross, the Croix de Guerre. She also landed the Russian Cross of St. George and English medal of the Most Distinguished Order of St Michael. After the war, Savić turned down a military pension in France so she could live in Serbia, finding work as a janitor. During World War II, Savić was tossed in a concentration camp for refusing to attend some bullshit ceremony honoring the Germans who had occupied her homeland. She survived that. After the war, Savić finally got her Serbian military pension and lived the rest of her life as a revered war hero.

3. HENRY JOHNSON
1918 - Argonne Forest, France

Five-foot-four 130-pound Henry Johnson badly wanted to serve his country in World War I. He enlisted in an all-black National Guard, only to find himself relegated to subservient tasks like digging latrines. But the French (whose troops were decimated by machine gun-shooting Germans) needed the help and enlisted Henry and his fellow "Harlem Hellfighters." While on watch in the Argonne Forest, Johnson was forced to fight off about twenty-five German soldiers by himself. Despite twenty-one wounds, Henry kept fighting and saved the lives of many fellow soldiers. For that, he was awarded France's top military honor and a New York City parade. Thanks to racism, it wasn't until 1996 that Johnson posthumously received his Purple Heart. In 2015, he was also awarded the Medal of Honor.

2. MARGARET SANGER
1916 - Brooklyn, New York

As a visiting nurse at a New York City hospital, Margaret Sanger saw her fair share of botched back-alley abortions. Between those horrors and the memory of her mother dying at an early age after giving birth to her eleventh child, Sanger made it her life's mission to help women avoid unwanted pregnancies. In open defiance to dildo inspector Anthony Comstock, Sanger sent diaphragms in the mail and was arrested. In 1916, she opened the first ever birth control clinic and was arrested. In 1921, she founded the American Birth Control League (an early version of Planned Parenthood). Sanger never backed down from a tussle and, in 1960, her lifelong dream was fulfilled when the FDA approved "the pill."

1. MOHANDAS GANDHI
1919 - Delhi, India

Gandhi completely flopped in his first case as a lawyer, so he moved to South Africa and found his calling as a leader and

1916	1917	1918	1918

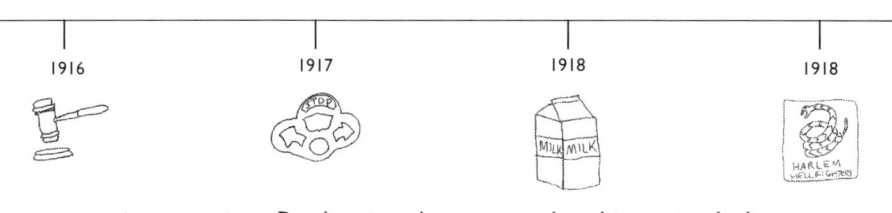

community organizer. By the time he returned to his native India in 1915, he was a civil rights force to be reckoned with. For the next three decades, Gandhi led his fellow Indian people through nonviolent protests in their push for independence from British rule. From boycotts of all things British (goods, government jobs, and state schools) to his 240-mile salt march to a well-publicized hunger strike, Gandhi let the Brits know he wasn't messing around. Finally, in 1947, after immense pressure, India was granted its freedom. While Gandhi had his flaws when it came to respecting other races and women, his peaceful dissension methods have been the blueprint for racial and gender equality protests for the past century. Mahatma (meaning "great soul") Gandhi, as he has become known, was one of the most important people in history.

Honorable Mentions: John McCrae - 1915 ("In Flanders Field"), Edith Cavell - 1917 (British nurse and spy), Jeannette Rankin - 1916 (first woman elected to Congress), Giuseppe Franco - 1915 (first hoagie), Emma Goldman - 1919 (women's rights), Norman Rockwell - 1916 (artist), Thomas Edward Lawrence - 1917 (the real *Lawrence of Arabia*), Nathan Handwerker - 1916 (Nathan's Famous Hot Dogs), T.S. Eliot - 1915 (poet), Sergei Rachmaninoff - 1917 (composer), Violet Jessup - 1916 (survived the sinking of both *Titanic* and *Britannic*)

WORST

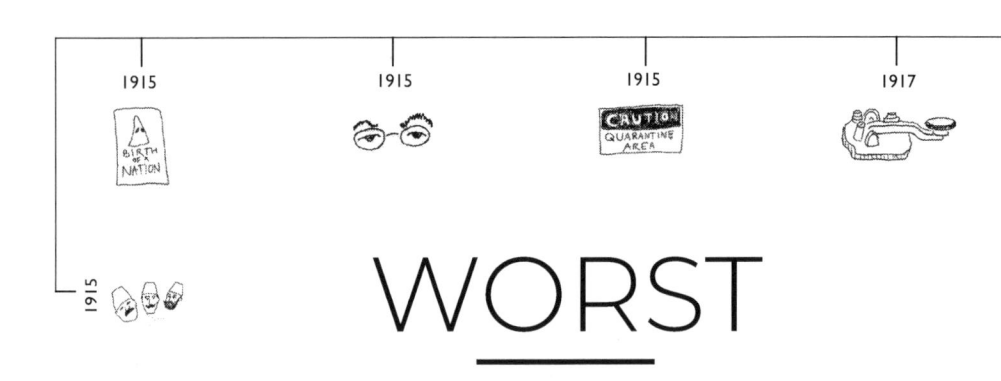

10. CHARLES COMISKEY
1919 - Chicago, Illinois

The owner of the Chicago White Sox was a stingy, racist dickhead. When he wasn't ratting out players for lying about their race, Comiskey was ripping off his talented team of baseball players. Gamblers and bookmakers like Arnold Rothstein seized the opportunity and convinced eight of the players to throw the 1919 World Series against the Cincinnati Reds so they could get money owed to them. They did—and the ensuing scandal ruined all of their careers.

9. MARY MALLON
1915 - New York, New York

After six of the eleven people living at a house where she worked (and one at each of her previous seven jobs) came down with typhoid, it was determined that cook Mary Mallon was the cause. While the Irish immigrant appeared healthy, she was a carrier. She was told to leave the food service industry to prevent any further contagion. Not long afterward, Sloane Maternity Hospital suffered a big outbreak of typhoid where twenty-three people got sick and two died. When they checked the kitchen, a cook named Mary "Brown" took off running. Typhoid Mary was caught and spent the rest of her life in quarantine.

8. ARTHUR ZIMMERMANN
1917 - Berlin, Germany

After the catastrophic losses suffered by the British and French in World War I on the Western Front (Somme, Verdun, Marne, Ypres, and others), the Allies desperately needed support from neutral

| 1919 | 1919 | 1919 | 1919 |

America. But the Yanks stayed out of it. Then, in January of 1917, British spies intercepted German General Arthur Zimmermann's telegram intended for a Mexican ambassador. In it, Zimmerman offered cash and help winning back the territory of Texas, New Mexico, and Arizona if Mexico were to join the Central Powers. The telegram was passed on to U.S. authorities and, by March 1, was on the front page of every major newspaper in America. On April 2, Woodrow Wilson stood in front of Congress calling for war.

7. GEORGES CLEMENCEAU
1919 - Versailles, France

Three men decided the fate of Germany after World War I: American President Woodrow Wilson, British Prime Minister Lloyd George, and French Prime Minister Georges Clemenceau. Wilson pushed for its entrance into the League of Nations (like the U.N.). George wanted to re-establish Britain's naval supremacy and make peace. But, since most of the war was fought on French soil and 15 percent of its male population had fallen casualty, Clemenceau was out for revenge. Well, luckily for him, Woodrow Wilson got the flu and conceded to most of the Frenchman's demands just so he could get the meeting over with. The result: crippling sanctions laid upon the Germans, which set the stage for an angry, us-against-the-world movement led by a fiery little fascist. The Treaty of Versailles ensured that "the war to end all wars" was pretty much a complete waste of time, effort, and millions of lives. Within twenty years, everyone was right back at war.

6. MITCHELL PALMER
1919 - Washington, D.C

After World War I, American labor conditions were poor. Work was hard to come by and, at the same time, an influx of recently immigrated Eastern Europeans had entered the workforce. These were also the years immediately following the Bolshevik Revolution. So, the Americans' fear of these Eastern Europeans was that they'd either take jobs or seek to overthrow the U.S.

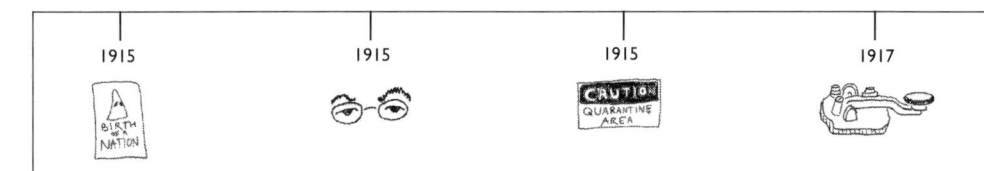

government. After a series of anarchist bombs went off in 1919, the Red Scare was in full effect. Attorney General Mitchell Palmer, a man with 1920 presidential aspirations, used his position to capitalize on xenophobia and arrest thousands of people through Constitution-violating arrests of foreign-born citizens. The over-the-top raids eventually led to the creation of the ACLU and the political downfall of Mitchell Palmer.

5. WOODROW WILSON
1915 - Washington, D.C.

From the moment he took office, President Woodrow Wilson did his best to give the South "home rule." In other words, he allowed white Southerners to turn back the clock to antebellum times in regards to treatment of people of color. Wilson's appointees were fellow racists, as well. He publicly endorsed D.W. Griffith's pro-KKK film *Birth of a Nation* ("it is all so terribly true") and did his best to put an end to all integration. When America entered World War I (just months after winning reelection by promising to keep America out of war), Wilson forcefully cracked down on anti-war protesters. He ignored requests for help fighting the worldwide flu epidemic in 1918 then, ironically, came down with it during the important Versailles Treaty. Woodrow Wilson was awful.

4. D. W. GRIFFITH
1915 - New York, New York

Before D. W. Griffith, movies were pretty much just recorded stage plays. Through his use of close-ups, crosscuts, dissolves, extensive set design, action footage, and intertwining stories, Griffith elevated the art form and realized the power of cinema. Unfortunately for the world, much like Darth Vader, he used his power for evil instead of good. In 1915, Griffith's *Birth of a Nation*, a three-hour Ku Klux Klan propaganda film, earned what would be an insane $1.8 billion in today's money. After *Birth of a Nation*'s release, the flagging Ku Klux Klan saw an immediate revival and lynching numbers across the South spiked.

3. HASEGAWA YOSHIMICHI
1919 - Seoul, Korea (South Korea)

In 1876, as Western powers gobbled up territories in Asia, Japan decided to beat them to the punch and gain control of Korea. After the Chinese (in 1894) and Russians (in 1904) tried to fight Japan for it and failed, Japan decided to annex Korea altogether. In 1919, Korean leaders assembled and declared their independence from Japan. In response, Hasegawa Yoshimichi, the Japanese governor-general of Korea, cited the anti-assembly rule and turned the military on the people. More than 7,500 protesters (or only 553, if you ask Japan) were killed on Yoshimichi's order. While the March 1 protest is celebrated each year as a national holiday, Korea didn't actually gain independence until after World War II.

2. CHARLES PONZI
1919 - Boston, Massachusetts

Lots of famous creations bear their inventor's name: braille (Louis Braille), graham crackers (Rev Sylvester Graham), Jacuzzi (Candido Jacuzzi), saxophone (Adolphe Sax)...and then there's the Ponzi scheme. After a few scams (and jail stints), Charles Ponzi moved on to a mail fraud pyramid scheme that would ever after bear his name. In a nutshell, Ponzi recruited investors and promised great returns but in reality was just borrowing from Peter to pay Paul. As long as new investors kept pouring in, things were okay. When the music stopped, 40,000 investors had lost between a total $15 and $20 million and six banks went belly-up.

1. THE THREE PASHAS (MEHMET TALAAT, AHMED DJEMAL, AND ENVER PASHA)
1915 - Constantinople, Ottoman Empire (Istanbul, Turkey)

In 1908, a group of malcontents in the Ottoman military (the Young Turks) seized power of their crumbling empire. The leaders

1915 — BIRTH OF NATION

1915

1915 — CAUTION QUARANTINE AREA

1917

1915

of this movement (the Three Pashas) were extremely wary of all non-Turks (i.e., Christians). After Mehmed Talaat failed to come to an agreement with the Russians in World War I, Enver Pasha worked out a deal with the Central Powers. Fearing that the Christian Armenian people would side with the Russians, the Three Pashas started a campaign to decimate them. On April 24, 1915 (Red Sunday), Ottoman authorities arrested and executed 250 Armenian intellectuals and community leaders. Soon thereafter, they unleashed killing squads and reduced the Armenian population from two million to under 400,000. To this day, the Republic of Turkey denies it was a holocaust and claims there were only about 300,000 deaths. Guess that makes it okay.

1919   1919   1919   1919   1919

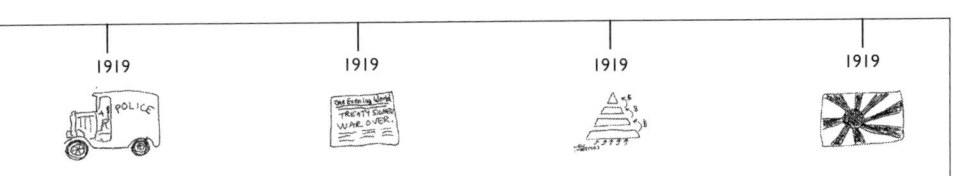

Dishonorable Mentions: Bela Kiss - 1916 (serial killer), Amy Archer-Landau - 1917 (nursing home killer), Henri Landru - 1915 (WWI widow murderer)

| 1920 | 1920 | 1921 | 1921 |

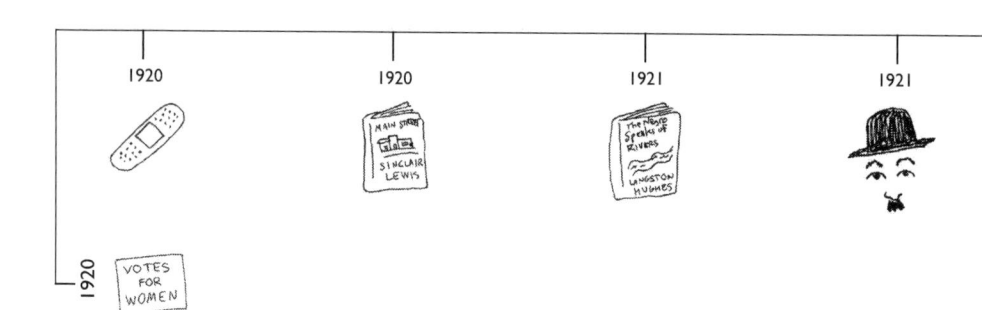

1920 VOTES FOR WOMEN

1920-1924

"If you can be the best, then why not try to be the best?"
-Garrett Morgan

B<u>E</u>ST

10. SINCLAIR LEWIS
1920 - Washington, D.C.

Sinclair Lewis was the prominent American novelist of the 1920s. In 1920, his novel skewering small-town life, *Main Street*, set off a firestorm of controversy. Prior to that point, small towns were considered the bastion of nobility (unlike the big, bad cities). But, in *Main Street*, Sinclair Lewis exposed them to be cripplingly provincial, smug, and lousy with gossip. For his brilliant work, he was awarded the Pulitzer Prize. Fearing backlash, though, the jurors at Columbia University later rescinded the award. Six years later, when that same jury tried to award Lewis another Pulitzer for his novel *Arrowsmith*, he told the committee (in terse but polite enough terms) that they could keep their award. In 1930, Sinclair Lewis became the first American author to be awarded the Nobel Prize for Literature.

9. CLARENCE BIRDSEYE
1924 - Gloucester, Massachusetts

Whether it's chicken nuggets for the kids, pigs in a blanket for a dinner party, or a frozen pizza for a lazy evening, everyone relies on frozen food at some point. The man to thank for the process of freezing food without sacrificing its taste is Clarence Birdseye. Birdseye, the biology student-turned-fur trader, noticed that local Inuits immediately froze the fish they caught, which kept it fresh until thawed and eaten. His scientific brain kicked in and, when he returned to America, he developed a process in which food would be quickly cooled inside of -25°F metal plates. The quicker it was frozen, the better it tasted when thawed. In 1924, he started the General Seafood Corporation. Clarence, we raise our Eggo waffle to you.

8. HARRY HOUDINI
1924 - Boston, Massachusetts

During a time when movies were mostly awful and nobody had television,

Harry Houdini entertained the world through daring escapes and public exhibitions. But his greatest contribution to society was his talent of debunking scam artists. In the years after World War I, as yellow fever was robbing the planet of millions of people, psychic mediums swooped in and offered to contact dead loved ones for a fee. One especially egregious con artist "medium" was a Boston woman named Mina Crandon. Houdini, a master of deception, saw right through her chicanery and published a pamphlet exposing all her tricks. Bet she didn't see that coming.

7. FRANZ KAFKA
1924 - Prague, Czech Republic

Franz Kafka had a tormented family life, a joyless career in insurance, intimacy issues (the guy was afraid to even get naked), a poor sense of self-worth, and fading health. Really, his only outlet was writing. His crippling self-loathing caused him to set most of his writings on fire and abandon 90 percent of his life's work. But, after his death at just forty-one years old, Kafka's friend, Max Brod, ignored his wishes to destroy the rest of the letters, diaries, and manuscripts and instead published them. In his three well-respected, highly influential, unfinished novels (*The Trial*, *The Castle*, and *Amerika*), Kafka tapped into darker human emotions and staunch portrayals of how we are all responsible for our own actions.

6. CAESAR CARDINI
1924 - Tijuana, Mexico

Salad is terrible. People pretend to love it but, really, the best salads are just the ones that make you the least sad. There is one exception: the Caesar salad. Tijuana restaurant owner Caesar Cardini was running low on food one night but didn't want to send his guests away hungry. So he took what was left in the kitchen (romaine lettuce, garlic, croutons, Parmesan cheese, boiled eggs, olive oil, and Worcestershire sauce) and whipped up a tableside concoction. Caesar salad was a big hit. Since Tijuana was a popular tourist destination for Americans looking for a boozy jaunt during Prohibition, soon celebrities like W. C. Fields and Clark Gable discovered this salad and loved it so much that they demanded it be brought to America.

5. CHARLIE CHAPLIN
1921 - Hollywood, California

Charlie Chaplin came to America and landed a gig as one of the Keystone cops. After a couple of years of pie-to-the-face/slip-on-a-banana-peel comedic roles, Chaplin wanted a bigger challenge. So he wrote, directed, starred in, and even composed his own films, eventually becoming the greatest silent film star of all time. When the crooked entertainment system shortchanged him, Chaplin used his influence to start his own studio (United Artists). In 1940, as America was trying its best to look the other way from Hitler committing atrocities in Europe, Chaplin made *The Great Dictator*, a movie that both humiliated Hitler and called for his countrymen to stand up to him. Charlie Chaplin was a force of nature. That is, until domestic villain J. Edgar Hoover pushed Chaplin out of the country during the Red Scare of the 1950s.

4. GARRETT MORGAN
1923 - Cleveland, Ohio

Garrett Morgan, the son of two former Kentucky slaves, had the Midas touch. At just fourteen years old the mechanically proficient Morgan started off as a sewing machine repairman and eventually opened up his own business with a few dozen employees. In 1916, Morgan used a gas mask he personally developed to rescue thirty-two trapped men in a tunnel 250 feet below Lake Erie. Soon, he was supplying gas masks to fire departments across the country as well as the army during World War I. He used that money to open his own newspaper (*Cleveland Call*) where black people could read positive stories about themselves and run ads. As the only car-owning black man in Cleveland, Morgan noted that many collisions were caused by traffic signals going from green to red with no warning, so he developed the first tricolor traffic light.

3. EARLE DICKSON
1920 - Highland Park, New Jersey

Earle Dickson's wife, Josephine, was a klutz. He would come home from his job as a cotton buyer for Johnson & Johnson and find that she had burned her finger on the stove or sliced it while preparing dinner. So, the devoted husband would cut some cotton gauze and tape it to her wounds. To save time and make it easier for Josephine to do it herself when he wasn't home, Earle prepared a bunch of ready-made bandages. After seeing them work, he took the idea to his boss, James Johnson. Johnson loved it and the company moved forward to mass-produce BAND-AIDS. For his multi-billion-dollar idea, Earle was promoted to vice president.

2. LANGSTON HUGHES
1921 - Harlem, New York

The 1920s Harlem Renaissance was a major step in the civil rights movement in America. After the Great Migration (a time when blacks moved from the South to Northern cities en masse), black people finally had an opportunity to publicly feel pride and celebrate their culture. The leading voice of the Harlem Renaissance was the poet and playwright Langston Hughes. Fresh out of high school, Hughes wrote his highly acclaimed poem "The Negro Speaks of Rivers," which called for black people to embrace their shared histories that go all the way back to the birth of civilization. The Harlem Renaissance reinforced pride within the black community and relaxed some of the ignorant bigotry coming from the whites.

1. ALICE PAUL AND CARRIE CHAPMAN CATT
1920 - Washington, D.C.

America took it quite literally when Thomas Jefferson wrote "all *men* are created equal." Women were decidedly second-class citizens and, since they weren't allowed to vote, things didn't look like they were about to change. Heroes like Elizabeth Cady Stanton, Lucretia Mott, Susan B. Anthony, Florence Kelly,

| 1923 | 1924 | 1924 | 1924 |

and Charlotte Perkins Gilman helped shift the narrative... but didn't clinch women's voting rights. Then Alice Paul made the issue impossible to ignore. After getting arrested for chaining herself to the White House fence, Paul went on a high-profile hunger strike. Meanwhile, Carrie Chapman Catt had organized the League of Women Voters, who demanded suffrage. Women had become essential to America during World War I, and now, with that newfound power, they were demanding to have a voice. On August 18, 1920, the Nineteenth Amendment was ratified. Women could vote.

Honorable Mentions: Bessie Coleman - 1920 (first black female pilot), George Gershwin - 1924 (Rhapsody in Blue), Jean Piaget - 1920 (cognitive development), Henry Gerber - 1924 (gay rights activist), Carl Jung - 1921 (psychiatrist), Frederick Banting - 1920 (insulin), William Butler Yeats - 1923 (poet), Edwin Hubble - 1924 (astronomer), Claude McKay - 1921 (poet), Grantland Rice - 1924 (sportswriter)

WORST

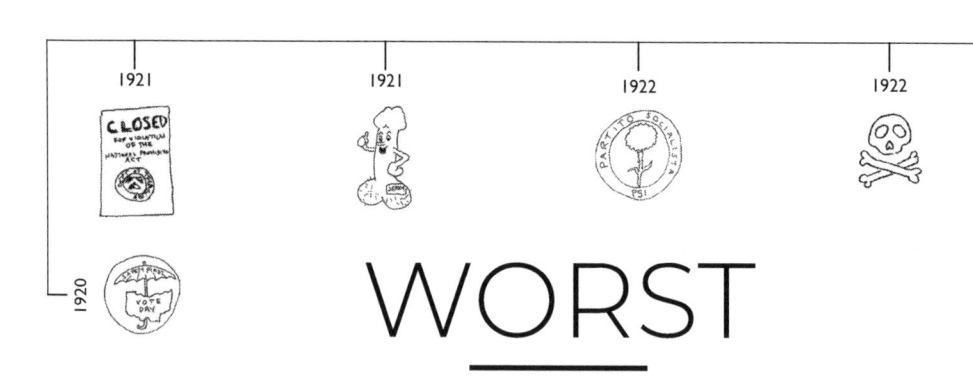

10. ALAN ALEXANDER MILNE
1926 - Sussex, England

A.A. Milne was already an accomplished author before his career was eclipsed by his fantastical story starring his son, Christopher Robin, and all his stuffed animals. In 1926, Milne unleashed the hell that is *Winnie-the-Pooh* upon the world. Never in the history of fictional characters has a greater collection of depressing dullards been assembled than in *Winnie-the-Pooh*. Pooh is a gluttonous moron—and not in a charming Homer Simpson/SpongeBob SquarePants way—whose sole ambition it is to eat endless amounts of honey. Everyone bends over backwards to enable his pathetic friend, Piglet. Tigger is exhausting. Eeyore constantly bums everyone out. And Rabbit is a dick. The whole ensemble sucks.

9. WARREN G. HARDING
1921 - Washington, D.C.

In a last-minute decision, the Republican Party made the presidential-looking Warren Harding their nominee in the 1920 election. He won the election and said the right things. He even spoke out against lynching and gave hope he'd be a good civil rights leader. But, in reality, Harding was just a guy who wanted to hit the golf course, play poker, and chase women while his unscrupulous cabinet appointments ripped off the government. In fact, Harding might have been the creepiest president in history. In love letters with his mistress (whom he knocked up), Harding constantly referred to his dick as "Jerry" and used terrible metaphors. "Wish I could take you to Mount Jerry. Wonderful spot." If Mount Jerry was anything like Harding's White House, it was impotent and disease-ridden.

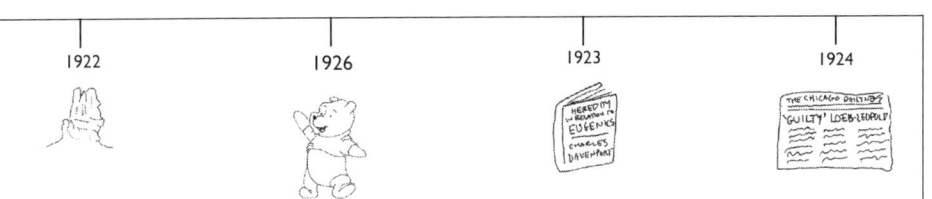

8. MABEL WALKER WILLEBRANDT
1921 - Washington, D.C.

When the Eighteenth Amendment went into effect on January 16, 1920, the entire United States of America went dry… at least in theory. The reality was that enforcement of Prohibition (as per the Volstead Act) was a task nobody really wanted, so people looked the other way for the most part. That is, until Warren Harding gave Mabel Willebrandt the job. Willebrandt was, by all accounts, a pretty solid person. But once she was handed the keys to the Volstead Act, she developed a God complex. With the law on her side, Willebrandt used the police, the navy, the coast guard, and lawyers to turn the nation into a no fun zone. Mabel Willebrandt was like the hall monitor from hell.

7. ALBERT FALL
1922 - Washington, D.C.

Warren Harding's "Ohio Gang" treated their cabinet positions like endless revenue streams. The worst of their offenses was the Teapot Dome scandal. In 1921, Secretary of the Interior Albert Fall lobbied to have the Elk Hills naval oil reserve in California and the Teapot Dome naval oil reserve in Wyoming transferred to the Department of the Interior's control. Once that was accomplished, Fall used his close relationships with Western developers to work out side deals to line his pockets. Fall's shady deals were exposed within a year and he was forced to resign in shame, pay a fine, and spend a year in the slammer.

6. AL WEININGER'S WIFE
1924 - Chicago, Illinois

After a tour in Germany with the U.S. Army, Henry Gerber returned to America to become its first gay rights advocate. He established the Society for Human Rights and published a couple copies of the newsletter *Friendship and Freedom* before his office was raided and he was arrested. Unfortunately, the Vice President of the Society for Human Rights was Al Weininger, a married father of two with an angry wife. Instead of simply ending their marriage,

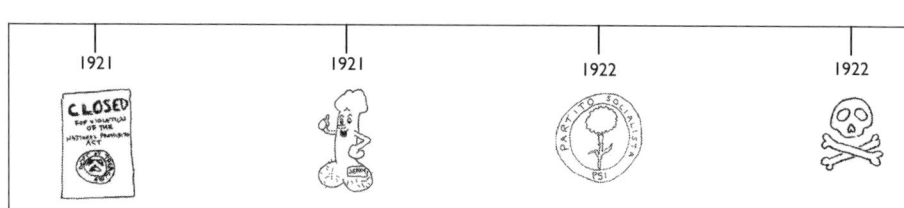

Weininger's wife decided to tear down the entire movement. The ensuing trials ruined Gerber financially and scared him from ever taking a public stance again. Gerber re-enlisted in the army and the gay rights movement was put on hold for another forty years.

5. NATHAN LEOPOLD AND RICHARD LOEB
1924 - Chicago, Illinois

Wealthy and intelligent University of Chicago students Nathan Leopold and Richard Loeb had Bonnie and Clyde-type fantasies of becoming famous criminals. But their larceny and arson crimes weren't making the newspaper headlines. So the two concocted an over-the-top crime—the kidnap and murder of a child. The psychopaths lured Loeb's fourteen-year-old cousin into their car, killed him, dumped his body in a swamp, and left a ransom note. The city was abuzz. In just a few days, the body was found along with Loeb's eyeglasses and a ransom note that was written with Loeb's typewriter. The trial for the so-called "crime of the century" (well, until O.J.) was a circus, ending with both getting ninety-nine years in the hoosegow.

4. CHARLES DAVENPORT
1923 - Cold Springs Harbor, New York

Charles Davenport, a highly respected biologist from New York, was inspired by the work of German scientist Gregor Mendel (who wrote about cross-breeding pea plants for optimal production). Davenport wanted to use those techniques to develop the best "racial stock," otherwise known as eugenics. With the financial backing of guys like Andrew Carnegie, people took Davenport's studies (which juxtaposed carnival freak shows and immigrants with healthy white people) seriously. One admirer, in particular, was enlightened by Davenport's plans for sterilization of criminals and the mentally inferior: Adolph Hitler. In his book *Mein Kampf*, Hitler stated that America's push for drumming out inferior offspring "represents the most humane act of mankind." Way to go, Chuck.

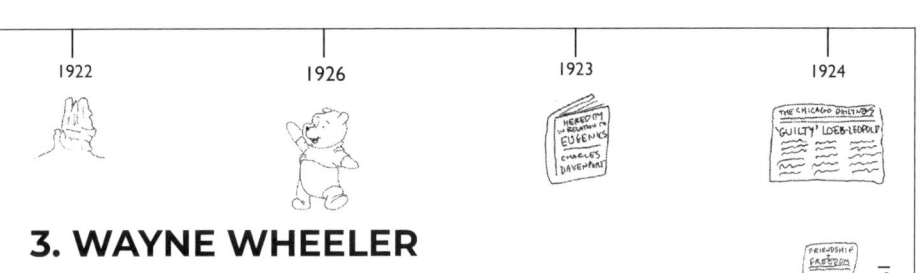

3. WAYNE WHEELER
1920 - Cleveland, Ohio

Wayne Wheeler took some rough alcohol-related childhood experiences and turned them into a lifelong crusade against booze. At the Anti-Saloon League in Ohio, Wheeler threw everything he had into getting pro-Prohibition candidates elected. As he moved around the country, Wheeler used any belief systems he came across (religion, xenophobia) to convince people to join him in the temperance movement. When Wheeler found out people were drinking industrial alcohol for the buzz, he had it poisoned, which led to blindness (hence, the term "blind drunk") and death. But Wheeler's lowest moment was courting the KKK's votes in exchange for letting them use whatever violence they deemed necessary to enforce the anti-alcohol agenda.

2. CARL PANZRAM
1922 - Salem, Massachusetts

Carl Panzram had a rough childhood and spent his entire adult life trying to bring the world down with him. At six feet tall and about two hundred pounds, he'd qualify as a big guy today. A hundred years ago, he qualified as a Hulk-like beast. Panzram went from town to town via boxcar. At each stop, he robbed, burned down buildings, and raped many young men and boys. In the 1920s, he added murder to his résumé. Finally, in 1928, Panzram was caught after some burglaries he committed in Washington, D.C. He confessed to over a hundred rapes and twenty-two murders.

1. BENITO MUSSOLINI
1922 - Rome, Italy

While the other Allied powers seemed to be enjoying the spoils of war after the Versailles Treaty, Italy got crumbs. Nationalists like Benito Mussolini were incensed. In 1919, Mussolini formed a fascist party (Italian Socialist Party) and called for a change in government. With a bunch of fiery "the people deserve better" speeches and promises to return Rome to its glory days, Mussolini quickly grew a big following. By 1922, his Black Shirts marched on

|1920| |1921| |1921| |1922| |1922|

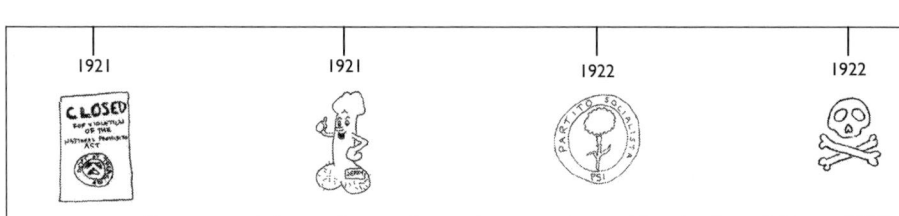

Rome and forced out the prime minister. He declared himself "Il Duce" ("the Leader"), dismantled all vestiges of democracy, and terrorized his country for the next thirteen years.

| 1922 | 1926 | 1923 | 1924 | 1924 |

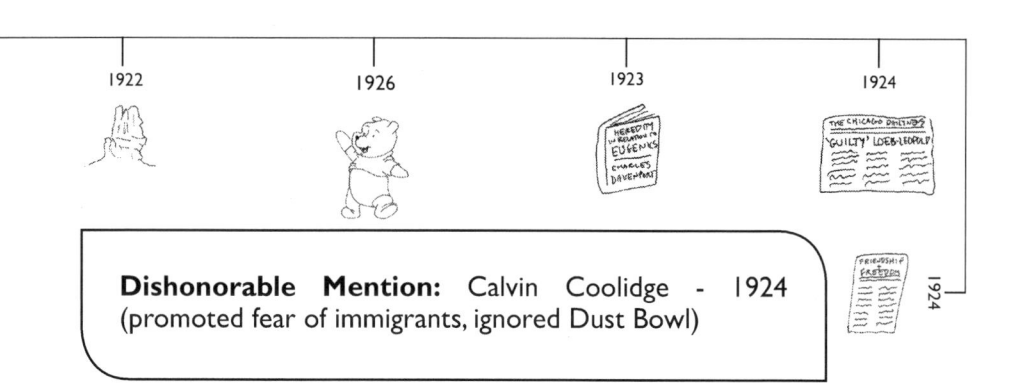

Dishonorable Mention: Calvin Coolidge - 1924 (promoted fear of immigrants, ignored Dust Bowl)

1925 1925 1925 1927 1927

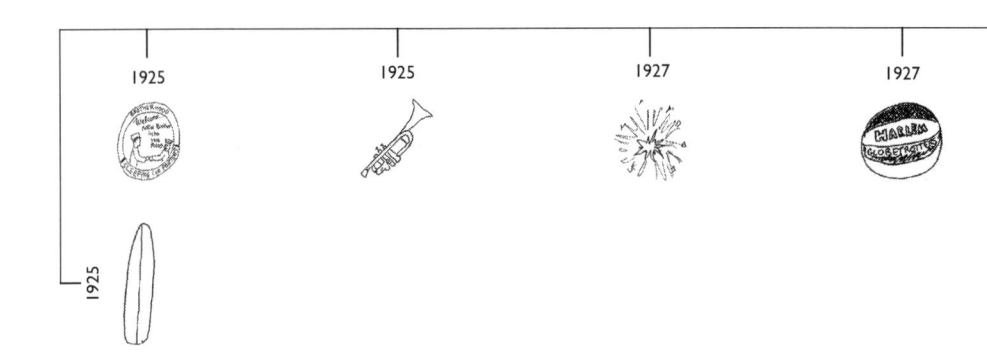

1925-1929

"Freedom is never granted; it is won. Justice is never given; it is exacted."
-A. Philip Randolph

BEST

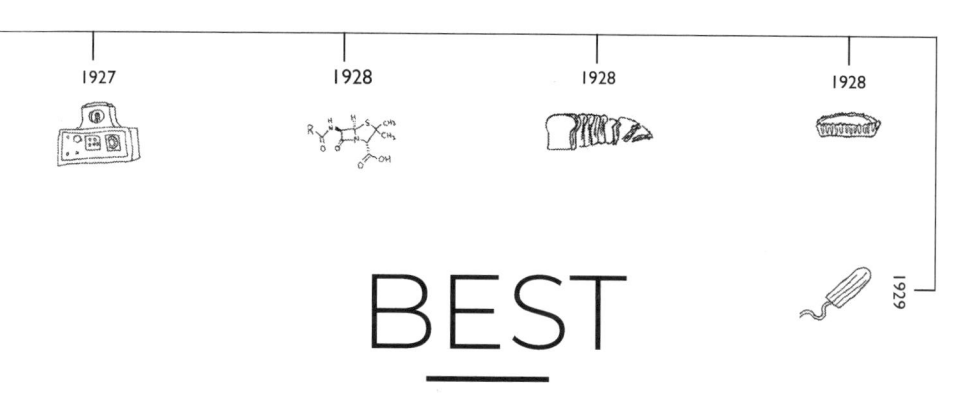

10. HARRY BURNETT REESE
1928 - Hershey, Pennsylvania

Given that he had sixteen kids, H. B. Reese was constantly looking for better-paying work. He had a decent job at the chocolate-making division at Hershey but supplemented his income by making his own chocolates in his basement. In 1928, Reese came up with his signature invention, the peanut butter cup. Orders flooded in for the "penny cup" (as they were known at the time), to the point where Reese was able to quit his job at Hershey and open his own factory down the street. They say necessity is the mother of invention. In the case of Harry B. Reese, a complete disregard for birth control was the grandmother of invention.

9. DUKE KAHANAMOKU
1925 - Newport Beach, California

In the mid-nineteenth century, white missionaries descended upon Hawaii and tried to make them live like white Europeans. After they condemned surfing as immoral, the sport almost completely disappeared. Thanks to Olympic super-swimmer Duke Kahanamoku, though, it was never completely abandoned. After winning multiple golds and silvers at the 1912, 1920, and 1924 Olympics, Kahanamoku used his celebrity to revive and promote surfing. In 1925, while out on the water in Newport Beach, California, Duke and a friend spotted a forty-foot fishing boat in bad shape. They paddled out to the wreckage and saved the lives of twelve fishermen. From that point on, surfboards became standard equipment for beach lifeguards. The "Ambassador of Aloha" was like a hybrid of Michael Phelps, Laird Hamilton, and Hasselhoff from *Baywatch*.

8. ABE SAPERSTEIN
1927 - Hinckley, Illinois

In 1927, Abe Saperstein was hired to coach and manage the Savoy Five, an all-black basketball team from Chicago. Saperstein renamed them the Harlem

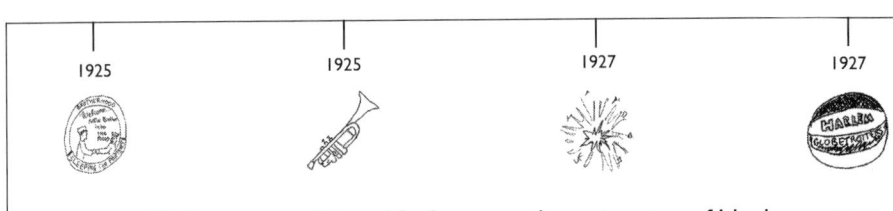

Globetrotters (since Harlem was the epicenter of black greatness in the 1920s) and sewed them snazzy new red, white, and blue uniforms. The Globetrotters destroyed just about every all-white team they played, so Saperstein encouraged them to have more fun with the game and show off cool tricks. Soon the team was playing to thousands of people and, in 1948, got a shot at the reigning all-white NBA Champion Minneapolis Lakers. Two years after that exhibition, the NBA fully integrated. At a time when people seriously doubted the merits of black athletes, a five-foot-five Jewish guy from London showed the world their greatness.

7. GEORGES LEMAÎTRE
1927 - Leuven, Belgium

Despite being one of the smartest people who ever lived, Albert Einstein was sometimes wrong. While he knew all about gravity, Einstein figured there was some mysterious equal force which evens everything out and keeps the universe static. Then, in 1927, Belgian priest (who studied at MIT) Georges Lemaître theorized that, based on science, the universe must be expanding constantly. Scientists passed the Catholic priest off as a kook. In 1929, Edwin Hubble published a report confirming Lemaître was right. Einstein nominated Lemaître for the Francqui Prize, the most prestigious award a Belgian scientist can get. So the next time someone argues the Book of Genesis and God creating Eve from Adam's rib and all that, remind them it was a Catholic priest who came up with the Big Bang Theory.

6. OTTO F. ROHWEDDER
1928 - Chillicothe, Missouri

People have been enjoying bread for a good 30,000 years. And for the first 29,910 of them, we had to cut or tear off a piece of it ourselves. Then a Missouri jeweler called Otto Frederick Rohwedder got to work on a contraption that would evenly slice a loaf. After a decade of working on it, Rohwedder sold his "power-driven, multi-bladed" bread slicer to the Chillicothe Baking Company. So, the next time someone says "the greatest thing since sliced bread," you know they're referring to the year 1928.

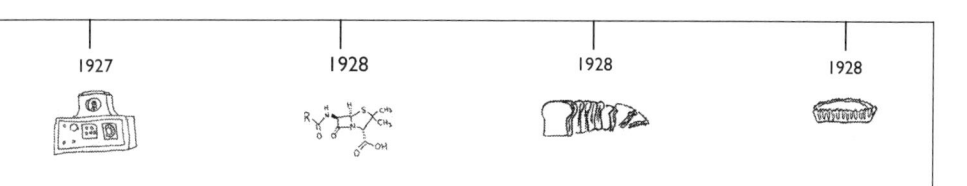

5. LOUIS ARMSTRONG
1925 - Chicago, Illinois

For the past fifty years or so, music has consistently crossed the color lines (well, except for maybe R.E.M.). But, before Louis Armstrong, white artists were released on white record labels and promoted to white audiences, and black artists were subjected to black labels. But when the New Orleans-born Armstrong burst on the scene in the mid-1920s with his infectious jazz style and his joyful, scratchy voice, all that went out the window. "Satchmo" crossed color lines. It was now cool for white people to be into black culture. Soon, stars like Frank Sinatra and Bing Crosby were shifting their styles to imitate Armstrong. There were many black artists that were key in the Harlem Renaissance (Duke Ellington, Billie Holiday, and more) but Louis Armstrong was the breakout star.

4. A. PHILIP RANDOLPH
1925 - Harlem, New York

With the rise of unions, labor conditions were slowly improving in America. But those improvements weren't extended to black workers. Blacks weren't allowed in the AFL. Then in 1925, A. Philip Randolph founded the Brotherhood of Sleeping Car Porters and led them in a fight against the railroads. The Sleeping Car Porters were eventually recognized by the AFL and later the CIO. After that, Randolph took his fight to Washington, where blacks were still barred from working for the Defense Department. Before Randolph could organize a protest march, Franklin Roosevelt conceded and banned discrimination in the defense industries, and later Harry Truman did the same with the army. In a final act of civil rights badassery, A. Philip Randolph was the originator of the March on Washington before handing the baton off to Martin Luther King.

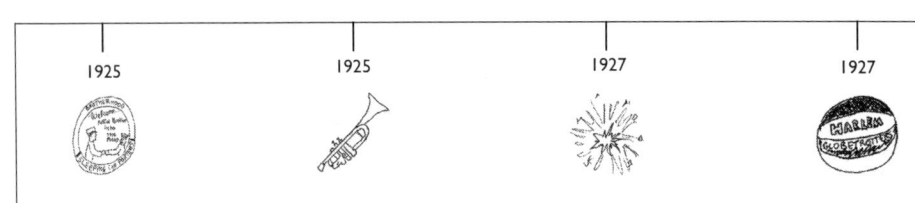

3. EARLE HAAS
1929 - Denver, Colorado

If men had periods, it would've been custom for every guy to take a week off from work each month. Women were never afforded that right. Since humanity's beginnings, they made do with whatever solutions they could think of (Ancient Egyptians—dirt, honey, elephant and crocodile feces; Romans—goose fat and opium; Indians—rock salt; Ancient Japanese—paper). Even in the early twentieth century, women still relied on uncomfortable belts and pads during that time of the month. Then, in 1929, Colorado Doctor Earle Haas created a contraption out of compressed cotton—the tampon. His company, Tampax (a combination of the words "tampon" and "vaginal packs"), never made Earle big money but its popularity soared during World War II, when women started taking over "male" jobs en masse. Today, it is estimated that a woman uses more than ten thousand tampons in her lifetime.

2. PHILO T. FARNSWORTH
1927 - San Francisco, California

Born in a Utah log cabin in 1906, Philo Farnsworth was a science prodigy. After reading about the quest to invent the television, the sixteen-year-old Farnsworth figured out what had eluded Edison, Tesla, and Marconi—the vacuum tube which made television possible. By the age of twenty, Farnsworth moved to California and brought his sketches to life. RCA came in with a lowball offer to buy it, but Farnsworth balked. For the next decade, they buried him with lawsuits until his television patent ran out. He never got the fame or money he deserved in his lifetime, but Philo Farnsworth is now considered one of the most important inventors in history.

| 1927 | 1928 | 1928 | 1928 |

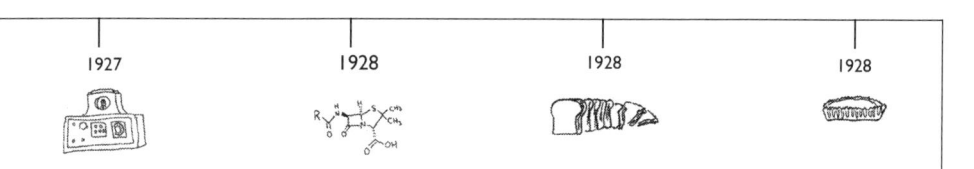

1. ALEXANDER FLEMING AND HOWARD FLOREY
1928 - Oxford, England

Bacteriologist Alexander Fleming returned from vacation and noticed mold had grown on certain Petri dishes where he was trying to grow germs. Instead of throwing them out, Fleming studied this mold (Penicillium notatum) carefully and noticed that it had created a bacteria-free radius around itself. Fleming tested the process several more times and found the penicillium continually inhibited the growth of the bacteria. So he took his discovery to Dr. Howard Florey at Oxford. Florey isolated the mold juice (amazingly, without vomiting), tested it on mice, and, in 1940, gave it to an actual person. Penicillin was ready just in time for World War II. During the previous world war, deaths from bacterial pneumonia were around 18 percent; during the second, penicillin lowered that rate to less than 1 percent. Fleming was hailed as the hero of this phenomenon, while Florey and his team were largely ignored.

Honorable Mentions: Amelia Earhart - 1928 (first woman to make transatlantic flight), Bernard Schimmel - 1925 (Reuben sandwich), Clarence Darrow - 1925 (Scopes monkey trial), Mikhail Bulgakov - 1925 (writer), Erich Maria Remarque - 1928 (*All Quiet on the Western Front*), John Logie Baird - 1928 (first transatlantic TV signal), George Jessel - 1927 (Bloody Mary), Virginia Woolf - 1927 (writer), William Faulkner - 1929 (writer), Daniel Frank Gerber - 1927 (baby food), Charles Lindbergh - 1927 (nonstop transatlantic flight), Babe Ruth - 1927 (baseball)

WORST

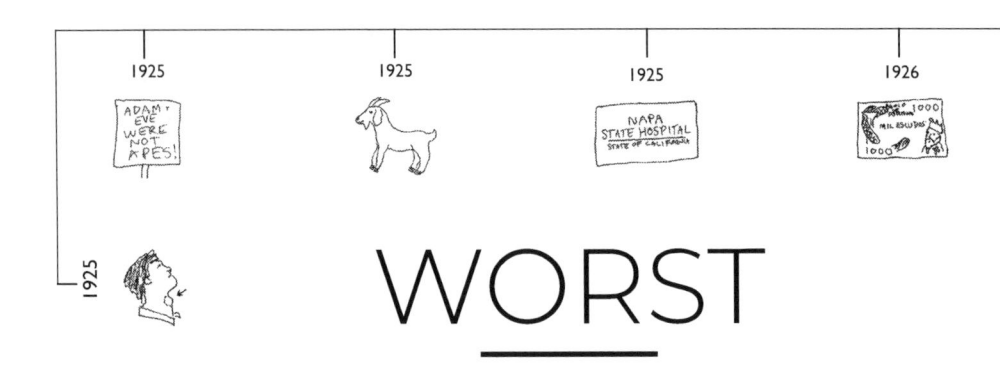

10. JOHN BRINKLEY
1925 - Milford, Kansas

John Brinkley got a degree from a sham college (Eclectic Medical University in Kansas City) and opened up a clinic in Brinkley, Kansas, which was one of those one-horse-town kinds of places from an old Western film. When a local patient complained of having sexual issues, Brinkley convinced the man to go through with his cure-all surgery: implanting goat testicles. He convinced the poor guy to go through with it. When the patient raved about the (placebo-effect) success of the procedure, people from all around paid $750 for Brinkley's wonder surgery. Over time, Brinkley's scam caught up to him, but not until at least forty-two patients died.

9. WILLIAM JENNINGS BRYAN
1925 - Dayton, Tennessee

In 1925, Tennessee Governor Austin Peay signed the Butler Act banning the teaching of evolution in schools. In protest, the ACLU announced they would defend any teacher in the Volunteer State who would teach evolution anyway. So the town of Dayton, in search of publicity, approached local substitute teacher John Scopes and convinced him to teach Darwin to a biology class. He agreed and was soon arrested, and Dayton got their circus trial. Clarence Darrow, the most famous defense lawyer in America, came down to defend Scopes and worked the prosecution's William Jennings Bryan like a heavy bag. While Bryan was progressive on peace and women's suffrage, he was also a Bible literalist and was badly exposed when subjects like Cain's miraculous wife or Jonah and the whale came up. Scopes was found guilty, but the evolution-versus-creationism (fact-versus-fairy tale) debate was pretty much over. The Butler Act was never again enforced and, over the next two years, anti-evolution proposals were defeated in twenty-two states.

8. THE ACADEMY OF MOTION PICTURE ARTS AND SCIENCES
1929 - Los Angeles, California

Louis B. Mayer was afraid of actors and directors forming unions and thereby becoming more expensive. So he had his show biz stars form a little club of their own and throw themselves a self-congratulatory party—the Academy Awards. For the first "best actor" award, the Academy chose to vote for a fucking dog. That's right. The overwhelming winner was Rin Tin Tin, a German Shepherd who had no idea what movies were. Eventually they overruled the vote and transferred the award to Emil Jannings, a German silent film star who went on to appear in Nazi propaganda films for his buddy Joseph Goebbels. Maybe the dog wasn't such a bad choice.

7. EARLE NELSON
1925 - San Francisco, California

Ten-year-old Earle Nelson was riding his bike when he was hit by a streetcar. When he awoke from a six-day coma, Nelson was never the same. For the rest of his childhood and early twenties, Nelson was in and out of jails and mental hospitals. In 1925, Nelson escaped Napa State Mental Hospital and the staff, tired of the havoc he caused, didn't bother to fetch him back. For the next year and a half, Nelson went on a nationwide killing spree, killing over twenty and earning the moniker the "Gorilla Man." He'd brandish a Bible, pose as a boarder, then brutally kill his landlady. Nelson was eventually caught and hanged in Winnipeg.

6. DAVID SARNOFF
1926 - New York, New York

RCA President David Sarnoff got word that some guy named Farnsworth had projected a television image in California. Knowing that if someone other than RCA invented the television,

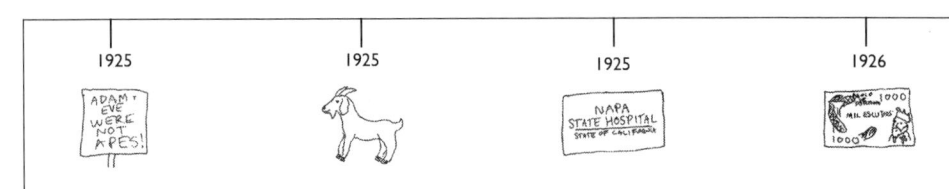

RCA would be crushed. Sarnoff sent his top engineer, Vladimir Zworkyin, to Farnsworth's lab to study his dissector tube. Next, RCA presented Farnsworth with a lowball offer for his invention. Farnsworth refused, so RCA just went ahead and copied his work. When Farnsworth sued, Sarnoff used his army of lawyers to bury the struggling entrepreneur until the patents had expired. The unethical corporate thug won. Sarnoff's corporate lawyer barrage continued, pulling off the same stunt with color television in 1945 and FM radio in 1948.

5. AL CAPONE
1929 - Chicago, Illinois

Al Capone's flashy ways, brazen disregard for ridiculous laws like Prohibition, and generosity to various charities had people thinking he was some sort of modern-day Robin Hood. But, make no mistake, Al Capone was a monster. In order to get his way, he strong-armed politicians, killed and bought police, rigged elections, and bullied law-abiding citizens. Al Capone was such a problem that he prompted Herbert Hoover into action—and that was a guy who couldn't be bothered to even do anything helpful during the Great Depression. When the law couldn't catch him on his violence, they nabbed him for tax evasion. Capone served six and a half years in Alcatraz before succumbing to syphilis.

4. ANDREW KEHOE
1927 - Bath Township, Michigan

Andrew Kehoe had a sick wife and was on the verge of losing his eighty-acre farm. When the town approved a tax increase to pay for a new school (a tax he fought hard against), Kehoe lost it. First he killed his wife and set the farm on fire as a distraction. When his fellow townspeople spotted the smoke and went to check out the situation, Kehoe went to the school and set off hundreds of pounds of dynamite, killing thirty-seven children between the ages of six and eight as well as several teachers. Then, he drove his truck loaded with more dynamite toward the superintendent and school officials. Within an hour, he had killed forty-five people.

3. ALVES DOS REIS
1926 - Lisbon, Portugal

Twenty-eight-year-old Alves dos Reis approached the British company that manufactured Portugal's bank notes and told them to print him $100 million escudos (the equivalent of one percent of Portugal's GDP). He gave them a bunch of fake paperwork, and they fell for the scheme. He received the money and set up a sham bank to launder it. When the government got involved and tried to recall the bank notes, a widespread panic ensued and the government fell to a military coup. Alves dos Reis served twenty years for his crime. The revolution he ignited led to a fascist dictator-style government (Salazar) in Portugal that lasted until 1974.

2. FRITZ HAARMANN
1925 - Hanover, Germany

Fritz Haarmann, the "Vampire of Hanover," was a thief-turned-police informant. In exchange for ratting on the underworld, Haarmann was allowed to continue lurking in the shadows. Under the protection of those shadows, Haarmann lured males between the ages of ten and twenty-two back to his place and killed them by biting their Adam's apples. By the time he was caught, Haarmann estimated he had given his "love bite" to as many as seventy victims.

1. JOSEF STALIN
1929 - St. Petersburg, Russia

After Lenin's death, Josef Stalin won a power struggle for the Communist party over Bolshevik Revolution architect Leon Trotsky. Once in charge, the thuggish Stalin murdered or jailed anyone in his path (including Trotsky). In an effort to rebuild the depleted Red Army, Stalin sent animal-breeding scientist, Ilya Ivanov, down to West Africa with a couple hundred thousand dollars and a bunch of sperm to try to artificially knock up chimps and create a *Planet of the Apes*-like ape-human hybrid army. But, instead of producing Doctor Zaius and Cornelius, the mission

| 1925 | 1925 | 1925 | 1926 |

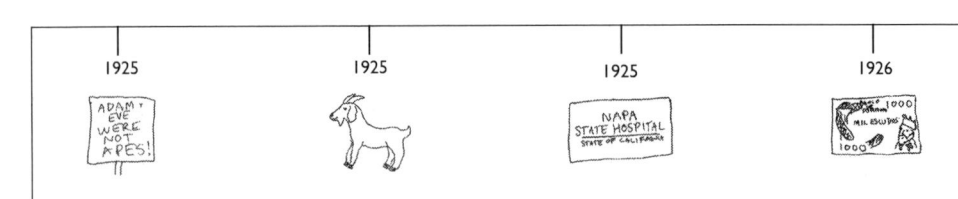

1925 begot nothing but ridicule and shame. By the way, his real name was Josef Jugashvili. "Stalin" means steel. The Soviet leader gave himself a porn star name: Joey Steel.

1926　　　　　1927　　　　　　　1929　　　　　　　1929

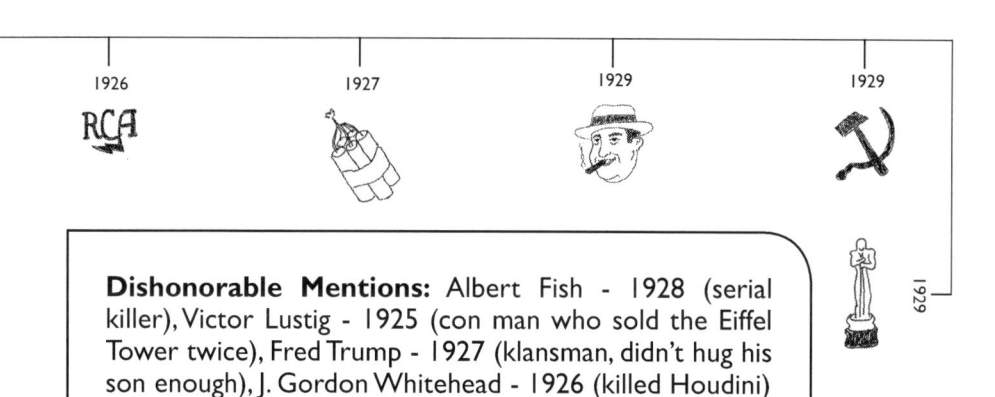

Dishonorable Mentions: Albert Fish - 1928 (serial killer), Victor Lustig - 1925 (con man who sold the Eiffel Tower twice), Fred Trump - 1927 (klansman, didn't hug his son enough), J. Gordon Whitehead - 1926 (killed Houdini)

1929

| 1930 | 1931 | 1931 | 1931 |

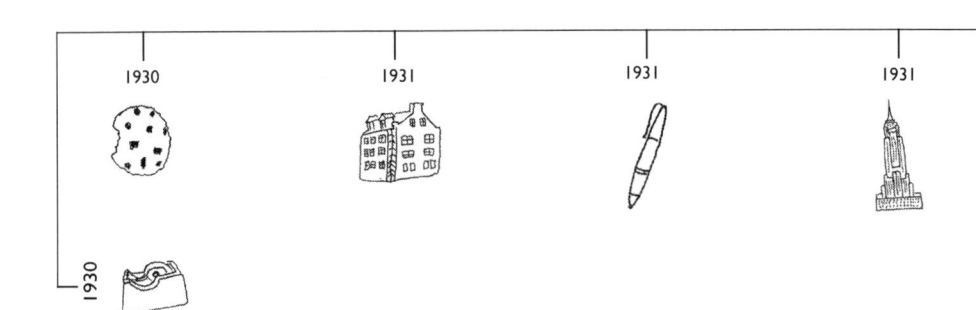

1930

1930-1934

"That men do not learn very much from the lessons of history is the most important of all the lessons of history."

-Aldous Huxley

BEST

10. RICHARD DREW
1930 - St. Paul, Minnesota

Richard Drew, a college dropout working for a small sandpaper company (3M), overheard car painters complaining about how hard it was to do two-tone paint jobs without having one side bleed into the other. Drew tried to tackle that problem by making a cellophane tape that left no sticky residue after removal. He tinkered with adhesives used in the company's sandpaper and came up with the clear, low-adhesive masking tape—Scotch tape. (It was dubbed "Scotch" because it was cheap and, apparently, trashing Scottish people was okay in those days.) Considering 3M now sells enough tape each year to circle the globe 165 times, Drew's invention kind of moved them out of the sandpaper business.

9. H. L. MENCKEN
1931 - Baltimore, Maryland

Henry Louis Mencken was armed with a brilliant wit and the ability to smell bullshit from a mile away. The longtime *Baltimore Sun* columnist and magazine editor critiqued everything from literature to the American people. If he liked something, like the works of Harlem Renaissance writers, he published it. If he didn't, like the South's debate over teaching evolution in schools, he sure as hell was going to let people know. Mencken detested narrow-minded provincialism ("the apex of moronia," he called it) and shoddy politicians. The "Sage of Baltimore" was one of the greatest columnists in American history.

8. KENNY SAILORS
1934 - Hillsdale, Wyoming

On a small farm in a forty-seven-person Wyoming town, Kenny Sailors came up with one of the great innovations in sports: the jump shot. Not surprisingly, whenever the five-foot-eight Kenny played basketball (using a hoop nailed to a windmill) against his six-foot-five brother, his shot was rejected. So, one time, Kenny charged at his brother and jumped as high as he could. At the apex of his jump, he bought his elbow to a ninety-degree angle and flung the ball with his wrist. Kenny went on to become a two-time all-American at the University of Wyoming and his shot was featured in *Life* magazine. Nobody, not even Michael Jordan, had a bigger impact on basketball than Kenny Sailors.

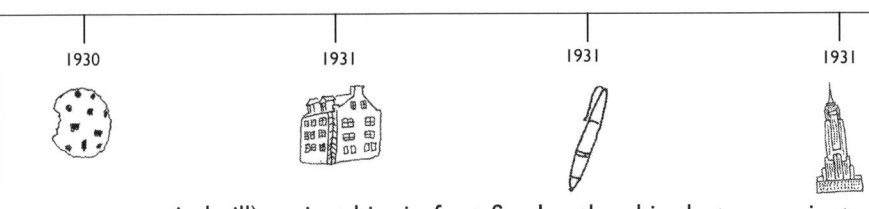

7. WILLIAM F. LAMB
1931 - New York, New York

In the late 1920s, the heads of Chrysler (William Chrysler) and General Motors (John Raskob) were having a pissing match. Both wanted to be owners of the world's tallest building. As Chrysler's shiny 1,046-foot building in New York City was being built, Raskob hired architect William Lamb to design one for him just eleven blocks away. With a pencil (as well as the Reynolds Building in Winston-Salem, North Carolina) as his inspiration, Lamb created one of the most iconic buildings in America—the Empire State Building. It was more than two hundred feet bigger than Chrysler's building. Built during the Depression, the art deco masterpiece employed up to 3,400 workers per day. Lamb followed that project up by providing low-income housing for poor families.

6. MOSES HORWITZ, JEROME HORWITZ, AND LOUIS FEINBERG
1934 - Hollywood, California

Vaudeville comedian Ted Healy tapped brothers Moses and Samuel Horwitz as well as Louis Feinberg to join his act, "Ted Healy and his Stooges." For show biz reasons, they changed their names to Mo Howard, Shemp Howard, and Larry Fine. Shemp dropped out and was replaced by the youngest Horwitz brother, Jerome ("Curly"). The Stooges broke off on their own and their physical comedy (three dumb guys beating the tar out of each other) was an instant hit. In 1940, while the rest of Hollywood tried not to piss off Germany (because of the foreign distribution money), Mo, Larry, and Curly slapped Hitler in the face with their short, *You*

Nazty Spy! The next year, America joined the war. Humanity was saved by eye-pokes.

5. RUTH GRAVES WAKEFIELD
1930 - Whitman, Massachusetts

When people think of the quintessential baker, they think Betty Crocker. But Betty Crocker wasn't even a real person. She was the creation of a bunch of dudes at the Washburn-Crosby Company. The greatest baker was Ruth Graves Wakefield. In 1930, Ruth and her husband were running the Toll House Inn. One night, Ruth went to make her famous chocolate cookies but realized she was out of chocolate. So instead she chopped-up a semi-sweet Nestle bar (that was given to her by Andrew Nestle himself) and mixed it in with the batter. The result was the first chocolate chip cookie. Ruth's creation was featured on a popular radio show, and the rest is delicious history.

4. LÁSZLÓ AND GYÖRGY BÍRÓ
1931 - Budapest, Hungary

Hungarian journalist László Bíró noticed that newspaper ink dried much quicker than fountain ink. Plus, the whole process of writing with a fountain pen was a huge pain in the ass. He tried pens filled with newspaper ink, but the ink flowed too slowly. So László went to his chemist brother, György, the brains of the family, for help with his idea. György helped him perfect the pen that had a small opening with a little ball that rolled the ink out of the pen onto the paper. Sadly, before the Jewish László could profit from his ballpoint pen, he was forced to flee for his life from the Nazis. So he sold his share of the company and helped his family escape to Argentina.

3. ELEANOR ROOSEVELT
1933 - Washington, D.C.

Much like her uncle Teddy, Eleanor Roosevelt had relentless drive. The First Lady visited Depression-era breadlines, wrote newspaper columns on helping the poor, promoted women's and children's rights, and fought against racial discrimination. During World War II, Eleanor boosted soldiers' morale, promoted women in the workforce, and advocated refuge for Europeans escaping tyranny. When people opposed black pilots' presence in the military, Eleanor went down to the Tuskegee Army Air Field and flew in the back of a plane flown by a black pilot. Anytime her husband was almost talked out of one of his New Deal programs, Eleanor got him back on track. Without ever picking up a weapon or winning an election, Eleanor Roosevelt was one of the great heroes in American history.

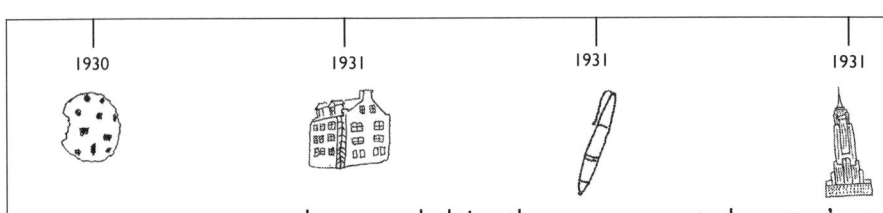

2. JANE ADDAMS
1931 - Chicago, Illinois

Inspired by a visit to London's Toynbee Hall, Jane Addams returned to Chicago and built a home for the underprivileged. Within a few years, Addams' Hull House was hosting over two thousand people a week. As her profile grew, Addams was asked for assistance by organizations in every imaginable area of service, from education to garbage collection. She also became a force in the suffrage movement, the NAACP, and the ACLU. Her vehement opposition to World War I got her labeled a traitor, but she never wilted. When the massive world war destroyed most of Europe (and pretty much proved her point that World War I was, in fact, bullshit), Addams provided assistance to women and children in enemy countries to help them get back on their feet. For her life of service, in 1931 Jane Addams became the first American woman ever to receive a Nobel Peace Prize.

1. FRANKLIN DELANO ROOSEVELT
1933 - Washington, D.C.

When FDR entered the White House, America was folding like an origami crane. A quarter of the population was out of work, most banks were closed, farmers were struggling mightily, and industrial production was way down. From his inauguration day—where he gave his famous "the only thing we have to fear is

| 1931 | 1933 | 1933 | 1934 |

fear itself" speech——he hit the ground running. Right away, he ended Prohibition. The country had a celebratory drink, and the government received an influx of tax revenue. Then he (with the help of Congress) put the New Deal into place, focusing on the three R's (Relief, Recovery, and Reform). Through handouts, the creation of new jobs, and changes to the way the economy was handled going forward, FDR quickly got America on track. The byproduct of these measures are institutions very much still in use today (FDIC, national parks, bridges, roads, schools, airports, better working conditions, unemployment insurance, and Social Security).

1934

Honorable Mention: Aldous Huxley - 1932 (Brave New World), Don Bradman - 1930 (cricket)

WORST

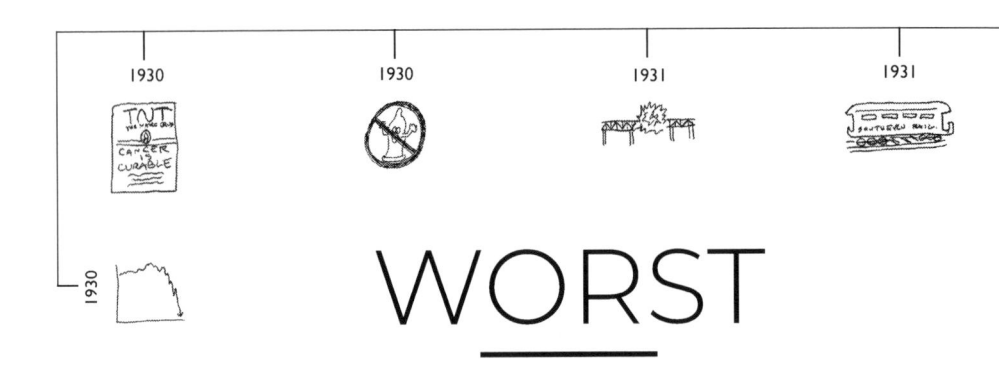

10. CHARLES DARROW
1933 - Germantown, Pennsylvania

Charles Darrow, a down-on-his-luck, unemployed salesman, approached Parker Brothers with an idea for a board game called Monopoly. When the game became a huge hit, Darrow got rich and Depression-era America got that grain of hope that anything was possible. One person didn't find that story quite so heartwarming, though—Lizzie Magie. In 1904, Magie had been granted a patent for her "Landlord's Game." Her game had seen modest sales around the country, including a purchase by a neighbor of Darrow's. One night, after an evening of playing the game, Darrow had asked his neighbor to give him a copy of the rules. He then changed the name to Monopoly and sold it to Parker Brothers. Magie's protests fell on deaf ears.

9. FRANCIS PASQUA, DANIEL KRIESBERG, TONY MARINO, JOSEPH MURPHY, AND HARRY GREEN
1932 - New York, New York

Every morning, unemployed Irish immigrant Michael Malloy would enter Tony Marino's Mermaid Speakeasy and get plastered. One day, Frank Pasqua convinced Marino (and Daniel Kriesberg) to take out an insurance policy on the friendless, family-less Malloy and let him drink himself to death. Joseph Murphy, of the speakeasy's bartenders, joined the plot and the four men got him obliterated every night. And each morning he'd be back, thirsty for more. After a while, Marino started cutting Malloy's booze with wood alcohol. Malloy kept going. When that didn't work, they served him oyster sandwiches full of broken glass and shrapnel. Lived through it. They took him outside in winter, drenched him in water, and let him freeze. Didn't kill him. They had taxi driver Harry Green drive over him. Survived. Finally, the gang just pinned him down and suffocated him. Word got out, Harry Green turned on his co-conspirators, and the whole gang was executed at Sing Sing.

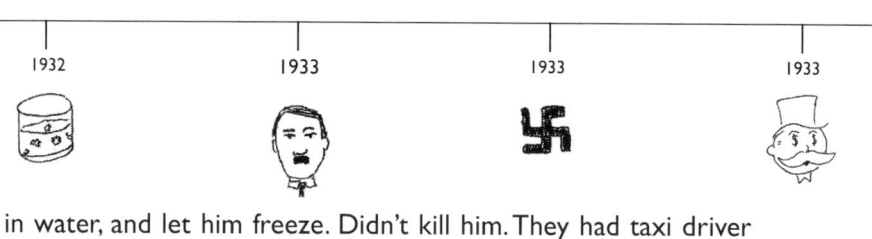

8. POPE PIUS XI
1930 - Rome, Italy

Pope Pius XI did some sensible things in his time as pope: he denounced Mussolini and opposed World War I. Unfortunately, he was a complete dope when it came to birth control. While the world was struggling with food shortages and widespread economic depression, Pius XI reminded everyone on New Year's Eve, 1930 that contraception was akin to murder. So if you're a good person, but use a condom or diaphragm… you can burn in hell with Attila the Hun and Caligula.

7. NORMAN BAKER
1930 - Muscatine, Iowa

Charismatic vaudeville performer Norman Baker constantly craved a bigger stage. He started his own radio station, charmed the pants off of Midwesterners, and helped influence Herbert Hoover's election in 1928. After getting an invite to the White House, the egomaniacal and populist Baker lost his mind. By 1929, he was taking shots at the American Medical Association and anyone who dared to question him. He then opened his own medical facility (the Baker Institute) to treat cancer patients with his alternative medicine (a mix containing watermelon seeds, corn silk, alcohol, and carbolic acid). Despite the fact that he had no medical training, patients paid Baker hundreds of thousands of dollars for cancer treatments. Bad idea. They all died and Baker was run out of town.

6. LENI RIEFENSTAHL
1934 - Nuremberg, Germany

From spectacular sweeping shots of the Alps to artfully shot scenes of everyday life, Leni Riefenstahl's films were all about beauty. And so, when Adolph Hitler needed someone to soften the edges of his hateful, murderous reputation as he rose in German politics, he went to Leni Riefenstahl. Funded by the tyrant, the German filmmaker made several films that extolled the virtues of the Aryan race and praised the strength of the Nazi party. She helped legitimize the worst person in history. When World War II was over, Riefenstahl escaped getting charged with war crimes but all was not forgiven. Despite her backpedaling and claims that she just thought Hitler was full of empty rhetoric just to get votes, Leni was blackballed for the rest of her life.

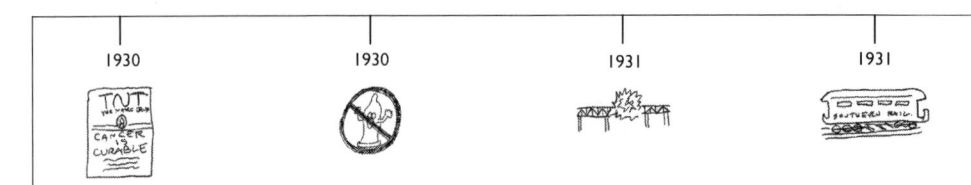

5. HERBERT HOOVER
1930 - Washington, D.C.

Just as businessman Herbert Hoover was sworn into office as president, the U.S. economy was collapsing. Manufacturing had slowed, farmers weren't selling enough, and banks were going under. The never-before-elected politician with the heavily gelled hair needed to enact some sort of economic stimulus. Instead, he signed the Smoot-Hawley Tariff Act, a bill that essentially told the world that America was going into isolationist mode. His new heavy tariffs on imports put a strain on exports, which brought the global economy to a screeching halt. Prices fell, companies lost tons of money, and the economy sputtered even more. Hoover did nothing to improve American morale and got destroyed in the next presidential election by FDR.

4. VICTORIA PRICE
1931 - Scottsboro, Alabama

On March 25, 1931, Victoria Price, a friend, and their boyfriends hopped on a Southern Railroad train full of young, black itinerant workers looking for the next job. A fight broke out between the whites and the blacks and, by the time the train pulled into Paint Rock, Arkansas, an angry white mob was waiting for them. Before she could get in trouble, Price claimed the black guys raped her. The thrice-married, sometimes prostitute twenty-one-year-old Price felt her virtue had been ruined by the nine black boys.

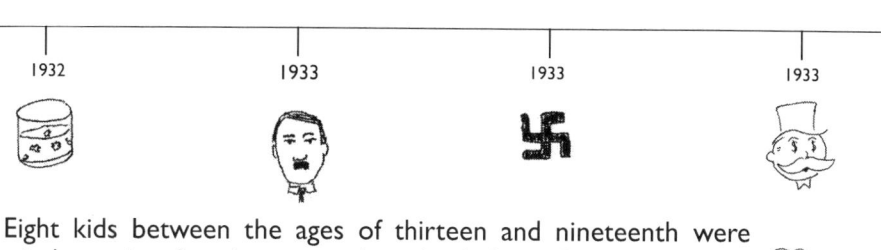

Eight kids between the ages of thirteen and nineteenth were tried, convicted, and sentenced to death (a ninth received a life sentence).

3. SEISHIRO IGATAKI AND KANJI ISHIWARA
1931 - Manchuria (China)

Japan was mired in a depression, had an expanding population, and was running low on resources. Adhering to a League of Nations sanction was pretty low on their priority list. So they decided to invade a country with more raw materials—Manchuria, a northeast province in China. Two colonels in the Kwantung Army (Igataki and Ishiwara) planted a bomb on Japanese railroad tracks and blamed it on China. Despite the fact that nobody even noticed the explosion, Japanese troops went into full "retaliation" mode. Calls to cease fire by the Japanese prime minister and League of Nations were ignored. For the next decade, Japan went rogue, raping Manchuria and plotting an attack on America.

2. HEINRICH HIMMLER, HERMAN GOERING, AND JOSEPH GOEBBELS
1933 - Berlin, Germany

It's one thing for a charismatic, pandering asshole to become popular. But for Adolph Hitler to become as powerful and dangerous as he did, he required the backup of the Third Reich's triumvirate of evil: Heinrich Himmler, Herman Goering, and Joseph Goebbels. Within a month of Hitler assuming power, Himmler announced the opening of Dachau, a concentration camp near Munich. Goering had his goose-stepping thugs round up Communists and Socialists. Through Goebbels' propaganda, disparaging lies were spread about the Jews, their businesses were boycotted, and their children were pulled out of public schools. By 1934, after Himmler's "Night of the Long Knives," somewhere between 150 and 200 political opponents were dead and Hitler was free to execute his aggressive, awful agenda.

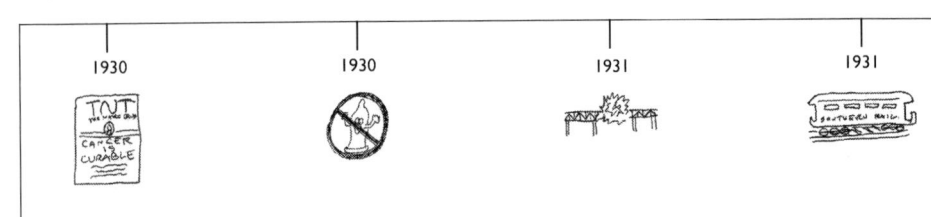

1. ADOLPH HITLER
1933 - Berlin, Germany

The worst guy ever rose to power via the age-old political strategy of pandering to angry dumbs. Germany was in the gutter after the unfavorable sanctions imposed by the Treaty of Versailles. Hitler promised to turn things around, and the uneducated lower and middle classes ate it up. After a failed bid to become German president in 1932 landed him in jail (where he produced his poorly written four hundred-page polemic, *Mein Kampf*, Hitler managed to pressure his way into becoming chancellor under President von Hindenburg. The following month, a suspicious fire burned down the parliament building. The fire was blamed on Communists and the government immediately sought to eliminate "enemies" at the expense of constitutional rights. Paul von Hindenburg died the next year and Hitler became the unopposed leader.

1932　　　　　1933　　　　　1933　　　　　1933

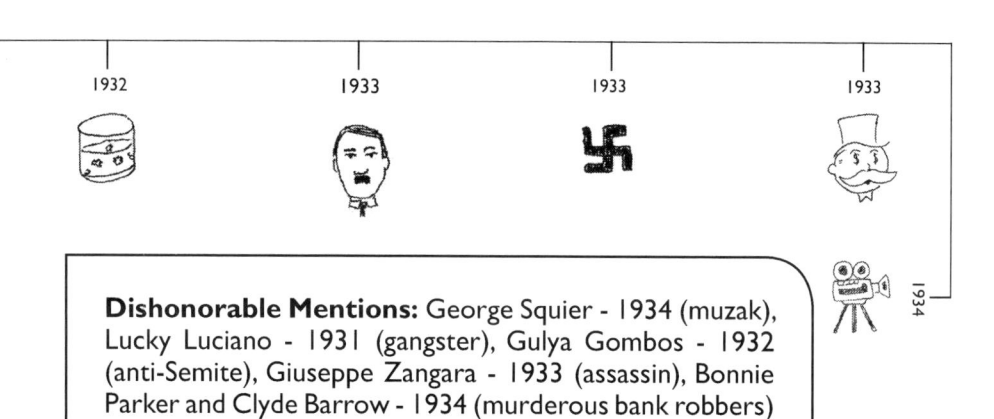

1934

Dishonorable Mentions: George Squier - 1934 (muzak), Lucky Luciano - 1931 (gangster), Gulya Gombos - 1932 (anti-Semite), Giuseppe Zangara - 1933 (assassin), Bonnie Parker and Clyde Barrow - 1934 (murderous bank robbers)

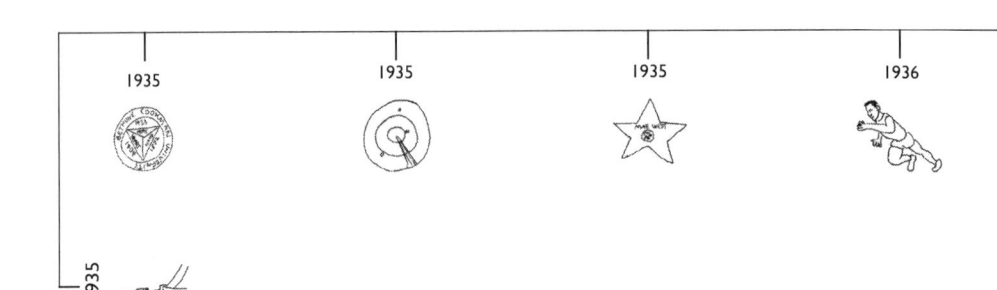

1935-1939

"All war is a symptom of man's failure as a thinking animal."
-John Steinbeck

BEST

10. MAE WEST
1935 - Hollywood, California

Sex symbol Mae West wanted creative control over her own movies. So she bucked the patriarchal Hollywood power structure and wrote and directed her own. Despite ridiculous morality charges and stints in jail, Mae West kept pushing boundaries (like her play about homosexuality, *Drag*). When the fun police forced her to revise her scripts, she just re-wrote them loaded with innuendo. At forty-two, an age by which pretty much every other Hollywood actress had long been put out to pasture, Mae West was the number two earner in America (second to only publisher William Randolph Hearst).

9. ZORA NEALE HURSTON
1937 - Eatonville, Florida

Even if it wasn't trying to, most literature of the time painted an unflattering portrait of black people and women in America. The "look how miserable and powerless their lives are" narrative wasn't working for Zora Neale Hurston, though. Sure, black people and women had their share of challenges in America, but they were also powerful forces. In her novel *Their Eyes Were Watching God*, Hurston shattered stereotypes about black people, women, sexuality, and the myth of the male savior. Unfortunately, the Harlem Renaissance writer was ahead of her time. Despite her influential writing, Hurston's work wasn't truly appreciated until the '60s and '70s, during the civil and women's rights movements.

8. ORSON WELLES
1938 - New York, New York

What passed for home entertainment in 1938 was profoundly sad. America's favorite radio program featured Edgar Bergen and his dummy, Charlie McCarthy. People were entertained by a ventriloquist... on the radio! Then came a brash twenty-three-year-old named Orson Welles with an update of

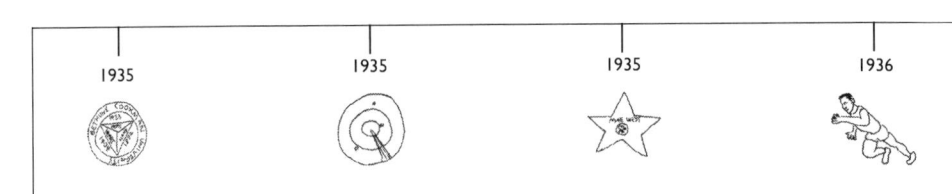

H.G. Wells' 1898 story *War of the Worlds*. Instead of the standard banter over a few microphones, Welles and his Mercury Theatre group treated the show as if it were a full stage production, with fake news reports interrupting fake music acts. The unique production did the unthinkable—it took listeners' minds off the Great Depression for an evening. Within a couple years, Welles was given carte blanche by RKO to write and direct what many consider one of the greatest movies of all time: *Citizen Kane*.

7. CARL VON OSSIETZKY
1936 - Berlin, Germany

In 1927, Carl von Ossietzky wrote a series of articles exposing the German army's blatant disregard for the Treaty of Versailles' armament limitations. For that, he was branded a traitor and thrown in jail for a year. When he was released, he went right back to blasting German militarization and extremism and was thrown in a concentration camp next. In 1935, a tuberculosis-stricken von Ossietzky won the Nobel Peace Prize, which the Nazis strongly advised him to publicly reject. He accepted it anyway. Hitler never let him travel to the awards ceremony in Norway, but Carl von Ossietzky's ultimate goal was achieved anyway—the budding monster in Germany had been exposed.

6. JOHN STEINBECK
1939 - Salinas, California

In the late 1930s, America was mired in the Great Depression. John Steinbeck wanted to properly document it. "I want to put a tag of shame on the greedy bastards who are responsible for this," he wrote. The Salinas, California native drew from his experience around migrant farmers and told the tale of America through their underrepresented eyes in his classics *Of Mice and Men* and *The Grapes of Wrath*. Steinbeck's novels tackled discrimination, racism, sexism, and classism head-on. The books served as both a rallying cry for struggling people in America and a great historical documentation for future generations. For his work, Steinbeck won both a Pulitzer (1940) and a Nobel Prize for Literature (1962).

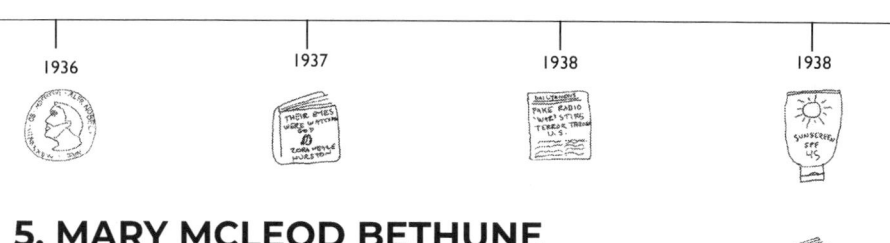

5. MARY MCLEOD BETHUNE
1935 - Washington, D.C.

Every day, Mary McLeod and her sixteen siblings worked long hours picking cotton in South Carolina. When a missionary opened up a school nearby for black children, Mary took full advantage and used it as a platform to escape her situation. From that point forward, Mary McLeod (eventually Bethune) spent the rest of her life improving black lives through education. After reading about a growing black population on the Gulf Coast of Florida, Mary opened up a school for girls in Daytona. The school merged with the Cookman Institute to form Bethune-Cookman College. Mary soon got the attention of Franklin Roosevelt who, in 1935, appointed her as director of the Division of Negro Affairs of the National Youth Administration.

4. WALLACE CAROTHERS
1935 - Seaford, Delaware

After reading one of his papers on synthetic fibers, DuPont recruited Wallace Carothers from Harvard down to its Delaware labs. For the next eight years, Carothers experimented with polymers (molecules linked together like paper clips) until he had the major breakthrough he was looking for: nylon. The synthetic, six-times-stronger-than-steel material was an instant success. First, nylon replaced hog hair as the preferred bristle in toothbrushes. Soon, it was used for women's stockings, parachutes, seat belts, and life rafts. Sadly, Carothers' depression got the best of him and he took his own life before he was able to see the effect of nylon on the world.

3. FRANZ GREITER
1938 - Piz Buin, Austria

In 1938, avid mountain climber Franz Greiter got severely sunburned while climbing the Swiss-Austrian border. Fed up with the constant skin damage, the Austrian chemistry student created a cream to shield himself. His first creation, Gletscher Crème, accomplished what ancient Greeks and Egyptians were never able to do—actually protect the skin from harmful rays. Unlike the Greeks' olive oil or the Egyptians' jasmine, Greiter's Glacier Cream had an SPF of two. Fellow hikers and skiers loved Greiter's product, and thus sunscreen was born. In the decades since, sunscreen has prevented millions of cases of sunburn, skin cancer, and people looking like leather bags by middle age.

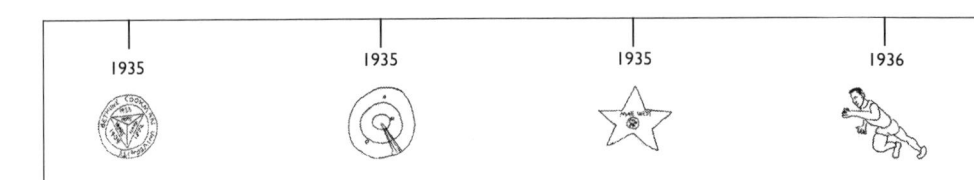

2. ALEXANDER WATSON-WATT
1935 - Dundee, Scotland

The idea for radar (RAdio Detection And Ranging) first came around in the mid-nineteenth century. It was never really practical until the 1930s when Alexander Watson-Watt, a descendant of steam engine inventor James Watt, was called upon to help the British Air Ministry develop a "death ray." While a death ray wasn't feasible, Watson-Watt was able to improve upon his technology which assisted airmen in avoiding dangerous storms. After he realized it could also detect other objects, a network of them was set up around Britain. Radar played a massive role in the Battle of Britain, helping the Brits to hold off and eventually push back the German Luftwaffe.

1. JESSE OWENS
1936 - Berlin, Germany

As a twenty-one-year-old college sophomore with a bad back, Jesse Owens accomplished more in forty-five minutes than just about any other athlete has in their entire career. At 3:15 p.m. at the 1935 Big Ten Championships, Owens tied the world record in the hundred-meter dash. At 3:25 p.m., he broke the world record in long jump. At 3:34 p.m., he broke the world record in the 220-meter dash. Finally, at 4:00 p.m., he broke the world record in the 220 low hurdles. Four world records in forty-five minutes. The next year, Owens took home four gold medals in front of Hitler at the 1936 Berlin Olympics, destroying Der Führer's wet dream of having an Aryan coronation on the world stage.

1936   1937   1938   1938

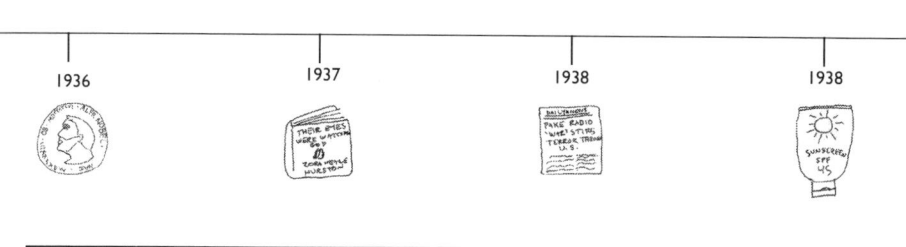

1939

Honorable Mentions: Hilary Fisher Page - 1939 (plastic building bricks), Jack LaLanne - 1936 (fitness pioneer), Lou Gehrig - 1939 (baseball), Scotty Kilpatrick - 1937 (photojournalist), Joe Louis - 1938 (boxer), Roy Plunkett - 1938 (Teflon), William Griffith Wilson - 1935 (Alcoholics Anonymous), Samuel Morse - 1938 (Morse code), Moms Mabley - 1939 (comic), Leon Blum - 1936 (labor protester), Chester Carlson - 1937 (photocopier), Charles Richter - 1937 (earthquake scale), Marian Anderson - 1939 (opera singer), J.R.R. Tolkien - 1937 (author)

WORST

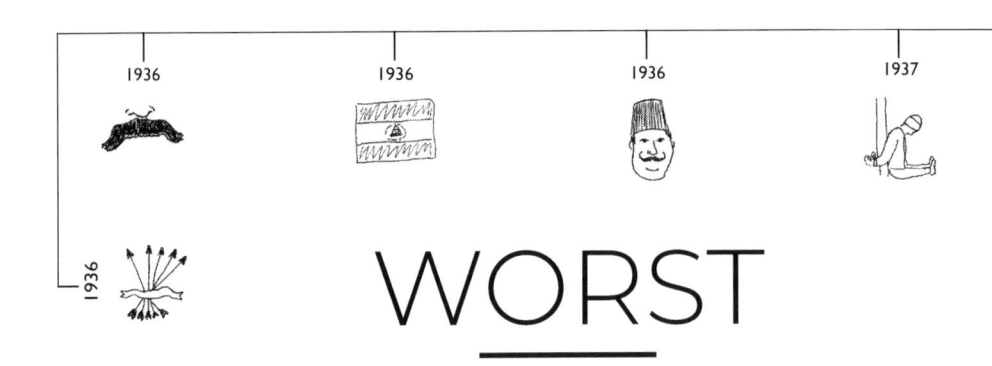

10. KING FAROUK
1936 - Cairo, Egypt

When sixteen-year-old Farouk was named King of Egypt, the beleaguered kingdom was optimistic. Being England's puppet country under Farouk's father hadn't been a good thing, so any change was good. But it was soon apparent that Farouk wasn't their savior. His entire reign seemed to be a quest to fill his bottomless pit of gluttony. Between round-the-clock visits from prostitutes, a staggering collection of pornography, the habit of shoveling food into his gullet as fast as humanly possible, and lavish overseas shopping sprees, Farouk couldn't be bothered to help his citizens struggling to make ends meet. Instead of making allies on the international stage, he robbed them… literally. The guy was a kleptomaniac. Fittingly, Farouk dropped dead in 1965 while stuffing his face in a restaurant in Italy.

9. DAUGHTERS OF THE AMERICAN REVOLUTION
1939 - Washington, D.C.

Singer Marian Anderson was in the middle of an exceptional career (Carnegie Hall, European tour) when she was invited by Howard University to perform at Constitution Hall. When her manager tried to book the black singer, the Daughters of the American Revolution (who owned the hall) said that no dates were available… at least, not for black people. Word got out and the most famous Daughter of the American Revolution of all, Eleanor Roosevelt, not only wrote about the injustice in her weekly newspaper column but also quit the D.A.R., along with thousands of others. On Easter Sunday 1939, the First Lady arranged for

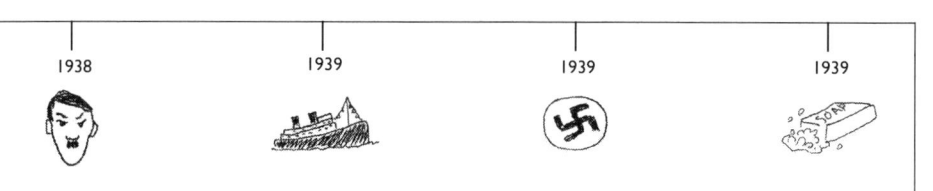

Anderson to sing in front of a crowd of 75,000 people at the Lincoln Memorial and on the radio for millions more.

8. LEONARDA CIANCIULI
1939 - Correggio, Italy

After a miserable childhood, Leonarda Cianciuli's adult life wasn't off to a good start. Her home had been destroyed by an earthquake, she had suffered several miscarriages and infant deaths, and a fortune teller had warned her that the rest of her kids would die. So she resorted to human sacrifice. Cianciuli drugged and axed three local middle-aged women who visited her shop. The first two were boiled in a vat then baked into chocolate tea cakes which she served to the community. Cianciuli turned her third victim into soap. When police tracked down the Italian shopkeeper, she gave them an unapologetic confession. The "Soap Maker of Correggio" spent her remaining years behind bars.

7. ANASTASIO SOMOZA GARCIA
1936 - Managua, Nicaragua

Tacho Somoza, the twenty-year dictator of Nicaragua, did a good job of minimizing his country's reliance on bananas. That's about all he did well. Taking full advantage of the United States' policy of "let's help the people in Central America who will threaten us the least," Tacho had his biggest rival assassinated and used the army to bounce his uncle out of the top job. He won an "election," then dramatically altered Nicaragua's constitution so he could be the country's richest person and top landowner. The next two decades were full of rigged elections, bribery, and intimidation. As FDR allegedly conceded, "Somoza may be a son of a bitch, but he's our son of a bitch."

6. FRITZ JULIUS KUHN
1939 - New York, New York

As head of the German-American Bund, Fritz Kuhn pledged loyalty to Der Führer and spread Nazi propaganda throughout the United States. The group held rallies, published hateful magazines and newspapers, and organized Hitler Youth camps complete with swastika-waving, goose-stepping children. By 1939, membership had climbed to 25,000 and the German-born Kuhn sold out Madison Square Garden (where he called the New Deal the "Jew Deal" and FDR "Frank D. Rosenfeld"). Thankfully, Kuhn proved to be his own undoing shortly thereafter. His weakness for trashy women had him dipping into the Bund's hate funds and thrown in jail for embezzlement.

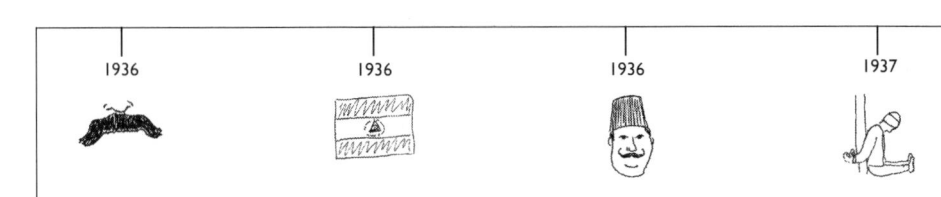

5. FRANCISCO FRANCO
1936 - Madrid, Spain

In the mid-1930s, Spain was a mess. The economy was crumbling and the right/left political divide had turned violent. In stepped Francisco Franco, the deposed right-wing general, to lead the Catholic Church-backed rebels in a civil war. Franco rode a wave of nationalism (and opened fire on those who disagreed with him) all the way to becoming Spain's commander-in-chief (Generalísimo). Anyone not with him was against him and was either thrown in prison or executed. As World War II heated up, Allied and Axis forces courted the geographically-important Spain. Of course, Franco, the evil dictator, chose to side with monsters Hitler and Mussolini. After the war, Franco continued to rule like a dick until his death in 1975.

4. CORDELL HULL
1939 - Washington, D.C.

After Kristallnacht, it was clear that conditions were not going to improve for Jews in Europe. Since they weren't being admitted as refugees in neighboring nations, 937 Jews boarded the *St. Louis*, a ship headed from Hamburg, Germany to Havana, Cuba. Most of the passengers applied for U.S. visas and planned to stay in Cuba until they got the stamp of approval to enter America. Franklin Roosevelt seemed willing to help the now world-famous refugees, but his Secretary of State, Cordell Hull, strongly opposed protecting them. In fact, Hull threatened that he and his fellow Southern Democrats would withdraw their support for FDR in the next election if the *St. Louis* were not turned away. So the ship was forced to return to the claws of the Third Reich, where more than a quarter of the Jews on board later died in the Holocaust.

3. MATSUI IWANE
1937 - Nanking, China

After about six years of sort-of elbowing their way into Chinese territories, Japan finally faced a unified resistance in 1937. The Japanese responded with brutal aggression. Following the ugly Battle of Shanghai, their forces marched on Nanking and took it with ease. But Japanese General Matsui Iwane wanted to break China's spirit. So he ordered a total destruction of the city. Disregarding the previously agreed-upon safety zone, his troops looted, burned down a third of the buildings, held contests to kill captive soldiers, committed between twenty and eighty thousand rapes, and tortured and executed entire families, including the elderly and children. Over the course of just six weeks, somewhere from two to three hundred thousand were killed in the Rape of Nanking.

2. JOSEF STALIN
1936 - Moscow, Russia

Josef Stalin was a paranoid asshole. The five-foot-four tyrant's three-decade dictatorship was marked by fear and consolidation of power. Initially, he went on a widespread purge throughout the government, complete with show trials, executions, and the Gulag (work camps in Siberia). After taking out political threats, Stalin moved over to the military, where he first took out officers, then low-ranking military members. By the end of the Great Purge, 93 of 139 Central Committee members were executed, 81 out of 103 generals and admirals were disposed of, and about three million Communist party members were murdered. When he ran out of people in those groups to kill, he turned on ordinary citizens, killing as many as thirteen million.

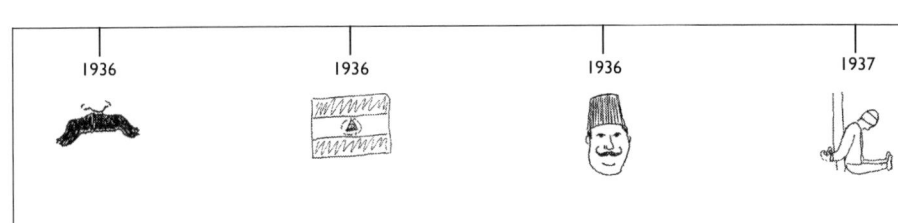

1. ADOLPH HITLER
1938 - Munich, Germany

Life for Jews in Hitler's Germany rapidly deteriorated—their businesses were boycotted, they were kicked out of schools, and many were exiled. After a seventeen-year-old son of two exiled Jews reached his breaking point, he retaliated towards a German official. The reaction was Kristallnacht ("Night of Broken Glass"). Nazi mobs set fire to Jewish synagogues, hospitals, businesses, schools, and homes, killing about a hundred Jews in the process. In the aftermath, thirty thousand Jews were sent to concentration camps, ushering in a new era of full-blown hostility and violence. The following year, Hitler invaded Poland, effectively starting World War II.

1938　1939　1939　1939

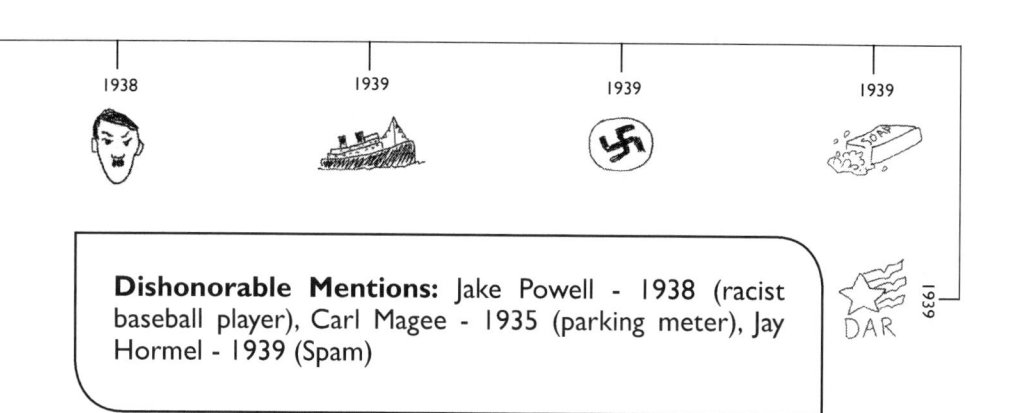

Dishonorable Mentions: Jake Powell - 1938 (racist baseball player), Carl Magee - 1935 (parking meter), Jay Hormel - 1939 (Spam)

DAR 1939

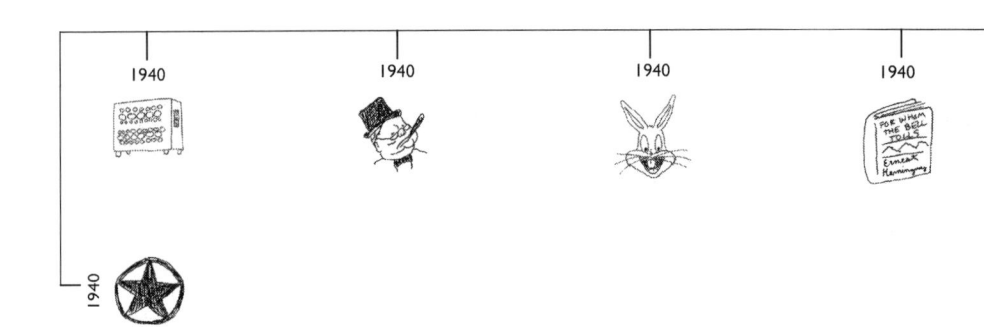

1940-1944

"The farther backward you can look, the farther forward you can see."
-Winston Churchill

BEST

10. IGNACIO ANAYA
1943 - Piedras Negras, Mexico

In 1943, Ignacio "Nacho" Anaya was trying to feed Texas-based army wives in his restaurant just across the border in Mexico. Since all he had in his kitchen were scraps of food, he took some tortillas, cut them into triangles, fried them up, piled all his ingredients on top, and cooked it some more. His creation ("Nachos Especiales") was an instant hit. The dish worked its way north of the border and has been a staple at restaurants and bars ever since. Sadly, this story isn't without its fair share of tragedy. In 1975, the Texas Rangers started selling chips smothered with some sort of nasty cheese blend at baseball games and called them nachos. Nacho Anaya passed away that same year. Coincidence?

9. JACQUES COUSTEAU
1943 - Paris, France

While rehabbing his arms by swimming in the Mediterranean, Jacques Cousteau got hold of some goggles and his life was changed forever. From that point forward, he was fascinated by life below the waves. Together with a friend, Cousteau created an "aqua lung," a twin-hosed breathing apparatus that allowed people to stay underwater and see parts of the ocean that nobody had ever seen before. The father of scuba shared his discoveries with the world in the form of photography and film, nabbing an Academy Award and Cannes Palm d'Or for his efforts. For the rest of his life, Jacques Cousteau was the sea's greatest advocate, fighting against commercial whaling and pollution. And, to top it all off, he rocked a pretty sweet red skull cap.

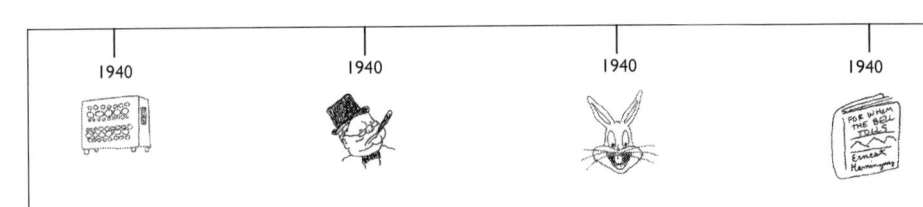

8. JACQUELINE COCHRANE, MILDRED MCAFEE, AND OVETA CULP HOBBY
1941 - America, Europe

Once the men left to fight in World War II, the women stepped into their places and kicked serious ass. From fundraising to factory work, women helped keep America running. Soon, through the persistence of women like Jacqueline Cochran, Mildred McAfee, and Oveta Culp Hobby, they were able to enter the military. As heads of their respective military outfits—the WASPs (Women Airforce Service Pilots), WAVES (Women Accepted for Volunteer Emergency Service), and WAAC (Women's Auxiliary Army Corps)—Jacqueline, Mildred, and Oveta shattered perceptions. Tens of thousands of women tested planes, helped with technology, and proved there's nothing women can't do. Their contributions during the war laid the foundation for the next phase of the women's rights movement.

7. ERNEST HEMINGWAY
1940 - Key West, Florida

Ernest Hemingway lived every day like it was his last and wrote about those life experiences in some of the most famous novels in history. Whether it was volunteering as an ambulance driver for the Italian army in World War I, hobnobbing with some of the greatest artists of the twentieth century (Picasso, Fitzgerald, Joyce, and others), hunting in Africa, deep-sea fishing, or attending bullfights in Spain, Hemingway always sought out great stories. His adjective-eschewing, cut-through-the-bullshit storytelling combined with his remarkable ability to examine human nature turned him into a star. For about a quarter century, Hemingway's brilliance was ignored by awards until his 1953 masterpiece, *Old Man and the Sea*, which nabbed him both a Pulitzer and a Nobel Prize.

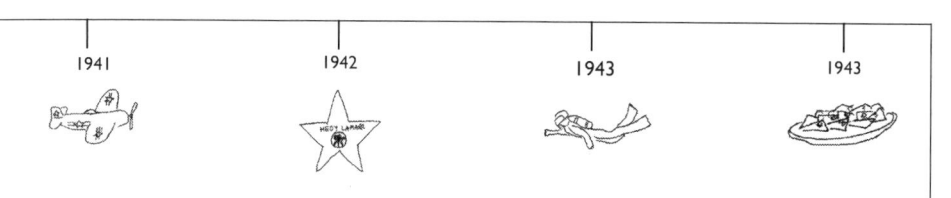

6. TEX AVERY, CHUCK JONES, AND MEL BLANC
1940 - Hollywood, California

At just twenty-seven years old, "Tex" Avery was overseeing every animated project at Warner Brothers, creating such iconic characters as Porky Pig, Elmer Fudd, and Daffy Duck. But, in 1940, Avery (along with the brilliant voice-over work of Mel Blanc and great directing of animation legend Chuck Jones) created the greatest cartoon character and, quite possibly, the greatest comedic character of all time: Bugs Bunny. Unlike that unfunny eunuch Mickey Mouse, and that asshole Woody Woodpecker, Bugs Bunny was actually cool. The wise-cracking, Brooklyn-accented, carrot-chomping, unflappable rabbit showed that cleverness and wit are far more effective than violence and intimidation.

5. HEDY LAMARR
1942 - Hollywood, California

One of the world's great brains was better known for her body. After appearing in the first ever full-frontal nudity and orgasm scene in movie history (as a teenager, no less), Vienna-born Hedy Kiesler married a rich Austrian dude who happened to be a Nazi-supporting arms dealer. So Kiesler changed her name to Lamarr, left her husband, and escaped to America, where she co-starred in movies with Clark Gable, Jimmy Stewart, and Spencer Tracy. But, every night, Hedy went home and worked on an idea that had been in the back of her mind since her marriage to that arms dealer—an encryption process which could control torpedoes. After some help from a Hollywood composer, in 1942, Lamarr was awarded the patent for frequency hopping. Hedy's invention eventually helped deescalate the Cuban Missile Crisis and laid the groundwork for cellular technology, Wi-Fi, and Bluetooth.

4. WINSTON CHURCHILL
1940 - London, England

Winston Churchill made some catastrophic decisions while

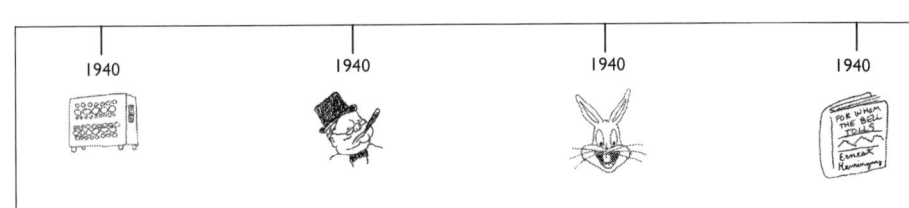

leading troops during World War I. His advocacy for use of poison gas doesn't put him in good company. His views on race were abysmal. He let the Bengal region of India starve to death and even cheered for Gandhi to die. But when the world needed him the most, Winston Churchill saved Western civilization. While the rest of Europe was rolling over for Hitler, Churchill dug in his heels, told the Nazis to piss off, and held the fort until he could coax the Yanks to join them in the fight across the pond.

3. ALAN TURING
1940 - Bletchley Park, England

By twenty-four, Alan Turing had written one of the most influential math papers the world has ever seen ("On Computable Numbers"), in which he outlined the principles of the modern computer. His idea was that a universal machine could be programmed to solve any problem that is mathematically solvable. That paper caught the attention of the British government, who tasked the brilliant mathematician with cracking the code of the German encryption device called Enigma. In only two years, Turing and his team at Bletchley Park cracked it and shortened World War II by as many as two to four years, thus saving the lives of millions. Sadly, instead of being treated like the hero he truly was after the war's end, Turing was persecuted for being gay and, in 1954, took his own life.

2. OSKAR SCHINDLER, CHIUNE SUGIHARA, IRENA SENDLER, MIEP GIES, AND NICHOLAS WINTON
1944 - Europe

Not all World War II heroes played their part on the battlefield. Oskar Schindler was initially just a guy looking for cheap factory workers but became the savior of over eleven hundred Jewish lives during the Holocaust. Japan's consul in Lithuania, Chiune Sugihara, risked his career by writing thousands of unauthorized visas for Jews to help them escape to safety. Irena Sandler led a group of young Polish women to provide medicine and food for Jewish children confined to a walled-off ghetto. British stockbroker Nicholas Winton arranged for eight trains carrying 669 children out of occupied Prague. Miep Gies, like many loving people across Europe, opened her home to a Jewish family (Anne Frank and her family) who were trying to hide from the Nazis. All these people and countless others, quietly proved that firing a gun was not the only way to beat the enemy.

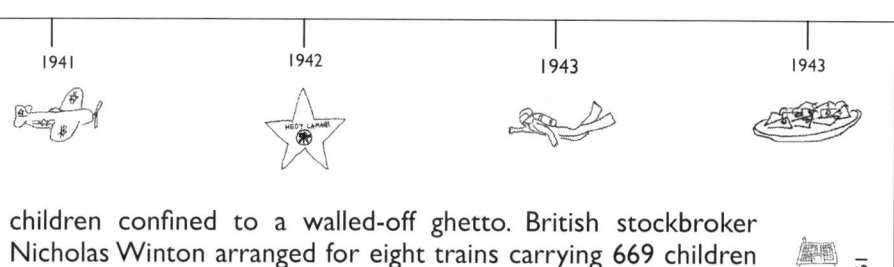

1. JOHN R. FOX, JOHN BUTTS, MACARIO GARCIA, AUDIE MURPHY, TOMMY PRINCE, LEO MAJOR, JOHN CHURCHILL, AND LEE ARCHER
1940-1944 - Europe

While guys like MacArthur, Montgomery, and Eisenhower get the lion's share of the credit for World War II heroics, the true heroes on the battlefield were the young men who went from being ordinary Joes to saviors of the world. To try to pinpoint one soldier would be pointless, so what follows is just a small sampling of the men who truly earned that "Greatest Generation" moniker. John R. Fox, a black guy from Ohio, called an airstrike against himself so his fellow soldiers could win a battle in Italy. Twenty-two-year-old Buffalo, New York native John Butts stormed the beaches in Normandy, then sacrificed himself so his men could take a strategically pivotal hill. French-Canadian Leo Major withstood broken bones in his back and a missing eye, also to help take Normandy. Macario Garcia, a Mexican immigrant, single-handedly stopped two gunners and took prisoners despite being badly wounded. Irish Texan Audie Murphy lied about his age after Pearl Harbor so he would be eligible to fight, then manned a machine gun on a burning tank and repelled German troops by himself on the French-Swiss border. Tommy Prince, a Canadian Aborigine, was a stealthy ninja-like badass who infiltrated German troops in the middle of the night. "Mad Jack" Churchill, a British archery champion in his late thirties, used his unusual skills on the battlefields from Dunkirk to an island in Yugoslavia. And Lee Archer, one of the Tuskegee Airmen, had to fight discrimination just to be allowed to fly a plane, then quickly proved himself to be

| 1940 | 1940 | 1940 | 1940 |

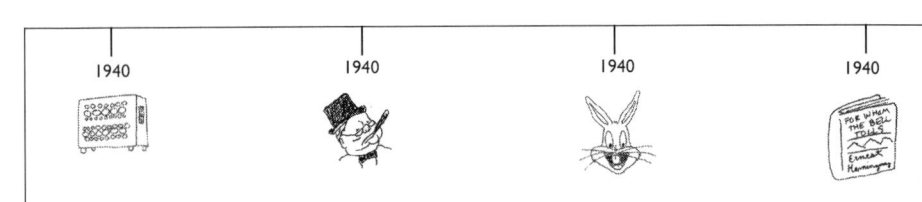

1940 an ace while escorting bombers over enemy territory. Greatness in World War II came in all forms. When Hitler made it seem like the world was caving in, these guys made sure that never happened.

1941   1942   1943   1943   1944

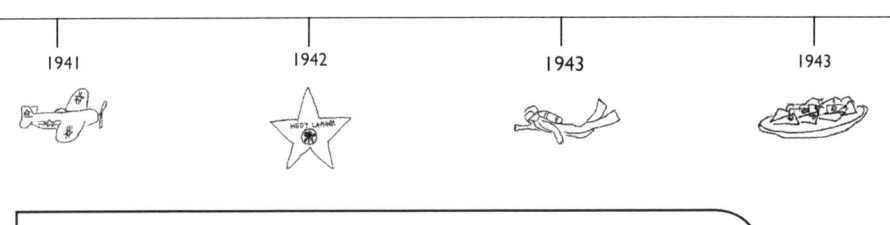

Honorable Mentions: Alfred Blaylock and Vivien Thomas - 1944 (pediatric heart surgeons), Recy Taylor - 1944 (civil rights and feminist hero), John Washington, Clark Poling, Alexander Goode, and George Fox - 1943 (sacrificed lives for soldiers), Olivia de Havilland - 1943 (actress, advocate), Joe DiMaggio - 1941 (baseball), Fred Korematsu - 1944 (internment camp protester), William Moulton Marston - 1941 (invented the polygraph and Wonder Woman), Pat Olivieri - 1941 (Philly cheesesteak), Harry Coover - 1942 (Super Glue), John Bumstead and Orvan Hess - 1942 (penicillin), Woodie Guthrie - 1944 ("This Land is Your Land"), Edward R Murrow - 1940 (journalist), Bielski brothers - 1941 (built forrest village to hide from Nazis)

WORST

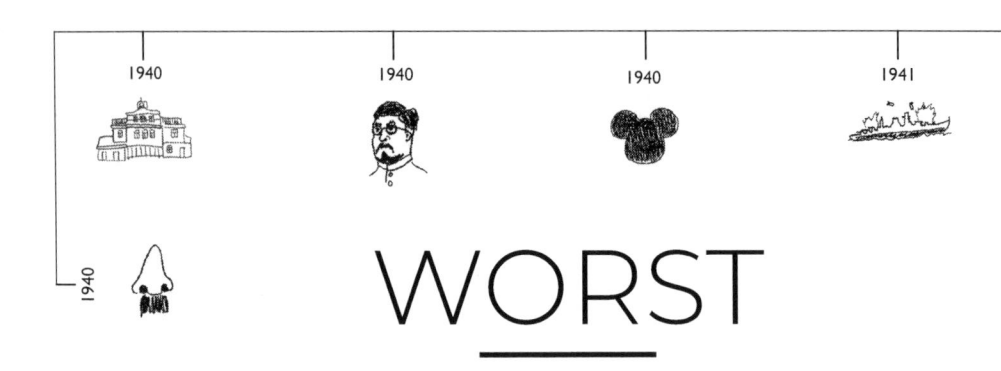

10. MILDRED GILLARS AND WILLIAM JOYCE
1942 - Berlin, Germany

Mildred Gillars (a.k.a. Axis Sally) and William Joyce (a.k.a. Lord Haw Haw) left their Allied countries and became propagandists for German radio. After a floundering acting and broadcast career in New York, Millard Gillars moved to Berlin and got radio work. William Joyce, on the other hand, was just an angry weirdo, not to mention a fascist and anti-Semite. He left Britain and got a job with the German equivalent to the BBC. Once the war started, both Gillars and Joyce taunted the Allied forces and dropped anti-Semitic rants. When their adopted homeland lost, it was curtains for the two traitors. The trash actress spent twelve years in a West Virginia prison. Lord Haw Haw was hanged at a London prison in 1946.

9. WALT DISNEY
1940 - Hollywood, California

Let's look past Walt Disney's overtly sexist employment policies and chalk them up to being a product of his time. And let's assume his black servant centaur in *Fantasia*, the peace-pipe smoking Indians in *Peter Pan*, the Jewish peddler in the *Three Little Pigs*, and the over-the-top black crows in *Dumbo* were coincidental characters. And let's pretend his comment about *Snow White's* dwarves being a "pile of niggers" and the whoa-this-whole-movie-is-racist-as-hell *Song of the South* never happened. You still have a guy who warmly embraced Nazi propagandist Leni Reifenstahl a month after Kristallnacht. And, during the Red Scare, he served as a snitch for Joseph McCarthy's House Un-American Activities Committee witch hunt. Mickey Mouse and his whole gang sucked anyway. Add it all up, and the founder of "the happiest place on Earth" was a real dick.

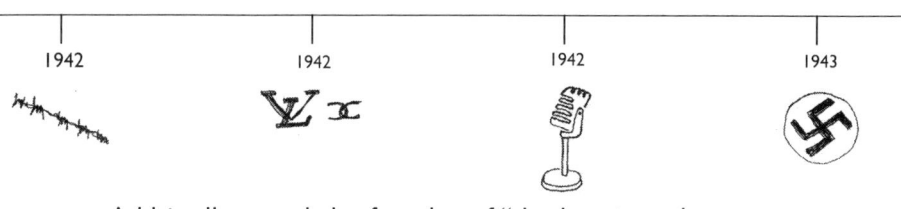

8. COCO CHANEL AND GASTON LOUIS VUITTON
1942 - Paris, France

Some saw Germany's invasion of France as an opportunity. Two prominent vultures, Coco Chanel and Gaston Louis Vuitton, actually assisted the sham Vichy government in any way they could in exchange for advancing their businesses. Instead of using her vast connections to help people out, the well-known anti-Semite Coco Chanel cited Aryan laws and assumed control of formerly Jewish-controlled businesses. Gaston Vuitton (grandson of founder Louis) set up a separate factory just to produce ass-kissing artifacts dedicated to puppet government head Philippe Petain. While everyone else was forced out, Vuitton got prime market share. But, by all means, enjoy that overpriced LV bag and Chanel perfume.

7. FRANKLIN ROOSEVELT
1942 - Washington, D.C.

With Hitler wreaking havoc in Europe, many stupid Americans used it as an opportunity to discriminate against people of German decent. Dopes even refused to use the words "frankfurter" and "sauerkraut." But, for Japanese-Americans on the West Coast, life was much, much worse. On February 19, 1942, President Franklin Roosevelt signed Executive Order 9066, which uprooted more than 120,000 Japanese-Americans and threw them into concentration camps. It didn't matter if they were shady individuals or upstanding doctors; anyone with Japanese heritage living on the West Coast was thrown into a camp. For the next three years, ordinary American citizens were treated like animals and subjected to emotional distress and physical disease. By the end of the war, more than 20,000 Japanese-Americans filed paperwork to go back to Japan, a place in complete turmoil. For all his accomplishments, FDR's legacy will forever have this stain.

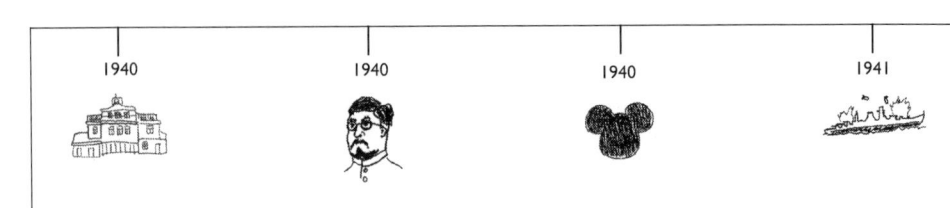

6. MARTIN DIES
1943 - Washington, D.C.

In the span of about six years, Martin Dies' promising career in the U.S. House of Representatives devolved into a hysterical, xenophobic, anti-Communist eyesore. As the first chair of the Committee to Investigate Un-American Activities, Dies tried to expose anyone he deemed not American enough. Despite wielding little to no proof, he repeatedly targeted labor unions and really anyone that didn't fit into his agenda. After the 1943 Detroit Race Riots, Dies used the tragedy as a way to blame... Japanese-Americans! According to Dies, they "had infiltrated Detroit's Negro population to spread hatred of the white man and disrupt the war effort." Martin Dies was a vomit bag of a human being.

5. HIDEKI TÔJÔ
1941 - Tokyo, Japan

Hideki Tôjô made a name for himself in the Kwangtung Army by killing lots of innocent Chinese people and was subsequently named prime minister in 1941. By the end of that year, "Razor" Tôjô initiated his plan to take over the world. On December 7, Japanese fighter planes and submarines attacked the U.S. port of Pearl Harbor in Hawaii, killing more than two thousand soldiers and civilians. This move kicked off a battle Japan really didn't want. After some early success, the U.S. pounded Japan and Tôjô was forced from power. Knowing he'd be tried for war crimes, he attempted suicide by shooting himself but didn't do a good enough job. He was nursed back to health, tried for war crimes, and then hanged.

4. ILSE KOCH
1940 - Buchenwald, Germany

Instead of accepting the cushy, hands-off role like most other Nazi officer wives, Ilse Koch opted to be an overseer at her husband's Buchenwald concentration camp. In no time, Ilse surpassed her husband's reputation in sadism and earned the label the "Bitch of

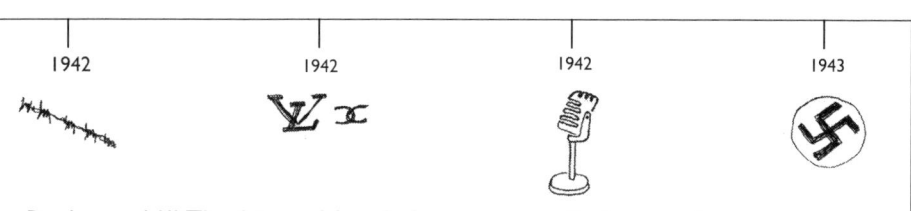

Buchenwald." The big, red-headed woman strolled around camp and whipped whomever she pleased, raped whenever it suited her, and collected lampshades, book covers, and gloves made from the tattooed skin of prisoners.

2. (TIE) SHIRO ISHII
1940 - Ping Fan, China

As Japan set out for world domination, evil political-ladder climber Shiro Ishii was put in charge of the notorious Unit 731. Unit 731 massacred thousands of Chinese and various prisoners of war under the guise of "research" through techniques like: spraying with flamethrowers, amputating limbs, frostbite, food and water deprivation, air-pressure torture, disease exposure, and a whole lot of other unconscionable stuff. Somehow, after the war, Ishii played the Americans and Soviets off each other and got clemency in exchange for information.

2. (TIE) JOSEF MENGELE
1943 - Oświęcim, Poland

In 1943, eugenics enthusiast Josef Mengele was promoted to S.S. captain by Heinrich Himmler and transferred to Auschwitz, where he became the chief camp physician. Each new prisoner was greeted by a white-gloved Mengele, who determined whether they were destined for hard labor or extermination. The latter ones were immediately sent to the gas chambers. The others were further sifted by the "Angel of Death" so he could experiment on them (until he had no use for them, then they were allowed to die). As the war wound down, he escaped to South America.

1. ADOLPH HITLER
1940 - Munich, Germany

Hitler's march across Europe came a little too easy. Poland had been toppled, Paris was under control of a Nazi-sympathizing puppet regime, and the Luftwaffe had reduced much of London to rubble. As Hitler's ego grew, so did the German army's agenda. Instead of just focusing on finishing off Britain (who proved to

| 1940 | 1940 | 1940 | 1941 |

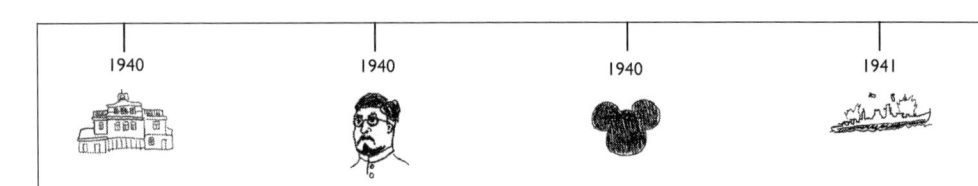

1940

be tougher than expected), Hitler sent troops into Russia and declared war on the United States. Suddenly he had a depleted army and millions of Allied troops closing in on him. By 1944, his regime was on the ropes and Der Führer descended into madness. In 1945, he ordered the "Nero Decree" (to burn everything) and retreated to a bunker with his girlfriend Eva Braun, his dog Blondi, and a handful of sycophants. Hitler killed himself just days before Allied forces took Berlin.

| 1942 | 1942 | 1942 | 1943 |

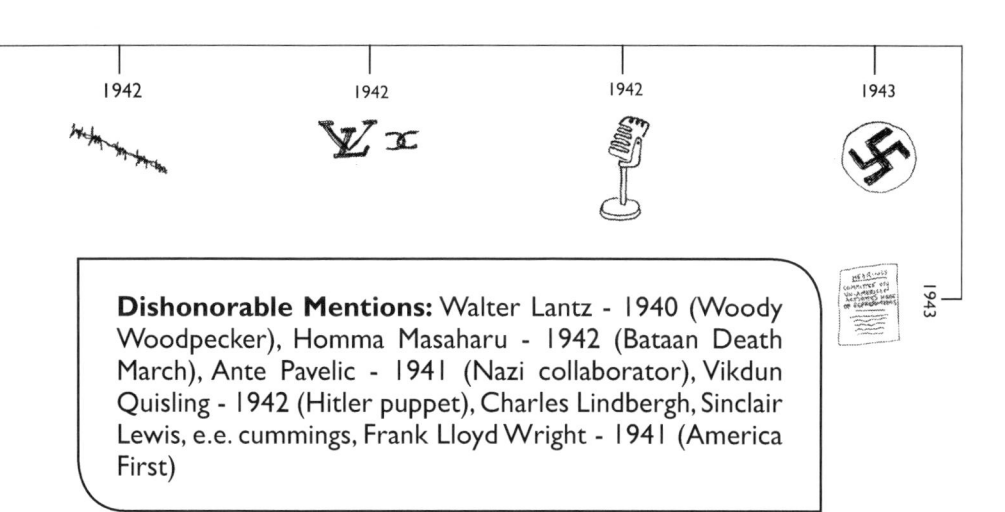

Dishonorable Mentions: Walter Lantz - 1940 (Woody Woodpecker), Homma Masaharu - 1942 (Bataan Death March), Ante Pavelic - 1941 (Nazi collaborator), Vikdun Quisling - 1942 (Hitler puppet), Charles Lindbergh, Sinclair Lewis, e.e. cummings, Frank Lloyd Wright - 1941 (America First)

1943

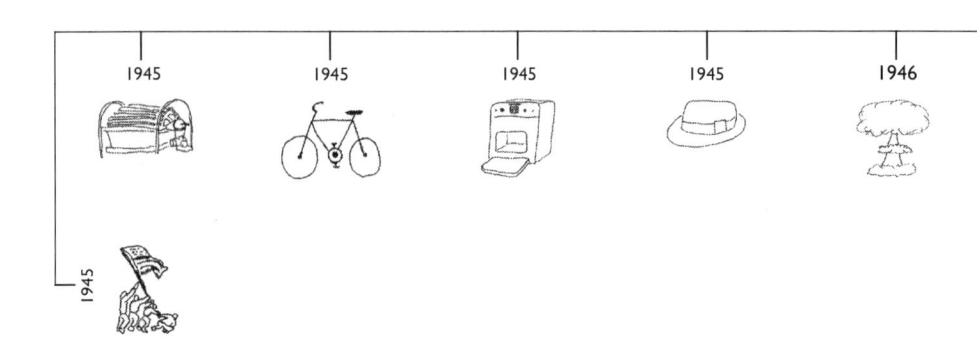

1945-1949

"The organizers and perpetuators of segregation are as much the enemy of America as any foreign invader."

-Bayard Rustin

BEST

10. (TIE) JAMES STEWART
1946 - Hollywood, California

Before Jimmy Stewart, movie acting was hot garbage. If you saw someone on the street behaving like Cagney, Bogart, or Gable did onscreen, you'd probably call the paramedics. And then director Frank Capra called on Jimmy Stewart, fresh off a harrowing five-year term of military service leading squadrons on bomber missions across Europe, to star in *It's a Wonderful Life*. Stewart powered through PTSD and gave the first truly great acting performance on the big screen. As his character George Bailey journeyed through frustration, fear, anger, confusion, relief, and joy, Jimmy Stewart gave that emotional complexity and more. For the rest of his diverse career (*Rear Window, The Man Who Shot Liberty Valance, Harvey, Vertigo*), Stewart was the gold standard for acting.

10. (TIE) FRANK SINATRA
1945 - New York, New York

For half a century, Hoboken, New Jersey native Frank Sinatra dominated the entertainment world. He was a pop idol and an Oscar-winning actor. Unfortunately, he was also an egomaniac, a womanizer, and a bully. But Ol' Blue Eyes was an important civil rights figure. As early as 1945, Sinatra spoke out in favor of school integration. He refused to play segregated clubs. He performed with virtually every prominent black singer of the era (Billie Holiday, Ella Fitzgerald, Nat King Cole, Sammy Davis, Jr., and more). In the 1950s, when Sinatra started doing his Rat Pack acts with Davis, he forced casinos to integrate. At a time when the black community needed a powerful ally, Frank Sinatra was their guy. Too bad he's now known for his two crummiest hits: "New York, New York" and "My Way."

9. BENJAMIN SPOCK
1946 - New York, New York

Dr. Benjamin Spock won a gold medal at the 1924 Olympics (in rowing), graduated from Yale, and finished at the top of his class at Columbia University's College of Physicians and Surgeons. Then he did something truly great. Spock realized most pediatric textbooks were impractical and outdated. So he interviewed parents, did studies, and wrote a book of his own called *Common Sense Book of Baby and Child Care*. His main message: Parents should trust their instincts and relax. Rigid schedules and harsh rules from doctors aren't making babies any healthier or happier. Despite textbooks' warnings, hugging and kissing your child is actually a good thing. To Spock, a happy baby becomes a more productive adult. During the Vietnam War, Nixon's VP Spiro Agnew called protesting hippies "the work of Spock." Hey, anyone who pissed off that asshole clearly did something right.

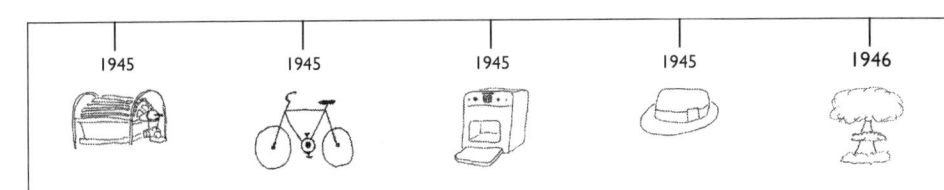

8. PERCY SPENCER
1945 - Waltham, Massachusetts

One day, while walking across an active radar set at work, Percy Spencer noticed that the chocolate bar in his pocket completely melted. The self-taught math and science whiz did some more tests and determined the chocolate liquefying was the result of electromagnetic waves. Spencer worked on harnessing those waves and, in 1945, filed the patent for the microwave. Over the years, the microwave went from six feet tall and 750 pounds to fitting nicely on the counter of nearly every kitchen. Besides the microwave, Percy Spencer was granted over three hundred other patents over the course of his highly decorated career. Not bad for a guy who didn't complete the seventh grade.

7. JOHN HERSEY
1946 - New York, New York

In 1946, *The New Yorker* sent Pulitzer-winning author and journalist John Hersey to Japan to report on the recently-bombed Japanese city Hiroshima. Hersey returned with a 31,000-word story chronicling the shattered lives of six survivors in the devastated city. The magazine dedicated an entire issue to it, it quickly sold out, and, for the first time, Americans had to face the harsh reality that the World War II-ending bombs had very real, lasting consequences. Although it had no editorializing, the conclusions drawn by "Hiroshima" were loud and clear—atomic bombs are awful and we should avoid using them at all costs.

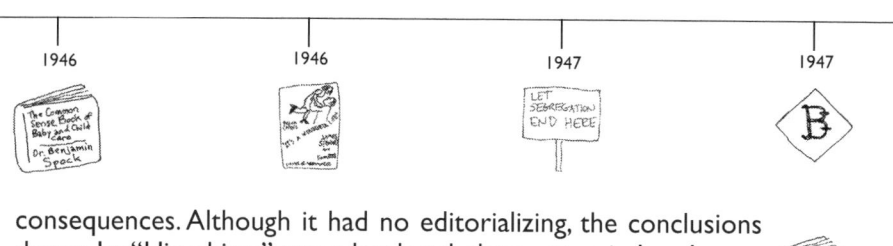

6. ALFRED KINSEY
1947 - Bloomington, Indiana

Alfred Kinsey, a biologist and one of the world's foremost experts on wasps, was asked to teach a course on marriage. From that point, his career took a completely different direction. After struggling to answer some of his students' questions about sex, Kinsey realized that, beyond old wives' tales like "If you masturbate, you go blind," there was no information out there on the subject. To save his students from suffering from the same repressed, confused feelings he had growing up in to regards to sex, Kinsey openly talked about it in his class and conducted student interviews where he collected sexual data. His groundbreaking book, *Sexual Behavior in the American Male* and its 1953 follow-up, *Sexual Behavior in the American Female*, changed the way people perceived sex and let everyone know they weren't weirdos for masturbating or having premarital sex.

5. WILLEM KOLFF
1945 - Groningen, The Netherlands

Hitler's takeover was terrible for the medical community in Europe on two fronts: first, the bombings and violence severely depleted resources, and second, since every doctor was performing mostly emergency services, very little effort was devoted to research and innovation. Dr. Willem Kolff was the rare exception. Besides risking his life to create Europe's first ever blood bank and providing alibis for many fleeing the Nazis, Kolff also developed the first successful kidney dialysis machine. What started as a collection of junkyard materials (car parts, orange juice cans, sausage casing, and other stuff) eventually became a machine that helped save a woman's life from kidney failure. After the war he moved to the United States, where he created portable dialysis machines, as well as a machine that kept patients alive during open-heart surgery.

| 1945 | 1945 | 1945 | 1945 | 1946 |

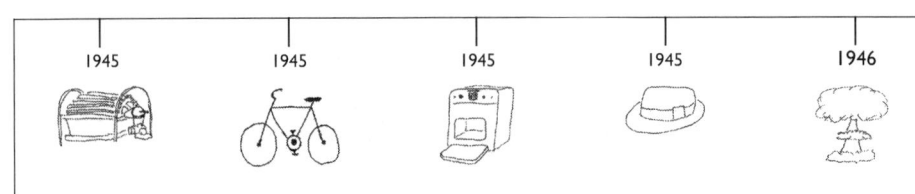

1945

4. JACKIE ROBINSON
1947 - Brooklyn, New York

Black guys were deemed good enough to fight for America in World War II but still not allowed to play baseball alongside white guys. Then, in 1946, Brooklyn Dodgers owner Branch Rickey took a chance on former UCLA star and current Negro Leaguer Jackie Robinson. Robinson didn't have to be just good, he had to be perfect. Besides excelling at the sport, Robinson had to endure a barrage of racism (from fans, players, and managers) on a daily basis and maintain his cool. If he fought back, he ran the risk of losing his and every other black baseball player's chance at playing in the league. Robinson withstood it all and easily won Rookie of the Year. Within a decade, ten percent of the league was black.

3. IRA HAYES, HAROLD SCHULTZ, MICHAEL STRANK, RENE GAGNON, FRANKLIN SOUSLEY, AND HARLON BLOCK
1945 - Iwo Jima, Japan

Fighting back against Japan was a logistical nightmare for America. One, it was really far away; and two, Japan controlled just about every strategic point of interest along the way. General Douglas MacArthur figured that to get to Japan, America had to win by "island hopping." In February 1945, Americans invaded the small-but-well-fortified island of Iwo Jima. After winning the bloody battle against Japanese soldiers in a network of tunnels and caves, six Marines planted an American flag on the top of Mount Suribachi. Photographer Joe Rosenthal's iconic photograph of that moment remains the most indelible image of the brave men who fought the Battle of the Pacific.

2. WALLY VAN HALL
1945 - Amsterdam, The Netherlands

When Nazis took over the Netherlands, the underground Dutch Resistance helped hide and protect Jews and those not

344

looking to fight for the Nazis. Feeding, hiding, and providing new identification for all these people took a lot of money. Operating under the code name Van Tuyl, banker Wally van Hall funneled eighty-three million guilders (about $480 million today) from the central bank and sent it on its way to an elaborate network of bicycle couriers (because, of course, it's Amsterdam) that got it to the Resistance. Instead of living a comfortable life as a banker, Wally van Hall risked (and sacrificed) everything to fight bad guys who weren't even after him. He was executed by a Nazi officer just a few months before the Netherlands was liberated.

1. BAYARD RUSTIN
1947 - Durham, North Carolina

Although he's rarely mentioned in the same breath as Martin Luther King and Rosa Parks, Bayard Rustin was every bit as important to the civil rights movement. Inspired by the pacifist teachings of Gandhi and the Quakers, Rustin organized rallies like the 1947 Journey of Reconciliation in the deep South and mentored future leaders like MLK. Unfortunately, as a gay man, Rustin was forced to do most of his work behind the scenes so his sexuality didn't undermine the overall mission. But when King was trying to organize his March on Washington, there was no question who one of his first calls would be—Bayard Rustin.

> **Honorable Mentions:** Bud Abbott and Lou Costello - 1948 (comedy), Desmond Doss - 1945 (war hero), Satchel Paige - 1948 (baseball), Louis Reard - 1946 (bikini), Chuck Yeager - 1947 (pilot), Bob Elliot and Ray Goulding - 1945 (comedy), Les Paul - 1945 (electric guitar), Fanny Blankers-Koen - 1948 ("Flying Housewife"), Dietrich Bonhoeffer - 1945 (helped Jews escape), Henri Charriere - 1945 (*Papillon*), Herman Hesse - 1946 (author), Gertrude Berg - 1949 (created the sitcom), Tennessee Williams - 1948 (*A Streetcar Named Desire*), Nikos Kazantzakis - 1946 (*Zorba the Greek*), Joseph Woodland - 1949 (barcode), Jack Cole - 1948 (Cliff's Notes), Earl Tupper - 1946 (Tupperware)

WORST

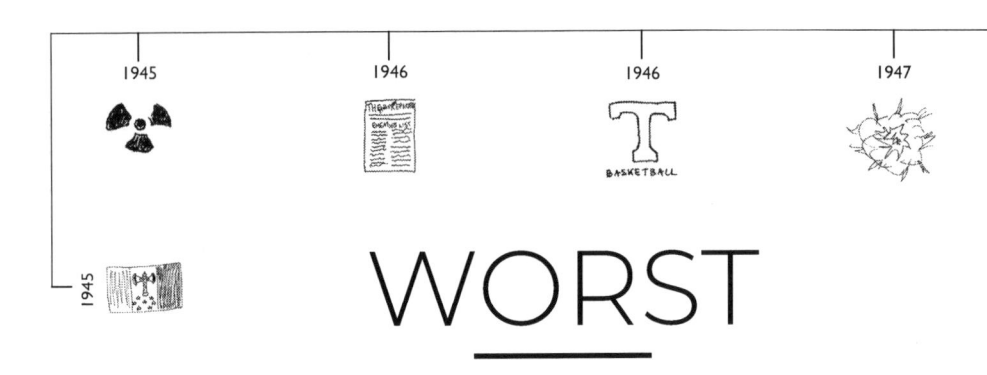

10. PAT MALONEY
1948 - Chicago, Illinois

On November 26, 1947, the printer's union in Chicago went on a twenty-two month strike. So instead of having fast, efficient printers do the job, *Chicago Tribune* staff had to cut and paste typewriter copy and arrange it into a newspaper format by hand. In order to meet their publishing deadline, all the work had to be undertaken hours earlier than usual. On election night in 1948, Pat Maloney chose to call the election early for Thomas Dewey (over his opponents, Harry Truman and third-party candidate Strom Thurmond) and write the headline *DEWEY DEFEATS TRUMAN*. In his quest to be first rather than right, Pat Maloney committed the biggest gaffe in headline history.

9. JOHN MAURER
1946 - McKeesport, Pennsylvania

Minutes before their basketball game, University of Tennessee Coach John Maurer informed Duquesne University Coach Chick Davies that his squad wouldn't play the game if Davies played black freshman Charles Cooper. Maurer's reasoning was some racist garbage about his team being a bunch of Southern boys who couldn't handle it. Davies and his Athletic Director Sammy Weiss didn't budge, so jackass Maurer chose to forfeit the game and take the next flight back to Knoxville.

8. ROBERT MAGEE
1947 - Los Angeles, California

When people exaggerate about their accomplishments, it's

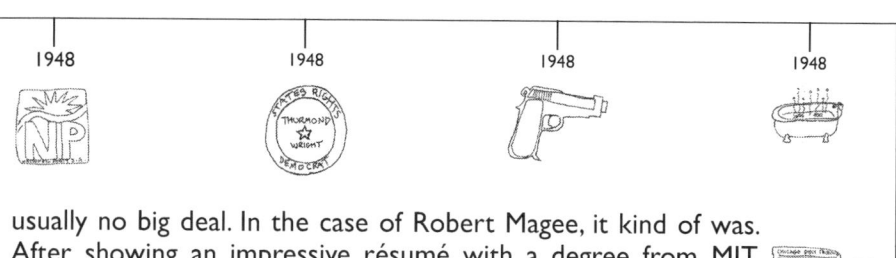

usually no big deal. In the case of Robert Magee, it kind of was. After showing an impressive résumé with a degree from MIT, Robert Magee was hired to be the chief engineer at chemical plant in Los Angeles. Magee got right to work on an aluminum-polishing concoction. One day, the refrigeration unit broke down. Magee inserted a plastic rack into the solution and KABOOM, the entire place exploded. Not only did it destroy the plant but also the entire neighborhood (116 buildings), killing fifteen people. Windows a mile away were blown out. As it turns out, his MIT degree was really just a high school diploma. And his previous work experience was at a dairy farm. Oops.

7. JOSEPH HAMILTON
1945 - San Francisco, California

As America ushered in the nuclear era, people like neurologist Joseph Hamilton were brought in to study the effects of radiology. After working with rats, Hamilton wanted to start testing on humans to see whether radiology could be used in warfare. So, in 1945, Hamilton convinced a house painter who thought he had stomach cancer to allow him to inject him with plutonium. It turned out to be an ulcer. Whoops! Then he injected plutonium into a boy with bone cancer. The army got creeped out and told him to stop. But Hamilton was hooked and found a few more unsuspecting patients. Luckily, before the entire Bay Area was injected with lethal doses of plutonium, Joseph Hamilton himself came down with a rare form of leukemia.

6. BILLY WILKERSON
1946 - Hollywood, California

Aside from *Avatar's* nomination for Best Picture, Hollywood's darkest moment was orchestrated by Billy Wilkerson, the owner and editor-in-chief of *The Hollywood Reporter* and right-wing asshole. In his "Tradeviews" column, Wilkerson regularly trashed pretty much anyone with views to the left of Harry Truman. The columns grew more and more crazed until it culminated with Wilkinson outing "Commies" and getting them blacklisted. What started with the "Hollywood Ten" (a group of actors and screenwriters like Dalton Trumbo, the writer of *Spartacus*) soon ballooned to over three hundred. Actors like Humphrey Bogart and Lauren Bacall tried to stand up for them but, due to pressure from Screen Actors' Guild President Ronald Reagan and studio heads like Walt Disney and Louis B. Mayer, the resistance proved useless.

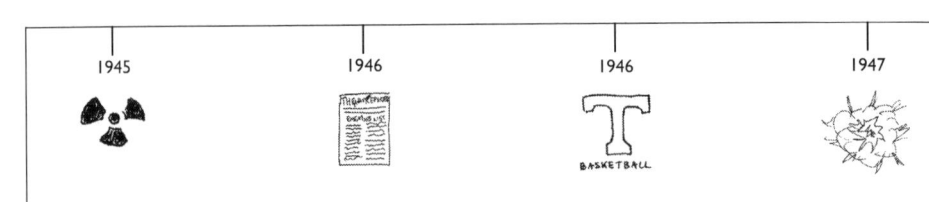

5. JOHN GEORGE HAIGH
1948 - London, England

John George Haigh was raised in a home where the only form of entertainment was Bible reading. Music, newspapers, books, sports—all forbidden. It was only natural consequence that, in adulthood, Haigh became the "Acid Bath Murderer." In the mid-1940s, Haigh murdered at least six people by bludgeoning them, drinking their blood, and dissolving their bodies in acid so the police couldn't find evidence, then sold their stuff for money. His "no bodies, no crime" defense with the police worked about as well as his parents' child-rearing techniques.

4. NATHURAM GODSE
1948 - New Delhi, India

Gandhi gave his blood, sweat, and tears for India. Literally. Through decades of non-violent protest, Gandhi helped the Indian people fight against excessive British taxation and unfair voting laws, and, ultimately, gain their freedom from British rule. But that freedom didn't bring about unity. Clashes between Hindus and Muslims caused Britain to break the region up into two separate states (India and Pakistan). In India the conflicts continued. When Gandhi tried to bring about compromise, Hindu fanatics were incensed. Gandhi's response? "If I am to die by the bullet of a madman, I must do so smiling." A couple weeks later, Nathuram Godse shot Gandhi three times. True to his word, Gandhi went out with a smile.

3. PHILIPPE PÉTAIN
1945 - Vichy, France

France's reputation for being soft can be traced back to Philippe

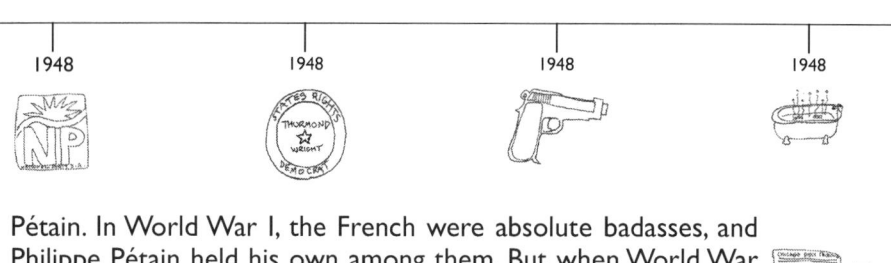

Pétain. In World War I, the French were absolute badasses, and Philippe Pétain held his own among them. But when World War II came along, Pétain's courage was nowhere to be found. When the Nazis invaded in 1940, not only did Vice Premier Pétain surrender; he also agreed to preside over a sham government in Vichy (southeast of Paris) which would collaborate with the Nazis. It's one thing to surrender, it's another to enthusiastically help the Nazis round up over 76,000 Jews. "The Savior of Verdun" was arrested after the war and died in jail.

2. STROM THURMOND
1948 - Washington, D.C.

For more than half a century, South Carolina Senator Strom Thurmond showed remarkable consistency. Whether it was staging a convention walk-out to protest President Truman's civil rights work in 1948, writing an anti-*Brown v. The Board of Education* manifesto, filibustering to stall the 1957 Civil Rights Act, trying to sabotage Martin Luther King's March on Washington, or switching parties after the Civil Rights Act of 1964, Thurmond remained an awful racist to the end. When he died at age 100 (those final years in the Senate, he was propped up like a racist version of *Weekend at Bernie's*), the world also learned he was a hypocrite. He had a black daughter! In the '20s, he had knocked up his dad's black maid (guessing that wasn't consensual) and kept her a secret.

1. DANIEL FRANCOIS MALAN
1948 - Cape Province, South Africa

After World War II, South African Prime Minister Jan Smuts was in the process of relaxing restrictions on African natives, recognizing black trade unions, and setting up programs that would help all his country's citizens. So D.F. Malan, the leader of the National Party, used it as an opportunity to stoke fear in the whites that their world was crumbling. If they didn't vote for him, Communism and the spread of minorities would lead to South Africa's downfall. And it worked. For the next half-century, Malan's National Party enacted and enforced increasingly harsh apartheid laws, including mandates on where people of color were allowed to live. D.F. Malan kicked off a terrible four decade stretch for South Africa.

1945 1946 1946 1947

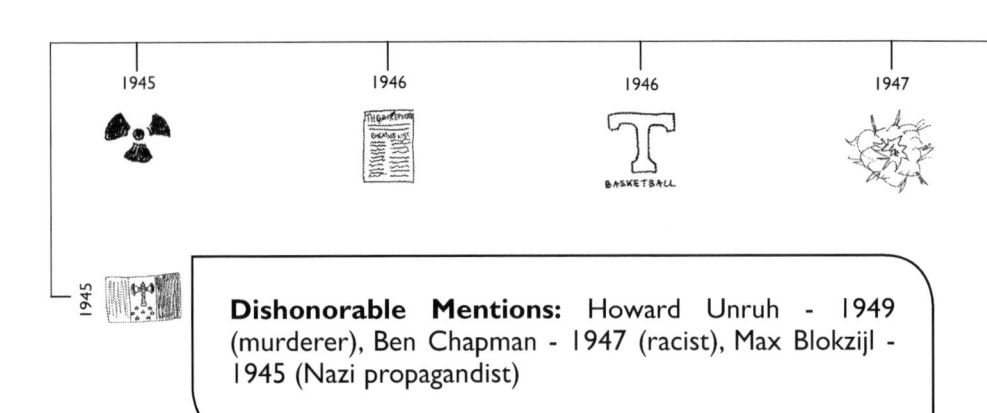

BASKETBALL

1945

Dishonorable Mentions: Howard Unruh - 1949 (murderer), Ben Chapman - 1947 (racist), Max Blokzijl - 1945 (Nazi propagandist)

1948　　　1948　　　1948　　　1948

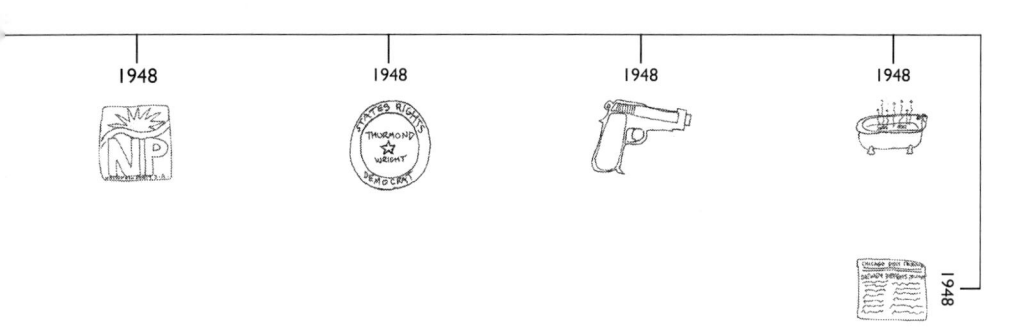

1948

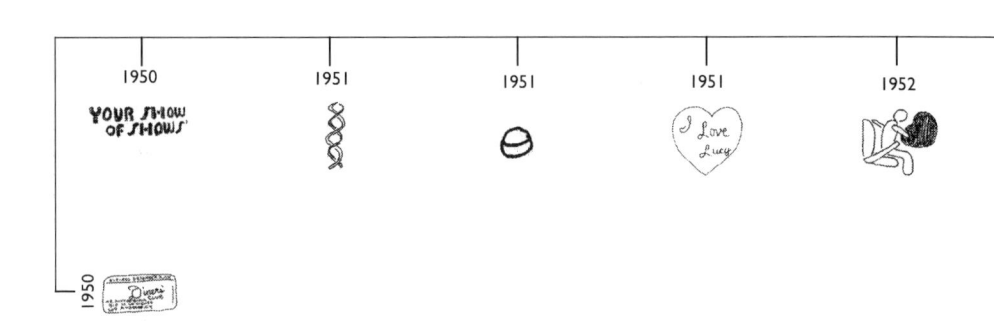

1950-1954

"The measure of a country's greatness is its ability to retain compassion in times of crisis."

-Thurgood Marshall

BEST

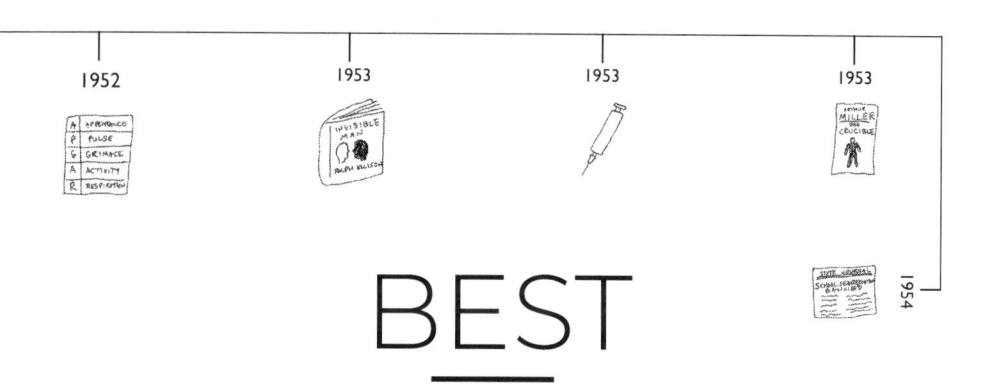

10. (TIE) JOHN HETRICK
August, 1952 - Newport, Pennsylvania

A deer jumped in front of industrial engineer John Hetrick's car, causing him to swerve. As the car was crashing, John and his wife reached their arms out to prevent their daughter from rocketing through the windshield. They were successful, but the incident got Hetrick thinking of ways to cushion car passengers for better safety in case of accidents. Then he remembered a mishap from his time in the navy during World War II. The torpedo air pressure was accidentally released and instantly filled a canvas bag to capacity. Hetrick applied it to the car and created the first airbag. He never made money off of it, but researchers believe his invention has reduced front-impact collision fatalities by 30 percent.

10. (TIE) ARTHUR MILLER
1953 - New York, New York

America's uneasiness with Communism had festered into full-blown hysteria. Senator Joseph McCarthy was on TVs everywhere screaming about the enemies within. Hollywood was blacklisting people left and right. After hearing his friend, the famous director Elia Kazan, rat out leftist-leaning people in the entertainment industry in front of the House Committee on Un-American Activities, Tony-winning playwright Arthur Miller fired back with *The Crucible*. Miller's play, which drew parallels between the Red Scare and the Salem Witch Trials, raised the ire of Joe McCarthy. Soon the senator was trying to pressure Miller, but the latter wouldn't budge. Eventually, McCarthy was drummed out of office and Miller was hailed as a hero. Oh, and he eventually married Elia Kazan's ex-girlfriend, Marilyn Monroe.

9. SID CAESAR
1950 - New York, New York

After a few years on Broadway, Sid Caesar was given his own show on television

| 1950 | 1951 | 1951 | 1951 | 1952 |

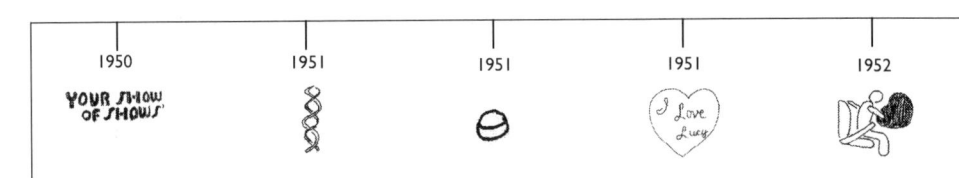

called *Your Show of Shows*. Besides absolutely owning Saturday nights in the '50s, Caesar's show boasted the most impressive writers' room in comedy history: Mel Brooks (*Blazing Saddles, Young Frankenstein*), Carl Reiner (*The Dick Van Dyke Show, The 2,000-Year-Old Man*), Neil Simon (*The Odd Couple*), Mel Tolkin (*All In the Family*), Larry Gelbart (*M*A*S*H, Tootsie*), Joe Stein (*Fiddler on the Roof*), Mel Ruben (*The Andy Griffith Show, Sanford and Son*), and Woody Allen (*Annie Hall, Hannah and Her Sisters*).

8. FRANCIS X. MCNAMARA
1950 - New York, New York

Frank McNamara was having dinner in New York City when he realized he forgot his wallet. So he called his wife, who drove to the restaurant with cash. Determined to never let that happen again, Frank came up with the idea of a credit card. Together with his lawyer and the grandson of the founder of Bloomingdale's, McNamara launched Diner's Club in 1950. Within a year, the first ever credit card company had ten thousand New Yorkers using it at twenty-eight different restaurants and two hotels around the city. Competitors quickly sprang up and, these days, paying cash at restaurants is usually left to people trying to avoid being detected by law enforcement.

7. LUCILLE BALL
1951 - Hollywood, California

When model-turned-B-movie-actress Lucille Ball's film roles started drying up, she got into broadcasting. After a successful run on the radio program *My Favorite Husband*, television executives pleaded with her to star in her own show. The redhead agreed, but with several demands: first, her real-life Cuban husband would play the same role in the show (even though it was the '50s and TV didn't show interracial couples); second, the show would be shot on film in Hollywood (instead of crappy live broadcasts in NYC like every other show); third, she'd get producer credit; and fourth, it would be shot with three cameras (instead of the usual one). Lucy's superb comedic timing and fearlessness made *I Love Lucy* an instant hit and the benchmark for all future television comedies. Later in her career, Ball became the first female studio head, producing shows like *Mission Impossible*, *The Untouchables*, *The Dick Van Dyke Show*, and *Star Trek*.

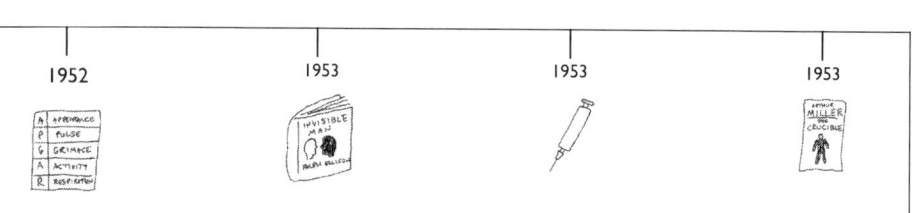

6. RALPH ELLISON
1953 - New York, New York

After graduating from the Tuskegee Institute in Alabama, Ralph Ellison moved up to New York in 1936 to work as a researcher and writer for the Federal Writers Program. Inspired by the great writers he met, such as Langston Hughes, and the thriving black community in Harlem, Ellison spent six years writing one of the definitive books on race in history: *Invisible Man*. Ellison's novel about a man dealing with stereotypes spent weeks on the bestseller list, won the National Book Award, and inspired future generations of writers and activists. Attempting to top perfection proved to be tough thing for Ellison, however. For the last forty years of his life, Ellison worked on a second novel, the 1,600-page *Juneteenth*.

5. ROSALIND FRANKLIN
1951 - London, England

The science world was pretty sure that DNA was the molecule of life but still didn't really know how it all worked. A team at Cambridge University (James Watson and Francis Crick) made models but kept coming up empty. Over at King's College in London, Rosalind Franklin experimented and took x-rays, one of which became the famous Photograph 51. Photograph 51 provided a clear picture of the double-helix, curving-ladder-shaped structure of DNA. One of Franklin's colleagues, Maurice Wilkins, took Photo 51 and gave it to the guys up at Cambridge. Watson, Crick, and Wilkins ran with the information, published their findings, and eventually were awarded the Nobel Prize. Franklin, who died from ovarian cancer in 1958, barely got a mention. But it was her DNA discovery that helped the world understand everything from hereditary diseases to crime scenes.

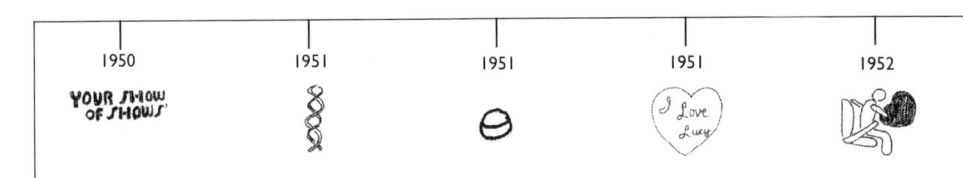

4. VIRGINIA APGAR
1952 - New York, New York

Before 1952, once a baby was delivered, the focus of the doctor lay chiefly in making sure the mother survived. The baby was swaddled up and laid down somewhere. Even if the baby had an issue that might have been treatable, they were often ignored until it was no longer so. Then Virginia Apgar, an anesthesiologist at Columbia University, developed her own test to help reduce the alarming infant mortality numbers. She developed a quick five-point system (skin color, heart rate, reflexes, muscle tone, and breathing) that a nurse could check twice: one minute and five minutes after a baby is born. The APGAR score soon became a standard test, and mortality rates dropped significantly because of it. The test is still used today.

3. THURGOOD MARSHALL
1954 - Washington, D.C.

Thurgood Marshall was told he couldn't attend University of Maryland Law School because he was black. So he went down the road to Howard, graduated first in his class, took the University of Maryland to the Supreme Court, and ended their racial discrimination policy. As an NAACP lawyer, Marshall won twenty-nine of the thirty-two cases he tried in front of the Supreme Court, including the monumental *Brown v. Board of Education of Topeka*. In the case, Marshall successfully argued 1896's *Plessy v. Ferguson* ("separate but equal") decision was completely unfair. The resources at black schools weren't remotely close to those at white schools. Marshall's star continued to rise and, in 1967, Lyndon Johnson named Thurgood Marshall the first ever black Supreme Court justice.

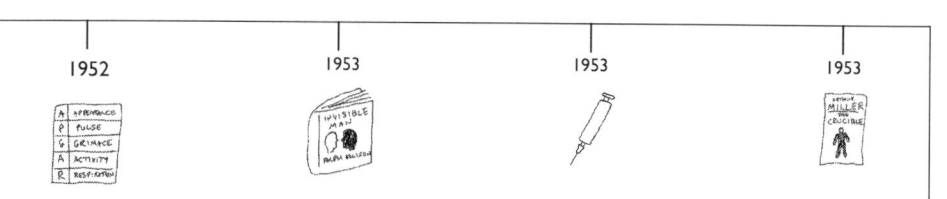

2. KATHARINE MCCORMICK, GREGORY PINCUS, CARL DJERASSI, AND JOHN ROCK
1951 - Worcester, Massachusetts; Mexico City, Mexico; San Juan, Puerto Rico

When Katherine McCormick's husband died and left her $15 million, the seventy-five-year-old turned to Margaret Sanger (also in her seventies) and asked where her money could be best spent. Sanger suggested she donate to Dr. Gregory Pincus, who was working on a birth control pill that could be taken as easily as aspirin. Meanwhile, down in Mexico City, chemist Carl Djerassi discovered that progesterone pills were an effective form of contraception. Pincus tested and confirmed Djerassi's findings. Fueled by further funding from McCormick and clinical trials of "the pill" by Harvard gynecologist John Rock (who performed them in Puerto Rico because it was illegal in Massachusetts), Pincus got the stamp of approval by the FDA in 1960. Sanger's lifelong dream was fulfilled and, within a few years, nearly a quarter of all couples were using the pill.

1. JONAS SALK
1953 - Pittsburgh, Pennsylvania

More than 50,000 new cases of polio (or "infantile paralysis") were diagnosed each year, killing 3,000 and leaving many more fully or partially paralyzed. While it affected small children the worst, it was also possible to catch it in adulthood (FDR got it when he was thirty-nine). Then Jonas Salk, a virologist at the University of Pittsburgh, announced on the radio that he had come up with a vaccine. Using a similar technique to the flu vaccine, Salk grew the live virus in a lab, killed it, then injected it into humans. Within two years, nearly two million American children were vaccinated and the number of polio cases dropped from 58,000 to 1,000. Today the virus is virtually nonexistent in the developed world.

1950 — YOUR SHOW OF SHOWS

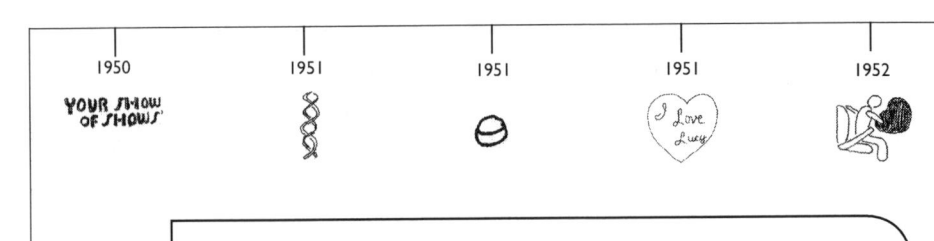

1951

1951

1951 — I Love Lucy

1952

1950

Honorable Mentions: James Baldwin - 1953 (*Go Tell It on the Mountain*), Alfred Hitchcock - 1954 (filmmaker), Abdul Sattar Edhi - 1951 (philanthropist), Abbe Pierre - 1954 (French priest, "uprising of kindness"), Helena Rubenstein - 1953 (philanthropist), Marlon Brando - 1954 (actor), Nat "Sweetwater" Clifton, Chuck Cooper, and Earl Lloyd - 1950 (first black NBA players), Barbara Johns - 1951 (civil rights pioneer), Harvey Kurtzman, William Gaines, Sergio Aragonés, Mort Drucker, Dave Berg - 1952 (*Mad Magazine*), Dr. Christian Hamburger - 1952 (performed first sex change), Ian Fleming - 1953 (James Bond), Marion Donovan - 1950 (disposable diaper), Tenzing Norgay - 1953 (Everest), Alan Freed - 1952 (rock and roll), William Golding - 1954 (*Lord of the Flies*), Steve Allen - 1954 (*Tonight Show*), Maria Tallchief - 1951 (ballerina), J. Hartwell Harrison and Joseph Murray - 1954 (first kidney transplant)

| 1952 | 1953 | 1953 | 1953 | | 1954 |

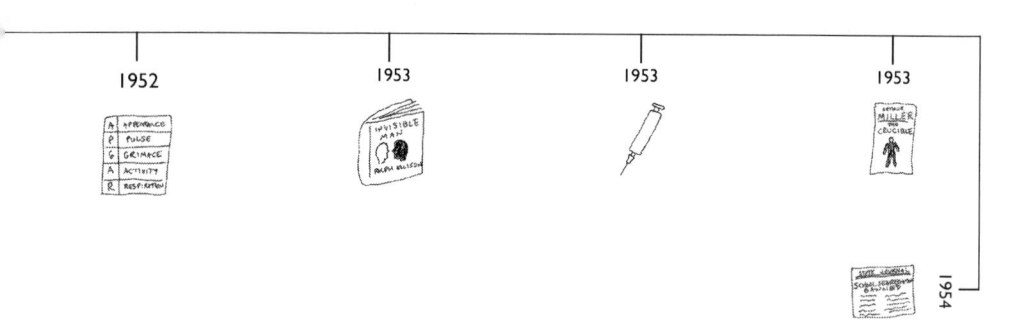

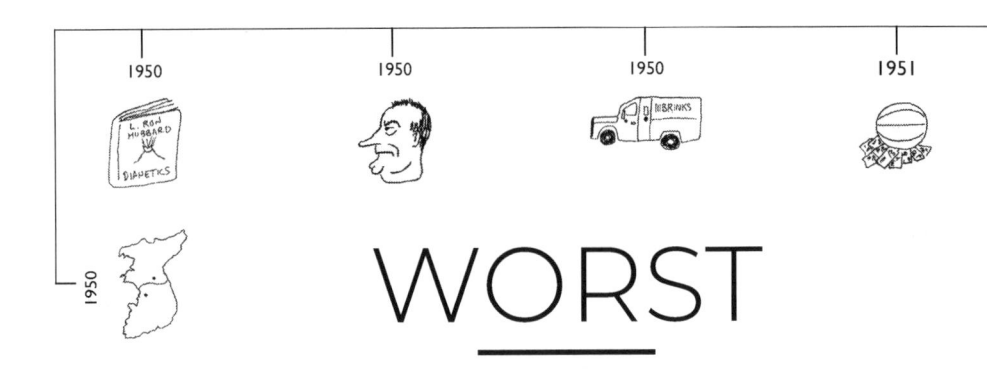

WORST

10. EDDIE GARD
1951 - New York, New York

Every summer, New York City basketball players were invited to work at the Catskills resort area as waiters and busboys. In reality, they were there to play basketball while old Jewish and Italian guys bet on the games. One of the players, Eddie Gard, realized he could get a cut of the action by altering the outcomes. So Gard approached small-time criminal Salvatore "Tarto" Sollazzo at the pool and worked out a deal. Soon, Gard's point-shaving graduated to college basketball, where he recruited thirty-two different players from seven schools to fix the games. Eventually they got caught. Careers were ended, reputations were ruined, and one program (CCNY) was decimated.

9. JOSEPH "SPECS" O'KEEFE
1950 - Boston, Massachusetts

In the movies, heist gangs are cool guys working for some noble cause. In reality, they're usually just goons. Despite plotting the perfect armed robbery of the Brinks Building for over a year, Boston career criminals Tony Pino and "Big Joe" McGinnis still had to rely on the erratic, bumbling Specs O'Keefe as a wingman. Thanks to fake keys, Brinks uniforms, and airtight alibis, the gang pulled off a record haul of $2.7 million. If they could just lay low until the statute of limitations ran out (in six years), they were set. Then Specs O'Keefe found a way to get arrested and lose his money. Just a few days before everyone would have been free, Specs ratted them out to the FBI.

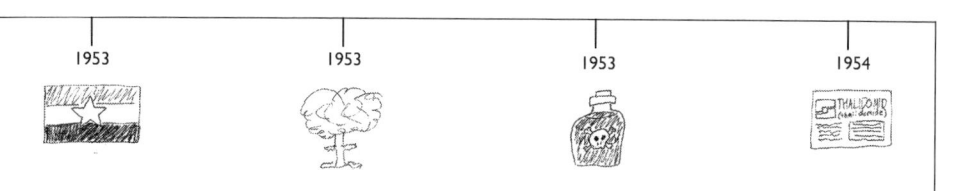

8. NANCY "NANNY" DOSS
1953 - Tulsa, Oklahoma

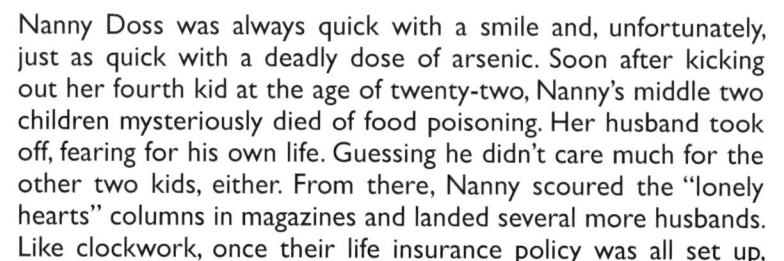

Nanny Doss was always quick with a smile and, unfortunately, just as quick with a deadly dose of arsenic. Soon after kicking out her fourth kid at the age of twenty-two, Nanny's middle two children mysteriously died of food poisoning. Her husband took off, fearing for his own life. Guessing he didn't care much for the other two kids, either. From there, Nanny scoured the "lonely hearts" columns in magazines and landed several more husbands. Like clockwork, once their life insurance policy was all set up, they died. When her arsenic-laced prune cake failed to finish off her fifth husband, the cops were alerted and Nanny's life of crime was over.

7. JULIUS ROSENBERG
1953 - Ossining, New York

In 1949, the Soviet Union showed off their nuclear capabilities by dropping a test bomb in Kazakhstan. Considering that they were nowhere close to that advanced only a few years earlier, American officials were convinced there was an internal leak and began extensive investigations. In February 1950, British officials intercepted decoded messages between former Manhattan Project physicist Klaus Fuchs and the Soviets. This set off a chain reaction of snitching which led authorities to Communists Ethel and Julius Rosenberg in New York. Julius' defense was weak. Ethel was also found guilty, mainly for having a rotten husband. So the end result of Julius' spy work: a wrongfully convicted wife, a step closer to a nuclear Armageddon, and two orphaned kids.

6. JOSIP BROZ TITO
1953 - Belgrade, Yugoslavia

Josip Broz Tito fought against Nazis. Despite being part of the post-World War II Communist bloc, he frequently clashed with Stalin. But, in this case, the enemy of your enemies is not your friend. Tito, the Yugoslavian president from 1953 until his death in 1980, was still a brutal dictator. When he didn't get what he wanted, he murdered. His death squads killed between five hundred thousand and two million people. While Yugoslavians had more freedom than people in other Communist countries, it was still Tito's way or the highway.

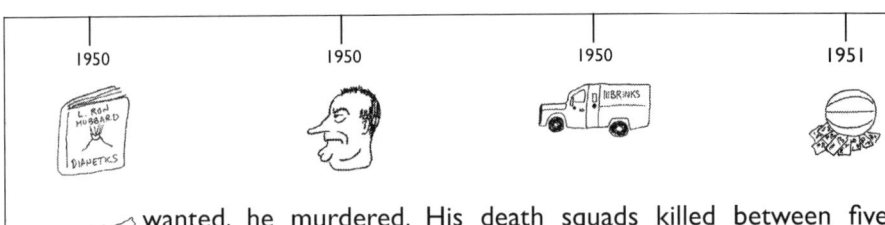

5. RAY KROC
1954 - San Bernadino, California

Ray Kroc was a dreamer, a hustler, and a sleazy, greedy son of a bitch. The former paper cup and milkshake-mixer salesman stumbled upon the first ever assembly-line burger joint in San Bernadino, California and knew it could be a national sensation. So he convinced Mac and Dick McDonald to allow him to franchise McDonald's and give them a cut of the profits. Eventually, Kroc figured out how to buy up the land beneath the franchises and force the brothers out of their own business. As Kroc once said, "If any of my competitors were drowning, I'd stick a hose in their mouth and turn on the water." Ray Kroc died in 1984, leaving behind a legacy of greed and excessive sodium, sugar, and fat.

4. JOSEPH MCCARTHY
1950 - Wheeling, West Virginia

After an unremarkable first term as senator, Joseph McCarthy needed to make a big splash. So the Wisconsin Republican played into America's biggest fear at the time, the Red Scare, and made wild accusations of Communist takeover plots which he would help bring down. McCarthy held up a piece of paper and screamed about having a list of 205 members of the State Department who were secret members of the Communist party. And people ate it up. Suddenly Joseph McCarthy was on the front page of every newspaper across the country, wielding real power (like getting all gay government employees fired). But, after calling out the U.S. Army on an alleged lack of patriotism, Joe McCarthy's house of cards came swiftly tumbling down.

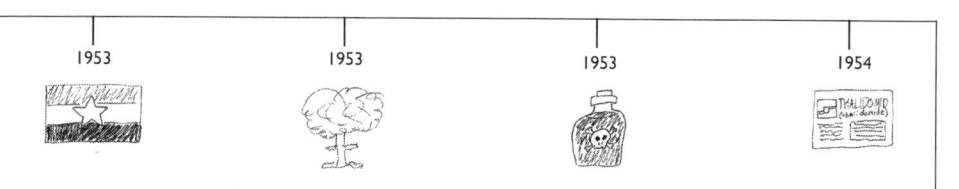

3. L. RON HUBBARD
1950 - Elizabeth, New Jersey

L. Ron Hubbard dropped out of college, wrote science fiction stories, got kicked out of the navy, joined a black magic cult, moved to New Jersey, wrote a book called *Dianetics*, then started a religion called Scientology. Its basic premise is that seventy-five million years ago, some tyrannical overlord named Xenu was concerned about an overpopulated planet that resembled 1950s America so he froze a bunch of people and sent them to Earth, which was a prison planet at the time. Despite sounding like the creation of some hack science fiction writer, lots of people joined this religion. When the government wanted Hubbard to pay taxes, he named himself commander of some fake navy and sailed the Mediterranean for several years. Hubbard, the tax-dodger, died before paying but his legacy lives on... in the form of a kooky, brainwashing, tax-avoiding religion.

2. SYNGMAN RHEE AND KIM IL-SUNG
1950 - Pusan, South Korea

While the Cold War was so called because the Soviets and Americans never officially declared war against each other, there was still plenty of bloodshed. They did their battling through other countries such as Korea. North Korea, under Supreme Leader Kim Il-sung, sided with the Soviets and Chinese. South Korea and its president, Syngman Rhee, opposed Communism and sided with America. Pretty much the only thing either leader seemed to be good at was antagonizing the other. Syngman Rhee slaughtered more than 100,000 North-leaning countrymen in a few weeks. Meanwhile, Kim il-sung, ignored the advice of Stalin and Mao and attacked the South in 1950. Battles were fought, hundreds of thousands of soldiers and more than a million civilians were killed, and, three years later, the two sides agreed to stop fighting and return to the way things were. Nothing was accomplished.

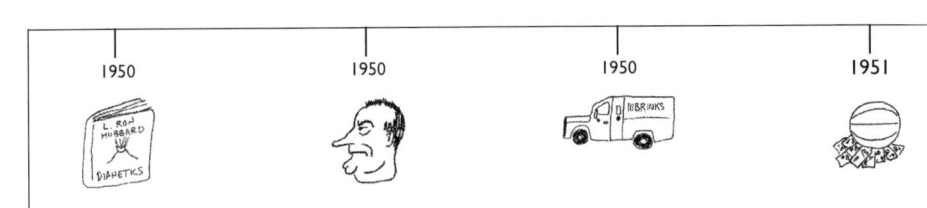

1. HEINRICH MÜCKTER
1954 - Aachen, Germany

In 1954, Chemie Grünenthal, a small German pharmaceutical company, started selling thalidomide, a sleep aid for pregnant women that could be "given with complete safety to pregnant women and nursing mothers without any adverse effect on mother and child." But Chemie Grünenthal's chief scientist and head of research, thirty-two-year-old Heinrich Mückter, knew that claim was a fallacy. The former Nazi Auschwitz "doctor" (who had tested vaccines and diseases by injecting concentration camp prisoners) just wanted to make his money before the jig was up. So he buried information about birth defects and kept selling. By the time thalidomide was pulled off the shelves in 1961, tens of thousands of babies around the world had been born with various ailments and missing limbs.

1953　1953　1953　1954

1954

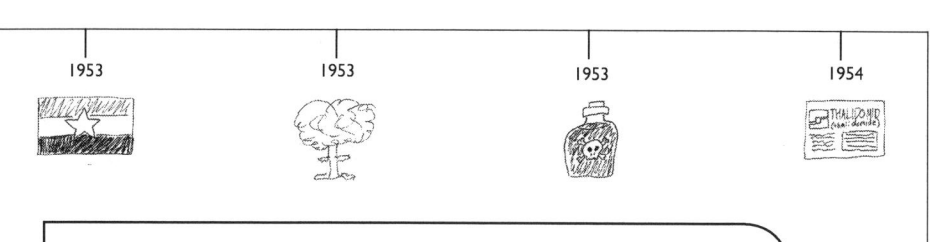

Dishonorable Mentions: Douglas MacArthur - 1950 (hawkishness helped cause Korean War), Oscar Collazo and Grisello Torrescola - 1950 (attempted assassins)

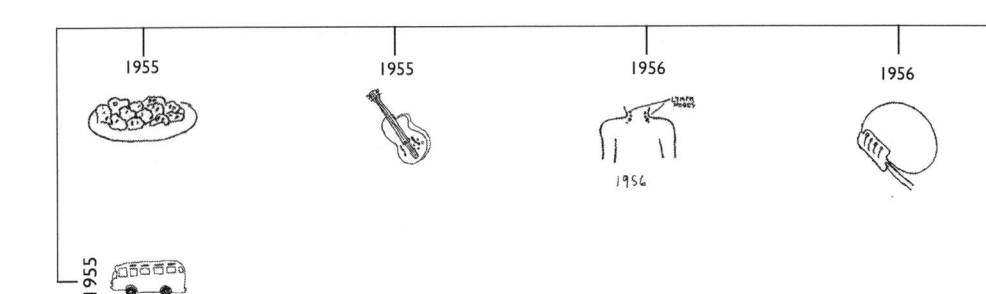

1955-1959

"No, the only tired I was, was tired of giving in."
-Rosa Parks

BEST

10. PENG CHANG-KUEI
1955 - Taipei, Taiwan

Tired of making the same old banquet food over and over again, chef Peng Chang-kuei decided to expand his menu. He named one of his new dishes (a breaded and stir-fried chicken in sweet and sour sauce) General Tso Chicken, after a famous general from Peng's native Hunan Province who quashed the Taipei Rebellion and never lost a battle. By the early 1970s, tensions between Taiwan and China had become bad enough that Peng moved to New York City and opened up a restaurant near the U.N. Within a couple years, the Hunanese general was conquering hearts and waistlines across America.

9. ELVIS PRESLEY
1956 - Memphis, Tennessee

Nineteen-year-old Elvis Presley wanted to make a record for his mom so he went into Sun Studios and paid the $4 fee. His song was unremarkable but Sam Phillips, the owner of the studio, saw the pompadoured kid's potential. So he called in some professional musicians and gave Elvis some better songs to sing. Within two years, the "white man with the Negro sound" was shaking his hips on national television and turning the younger generation, for the first time ever, into powerful consumers. In his career, Elvis had 114 top-forty hits, 40 top-ten, and 18 number-one hits. Elvis was so big that, after he was spotted getting the polio vaccine at a press conference, teenager immunization numbers exploded. Poor management and excess everything derailed his career but, without question, Elvis was the single biggest music star of all time. While many credit his success to "cultural appropriation," the reality was that his success opened the door for underappreciated black artists like Little Richard, Muddy Waters, James Brown, and Fats Domino and set the table for future stars like the Beatles, Michael Jackson, and Madonna.

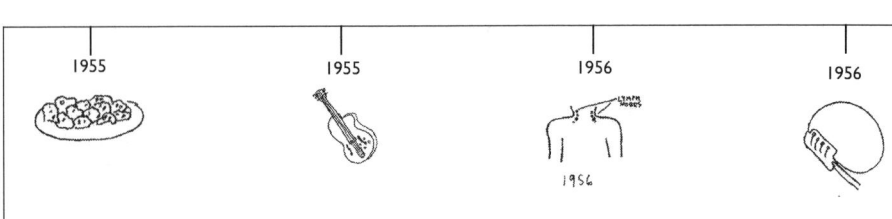

8. JAMES B. DONOVAN
1957 - Brooklyn, New York

Like John Adams, James Donovan was put in the unenviable position of having to defend an enemy during tense times. In 1957, the United States arrested Soviet spy Rudolf Abel and Donovan, an insurance lawyer, was chosen to defend him. After a pretty cut-and-dry trial, Donovan was successful in arguing that executing Abel was a bad idea. A few years later, his sentencing argument proved prophetic. When an American spy plane pilot was shot down over the USSR, JFK called upon Donovan to execute a swap. From that point forward, Donovan got the reputation as a deal maker. Over the course of his career, he negotiated the release of more than nine thousand prisoners. Basically the insurance lawyer version of James Bond.

7. MARY LEAKEY
1959 - Olduvai Gorge, Tanzania

One day while her husband Louis was sick with the flu, British paleontologist Mary Leakey went on one of her daily digs at Olduvai Gorge, a steep ravine in what is now Tanzania. She found an ape-like skull with large teeth and a small brain (*Zinjanthropus boisei*). Louis got most of the credit and went on a fundraising tour to support further digging efforts. Meanwhile, Mary stayed at the site and kept digging. The following year she found another skull and bones but, this time, it had a larger brain and more human features. The 1.4 million-year-old *Homo habilis* (or "handy man") was the breakthrough they were looking for—it used tools, had modern foot arches, and walked in a more upright position. Mary Leakey helped the world understand evolution.

6. FRANK LLOYD WRIGHT
1959 - New York, New York

Frank Lloyd Wright grew up exploring the green landscape of Wisconsin and became determined to bring some of its beauty to the medium of architecture. After getting his start working

| 1956 | 1956 | 1957 | 1959 |

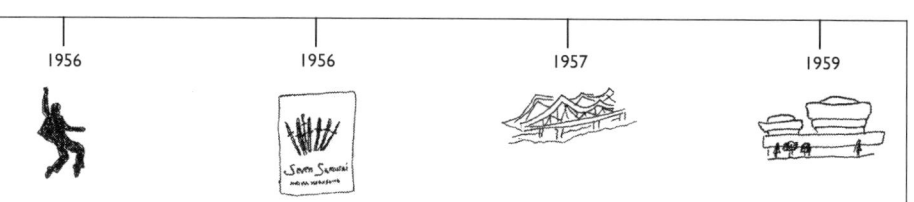

for Louis Sullivan ("father of skyscrapers"), Wright branched off on his own, gaining recognition for his simple yet perfect Prairie Houses. For the next six decades, Wright designed hundreds of iconic buildings, stuck to his "form follows function" ideals and established himself as the premier architect in American history. Over the final sixteen years of his life, Wright designed the building for which he's most famous in the most chaotic, noisiest, most un-Frank Lloyd Wright-like city of them all—New York. Six months after Wright's death, the doors were opened to the Guggenheim Museum, his spiraling concrete masterpiece.

5. AKIRA KUROSAWA
1956 - Tokyo, Japan

During the post-World War II American occupation years in Japan, director Akira Kurosawa exposed himself to everything Western popular culture had to offer, from Shakespeare to American pulp novels. When he re-emerged onto the film scene, he set off on an unparalleled run of movies that still very much resonate with today's audiences. Kurosawa's Japanese-Western hybrid filmmaking, which produced classics like *Rashomon*, *The Seven Samurai*, *The Hidden Fortress*, and *Yojimbo*, won him many awards and inspired just about every subsequent filmmaker of note (Scorsese, Woody Allen, Coppola, George Lucas, and Tarantino, to name a few). Akira Kurosawa was the first great modern film director.

4. CHUCK BERRY
1955 - St. Louis, Missouri

On New Year's Eve 1952, Chuck Berry, the troubled-kid-turned-beautician, was asked to fill in for a sick member of his buddy's band. Berry's high-energy, up-tempo style was a big hit. Within a couple years, the great Muddy Waters introduced him to mega-producer Leonard Chess. Shortly thereafter, he was kicking out some of the most famous and influential songs in rock and roll history: "Maybellene," "School Days," "Rock and Roll Music," "Johnny B. Goode," "Memphis, Tennessee," "Roll Over, Beethoven," and "Brown-Eyed Handsome Man." In 1959, he was charged with violating the controversial Mann Act (a.k.a. the "White Slave Traffic Act") and was sentenced to twenty months in the clink. By the time he was out, the British invasion (who were massively influenced by Berry) had transformed the music industry and relegated Chuck to elder statesman territory. Chuck Berry was as important to rock and roll as the Wright brothers were to flight.

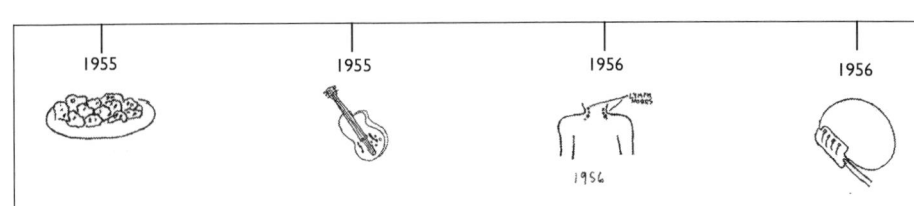

3. WILSON GREATBATCH
1956 - Buffalo, New York

Medical researcher Wilson Greatbatch was trying to build a device to record heart sounds but accidentally utilized a wrong part which caused the contraption to give off a pulse of its own. Inspired, Greatbatch shifted focus to the possibility of creating an electric heartbeat. So he made the device smaller and created the world's first fully functional implantable pacemaker (there was already a Swedish version that lasted a couple days and a Uruguayan version that lasted a few months). Today, more than three million people rely on Greatbatch's monumental invention. After that, he devoted his efforts to improving the batteries of pacemakers, contributing to environmental causes, and AIDS research.

2. MILDRED VERA PETERS
1956 - Toronto, Canada

Before Dr. Vera Peters, when someone was diagnosed with Hodgkin's Disease, doctors cut out the affected area and told them to enjoy what little time they had left. Then, in 1947, Peters' mentor Dr. Gordon Richards asked her to study the effects of radiology on patients suffering from the disease. A few years later, she concluded that high doses could, in fact, stop its progression. For the next six years, Peters produced more research and beat the drum about her findings. Today the cure rate is around 90 percent. Later in her career, Peters shifted her focus to breast cancer. She worked with affected patients and championed alternative treatments to mastectomies (like lumpectomies and

| 1956 | 1956 | 1957 | 1959 |

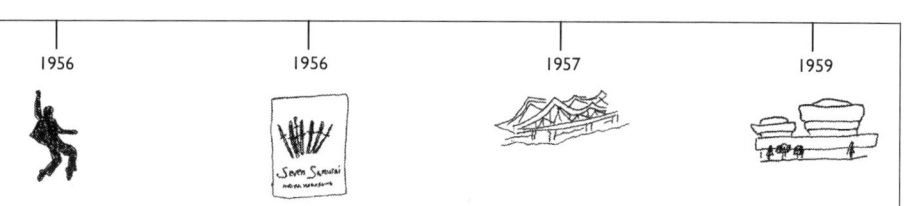

radiation treatment). In 1975, she was named Officer of the Order of Canada.

1. CLAUDETTE COLVIN AND ROSA PARKS
1955 - Montgomery, Alabama

Pregnant, black fifteen-year-old Claudette Colvin was told to move to the back of the bus. She refused and was arrested. While the NAACP admired her stance, they knew that if they publicized it, their message would get dismissed by many as just some pregnant teenager from a low-income neighborhood causing trouble. In stepped Rosa Parks, a forty-two-year-old seamstress and upstanding member of the black community. Nine months after Colvin's stand, Parks did the exact same thing. Right away, the NAACP organized a mass boycott of the Montgomery buses. For the next 381 days, forty thousand black citizens in Montgomery carpooled and walked long distances but never took the bus. By December of 1956, thanks to court sanctions and the crippling economic impact of the boycott, the racist policy was changed.

Honorable Mentions: Pelé - 1958 (King of Futbol), Don Rickles - 1959 (Mr. Warmth), Sydney Lumet - 1957 (*Twelve Angry Men*), Red Foxx - 1956 (comic), Fats Domino - 1955 (rock and roll), Pete Seeger - 1955 (folk singer), Heile Selassie - 1955 (equal rights in Ethiopia), Wilma Rudolph - 1956 (track and field), Robert Adler - 1955 (wireless TV remote), Jorn Utzon - 1957 (Sydney Opera House), Bill Richards - 1958 (skateboard), Dalai Lama - 1959 (spiritual leader), Ella Fitzgerald - 1955 (singer), Phyllis Diller - 1955 (comic), Nils Bohlin - 1959 (three-point seatbelt), George De Mestral - 1955 (Velcro), Momofoku Andu - 1958 (ramen), Mamie Till - 1955 (civil rights hero), Little Richard - 1955 (rock and roll)

WORST

10. GEORGE METESKY
1957 - New York, New York

Between 1940 and 1957, disgruntled ex-Con Edison employee George Metesky bombed thirty-three different locations throughout New York City (among them theaters, train stations, and libraries) with the message, "Con Edison crooks, this is for you!" The NYPD was stumped. Then they turned to private psychologist James Brussel for help. Pretty quickly, Brussel came up with a fairly accurate profile of the Mad Bomber of New York: an unmarried, clean-shaven, middle-aged man of Eastern European descent who lives with female relatives and wears double-breasted suits. Con Ed checked their records and came up with Metesky. Dr. Brussel's successful profiling efforts gave birth to a completely new way of crime fighting and inspired the CBS network with over twenty years' worth of ideas for new series.

9. ART CLOKEY
1959 - Los Angeles, California

In 1959, the Lutheran Church approached Art Clokey, the creator of the trippy stop-motion animated show *Gumby*, about making a show with religious messages. So, in 1959, Clokey created *Davey and Goliath*, a heavy-handed bummer of a show about a boy and his crummy dog. While the show may have had its heart in the right place, the end result was dreadful. Every episode was the same: Davey would try to have fun and his sad-sack dog would remind him that the big guy upstairs wouldn't approve of the activity. Everything from alone time with his dad to playing with a toy robot became some sort of moral quandary. Seventy-two doleful episodes were jammed into Saturday mornings before God, mercifully, pulled the plug.

8. JOACHIM KROLL
1955 - Ludighausen, Germany

Joachim Kroll had no friends, an awful family life, no money, and an ugly face. Even when he picked up hookers, he was unable to perform. Then, while working as a farm hand, he found his purpose in life: killing. From the moment he was put on slaughterhouse duty, he felt sexually aroused. By 1955, he escalated his killing to humans. He'd kill, have sex with, and then eat his victims. Finally, in 1976, Kroll's neighbors complained that the drainage pipe for the building was blocked. The cops came and found it was a missing four-year-old girl. The Duisberg Cannibal spent the rest of his miserable life in jail.

7. ED GEIN
1957 - Plainfield, Wisconsin

People in real life inspire movie characters all the time. Ed Gein inspired three. Unfortunately for him (and his victims), those characters were Norman Bates from *Psycho*, Leatherface from *Texas Chainsaw Massacre*, and Buffalo Bill from *Silence of the Lambs*. Gein was a deranged Wisconsin farm boy obsessed with his dead mother. When a local store owner went missing, police checked with the town creep (Gein) and found a house of horrors: the store owner hanging upside down from a hook, chairs upholstered with human skin, organs in his fridge, heads on bed posts, a heart on the stove, lips hanging from a window shade, soup bowls made from human heads, and nine human faces turned into masks. Gein spent the rest of his life in mental hospitals.

6. AYN RAND
1957 - New York, New York

In 1957, *Atlas Shrugged*, a 1,000-page screed about a bunch of industrialists creating a utopia, brought Ayn Rand a cult-like following from a group of people called "the Collective." For the rest of her life, Rand did her best to dump on anyone who wasn't a selfish asshole. If a person wasn't a titan of industry, they must be a bloodsucking leech. Worrying about others' feelings was a weakness. Native Americans were being wiped off the map because they never became capitalists. She trashed homosexuality as "disgusting." She belittled medical opinions that weren't convenient for her. She regularly bragged that "no one helped me." That would be true... if you conveniently forget those times when she was taken in by charitable relatives upon leaving Russia, watched tons of free movies at her uncle's theater, got a script reading job from Cecil B. DeMille despite not having any qualifications, was treated by scores of doctors and nurses when she got lung cancer, and had her assistant collect her Social Security and Medicare payments which Ayn received under the name of Ann O'Connor. Then, yes, you could say "no one" helped her.

5. ORVAL FAUBUS
1957 - Little Rock, Arkansas

Three years after *Brown v. Board of Education*, "the Little Rock Nine" were set to enter Little Rock High School. So Arkansas Governor Orval Faubus called in the Arkansas National Guard and told them to block its entrance. Eisenhower called Faubus and ordered him to have the National Guard protect the black students' safety instead. Faubus hung up, then defied the president by telling the guards to not bother showing up. Predictably, the students faced angry, brick-throwing hayseeds and the school had to be evacuated. Again, Eisenhower had to step in—he sent paratroopers to establish order and protect "the Little Rock Nine" for the rest of the school year. By 1965, black people were able to vote and Faubus was on a career path towards managing an amusement park called Dogpatch U.S.A. Even cleaning vomit off the tilt-o-whirl was too good a job for that turd.

4. FIDEL CASTRO
1959 - Havana, Cuba

In his forty-nine years running Cuba, Fidel Castro dramatically improved the island's education and healthcare systems, put people to work, and helped fight against apartheid in South Africa. Also over that half century in charge, he was the target of more than six hundred assassination attempts. And for good reason—despite some positive accomplishments, the man was awful. Once the dust settled from the revolution (in which he and Che Guevara toppled brutal dictator Fulgencio Batista), Castro become just another oppressive dictator. His firing squads murdered tens of thousands of political opponents. Journalists and human rights defenders were routinely jailed. Homosexuals were rounded up and thrown into prison work camps. Over the years, hundreds of thousands of Cubans escaped to Florida looking for a better life. Sure, they had great healthcare and full literacy, but at what cost? Fidel Castro did win one human rights award, however: the Muammar Qaddafi Human Rights Prize in 1998.

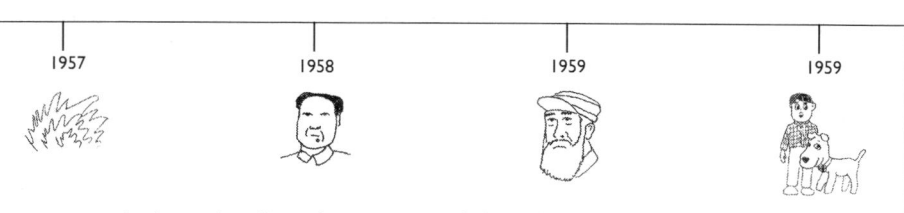

3. CAROLYN BRYANT, ROY BRYANT, AND J.W. MILAM
1955 - Money, Mississippi

While visiting relatives in Mississippi, black fourteen-year-old Emmett Till went into a general store for some bubble gum. The woman behind the counter, Carolyn Bryant, went home and told her husband and brother-in-law that Emmett had grabbed her hand and whistled at her. So, two nights later, Roy Bryant and J.W. Milam kidnapped Emmett from his uncle's house, beat, tortured, and shot him, then threw him in the Tallahatchie River. The body was recovered and Bryant and Milam were tried in front of a jury of their peers (i.e., racist white guys). Predictably, they were found not guilty, but Till's open-casket funeral back home in Chicago reminded the country that it had miles to go for racial equality. More than fifty years later, Bryant's wife admitted she'd made the whole thing up.

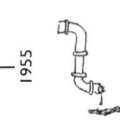

2. FRANCOIS "PAPA DOC" DUVALIER
1957 - Port-au-Prince, Haiti

For fourteen years, black nationalist Francois "Papa Doc" Duvalier ruled the destitute island of Haiti into the ground. He proclaimed himself president for life, had voodoo priests declare him an "immaterial being," and had the Lord's Prayer ("Our Father") rewritten in Haiti as, "Our Doc, who art in the National Palace, hallowed be thy name…" If people didn't go along with his plans, Duvalier sent his secret police, the Tontons Macoutes (Creole for "boogeymen"), to murder them. He killed over thirty thousand during his reign. Despite an influx of money from the United States ("thank you for not being Communist" money), Papa Doc found ways to spend it on himself while strengthening Haiti's status as the poorest nation in the Western hemisphere. He was succeeded in 1971 by his son Baby Doc, who left his own mark with a decade and a half of political repression, human trafficking, and turmoil.

1. MAO ZEDONG
1958 - Beijing, China

In an attempt to catch up to (and surpass) the Western world, in 1958, Mao Zedong announced the "Great Leap Forward." Overnight, a country of 700 million people—mostly farmers — was told that everyone needed to share just about everything. Mao's plan was to consolidate an eighty-year industrial revolution into just fifteen. Many were told to stop farming and instead make steel in their backyards, while the remaining farmers would have to increase production for the good of society. The steel-makers didn't know what they were doing and used up all of China's coal supply, which meant the trains couldn't run. Also, thanks to fewer farmers and meager harvests due to floods and droughts, there wasn't nearly enough food. To make matters worse, Mao tried to keep up appearances on the international stage by exporting a huge chunk of China's crop production. People starved. Food hoarders were tortured and murdered. Some even turned to

1957	1958	1959	1959

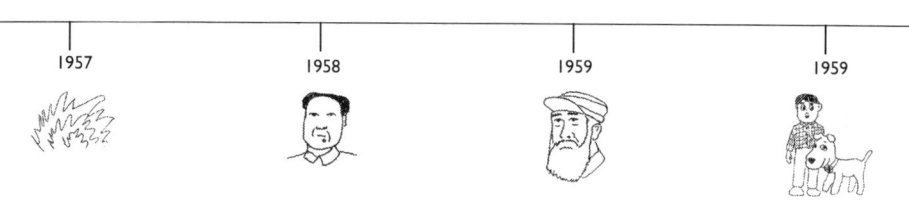

cannibalism. Scholars estimate Mao's grand plan to have cost anywhere from 36 to 45 million lives. More like, the "Great Leap Off the Cliff."

1955

Dishonorable Mentions: Kenneth Adams - 1956 (Nat King Cole assaulter), Richard Peterson - 1959 ("The Day the Music Died" pilot), Ross Bagdasarian - 1958 ("The Chipmunk Song"), Charles Starkweather - 1957 (teenaged serial killer), Dick Whittinghill - 1957 (prudish DJ), Albert Freidman - 1957 (game show fixer), Jimmy Hoffa - 1956 (mobbed-up Teamsters leader), Reg Smythe - 1957 (*Andy Capp*)

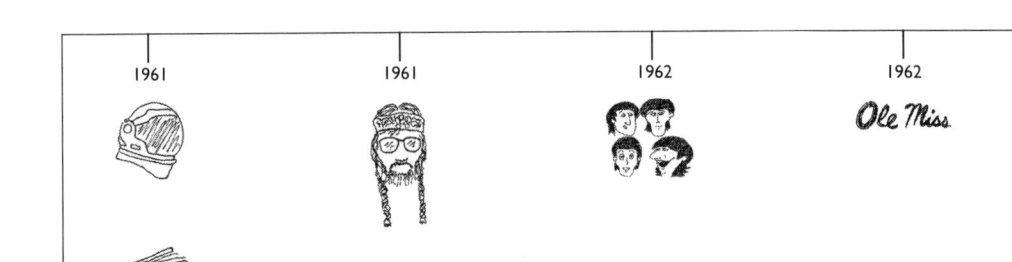

1960-1964

"The time is always right to do what is right."
-Martin Luther King

BEST

10. MERV GRIFFIN
1964 - New York, New York

In the late 1950s, three trivia game shows got caught rigging the outcomes so their more intriguing contestants would win. Feeling betrayed, America turned its back on the genre and took to Westerns. But Merv Griffin, the singer, actor, and talk show host, believed there was still some value in the trivia game show. In order to revive it, though, there had to be a twist. If nobody wanted to hear questions, what if... they heard the answers first and had to come up with the questions themselves? From the moment it aired in 1964, *Jeopardy* was a hit. Over the past half-century, it has faced many competitors (including Merv's own glorified hangman show, *Wheel of Fortune*), but Jeopardy is still the king.

9. TERESSA BELLISSIMO
1964 - Buffalo, New York

Late one Friday night in 1964, Catholic patrons were gutting out yet another self-imposed no-meat Friday at Teressa Bellissimo's Anchor Bar in Buffalo, New York. So bartender Dom Bellissimo asked his mom to whip something up for them when the clock struck midnight. However, earlier that day, the food delivery truck had screwed up their order and given them chicken wings by mistake. So the crafty Teressa cut each wing in half to produce a "drumstick" and a "flat," and threw them in the deep-fryer. When cooked, she doused them with hot sauce and served them with blue cheese and celery. Within a decade, Buffalo wings were a staple in bars across America.

8. JOHNNY CARSON
1962 - New York, New York

In 1962, NBC tapped Nebraska native Johnny Carson to replace Jack Paar on *The Tonight Show*. Every weeknight for the next thirty years, America tuned in to watch the coolest guy in the room rub elbows with Hollywood royalty and make viewers laugh. Whether it was turning around a monologue joke that bombed or letting Don Rickles go off on a tangent, Carson was the master of maximizing the laughs out of every situation. Because of that, he was a kingmaker when it came to comedy. For just about every comedian of note in that three-decade span (Joan Rivers, David Letterman, Jerry Seinfeld, Garry Shandling, Robin Williams, Roseanne Barr, Jim Carrey, Ellen DeGeneres), Johnny's approval was the launchpad to stardom.

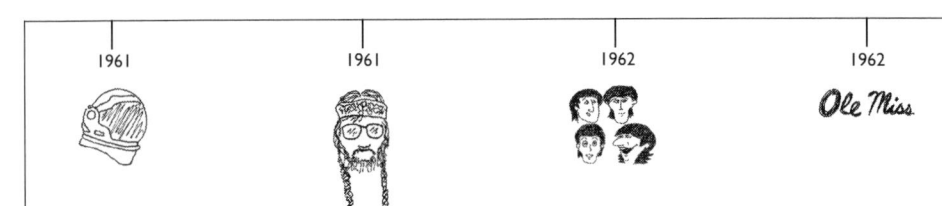

7. WILLIE NELSON
1961 - Nashville, Tennessee

Willie Nelson, a clean-cut, door-to-door encyclopedia salesman-turned-songwriter from Texas convinced the owner of Tootsie's Orchid Lounge in Nashville to put a couple of his forty-five records in her jukebox. After a night of boozing with Patsy Cline's husband, Charlie Dick, Willie played one of the records for him. Charlie loved the song "Crazy" so much that the two drove back to his house, woke up Patsy, and played it for her. Within a week, the star singer recorded it. Two months after that, "Crazy" became one of the biggest country/pop crossover hits of all time. Although he only got $25 for his work on the song, it launched Willie's prolific, beloved, charitable, half-century career.

6. ED ROBERTS
1962 - Berkley, California

Just two years before Jonas Salk's vaccine was available, fourteen-year-old Ed Roberts contracted polio and was paralyzed from the neck down. While most believed his wheelchair and iron lung-bound existence meant the negation of any chance at a fulfilling life, Ed spent every day shattering perceptions. What started as a personal fight to get a high school diploma and then admission at Cal-Berkeley soon turned into leading the independent living movement for people with disabilities everywhere. By arguing for amenities as simple as wheelchair ramps, Ed Roberts helped reshape the lives of millions over the years. His wheelchair is now on display at the Smithsonian.

| 1962 | 1962 | 1963 | 1964 |

5. YURI GAGARIN, ALAN SHEPARD, AND JOHN GLENN
1961 - Space

The Cold War was essentially a big pissing match. Since the existence of nuclear weapons made outright conflict too costly a proposition, the Soviet Union and United States tried to outdo each other with things like the Space Race. The Soviets struck first in 1957 with the first satellite, Sputnik. In April of 1961, the Soviets again led the way by sending the first man into orbit, Yuri Gagarin. A few weeks later, the United States sent Alan Shepard into space for about fifteen minutes, then John Glenn into orbit three times the following February. In the span of about seventy-five years, humans went from relying on horses for transportation to sending men to outer space!

4. HARPER LEE
1960 - New York, New York

For Christmas in 1956, two friends of Truman Capote (lyricist Michael Martin Brown and his wife Joy) gave Capote's childhood pal Harper Lee money to quit her job at the Eastern Airlines reservations desk so she could write for a year. In that time, Lee put together the manuscript that would become her first (and, kind of, only) novel, *To Kill a Mockingbird*. The book took on a difficult subject matter (Southern racism and integration) and explored it through the simplistic and innocent eyes of a child. *Mockingbird* won the Pulitzer in '61 and is one of the most successful and well-reviewed novels in American history. The following year, it was made into an Academy Award-winning film.

3. JAMES MEREDITH
1962 - Oxford, Mississippi

James Meredith served in the U.S. Air Force for nine years, then attended the all-black Jackson State University. After a couple of years, he applied to transfer to the University of Mississippi. When he was denied entry, Meredith went to the NAACP and fought it in court. Even after he was granted the right to attend in 1962, Governor Ross "I'm a Mississippi segregationist and I am proud of it" Barnett stepped in and blocked Meredith. Thanks to President Kennedy and national guardsmen, Meredith got his degree from Ole Miss and embarked on a life courageously fighting for civil rights.

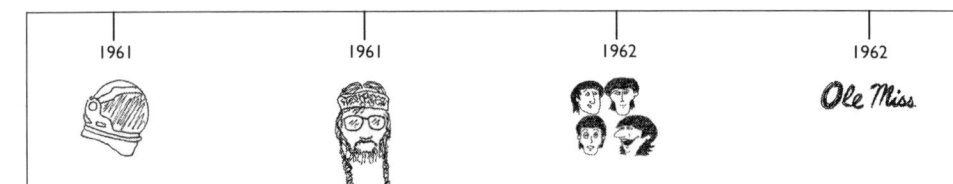

2. JOHN LENNON, PAUL MCCARTNEY, GEORGE HARRISON, AND RINGO STARR
1962 - Liverpool, England

In 1960, a Chuck Berry/Buddy Holly cover band was discovered by record store manager Brian Epstein. He helped the Beatles develop their style, hooked them up with real producer (George Martin), and had them switch drummers. By 1962, Lennon, McCartney, Harrison, and Starr were kicking out number-one hits. After seventy million Americans tuned in to watch them perform on *The Ed Sullivan Show* in 1964, the band changed just about everything in music and culture. Instead of ordinary pre-programmed record label performers, the Beatles did things their own way: they wrote their own songs, they chose their own style, they grew long hair, they protested segregation and war. They ushered in a new era of consciousness. Suddenly it was cool to care about humanity and the planet. By the time they split up in 1969, they were the gold standard by which all future musical groups would be judged.

1. MARTIN LUTHER KING
1963 - Washington, D.C.

On an 83°F day, more than 250,000 people marched on Washington to remind the nation that America was founded on the principle that "all men are created equal." The guy behind that march (and, seemingly, every major significant civil rights event of the era) was Martin Luther King. Starting in the mid-fifties, the twenty-six-year-old Gandhi-inspired King organized major nonviolent protests (like the Montgomery Bus Boycott) across the South.

| 1962 | 1962 | 1963 | 1964 |

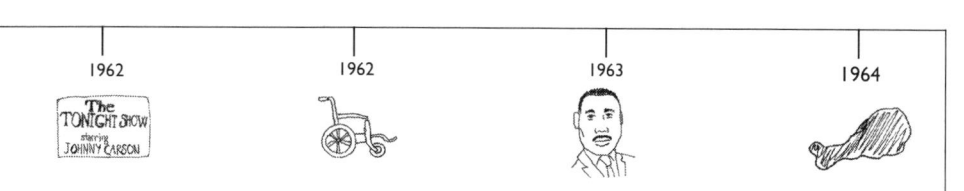

But, in 1963, after having firehoses and dogs turned on them during a demonstration in Birmingham, King brought the fight to the nation's capital. He protested with the help of countless volunteers and major celebrities (Harry Belafonte, Sydney Poitier, Paul Newman, Marlon Brando, Sam Cooke, Bob Dylan, and Joan Baez). All eyes were on King as he delivered the single greatest oration in history. His sixteen-minute "I have a dream" speech was the hammer the movement needed. Within a year, sweeping changes came in the form of the Civil Rights Act of 1964.

1964

Honorable Mentions: Estelle Griswold - 1963 (Planned Parenthood), Sam Cooke - 1964 (civil rights, soul legend), Ken Kesey - 1962 (*One Flew Over the Cuckoo's Nest*), Betty Friedan - 1963 (The Feminine Mystique), Dick Gregory - 1963 (comic, civil rights), Diana Vreeland - 1963 (fashion columnist), Michael Apted - 1964 (documentarian, *Up* series), Medger Evers - 1963 (civil rights), Walter Cronkite - 1963 (anchorman)

WORST

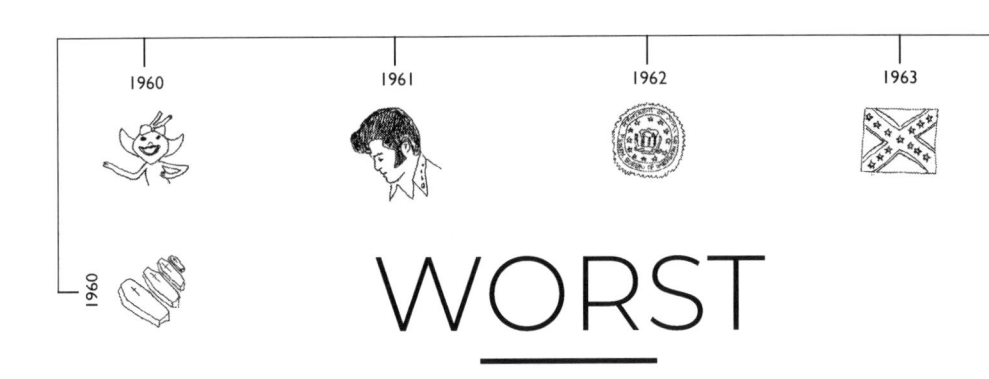

10. RICHARD KUH
1964 - New York, New York

Lenny Bruce's act doesn't hold up so well. He'd take the stage, do some wordplay, drop a bunch of f-bombs and sexual innuendo, and call it a night. Nonetheless, by challenging the prudish status quo of the times, Bruce ruffled quite a few feathers, including those of Manhattan prosecutor Richard Kuh. Instead of treating Bruce's law-breaking like the thousands of cases of jaywalking that go unchecked every day, joy-killer Kuh went out of his way to prosecute Bruce and even managed to have him sent to Rikers Island for four months. Four months for salty language! The Lenny Bruce obsession was a black mark on the quality career (pro-gay rights, anti-harsh drug laws) of an otherwise good man.

9. COLONEL TOM PARKER
1961 - Memphis, Tennessee

In 1929, a witness saw a man he believed to be Andreas van Kuijk at a murder scene in Breda, the Netherlands. That same night, van Kujik left the country and never returned. He resurfaced in the U.S. Army, stole the name of a guy in the registration office (Tom Parker), and was soon discharged for being a psychopath. He managed small country music acts throughout the South then, in the mid-fifties, a gift fell into the huckster's lap: Elvis Presley. Parker quickly signed the rising star to an egregious contract (50 percent management fees instead of the standard 10 percent), turned down all overseas appearances for "the King" (maybe because of that murder?), and pushed Presley into crappy-yet-profitable musicals that drove the once-promising star's career

| 1963 | 1963 | 1963 | 1964 |

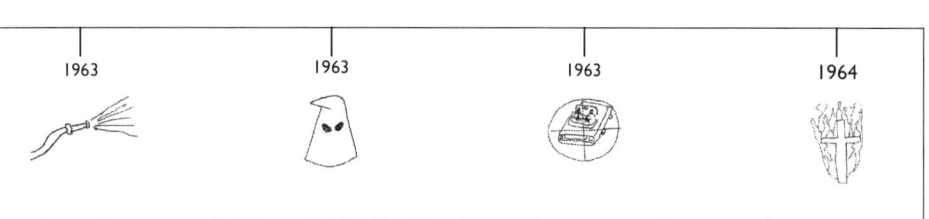

into the ground. When Elvis died in 1977 his net worth was only $10 million, despite generating more than a billion dollars over the span of his career. Parker had been ripping him off for years.

1964

8. HAROLD VON BRAUNHUT
1960 - Bryans Road, Maryland

In the early 1960s, Harold von Braunhut invented Sea Monkeys (and a bunch of other back-of-the-comic-book scam products like X-Ray Spex and Invisible Goldfish). Then he took the money he gained from ripping off kids and funded Nazis. Yup, Mr. Sea Monkey was a white supremacist. Every year, he could be found burning crosses at the Aryan World Congress in Hayden Lake, Idaho. He collected Nazi memorabilia, believed that Hitler just suffered from "bad press," bought guns for the KKK in Ohio, contributed to the legal defense of the leader of the Aryan Nation, and even published a hate-spewing newsletter under the name Hendrik von Braun. The only thing with less character than those sad translucent shrimp brine they call Sea Monkeys was Harold von Braunhut.

7. LEE HARVEY OSWALD
1963 - Dallas, Texas

Lee Harvey Oswald was always kind of a mess. After his mom abandoned him, he got really into the works of Karl Marx. At seventeen, he joined the Marines and showed promise as a sharp-shooter yet was court-martialed twice for breaking rules. In 1959, he went AWOL and tried to become a Soviet citizen. When they turned him down, he tried to kill himself. Then he went to Cuba to pledge allegiance to Castro but was rejected again. Finally, in November of 1963, the sharp-shooter took his rifle to a book warehouse and shot JFK through the window while he was driving through Dallas, sending the nation into a tailspin and whipping tinfoil-hat conspiracists into a frenzy.

6. BYRON DE LA BECKWITH
1963 - Jackson, Mississippi

Much like Medgar Evers, Byron De La Beckwith fought for the United States in World War II. But when they returned, their lives went in different directions. Edgars took advantage of his G.I. Bill, graduated from college, and became a civil rights hero. De La Beckwith, on the other hand, joined the KKK and felt threatened by Evers' successes. So, like the coward he was, De La Beckwith hid across the street from Evers' house and shot the activist in the back as he got out of his car one evening. Despite overwhelming evidence, it took three trials to finally convict De La Beckwith in 1994. In 2001, the eighty-year-old pile of excrement died in a prison hospital.

5. EDGAR RAY KILLEN, SAM BOWERS, LAWRENCE RAINEY, CECIL PRICE, WAYNE ROBERTS, JIMMY SNOWDEN, BILLEY WAYNE POSEY, HORACE BARNETT, JIMMY ARLEDGE, AND JUDGE WILLIAM COX
1964 - Philadelphia, Mississippi

In 1964, three civil rights workers were pulled over by Neshoba County Deputy Sheriff Cecil Price, arrested on cooked-up charges, subjected to seven hours in jail, denied a phone call, released on bail later that night, and escorted to the edge of town. They were never heard from again. The reason for that disappearance was that civil rights workers were a thorn in the side of the Mississippi KKK. And, while the three activists were in jail that night, preacher (and klansman) Edgar Ray Killen organized a plan to murder them. RFK-led FBI agents eventually found the tortured and murdered bodies in a swamp. An all-white jury and racist judge gave out light sentences to only seven of the twenty Klansmen who were involved in the "Mississippi Burning" murders. Until 2005, that is—

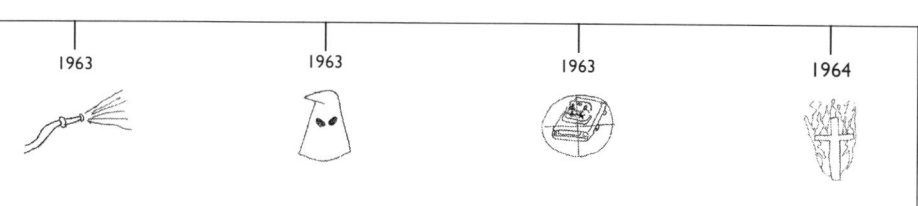

when new evidence nailed eighty-year-old Killen for the crimes. He was sentenced to sixty years in the pokey.

4. EUGENE "BULL" CONNOR
1963 - Birmingham, Alabama

Every American civil rights history montage features images of firehoses and dogs turned on black people. That was the work of Birmingham's commissioner of public safety, Bull Connor. For years, Connor famously looked the other way as the Klan attacked black churches, houses, and schools. But in 1963, when Martin Luther King's massive segregation protests across Birmingham were starting to get business owners ready to concede, Connor instructed his officers to go on the offensive with violence and mass arrests. For many Americans, Connor's firehose and dog attacks appearing on the front page of the newspapers were the catalyst for joining the civil rights movement. After being locked up by Connor's men, Martin Luther King wrote his famous "Letter From Birmingham Jail." A few months after that, he was leading the March on Washington.

3. GEORGE WALLACE
1963 - Tuscaloosa, Alabama

Unlike politicians who hid behind the whole "state's rights" argument for implementing institutional racism, Alabama Governor George Wallace put himself front and center while carrying out overtly racist policies. After an ordinary gubernatorial campaign got him nowhere, in 1962, Wallace openly courted segregationist and KKK voters. At his inauguration, he spewed his infamous hateful line, "Segregation now, segregation tomorrow, segregation forever." When courts ruled that black students could attend white schools, it was Governor Wallace who blocked the door. The "head racist in America" tried running for president a few times but the rest of the country never embraced him like his racist Alabaman supporters did. In fact, someone in Maryland shot and paralyzed him in 1972.

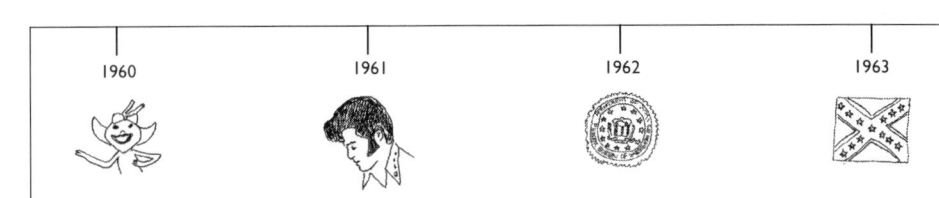

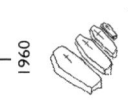

2. J. EDGAR HOOVER
1962 - Washington, D.C.

There's a reason why J. Edgar Hoover kept his job as head of the FBI through ten different presidential administrations—everyone was afraid of him. He spied on and tried to blackmail everyone from Eleanor Roosevelt to JFK to maintain that power. He routinely broke the law to apply pressure on the leaders of any movement he disagreed with (Marcus Garvey, Martin Luther King, and others). He abused his power for personal gain as well, using FBI guys to paint and remodel his house. But his most deplorable moment came in the aftermath of the Selma march in 1965, when Viola Liuzzo was murdered by the KKK. Since someone involved in the killing was an FBI informant, Hoover covered his ass by trashing the legacy of the heroic Liuzzo. The fact that he's now known to have been a closeted gay cross-dresser is a shame; that revelation is the only thing that makes him seem human. J. Edgar Hoover was a monster.

1. D. H. PIENNAR
1960 - Sharpeville, South Africa

In South Africa, if you weren't white, you needed a "passbook" to go anywhere. That way whites could control non-whites' every movement (where they could live, where they could work, and so forth). And people were sick of it. In March of 1961, between five and twenty thousand protesters descended upon the Sharpeville police without their passbooks. On the signal of Colonel D. H. Piennar, three hundred officers opened fire on the crowd. In two minutes, the all-white officers fired more than 1,300 bullets at unarmed, nonviolent black protesters who were running away, killing 69 and wounding another 180. Another 11,000 were arrested in the aftermath. The Sharpeville Massacre was the violent start to a brutal thirty-year struggle to end apartheid in South Africa.

1963   1963   1963   1964

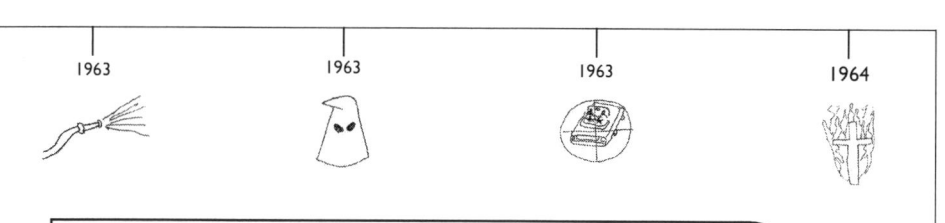

Dishonorable Mentions: Albert DeSalvo - 1962 (Boston Strangler), Barry Goldwater - 1964 (unhinged politician), Ngo Dinh Diem - 1961 - Vietnam (murderous dictator), Joseph Kennedy - 1961 (racist), Sam Panopoulos - 1962 (created Hawaiian pizza), Myra Hindley - 1963 (killer), Dick Rowe - 1962 (turned down the Beatles), Ross Barnett - 1962 (racist)

1964

1965 — UFW

1965 — Boycott Grapes

1965 — Unsafe at Any Speed / Ralph Nader

1965 — Confederacy of Dunces

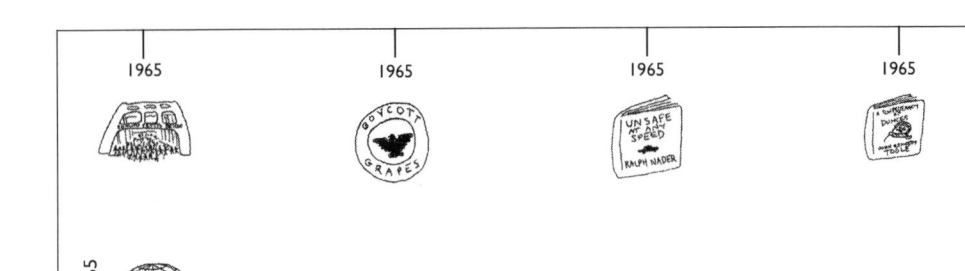

1965 — DARPA

1965-1969

"I am at the moment writing a lengthy indictment against our century. When my brain begins to reel from my literary labors, I make an occasional cheese dip."

-John Kennedy Toole *(A Confederacy of Dunces)*

| 1965 | 1967 | 1969 | 1969 |

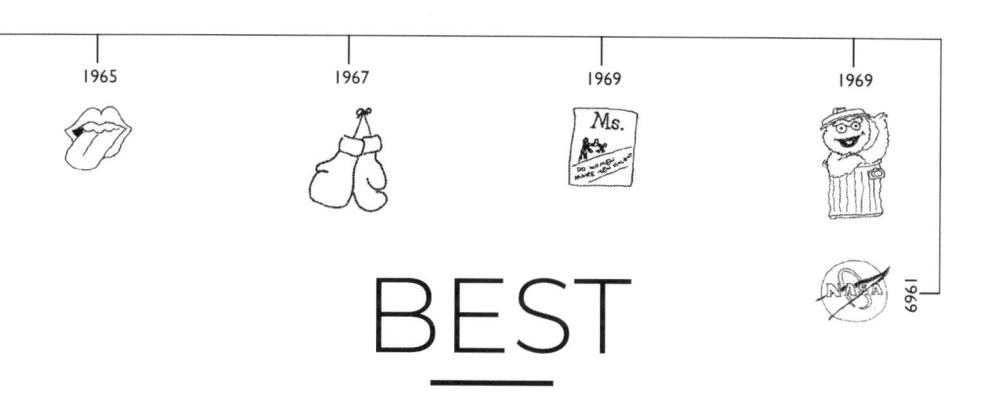

BEST

10. KEITH RICHARDS, MICK JAGGER, BRIAN JONES, BILL WYMAN, AND CHARLIE WATTS
1965 - Hollywood, California

After the Beatles broke the door down in America in 1963, they were soon followed by pretty much anyone with a British accent and a musical instrument. Most were pretty bad, some were great (The Kinks, The Who), and the cream of the crop was the Rolling Stones. The band named after a Muddy Waters song got their start covering black musicians like Howlin' Wolf and Chuck Berry. By the mid-sixties, they were writing their own stuff, like Keith Richards' guitar masterpiece "Satisfaction." Unlike the "peace and love" bands of the era, the Stones were dangerous. They were aggressive. With songs like "Paint It Black," "Sympathy for the Devil," and "Gimme Shelter," Jagger and Richards ushered in an edge to the music scene that would define the ensuing decades. There can only be one "World's Greatest Rock 'n' Roll Band," and they are the Rolling Stones.

9. JOHN KENNEDY TOOLE
1965 - New Orleans, Louisiana

Ken Toole was a brilliant, gifted writer who graduated with honors from Tulane and got a master's from Columbia. In adulthood, he struggled to find inner peace and bounced around jobs. On the side he worked on a novel about an intelligent, misanthropic New Orleans resident named Ignatius J. Reilly, who happened to live at home and couldn't hold a job. Toole finished his novel in 1964 and sent it out to publishers. Despite some initial interest from Simon & Schuster, ultimately, the very personal novel found no suitors. Toole's life began to crumble. He drank heavily, became paranoid, and ultimately took his own life in 1969 at the age of thirty-one. After a couple years of grieving, his mother Thelma took his beloved manuscript to the author Walker Percy, who was teaching at nearby Loyola College. Percy wanted to automatically reject it but read it anyway to be polite. What he discovered was the funniest novel ever written. Percy helped get *A Confederacy of Dunces* published. The following year, it won the Pulitzer Prize and today has sold almost two million copies.

8. KATHERINE JOHNSON, GENE KRANZ, NEIL ARMSTRONG, BUZZ ALDRIN, AND MICHAEL COLLINS
1969 - Langley, Virginia; Houston, Texas; and the Moon

An iPhone today is 120 million times faster than a NASA computer in 1960. So, if America was going to get to the moon (and win the Space Race against the Soviets), it would take a team effort. In Houston, Flight Director Gene Kranz oversaw everyone's jobs on the ground. Katherine Johnson, a brilliant woman from Virginia, crunched key numbers at her desk to keep the mission on track. Armstrong, Aldrin, and Collins piloted Apollo 11. Then, on July 20, 1969, because of all their amazing work, man walked on the moon. Mankind made that giant leap and truly anything seemed possible.

7. MUHAMMAD ALI
1967 - Houston, Texas

Muhammad Ali was rich, famous, and made lots of powerful people lots and lots of money. If the heavyweight champion of the world wanted to use connections to avoid fighting in Vietnam, he could have. But he didn't. In 1967, Ali outright refused to join the military. Fighting in war was against his Muslim beliefs. So, in the words of the great comedian George Carlin: "And the government said, 'Well, if you won't kill people, we won't let you beat 'em up.'" Just like that, Muhammad Ali was barred from the sport and became the most hated man in America. Ali never buckled during his three-year banishment and, over time, people realized he was right. He returned to the ring in 1970 and quickly regained his title and popularity.

6. JOAN GANZ COONEY, LLOYD MORRISETT, AND JIM HENSON
1969 - New York, New York

At a 1966 dinner party, Lloyd Morrisett, the vice president of a philanthropic branch of the Carnegie Corporation, bemoaned that there was a severe preparedness gap between rich and poor children when it came to starting school. There didn't seem to be an alternative to catch up the kids who couldn't afford to attend preschool. Another guest at the party, Joan Ganz Cooney, a public television producer, believed that they should collaborate and find a solution. She consulted with psychologists and educators and brought in puppeteer Jim Henson to create characters for a TV program, while Morrisett arranged for the funding. In November 1969, *Sesame Street* premiered. The show, which taught everything from social interaction to A-B-Cs and 1-2-3s, was an instant success. Within the first year *Sesame Street* was seen by half of the nation's three- to five-year-olds and educators soon noticed a big difference. Three years after that fateful dinner party, Cooney and Morrisett had created the most meaningful television show of all time.

5. RALPH NADER
1965 - Washington, D.C.

A few decades before messing up the 2000 presidential election, Ralph Nader singlehandedly took on the entire American auto industry and won. After a short stint at the Department of Labor, Nader wrote the book *Unsafe at Any Speed: The Designed-In Dangers of the American Automobile*. Right when it hit the shelves, it was a media sensation. Big car manufacturers tried to bribe and harass Nader but the consumer advocate never budged. After a Senate subcommittee hearing, not only were car manufacturers forced to make sweeping changes to auto production but also they were forced to apologize to Nader. David whipped Goliath's ass then made Goliath apologize. Thanks to *Unsafe at Any Speed*, our cars now have mandatory seat belts, air bags, antilock brakes, and other safety features; and, despite more cars on the road each year, highway fatality numbers have steadily declined since the mid-sixties.

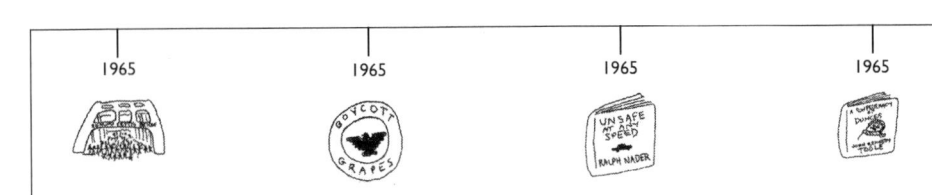

4. GLORIA STEINEM
1969 - New York, New York

Raised by a struggling single mom, Gloria Steinem saw firsthand how much the deck was stacked against women. After nearly two centuries, women in America were still viewed as sex objects, wives, mothers, and little else. Sexual harassment wasn't even an acknowledged thing. After finishing first in her class at Smith College, Steinem became a force in journalism, writing scathing exposés on misogyny and double standards in the workplace. As one of the early columnists at *New York* magazine, Steinem's unflinching takes on abortion and equal rights for women brought her to the forefront of the feminist movement. In 1972, she launched *Ms.* magazine, which focused on important yet underreported topics for women like domestic violence. Every movement needs an unrelenting hero in their corner. For the past half-century in women's rights, it has been Gloria Steinem.

3. CESAR CHAVEZ
1965 - Delano, California

California grape vineyard owners treated their Mexican and Filipino laborers terribly. In 1965, when the Filipino packers finally walked out, the growers turned to the Mexicans to take on their jobs. Even though it would mean more work for his fellow Mexicans, Cesar Chavez knew the only way for conditions and wages to improve was to show solidarity. Inspired by Gandhi and Martin Luther King, Chavez led the merged unions through organized marches, boycotts, and hunger strikes. When growers brought in scabs, Chavez led a three hundred-mile march along Highway 99 to the state capital in Sacramento, attracting national attention and, eventually, improving conditions and wages for his union. Despite being rather ordinary looking and lacking the powerful oratory skills of MLK, Cesar Chavez was a titan for farm workers. His unrelenting dedication to improving conditions in California led to sweeping improvements for farm workers across the nation. His famous black nylon union jacket now hangs in the Smithsonian.

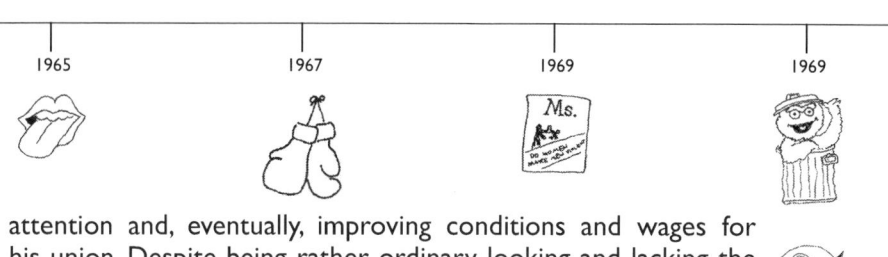

2. JOHN LEWIS, AMELIA BOYNTON, AND HOSEA WILLIAMS
1965 - Selma, Alabama

The Civil Rights Act of 1964 was a great start but, as long as racist politicians with discriminatory agendas were in place, it would be extremely difficult to dramatically improve life for black people. The only way to truly move forward was to vote those monsters out. And even though the Fifteenth Amendment states that race cannot prevent someone from being able to vote, it was nearly impossible for black people in the South to do so. Whether it was misleading polling information, application rejections over technicalities, or literacy tests, black votes were being denied. Ground zero for voter suppression was Selma, Alabama, where the racist governor (George Wallace) and county sheriff (Jim Clark) did everything in their power to stop black voters. After failed attempts to get the possible fifteen thousand black voters registered, local civil rights hero Amelia Boynton, Hosea Williams and the Southern Christian Leadership Council (SCLC), and John Lewis and the Student Nonviolent Coordinating Committee (SNCC) led a march of six hundred protesters from Selma to the state capital in Montgomery. They got as far as the Alabama River before Sheriff Clark and his crew brutally attacked the nonviolent marchers with billy clubs—all while a horrified nation watched on TV. Within a couple weeks, Martin Luther King and 25,000 others joined Lewis, Boynton, and Williams and continued the protest, this time making it all the way to the capital. Less than six months later, President Johnson signed the Voting Rights Act into law.

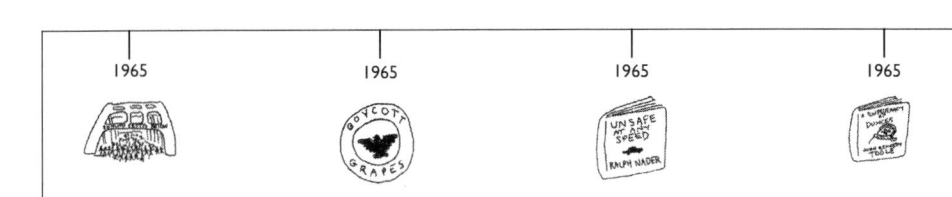

1. J. C. L. LICKLIDER, LAWRENCE ROBERTS, AND LEONARD KLEINROCK
1969 - Washington, D.C.

After the Soviets launched Sputnik in the late 1950s, the United States responded by assembling a bunch of brilliant minds—the Defense Advanced Research Projects Agency (DARPA)—and tasked them with ensuring America would never be at a technological disadvantage to the Soviets again. In the early sixties, DARPA's J. C. L. Licklider wrote memos about a network of computers that could share information. Until that point, computers were just big machines that could do math quickly. In stepped MIT's Larry Roberts and UCLA's Leonard Kleinrock. The men worked with the government and, in 1969, made Licklider's idea become reality. DARPA connected computer systems in four different places (UCLA, Stanford, University of Utah, and UC Santa Barbara) and called it ARPANET, which formed the basis for the internet. There were a lot of world-changing events going on in the late 1960s. A bunch of nerds in a lab created the biggest change of all.

| 1965 | 1967 | 1969 | 1969 | 1969 |

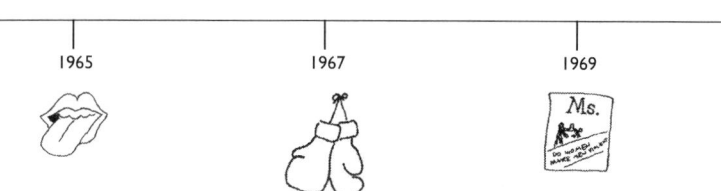

Honorable Mentions: Otis Redding - 1967 (singer-songwriter), Hugh Thompson - 1968 (My Lai massacre hero), Stephanie Kwolek - 1965 (Kevlar), George Romero - 1968 (zombie movies), Jim Brown - 1967 (civil rights, football), John Carlos and Tommy Smith - 1968 (Olympians, activists), Charles Portis - 1968 (*True Grit*), Philip Roth - 1969 (author), Mary Quant - 1968 (fashion: miniskirt, hot pants), Johnny Speight - 1965 (TV writer), Rachel Carson - 1969 (*Silent Spring*), Frank Kameny - 1969 (gay rights), James Brown - 1965 (singer), Curt Flood - 1969 (baseball pioneer), Katherine Switzer - 1967 (first woman to run Boston Marathon), Brian Wilson - 1966 (singer-songwriter), Bob Dylan - 1965 (singer-songwriter), Iggy Pop - 1969 (punk), Gene Roddenberry - 1966 (*Star Trek*), Truman Capote - 1966 (author), Katherine Hepburn - 1968 (acting), Max Yasgur - 1969 (Woodstock), John Shepherd-Barron - 1967 (ATM), Dennis Hopper (acting, directing), Texas Western basketball team - 1966 (first all-black NCAA champions), Arthur Penn (*Bonnie and Clyde*), Viola Liuzzo - 1965 (Selma hero), Helen Gurley Brown - 1965 (Cosmo), Malcolm X - 1965 (activist), Spencer Silver, Arthur Fry - 1968 (Post-Its), Jimi Hendrix - 1967 (guitarist), Dick and Tommy Smothers - 1967 (socially conscious variety show hosts), Aretha Franklin - 1967 ("Queen of Soul"), Kareem Abdul-Jabbar - 1969 (basketball, activist)

WORST

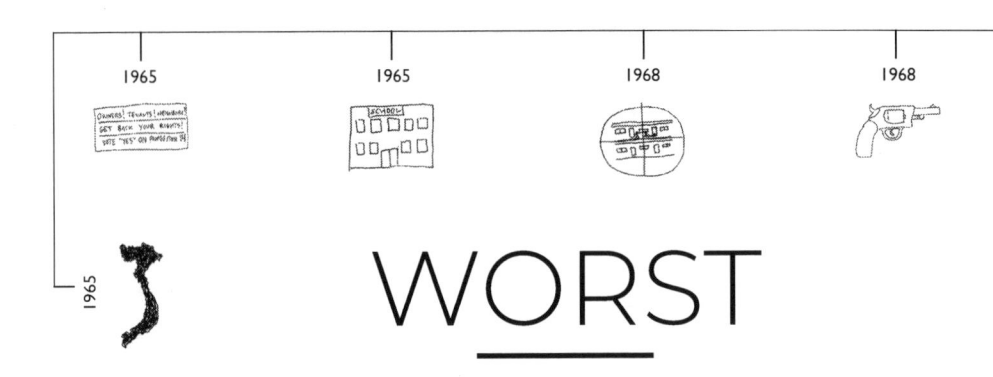

10. HELLS ANGELS
1969 - Livermore, California

The Rolling Stones missed out on Woodstock but wanted to close out their U.S. tour in 1969 with a festival of their own. So they had some organizers quickly set something up in California. A couple other bands (Grateful Dead, Jefferson Airplane) joined the cobbled-together festival at the Altamont racetrack and the Hells Angels were hired to work security. It was apparent from the start: a few dozen members of a motorcycle gang (who had been paid in beer) were going to struggle to contain 300,000 concert-goers. These weren't the friendly Hells Angels from London, either. These were scary motherfuckers itching for a fight. During Jefferson Airplane's set, one of the Hells Angels knocked out one of the lead singers. By the time the Stones took the stage, tensions were high and security was drunk. As Jagger and Richards performed, the Angels stabbed and killed someone in the crowd, marking a sad end to the "peace and love" decade.

9. EDWARD KENNEDY
1969 - Chappaquiddick Island, Massachusetts

Despite getting kicked out of Harvard for cheating, several driving arrests, and a drunken incident on a flight from Alaska, it was still assumed Ted Kennedy would ride a wave of sympathy for his assassinated brothers and become the president in 1972. The plan got derailed after a day of drinking in the summer of '69. The married father of three was kind enough to offer his twenty-eight-year-old staffer Mary Jo Kopechne a ride "back home" (even though her purse and room key were left back at the party). After a wrong turn on the road to a secluded beach, Teddy drove his car right into Poucha Pond. Ten hours after the crash, a sober and freshly showered Ted Kennedy decided to report the accident and mention that Mary Jo was still trapped in the car. He was charged for leaving the scene of an accident but, since he was a Kennedy in Massachusetts, was only given a slap on the wrist. The presidential dream might've died that night, but chin up, Ted! You got away with killing a woman!

8. WILLIAM CALLEY
1968 - My Lai, Vietnam

A little more than a century after saying, "war is hell," then promptly burning Atlanta to the ground, William Tecumseh Sherman's famous phrase rang true in Vietnam. Four years into America's soulless slog of fighting a winless war, the Charlie Company of the Eleventh Infantry Brigade was on an aggressive search-and-destroy mission (Task Force Barker) to a small town allegedly teeming with Viet Cong (VC). When the Lieutenant William Calley-led troops got to My Lai, there was nobody but ordinary civilians ranging from one to eighty-two years old. Despite encountering no violent hostility, Calley gave the order to rape, torture, and slaughter the civilians. Luckily, Army helicopter pilot Hugh Thompson stumbled upon the massacre while on a reconnaissance mission and stopped further bloodshed. The Army tried to cover it up, but eventually the story leaked and Calley went to jail. In 1974, Nixon pardoned him.

7. CHARLES MANSON
1969 - Los Angeles, California

Abandoned by his prostitute mother at an early age, Charles Manson turned to a life of crime. After spending half of his first thirty-two years in the hoosegow, Manson read the book How to Win Friends and Influence People and felt inspired to become famous. He moved to California, became friends with some of the Beach Boys, sold drugs, and tried to make it in the music business. After failing to land a record deal, he pivoted towards a career as an evil cult leader. Manson proclaimed himself Jesus and ordered his followers to commit a series of murders in the world that had rejected him—Hollywood. By the time police finally locked him away, Manson's cult was responsible for thirty-five killings, including, the famed pregnant actress, Sharon Tate.

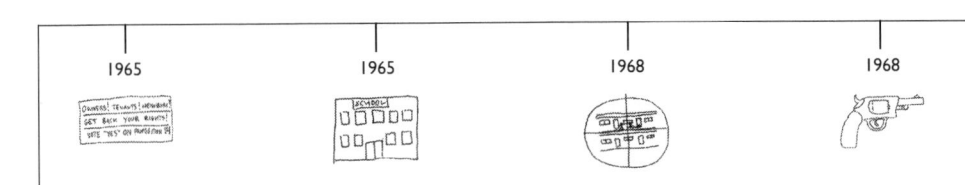

6. BRUTALIST ARCHITECTS
1965-1969 - Everywhere

Swiss-born architect Le Corbusier kicked off the twentieth-century building trend of function over style. Some architects from that school of thought, like Frank Lloyd Wright and Walter Gropius, still made some impressive-looking buildings. But, as the 1950s shifted into the 1960s, that Brutalist style grew out of control. Hideous concrete abominations started popping up everywhere—public housing, libraries, courthouses, multipurpose stadiums, and schools. Seemingly everyone has attended classes in one of those rectangular blocks of sadness. Not every building has to be the Taj Mahal but, for the love of God, does it have to look like it was designed in a 1981 video game?

5. JOHN BIRCH SOCIETY
1965 - Los Angeles, California

On a hot summer day in the Watts section of Los Angeles, two white cops pulled over a black driver, an argument ensued, and a few people were hauled off to jail. This prompted a four-day riot that left thirty-four dead, more than 1,000 injured, 4,000 arrested, and more than $50 million worth of property damage. Why were people so pissed off? Because the system was rigged against them. After the Civil Rights Act of 1964, conservative groups like the John Birch Society and the California Republican Assembly (led by prominent guys like Ronald Reagan) pushed for things like Proposition 14, which gave property owners the ability to discriminate when renting or selling. This was yet another way to keep things segregated. For the people confined to the Watts area, joblessness was soaring, housing conditions were terrible, and the schools sucked. Unrest was bound to happen. Institutional racism caused the Watts riots, just like it did in Newark and Detroit in 1967 and Chicago in 1968.

| 1968 | 1969 | 1969 | 1969 |

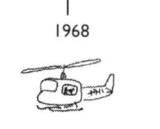

4. SIRHAN SIRHAN
1968 - Los Angeles, California

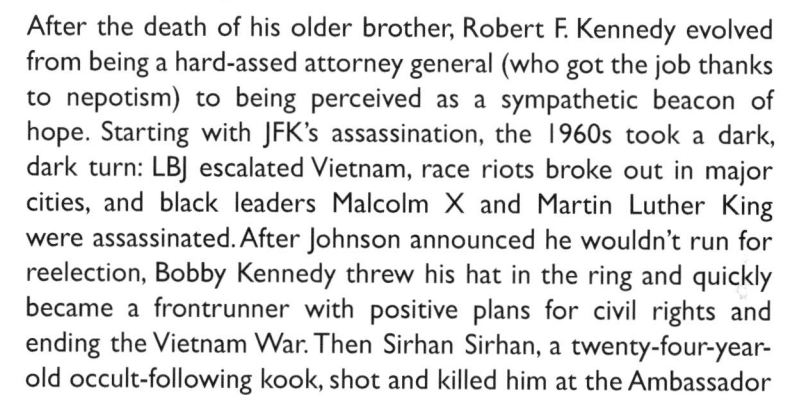

After the death of his older brother, Robert F. Kennedy evolved from being a hard-assed attorney general (who got the job thanks to nepotism) to being perceived as a sympathetic beacon of hope. Starting with JFK's assassination, the 1960s took a dark, dark turn: LBJ escalated Vietnam, race riots broke out in major cities, and black leaders Malcolm X and Martin Luther King were assassinated. After Johnson announced he wouldn't run for reelection, Bobby Kennedy threw his hat in the ring and quickly became a frontrunner with positive plans for civil rights and ending the Vietnam War. Then Sirhan Sirhan, a twenty-four-year-old occult-following kook, shot and killed him at the Ambassador Hotel in Los Angeles. America went on to elect Dick Nixon and was subjected to his trash presidency.

3. LYNDON B. JOHNSON
1965 - Washington, D.C.

There are three things to know about the Vietnam War: one, it inspired some good music; two, it was never actually a war (a "declaration of war" never happened); and three, LBJ really messed up. What started as a "let's keep our eye on the Communists" presence in the region quickly escalated when the big ol' tough-talkin' Texan Lyndon Baines Johnson took over. He wanted to squash the Commies from the North but needed a way to escalate the conflict without the public calling for his head. In an effort to not seem like a pussy, LBJ sent a fleet deep into North Vietnamese territory (the Gulf of Tonkin) kind of looking for a fight. When the *U.S.S. Maddox* was attacked, LBJ got a blank check to send in however many troops he needed. So he threw money and humans and more money at the problem, and it kept getting worse. The Vietnam War ended with 58,000 Americans and millions of Vietnamese soldiers and civilians dead and absolutely nothing accomplished. As soon as troops pulled out, the whole place became Communist anyway. Death upon death upon death, all because LBJ didn't want to be "the first American President to lose a war." Well, you certainly did, Lyndon.

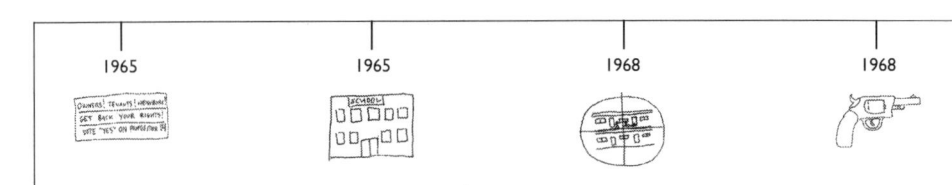

2. RICHARD M. NIXON
1969 - Washington, D.C.

While opening up trade with China and starting the EPA should be lauded, Richard Nixon's presidency was most certainly dogshit. Sure, LBJ made the situation in Vietnam worse by sending troops in 1965, it was Nixon who sent it spiraling out of control. Nixon and National Security Advisor Henry Kissinger's grand plan was sending hundreds of thousands of B-52 bombing missions over Laos, Cambodia, and Vietnam. America dropped more bombs on tiny Laos than it had on Japan and Germany combined during World War II, killing thousands of innocent people and paving the way for monsters like Pol Pot to take over and murder millions more. Nixon was also responsible for giving tons of weapons to the Shah of Iran (which is still biting us in the ass) and for helping fascist Pinochet overthrow the democratically elected government in Chile. In June of 1972, despite a commission led by a Republican senator deeming that marijuana should be decriminalized, Nixon pushed for harsher penalties, kick-starting "the War on Drugs." Decades later, drug use is no lower than in 1971 but prison populations have exploded. The United States has 5 percent of the world's people and 25 percent of its prisoners. Black men in America are incarcerated at a rate four times the rate of black men in South Africa under apartheid. These racist consequences shouldn't be surprising to anyone. One of Nixon's closest aids at the time, John Ehrlichman, told author Dan Baum marginalizing black people was the intention all along. Nixon sucked. His legacy is trash. And let's not forget that whole Watergate thing.

1. JAMES EARL RAY
1968 - Memphis, Tennessee

Martin Luther King was committed to nonviolence. Even when the situation begged for it, he would never throw a punch. He

| 1968 | 1969 | 1969 | 1969 |

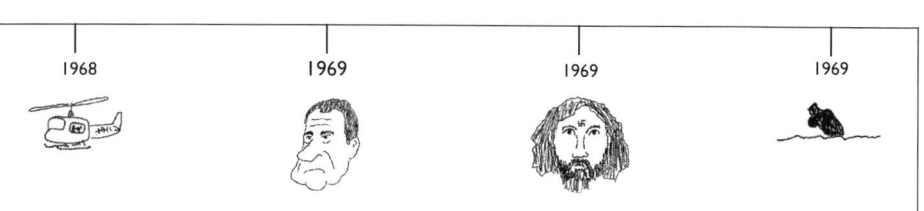

didn't let his entourage carry weapons, either. His motto was, "If someone wants to kill me, there's nothing I can do about it." And by sticking to those principles, he was able to change America in more positive ways than just about anyone in history. James Earl Ray, on the other hand, was just a racist asshole with a gun.

Dishonorable Mentions: Neil Diamond - 1969 ("Sweet Caroline"), Charles Joseph Whitman - 1966 (University of Texas shooter), Fred Hartley - 1969 (Union Oil spill), Donald Elbert - 1965 (AstroTurf), Thomas Hagan - 1965 (assassinated Malcolm X), Fred West - 1967 (serial killer), Leonid Brezhnev - 1968 (crushed "Prague Spring"), Jim Delligatti - 1967 (the Big Mac)

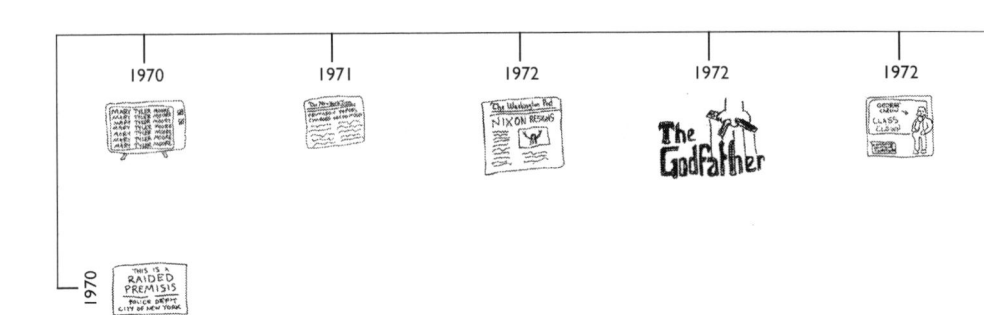

1970-1974

"The very existence of flame-throwers proves that some time, somewhere, someone said to themselves, 'You know, I want to set those people over there on fire, but I'm just not close enough to get the job done.'"

-George Carlin

BEST

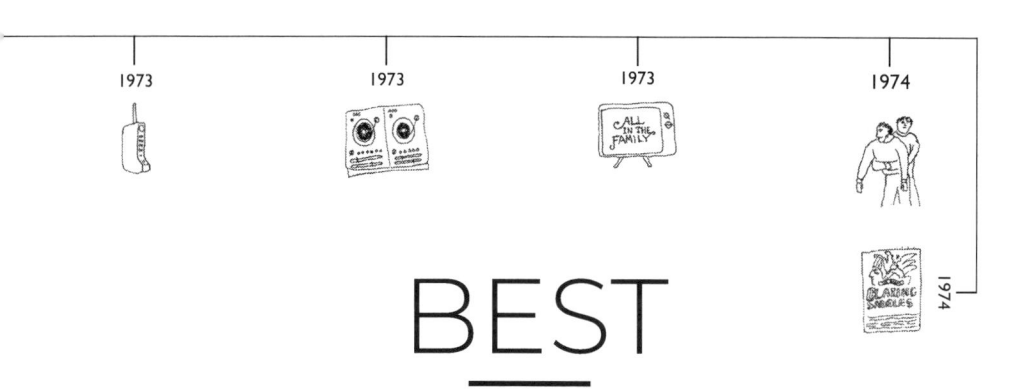

10. (TIE) MEL BROOKS
1974 - Hollywood, California

Melvin Kaminsky always had a huge set of balls. Whether it was bravely fighting in World War II's Battle of the Bulge or squeezing laughs out of history's greatest monster (Hitler), the man now known as Mel Brooks never backed down. After returning from war, he got into comedy and eventually landed in the greatest writer's room in comedy history at Sid Caesar's *Your Show of Shows*. Brooks then branched out with a hit comedy album with his friend Carl Reiner (*The 2,000-Year-Old Man*) and a sitcom (*Get Smart*) before making a movie that took the piss out of Nazis (*The Producers*). Despite good reviews, *The Producers* was a flop. So, with his Hollywood career in the balance, Brooks responded by going right back to touchy subjects and created the race-baiting 1974 classic *Blazing Saddles*. That same year, he also created the great *Young Frankenstein*. For decades, Brooks churned out comedy hits and later created his own production company to support other unconventional artists and projects (like *Elephant Man* and *The Fly*). Not that he needs awards to cement his legendary status, but there's a reason he's one of very few people in history to win the EGOT (Emmy, Grammy, Oscar, Tony).

10. (TIE) GEORGE CARLIN
1972 - Santa Monica, California

Even as a clean-cut, safe-topic comic, Carlin was brilliant. But, as society changed in the late sixties, so did Carlin. He grew his hair long and turned his focus to some not so safe subjects, such as religion and government. Carlin reached his apex in 1972 with "Seven Dirty Words," a routine that pointed out how the world is full of violence and suffering, and yet seven magical words (out of the 400,000 in the English language) are just too much for people to handle on television. Carlin never backed down from a chance to shine a light on life's hypocrisies, no matter how touchy the subject. Lenny Bruce may have loosened the puritanical vulgarity laws, but it was George Carlin who stretched the canvas for future comics to work with.

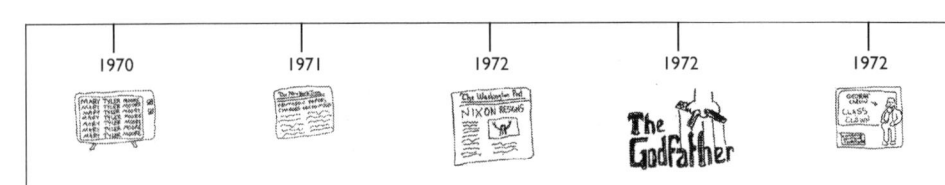

9. SYLVIA RIVERA AND MARSHA P. JOHNSON
1970 - New York, New York

In 1969, the NYPD raided the Stonewall Inn, a gay club in New York's Greenwich Village, for nonsensical violations. The incident, which involved three drag queens and a lesbian getting thrown in jail, set off a series of riots in the gay community. Led by two transgender women of color, Sylvia Rivera and Marsha P. Johnson, the Stonewall Riots marked the start of the LGBT movement. Unfortunately, as the gay rights movement went a bit more mainstream, the transgender community was somewhat marginalized. So, in 1970, Sylvia and Marsha established STAR (Street Transvestite Action Revolutionaries) and a shelter for homeless transgender youth. While STAR only lasted a few years, the foundation was laid for the LGBT movement in the decades to come.

8. FRANCIS FORD COPPOLA
1972 - Hollywood, California

When he was ten, Francis Ford Coppola contracted polio and was paralyzed on his left side. For the next nine months, the bedridden boy was forced to entertain himself, usually with puppet shows. He then took that love of entertaining to film school and worked as an assistant to B-movie king Roger Corman. After he won an Oscar for writing the movie Patton, Coppola was asked to direct the film adaptation of Mario Puzo's bestselling novel, *The Godfather*. Right away, studio executives were up Coppola's ass about his decision to cast the unknown Al Pacino instead of the dreamy Ryan O'Neill. But Coppola held firm to his choice and eventually was allowed to finish. The end result? Two of the finest movies ever made (*The Godfather* and *The Godfather: Part II*). Coppola also went on to make classics *The Conversation* and *Apocalypse Now* as well as mentor two up-and-comers in Hollywood: Steven

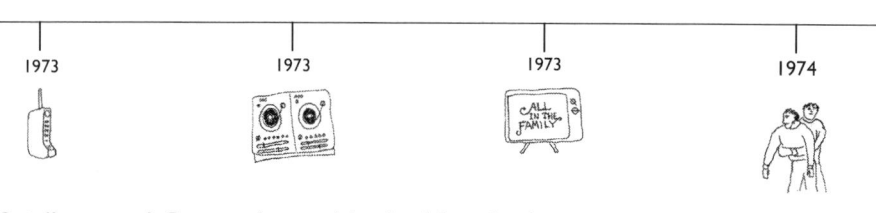

Spielberg and George Lucas. Not bad for the former assistant to the guy who directed *Bloody Mama* and *Teenage Cave Man*.

7. NORMAN LEAR
1972 - Los Angeles, California

Before Norman Lear, comedy on television ignored real life. You turned on the TV, and, to quote Lear himself, "...if the roast was ruined and the boss was coming to dinner, that was one of the biggest problems in the history of human families." In 1971, Norman Lear defied the wholesome model with All in the Family, a show he adapted from the British sitcom *Till Death Do Us Part*. By addressing race, sexuality, and integration, *All in the Family* was the first American sitcom to resemble real life. Lear followed that up with shows about people rarely featured on television: middle-aged women (*Maude*), poor black people (*Sanford and Son*, *Good Times*), rich black people (*The Jeffersons*), and single moms (*One Day at a Time*). By the mid-seventies, Lear produced six of the top ten shows on television. When he left TV in 1981 to get into political activism (and fight Bible-thumping pricks like Jerry Falwell), television viewers not only embraced shows that dealt with difficult, authentic subject matter; they expected them.

6. CLIVE "DJ KOOL HERC" CAMPBELL
1973 - Bronx, New York

Cindy Campbell wanted to throw a back-to-school party. So she reserved the rec room of her apartment building in the Bronx, handed out some flyers, and got her brother Clive (aka "DJ Kool Herc") to agree to play music. Clive noticed how people seemed to go crazy on the dance floor for the parts of songs that included a unique drumbeat—the break. So he set up two turntables and switched back and forth between them to extend those breaks, calling it "the merry-go-round." People went nuts. Herc's buddy, Coke La Rock, shouted out people's names during the breaks and, just like that, hip hop was born.

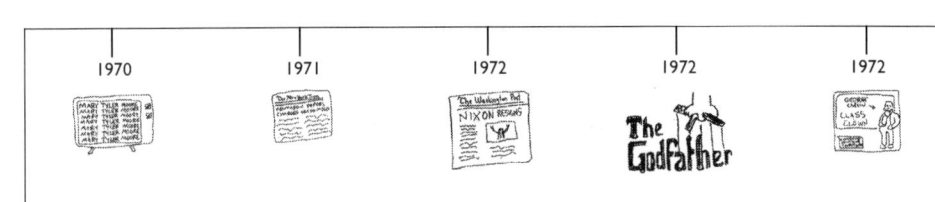

5. MARTIN COOPER
1973 - New York, New York

Before AT&T announced they were going to create phones that could be used in cars, the only way to talk on a phone was to use a rented, connected line from Ma Bell. But Marty Cooper, a researcher for Motorola, thought that idea still seemed too limiting. Why confine it to a car? For the next three months, he and his team worked on a prototype that Cooper demonstrated by walking out on the street in New York City and calling his rival at AT&T. How do you like them apples, Ma Bell? The first cell phone hit the market eleven years later. Motorola's DynaTAC 8000X (aka "the Brick") weighed two pounds, cost four grand, and was about as comfortable to use as holding a dictionary up to your head. But they worked out the kinks and now there are more cell phones on Earth than people.

4. MARY TYLER MOORE
1970 - Hollywood, California

In theory, lots of people understood that women didn't belong only in the kitchen... they just struggled to envision women in different roles. Then *The Mary Tyler Moore Show* premiered and changed everything. Mary Tyler Moore played Mary Richards, a working woman in her thirties, single, and not looking for a man to make her life complete. As producer of the show, Moore ensured that women were involved behind the scenes as well in front of the camera. She employed dozens of female writers who examined real issues that women could relate to (like the pill), not just stories about a woman landing a man. Mary's independence, wit, and spunk won the show multiple Emmys and millions of viewers every week for seven seasons. *The Mary Tyler Moore Show* was one of the best champions the women's rights movement ever had.

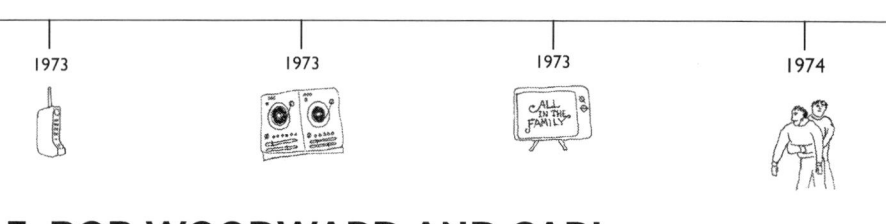

3. BOB WOODWARD AND CARL BERNSTEIN
1972 - Washington, D.C.

Democracy doesn't really work if the people don't have all the facts. In 1972, the highest office in America tried outright to suppress facts, but two young reporters at *The Washington Post* wouldn't let it happen. What started with a break-in at the Democratic National Committee headquarters ended with the president of the United States resigning in shame two years later. Bob Woodward and Carl Bernstein set the standard for investigative journalism in the early '70s by relentlessly pursuing the truth. They followed every lead, uncovered (but protected) informants, followed the flow of money, and learned that President Nixon was a paranoid lunatic who used a slush fund to commit crimes and attack perceived enemies. Eventually their mountain of evidence got the rest of the government involved, and Tricky Dick was forced to quit.

2. HENRY HEIMLICH
1974 - Cincinnati, Ohio

Doctor Henry Heimlich thought the widely-accepted whack-on-the-back method to help people choking on food was garbage. Often, it just knocked the food further down the windpipe and made the choking worse. So he developed a technique of pressing up on the diaphragm. He approached *Chicago Daily News*' medical writer, Arthur Snider, to have him publicize it in his syndicated column. A week later, someone used the technique on a choking diner in a restaurant and word quickly spread. Within two months, the American Medical Association dubbed it "the Heimlich Maneuver." Over the years, Heimlich's discovery has been credited for saving more than a hundred thousand lives, including high profile people like Carrie Fisher, Walter Matthau, Jack Lemmon, and Liz Taylor.

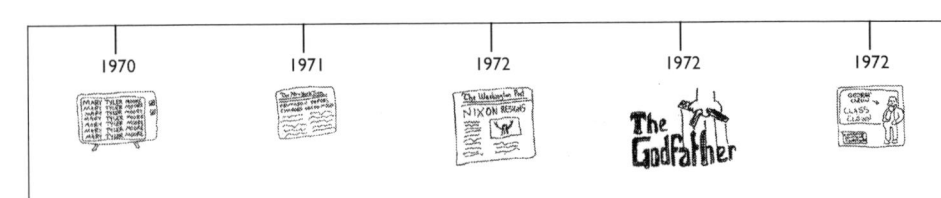

1. DANIEL ELLSBERG
1971 - Washington, D.C.

In 1967, military analyst Daniel Ellsberg worked on an extensive study on the United States' involvement in the Vietnam War (nicknamed "the Pentagon Papers"). Ultimately, the 3,000-page report indicated that Presidents Truman, Eisenhower, Kennedy, and Johnson had misled the public about what exactly America was doing in Vietnam and how it was escalating a pointless war. Despite those findings, in the years following the report's completion, Ellsberg saw the Nixon administration continue to escalate the Vietnam situation. So he photocopied the entire thing and gave it to a reporter at *The New York Times*. The government filed an injunction and did everything possible to discredit Ellsberg, but his goal was accomplished. After Ellsberg's leak, public support of the indefensible war completely eroded. The United States had lost its way during the Vietnam War. Daniel Ellsberg's Pentagon Papers leak helped us find it.

1973　　　　　1973　　　　　1973　　　　　1974

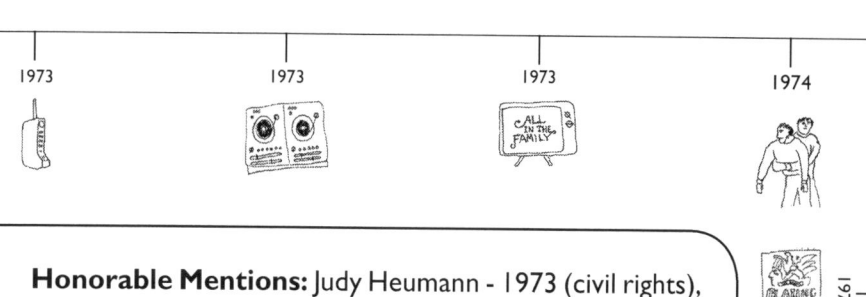

1974

Honorable Mentions: Judy Heumann - 1973 (civil rights), Hank Aaron - 1974 (baseball), Norman Borlaug - 1970 (Green Revolution), Jocelyn Bell Burnell - 1974 (physics), Fazlur Rahman Khan - 1973 (structural engineering), Richard Oakes - 1972 (Native American activist), Michael O'Donohue - 1973 (*National Lampoon*), Hunter S. Thompson - 1971 (journalist), Carol Burnett - 1972 (comedy), Billie Jean King - 1973 (tennis), Elton John - 1972 (singer-songwriter), Ray Tomlinson - 1971 (email), Bruce Lee - 1972 (*Enter the Dragon*), David S. Ward, George Roy Hill - 1971 (The Sting), Mark Spitz - 1972 (swimming), Mark Felt - 1972 ("Deep Throat"), Bill Walton - 1973 (basketball), Arthur Ashe - 1973 (tennis, activism), Marvin Gaye - 1971 (singer-songwriter), Dan Gable - 1972 (wrestling)

WORST

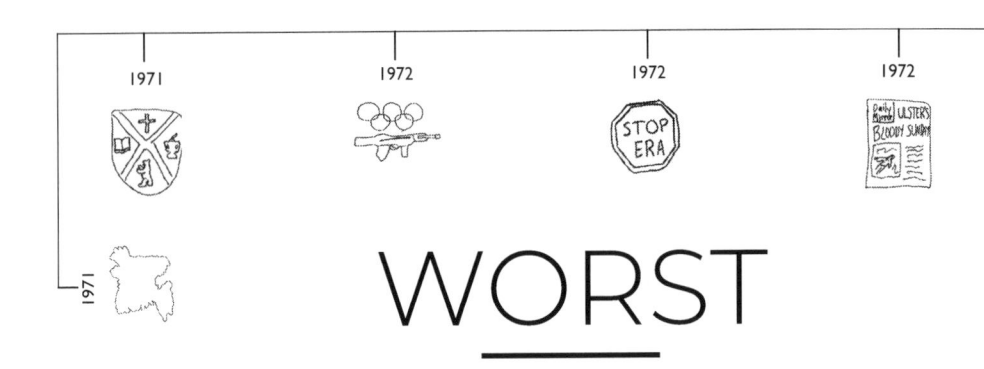

10. HENRY B. WADE
1973 - Dallas, Texas

One could argue that Dallas County prosecutor Henry Wade was just doing his job when he enforced the anti-abortion law against a pregnant carnival worker in the famous *Roe v. Wade* case. One could also argue that Henry Wade couldn't care less about the law. In his thirty-six years on the job, the cigar-chewing Texan known as "the Chief" valued winning cases more than preserving justice. Wade bragged about his over-90 percent conviction rate. His secret? All-white juries. His policy to "…not take Jews, Negroes, Dagos, Mexicans, or a member of any minority race on a jury, no matter how rich or how well educated" got him his coveted convictions although, predictably, many of them were wrongful. Filmmaker Errol Morris easily poked holes in a 1977 Wade murder conviction in his documentary *The Thin Blue Line*, which led to Randall Dale Adams being released from death row. Another nineteen convictions (murder, rape, and burglary) won by Wade and two successors who trained under him have been overturned after DNA evidence exonerated the defendants.

9. DONALD DEFREEZE
1973 - Oakland, California

A bunch of white, middle class left-wing kooks grew up during the sixties, saw youth taking a stand, and wanted to form their own protest group. So they formed the Symbionese Liberation Army (SLA), an organization committed to fighting the United States government and bringing about change. Too bad the Berkeley, California group had no clue what they were doing. First of all, "Symbionese" doesn't mean anything. Second, they weren't liberating anyone. Third, their "army" had like ten people.

When they allowed violent escaped convict Donald De Freeze to take over their group, the SLA went from a rudderless ship to a dangerous rudderless ship. Their first action was murdering Marcus Foster, the first ever black superintendent in Oakland, because he wanted students to have ID cards. A few months later, they became nationally famous for kidnapping nineteen-year-old heiress Patty Hearst and then robbing banks with her as an accomplice. DeFreeze eventually was killed in a shootout and the SLA had still liberated no one.

8. ROBERT FORD
1972 - Londonderry, Northern Ireland

What started as peaceful protests of institutional discrimination against Catholics in Northern Ireland in the late sixties soon devolved into rock-throwing violence throughout the country. On Sunday, January 30, 1972, British World War II hero General Robert Ford planned to shut down a protest in Londonderry with the notoriously super-aggressive paratrooper force, 1 Para. After Ford said, "Go on Paras, go on and get them," the soldiers fired haphazardly into the crowd, killing thirteen and wounding another seventeen. They claimed they were shot at first, but it was determined that none of the dead or wounded protesters had any weapons. If things were bad before, "Bloody Sunday" made them a whole lot worse. The Irish Republican Army (IRA) responded a few months later by setting off twenty bombs, killing civilians and British soldiers. The Troubles would last until a ceasefire in 1998.

7. ILICH RAMÍREZ SÁNCHEZ
1973 - London, England

Ilich Ramírez Sánchez was a rich Venezuelan kid. Naturally, after getting kicked out of school in 1970, he joined the Popular Front for the Liberation of Palestine and became a terrorist. His first assignment was to go to London and murder the Jewish president of a retail chain. For the next quarter-century, "Carlos the Jackal" committed more than eighty murders as a self-proclaimed "professional revolutionary." In reality, he was just a mercenary who worked for such bulwarks of freedom and humanity as

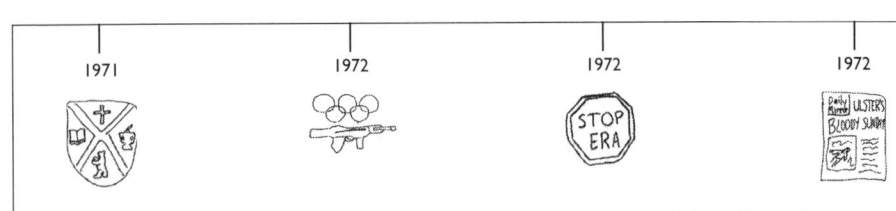

Saddam Hussein and Muammar Qadaffi. In 1994, French agents captured him in Sudan. He now is serving multiple life sentences.

6. PHYLLIS SCHLAFLY
1972 - Alton, Illinois

The strides made by the women's rights movement in the late sixties and early seventies threatened deeply conservative housewife and author Phyllis Schlafly. In her twisted mind, women seeking to do anything but be a wife or mother was a threat to wives and mothers. So when the Equal Rights Amendment (ERA) was proposed (in an attempt to clarify that sexual discrimination is unconstitutional), Schlafly went nuts. She believed this amendment would open the door for gay marriage, unisex bathrooms, a surge in abortions, women in combat, dogs and cats living together, MASS HYSTERIA! The ERA passed easily in both the House and Senate. All that needed to happen was for it to be ratified by at least three quarters of the states within a ten-year stretch. Schlafly spent the next decade smearing the ERA, which fell three states short of its goal. From there, she became a gay and women's rights-bashing writer. Her miserable life fighting progress and joy finally ended in 2016. Good riddance.

5. TED BUNDY
1974 - Seattle, Washington

While it's still unclear when it all started (some think he killed in his paperboy days), by 1974 Ted Bundy had established himself as one of America's worst serial killers. After getting dumped by his college girlfriend, Bundy went on a five-year tear after women who resembled her. He got away with it for so long because he was a clean-cut, good-looking white guy. When word got out a handsome guy named Ted was murdering women in the Pacific Northwest (and having sex with their corpses), he moved to Utah. He was caught the following year but escaped and continued his murderous rampage across the country. Finally, in 1978, Bundy was caught in Florida and properly jailed. He received the death penalty for committing over thirty murders (but possibly more than a hundred).

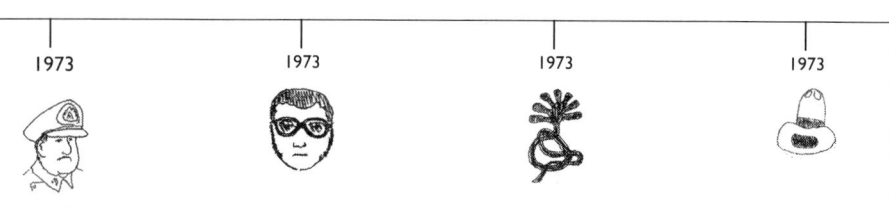

4. BOB JONES III
1971 - Greenville, South Carolina

Founded by Bob "I say the colored people should have been left over in Africa" Jones in 1927, Bob Jones University was a school designed for white people. Their admissions office practiced overt racism for decades, claiming it was their First Amendment right. Then, in 1971, the IRS said that if they wanted to be racists, they'd lose their tax exempt status which is normally given to religious organizations. The school fought the ruling all the way to the Supreme Court. Conservatives like Paul Weyrich used this fight to rally Southerners to start voting for the GOP so they could protect their eroding way of life. On a macro level, it worked. The South has been solidly GOP ever since. On a micro level, it didn't. In 1971, Bob Jones was forced to begrudgingly admit black people to its mediocre university. They even started to allow interracial dating in 2000. What a school!

3. ALI HASSAN SALAMEH
1972 - Munich, Germany

In the late 1950s, Yasser Arafat founded the Fatah, an organization dedicated solely to toppling Israeli control of Palestine through guerrilla warfare. Then, in 1971, a militant subsection of Fatah called Black September formed with the explicit goal of spreading mayhem to other countries. After trying to assassinate King Hussein in Jordan, they moved on to terrorizing various other Western countries (the Netherlands, Belgium, Greece, England, and others). The highest-profile attack of Black September's three-year reign of terror was at the 1972 Munich Olympics. While athletes Mark Spitz and Olga Korbut were kicking ass in competition, Ali Hassan Salameh sent ski mask-wearing Palestinian terrorists to Olympic Village to kidnap, torture, and, eventually, murder Israeli athletes. The incident, which achieved nothing, only led to more bloodshed (like Mossad agents retaliating against Black September)

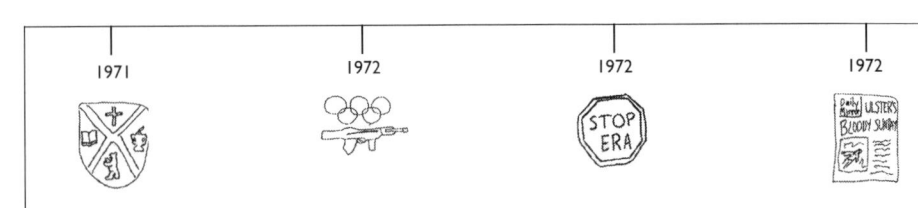

2. AUGUSTO PINOCHET.
1973 - Santiago, Chile

In 1973, Chilean President Salvador Allende promoted Chilean Army leader Augusto Pinochet to be his Commander in Chief. A month later, Pinochet led a coup that overthrew the elected leader. While the United States still maintains they never had anything to do with the military coup, they acknowledge that their objective in Chile at the time "was to discredit Marxist-leaning political leaders, especially Dr. Salvador Allende, and to strengthen and encourage their civilian and military opponents." In other words, they helped. Allende was a socialist leader during the Cold War and the U.S. wanted him out. Instead, they supported a monster like Pinochet, who spent the next twenty five years imprisoning, torturing or killing over 40,000 people. He was an evil dictator until his arrest in 1998. Pinochet died before being tried for war crimes.

1. YAHYA KHAN
1971 - Dhaka, East Pakistan (Bangladesh)

In 1970, the Awami Party of East Pakistan defeated Yahya Khan's central government and demanded autonomy in their region. Before they could take power, Khan visited the region, told his military, "Kill three million of them," and returned to the West. When he was confirmed safe, the West Pakistani military unleashed hell. Hundreds of thousands (possibly millions) of Bengali people in East Pakistan were murdered or fled to India. At least two hundred thousand women were raped. Nixon and Kissinger were aware of the situation but, to them, Khan was easier to deal with than the Awami Party so they looked the other way as he committed genocide. When India eventually got involved, West Pakistan had to stand down. East Pakistan declared independence and became Bangladesh while Khan was placed under house arrest.

1973   1973   1973   1973

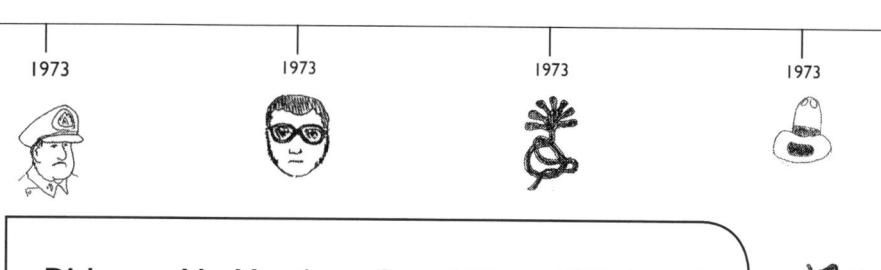

1974

Dishonorable Mentions: Steve Miller - 1973 (music), Muhammad Ali - 1971 (awful friend to Joe Frazier), Frank Lucas - 1970 (gangster), Dennis Rader - 1974 (BTK), Dennis Hastert - 1974 (pederast), Sun Myung Moon - 1970 (cult leader), Jean-Claude "Baby Doc" Duvalier - 1971 (dictator), R. William Jones, Renato Righetto, Artenik Arabadjian - 1972 (terrible Olympic basketball refs)

417

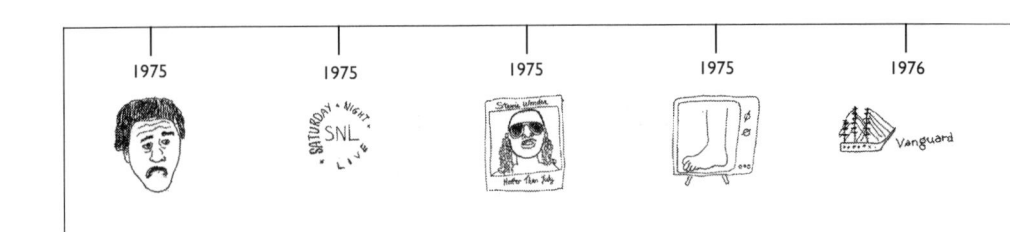

1975-1979

"Hope is never silent."
-Harvey Milk

BEST

10. (TIE) GLENN BURKE
1977 - Los Angeles, California

One of the world's great pioneers created something in front of 46,000 people and, yet, barely anyone knows it. After Glenn Burke's Los Angeles Dodgers teammate, Dusty Baker, had just cranked his thirtieth home run on the last day of the season, Burke raised his hand up in the air for Dusty to slap. He did. Then, Glenn Burke stepped to home plate and hit his first career home run. Dusty Baker returned the favor with yet another high-five. Ever since, the high-five has been the universal celebration for athletes (and awkward adults) everywhere. Burke played only four seasons and had 124 career hits (only two of which were homers) but his contribution, in many ways, is bigger than that of nearly any other professional athlete. High-five, Glenn.

10. (TIE) WOODY ALLEN
1977 - New York, New York

The greatest screenwriter of all time certainly has his personal baggage, but his career achievements are astonishing. After an early career of being a TV comedy writer, stand-up, and author, Woody Allen found his true calling in the late sixties with *Take the Money and Run*, a mockumentary about a pathetic bank robber. From that point forward, Allen has made about one movie a year for over fifty years. His work has garnered a staggering number of Academy Award nominations (twenty-five, of which he won five), including 1977's *Annie Hall*, which is widely considered the greatest romantic comedy of all time. Actors in his movies have been nominated for another eighteen Oscars (of which they have won seven). From *Bananas* to *Hannah and Her Sisters* to *Match Point* to *Midnight in Paris*, Woody Allen has covered all genres and killed it. As the great Chris Rock pointed out, "he is peerless... Most people last twenty years. He's been doing this for over forty."

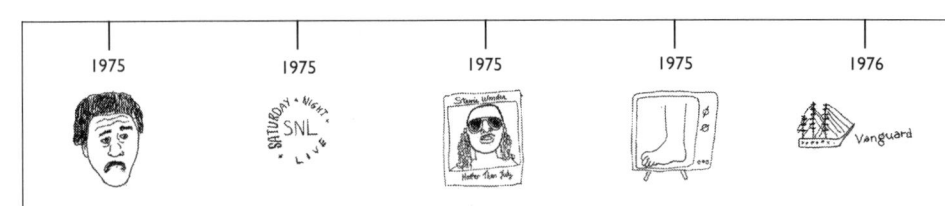

9. LORNE MICHAELS
1975 - New York, New York

In 1974, Johnny Carson wanted NBC to stop showing his reruns every Saturday night at eleven-thirty. So the network tapped thirty-year-old Canadian comedy writer, Lorne Michaels, to create a sketch show. Michaels dipped into *National Lampoon*'s talent pool (Michael O'Donohue, John Belushi, Gilda Radner, Chevy Chase), found a few other sketch performers (Garrett Morris, Jane Curtin, Laraine Newman), and got his Toronto buddy Dan Ackroyd to join the cast. From its first show, *Saturday Night Live* was a big hit. Each new season has brought cast changes, but that means more opportunities for Michaels to discover great new talent. For the past four-plus decades, *Saturday Night Live* has served as a launchpad for the careers of a who's who in the comedy world (Dana Carvey, Chris Farley, Will Ferrell, Tina Fey, Bill Hader, Phil Hartman, Jon Lovitz, Norm MacDonald, Kate McKinnon, Tracy Morgan, Eddie Murphy, Mike Myers, Conan O'Brien, Amy Poehler, Chris Rock, Andy Samberg, Adam Sandler, David Spade, Kristin Wiig, and many others).

8. JACK BOGLE
1976 - Philadelphia, Pennsylvania

In the mid-seventies, overpaid money managers weren't getting enough of a return to justify their fees. So Vanguard Group founder Jack Bogle came up with a lower cost approach for investors—a mutual fund that would match the performance of the Standard & Poor's 500 stocks. Money managers argued that if you're not choosy, you're adding a bunch of bottom-of-the-barrel stocks that will bring down the value of the good ones. Bogle persevered, and the first ever index fund outperformed most managed money in the eighties... by a lot. One analyst argued that Bogle's creation has probably saved investors around $175 billion in fees since it launched. Those are fees that would've just lined Wall Street pockets at the expense of investors. Warren Buffet calls Jack Bogle a hero, and so should you.

7. JOHN CLEESE, MICHAEL PALIN, ERIC IDLE, TERRY JONES, GRAHAM CHAPMAN, AND TERRY GILLIAM
1975 - London, England

In 1969, a group of Oxford and Cambridge University graduates (and one American) got together and formed "the Beatles of Comedy" —a.k.a. Monty Python. Unlike other single-themed television shows of the era, *Monty Python's Flying Circus* was just a series of comedy sketches mashed together. It didn't matter if it was highbrow or slapstick, just as long as it got a laugh. After its successful run in the U.K., the show was picked up in 1974 by PBS in America and gained a whole new audience. So they got back together and made a feature-length King Arthur-themed movie which pretty much just made fun of everything, and called it *Monty Python and the Holy Grail*. Monty Python had a major influence on all sketch comedy (*Saturday Night Live*, *SCTV*, the Groundlings, *Key & Peele*), absurd late night talk show hosts (David Letterman, Conan O'Brien), *The Simpsons*, *Jackass*, and more. If it's funny and not afraid to get weird, chances are Monty Python played a big role in its inspiration.

6. RICHARD PRYOR
1975 - New York, New York

Safe, one-liner comic Richard Pryor stared out at his audience at the Aladdin Hotel in Las Vegas, thought, "Fuck this," and walked off the stage. Born the son of a pimp and hooker and raised in a brothel, Richard Pryor had real stuff to talk about. So he reinvented himself and launched a new routine full of stuff people weren't comfortable talking about (race, poverty, social issues) and presented it just like how real people talked. He dropped N-bombs. He made fun of white people. If the situation called for profanity, Richard Pryor didn't shy away from it. And audiences absolutely loved it. Pryor told stories and brought everyone along for the ride. And, as if being one of the great stand-up comics of all time wasn't enough, the man co-wrote *Blazing Saddles*!

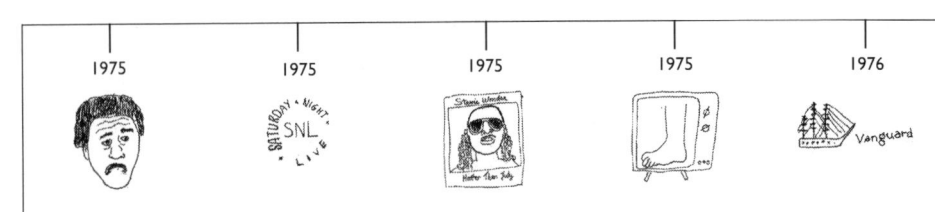

5. STEVEN SPIELBERG
1975 - Los Angeles, California

In just a few years at Universal, Steven Spielberg went from being an unpaid intern to a TV director to *Jaws*. Right away, it seemed the twenty-seven-year-old was in over his head: the mechanical shark didn't work, the shooting schedule nearly tripled in duration, and he was 300 percent over budget. Since major flops can lead to studio shakeups, the head of Universal thought they might as well go all in and promote the hell out of this runaway train, by buying commercial spots and putting it in as many theaters as possible (instead of the usual slow trickle-out strategy). Within two weeks, the studio had made its money back and, within seventy-eight days, *Jaws* had surpassed *The Godfather* at the all-time box office. *Jaws* created the summer blockbuster and launched the career of the greatest storyteller of the past half-century. From aliens and dinosaurs to the Holocaust and Civil War, Steven Spielberg has contributed some of the most compelling movies in the industry's history.

4. HARVEY MILK
1978 - San Francisco, California

While he became increasingly active in San Francisco's gay community (he was nicknamed the "Mayor of Castro Street"), Korean War vet Harvey Milk knew that if he wanted to make meaningful change, he would need to run for political office. After a couple of failed runs, in 1977, he became America's first (openly) gay elected official. In his first (and, sadly, only) year in office, Milk got a lot done. What started with ending the no-gay-teachers-in-schools Proposition 6 led to a chain reaction which eliminated sexual orientation discrimination at the airport and the airlines that operated there. Plus, he made sure San Francisco was the first city with a pooper scooper law. Unfortunately, former city supervisor Dan White, a homophobic former cop, snuck into city hall and murdered Milk in November 1978. To honor his inspirational legacy, the United States Navy announced in 2016 that they would be naming a tanker the USNS *Harvey Milk* in his honor.

3. STEVIE WONDER
1976 - Detroit, Michigan

In 1961, Gerald White asked his brother Ronnie (who was in the musical group The Miracles) to come check out a performance of a buddy of his, Stevland Morris. Despite being only ten years old (and blind), Stevie Morris had a powerful voice and played piano, harmonica, and drums. An impressed Ronnie brought him to Berry Gordy, who dubbed him "Wonder." Thus, the legend was born. After successful teenage years with hits like "Uptight," "For Once in My Life," and "My Cherie Amour," Stevie fought for (and got) more artistic freedom from Motown Records. Instead of chasing poppy, chart-topping hits, Stevie Wonder focused solely on creating great music, resulting in one of the most impressive runs the music industry has ever seen—groundbreaking, socially conscious, innovative hits that netted him fifteen Grammys (including Album of the Year in 1974, 1975, and 1977). His 1976 masterpiece, *Songs in the Key of Life* ("Sir Duke," "Isn't She Lovely," "Pastime Paradise") is the gold standard album for one of the gold standard musicians in history.

2. GEORGE LUCAS
1977 - Los Angeles, California

In 1973, a young director named George Lucas came out with American Graffiti, a nostalgic 1950s-era film that made tons of money and reminded audiences of simpler times (before Vietnam and Nixon, that is). This led to two things: first, the TV show Happy Days; and second, the freedom for George Lucas to do whatever the hell he wanted. So he did. Again, Lucas tapped into the simpler stories of his youth (right versus wrong) and incorporated his wild, groundbreaking filmmaking techniques into the movie Star Wars. From the moment it was released, the movie starring

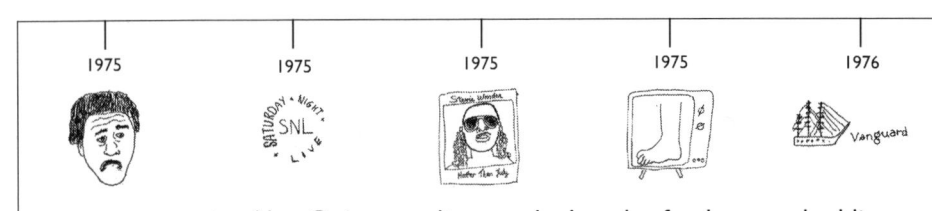

starring Alec Guinness, aliens, and a bunch of unknowns had lines around the block of excited fans. Star Wars earned over $513 million during its original run (it cost $11 million to make) and raised the bar for special effects, sound effects, and moviemaking in general.

1. ROBERT EDWARDS AND PATRICK STEPTOE
1978 - Cambridgeshire, England

As a side job while in school, Robert Edwards worked in a laboratory with mice and experimented with fertility drugs. He stayed in the science field, got married, and started a family. In 1960, friends of the Edwardses came by to see their young daughters and bemoaned the fact that they were unable to have kids of their own. This got Edwards thinking. In school, he had experimented with implanting embryos into mice. What if he tried the same thing with humans? He threw himself into the cause and, within a few years, hooked up with gynecologist Patrick Steptoe, a pioneer of laparoscopy. The two committed to the painstaking process together for the next dozen or so years. Finally, in 1977, Edwards and Steptoe were able to successfully impregnate a woman through in vitro fertilization (IVF) and delivered the world's first test-tube baby on July 25, 1978. Today, as many as six million babies have now been born, thanks to IVF.

| 1977 | 1977 | 1977 | 1978 |

Honorable Mentions: Albert Brooks - 1979 (comic, filmmaker), Mikhail Baryshnikov - 1977 (ballet), Ralph Baer - 1978 (video games), Steve Biko - 1977 (anti-apartheid activist), Stephen King - 1977 (author), Bruce Springsteen (singer-songwriter), Henry Edward Roberts - 1975 (first PC), Joe Strummer, Mick Jones, Paul Simonon - 1978 (The Clash), Nobutoshi Kihara - 1979 (walkman), Steve Martin - 1979 (comic), Nadia Comaneci - 1976 (gymnast), Sylvester Stallone - 1975 (*Rocky*), Bruce Jenner - 1976 (decathlete), Ben Cohen and Jerry Greenfield - 1978 (ice cream), Alex Haley - 1977 (*Roots*), John Landis - 1978 (comedy director), Freddie Mercury - 1975 (rock god), Robin Williams - 1978 (comedy), Al Pacino - 1975 (actor), Robert DeNiro - 1976 (actor), John Cazale - 1975 (actor), John Wooden - 1975 (basketball coach), Jimmy Iovine - 1975 (producer), Deborah Harry - 1978 (Blondie)

1978

WORST

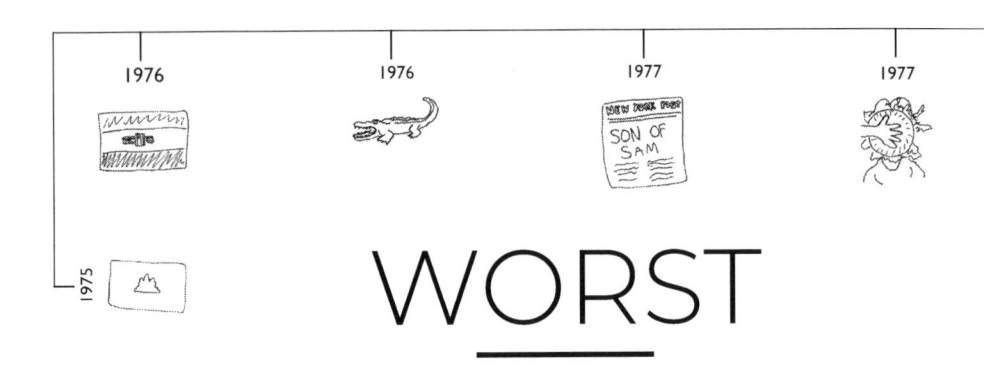

10. DAVID BERKOWITZ
1976 - New York, New York

In January 1977, NYPD detectives linked the murder of a couple to several other similar unsolved killings. New York City had a serial killer. Tabloids (led by Rupert Murdoch's *New York Post*) had a field day with the story using outlandish headlines in order to sell more papers. The city was paralyzed. People stopped going out after dark. The "Son of Sam" (as he later called himself in taunting notes left for the police) was finally caught in August. But who was he? A devious mastermind like the Zodiac Killer? A guy trying to start a race war like Charles Manson? Nope, just a twenty-three-year-old loner who claimed his neighbor's dog told him to do it. For his six murders and seven more attempts, David Berkowitz was sentenced to 365 years in prison. America was sentenced to a lifetime of race-baiting shitbirds like Rupert Murdoch. Yellow journalism had been, for the most part, shamed out of existence after the Spanish-American War fiasco. Son of Sam brought it all back.

9. ANDREI CHIKATILO
1978 - Rostov, USSR (Russia)

After being chased out of several schools for rage issues, schoolteacher Andrei Chikatilo settled in Rostov, a town about six hundred miles south of Moscow. In Rostov, he befriended dozens of kids at the train station, got them alone by promising them food or candy, and then killed them, using their bodies for sex or food. Since the official ideology in the Soviet Union at the time didn't accept the possibility of serial killers existing in their communist society, the police had to quietly treat the murders like small investigations, which enabled Andrei to literally get away with murder. Finally, in 1990, police caught up to Chikatilo. The "Butcher of Rostov" was put on in a cage in the middle of the courtroom, found guilty on thirty-six counts, and executed in 1994.

8. JOHN WAYNE GACY
1978 - Norwood Park, Illinois

The warning signs were all there for John Wayne Gacy. After serving only a year and a half for molesting a couple of teenage boys in Iowa, Gacy was released and moved to the Chicago area. He got married, went to church, and, despite the fact that he appeared at birthday parties as Pogo the Clown, was relatively well liked in the community. Then, in December of '78, a woman reported to the police that her fifteen-year-old son was missing. When the police showed up at Gacy's house, they found a bunch of pictures of sad clowns, sex toys, and some old man-on-young-boy pornography. When they checked his foul-smelling crawlspace, they found the decomposing remains of dozens of boys.

7. JIMMY BUFFETT
1977 - Key West, Florida

Jimmy Buffett has invested lots of time and money into important environmental and humanitarian causes. By most measures, he's been a solid citizen and all-around decent person. But there's a problem with the estimated half-billion dollars he has made over the course of his singer-songwriter career: his music is just the worst. The super chill dude cobbled together a bunch of lazy songs ("Margaritaville," "Cheeseburger in Paradise") about beer, mixed drinks, beaches, and hammocks, and just like that became a superstar. Buffett essentially played Mad Libs while holding a guitar. Rhymes like, "But there's booze in the blender, and soon it will render" are about as fun as getting that "lost shaker of salt" poured into your eyes.

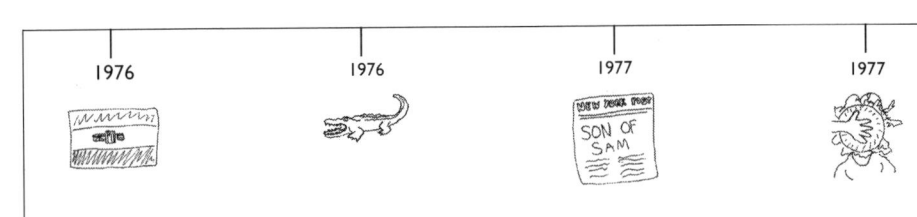

6. ANITA BRYANT
1977 - Des Moines, Iowa

Anita Bryant, the former Miss Oklahoma-turned-pop star and Florida Citrus Commission spokesperson, was asked by her Miami pastor to help him fight against homosexuality. Earlier that year in South Florida, a homosexual nondiscrimination ordinance had been passed which, essentially, granted gay people the right to be teachers. So Anita Bryant and her manager husband started a nationwide "Save Our Children" crusade. Bryant held press conferences and spouted off fear-mongering flummery like, "Gays can't reproduce so they have to recruit," and warned that giving rights to gay people would lead to giving rights to people with "sexual preference for the dead or who want to have sex with a Saint Bernard." The backlash was swift and severe. In Iowa, someone hit her in the face with a pie. The Florida Citrus Commission dumped her as a spokesperson and her marriage crumbled soon thereafter. Maybe she should've just stuck to tiaras and abominable music.

5. JIM JONES
1978 - Jonestown, Guyana

When people use the phrase "drinking the Kool-Aid," they're talking about this guy's legacy. In the mid-sixties, when lots of bewildered Americans were trying to find themselves, Jim Jones spewed a bunch of spiritual bunkum about "healings" and soon amassed a huge following in San Francisco. When the media and politicians started sniffing around Jones' cult for fraud and child abuse, he relocated his church to the middle of the jungle in Guyana. But instead of the utopia Jones had promised, cult members found themselves in hell surrounded by armed gunmen. In 1978, after a former member begged the government to help her get her son back, California congressman Leo Ryan flew down to investigate along with a few reporters. Jones had his goons murder them and, since retaliation from the U.S. government would surely soon be coming, had everyone drink Kool-Aid spiked with poison in a mass suicide, killing 909 people (276 of whom were children) before shooting himself.

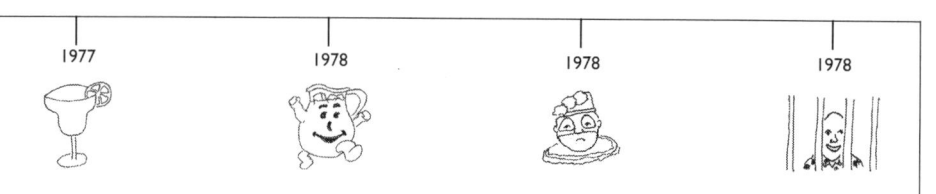

4. GIDEON NIEUWOUDT
1977 - Johannesburg, South Africa

After Nelson Mandela was sent to prison, several leaders stepped up to lead the resistance against apartheid. One of the brightest of the bunch was the young Steve Biko. In 1977, police arrested the activist and brought him to the Walmer Police Station, where Colonel Gideon Nieuwoudt ordered Biko to be stripped naked, chained, and beaten for the next three weeks. Afterward, his body was found a few miles away in Pretoria. His funeral attracted more than fifteen thousand people and ignited an even stronger sense of outrage, which would propel the Black Consciousness Movement into the 1980s. The villainous officers later confessed and applied for amnesty in 1997. Amnesty was denied. To hell with them. Gideon Nieuwoudt died of lung cancer in 2005.

3. JERRY FALWELL
1979 - Lynchburg, Virginia

You know those mouth-breathers who twist things they read in the Bible so they can justify being complete assholes? Jerry Falwell was the king of those people. Unlike his contemporary Reverend Billy Graham, who preached what he believed but pretty much stayed out of politics, Falwell saw his status as a reverend as his right to tell people what to do politically and to justify hatred of others. Jerry Falwell wasn't some intellectual or policy expert or even someone who gave a rat's ass about civil rights. He was a hate-spewing, exclusion-promoting moron. Whether it was Martin Luther King, Gloria Steinem, Harvey Milk, Jimmy Carter, or the *Teletubbies*, Jerry Falwell had a problem with them. After the September 11th attacks, he blamed feminists and gays. Finally, in 2007, Jerry Falwell was found in a lump on the floor of his Liberty University office. Jimmy Carter was right. If there's a hell, Jerry Falwell is there.

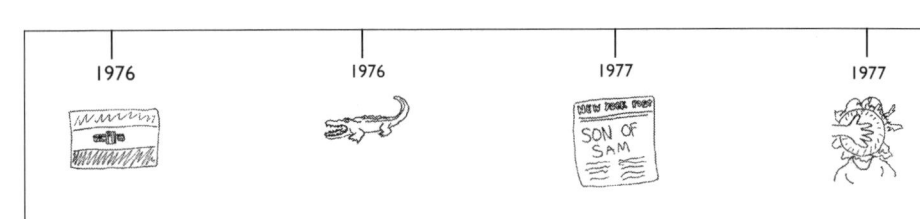

2. IDI AMIN
1976 - Entebbe, Uganda

In 1971, when Ugandan President Milton Obote was away on a trip to Singapore, his brutal head of the military, Idi Amin, led a coup. Once in charge, Amin had all Obote supporters killed, forced Obote to flee to Tanzania, banned all Asians from Uganda (which soon led to a complete economic collapse), and gave himself lots of new titles. After the first wave of murders were done, His Excellency President for Life, Field Marshal, Lord of all the Beasts of the Earth and Fishes of the Sea, and Conqueror of the British Empire in Africa in General and Uganda in Particular still had bloodlust. So he had death squads kill journalists, lawyers, homosexuals, students, old people, or whoever else suited the increasingly erratic leader on any given day. Once they ran out of grave sites, Amin had his troops feed the bodies to crocodiles in the Nile. Even there, supply outweighed demand and intake ducts at the Ugandan hydroelectric plant were blocked by corpses. When the rest of the world turned their backs on the man who killed 500,000 of his own people, Amin turned to the only people who didn't mind him—terrorists. In 1978, after a failed invasion of Tanzania, "the Adolph Hitler of Africa" was forced to flee to Saudi Arabia, where he would spend the rest of his miserable life.

1. POL POT
1975 - Phnom Penh, Cambodia

Cambodia's Communist party (Khmer Rouge) lacked enough members to become a force. Then, after Richard Nixon dropped 500,000 tons of bombs on Cambodia (which was more than three times the amount dropped on Japan in World War II), suddenly they were flush with rural supporters. Khmer Rouge leader Pol Pot mobilized his troops, instigated a civil war, and, in 1975, was able to take over the capital city. Once in charge, Pol Pot declared massive changes—Cambodia would become a classless, agrarian society immediately. If anyone resisted, they were jailed and killed. In order to save bullets, soldiers were told to beat people to

| 1977 | 1978 | 1978 | 1978 |

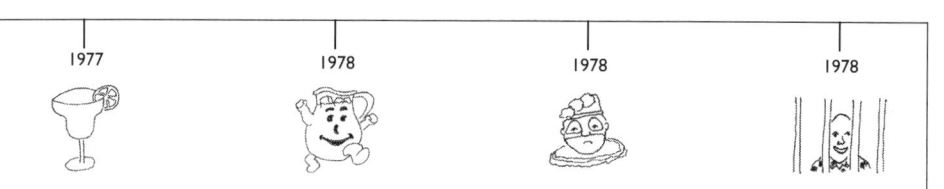

death. Between the slaughters and inevitable famine, around 1.7 million people were killed in a four-year span. That's about one out of every five Cambodians. In 1979, Pol Pot was toppled and placed under house arrest for the last two decades of his life.

1979

Honorable Mentions: William Luther Pierce - 1978 (*The Turner Diaries*), Paul McCartney - 1979 (Wonderful Christmastime), Eric Clapton - 1976 (racist), Jimmy Burke - 1978 (mob thug), Dan White - 1978 (murderer), Sid and Marty Kroft - 1976 (*H.R. Pufnstuf*), Sara Jane Moore - 1975 (failed assassin), Harlon Carter - 1977 (murderer, "Mr. NRA")

| 1980 | 1981 | 1982 | 1982 |

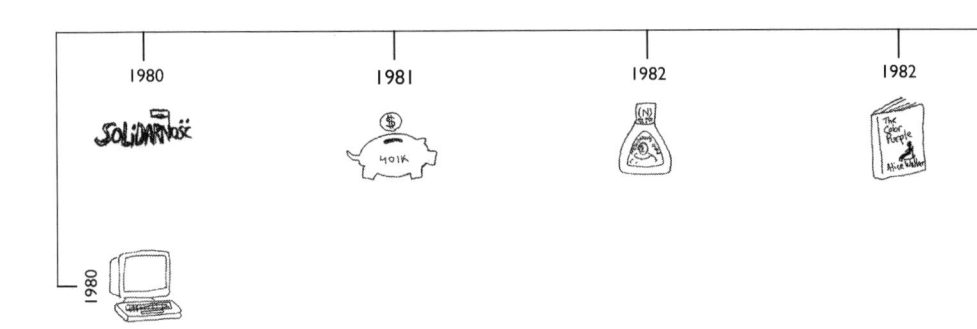

1980

1980-1984

"I think you can be defiant and rebellious and still be strong and positive."
-Madonna

BEST

10. TED BENNA
1981 - Philadelphia, Pennsylvania

In the seventies, when people retired, their companies gave them big, fat pensions. But, over time, business owners kept trying to tweak things to line their own pockets while giving less and less to employees. It was Ted Benna's job to help them do exactly that. And he hated it. Then one September Saturday, Benna was in his quiet office in the Philly suburbs working on redesigning the retirement program for one of his clients when he had an idea. In 1978, Congress passed an addendum to tax code section 401. In paragraph "K" there was a tax break for companies which allowed workers to put away cash on the side for their future. To get them to do that, employers could be incentivized to match their contributions—truly an "everybody wins" scenario. When no employer wanted to try it out, Benna started his own company. It worked and, soon, just about everybody copied the idea. Ted Benna's 401K has helped lots of people save.

9. DAVID BOWIE
1983 - New York, New York

From the moment it launched in 1981, MTV had a massive impact on the music business. Careers were made and broken by the new network. Then, in 1983, David Bowie stopped by MTV for an interview. Instead of promoting his *Let's Dance* album, Bowie took the opportunity to chastise the network for only playing black artists in the middle of the night. And that was David Bowie. Throughout his career, he never had the stomach for posturing or compromising himself for the good of record sales. His 1969 breakout album, *Space Oddity*, kicked off what *Rolling Stone* called "one of the longest creative streaks in rock history." The only constant in his career was change. When people dressed like hippies, Bowie dressed like a Martian and sang about space. He did rock. He did disco. He did punk. He wore dresses. And when he called out MTV for whitewashed programming, they listened. Shortly thereafter, Prince and Michael Jackson were all over the network pushing the art form to new heights.

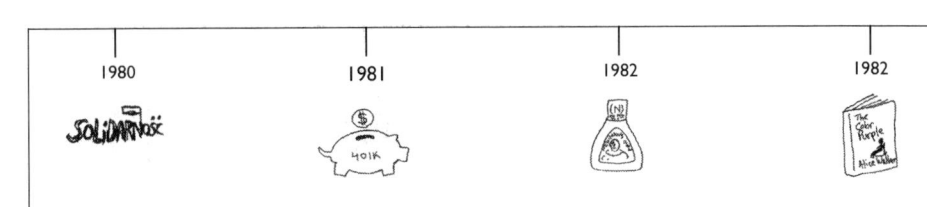

8. ALICE WALKER
1982 - Berkeley, California

In 1982, author and civil rights activist Alice Walker had her big breakthrough. In her novel *The Color Purple*, readers follow the hardships and perseverance of a poor black girl in the early twentieth-century South. The book explores racism, sexism, and love and, in the words of Victoria Bond, "disassembles the myth of the strong black woman." The idea that you can heap endless hardships on black women and they're expected to simply take it is nonsense. Every living person thrives on happiness and love. The book was a smashing success, selling over five million copies and earning Walker the Pulitzer Prize in 1983. In 1985, Steven Spielberg turned Walker's novel into an Academy Award-winning movie.

7. PAUL NEWMAN
1982 - Westport, Connecticut

By the early eighties, Paul Newman was already a legend. He had played some of the most iconic roles in cinema history (Cool Hand Luke, Fast Eddie Felson, Butch Cassidy, Henry Gondorff, Brick, Frank Galvin), become an award-winning race car driver, and managed to piss off Richard Nixon enough to land at number nineteen on his enemies list (a list Newman fondly framed). Then, he and his friend, writer A.E. Hotchner, made salad dressing, put it in wine bottles, and gave it out to all their friends as holiday gifts. After enough urging, they decided to sell it in stores. In just the first year, Newman's Own made $350,000. When asked what to do with the profits, Newman replied, "Let's give it all away to those who need it." So they did. The company expanded and, without pocketing a dime, Newman gave it all to handpicked charities. To date, Newman's Own has raised nearly half a billion dollars. As it turns out, the guy with the famous blue eyes was even more beautiful on the inside.

6. EDDIE MURPHY
1984 - New York, New York

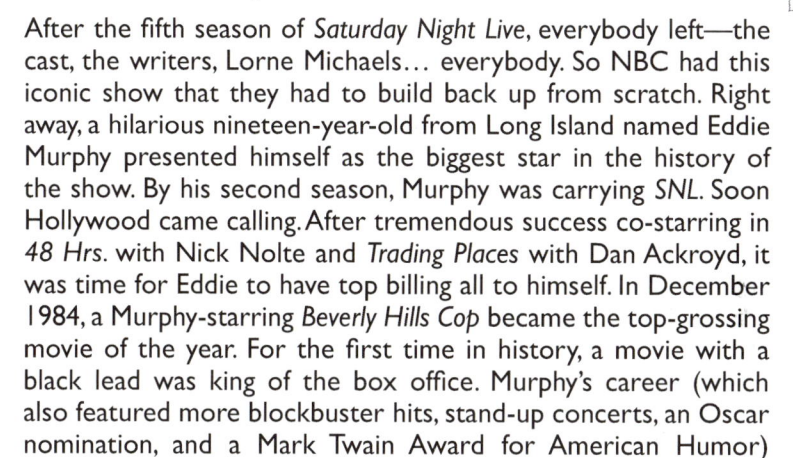

After the fifth season of *Saturday Night Live*, everybody left—the cast, the writers, Lorne Michaels… everybody. So NBC had this iconic show that they had to build back up from scratch. Right away, a hilarious nineteen-year-old from Long Island named Eddie Murphy presented himself as the biggest star in the history of the show. By his second season, Murphy was carrying *SNL*. Soon Hollywood came calling. After tremendous success co-starring in *48 Hrs.* with Nick Nolte and *Trading Places* with Dan Ackroyd, it was time for Eddie to have top billing all to himself. In December 1984, a Murphy-starring *Beverly Hills Cop* became the top-grossing movie of the year. For the first time in history, a movie with a black lead was king of the box office. Murphy's career (which also featured more blockbuster hits, stand-up concerts, an Oscar nomination, and a Mark Twain Award for American Humor) completely changed perceptions in Hollywood.

5. MADONNA CICCONE
1984 - New York, New York

Although she's had a very different life path than Susan B. Anthony or Gloria Steinem, Madonna has also been a towering force in the feminist movement. After the former club singer sold five million copies of her debut album, she was officially a pop star. But she aimed much higher than that. In 1984, she followed it up with "Like a Virgin," the first of her twelve number-one hits. For the first time ever, a female singer fully embraced her sexuality and spoke her mind. Madonna pushed boundaries. She was a fashion icon. She ran her own record label. Pretty much the only thing she never really conquered was Hollywood. Then again, she still won an Oscar for *Evita*. Madonna has had the career that every pop star dreams of.

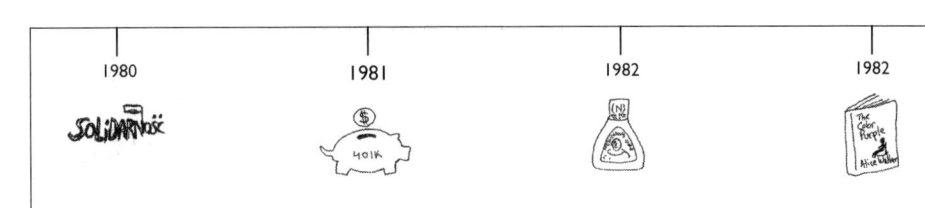

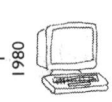

4. RICK RUBIN
1984 - New York, New York

Rick Rubin was a twenty-year-old heavy metal fan studying philosophy at NYU. After being exposed to rap at a local club, he fell in love with the new music style and bought some singles. When those singles sounded nothing like what he'd heard in the club, he decided he wanted to make his own. So he approached some DJs and rappers he liked and recorded singles under his new label Def Jam. Twenty-six-year-old Russell Simmons, a hustler and promoter, heard these singles and soon joined the dorm room record label. Simmons brought in guys like Kurtis Blow and Run-DMC (starring Simmons' brother, Joseph) and helped grow the business. Then, after Rubin's buddy Adam Horovitz (Ad-Rock from the punk group Beastie Boys) brought him a demo from a sixteen-year-old kid who called himself LL Cool J, the label had its new star. Rubin dropped some beats while LL rapped what would be "I Need a Beat." The song sold more than a hundred thousand copies and the rap industry, for all intents and purposes, was born.

3. DAVID LETTERMAN
1982 - New York, New York

In 1981, David Letterman was given the 12:30 a.m. post-Johnny Carson time slot with a ridiculous set of rules (no big band, no topical monologue, no Carson guests, and so on). Essentially, he was challenged to produce a successful talk show without using most of the models that had worked for the past quarter century. So he (and head writer Merrill Markoe) had to get creative. The whole concept of a television talk show was ridiculous, and Letterman embraced the absurdity of it all. He experimented with suits made of magnets, Rice Krispies, Alka-Seltzer, and Velcro. He gave the camera to a roller-skating monkey named Zippy. He smashed stuff. If the vapid star/starlet-of-the-month wasn't interesting enough, Letterman would cut the interview short to spend more time with weirdos like unhinged comic book writer Harvey Pekar. Thanks to his unbelievably quick wit, Dave got the absolute best out of guests. There is nothing less funny than playing it cool. David Letterman never tried to. And, for that, he was the coolest.

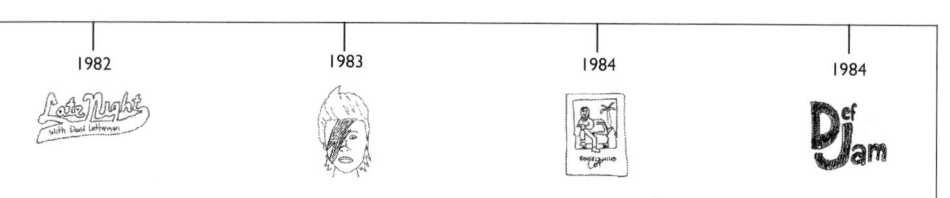

2. LECH WAŁĘSA
1980 - Gdańsk, Poland

Lech Wałęsa saw police kill several protesters during food riots at the Lenin Shipyard and decided to commit his life to pushing back against Poland's oppressive government. With each protest, he was tossed in jail or fired from his job. But, ultimately, the government knew an unemployed Walesa would stir up even more trouble so he kept getting rehired. After successfully negotiating a strike to counter rising food prices in 1980, other unions joined Walesa in the Solidarity movement. But the mother ship (USSR) didn't take kindly to a ten million-person trade union and placed the country under martial law. For the rest of the decade, Walesa was forced to lead the Solidarity movement from underground. Little by little, the union chipped away while the Polish economy crumbled. In 1988, they held free elections for open parliament seats, which were nearly all won by Solidarity members. By 1990, Wałęsa was named president of Poland. Lech Wałęsa: 1. Communism: 0.

1. TIM BERNERS-LEE
1980 - Geneva, Switzerland

As the son of two people who worked on the first commercial computer (Ferranti Mark I), Tim Berners-Lee was knowledgeable of the fledgling industry from an early age. After Oxford, he got a consulting gig at CERN, a particle physics lab in Geneva. A big part of the job was sharing information with other researchers around the world. So, to make it easier, Berners-Lee created the ENQUIRE system, which combined hypertext with internet nodes and domains. (This, hopefully, makes sense to nerds.) It eventually became the all-consuming behemoth we now know as the World Wide Web. By 1991, with the help from Robert Cailliau, he created the first ever website. What started as a research information-sharing platform has ballooned into something society can no longer do without (i.e., our source of cat videos and porn).

1980 1981 1982 1982

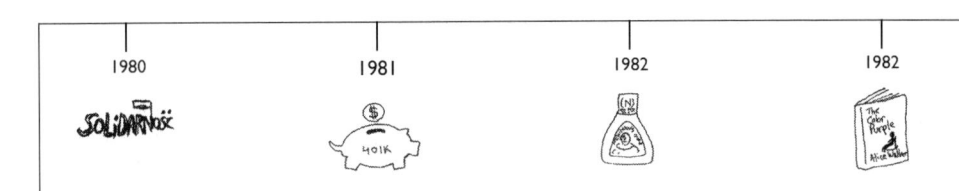

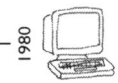

1980

Honorable Mentions: Rob Reiner, Christopher Guest - 1984 (*This is Spinal Tap*), Frank Shankwitz - 1980 (Make-A-Wish Foundation), Merrill Markoe - 1982 (comedy), James Todd Smith - 1984 (LL Cool J), Joe Delaney - 1983 (hero, NFL player), Phoebe Cates - 1983 (*Fast Times at Ridgemont High*), Rodney Dangerfield - 1980 (comedy), Vigdís Finnbogadóttir - 1980 (first democratically elected female leader), Russell Simmons - 1984 (Def Jam), Haruki Murakami - 1982 (author), Robert Pearson - 1983 (pilot, hero), Bill Cosby - 1984 (comic, actor), Christine Craft - 1981 (activist), Sallie Ride - 1983 (first American woman in space), Harold Ramis - 1983 (comedy), Les Charles, Glen Charles, Jim Burrows - 1983 (*Cheers*), Jim Craig - 1980 (hockey), Michael Jackson - 1983 ("King of Pop"), Carl Lewis - 1984 (track and field), Alec Jeffreys - 1984 (DNA fingerprinting), Martin Short, Eugene Levy, John Candy, Catherine O'Hara, Joe Flaherty, Andrea Martin, Dave Thomas, Rick Moranis - 1981 (*SCTV*), John McEnroe, Björn Borg - 1980 (tennis), Grandmaster Flash - 1981 (DJ), Alex Trebek - 1984 (game show host)

1982 | 1983 | 1984 | 1984 | 1984

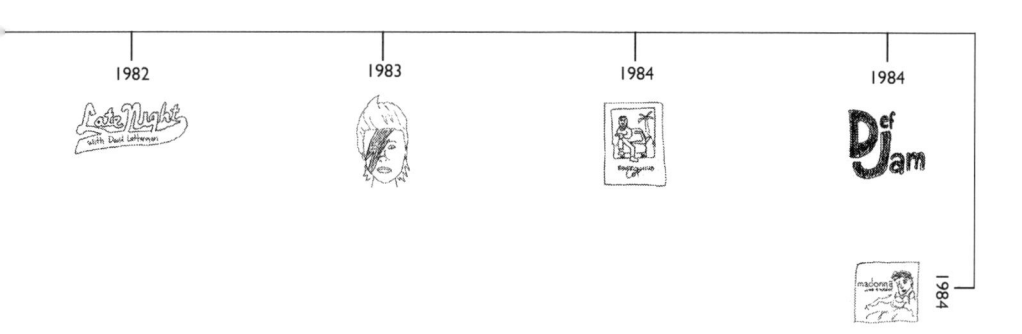

WORST

10. RICH SKRENTA
1982 - Mt. Lebanon, Pennsylvania

One day in 1982, fifteen-year-old Pittsburgh-area nerd Rich Skrenta found some holes in one of his Apple II computer applications. So he designed the Elk Cloner virus to expose the weakness, put it on a floppy disc, and passed it to all his friends. The virus made the screen show a really dumb poem then forced the user to reboot. Sure, Skrenta's virus was benign, but it set an example for creeps everywhere to torture the lives of millions of innocent people who don't really want to be thinking about the holes in an application language. Computer viruses now cost the world $55 billion annually and countless headaches. Cool legacy, Rich.

9. JARNAIL SINGH BHINDRANWALE
1984 - New Delhi, India

In the same country where Mahatma Gandhi showed the world how to bring change nonviolently, an obscure preacher from Punjab tried to do it the completely opposite way. Sikh leader Jarnail Singh Bhindranwale detested the direction India was going. Unhappy that Sikhs were doing things like drinking, using tobacco, and cutting their hair, Bhindranwale demanded Sikhs purify themselves and be given a separate Sikh state of Khalistan. Anyone who opposed that view (politicians, journalists, Hindu citizens) was targeted. In 1984, the bandolier-wearing Bhindranwale led his followers in a storming of the sacred Golden Temple in New Delhi. The ensuing gunfight left Bhindranwale and hundreds more dead and many more angry. A few months later, Indian Prime Minister Indira Gandhi was assassinated in retaliation, which only led to even more violence—tens of thousands of Sikhs were killed in the aftermath. Lots of people died, and to this day no separate Sikh state has been established.

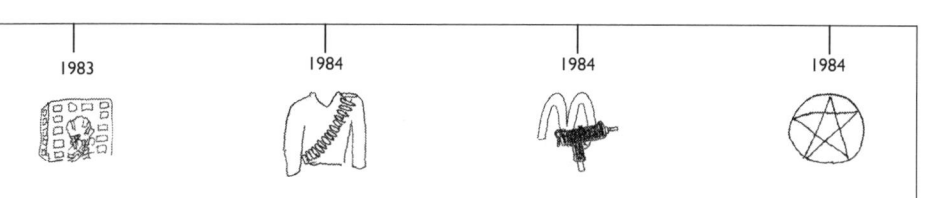

8. BILL COSBY
1984 - Los Angeles, California

There were whispers about Bill Cosby's dark side for many years. After all, he had settled out of court with sexual assault accusers in the past. But, since he was a beloved stand-up comic, pitchman, and television dad, people chose to block it from their minds. Bill Cosby was a towering figure in America. People wanted to believe the best in him. So Cosby went back to being the revered elder statesman of comedy who critiqued other comics (everyone from Eddie Murphy to John Stewart) for not following his arbitrary set of PG-rated comedy rules. Then, in 2014, comedian Hannibal Burress pointed out the rapey old comic's hypocrisy. The clip went viral and, suddenly, dozens of women spoke out about Cosby's sexual assaults. When *The New York Times* went through Cosby's deposition of his 2005 civil trial, he fully admitted to drugging women. But let's say all fifty-seven (!) of them made the story up and he was wrongly convicted. Still, should a guy responsible for the movies *Leonard Part 6* and *Ghost Dad* be lecturing anyone about comedy?

7. RICHARD RAMIREZ
1984 - Los Angeles, California

After a one-year stint in prison, Ramirez had rotten teeth and a thirst for murder. He attacked women of all ages (his first victim was seventy-nine) in the middle of the night, often raping and killing them, then leaving a satanic pentagram sign as his signature. For two years, the "Night Stalker" terrorized Southern California. He even murdered Peter Pan (a sixty-six-year-old accountant, not the ageless gatekeeper to Neverland). Eventually, some Mexican immigrants in East L.A. caught the "Night Stalker" trying to jack one of their cars and roughed him up until the police arrived. The defiant Ramirez yelled "Hail Satan!" throughout his trial before he was convicted of forty-three charges.

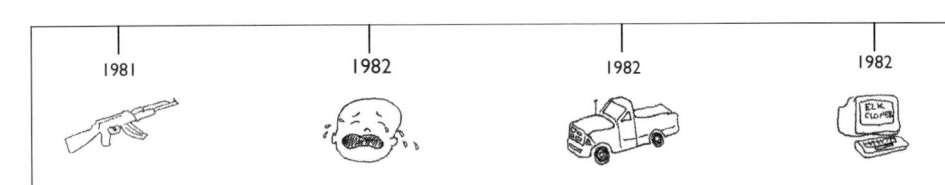

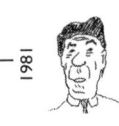

6. JAMES HUBERTY
1984 - San Ysidro, California

James Huberty's rampage should have been the wake-up call America needed. The unhinged forty-one-year-old entered a California McDonald's strapped with an uzi, a shotgun, and a handgun and opened fire on everyone in sight (a baby, grandmothers, kids on bikes, teenagers), killing twenty-one and wounding twenty more. After an hour of mayhem, a police sniper took him out. Sadly, America's only official response was to more heavily arm the police. And, in the most American of all twists, Huberty's wife sued McDonald's claiming their food additives caused him to go crazy. Automatic weapons, fast food, and lawsuits! U-S-A! U-S-A! U-S-A!

5. GARY RIDGWAY
1982 - King County, Washington

No American serial killer amassed a bigger body count than Gary Ridgway. The warning signs were there. The thrice-divorced Ridgway regularly wept in church, gave unwelcome massages to coworkers, and used a squirt bottle and comb to straighten his hair and mustache constantly. In 1982, he started killing. He'd drive his truck to the Sea-Tac strip (between Seattle and Tacoma), pick up prostitutes and runaways, have sex with them, strangle them, and then have sex with their corpses. In 1991, when DNA testing became more advanced, police were able to charge him with four murders. He confessed to forty-eight. In 2013, that number grew to eighty.

4. RONALD REAGAN
1981 - Washington, D.C.

Ronald Regan has been put on a pedestal by conservatives in the decades following his presidency. After all, "the Great Communicator" resuscitated the GOP from the Nixon years, helped drag America out of the malaise of the Carter years, and did it all with snappy slogans. And, if you were a rich, white guy or an arms manufacturer? He really was great. But if you were black? Reagan fought affirmative action, even though, only seventeen years earlier, blacks were legally allowed to be treated like second-class citizens in America. Then again, Reagan opposed the Civil Rights Act of 1964 and the Voting Rights Act of 1965 and was recorded calling black people "monkeys," so that shouldn't have really surprised anybody. If you were poor? Reagan tried his best to dismantle social welfare programs and falsely portray poor people as lazy freeloaders. Gay? As the gay community was ravaged by the AIDS epidemic, Reagan didn't even address the issue until far into his second term (after over 36,000 Americans had been diagnosed and more than 20,000 had died). And, even then, he just preached abstinence as if that suggestion ever, in the history of mankind, got people to stop having sex. His second term was ravaged by his administration illegally selling arms to Iran to fund rebels in Nicaragua. But, it is mostly assumed that the "Great Delegator" didn't know about it. At best, he was asleep at the wheel. So, yeah, not so great.

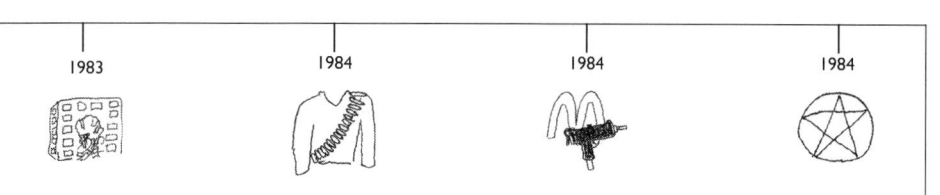

3. ABOUD AL-ZOMOR AND KHALID ISLAMBOULI
1981 - Cairo, Egypt

Unlike other Arab nation leaders, Anwar Sadat made decisions based on what he thought was best for Egypt, not necessarily what was best for the Arab world. From a distance, seeing Sadat meet with Israeli Prime Minister Begin to discuss peace just a decade after the Six-Day War seemed like a good thing. But to Aboud Al-Zomor, the Camp David Accords were a slap in the face. The founder of the Egyptian Islamic Jihad supplied assassins with ammunition and plotted Sadat's death. While posing as a soldier in a parade, Khalid Islambouli opened fire, killing Sadat and eleven others and injuring twenty-eight more. Besides murdering a Nobel Peace Prize winner, Islambouli's bullet ushered in the oppressive and corrupt thirty-year Hosni Mubarak regime.

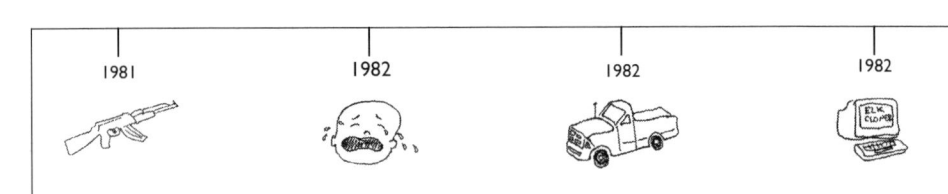

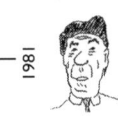

2. NICOLAE CEAUSESCU
1982 - Romania

Nicolae Ceausescu rose through the ranks of the Politburo in Romania and, in 1965, took charge. Like every evil leader, he surrounded himself with sycophants and locked up or killed people who didn't agree with him. Women in his regime were subjected to a horrendous baby mandate. Inspired by the Stalinist theory that population growth leads to economic growth, Ceausescu issued Decree 770. Essentially, women had to have four children or be punished. The marriage age was lowered to fifteen, birth control was outlawed, and a tax was levied on childless couples. Living conditions plummeted, AIDS cases ballooned, there were massive food shortages, poverty skyrocketed, and hundreds of thousands of babies were abandoned. He ruled with an iron fist until he met his demise in front of a firing squad in 1989. His terrible legacy still persists to this day as many of those abandoned children from the '70s and '80s have struggled as adults.

1. ALI AKBAR MOHTASHEMIPOUR
1983 - Beirut, Lebanon

It's a terrible idea to try to sum up any Middle East conflict in just a few sentences, but let's give it a shot. After World War I, the Ottoman Empire crumbled, the British took control of Palestine and (what is now) Iraq, and the French took control of (now) Syria and Lebanon. Aiming to make it a mountain home away from home, the French established Lebanon as a Christian country. By the time Lebanon achieved independence in 1943, it contained a fairly even mix of Christians and Muslims. Well, after Israel was given an independent state in southern Palestine, about 100,000 Palestinians flooded Lebanon. That number climbed and, by the mid-seventies, there were more than 400,000 Palestinians living in Lebanon, which tipped the Christian-Muslim scales in a big way. Predictably, religious nuts on both sides got militant and a civil war broke out. In 1982, the Palestine Liberation Organization attacked Israel from Lebanon, so Israel invaded Lebanon. Then American

| 1983 | 1984 | 1984 | 1984 |

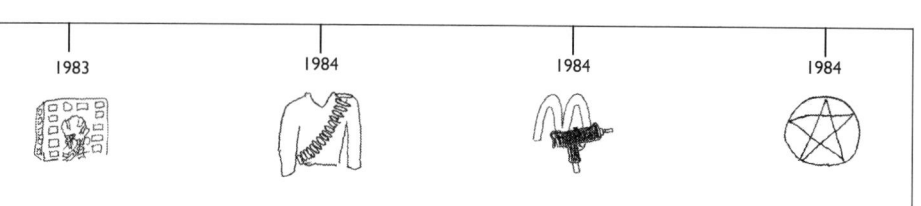

and French peacekeeping forces were sent in. The Shiite Muslims saw the new Christian presence as a threat. Also, Iran was pissed at America for backing Iraq. All of this led to the complete clusterfuck known as 1983 Beirut. At this point, the founder of Hezbollah (a militant Shia Muslim group backed by Iran), Ali Akbar Mohtashemipour, organized attacks on the U.S. embassy (killing 63), Marine barracks (killing 241), and a French Army compound (killing 58). Violence continued in Lebanon for another six years, killing over 200,000 total and displacing a million people in the process

1984

Dishonorable Mentions: Tipper Gore - 1984 (fun police), Samuel Little - 1984 (serial killer), Bob Mathews - 1984 (white supremacist), Wai-Chiu "Tony" Ng, Kwan Fai Mak, Benjamin Ng - 1983 (murderers), George Banks - 1982 (murderer), Mark David Chapman - 1980 (murdered John Lennon), Klaus Barbie - 1983 (Nazi), Peter Chapman - 1981 ("Yorkshire Ripper"), John Hinkley, Jr. - 1981 (attempted assassin), Marvin Gaye, Sr. - 1984 (murdered son), Dorothea Puente - 1982 ("Death House Landlady"), Bernhard Goetz - 1984 (subway shooter), Nick Perry - 1980 (fixed lottery), Buckner and Garcia - 1981 (Pac-Man Fever), John Schnatter - 1984 (terrible pizza), Angelo Erricheti, Mel Weinberg, Harrison Williams, Frank Thompson - 1980 (Abscam), Genene Jones - 1984 (child-killing nurse), Ferdinand Marcos - 1983 (evil Philippines prez), Jack Valenti - 1982 (MPAA head, fought VCRs)

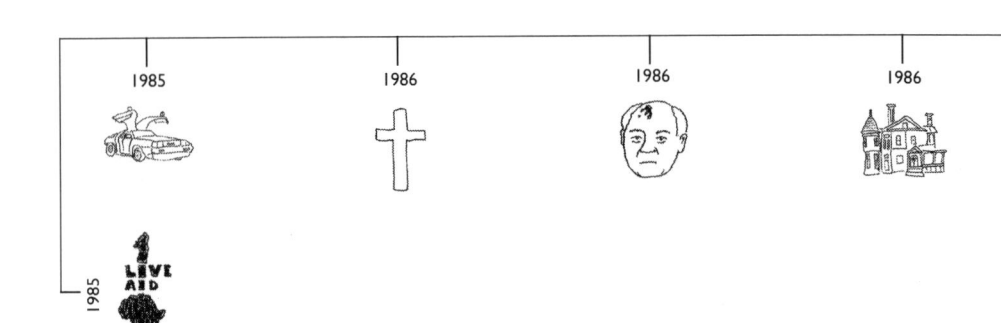

1985-1989

"Without forgiveness, there's no future."
-Desmond Tutu

BEST

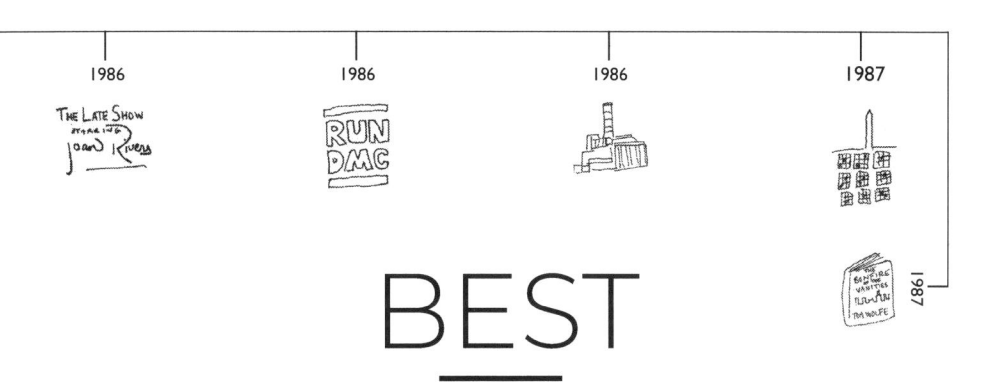

10. TOM WOLFE
1987 - New York, New York

While it should come as no surprise that a guy who spent most of his adult life wearing a white suit was obnoxious and had his share of detractors (John Irving, Leonard Bernstein, Hunter S. Thompson), it should also be noted that Tom Wolfe was a spectacular writer. As one of the pioneers of the "New Journalism" movement in the late sixties, Wolfe showed an incredible ability to immerse himself in different communities (1960s counterculture movement, early days of NASA, and others) and vividly describe them for the reader. In the mid-eighties, Wolfe took aim at the ridiculous, greedy Yuppie Decade his first novel, *Bonfire of the Vanities*. His hilarious but blistering takes on Wall Street, grandstanding media whores, and social injustice, all woven together in a silly story, was perfection.

9. JOSEPH "RUN" SIMMONS, DARRYL "DMC" MCDANIELS, AND JASON "JAM MASTER JAY" MIZELL
1986 - New York, New York

Rap music had reached a crossroads. Would it be a short-lived fad like disco or grow into something bigger? Run-DMC was mildly popular… but still not getting any pop radio airtime. Producer Rick Rubin thought if he could somehow merge rap and rock, he could push rap into the mainstream. So he approached Simmons, McDaniels, and Mizell with the idea of them doing a song with '70s rock group Aerosmith. The beat from their 1975 song "Walk This Way" had already been used in the rap community by greats like Grandmaster Flash, but nobody had ever done a full rock/rap collaboration. Simmons and McDaniels hated the idea, while Aerosmith was coming off a couple flops and not really in a position to refuse. Jam Master Jay talked them all into it and they gave it a shot one March afternoon in NYC. A couple months later, the song shot all the way up to number four on the Billboard 100 and became a radio staple. "Walk This Way" changed music forever.

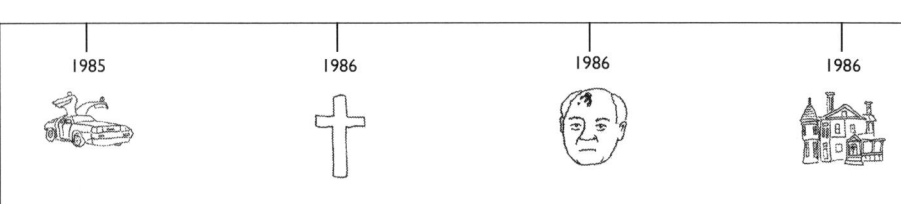

8. JOAN RIVERS
1986 - Los Angeles, California

Joan Rivers burst onto the male-dominated comedy scene in the 1960s and unapologetically said whatever was on her mind. Through razor-sharp wit and sheer force of will, Rivers shattered preconceived notions of women in comedy and, by 1983, was anointed the permanent guest host of The Tonight Show. In 1986, the Fox network chose her to be its first ever late night talk show host. Rivers paved the road for generations of women in comedy.

7. MICHAEL J. FOX
1985 - Hollywood, California

When he maxed out at five-foot-four, Michael Fox dropped the Canadian dream of becoming a professional hockey player and shifted his focus to acting. Good move. By the time he was twenty-one, Fox was starring on the NBC sitcom, *Family Ties*, a show with thirty million viewers each week. And in 1985, Fox played Marty McFly in *Back to the Future*, the top grossing movie of the year. He continued to work in movies and television until 1998, when he publicly announced he had Parkinson's disease and would step away from acting. But, instead of retreating, Fox used his celebrity platform to launch the Michael J. Fox Foundation for Parkinson's Research. Since 2000, the Fox Foundation has raised over $700 million dollars and helped the medical community make great strides in identifying and treating the degenerative disease. Through optimism, hard work, and charm, Michael J. Fox has given hope to millions of people.

6. CLARA HALE
1986 - New York, New York

Clara Hale was twenty-seven years old when her husband died, leaving her with three young children to raise by herself. If she were to have worked a bunch of jobs, she'd never see them. So, instead, she turned her apartment into a daycare. Over the years, the Hale House morphed into a place for addicts to drop off babies whom they couldn't care for themselves. Word of Clara's generosity got out and philanthropic organizations (and even John Lennon) raised enough money for the Hale House to move to a large renovated brownstone. When the AIDS epidemic hit in the 1980s, Clara cared for hundreds of babies and toddlers inflicted with the disease. For more than three decades, over a thousand children without much of a chance got one, thanks to Mother Hale.

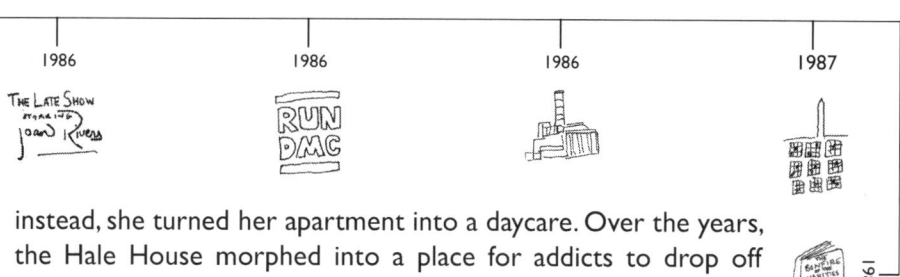

5. MIKHAIL GORBACHEV
1986 - Moscow, USSR (Russia)

After three old Soviet leaders died in a little more than three years, the Politboro opted to go with its youngest member, Mikhail Gorbachev. Rather than plow forward with the same old policies, Gorbachev introduced dramatic reforms to fix the downtrodden country and its stagnant economy. Gorbachev's Perestroika ("restructure") and Glasnost ("openness") movements were massive departures from the norm in Moscow. Gone were the days of people disappearing in the middle of the night for saying the wrong thing or practicing the wrong religion. And, most importantly, he reached out to and showed a real willingness to work with Western leaders. All of these changes led to an end to the Cold War, a unified Germany, and a Nobel Peace Prize for Gorbachev in 1990. Unfortunately for Gorbachev, all these changes also led to his political downfall. Well, that and Chernobyl. The Soviet Union collapsed and he was out of a job.

4. BOB GELDOF
1985 - London, England

In 1984, singer Bob Geldof saw a BBC report about the atrocious living conditions in Africa. Geldof felt so moved that he rounded up a bunch of famous musicians from England and Ireland (including Bono, George Michael, and Sting) to collaborate on the song "Do They Know It's Christmas?" for charity. Inspired by Geldof's song which raised $10 million, Harry Belafonte gathered an even bigger group of musicians (Stevie Wonder, Michael Jackson, Ray Charles, Lionel Richie, Bruce Springsteen, Willie Nelson, Bob Dylan, Tina Turner, Cyndi Lauper, Billy Joel, and others) and created "We Are the World," which raised over $63 million for Ethiopia. That summer, Geldof organized the biggest charity concert of all time: Live Aid. The concert, which featured Madonna, Jagger, Richards, McCartney, Bowie, Queen, Dylan, Led Zeppelin, Run-DMC, The Who, Sting, Elvis Costello, Pretenders, Tom Petty, Hall & Oates, and many more, was watched by a quarter of the planet and raised over $80 million. More importantly, it got the world thinking about helping a forgotten continent. In the decades since, the percentage of African people living in extreme poverty (while still a massive problem) has steadily dropped and Ethiopia's economy is now one of the fastest growing in the world.

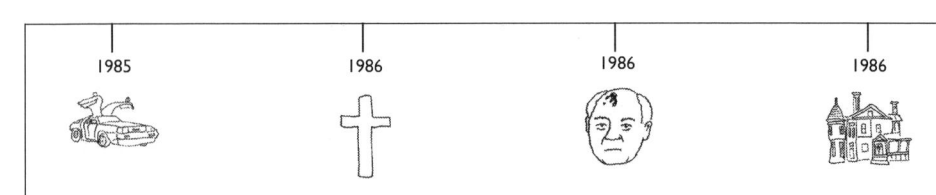

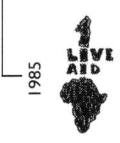

3. CLEVE JONES
1987 - Washington, D.C.

By 1985, more than 15,000 Americans had contracted AIDS and nobody in the government was talking about it. So Cleve Jones, a gay rights activist from San Francisco, asked people to write the names of loved ones they had lost to AIDS on a notecard. He then taped the cards to the San Francisco Federal Building, making the outer wall look like a patchwork quilt. Then Jones had a bigger idea—what if they were to make an actual quilt where people could honor those who died? So he and some fellow activists created the NAMES Project Foundation. People were asked to create three-by-six-foot panels honoring loved ones, and the foundation sewed them together. In 1987, the giant quilt containing 1,920 panels was displayed on the national mall in Washington. The quilt then went on a twenty-city tour, raised more than $500,000 for AIDS-related organizations, and got much needed media coverage, helping to make the disease impossible to ignore.

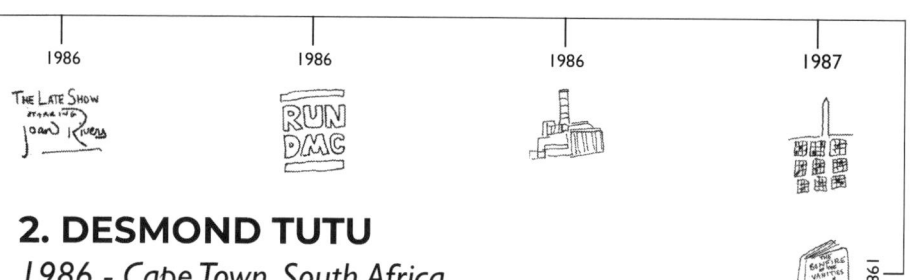

2. DESMOND TUTU
1986 - Cape Town, South Africa

Desmond Tutu wanted to be an educator. But, thanks to oppressive politics, he found South Africa's education system completely broken. So, in 1957, he quit and studied theology. Over the next decade, he moved up the ranks and became the first black dean of St. Mary's Cathedral in Johannesburg. Desmond Tutu passionately spoke out against South Africa's unconscionable apartheid at every opportunity. On numerous occasions, he broke up potentially deadly situations with his calming influence. Not only did South Africans take notice but so did the world. Thanks to the work of Desmond Tutu, South Africa came under constant global pressure to change their overtly racist policies. His 1984 Nobel Peace Prize was profoundly earned. When apartheid finally crumbled, Nelson Mandela appointed Archbishop Tutu to a role where he could help heal relations in the unstable new era.

1. ALEXEI ANANENKO, VALERI BEZPALOV, AND BORIS BARANOV
1986 - Pripyat, USSR (Ukraine)

On April 25, 1986, a group of imbecilic engineers did a ridiculously dangerous test on one of Chernobyl's nuclear reactors, causing an explosion that released four hundred times as much radiation as Hiroshima. The local fire brigade (with heroes like twenty-three-year-old Volodymyr Pravik) rushed to the scene knowing they'd probably die from the incredible exposure and, sadly, did. One report said the exposure turned Pravik's brown eyes blue. But the bigger issue arose a few weeks later. A slab of concrete below nearly 400,000 pounds of nuclear material was on the verge of cracking, which would set off a second explosion that had the potential to wipe out half of Europe. So two plant workers (mechanical engineer Alexei Ananenko and Valeri Bezpalov) and a soldier (Boris Baranov), put on wetsuits, waded into radioactive water in a pitch-black basement underneath a nuclear reactor, and shut off key valves. Three brave men saved half a continent. Despite severe radiation poisoning, all three miraculously survived. Boris Baranov died of a heart attack in 2005. The other two stayed in the industry.

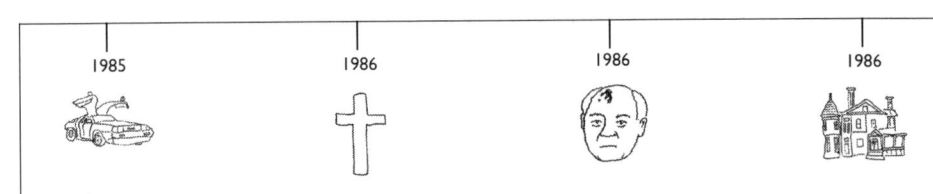

Honorable Mentions: Dalai Lama - 1989 (spiritual leader), "Tank Man" - 1989 (Tiananmen Square hero), Tim Keck, Christopher Johnson - 1988 (*The Onion*), Jackie Joyner-Kersee - 1988 (track and field), Adam Yauch, Adam Horovitz, Michael Diamond - 1989 (Beastie Boys), Michael Jordan - 1988 (baskeball), Toni Morrison - 1988 (*Beloved*), Steven Hawking - 1988 (*A Brief History of Time*), John Hughes - 1986 (writer/director), Roy Jones - 1988 (boxing), Tracy Marrow - 1986 (Ice-T), Bill Raftery - 1988 ("Send it in, Jerome!"), Alan Rickman - 1988 (Hans Gruber), Florence Griffith-Joyner - 1988 (track and field), Kelvin Mercer, David Jude Jolicoeur, Vincent Mason - 1989 (De La Soul), Wayne Gretzky - 1988 (hockey), Eric Barrier and Rakim Allah - 1988 (Eric B. & Rakim), Diego Maradona - 1986 (football), Phil Hartman - 1988 (comedy), Paul Reubens - 1985 (Pee-wee Herman), Danny DeVito - 1988 (actor), Bo Jackson - 1989 (athlete), Carlton Ridenhour, William Drayton - 1987 (Public Enemy), Cheryl Miller - 1985 (basketball), Len Bias - 1986 (basketball)

| 1986 | 1986 | 1986 | 1987 |

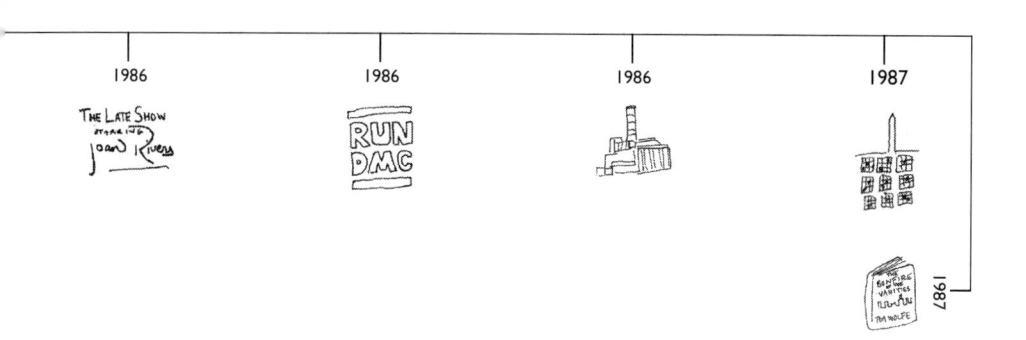

THE LATE SHOW
starring
Joan Rivers

RUN
DMC

1987

WORST

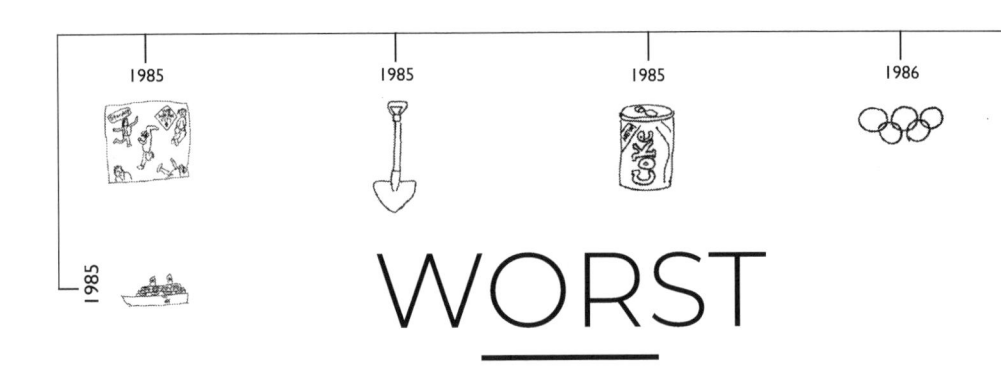

10. ROBERTO GOIZUETA
1985 - New York, New York

By 1984, Coca-Cola's market share, which had been nearly two-thirds in 1948, had shrunk down to 21.8 percent. Pepsi was nipping at its heels. So, in a New York City press conference, CEO Roberto Goizueta and President Donald Keough announced Coca-Cola was scrapping the original formula that had made them filthy rich over the years and replacing it with "New Coke," a sweeter substitute that would surely be a hit with those super hip young kids. People hated it. Sure, their market share was shrinking, but they were still number one. Pepsi gave its employees the day off and congratulated themselves in newspaper ads, and morons took to the streets in protest. Goizueta's plan to kill the golden goose ended after just seventy-nine days, when Coca-Cola announced the old formula would return.

9. JIM BROWN
1985 - Los Angeles, California

Jim Brown was a giant in the civil rights movement in America and one of its greatest-ever athletes. Too bad he was run-of-the-mill goon when it came to women. From 1965 to 2000, Brown was investigated or charged with assaulting six different women. In '68, West Hollywood police found Brown's twenty-two-year-old girlfriend semi-conscious underneath his second floor balcony. When police arrived, Brown threw one of the cops through the closet door. Charges were dropped when the girlfriend said she fell. Two years later, Brown was charged for throwing a couple other twenty-two-year-old women down the stairs for not participating in a three-way. Luckily for Jim, charges were dropped due to lack of witnesses. In '78, Brown served a day in jail for choking his golfing partner. In '85, a friend of his claimed he beat and raped her. The next year, yet another twenty-two-year-old claimed he assaulted her. In '99, Brown's wife hid in her car as Brown smashed it with a shovel. But maybe he was just really unlucky and none of it was true. Nope. In his autobiography, Brown freely admitted to hitting women and offered a weak line or two about how it's a bad thing to do.

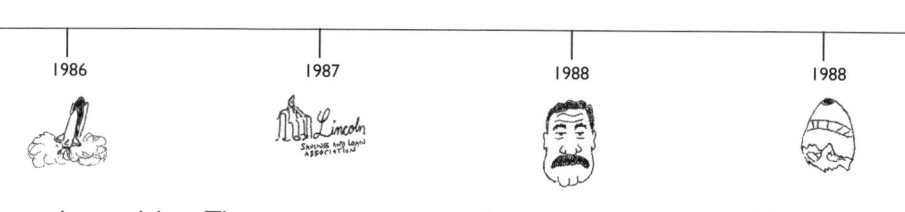

8. LAWRENCE MULLOY, JOE KILMINSTER, JERRY MASON, CALVIN WIGGINS, AND ROBERT LUND
1986 - Cape Canaveral, Florida

In the days leading up to the latest space shuttle launch (the Challenger), engineers at Morton Thiokol noticed that there was a cold front approaching Florida and Cape Canaveral could be experiencing record-low temperatures on the morning of the launch. If temperatures got too cold, the rubber O-rings (the things that keep the boosters together) would become brittle and largely useless. So these engineers voiced their objection. NASA was pissed. "My God, Thiokol, when do you want me to launch—next April?" whined NASA manager Larry Mulloy. Feeling the heat from NASA and, most likely, worried about how delaying the launch could affect future business contracts, Morton Thiokol higher-ups Joe Kilminster, Jerry Mason, Calvin Wiggins, and Robert Lund signed off on the launch. Sure enough, it was too cold, the brittle O-rings gave out, and the shuttle exploded, killing seven people and wasting about a billion dollars' worth of technology. The lesson? Never ignore science.

7. GRACE SLICK, MICKEY THOMAS, PETER WOLF, AND BERNIE TAUPIN
1985 - San Francisco, California

In a decade that featured such auditory assaults like "Lady in Red" and "Kokomo," one '80s song was the absolute worst: "We Built This City." On paper, it should've worked. It was co-written by Bernie Taupin, one of the great songwriters in history ("Tiny Dancer"). It was performed by Starship, a group that emerged from the great '60s band Jefferson Airplane. But this song was awful. Maybe he was saving his best for Elton John, but Bernie Taupin's lyrics here were straight up terrible (rhyming "corporation names" with "corporation games"). Grace Slick and Mickey Thomas' duet sounded less like music and more like two parents fighting. And, if it's a song about getting back to good ol' fashioned rock and roll, why does it sound like it belongs in a crummy video game? Fuck this song and everyone associated with it.

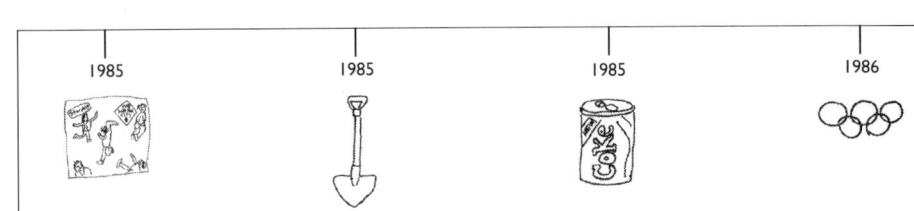

6. LI PENG
1989 - Beijing, China

Witnessing the push for democracy in the Soviet Union and neighboring Eastern European nations, many in China felt inspired to follow their lead. So thousands of students and workers gathered in Tiananmen Square, Beijing's symbolic heart, to protest. With Soviet leader Mikhail Gorbachev's highly publicized visit scheduled, Chinese Prime Minister Li Peng desperately wanted to make it all go away. So, between June 3 and 4, he sent thousands of troops to confront the now million protesters in Tiananmen Square. Bullets were fired into the crowd, killing hundreds, possibly thousands. Protesters were arrested and thrown in jail or executed. Li Peng tried to pass the blame off on party elders but, ultimately, it was his call.

5. CHARLES KEATING
1987 - Phoenix, Arizona

In 1987, five senators (including Ohio Democrat John Glenn and Arizona Republican John McCain) vouched for Lincoln Savings and Loan boss Charles Keating. After all, he was the religious crusader who campaigned against Larry Flynt and *Playboy* magazine. He even vilified the Ramada Inn hotel chain for showing pornography in its rooms. Sure, Keating had some missteps (like when he was fined by the Securities and Exchange Commission in the midseventies for profiting from illegal loans). But he was a "good guy" (and a key donor to their campaigns). In reality, the Keating Five were just buying more time for a monster to convince people to swap their safe holdings for his rotten American Continental

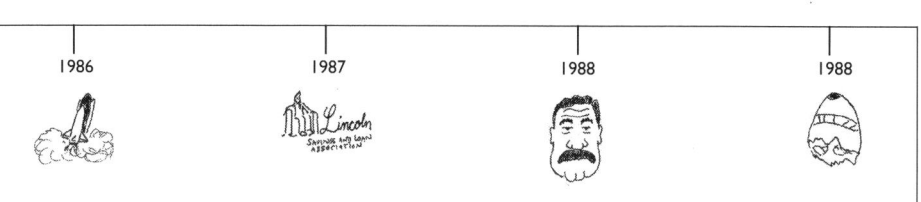

Corp junk bonds. Keating then took that money and gambled on the market. The Savings and Loan collapse cost 23,000 investors a total of $285 million and taxpayers $3.4 billion. For many elderly investors, it was their life savings. In 1993, a federal jury convicted Keating of seventy-three counts of wire and bankruptcy fraud. He served fifty months in jail. Inexplicably, McCain and Glenn kept their jobs.

4. ABU AL-ABBAS
1985 - Alexandria, Egypt

In October 1985, Palestinian terrorists led by Abu al-Abbas hijacked the Italian cruise ship *Achille Lauro*, in the process murdering Jewish-American retiree Leon Klinghoffer and dumping his body overboard. Afterward, the group promised no one had been harmed and worked out a deal for their freedom. When it was discovered they had murdered Klinghoffer, al-Abbas went on television and smugly suggested that the wheelchair-bound sixty-nine-year-old might have swum for it. This awful incident was one of many terrorist attacks throughout 1985 (like the killing of Israelis in Cyprus, Barcelona, and near the West Bank) and, really, the entire decade, committed by a Palestinian group that was loosely linked to PLO chief Yasser Arafat. Abu al-Abbas continued his life of violence until he was finally apprehended in Iraq in 2003.

3. CHUN TOO HUAN AND PARK IN-KEUN
1986 - Seoul, South Korea

In September of 1988, South Korea hosted the twenty-fourth Summer Olympics and put their newfound embrace of democracy on display. Aside from Canadian Ben Johnson's hundred-meter doping scandal, the Olympics seemed to be a big success. But, after some serious digging by the Associated Press in subsequent years, the world learned that something much more sinister went on behind the scenes. In an effort to clean up the streets before the Olympics put Seoul on the world stage, Dictator Chun Too

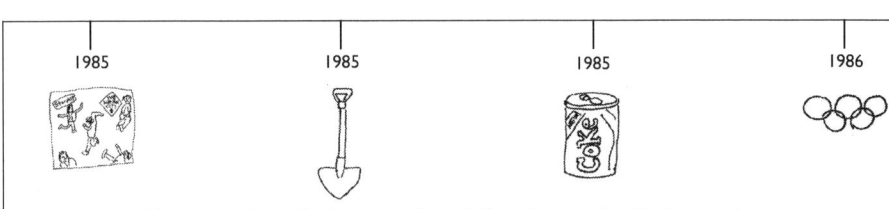

Huan ordered thousands of "undesirables" (homeless, vagrants, drunks, disabled people, and children) to be rounded up and sent to slave labor camps. Innocents (mostly children) were beaten, raped, and forced to work for free while monsters like Park In-keun, the owner of one of these facilities, got insanely wealthy selling the products made by his prisoners.

2. MUAMMAR QADAFFI
1988 - Tripoli, Libya

At first, it seemed like Muammar Qadaffi would actually be a positive force for Libyan people. Right away, he stood up to the oil companies and Libya became the first developing country to keep the majority of its oil profits. But it was pretty much downhill from there. In 1970, he expelled tens of thousands of Jews and Italians, got filthy rich from all the oil profits, and treated everyone horribly. Since most of the international community disliked the eccentric dictator, he sided with terrorist groups. In 1986, he supported the bombing of a Berlin nightclub frequented by U.S. soldiers. Two years later, Qadaffi-backed terrorists put a bomb on a New York-bound Pan Am flight, killing all 259 aboard and 11 on the ground in Scotland. In 2011, as revolts spread across the Arab world, Qadaffi tried to disappear. He was found in a drain, killed, and dragged through the streets.

1. SADDAM HUSSEIN
1988 - Halabja, Iraq

By 1979, Saddam Hussein had ruthlessly risen up the ranks in Iraq's Ba'ath Party to become president. After eliminating any potential dissenters in his cabinet, Hussein focused on attacking Iran's oil-rich area of Khuzestan with chemical weapons. But, since the United States and Western allies were more afraid of Iran's Ayatollah Khomeini and the spread of radical Islam than of Saddam, they looked the other way. The eight-year Iran-Iraq War left more than a million dead with no victor. Towards the end of that war, Hussein even used chemical weapons on his own people, the independent-leaning Kurds in the north; he killed 12,000 of them in 1988 with sarin and mustard gases. Also in 1988, over 100,000

| 1986 | 1987 | 1988 | 1988 |

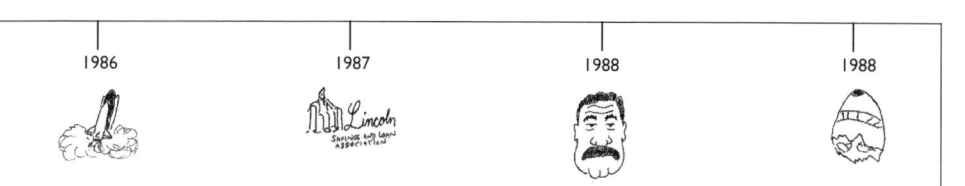

Kurdish men and boys were taken to the middle of nowhere and murdered by Saddam's troops. People just went missing during Saddam's three-decade regime—we're talking nearly *300,000* people. In 1990, he set his sights on invading another one of his neighboring countries—the wealthy Kuwait—which led to a lost war and countless dead. Ironically, Saddam Hussein's ultimate downfall was due to something he wasn't actually guilty of (possessing weapons of mass destruction). In 2003, he was found hiding in a hole and was executed.

| 1985 | 1985 | 1985 | 1989 |

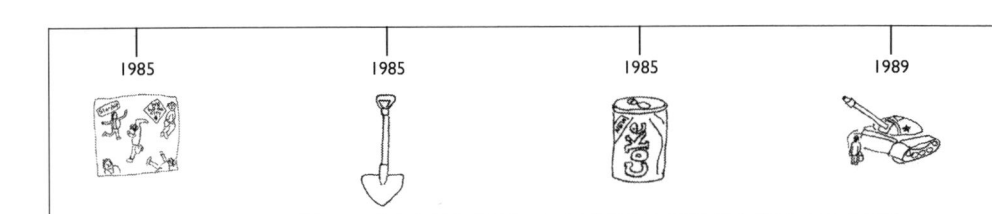

1985

Dishonorable Mentions: Evan Mecham - 1987 (cancelled MLK Day in Arizona), Aldrich Ames - 1985 (spy), Jim Bakker and Jimmy Swaggert - 1987 (crooked televangelists), Richard Kuklinski - 1986 ("The Iceman"), Kurt Waldheim - 1986 (Nazi), Patrick Henry Sherrill - 1986 ("going postal"), Robert Bork - 1987 (opposed civil rights), Arthur James Walker - 1985 (spy), Don King - 1988 (con artist, killer), Michael Milken - 1989 (fraud), Brian Lee Tribble - 1986 (sold Len Bias coke), John Gotti - 1985 (mob boss), Jimmy "the Greek" Snyder - 1988 (racist), Manuel Noriega - 1989 (brutal dictator), Joseph Hazelwood - 1989 (Exxon Valdez), Oliver North and John Poindexter - 1986 (Iran-Contra affair), Aileen Wournos - 1989 (serial killer), Gwendolyn Graham and Catherine May Wood - 1987 ("Lethal Lovers"), Leona Helmsley - 1989 ("Queen of Mean"), Giraldo Rivera - 1986 (dingbat)

1987 1985 1986 1988

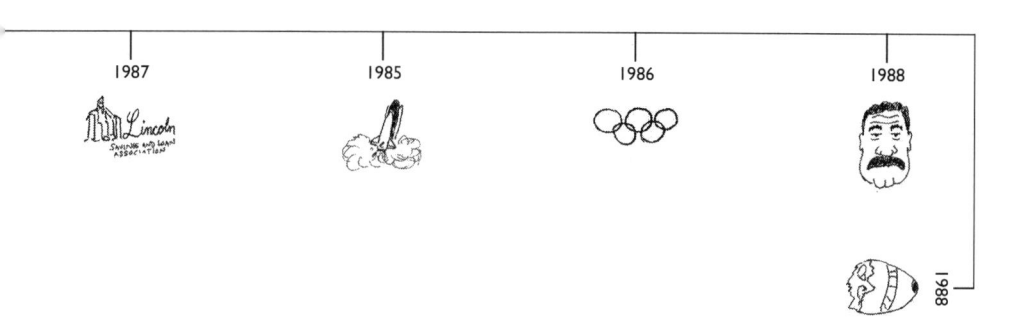

1988

461

| 1990 | 1990 | 1990 | 1993 |

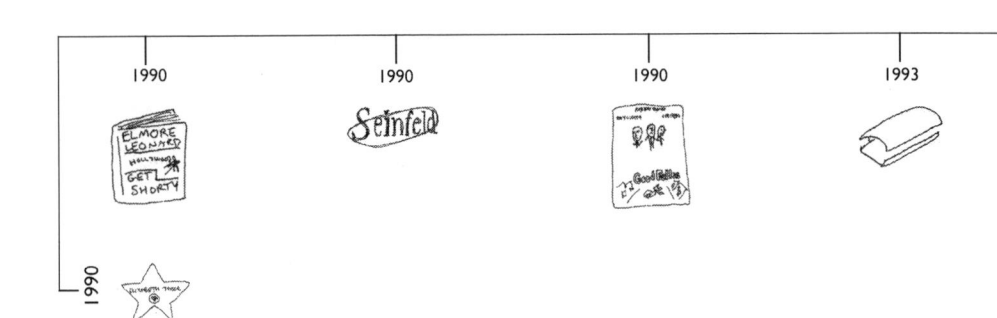

1990

1990-1994

"I learned that courage was not the absence of fear, but the triumph over it. The brave man is not he who does not feel afraid, but he who conquers that fear."

-Nelson Mandela

BEST

10. MARTIN SCORSESE
1990 - New York, New York

After briefly flirting with the idea of becoming a priest, Martin Scorsese got into filmmaking. He taught at NYU film school (one of his students was Oliver Stone) while honing his craft then, in 1973, unleashed the Martin Scorsese we all know and love. *Mean Streets* hit every Scorsese mark—unique, stylish shots, great acting performances, powerful use of pop music, and a healthy dose of gritty violence. But gritty wasn't all he could do. Over his career, Scorsese proved greatness at epics, family movies, dramas, comedies, horror, and music. There has never been a better director than Martin Scorsese. Despite kicking out some of the best movies of all time (*Raging Bull*, *Goodfellas*), Scorsese was held to a higher standard and awards escaped him. Finally, in 2007, the Academy righted its wrongs and gave Martin Scorsese his long overdue Oscar for *The Departed*. Congratulations, Academy. Now find a way to give him the nine more you owe him.

9. JERRY SEINFELD AND LARRY DAVID
1990 - Los Angeles, California

Before the show *Seinfeld*, TV shows revolved around the premise that their main characters were, deep down, likable people. People were always told to cheer for the guy in the white hat. That all changed in 1990 (well, the pilot was in '89 but nobody watched). Larry David and Jerry Seinfeld's show about a stand-up comic and his selfish, narcissistic friends consistently got thirty million viewers each week. Yes, it was the funniest show of all time but, on a more macro level, *Seinfeld* showed executives it's okay to focus on the bad guy. A character like George Costanza made it possible for lovable villains like Tony Soprano, Don Draper, and Walter White to exist. After the hugely successful nine-season run, Jerry Seinfeld went back to being one of the best comics in America and Larry David moved on to create another tremendous sitcom, *Curb Your Enthusiasm*… about an abrasive, neurotic main character named Larry David.

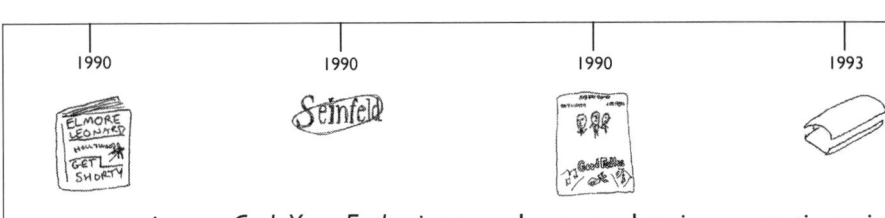

8. ELMORE LEONARD
1990 - Detroit, Michigan

Thanks to the over-saturation of Westerns on television, nobody wanted to read them in book form. So, former advertising copywriter-turned-Western writer Elmore Leonard pivoted to crime novels and became the best there ever was. Rather than doing writer-y things like dropping a bunch of twenty-five-cent words, Leonard wrote each story in the style of a guy talking to his buddy at a bar. In 1984, "the Dickens of Detroit" appeared on the cover of Newsweek and his novel LaBrava was chosen as the year's best by the Mystery Writers of America. The following year, The New York Times dubbed the sixty-year-old Leonard "the greatest living crime writer." And that was just the start. Between the ages of sixty and eighty-five, Leonard kicked out another twenty-three books, ranging from very good to fantastic. Hollywood eventually figured out how to turn them into great movies (Get Shorty, Jackie Brown, Out of Sight) and television shows (Justified). If he's not the single greatest American author, Elmore Leonard's surely in the top two or three.

7. HOWARD STERN
1993 - New York, New York

For decades, talk radio fell into one of two categories: serious or lame. Then word spread about this hilarious six-foot-five, long-haired force of nature in New York. Critics derided him as a vulgar, talentless "shock jock" but audiences clearly didn't agree. Look past the eye-opening subject matter, and the Stern radio show was the only authentic show on the air. Rather than relying on goofy sirens and peppy talk, Stern gave probing interviews and talked about real-life topics. If the show took an R-rated turn, so what? Life can be R-rated. Stern dominated the ratings in New York and, soon, his radio show was syndicated all over the country (reaching a daily audience of twenty million spanning just about every socioeconomic background). Over the years, Howard (and the show) has evolved but the core conviction has remained the same: deep down, we're all weirdos. Might as well embrace it. Baba Booey!

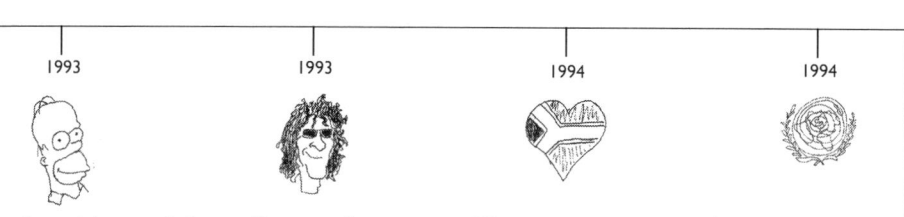

6. ELIZABETH TAYLOR
1990 - Los Angeles, California

By the mid-eighties, Liz Taylor was Hollywood royalty and could've spent the rest of her life getting her ass kissed. But in 1985, as her friend Rock Hudson was dying from AIDS, she saw Hollywood (and Hudson's old pal, Ronald Reagan) turning its back on the disease ravaging the country. So Elizabeth Taylor got to work. She hosted benefits, badgered other A-listers to support the cause, pleaded with Congress, and started foundations. Her star-studded Commitment to Life dinner raised over $1.3 million and was covered by network television. Finally, in 1987, she browbeat the president into publicly speaking about the disease for the first time. In the nineties, she even ran a *Dallas Buyers Club*-like program out of her Bel Air mansion, procuring experimental AIDS medication for people who were running out of options. Liz Taylor was so much more than seven husbands and *Cleopatra*. She was the real deal.

5. MATT GROENING
1993 - Los Angeles, California

At first, Matt Groening's cartoon family the Simpsons were just animated bumpers during *The Tracey Ullman Show*. Pretty soon, though, these characters became more popular than the show itself. So, in December 1989, *The Simpsons* got its own time slot. Along with the help of Jim Brooks and producer Sam Simon, the show hired a bunch of former *Harvard Lampoon* writers and hit the ground running. Fairly quickly, *The Simpsons* became a cultural hit. The show was a perfect balance of goofiness and highbrow humor. For every slapstick fall, there would be an Ayn Rand or *Rashomon* reference. In 2009, the show surpassed *Gunsmoke* as the longest running scripted primetime show in American history.

The Simpsons are as much an American institution as the Model T and apple pie.

4. QUENTIN TARANTINO
1994 - Los Angeles, California

While working as a video store clerk, Quentin Tarantino wrote two of the best screenplays of the 1990s (*Reservoir Dogs* and *True Romance*). He hooked up with producer Lawrence Bender, who got the scripts in the right hands. Suddenly, Quentin Tarantino wasn't working at a video store anymore. Tony Scott liked True Romance and bought it. Harvey Keitel loved *Reservoir Dogs* so much that he signed on to star in and produce it (while allowing QT to direct for the first time). While the violent heist-gone-wrong movie didn't make a ton of dough at the box office, it put Tarantino on the map. Big-time actors (Christopher Walken, Bruce Willis) signed up to work with him on his next project, the Cannes Film Festival-winning *Pulp Fiction*. While the action-packed, mold-breaking *Pulp Fiction* did spawn a bunch of terrible copycats, it also raised the bar for the entire industry. Actors weren't afraid to do more creative independent movies. Writers improved dialogue in mundane scenes to more closely resemble real life. Studios were willing to take more chances. Quite simply, *Pulp Fiction* is the greatest movie ever made.

3. ASHOK GADGIL
1993 - Berkeley, California

Growing up in Mumbai, India, Ashok Gadgil saw firsthand how difficult finding clean water could be. So, in 1993, when he learned of 10,000 people dying from "Bengal cholera," he decided to focus his efforts on coming up with a cheap and simple water purification design for his home country. After a few years, Gadgil came up with a UV lamp that, for just $2, could kill bacteria and purify water for two thousand people a year. WaterHealth International now uses his design to provide safe drinking water for more than five million people in developing countries. Rather than bask in his many accolades, Gadgil then turned his focus to war-torn Darfur, where women risked their lives on a daily basis just by gathering firewood. So, Gadgil designed a stove that ran on half the fuel. Today, Gadgil's Berkeley-Darfur Stoves are helping more than 125,000 families.

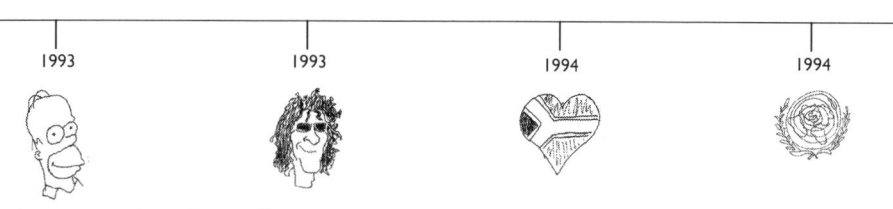

2. MBAYE DIAGNE
1994 - Kigali, Rwanda

Once the Rwandan genocide began in the spring of 1994, French, Belgian, and Italian governments sent in their troops, but only to get their nationals out safely. The United States was only six months removed from the Black Hawk Down debacle in Somalia, so there was no chance they were going to get involved. That left some random U.N. troops, who were told to surrender and get the hell out of Dodge. But Captain Mbaye Diagne, a young U.N. officer from Senegal, wasn't about to do that. For a couple months, Diagne bravely went on solo missions in his vehicle to rescue four or five Tutsis at a time and deliver them to safety (the U.N.-guarded Hotel des Mille Collines of *Hotel Rwanda* fame). To get past the constant checkpoints, the devout Muslim loaded up his car with booze, cigarettes, and cash to bribe soldiers. Sadly, after months of saving hundreds, possibly thousands of lives, Diagne's car was hit by a mortar shell. He was killed instantly.

1. NELSON MANDELA
1994 - Pretoria, South Africa

No matter what Nelson Mandela tried to do to help improve South Africa (law school, politics, nonviolent protest), he was met with brutality by the Afrikaner government. So, after the Sharpeville massacre, he decided to change course and blow things up, literally. If peaceful protests were going to be met with brutality, Mandela believed he was going to have to get violent as well. In 1961, Nelson Mandela founded the Umkhonto we Sizwe

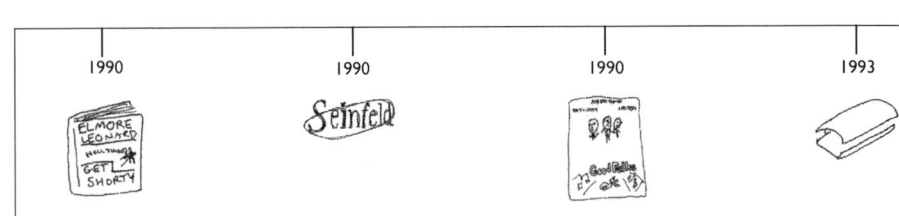

("Spear of the Nation"), a protest group that used guerrilla war tactics to fight apartheid. By 1963, he was arrested and given a life sentence. For eighteen of the next twenty-seven years, Mandela was confined to a small cell without a bed, plumbing, or adequate medical care on former leper colony Robbin Island. He could've gotten out sooner but he refused to relinquish his right to protest. Then, as apartheid was collapsing in the early '90s, the seventy-one-year-old Mandela was finally freed. And, right away, he got back to work. He worked tenaciously with President F.W. de Klerk on improving life for all in South Africa, earning the 1993 Nobel Peace Prize. The following year, Mandela became president with de Klerk as his deputy. Nelson Mandela improved the lives of millions. Maybe that's why nobody had the heart to tell him he was wearing ugly shirts.

| 1993 | 1993 | 1994 | 1994 |

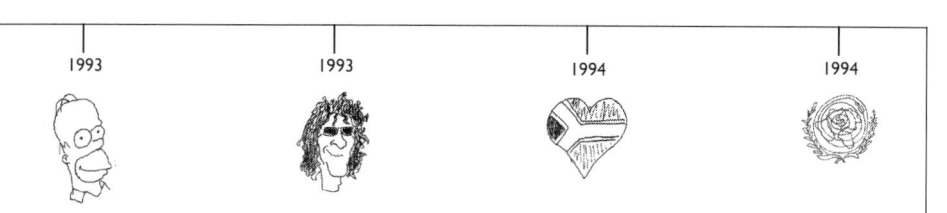

Honorable Mentions: Bill Murray - 1993 (comedy), Benazir Bhutto - 1993 (first female head of Muslim state), Kenan Ivory Wayans - 1990 (*In Living Color*), Kirk Cobain, Dave Grohl, Krist Novoselic - 1991 (Nirvana), Mario Lemieux - 1993 (hockey), Bob Newhart - 1990 (comedy), Conan O'Brien - 1993 (comedy, "Marge vs the Monorail"), Ron Chernow - 1990 (biographer), Eddie Vedder, Stone Gossard, Jeff Ament, Mike McCready, Matt Cameron - 1991 (Pearl Jam), Kelly Slater - 1994 (surfing)

1994

WORST

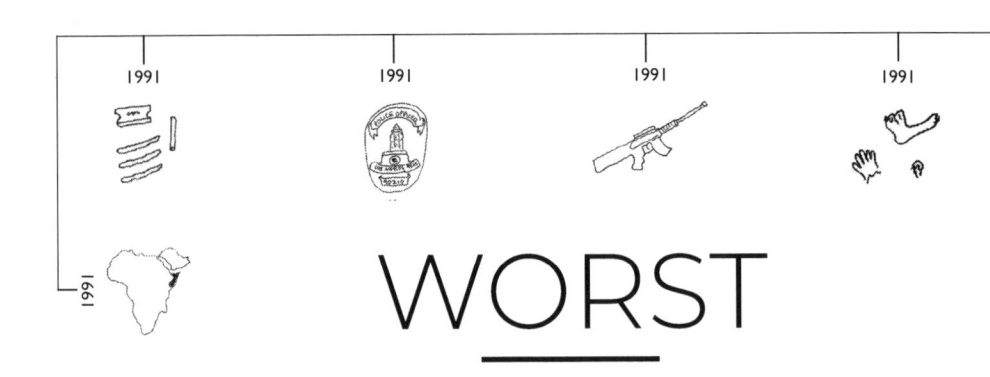

10. (TIE) ORENTHAL JAMES SIMPSON
1994 - Brentwood, California

In 1989, O.J. Simpson beat his wife Nicole Brown Simpson and threatened to kill her. But it was before the existence of social media, so everyone conveniently forgot about it. The charming football great/movie star/pitchman was back on TV and movie screens in no time. Then, a few years later, Nicole Brown Simpson and her special friend, Ronald Goldman, were found stabbed to death and nearly decapitated outside Nicole's home. Things didn't look so good for "the Juice" —he had a wound on his hand, his blood was found at the crime scene, footprints at the murder site matched his shoe size, he had recently purchased a knife that was consistent with the wounds (but, mysteriously, went missing), and he had no alibi for the time of the crime. And, when authorities were about to arrest him, O.J.'s bootlicker buddy Al Cowlings helped him take off on the world's slowest police chase. He eventually surrendered (with a fake beard and passport) and the "trial of the century" finally got started in January of 1995. O.J. hired the best lawyers money could buy, the L.A. prosecutor's office screwed up in a hundred different ways, and a group of L.A.P.D.-wary jurors voted "not guilty." Since then, Simpson has taken his time looking for "the real killer."

10. (TIE) JAY LENO
1993 - Burbank, California

It was widely assumed that David Letterman was the heir apparent to *The Tonight Show* when Johnny Carson retired. So, in 1991, Jay Leno's bulldog manager, Helen Kushnick, floated a story in the *New York Post* about NBC trying to push Johnny Carson into retirement so Jay Leno could be the host. The specious story was effective and Leno got the job. For the next quarter-century, Leno sold his soul (and once promising comedic ability) just to have *The Tonight Show*. Instead of trying to be funny, Leno played it safe with a steady dose of inoffensive, flaccid jokes and bland, suck-up celebrity interviews. In 2009, after wasting a chance to redeem himself, Leno went back to his back-stabbing ways and pushed out the next *Tonight Show* host (Conan O'Brien) to buy himself a few more years. One of the best comics in America turned out to be a run-of-the-mill office weasel.

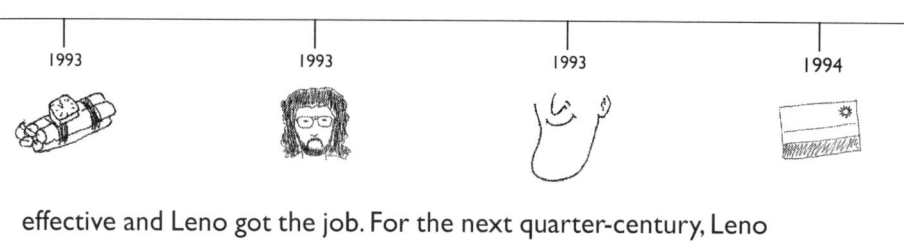

9. JOSEPH NICOLOSI, BENJAMIN KAUFMAN, AND CHARLES SOCARIDES
1992 - New York, New York

Until 1987, the American Psychiatric Association still considered homosexuality to be some sort of disorder (an opinion the World Health Organization also had until 1992). So, in 1992, three men—Charles Socarides, Joseph Nicolosi, and Benjamin Kaufman—decided the world was getting too gay for their tastes and formed the National Association for Research and Therapy of Homosexuality (NARTH). Together the three psychotherapists fought against the (in Socarides' words) "purple menace that is threatening the proper design of gender distinctions and society." What they were doing was performing gay conversion therapy (*Clockwork Orange*-nonsense where a patient is put through a battery of tests designed to drum the homosexuality out). It would be easy to just call these three "kooks," but NARTH's "medical" opinions are still used today by right wing homophobes in the highest offices in America.

8. JEFFREY DAHMER
1991 - Milwaukee, Wisconsin

Jeffrey Dahmer's probation officer had a lot on her plate, so she stopped making house visits. She knew the thirty-one-year-old Milwaukee man who had served ten months in the slammer for fondling a thirteen-year-old Laotian boy in 1988 had his demons.

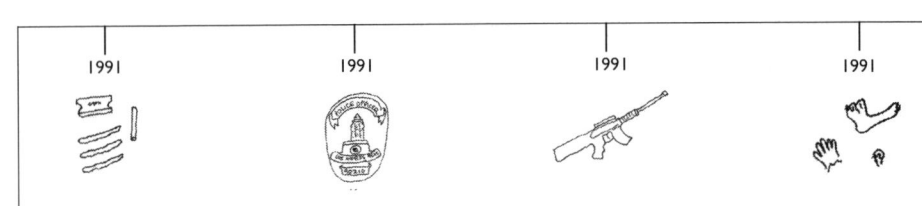

But, at the same time, he checked in with her regularly and held a stable job at the Ambrosia Chocolate Company. Bad idea on her part. On July 22, 1991, police encountered a handcuffed thirty-two-year-old man running down the street telling them a man named Dahmer was trying to kill him. When officers went to Jeffrey Dahmer's apartment to investigate, they found pictures of decaying bodies and actual human remains all over—in the fridge, the freezer, in a file cabinet. They even found a couple hands and a penis in a kettle on the stove. For thirteen years, Dahmer had targeted poor black, Asian, or Latino men and boys, the most ignored demographic in America, and lured them back to his place by offering them money to model for pictures. Then he'd drug, strangle, and cut them to pieces. Lastly, he'd have sex with and eat them. He was murdered in prison.

7. GEORGE HENNARD
1991 - Kileen, Texas

George Hennard had no friends and no job. But, since his parents were wealthy, he was able to live for free in his mom's spare house. He creepily tried to hook up with his neighbor's teenaged daughters but was rejected. Then he filed civil rights charges with the FBI against women for plotting against him. Nothing happened. Finally, the day after his thirty-fifth birthday, Hennard loaded a couple semiautomatic weapons, got in his truck, and drove it straight through the window of Luby's Cafeteria at lunchtime. He then got out of the truck with a smile on his face and opened fire on the crowd for ten minutes while shouting, "This is for the women of Bell County." Hennard killed twenty-three people, wounded another twenty, and then shot himself in the head. No official gun control measures were taken in response to this incident.

6. DAVID KORESH
1993 - Waco, Texas

When Vernon Wayne Howell's Hollywood rock star dreams didn't pan out, he moved to Waco, Texas and joined the Branch Davidians, who are kind of an intense spinoff of the already pretty intense Seventh-Day Aventists. He shacked up with the "prophetess" Lois Roden, who was in her late sixties, then took over when she died. He changed his name to David Koresh (which loosely translates to Cyrus, the name of a Persian king), then informed the Branch Davidians that, as their leader, he was allowed to have "spiritual weddings" with female followers. In other words, he could bang whomever he pleased. Koresh ended up fathering a dozen children. He told his followers about an impending Armageddon and that they should build an "Army of God" to prepare for it, so they started stockpiling weapons. When the Bureau of Alcohol, Tobacco, and Firearms (ATF) tried to investigate, a four-hour shootout erupted, leaving six Branch Dravidians and four ATF agents dead. This led to a fifty-one-day standoff. When the feds tried to smoke them out of their fortress, Koresh seized upon the opportunity to die a martyr and set the place on fire. More than seventy men, women, and children were killed on national television. Right-wing extremists jumped on the opportunity to paint the government as a villain who will kill you and take your guns.

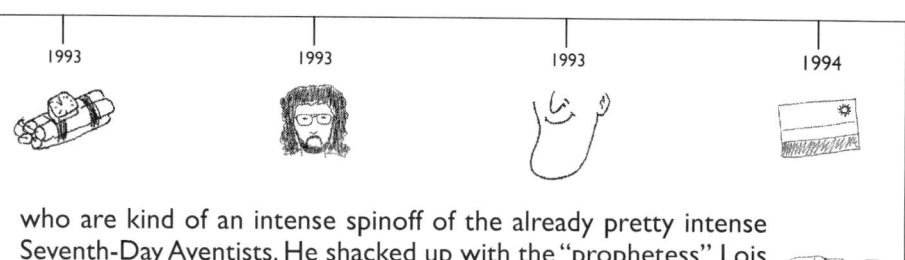

5. JOHN BURT AND MICHAEL GRIFFIN
1993 - Pensacola, Florida

Former KKK member-turned-minister John Burt printed out wanted posters featuring Alabama fertility Doctor David Gunn and encouraged people to harass him. One of Burt's followers, Michael Griffin (a fundamentalist Christian whose biggest life highlight up to that point was getting fired from a roller skating rink for hitting a customer) followed Burt's directive and murdered Gunn in 1993. The shooting galvanized the radical anti-abortion movement. The following year, a former Christian minister murdered another two doctors at a Pensacola clinic. Later in 1994, a man opened fire in a Planned Parenthood in Massachusetts. To this day, the same senseless acts of terrorism continue. It all started with Burt and his vacuous follower, Griffin. Griffin still sits in jail while Burt... well... he, too, found his way into the clink, but for child molestation. Apparently he just wanted to save the babies so there would be more for him to prey upon.

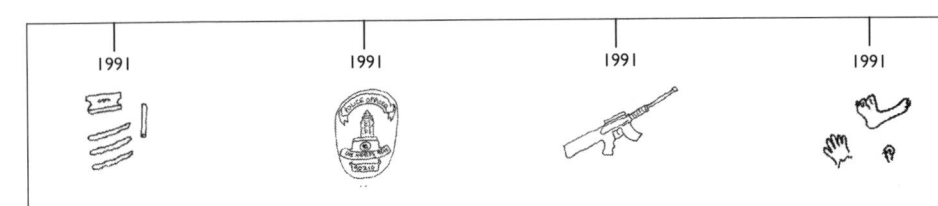

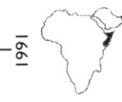

4. DARYL GATES, STACEY KOON, LAURENCE MICHAEL POWELL, TIMOTHY WIND, AND THEODORE BRISENO
1991 - Los Angeles, California

When Los Angeles was chosen to host the 1984 Summer Olympics, Chief Daryl Gates was tasked with cleaning up the city. He responded by turning beaten-down, minority-heavy areas like South Central and East L.A. into militarized zones. Mass arrests were made under the guise of breaking up gangs, the Olympics went off without a hitch, and Gates was hailed as a hero. After the Olympics, police brutality complaints surged by over 33 percent, and yet, nothing was done. Finally, in 1991, someone caught the brutality on tape. After police pulled over intoxicated motorist Rodney King, Sgt. Stacey Koon instructed his officers Laurence Powell, Timothy Wind, and Theodore Briseno to beat him senseless while seventeen other officers watched. The officers were charged but, ultimately, were acquitted. Much like the Watts Riots in 1965, the people reached their boiling point. For the next few days, rioting claimed the lives of more than sixty people, thousands more were injured, seven thousand-plus were arrested, and three thousand buildings were set on fire.

3. PABLO ESCOBAR
1991 - Medellín, Colombia

Pablo Escobar lived in the perfect time and place to become a drug kingpin. Colombia was right near the coca plant-rich Peru and Bolivia and on the northern tip of South America, just a short trip removed from America. Plus, this was the Studio 54-era in America. Booger sugar was as much a part of nightlife as dancing. Pablo's Medellín cartel dominated 80 percent of the U.S. cocaine market and was raking in $420 million per week. With a net worth around $30 billion, *Forbes* had Pablo Escobar pegged as one of the ten richest people in the world. By taking some of that money and giving that back to the community, Escobar endeared himself to the people and even got elected to Colombia's congress. When he was kicked out, Escobar turned full villain. Everyone became a target, even ordinary citizens. The death toll climbed but nothing, not even sending him to jail, could slow down Pablo Escobar. Finally, in 1993, the United States' DEA, a mysterious group called Los Pepes (*Perseguidos por Pablo Escobar*, or "People Persecuted by Pablo Escobar") and the non-bought-and-paid-for members of Colombia's military tracked down Escobar and killed him.

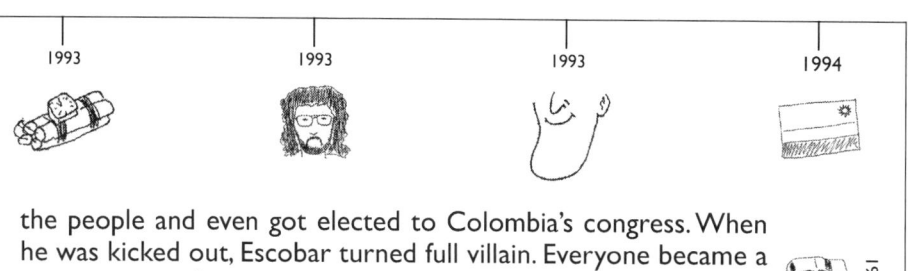

2. MOHAMED SIAD BARRE, MOHAMED FARRAH AIDID, AND ALI MAHDI MUHAMMAD
1991 - Mogadishu, Somalia

At the pointiest part of the Horn of Africa lies Somalia, a country so messed up that piracy is a reasonable career choice. Much of that blame for the downfall of the once proud "nation of poets" falls upon Siad Barre. The former general overthrew the government in 1969, and then spent the next two-plus decades consolidating power and oppressing his people through a myriad of human rights violations. As Siad's bloodsucking family and friends got rich, the Somali people starved. Major droughts in the '80s and '90s brought outright mayhem. Siad fled to Nigeria, leaving a completely shattered government and an open door for warlords Mohamed Farah Aidid and Ali Mahdi Muhammad to take over. The two leaders of rival clans engaged in a brutal civil war as ordinary citizens were completely neglected and starved. George H.W. Bush tried to send some humanitarian aid and Bill Clinton tried to take out warlord Aidid. But, after the Black Hawk Down disaster, dozens of other American deaths, and billions spent, the U.S. decided to abandon the region altogether. Things have only gotten worse. Somalia still has no real government. The only constants are famine, disease, and war.

1. THEONESTE BAGOSURA
1994 - Kigali, Rwanda

When the rich European countries divided up previously German territories after World War I, Belgium got Rwanda. Belgian officials then traveled to the East African nation and determined the Tutsi people would be the ruling class. This relegated 85 percent of Rwanda's population, the Hutu, to working class status. Then, in 1959, the Hutu rebelled and took over the government, pushing the Tutsis to scramble to other countries (like Uganda) or else stay in Rwanda and have the tables turned on them. Over the next few decades, the Tutsis fought to, once again, have some sort of voice in the government. Just as President Juvenal Habyarimana was set to grant the Tutsis a seat at the Hutu-controlled table, Hutu extremist military leader Theoneste Bagosura shot down Habyarimana's plane and blamed it on the Tutsis. The following day, Bagosura got on the radio, called the Tutsi "less than human," and ordered citizens help him in exterminating the "enemy." Over the next hundred days, 800,000 Rwandans were slaughtered. Neighbors attacked neighbors. Hutu priests murdered refuge-seeking Tutsis. Bagosura's troops were eventually subdued and he escaped to Cameroon. He was caught in 1996 and tried for genocide and crimes against humanity.

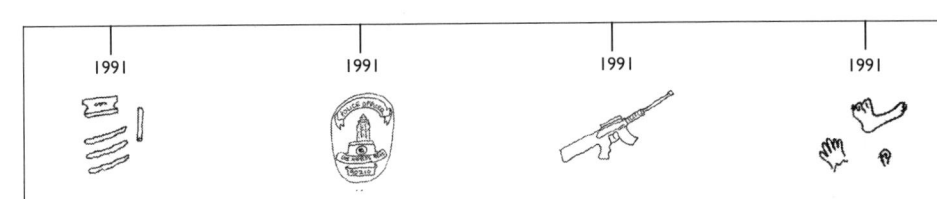

1993   1993   1993   1994

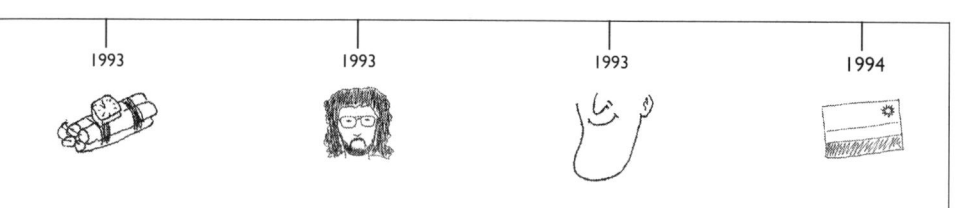

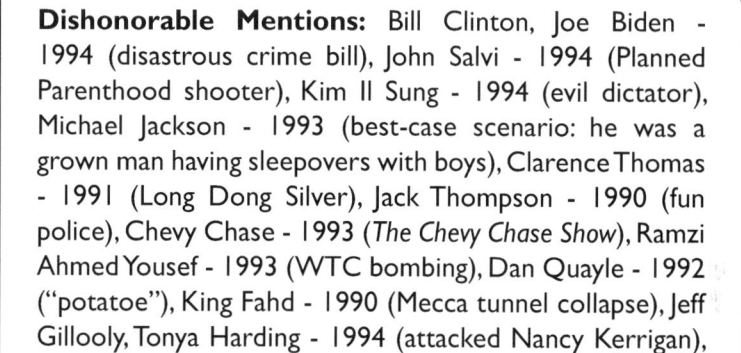

Dishonorable Mentions: Bill Clinton, Joe Biden - 1994 (disastrous crime bill), John Salvi - 1994 (Planned Parenthood shooter), Kim Il Sung - 1994 (evil dictator), Michael Jackson - 1993 (best-case scenario: he was a grown man having sleepovers with boys), Clarence Thomas - 1991 (Long Dong Silver), Jack Thompson - 1990 (fun police), Chevy Chase - 1993 (*The Chevy Chase Show*), Ramzi Ahmed Yousef - 1993 (WTC bombing), Dan Quayle - 1992 ("potatoe"), King Fahd - 1990 (Mecca tunnel collapse), Jeff Gillooly, Tonya Harding - 1994 (attacked Nancy Kerrigan), Gunter Parche - 1993 (stabbed Monica Seles)

1994

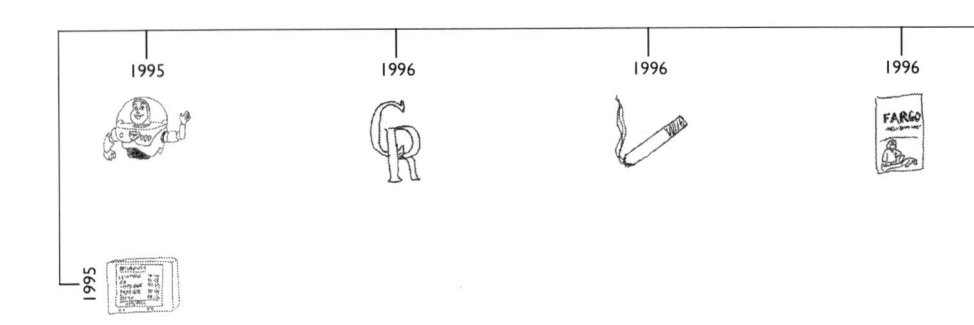

1995-1999

"Black people yelling "racism!" White people yelling "reverse racism!" Chinese people yelling "sideways racism!" And the Indians ain't yelling shit, 'cause they dead. So everybody bitching about how bad their people got it: nobody got it worse than the American Indian. Everyone needs to calm the fuck down."

-Chris Rock

BEST

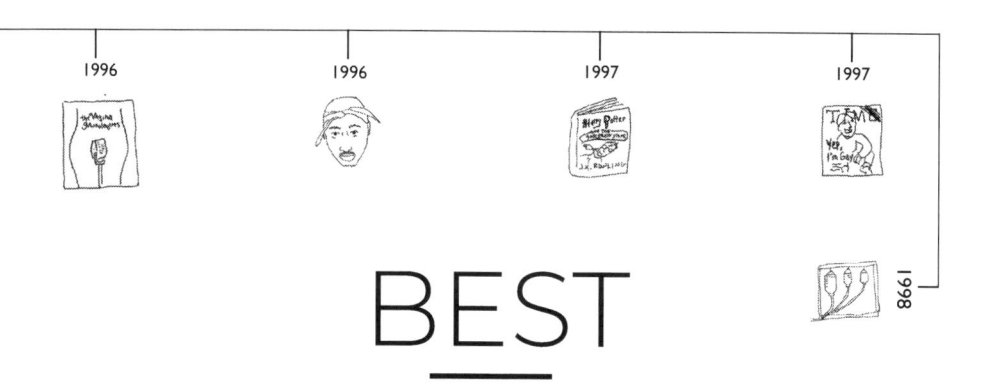

10. JACK KEVORKIAN
1998 - Oakland County, Michigan

Doctors in America are trained to keep people alive as long as they can. But Jack Kevorkian thought some of his patients were just ready to go. When he wrote about assisted suicide in medical journals, everyone just wrote him off as a kook and nicknamed him "Doctor Death." Then, in 1990, Kevorkian made national news by assisting the suicide of an Oregon woman suffering from Alzheimer's. He was charged with murder but, since the laws were still kind of vague, charges were dropped. They clarified the law, but that didn't stop Kevorkian from helping more than a hundred people end their suffering. In 1998, he even assisted a suicide on national television (*60 Minutes*) and was convicted for second-degree murder. Most seventy-year-olds are looking for a soft landing spot for their twilight years. Jack Kevorkian chose prison for his beliefs.

9. TUPAC SHAKUR
1996 - Los Angeles, California

If you could create a rapper in a laboratory, the end result would be Tupac Shakur. He had a hardscrabble background, so he could connect to the streets. He was highly educated in the arts, so he was able to draw from different inspirations in different genres. His parents were Black Panthers and drug addicts, so he was acutely aware of the injustices and problems facing the black community. In high school, he sold drugs and performed in a theater group. He rapped about the need for black men to break out of the vicious circle and yet did several stints in jail for various assaults. As an actor, he played a great menacing thug in *Juice* and *Above the Rim* but also received strong reviews for playing vulnerable characters in *Poetic Justice* and *Gridlock'd*. Tupac Shakur was a walking contradiction and a ridiculously talented artist. His inability to shake the street caught up to him when he was murdered in Las Vegas in 1996. But, thanks to an insane work ethic, after only twenty-five short years on earth, Tupac Shakur left a massive music catalog and unmatched legacy.

8. EVE ENSLER
1996 - New York, New York

In 1994, Eve Ensler told her friend a story about her vagina. Her friend responded in kind. Eve got to thinking. Why are vaginas never really talked about? Guys talk about their penises all the time. What was the big deal? You never even saw the word. Not in print. Not on TV. Nowhere. So she asked more friends and heard their stories (sex, puberty, assault) and wrote a forty-minute show called *The Vagina Monologues*. After great struggles to advertise it anywhere (nobody wanted the word "vagina" in big font), it turned out to be word of mouth that made the show possible and, soon, celebrities like Calista Flockhart, Alanis Morissette, Joanne Woodward, and Paul Newman were advocating for it. Within a few years, *The Vagina Monologues* was performed in over 140 countries in 48 different languages, raising $100 million for charity in the process. Never underestimate the power of the vagina.

7. JOEL AND ETHAN COEN
1996 - Hollywood, California

While they have bounced across different genres throughout their career, filmmakers Joel and Ethan Coen have stayed remarkably consistent. Regardless of the movie itself, a Coen brothers' creation is always full of rich characters played by actors at the absolute top of their game. Since they usually are not working with a crazy budget, studios have given them lots of creative freedom. Whether it's a gangster film, a black comedy, neo-noir, Western, drama, or just absurd comedy, the brothers have steadily kicked out meticulously made gems (*Blood Simple, Raising Arizona, Fargo,*

The Big Lebowski, No Country For Old Men, True Grit). Their movies all sound characteristically terrific, as they diligently ensure proper timing for music and silence within dialogue. They write together, they direct together, they edit together, and nobody really understands how it all works. But it's worked for more than three decades, so it's probably best to not question it.

6. CHRIS ROCK
1996 - Washington, D.C.

At thirty-one years old, Chris Rock was in the middle of a solid but not great show biz career. He had some small roles in movies, a pretty good three-year run on *Saturday Night Live*, and moderate stand-up success. To be great, he knew he had to rededicate himself to his first love: comedy. For two years, Chris Rock hit the road and fine-tuned his stand-up act. By 1996, it was good enough for HBO to give him his own one-hour special, *Bring the Pain*. Rock's special took the audience to uncomfortable places—race, infidelity, domestic abuse, and more—and he had people howling at every step of the way. *Bring the Pain* was the greatest stand-up special in history. We're talking better-than-Richard-Pryor's-*Live-on-the-Sunset-Strip* good. Better than *Carlin at Carnegie*. From that point forward, Chris Rock was great.

5. JOHN LASSETER
1995 - Burbank, California

Even though they were making some cool breakthroughs, Lucasfilm's computer graphics department was hemorrhaging money. Considering that the final *Star Wars* movie (in the original trilogy) was already completed, cash flow would be minimal. So George Lucas sold the company to recently-out-of-work Steve Jobs for five million. The new company (now called "Pixar," which was a made-up Spanish-sounding word for "to make pictures") would focus on providing computer animation for the government and the medical community. But it still lost money. So Jobs called on his team to make some short films and drum up interest.

Animator John Lasseter proved to be a brilliant storyteller. His second short film (*Tin Toy*) won an Oscar. Soon Disney approached Pixar to do a full-length version of *Tin Toy*. Lasseter and his crew (with the help of about 800,000 computer hours) created *Toy Story*, the game-changing top-grossing movie of 1995. In the two-plus decades since, Pixar has been the undisputed top family movie studio. Unfortunately, Lasseter never practiced the family values that his movies preached and was dismissed by the studio for being a grabby creep.

4. ELLEN DEGENERES
1997 - Los Angeles, California

Up until the late 1990s, nobody on television was gay. Sure, Liberace had his own show and Paul Lynde was a regular on *Hollywood Squares*, but nobody was officially "out." Then, Ellen DeGeneres, comedian and star of her own TV show (*Ellen*), changed everything. Tired of being in the closet in her personal life, DeGeneres decided to come out to the world and have her character on the show to do the same. As word got out, interest in the story grew. By the time "The Puppy Episode" aired on April 30, 1997, more than 42 million people tuned in to hear Ellen say the words no main character on television had ever said: "I'm gay." Predictably, there was blowback from the religious right, like sentient bag of feces Jerry Falwell and by advertisers, like greasy, artery-clogging, square burger-peddler Wendy's. Her show was soon canceled and her career was left in shambles. But after the initial outrage, Americans collectively stopped thinking of it as that big of a deal. Ellen DeGeneres helped normalize homosexuality. Today, nobody under the age of twenty-five cares whether you're gay or straight. Ellen clawed her way back and is now the host of a hugely successful syndicated talk show.

3. JOANNE ROWLING
1997 - Edinburgh, Scotland

| 1996 | 1996 | 1997 | 1997 |

1998

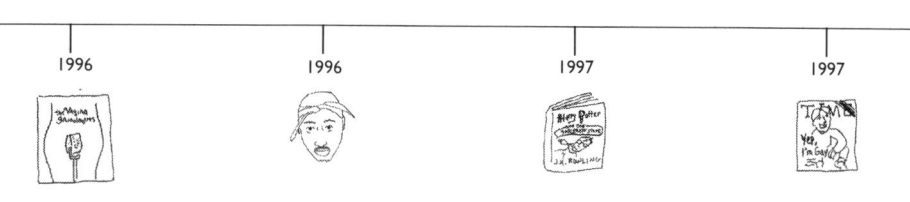

In the winter of 1994, single mom Joanne Rowling was struggling to make ends meet while coping with the crushing loss of her mother. The one thing that helped was writing a story about a boy wizard she had been kicking around in her head. After she completed her first novel, she shopped it around to numerous agents and publishers before a small independent publisher bought the rights for the equivalent of about $4,000. The first Harry Potter book was an incredible success. By 1999, the first three novels in the series were occupying the top three spots on The New York Times bestseller list. Rowling's seven-book series (full of eight and nine-hundred page books) has sold more than 450 million copies and inspired a multi-billion-dollar film franchise. Psychologists have praised the Harry Potter series for helping promote empathy and social skills in children. What Sesame Street is to preschoolers, Harry Potter is to ten-year-olds.

2. ANTHONY WOOD
1995 - Santa Clara, California

Tired of watching old episodes of Star Trek: The Next Generation on clunky, low-quality videotapes, Anthony Wood wondered if he could record shows on a hard drive. Hard drives were getting cheaper every day. Surely there was a market for this. Within a couple years, Wood was able to raise enough cash to launch ReplayTV, the world's first DVR. ReplayTV might not have lasted long, but the DVR completely changed the entire television industry. Aside from sporting events, people stopped planning their schedules around watching a specific program. The DVR allowed people to be choosier with their entertainment and inspired streaming services to produce their own high-quality content. Everyone has had to raise their game to stay relevant and, as a result, television is better than ever.

1. JEFFREY WIGAND
1996 - Louisville, Kentucky

| 1995 | 1996 | 1996 | 1996 |

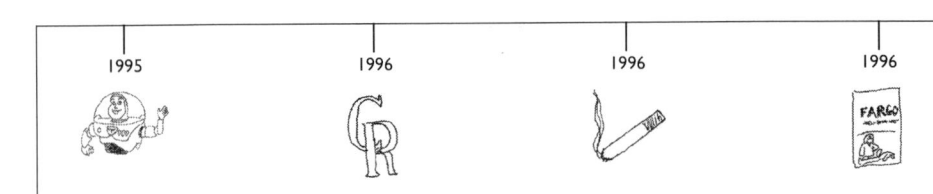

In 1989, Wigand was hired to develop a "safer" cigarette at Brown & Williamson (America's third-largest cigarette manufacturer at the time). After only about a year, the company dropped the project and sent Wigand into R&D. A few years later, he read a report about the dangers of coumarin, a substance used in the company's tobacco. He voiced concerns about the rat poison-like substance full of carcinogens but management ignored and, ultimately, fired him. So Wigand took a high school teaching job (at a tenth of his former salary) and began a crusade against his deceitful former employer. After an appearance on **60 Minutes**, the tobacco industry fired back with a smear campaign that destroyed his home life. But he stuck to his guns and, in 1998, helped bring about the Master Settlement Agreement where tobacco companies agreed to pay billions of dollars to states for smoking-related medical costs and, more importantly, raised awareness about the health hazards.

| 1996 | 1996 | 1997 | 1997 |

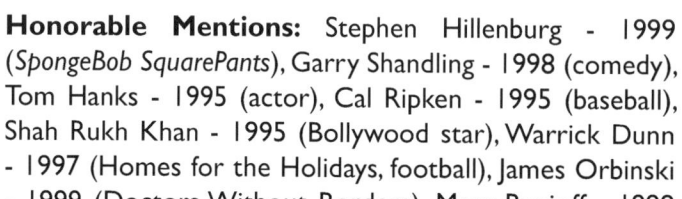

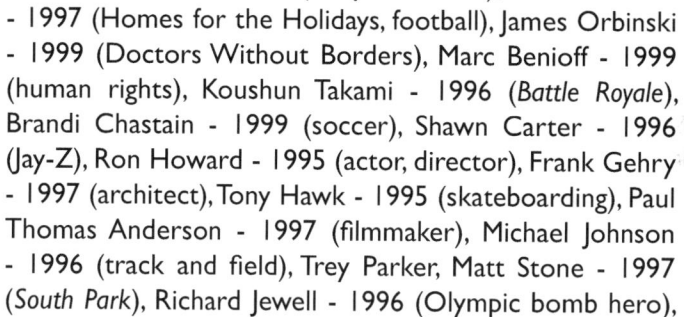

1998

Honorable Mentions: Stephen Hillenburg - 1999 (*SpongeBob SquarePants*), Garry Shandling - 1998 (comedy), Tom Hanks - 1995 (actor), Cal Ripken - 1995 (baseball), Shah Rukh Khan - 1995 (Bollywood star), Warrick Dunn - 1997 (Homes for the Holidays, football), James Orbinski - 1999 (Doctors Without Borders), Marc Benioff - 1999 (human rights), Koushun Takami - 1996 (*Battle Royale*), Brandi Chastain - 1999 (soccer), Shawn Carter - 1996 (Jay-Z), Ron Howard - 1995 (actor, director), Frank Gehry - 1997 (architect), Tony Hawk - 1995 (skateboarding), Paul Thomas Anderson - 1997 (filmmaker), Michael Johnson - 1996 (track and field), Trey Parker, Matt Stone - 1997 (*South Park*), Richard Jewell - 1996 (Olympic bomb hero), Ira Glass - 1995 ("This American Life"), Laird Hamilton - 1996 (surfing)

WORST

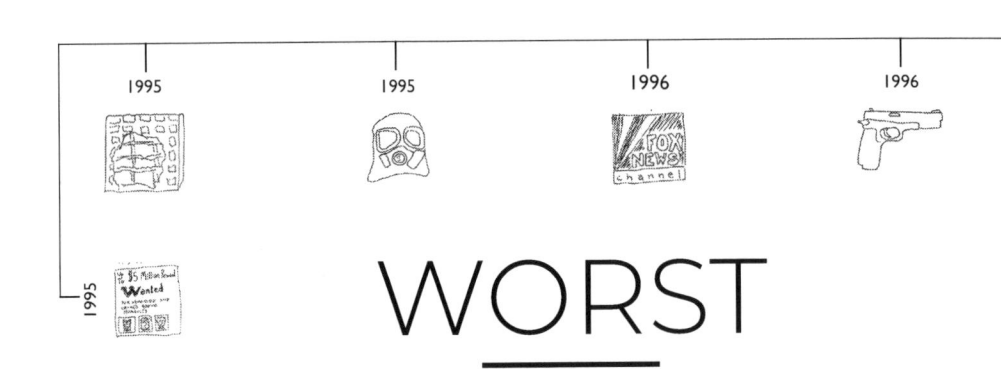

10. TED KACZYNSKI
1996 - Lincoln, Montana

Ted Kaczynski was such a smart kid that he skipped two grades and enrolled at Harvard when he was just sixteen. Socially, on the other hand, Kaczynski was a mess. After failing to coexist with the rest of society, the angry math genius took to a cabin in the Montana woods and started a nearly-two decade crusade against the government and technology. Starting in 1978, Kaczynski sent bombs to university professors and airlines, earning him the name "Unabomber" (UNiversity and Airline) from law enforcement. But nobody could figure out who was doing it. Then, in 1995, Kaczynski sent a 35,000-word manifesto to the FBI bitching about society. When Kaczynski's brother read it in *The New York Times*, he recognized the writing style and told the FBI. When the FBI raided his cabin in 1996, they found bomb equipment and 40,000 pages of journals detailing his crimes. Now he enjoys three hots and a cot in a cell not much smaller than his Montana cabin.

9. PAPARAZZI
1997 - Paris, France

It's easy to resent the British royal family. They're just a bunch of people who were born into wealth and status. But Princess Diana, in many ways, was different. Rather than be content with a life of luxury, she used her privileged platform to call attention to important issues that were going unreported (land mines, AIDS, and other such stuff). Even after divorcing out of the royal family, her social life was highly sought-after tabloid fodder. One night in Paris, she and her boyfriend tried to sneak away from the relentless paparazzi. Unluckily for them, their driver was three-sheets-to-the-wind drunk, lost control, and got everyone in the car killed. What did the paparazzi do as the badly injured princess was struggling for her life? They climbed onto the car and kept taking pictures. In the decades since, the morally bankrupt profession has only grown in stature.

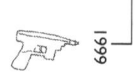

8. SHOKO ASAHAR
1995 - Tokyo, Japan

As consumerism was devouring Japan in the late '80s, some people felt a spiritual void. Along came Shoko Asahar, a long-haired, bearded guy in pajamas, who claimed he was the second coming of both Jesus Christ and Buddha, could levitate, and didn't need to eat, drink, or bathe. He opened the Aum Shinrikyo (Aum Supreme Truth) yoga studio, which quickly morphed into a doomsday cult. Shoko Asahar convinced his thousands of followers that the government was coming to get them and recruited scientists to help them build an arsenal of biochemical weapons. When politicians or judges opposed them, they became targets. In 1994, the Aum cult released sarin gas at a dormitory that housed judges in a town west of Tokyo, killing seven and injuring another 150. Then, in March of 1995, Shoko Asahar instructed his cult that World War III was to begin. Aum Shinrikyo teams boarded separate subway cars during morning rush hour in Tokyo armed with sarin gas, killing twelve and badly injuring thousands more. Shoko Asahar was arrested and sentenced to death. Aum Shinrikyo had its religious tax privileges stripped and lost lots of members, but the doomsday cult still isn't completely dead. The now renamed Aleph cult still boasts thousands of followers. If the world has taught us anything it's that there is no low point for morons.

7. ERIC RUDOLPH
1996 - Atlanta, Georgia

During the 1996 Summer Olympics in Atlanta, a forty-pound pipe bomb exploded, injuring more than a hundred people and killing one woman (and also causing a fatal heart attack). Six months later, a couple of similar nail-laden pipe bombs blew a hole through the wall of an Atlanta abortion clinic. Five days after that, a bomb blew up outside a gay nightclub. Police knew it was the same person but had no leads. Then, in January of 1998, a bomb exploded outside a Birmingham, Alabama women's clinic. This time, people spotted the culprit's pickup truck so the police had their suspect: Eric Rudolph, a self-employed carpenter. Rudolph confessed but showed zero remorse for the abortion clinic or gay club bombings because that wouldn't jive with God's plan… you know, the plan which the Lord personally divulged to some cretin with a creepy mustache.

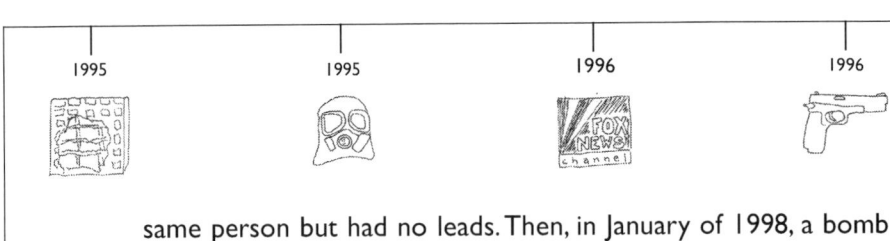

6. ERIC HARRIS AND DYLAN KLEBOLD
1999 - Littleton, Colorado

At around 11:00 a.m. on a Tuesday morning in April, eighteen-year-old Eric Harris and seventeen-year-old Dylan Klebold planted propane bombs in their Columbine High School cafeteria, hoping to cause the greatest mass murder of all time. They went back to their cars and waited for the explosion. When it never came, they picked up their guns instead and headed inside. They laughed and tormented students as they shot them, killing twelve of them (and a teacher) and injuring another twenty. Then they killed themselves. There had been plenty of warning signs but, still, a friend was able to easily buy them the guns at a gun show. Afterwards, there was a lot of talk to close loopholes and put greater restrictions on guns but, ultimately, politicians took their marching orders from the National Rifle Association and shot down any proposed restrictions. America has had more than ninety mass shootings in the twenty years since.

5. THOMAS HAMILTON AND MARTIN BRYANT
1996 - Dunblane, Scotland; Port Arthur, Australia

In the spring of 1996, two communities in different countries were devastated within the span of just a few minutes by two disturbed armed men. Forty-three-year-old Thomas Hamilton walked into a Scottish primary school with 743 rounds of ammunition and opened fire on a group of five- and six-year-olds and their teacher, killing seventeen and wounding another fourteen. A month later in Australia, twenty-eight-year-old Martin Bryant walked into a cafe with an automatic weapon and opened fire, killing a total of thirty-five people. Both countries responded with strict gun control measures. Neither has had another mass shooting since.

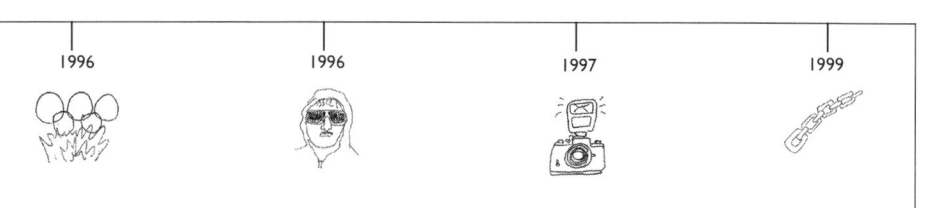

4. JAVED IQBAL
1999 - Lahore, Pakistan

Javed Iqbal targeted beggar and street children between the ages of six and sixteen, sodomized them, strangled them with a chain, cut them into pieces, and then dissolved them in a vat of acid. Police had heard some complaints about him but took no action. Then, in December 1999, the police received an anonymous letter stating, "I have killed 100 beggar children and put their bodies in a container." This set off a month-long manhunt which ended fruitlessly. Finally, Iqbal walked into a newspaper office and declared that he, in fact, was the guy who wrote the letter. When police checked out his place, they found vats of acid, human bones, children's clothing, and a thirty-two-page journal containing victim details. Guess they should've followed up on those early complaints.

3. ROGER AILES
1996 - New York, New York

For decades, Australian billionaire huckster Rupert Murdoch kept acquiring media outlets and turning them into salacious trash. But, during the media boom of the '90s, Murdoch wanted the biggest cash cow of them all—a cable news network. So he hired former daytime TV producer and political strategist Roger Ailes to launch the Fox News network. The strategy was pretty simple: don't spend money actually breaking news but rather just hire a bunch of good-looking talking heads to react to it. He filled studios with alpha males and attractive women and had them play to the most under-targeted and rapidly expanding demographic in America—old white people. Pretty much every old white person loves two things: conspiracy theories and longing for "the good ol' days." So

489

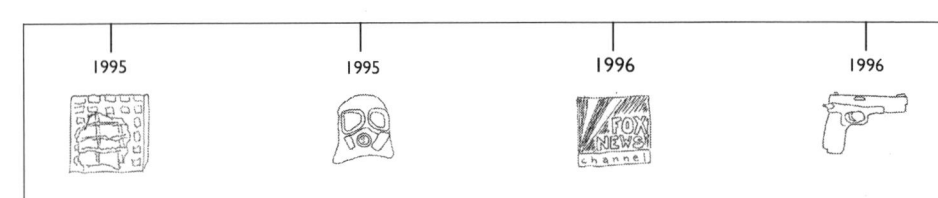

that's what Ailes gave them on a daily basis. By calling Fox News "fair and balanced," it implied that every other source of media had some sort of agenda. People actually breaking stories? They were trying to manipulate you. Ailes creation quickly became Frankenstein's monster (a.k.a. hyper-partisan America). You were either with Fox News or against America. Oh, and Ailes also happened to be a sexual predator who was forced to resign in 2016. Apparently looking like Jabba the Hutt wasn't enough for Roger Ailes. He had to act like him too.

2. TIMOTHY MCVEIGH
1995 - Oklahoma City, Oklahoma

After serving in the U.S. Army, Timothy McVeigh began a nomadic lifestyle and bounced from state to state, attending endless gun shows. At each show, McVeigh became closer with right-wing militia members and his resentment for the government grew. After the 1992 Ruby Ridge and 1993 Waco incidents, McVeigh's anger reached a boiling point. By the fall of 1994, with help from some old army buddies, McVeigh plotted a massive attack on the Alfred P. Murrah Federal Building in Oklahoma (because it would provide great camera angles for the inevitable media coverage). On the two-year anniversary of Waco, McVeigh parked a rented truck filled with tons of fertilizer and gallons of fuel and blew the north side off the building, killing 168 people (including nineteen young children in a daycare center) and wounding another 450. He was eventually caught and executed. And for what? Did he prove any profound point? No. He was just an angry blockhead who loved guns too much.

1. SLOBODAN MILOSEVIC, RADOVAN KARADZIC, AND RATKO MLADIC
1995 - Srebrenica, Bosnia-Herzegovina

Yugoslavia was breaking up and the mostly Muslim Bosnia wanted to split off into its own territory. The 30 percent Serbian population of Bosnia-Herzegovina wanted to stay with Serbia, though. So, when the split officially happened in 1992, Serbian President Slobodan Milosevic had Bosnian Serb leader Radovan

| 1996 | 1996 | 1997 | 1999 |

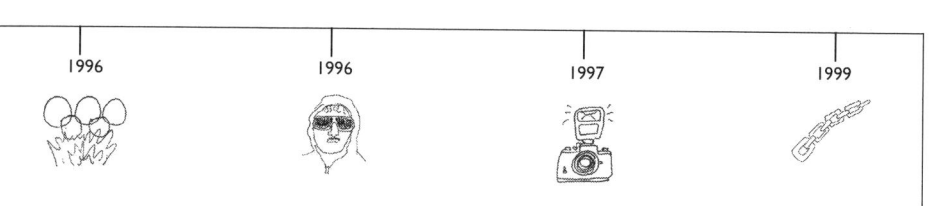

Karadzic lead troops into the Bosnian capital, Sarajevo, and bomb it to smithereens, killing thousands of Muslims and Croats. Serbian military leader Ratko Mladic quickly earned the moniker "the Butcher of Bosnia" by carrying out Milosevic and Karadzic's plan of ethnic cleansing. In 1995, the U.N. war crimes tribunal officially charged Karadzic and Mladic with genocide. NATO air strikes were called in. The men were removed from their roles and, eventually, were thrown in the iron city. Milosevic died in custody during his trial.

1999

Dishonorable Mentions: Charles and David Koch - 1999 (environmental destroyers), Kenneth Starr - 1998 (blowjob investigator, university sexual assault enabler), Rae Carruth - 1999 (NFL murderer), Yigal Amir - 1995 (assassinated Rabin), Aaron McKinney and Russell Henderson - 1998 (murdered Matthew Shepard), Whitey Bulger - 1995 (Boston crime boss), Bernard Parks - 1998 (Rampart scandal), Yolanda Saldivar - 1995 (murdered Selina), Newt Gingrich - 1997 (crooked politician), Mark Barton - 1999 (murderer), Andrew Cunanan - 1997 (murdered Versace), Luis Garavito - 1999 (serial killer), George Lucas - 1999 (Jar Jar Binks), Michael McKevitt - 1998 (Real IRA, terrorist)

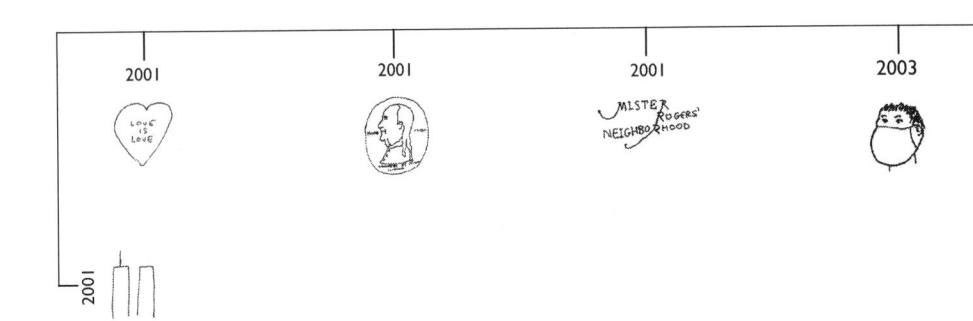

2000-2004

"The generation that destroys the environment is not the generation that pays the price. That is the problem."

-Wangari Maathai

BEST

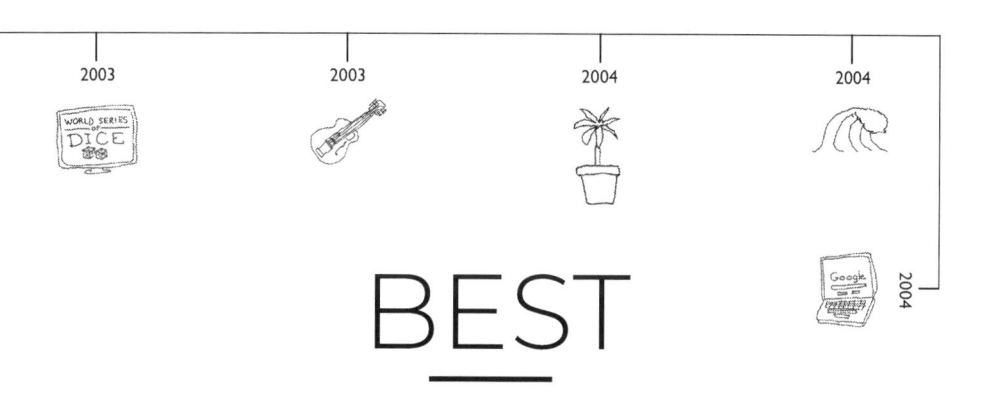

10. JACK WHITE
2003 - Detroit, Michigan

While doing a sound check before a White Stripes show in Australia, Jack White messed around with a few chords on his guitar. He wrote it down and saved it in his notes as "Bond Theme" (in case he was ever asked to write one). When it was time to create the next White Stripes album, *Elephant*, White shelved the whole Bond idea and decided to use the tune for himself under the title "Seven Nation Army." Ever since 2003, the most famous guitar riff of all time can be heard just about anywhere—movies, sports stadiums and arenas, even during Arab Spring in Egypt. Usually, even the biggest songs fall out of favor or slip into a nostalgia category. "Seven Nation Army" has been on constant rotation for over a decade and a half and shows no signs of slowing down.

9. DAVE CHAPPELLE
2003 - New York, New York

At just twenty-nine years old, Dave Chappelle was already a fifteen-year veteran in the stand-up comedy world. By then he had a finely-tuned act and clear comedic voice. After a series of hugely successful hour-long specials, Comedy Central gave him the platform to do his own sketch comedy show. Much like his stand-up act, the show was silly, didn't follow any particular pattern, and regularly stomped on third-rail topics like race. The cultural phenomenon soon had executives throwing insane sums of money at him for a third season. But, instead of letting the show become a parody of itself, Dave Chappelle walked away and went back to stand-up, where he once again reached legendary status.

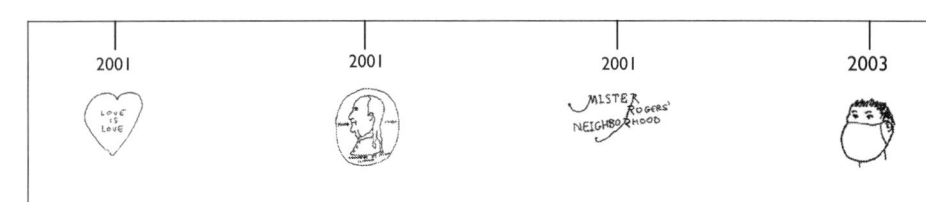

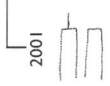

8. SARI HORWITZ, SCOTT HIGHAM, AND SARAH COHEN
2001 - Washington, D.C.

The thing people don't like addressing when it comes to capitalism is that there's only so much room at the top. Some people, quite simply, get run over and need government assistance to survive. Between 1993 and 2000 in the nation's capital, the government failed those people and 229 children died while in protective care. Since they were poor kids, nobody seemed to notice. Then, Washington Post investigative reporters Sari Horwitz, Scott Higham, and Sarah Cohen did a multipart series about the blatant neglect by D.C.'s child welfare system, which led to sweeping top-to-bottom reforms. The Pulitzer Prize-winning series was a shining example of how important great journalism is to a democracy. Horwitz, Higham, and Cohen gave a loud voice to those who had none.

7. TILLY SMITH
2004 - Phuket, Thailand

If you're looking for someone to demonstrate a cannonball at the pool or give you a ranking of Harry Potter characters, a ten-year-old would be an excellent choice. If you're looking to save the lives of a hundred people, probably not. In 2004, Tilly Smith proved to be atypical of her age group. While vacationing with her family on the beaches of Phuket, Thailand, ten-year-old Smith noticed the beach shrinking and being swamped with bubbling water (like the froth on a beer). It seemed a little odd to others but Tilly Smith knew it was serious. She started freaking out and got everyone off the beach. Just a few weeks earlier, Tilly had learned about tsunami warning signs in Andrew Kearney's geography class in Surrey, England. People quickly rushed to higher ground and, within minutes, a tsunami crushed the Thailand resort city. The tsunami ended up killing a quarter million people that day, ten thousand of them in Thailand. Thanks to the "Angel of the Beach," none of them were staying at Tilly Smith's resort.

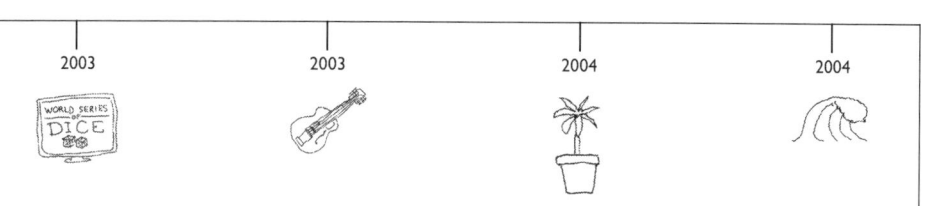

6. FRED ROGERS
2001 - Pittsburgh, Pennsylvania

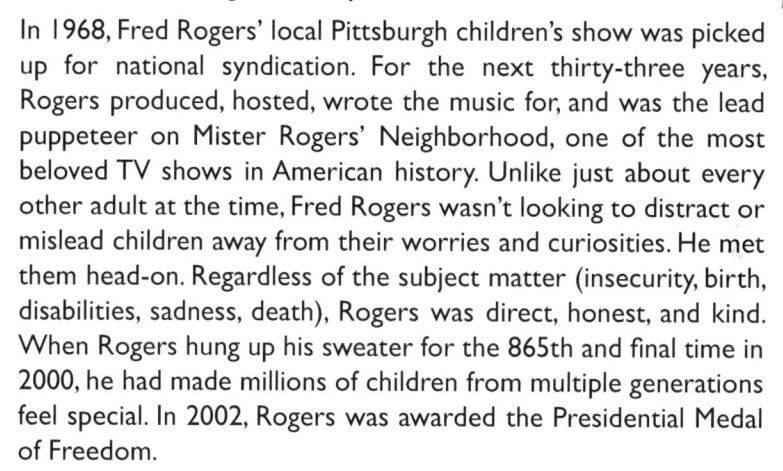

In 1968, Fred Rogers' local Pittsburgh children's show was picked up for national syndication. For the next thirty-three years, Rogers produced, hosted, wrote the music for, and was the lead puppeteer on Mister Rogers' Neighborhood, one of the most beloved TV shows in American history. Unlike just about every other adult at the time, Fred Rogers wasn't looking to distract or mislead children away from their worries and curiosities. He met them head-on. Regardless of the subject matter (insecurity, birth, disabilities, sadness, death), Rogers was direct, honest, and kind. When Rogers hung up his sweater for the 865th and final time in 2000, he had made millions of children from multiple generations feel special. In 2002, Rogers was awarded the Presidential Medal of Freedom.

5. AXEL AND EIGIL AXGIL
2001 - Copenhagen, Denmark

In 1948, Axel Lundahl-Madsen established one of the first gay rights organizations in Europe. The following year he met and fell in love with a man named Eigil Eskildsen. The two changed their surname to Axgil (a combination of both their first names) and spent the next four decades openly living their lives, running a gay modeling agency, lobbying for gay rights in their country, and risking jail time. Finally, in 1989, Denmark became the first country in the world to legalize same-sex civil unions. The seventy-four- and sixty-seven-year-old Axgils were awarded the first ever civil union. Within a few years, fellow Scandinavian countries Norway and Sweden followed suit. About ten years after that, the Dutch Catholic Church was dealing with so many self-inflicted wounds in their hospitals by depressed gay people that they defied the Vatican and lobbied the Netherlands to change its laws to match those in Scandinavia. On December 21, 2000 Queen Beatrix ratified the law allowing gay marriage. Soon, gay marriage was legal in most of the Western world. It may have taken half a century, but the brave persistence of Axel and Eigil Axgil paid off. Love won.

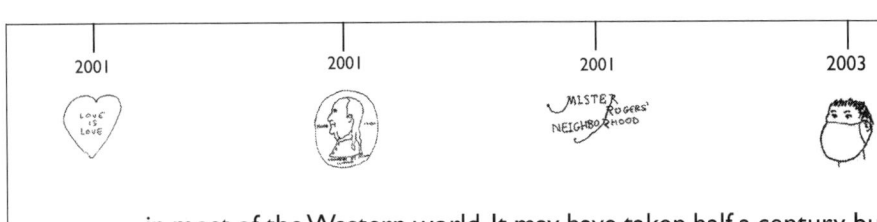

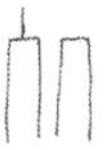

4. WANGARI MAATHAI
2004 - Nairobi, Kenya

Between a population explosion and excessive deforestation, by 1978, Kenya was becoming a barren wasteland. That's when Wangari Maathai, a professor at the University of Nairobi, said enough was enough. Maathai launched the Green Belt Movement, a women-run tree-planting program. Since women were expected to protect their children, the women of Kenya would think ahead by protecting the forests. By 1987, more than 50,000 women had planted a total of more than ten million trees. Not only did the campaign reverse the trend of eroding fertile ground and food shortage; it also empowered women in a culture where they had no voice. The Green Belt Movement took on a second life, fighting environment-killing building projects and improving life for women in her country. Maathai suffered harassment and assaults for her cause by the patriarchal government on many occasions but never wavered. In 2004, she was awarded the Nobel Prize. Towards the end of her life, she spouted some bonkers theories about AIDS but, undeniably, Wangari Maathai was one of the most important environmentalists and women's rights activists in history.

3. JIANG YANYONG
2003 - Beijing, China

In November 2002, a Chinese businessman became sick with a weird case of pneumonia. The four people who treated him at the hospital also became sick. Over the next few months, thousands of cases of severe acute respiratory sickness (SARS) popped up all over China. The government was puzzled by it but, at the same time, didn't want anyone to freak out about it. So they covered up the story. SARS was a killer and nobody really knew. Finally, a semiretired doctor named Jiang Yanyong wrote a letter about the cover-up to the Chinese media. The letter found its way to *Time*

Magazine, who then blasted it out to the Western world. The World Health Organization went into crisis mode and the rest of the world poured resources into finding a cure. By the following July, the mysterious killer had been stopped.

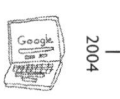

2. SERGEY BRIN AND LARRY PAGE
2004 - Mountain View, California

For a master's assignment at Stanford, Sergey Brin and Larry Page teamed up and developed a search engine that listed results by the popularity of the pages. The project, called Google (a play on the word "googol," which is a number equal to one with a hundred zeros after it), was a big success. So they raised money and launched it as a business. At the time, the honeymoon phase of the internet was wearing off a little. It was cool but not very user-friendly. People would go to search engines with slow-loading ads and irrelevant results and have to sift through a mess with every search. Google took out the unnecessary garbage and made the search process dramatically faster. Users flocked to the site in droves and, within a couple of years, Google had become a commonly used verb.

1. RICK RESCORLA, BRIAN MASTERSON, DAVID MAHMOUND, WELLES CROWTHER, TOM BURNETT, ERIC JONES, AND STEVE DE CHIARO
2001 - New York, New York; Washington, D.C.

September 11, 2001 will always be one of the darkest days in American history. But it would've been much, much worse if not for the heroic efforts of many. Instead of running away from the horror, some charged into danger in hope of saving others' lives. Following are just a few. Morgan Stanley's head of security (and decorated Vietnam veteran) Rick Rescorla ignored warnings to stay put after the first plane hit the North Tower and marched 2,700 employees out of the building before the second plane hit.

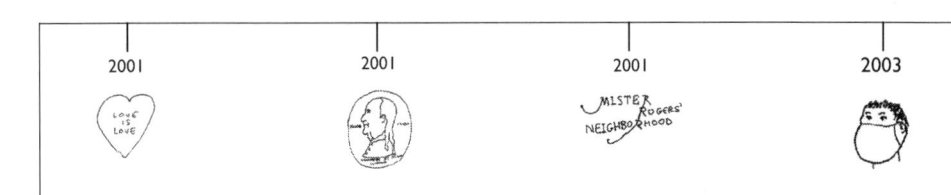

He was last seen looking for stragglers on the tenth floor. Twenty-four-year-old equities trader Welles Crowther covered his mouth with a bandana and helped disoriented people struggling to find the exits. The building collapsed as he tried to help more. Tom Burnett and fellow passengers fought to ensure their plane crashed into a Pennsylvania field rather than another building. At the Pentagon, heroes Eric Jones and Steve De Chiaro went into the burning building and risked their lives to save others. Both were awarded the Medal of Valor. And between the groups that lost the most—the N.Y.F.D., N.Y.P.D., and Port Authority P.D.—there are too many heroic stories to mention here. Even many of those involved who didn't lose their lives on that day were not left unscathed; their efforts to help others eventually led to cancer and respiratory diseases caused by the toxic fumes inhaled at the site (as was the case with heroes like firefighter Brian Masterson and police officer David Mahmound). It was a day that showcased both the depths of evil and the great, great heights of humanity.

| 2003 | 2003 | 2004 | 2004 |

2004

Honorable Mentions: Sharon Watkins - 2001 (Enron whistleblower), Johnny Knoxville - 2000 (*Jackass*), Ben Kingsley - 2000 (actor), Matt Carroll, Sacha Pfeiffer, Michael Rezendes, Walter V. Robinson - 2002 (Boston Globe Spotlight team), Sasha Baron Cohen - 2001 (Ali G), David McCullough - 2001 (historian, author), Bono - 2004 (ONE Campaign), Chuck Klosterman - 2003 (writer), Bill Simmons - 2001 (sportswriter), Jimmy Carter - 2002 (humanitarian), Ricky Gervais, Stephen Merchant - 2001 (*The Office*)

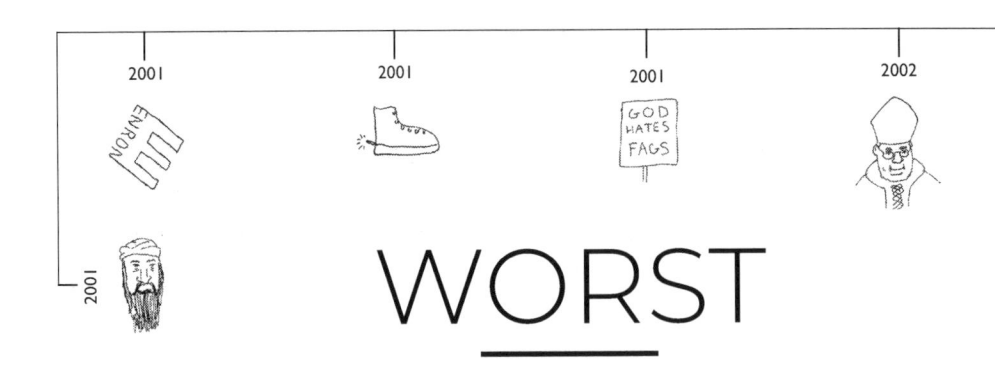

WORST

10. DAVE BLISS
2003 - Waco, Texas

In the shady, unethical world of college athletics, men's basketball coach Dave Bliss stood out for his terribleness. Despite being known as a cheater at previous gigs, strict Baptist school Baylor University hired Bliss to turn their program around. Instead he made it worse. One of his players (Patrick Dennehy) was murdered by another one (Carlton Dotson). Since the murdered guy happened to be getting paid by boosters, any investigation would've looked bad for Dave Bliss. So, to justify how Dennehy got that money, he instructed coaches and teammates to tell investigators that Dennehy was a drug dealer on the side. Fortunately, one assistant recorded Bliss making the story up and the shady coach was ruined. Dave Bliss was a bad basketball coach and a much, much worse human being.

9. FRED PHELPS
2001 - Topeka, Kansas

Despite that he was a lawyer who fought for civil rights in the 1960s, Fred Phelps was an unredeemable piece of garbage. Starting in 1991, Phelps made it his life's mission to protest homosexuality. Hung up on one line from Leviticus in the Bible ("You shall not lie with a male as with a woman; it is an abomination"), Phelps picketed places which he believed were havens for immoral activity, like Gage Park in Topeka, Kansas. When Councilwoman Beth Mechler doubted his claims that Gage Park was the second coming of Sodom and Gomorrah, Phelps called her a "Jezebelian switch-hitting whore," stole her blood bank records, revealed to everyone that she had hepatitis, and caused her to lose the next election. Emboldened by his victory, Phelps and his Westboro Baptist Church (i.e., Phelps and his kids), started showing up at high-profile funerals with signs that read, "GOD HATES FAGS." Didn't matter if it was a school shooting or a military funeral, Phelps was there waiting with his hateful signs. Finally, 2014, he took his long overdue dirt nap. Rest in misery, Fred.

8. JOHN ASHCROFT
2002 - Washington, D.C.

In 2000, John Ashcroft lost his U.S. Senate race to a dead guy. After giving the people of Missouri six years of service in the Senate, they thought a rotting corpse would do a better job than John Ashcroft. They were probably right. As luck would have it, George W. Bush was filling out his cabinet and needed to appease the religious right, so he chose John Ashcroft to be the United States' top law and order guy—the attorney general. For seven months on the job, Ashcroft set his sights on super dangerous things like busting illegal marijuana dispensaries while placing a low priority on terrorism. When Ashcroft got a tip that an airline attack was imminent, he stopped flying commercial. Then, after 9/11, an emboldened Ashcroft used the Patriot Act to turn back the clock in America to the Palmer Raids—throwing due process to the wind and imprisoning men indefinitely because they fit a certain racial / cultural profile. Besides chasing away brown people, John Ashcroft also found it in his heart to restrict gay rights and to spend $8,000 covering up the statue *Spirit of Justice*'s naked breast with velvet drapes in the Justice Department building. What a guy!

7. JOHN ALLEN MUHAMMAD AND LEE BOYD MALVO
2002 - Wheaton, Maryland

In a three-week stretch in autumn 2002, thirteen people were shot by a sniper while going about mundane activities in the Washington, D.C. metro area. The entire region was in a panic while law enforcement was perplexed. There was no real pattern or link between the victims. Then, the FBI received a phone call from somebody bragging about a murder. At the corresponding crime scene, police found a fingerprint belonging to a seventeen-year-old kid named Lee Boyd Malvo. They discovered that Malvo had a mentor named John Allen Muhammad, a former army sharpshooter in the service during the Persian Gulf War. Two days later, the pair were spotted sleeping at a Maryland rest stop and were arrested. Apparently, the master plan was to extort the government for $10 million in exchange for not killing anymore. They'd then use that money to set up a utopia in Canada where they would train seventy boys and seventy girls to become super-people. What they got instead was plan B: Muhammad was executed and Malvo spends twenty-three hours a day in solitary confinement.

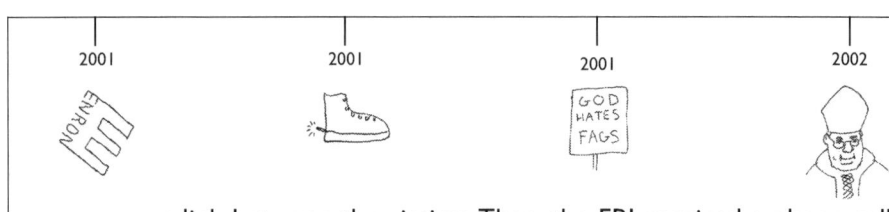

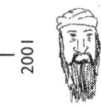

6. RICHARD REID
2001 - Boston, Massachusetts

Ever wonder why you have to take your shoes off before walking through security in an airport? It's this asshole's fault. A few days before Christmas in 2001, the British-born Richard Reid tried to light a fuse attached to his shoe (which contained a plastic explosive). A flight attendant noticed and he was beaten senseless by fellow passengers. Reid will spend the rest of his days in a supermax prison in Colorado. The rest of us are doomed to an eternity of taking off our shoes and putting them in a germ-ridden plastic bucket every time we fly.

5. KENNETH LAY, JEFFREY SKILLING, ANDREW FASTOW, LOU PAI, AND DAVID DUNCAN
2001 - Houston, Texas

In 1985, Ken Lay founded Enron, a natural gas provider in Houston, Texas, and brought in Jeff Skilling to be his hatchet man. Skilling's "rank and yank" system (where employees review their coworkers each year and the bottom twenty percent get the axe, while the top get hefty bonuses) encouraged a "win at all costs" attitude. Throughout the nineties, Enron exploited every corporate loophole and shifted its focus away from just being a supplier to making even more money as an energy trader. Led by savages like Andy Fastow and Lou Pai, the company got even more aggressive. Enron faked the sale of Nigerian power barges to inflate profit, lobbied for deregulation allowing them to trade gas and energy, created a bunch of fake companies to make it seem like money was pouring in, and purposefully toyed with the public's power supply to help drive up demand. Anytime their business was questioned, Enron leaned on powerful friendships (like George H.W. and George W. Bush) to help legitimize themselves. Really, the only hope for consumers to expose this fraud was the reputable accounting firm, Arthur Anderson, which had full access to their books. Just kidding, there wasn't any hope there either. David Duncan, the lead auditor, was helping Enron shred incriminating evidence. Eventually, the sixth-largest company in the world took a nosedive and all the major players went to jail. (Well, except for Lou Pai, who cashed out a few months before the crash because he knocked up a stripper.) Thousands of life savings were destroyed by a small handful of creeps in Houston, Texas.

4. DONALD RUMSFELD AND DICK CHENEY
2003 - Washington, D.C.

On September 10, 2001, Donald Rumsfeld warned at the Pentagon that bureaucracy was the biggest threat to America. Less than a day later, we learned it wouldn't crack the top three. The number one threat was Osama bin Laden. Numbers two and three? That would be Donald Rumsfeld and Dick Cheney, George W. Bush's secretary of defense and vice president, respectively. The day the planes hit the twin towers, Rumsfeld and Cheney looked for a link between Osama bin Laden and Saddam Hussein. Whether it was for oil, bloodlust, or just cockiness that the weak Iraqi military could be easily toppled, the duo spent much of the next year building a case both within the White House and with the American people that Saddam had weapons of mass destruction (WMDs). While the information they had was dubious at best (top intelligence officers in France, Germany, and Russia didn't believe it to be true), the United States and Britain listened to some convicted sex offender source called "Curveball" and invaded Iraq. This kicked off an eight-year war that killed more than a half-million Iraqi people and five thousand American and British troops, cost about two trillion dollars, and led to the rise of ISIS. But, besides all that… good idea, guys.

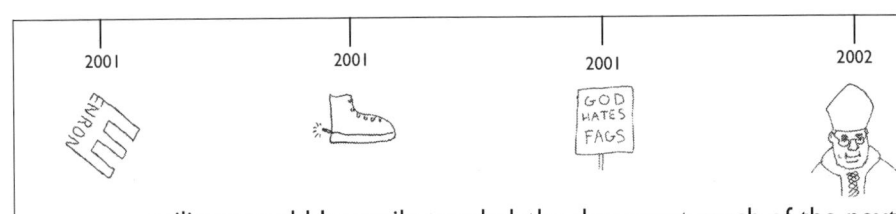

3. BERNARD LAW AND JOHN GEOGHAN
2002 - Boston, Massachusetts

Father John Geoghan was a pederast. Cardinal Bernard Law knew it and let him continue. In over three decades, the Catholic priest molested more than 130 young boys (the youngest was only four years old). He got to a parish, found the poorest and most vulnerable kids, befriended them, and assaulted them. Whispers became open complaints, so Cardinal Law sent Father Geoghan to a new parish. Then the cycle would repeat. Finally, in early 2002, the *Boston Globe* Spotlight team published a story that brought the whole disgusting situation to light. Geoghan was sent to jail and was beaten to death within a year. Law, on the other hand, got a cushy transfer to the mother ship in Vatican City. Guess that's not an altogether surprising response from an organization that was forced to defrock 848 priests and reprimand another 2,572 for molestation between 2004 and 2014.

2. OMAR AL-BASHIR
2003 - Khartoum, Sudan

In more than six decades of Sudanese independence, only about eleven years have been peaceful. In short, the 52 percent black Christian population in the south and the 39 percent Arab Muslims in the north don't get along. Then, in the west, there is a region about the size of Texas called Darfur, which is dominated by black Muslim farmers. These farmers are constantly at odds with the Arab herders in their rapidly shrinking region (the growing Sahara desert gives Sudan a smaller piece of inhabitable land with each passing year). So, in 2003, after being ignored blatantly for years by President Omar al-Bashir, the non-Arabs in Darfur reached a boiling point and attacked a Sudanese Air Force base. With the help of Chinese weapons and bombers (because China is the major consumer of Sudan's oil), President al-Bashir responded by bombing Darfur villages. Then, he supplied the Janjaweed militia (Arabs in Darfur) with even more weapons and told them to rape, pillage, and exterminate all non-Arabs. At least 300,000 non-Arabs have been killed in Darfur since 2003 and another two million displaced from their homes. In 2011, South Sudan was able to break away from the north but, before anyone gets out the party hats, they soon had their own civil war and are on the brink of collapse. Thanks to his vast oil reserves, genocidal monster Omar al-Bashir is still doing just fine.

1. OSAMA BIN LADEN
2001 - Eastern Afghanistan

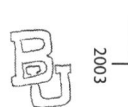

In 1979, right in the middle of the Cold War, the Soviet Union invaded Afghanistan. The United States, naturally, tried to prop up the resistance (the mujaheddin). Through Operation Cyclone, America spent hundreds of millions (possibly billions) of dollars on weapons and training for guerrilla fighters. One of the trained mujaheddin was Osama bin Laden, the highly educated son of a Saudi construction billionaire. When the Soviets left in '89, bin Laden and the mujaheddin focused their efforts on driving non-Muslim governments out of the Middle East. Well, just two years later, the Gulf War broke out and as a result, the area was full of Americans. So, in 1993, bin Laden gathered a bunch of militant Muslims and formed al Qaeda (Arabic for "the base"), a group dedicated to carrying out attacks around the world until the Middle East was run by Taliban-like governments. With a mountain of money, a stockpile of weapons, and highly trained soldiers, bin Laden's al Qaeda caused worldwide terror. The deadliest of his attacks happened on September 11, 2001, when terrorists hijacked four commercial jets, damaged the Pentagon in Washington, DC, and destroyed the World Trade Center in New York City. About three thousand people were killed and the U.S. economy took a major hit. While bin Laden's 9/11 plan initially worked out well for his terrorist group, ultimately it was a big mistake. Instead of driving American military presence out of Middle Eastern countries, his attacks kicked off endless wars and brought exponentially more U.S. troops into the region. After a decade on the run, Osama bin Laden was killed by Navy Seals in Pakistan and dumped in the ocean. He won't be missed.

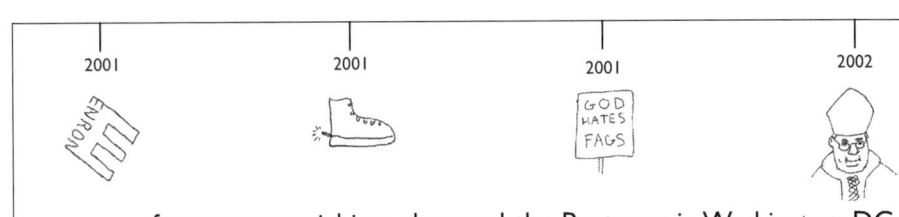

Dishonorable Mentions: Erik Prince - 2003 (Blackwater), Thomas Lubanga - 2002 (Congo child soldier trainer), Bruce Ivins - 2001 (anthrax), Rush Limbaugh - 2003 (white supremacist), Alexander Pichushkin - 2001 (Chessboard Killer), Colin Powell - 2003 (Iraq War), Jeffrey Epstein - 2000 (pedophile), Alan Dershowitz - 2000 (pedophile's friend, questionable views on what constitutes statutory rape), Andrea Yates - 2001 (murderer), Robert Hanssen - 2001 (spy), Friedrich Leibacher - 2001 (murderer), Jemaah Islamiyah - 2002 (bomber), Jack Abramoff - 2004 (crooked lobbyist), Heather Wilson - 2004 (nipple crusader)

| 2002 | 2002 | 2003 | 2003 | 2003 |

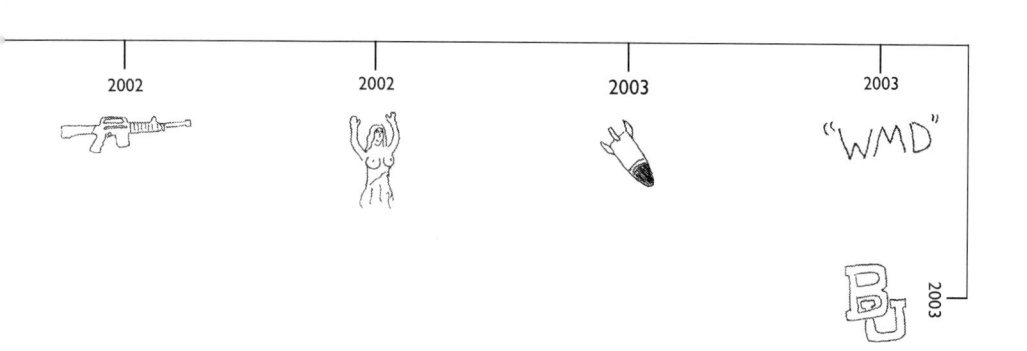

2005　　　　2005　　　　2006　　　　2006
　　　　　　YouTube

2005

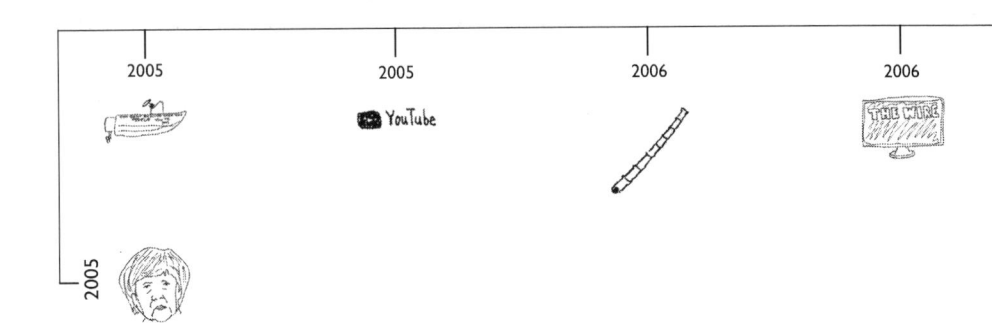

2005-2009

"The drug war is a holocaust in slow motion."
-David Simon

BEST

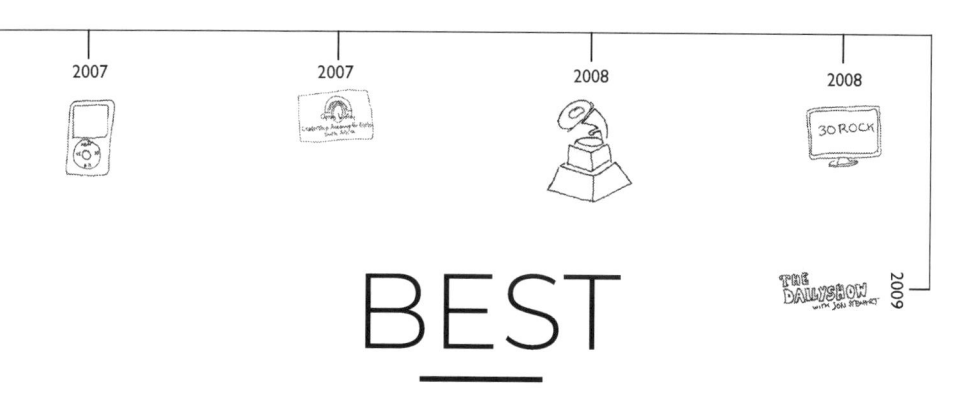

10. CHAD HURLEY, STEVE CHEN, JAWED KARIM
2005 - San Mateo, California

Chad Hurley, Steve Chen, and Jawed Karim had a new idea for an online dating service: people could film and upload videos of themselves, sit back, and let the dates pour in. They even had a catchphrase: "Tune in, hook up." The next step was getting people to actually post videos of themselves. So they went on Craigslist and offered women $20 to upload videos of themselves. Whether it was because this request seemed super pervy or possibly posted by a serial killer, nobody took the bait. So, instead the trio just put up a video of Karim at the San Diego Zoo. Word spread of this new site where people could upload their videos for free and, within a year, more than twenty million YouTube videos were being watched per day. Instantly, the world became a much smaller place. Sure, it spreads way too many cat and conspiracy theory videos but, over time, YouTube has launched singing and comedy careers, exposed injustices, and, yes, given the world the joy of watching guys getting hit in the nuts on endless loops.

9. DAVID SIMON
2006 - Baltimore, Maryland

As the newspaper industry took a nosedive, David Simon was a reporter without a paper. So the former police beat guy for The Baltimore Sun, who had previously found success turning his experiences into a book and television series (*Homicide: A Year on the Killing Streets*), turned back to the small screen. Along with his cop buddy, Ed Burns, Simon wrote another book about Baltimore's inner city but, this time, told it from the perspective of the citizens those cops are sworn to protect and serve. Once again, his book (*The Corner: A Year in the Life of an Inner-City Neighborhood*) was made into a TV series which garnered critical acclaim. HBO approached Simon and asked him to

2005 | 2005 | 2006 | 2006
YouTube

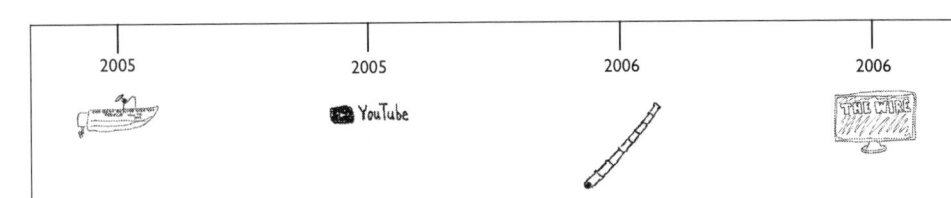

2005

create an entire series (*The Wire*) about the things he knew best (cops and the city of Baltimore). Unlike an ordinary cop show, *The Wire* played out like a serialized Dickens novel. Layer by layer, the show explored the struggles of a community run over by capitalism, a corrupt political system, a failing drug war, an out-of-touch education system, and a decaying journalism business. *The Wire* was complex and difficult and sad but also exciting and touching and funny. David Simon never stopped being a reporter. He just found a different medium. The end result was the greatest television show in history.

8. TINA FEY
2008 - New York, New York

To say the world of comedy writing has been kind of a boys' club is kind of like saying New Balance sneakers are kind of a white people thing. There have been women who have been giants in comedy writers' rooms (Merrill Markoe, Carol Leifer, Paula Pell), but they were mostly treated as anomalies. The rooms were still dominated by men into the nineties and, as a result, men got all the credit. Starting in 1995, things began to shift. Tina Fey, a talented writer from Chicago's Second City sketch group, was hired to write for *Saturday Night Live* and, four years later, emerged from the lion's den as the head writer, the first woman to do so in the show's twenty-five-year history. After the success of *SNL*, Fey created and starred in *30 Rock*, a sitcom revolving around a female head TV writer. Much like *The Dick Van Dyke Show* four decades earlier, *30 Rock* gave viewers a peek at a writers' room except, this time, it was run by a woman. While the successful, funny show didn't suddenly turn comedy writers' rooms to a fifty-fifty men/women ratio, it is clear a shift is happening. More women-run shows are premiering each year and the comedy world is better for it.

7. JON STEWART
2009 - New York, New York

When comedian Jon Stewart took over *The Daily Show*, it morphed from a "let's just take the piss out of someone" kind of show to a "let's call politicians and television personalities out on their bullshit" one. Compared to the embarrassingly partisan hosts on Fox News, MSNBC, CNBC, and even CNN, the affable Stewart quickly turned into the hyper-intelligent voice of reason. Whether it was blowing the whistle on politicians talking out of both sides of their mouths, eviscerating political hosts and networks for selective outrage, or humiliating CNBC hosts for being puppets for Wall Street, Jon Stewart pulled no punches and was the perfect antidote for the bombastic world of cable news. Plus, as a judge of talent, Stewart was incredible (he helped launch the careers of Stephen Colbert, Steve Carell, John Oliver, Ed Helms, Rob Corddry, Samantha Bee, Josh Gad, and Olivia Munn).

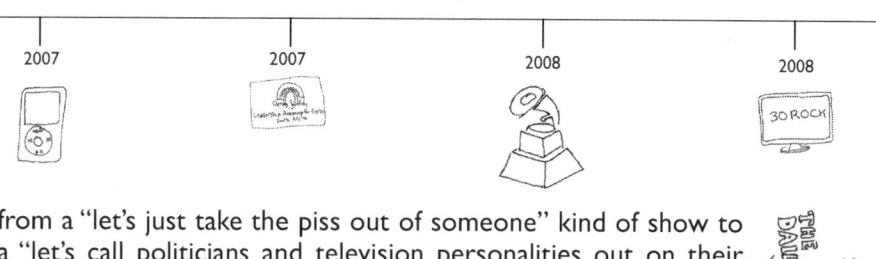

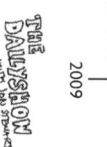

6. BEYONCÉ
2008 - New York, New York

Throughout history, for a woman to be really successful, she usually had to pick a particular angle. Either she's an artist, a sex symbol, a provocateur, a feminist, an activist, or a mogul. Beyoncé picked all of the above. From her early days as a member of Destiny's Child in the late '90s to her solo career, which launched in 2003, Beyoncé has been an enormous success (sixty-four gold and platinum records; a boatload of Grammys; performed at Obama's presidential inaugurations and at Super Bowl halftime; was named *Billboard*'s "artist of the decade"). While a lot of her early success was due to more mainstream pop hits, Beyoncé took risks by singing about heavier topics like feminism, race, politics, infidelity, and identity. For the first time, really ever, in pop history, Beyoncé's albums spoke out to one of the most marginalized group of people in America—black women. Despite increased public scrutiny of every career move, Beyoncé has fearlessly pushed herself further with each artistic endeavor (well, except for that crummy *Austin Powers* sequel).

5. OPRAH WINFREY
2007 - Henley-on-Klip, South Africa

Despite looking nothing like the other pencil-thin, lily-white television hosts at the time, local talk show host Oprah Winfrey routinely beat nationally syndicated Phil Donohue in the Chicago market. Whether it was discussing eating disorders, sexual abuse, or just everyday insecurities, Oprah gave women a voice and, within a couple years, was given her own syndication deal and even an acting role in Spielberg's *The Color Purple* (for which she was nominated for an Oscar). By 1994, Oprah distanced herself from trashy, ratings-grabbing talk show controversies and instead promoted books, important issues, and inspirational people. In 2003, *Forbes* announced that Oprah Winfrey was the first black woman billionaire. Over the years, Oprah has spent hundreds of millions of dollars on a variety of charities and, in 2007, launched the Oprah Winfrey Leadership Academy for Girls in South Africa. In its decade in existence, the boarding school has transformed the lives of hundreds of girls who wouldn't otherwise have had much of a chance in the world and sent them to college.

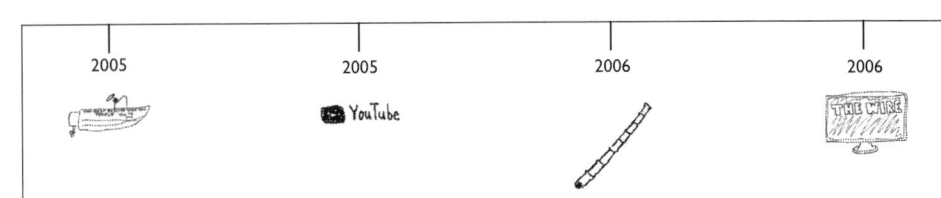

4. KEN BELLAU
2005 - New Orleans, Louisiana

On August 29, 2005, Hurricane Katrina pounded New Orleans, leaving the six-feet-below-sea-level city 80 percent underwater. Two days later, New Orleans native Ken Bellau loaded up his car (he was in Mississippi at the time), threw on camouflage and a gun (so he could get past military checkpoints), and drove down to the Crescent City. He posted his phone number on a local website and helped anyone he could. When his gas ran out, Bellau joined some guys with a twenty-four-foot motorboat on rescue missions. By morning, the rest of the guys had given up, but Bellau kept going. Fighting off exhaustion and people trying to take his boat, Bellau powered through until the National Guard was ready to help. When the city finally drained a week later, Ken Bellau abandoned the boat and wrote a message on the hull: "This boat rescued over 400 people. Thank you!"

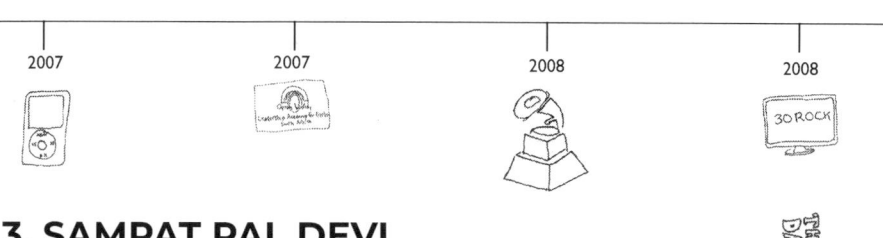

3. SAMPAT PAL DEVI
2006 - Uttar Pradesh, India

Sampat Pal Devi, a twenty-year-old mother of five, saw a guy beating his wife on the street. She begged for him to stop but he refused. This was India, a country where violent crimes against women are rarely reported and, even if they are, the police almost never do anything about it. Well, Sampat Pal returned the next day with a gang of bamboo stick-carrying women and beat the shit out of the guy. From that point forward, Sampat Pal Devi would dedicate her life to leading the Gulabi ("Pink") Gang and helping women fight back. If she received word of violence or repression, Devi got on her bike and delivered justice. Over time, that group has grown to 400,000 and their reach has dramatically expanded. As long as there's a dowry system, an education gap, or women are being attacked, there's a superhero looking out for them. Just trade the cape for a pink sari and a bamboo stick.

2. ANGELA MERKEL
2005 - Berlin, Germany

After the fall of the Berlin Wall in 1989, Chancellor Helmut Kohl was looking for a dynamic Eastern woman for his cabinet that would help connect East and West Germany. Merkel, a politically-minded scientist, filled the bill. After an impressive start working on environmental causes, Merkel ascended the political ladder and became Germany's first ever female chancellor in 2005. Despite her folksy, motherly style (many Germans refer to her as "Mutti," meaning "mother"), Merkel quickly proved to be a remarkably decisive and effective leader. As the crumbling global economy led to the euro crisis in 2010, it was Merkel who calmly led the entire European Union back from the brink. When Vladimir Putin tries to bully others, it is Angela Merkel who calls him out on it (standing up for EU sanctions on Russia for Ukraine crisis, denouncing his horrible gay rights record, and such). As anti-globalists turn their backs on those human beings who need the most help, it's Angela Merkel who has set the shining example for supporting refugees. In the past two-plus decades, Germany has had probably the

| 2005 | 2005 | 2006 | 2006 |

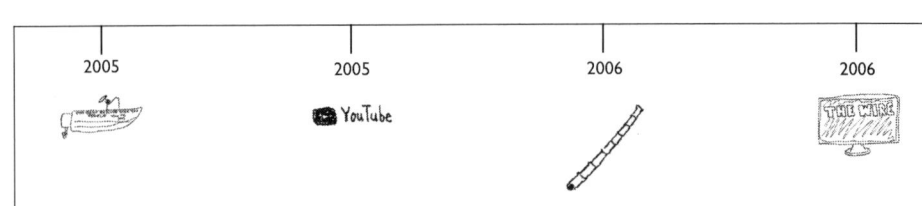

world's strongest leader. Germany! To quote Norm MacDonald, "I don't know if you guys are history buffs or not… but…"

1. STEVE JOBS
2007 - Cupertino, California

Steve Jobs was a modern-day Thomas Edison. His creations changed the world and made him a beloved icon. Also like Thomas Edison, he was kind of a dick. At just twenty-one, Jobs and his friend Steve Wozniak started Apple Computer and quickly turned it into a billion-dollar business. Unlike the tougher-to-navigate PCs, Jobs' products seemed to always be the user-friendlier option. After some ups and downs and time away from the company in the late '80s and early '90s, Jobs returned to Apple in 1996 and completely turned the industry on its head. First it was the colorful iMac. Then, in 2001, Jobs saw an opportunity in digital music and his company created the iPod and iTunes. This completely changed the music business and gave everyone the ability to carry their entire music collections around in their pocket. Then, in 2007, Jobs revolutionized the cell phone industry with the iPhone. While not the first phone with a keyboard or camera, the game- changing iPhone combined those things along with an iPod and a millions-of-times-more-powerful-than-the-ones-NASA-used- to-send-man-to-the-moon-in-1969 computer. Today, more than a quarter of the world's population has a smartphone. Yes, he was a backstabber, a crummy dad (to his first kid, at least), and a greedy, corner-cutting wealth-hoarder, but you'd be hard-pressed to find someone who's had a societal impact equal to Steve Jobs'.

| 2007 | 2007 | 2008 | 2008 | 2009 |

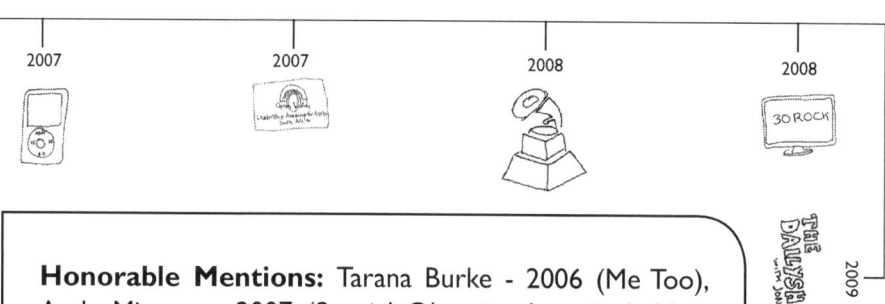

Honorable Mentions: Tarana Burke - 2006 (Me Too), Andy Miyares - 2007 (Special Olympic champion), Matt Taibbi - 2005 (journalist), Patton Oswalt - 2007 (comic), Salman Khan - 2009 (online educator), Michael Phelps - 2008 (swimmer), Jim Gaffigan - 2006 (comic), Chinua Achebe - 2007 (*Things Fall Apart*), Anna Politkovskaya - 2006 (reporter), Usain Bolt - 2008 (sprinter), Jong-rak Lee - 2009 (humanitarian), Lisa Randall - 2007 (theoretical physicist), Daniel Day Lewis - 2007 (actor), Roger Federer - 2008 (tennis), Harald Zur Hausen - 2008 (virologist)

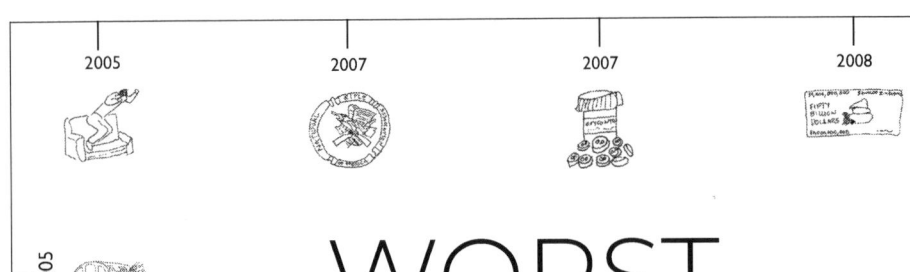

＃ WORST

10. TOM CRUISE
2005 - New York, New York

Tom Cruise was doing the talk show circuit to promote his upcoming film, *War of the Worlds*. When he got to the *Today* show, instead of talking about aliens and special effects, he opted to disparage the profession of psychiatry. He denounced fellow celebrity Brooke Shields' book about dealing with postpartum depression, saying chemical imbalances aren't real and her use of anti-depressants was "irresponsible." Never mind the Andrea Yateses of the world. The guy who believes in a religion that claims humans evolved from clams has all the answers. Hey Tom, if we need an expert on acting in homoerotic beach volleyball scenes, you're our guy. If we need an expert of psychiatry, we'll look to people who went to medical school.

9. BERNIE MADOFF
2008 - New York, New York

In 1999, Harry Markopolos, a quantitative financial whiz at a Boston-based financial services firm, was asked to figure out a way to come up with similar returns to the ones achieved by Bernie Madoff. Every month, Madoff's investors clipped a consistent one- to two-percent return. After trying just about every possibility, Markopolos concluded it was impossible and wrote to the SEC to tell them their golden boy was a fraud. They ignored him. He reached out to politicians and journalists. They, too, didn't seem to care. Madoff was a legend. He went from a lifeguard to a titan on the Exchange. He launched NASDAQ. He was an advisor to the SEC. Everyone respected Madoff. But Markopolos was right. It was all a lie. Bernie Madoff was running the biggest Ponzi scheme in history. And, once Lehman Brothers collapsed in 2008, everyone started asking for their money back. When Madoff didn't have it (the $65 billion-dollar portfolio was down to a couple hundred million), he was sentenced to 150 years in prison.

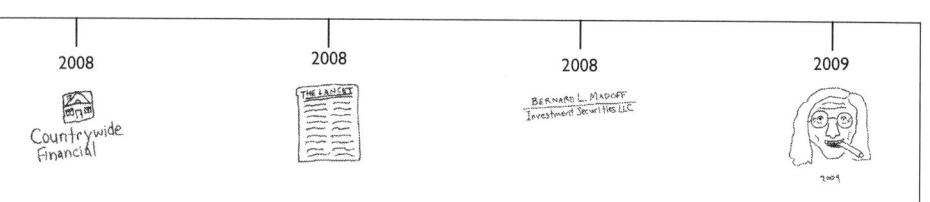

As the old adage goes, if it seems too good to be true, it probably is. Also, never invest with a sociopath.

8. ANDREW WAKEFIELD
2008 - London, England

In February of 1998, British medical journal *The Lancet* published a groundbreaking study by Andrew Wakefield, which suggested the measles, mumps, and rubella (MMR) vaccine may lead to "behavioral regression and pervasive developmental disorder in children." In other words, the MMR vaccine could give your kid autism. The news spread and panicked, well-meaning parents started avoiding giving their kids the vaccine. The problem with Wakefield's study was that it was garbage. His sample size was way too small and it was determined that he altered the results which led to false conclusions. Predictably, cases of the previously dormant measles shot up everywhere. By the time *The Lancet* retracted the story in 2010, irreparable damage had been done. Andrew Wakefield's study was one of the most irresponsible medical conclusions in history.

7. ANGELO MOZILO
2008 - Callabassas, California

There are plenty of people to blame for the 2008 economic crisis that brought the world to its knees but, if you had to pick just one, it would be tough to find a better candidate than the tangerine-hewed ghoul who co-founded Countrywide, the largest mortgage lender in America. Essentially, Angelo Mozilo realized he'd make a shitload of money if he delivered Wall Street as many loans as possible, which would then be packaged and cut up into complicated bonds, which would then be sold to investors who had varying degrees of knowledge about what was inside those bonds. For Mozilo and Countrywide, the more loans the better. A bartender in the Rust Belt? By all means, give that woman a

$600,000 loan for a vacation home in Jupiter, Florida! They gave loans to everybody. And executives on Wall Street knew it and played a game of hot potato with those terrible loans, getting paid as much as possible before the mortgage time bomb exploded. Between 2000 and 2008, Angelo Mozilo made over a half billion dollars for steering the Countrywide Titanic towards the iceberg. Meanwhile, the orange pile of shit in the Armani suit was unloading his shares at an alarming clip. Then it all collapsed. Bear Stearns, who was bursting at the seams with ugly subprime loans, was sold for pennies on the dollar (as their out-to-lunch CEO Jimmy Cayne was on one of his usual three-and-a-half-day bridge-playing weekends). Lehman Brothers (led by their unapologetic jerkoff of a CEO Dick Fuld) filed for Chapter 11. AIG, America's largest insurance company, was the next to go down. The Dow Jones lost a third of its value in 2008 and the world (Germany, Japan, China, and many more) joined America in an economic tailspin.

6. JERRY SANDUSKY
2009 - State College, Pennsylvania

For decades, the football team at Penn State University won a lot of games and made a lot of money. Because of that, anyone associated with the program was given a lot of trust and treated like a hero. Assistant Coach Jerry Sandusky took full advantage of that trust and worship by becoming one of the most notorious sexual predators in American history. In 1998, he was caught showering with an eleven-year-old boy. He apologized and promised to never do it again so the police let him go. A few years later, an assistant coach caught Sandusky molesting a ten-year-old boy in the showers. The coach notified Head Coach Joe Paterno, who then let Athletic Director Tim Curley know. Again, nobody did a thing. Finally, in 2008, a high school football player accused Sandusky of abusing him. The ensuing investigation led to nearly fifty charges. Sandusky was thrown in jail for life, Paterno was fired, and the school president, AD, and VP all did time for child endangerment after failing to report the crime. Good job, meatheads.

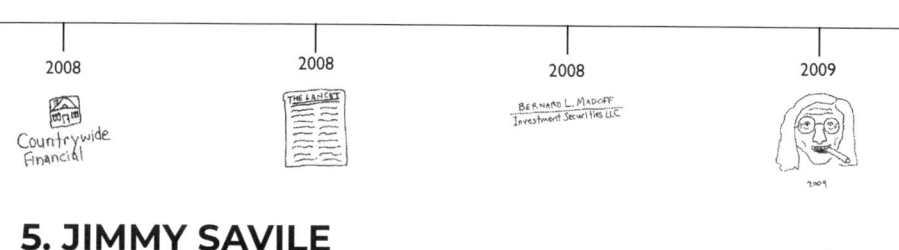

5. JIMMY SAVILE
2009 - Surrey, England

We're always told to never judge a book by its cover but, in the case of super creepy-looking Jimmy Savile, it would've been prudent. For more than five decades, Britain's version of Dick Clark (if Dick Clark looked like a white-haired, bug-eyed zombie) abused vulnerable kids throughout England. The host of BBC's *Top of the Pops* made frequent appearances at children's hospitals and schools for troubled girls, then molested them. Boys, girls, five-year-olds, seventy-five-year-olds… even corpses were in play for Jimmy Savile. There were whispers following him, but it wasn't until after his death in 2011 that the floodgates opened. Within a month of his death, hundreds of reports on Savile's abuse surfaced. As hard as it is to believe, Jimmy Savile was even uglier on the inside.

4. RASHID RAUF, MOHAMMAD SIDIQUE KHAN, SHEHZAD TANWEER, GERMAINE LINDSAY, AND HASIB HUSSAIN
2005 - London, England

In 2002, Rashid Rauf moved from Pakistan to Birmingham, England, where he became a bakery delivery boy. Within a few years, the twenty-four-year-old was plotting devastating acts of terrorism for al Qaeda. He recruited fellow radicalized British citizens (Siddique Khan, Shehzad Tanweer, Germaine Lindsay, and Hasib Hussain), trained them, and on July 7, 2005 had them execute coordinated suicide bombings on London Underground trains and a double decker bus. In total, fifty-two people were killed and more than seven hundred were injured. He planned another attack just two weeks later but, fortunately, the detonator never went off. Rauf was killed by a drone strike in 2008.

3. RICHARD, MORTIMER, AND RAYMOND SACKLER
2007 - Stamford, Connecticut

With a combined wealth of over thirteen billion dollars and their name on noteworthy museums and universities across the country, the Sacklers are one of America's richest and most powerful families. Where'd all that money come from? From being the baddest drug dealers on the planet. After a troubling history of pushing stuff like Valium, the Sackler-owned Purdue Pharma kicked their wealth into overdrive in the mid-nineties with their super-opiate OxyContin. The Sackler clan wined, dined, and lied to doctors about the safety of their heroin-like pill, then bought a puppet at the FDA (and future Purdue employee) to give it his stamp of approval. Soon doctors were prescribing the drug that was twice as powerful as morphine to everyone with an ache or a pain. In the two decades since, America has suffered from an out-of-control opioid crisis: 145 people dying a day from overdoses while heroin usage and opioid-related crime is on the rise. Purdue was forced to pay a $600 million fine in 2007 for lying, which would be pretty crippling for most companies. Not for the Sacklers. Oxy has netted those ghouls over $35 billion in profits.

2. WAYNE LAPIERRE
2007 - Washington, D.C.

After the Columbine High School massacre in 1999, it was widely assumed by reasonable people that it shouldn't be quite so easy to acquire a gun. Even Wayne LaPierre, head of the National Rifle Association (NRA), thought a universal background check might be a good idea. But, after extreme members of the powerful gun club threatened to oust LaPierre for giving an inch, he changed his tune and went back to being a soulless lobbyist. Thanks to LaPierre's fear mongering and political extortion, any and all gun restrictions (even the most reasonable loophole changes) and background checks were voted down. Eighty percent of Americans want stricter gun control, and yet no new legislation has been passed since 1994. All credit for that falls on Wayne LaPierre, the biggest asshole in America.

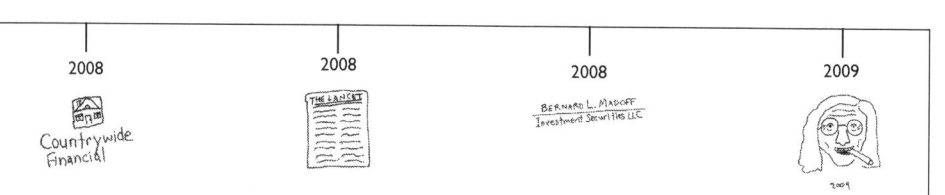

1. ROBERT MUGABE
2008 - Harare, Zimbabwe

After the British pulled out of Rhodesia, it changed its name to Zimbabwe, and the guy revered for helping the country gain its independence, Robert Mugabe, was named prime minister. Too bad Mugabe also happened to be a monster. He murdered tens of thousands of dissenters, bankrupted the country while interfering with Congo's civil war (presumably to steal their diamonds), seized land when it suited him and his friends, and changed the constitution to increase his powers. Then, when all of Zimbabwe's money ran out, Mugabe used the logic of an eight-year-old and just printed more cash. Soon people were using currency like the $50 billion note (which could buy two loaves of bread). By 2008, inflation had reached 500 billion percent. Since buying the simplest of objects required high-level math, the country just started chopping off zeroes. One day something cost 10 billion. The next it was worth a dollar. Finally, in 2017, after thirty-seven years of diminishing average lifespan, increasing AIDS population, and crippling poverty, Robert Mugabe was forced out.

Dishonorable Mentions: Seung-Hui Cho, Nidal Hasan, Jennifer San Marco, Jiverly Wong - 2006-2009 (mass murderers), Lyndie England - 2005 (Abu Ghraib), Jeb Bush - 2005 (Terry Schiavo), Jenny McCarthy - 2007 (anti-vaccination "expert"), Andal Ampatuan - 2009 (Maguindanao Massacre), Conrad Murray - 2009 (bad doctor), Johannes Mehserle - 2009 (Oscar Grant murder), Mahmoud Amadinejad - 2009 (human rights destroyer), Chris Brown - 2009 (domestic abuser), Najib Razak, Rosmah Mansor, Jho Low - 2009 (1MDB scandal, ripped off billions from Malaysia)

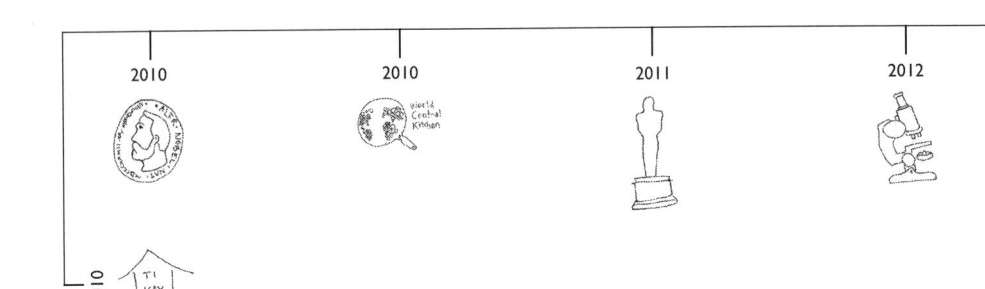

2010-2014

"The extremists are afraid of books and pens, the power of education frightens them. they are afraid of women."

-Malala Yousafzai

BEST

10. SARAH KOENIG
2014 - Baltimore, Maryland

A couple years after the iPod brought massive change to the music industry, broadcasters started using the MP3 player explosion to their advantage in the form of podcasts. As interest in the medium increased, so did the flow of money and quality of shows. In late 2014, Sarah Koenig and Julie Snyder (from *This American Life*) created *Serial*, a twelve-part podcast that examined a fifteen-year-old murder case. Koenig, the show's host and co-producer, gave listeners an inside-look into investigative journalism as she deconstructed a murder investigation. She asked the questions everyone wanted asked and vented her frustrations and concerns, which added a layer of humanity to the investigation. Public interest exploded and the show saw over eighty million downloads. Podcasts went from niche entertainment to genuine water cooler discussion. Aside from Howard Stern, people hadn't talked about the audio programs they were listening to since the 1950s. Sarah Koenig's *Serial* was for podcasts what *The Honeymooners* was for television.

9. BARACK OBAMA
2012 - Washington, D.C.

Barack Obama inherited a nation embroiled in two pointless wars and an economy circling the drain. The opposing political party was moving Heaven and Earth in their attempts to keep him from a second term as president. By the time he left office eight years later, the "misery index" (unemployment plus inflation rates) had dropped from about 13 percent to just over 6 percent, the Dow Jones had more than tripled, the deficit had shrunk by nearly $1 trillion, the failing auto industry was turned around, both U.S. combat missions in Iraq and Afghanistan had ended, gays were allowed to openly serve in the military, energy usage had been reduced by one percent, emissions were cut, foreign oil consumption had dropped 60 percent, universal healthcare was added, student loan jackals were reigned in, and, in 2012, gay marriage was legalized in America. Like any presidency, there were missteps (failed to prosecute Wall Street crash villains, excessive use of drones, never stood up to Big Pharma, and never stabilized Syria. But, overall, it was eight years of progress with zero bullshit wars, staff arrests, or sex scandals. Oh, yeah, he also happened to be the first black president.

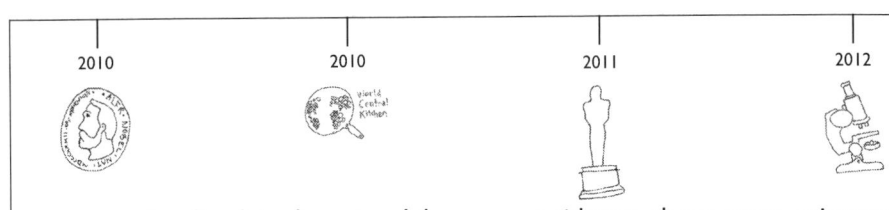

8. MEGAN COFFEE
2010 - Port-au-Prince, Haiti

Like the rest of the world, Megan Coffee was horrified by the devastating news footage of the January 2010 earthquake in Haiti. Sure, the Red Cross did its thing and some charity concerts and collections were held but, eventually, the rest of the world moved on with their lives. But the thirty-three-year-old Harvard- and Oxford-educated doctor and infectious disease expert felt compelled to do more. Less than a month after the quake, Coffee left her research position in Berkeley, got on a plane, and flew down to the poorest country in the Western hemisphere to lend a hand. Right away, Coffee helped turn around a floundering hospital's tuberculosis treatment unit, cooked pots upon pots of spaghetti to fight malnutrition, and helped medical staffers learn how to maximize supplies and medicine. Nearly a decade later, Dr. Megan Coffee is still there, helping the people and raising money through her Ti-Kay Haiti foundation. The world needs more Megan Coffees.

7. MERYL STREEP
2011 - Los Angeles, California

In just her second film role (*The Deer Hunter*), Meryl Streep was nominated for an Academy Award. She'd only accepted the gig because it allowed her to work closely with her dying boyfriend, John Cazale. In the decades since, Streep has played some of the most iconic roles in history in such movies as *Kramer vs. Kramer, Sophie's Choice, Silkwood, Defending Your Life*, and *Adaptation*, garnering a record twenty-one Oscar nominations (winning three). Even when the movies weren't so great, like 2011's *The Iron Lady*, Streep managed to deliver an award-winning performance. Meryl Streep has been better at acting than anyone has been at pretty much anything. From silly comedies to bleak dramas (and just about everything in between), Streep elevates every movie she appears in.

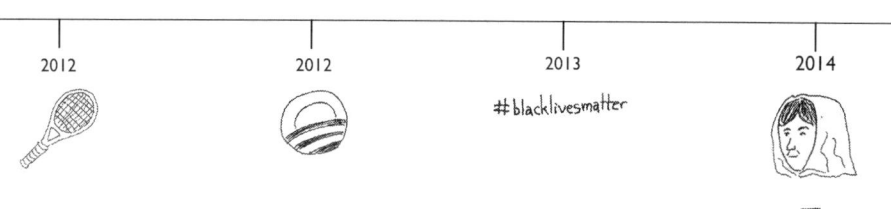

6. SERENA WILLIAMS
2012 - London, England

Like many tennis pros, Serena Williams started playing the sport at an early age. And that's where most of the comparisons end. Unlike the lily white, country club world where most of her competitors emerged, Serena and her sister Venus honed their craft on public courts in Compton, California. When she turned pro at fourteen, she was kind of dismissed as a novelty. When she started winning big, Williams had to deal with discrimination within the tour, racist taunts, and media coverage that frequently featured coded language emphasizing her body type and style as "pummeling" and "overwhelming." But the determined and charismatic Williams overcame it all and became the best athlete since Jim Thorpe. Along with multiple number-one rankings, Olympic gold medals, and a record 23 Grand Slam titles, Serena has become a role model for women everywhere. Off the court, Serena is a fashion icon and a women's right's advocate. She is heavily involved with charities including building special needs schools in Jamaica, Zimbabwe, Uganda, and Kenya, and serves as a Goodwill Ambassador for UNICEF.

5. JOSÉ ANDRÉS
2010 - Washington, D.C.

Credited with creating the "Spanish food boom in America," chef José Andrés racked up awards and Michelin stars over the course of his career. After a 7.0-magnitude earthquake hit Haiti in 2010, he traveled there and worked with some other charitable organizations to install clean cookstoves for residents. While there, he felt inspired to create a dedicated organization that could feed troubled areas like Haiti. World Central Kitchen is kind of like Doctors Without Borders, but for chefs. Wherever disaster hits (Houston's Hurricane Harvey, Puerto Rico's Hurricane Maria, California's wildfires, Trump's government shutdown), Andrés and his crew are there, serving as many as 10,000 meals a day to those in need. In 2018, *Fast Company* named World Central Kitchen as one of the most innovative companies in the world.

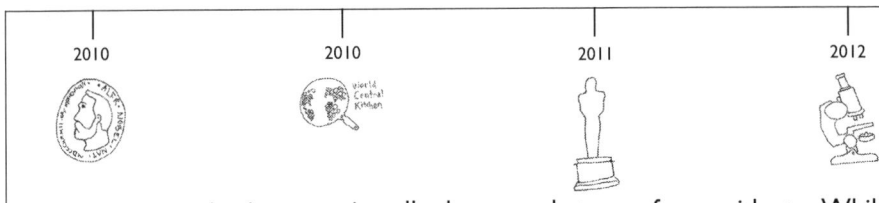

4. LIU XIAOBO
2010 - New York, New York

University professor Liu Xiaobo was giving a lecture in New York in 1989 when pro-democracy protests broke out in China. He immediately returned back home and joined the movement. When the government opened fire on dissidents, Liu helped hundreds escape. For his role in the protests, he was sentenced to three years of hard labor. When he was released, he got right back to fighting for democracy in China and getting thrown in jail. After publishing the first public document in sixty years to question China's one-party system, Liu was sentenced to eleven years in prison and his wife was placed under house arrest. In 2010, Liu received the Nobel Peace Prize. He died of liver cancer in 2017 while in custody. Liu Xiaobo was a beacon of light for the human rights and democracy movement in China.

3. MALALA YOUSAFZAI
2014 - Swat Valley, Pakistan

When the Soviet Union pulled out of Afghanistan in the early '90s, in stepped the Taliban. Preaching a hardline (and bastardized) form of Islam—beyond taking a firm stance on traditions like men having beards and women wearing burkas—things like movies, music, and television were banned. Girls over the age of ten were prohibited from attending school. That last rule was unacceptable for eleven-year-old Malala Yousafzai, the daughter of an anti-Taliban activist. Instead of retreating when she saw girls getting attacked for going to school, Malala gave a speech entitled, "How dare the Taliban take away my basic right to education?" The following year, Malala was writing a column (under a pen name) for the BBC, exposing the misery under Taliban rule. Even after her identity was exposed, the girl remained undeterred and kept speaking out. While she was awarded internationally for her bravery, the Taliban decided to put an end to someone promoting their biggest kryptonite: education. So, on October 9, 2012, masked gunmen boarded fifteen-year-old Malala's bus and shot her in the head. Miraculously, after several operations in Pakistan and the UK, she recovered and continued fighting for her cause. In 2014, Malala Yousafzai became the youngest Nobel Peace Prize winner in history.

2. ALICIA GARZA, PATRISSE CULLORS, AND OPAL TOMETI
2013 - San Francisco, California

When Barack Obama was elected president, many people assumed the racial playing field had been leveled. Nope. After the unconscionable acquittal of George Zimmerman's murder of Trayvon Martin, Alicia Garza went on Facebook and affirmed that "black lives matter." Her friends Patrisse Cullors and Opal Tometi soon helped turn those three words into a movement with the hashtag #blacklivesmatter, shining a light on the injustices black people face in the U.S. on a daily basis. Now, more than 60 percent of Americans realize more needs to be done for racial equality (versus the 46 percent that believed that in the year before #blacklivesmatter).

1. JOHN GURDON AND SHINYA YAMANAKA
2012 - Cambridge, England, Kyoto, Japan

When he was fifteen, John Gurdon's biology teacher thought his dreams of becoming a scientist were a "sheer waste of time." He stuck with it anyway and, by his mid-twenties, proved that you could take a cell from the intestines of an adult frog, place it in a frog egg, and turn it into a whole new frog. Gurdon had invented stem cells and cloning. But, even after his paper came out in 1962, nobody really believed him and it took more than forty years for his conclusions to become practical for humans. Japanese medical researcher Shinya Yamanaka adapted Gurdon's work and, instead of taking an old cell and putting it back into an egg, simply reset the cell and made it pluripotent (i.e., able to form into any type of cell). Skin cells could help generate a new liver, for example. In 2012, fifty years after John Gurdon's paper, he and Yamanaka were awarded the Nobel Prize for Medicine for one of the biggest medical breakthroughs of the past century.

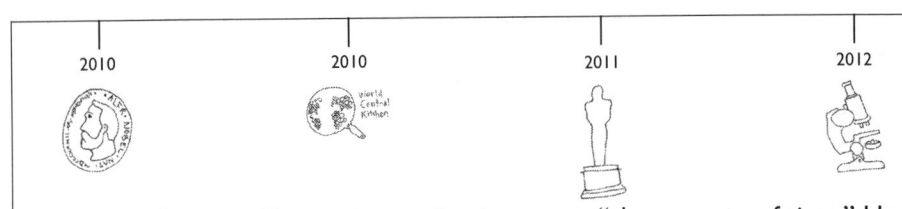

2012

2012

2013
#blacklivesmatter

2014

SERIAL
2014

Honorable Mentions: Edie Windsor - 2013 (LGBT rights activist), Jorge Munoz - 2015 ("Angel of Queens"), Anita Sarkeesian - 2012 (gaming feminist), Adam Resnick - 2014 (comedy writer), Dwyane Wade, LeBron James - 2012 (basketball, "Don't Shoot"), Emma Watson - 2014 (actress, HeForShe), Chimamanda Ngozi Adichie - 2014 (author, feminist)

WORST

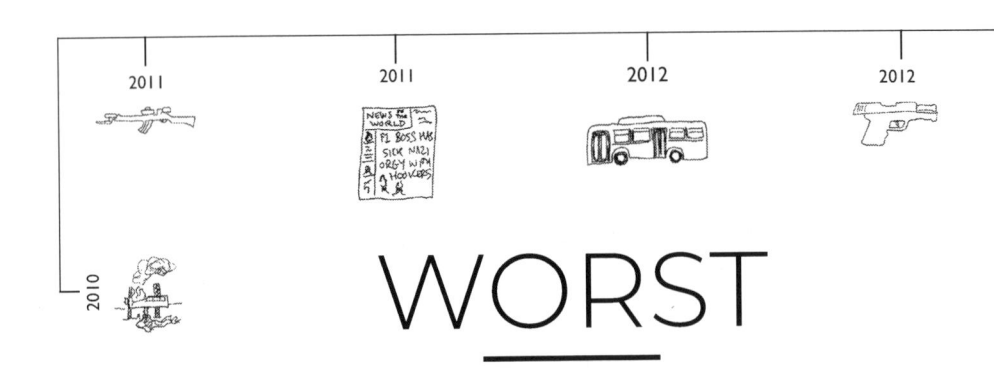

10. GEORGE ZIMMERMAN
2012 - Sanford, Florida

On February 26, 2012, racist neighborhood watch captain George Zimmerman spotted a black seventeen-year-old kid on the street wearing a hoodie and called the police. Since this was (at least) the forty-sixth time he had called for racial profiling situations (once even questioning a seven-year-old), the 9-1-1 operator just told him to stay in his car. Zimmerman didn't listen and approached the unarmed Trayvon Martin with his gun, a fight broke out, and Zimmerman shot and killed the teenager. Then he claimed self-defense. Since it was Florida, all Zimmerman had to show were his few scrapes (even though he had initiated the confrontation) and he was found not guilty due to the "stand your ground" rule. In the years since, Zimmerman has made a multitude of racist statements and actions, beaten family members and girlfriends, and taunted Trayvon Martin's family.

9. TAMERLAN AND DZHOKHAR TSARNAEV
2013 - Boston, Massachusetts

At the 2013 Boston Marathon, a couple of pressure-cooker bombs full of shrapnel and nails exploded near the finish line, killing three people and injuring another 264. The FBI and police went on a four-day manhunt. Finally, on the morning of April 19, police found themselves in a shoot-out with brothers Tamerlan and Dzhokhar Tsarnaev. In the chaos, the nineteen-year-old Dzhokhar ran over and killed his twenty-six-year-old brother. He was caught later that night when a guy reported someone hiding in his backyard. So why did the Chechen-born U.S. residents do it? Well, older brother Tamerlan was kind of a zero. When life didn't work out for him, he became radicalized and recruited his promising college-student brother to join in planting bombs in protest of American wars in Muslim countries. The only thing the bombing accomplished was stoking the fire of xenophobia and anti-Muslim sentiments in America.

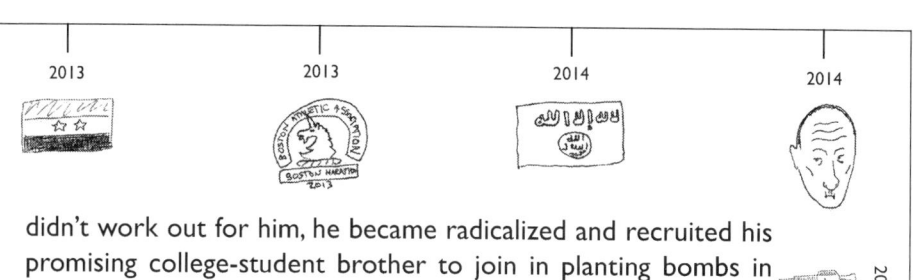

8. DONALD VIDRINE AND ROBERT KALUZA
2010 - Gulf of Mexico (near Louisiana)

If you had to narrow the blame for the worst oil spill in United States' history, you'd come down to the names Donald Vidrine and Robert Kaluza. Regardless of whether British Petroleum executives in Houston were putting heat on the Deepwater Horizon rig to drill despite tests indicating that wasn't such a good idea, it was Vidrine and Kaluza who were on site and, ultimately, concluded that the risk was worth it. On April 20, 2010, they were proven wrong. A surge of natural gas broke through a weak layer of concrete and shot straight up to the Deepwater Horizon platform, which caused an explosion that killed eleven workers, injured seventeen more, and dumped 60,000 barrels of oil into the gulf, killing hundreds of thousands of birds, turtles, and other animals. Ultimately, BP was forced to pay more than $60 billion in penalties. Vidrine and Kaluza chose to disregard safety and the environment to protect their six-figure job status and it cost the Earth dearly.

7. MUKESH SINGH
2012 - Delhi, India

India's huge rape problem was put on the global stage in 2012 with the rape and murder of a twenty-three-year-old recent college graduate on the way home from a movie. Five men and a boy followed the woman and her friend onto a bus, beat up the friend, then took turns raping her. Bus driver Mukesh Singh believed nice girls shouldn't be out at that hour, so he unconcernedly sat by. When she died a few weeks later, mass protests erupted across India. A woman is raped every fifteen minutes in India yet few are ever reported. Even if they are, it rarely ends in prosecution. Thankfully, in this egregious case, the rapists were convicted and sentenced to death.

6. ANDERS BEHRING BREIVIK
2011 - Oslo, Norway

Right-wing ghoul Anders Breivik felt Norway was getting too soft and too Muslim. So he wrote a rambling 1,500-page document about how he and fellow members of an organization that didn't even exist would execute a series of uprisings and take the continent back by the year 2083. Then he detonated a 2,000-pound fertilizer bomb outside a government building in Oslo. While law enforcement investigated the blast (which killed eight), Breivik made his way to an island twenty-five miles southwest of Norway's capital that was hosting a summer camp for liberal political activists. When he got to the island Breivik shot ninety-nine people (mostly teenagers), killing sixty-nine. It was the worst atrocity in Norway since World War II. While rotting in prison, Breivik, the guy who felt Norway was too soft, has threatened to go on hunger strikes because he wants more butter, warmer coffee, and better video games in his cell.

5. ADAM LANZA
2012 - Newtown, Connecticut

Twenty-year-old Connecticut resident Adam Lanza grabbed three of his mom's (legally purchased) guns, shot her in the head, and then went to the school where she taught (Sandy Hook Elementary School) and murdered twenty six- and seven-year-old children and six adults. Gun culture in America, seemingly, had gone too far. People wanted change. But nope. NRA chief Wayne LaPierre held a press conference in which he scolded America for not allowing guns in schools. Every teacher should be strapped in order to prevent such situations, he suggested. Politicians cowered to the gun lobbyists and nothing ever came of it. No attempts at better background checks. No attempts at restricting the sale of mass-murder machine AR-15. Nothing. The occasional dead children are now just the cost of living in America. Fuck Adam Lanza. Fuck

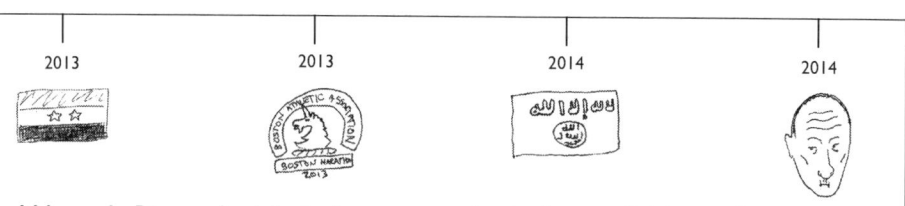

Wayne LaPierre. And fuck the scores of spineless politicians who sat on their hands when change was badly needed.

4. RUPERT MURDOCH
2011 - London, England

Rupert Murdoch relied on his two biggest personality traits to become an international media mogul: first, incredible drive; and second, moral bankruptcy. For more than six decades, Murdoch has lived by the principle that people react strongly to tabloids, sex, and fear. Turning the media into a circus has paid handsomely. Australian tabloid success led to his purchase of bigger papers around the world like The Sun and The New York Post. Once he bought them, he turned them into trash as well. Finally, in 2011, the world learned just how sleazy Murdoch's papers were. For the previous decade, his minions had been hacking people's phones—celebrities, members of the royal family, loved ones of dead soldiers, and even a teenager who had been murdered. When it was found out, people went to jail and Murdoch was forced to shut down his embarrassment of a publication, *The News of the World,*. Not even launching the network that gave us The Simpsons will bump Rupert Murdoch from his spot on the all time shit heel list. His legacy will always be irresponsible hysteria, shattered privacy, and a lax attitude towards the truth. Rupert Murdoch has been a festering carbuncle on the neck of society for the better part of a century.

3. ABUBAKAR SHEKAU
2014 - Chibok, Nigeria

For more than a century and a half, the British ruled Nigeria. Really, they only cared about southern Nigeria (where the oil was) and brought Christianity to the people there. As for the North? As long as they followed the rules (and didn't complain about their rampant poverty and disease), they could remain Muslim. Nigeria gained independence in 1960, but things didn't really change for the North for the next four decades. The door was wide open for an organized group to do away with the practice of Christianity in the South. So, in 2002, Mohammed Yusuf formed a group aiming to create an Islamic state and called it Boko Haram (which translates to "Western education is a sin"). The group attacked buildings and police stations and killed government officials. When their leader (Yusuf) was executed, a man named Abubakar Shekau took over and turned Boko Haram into a large-scale terrorist organization which performed suicide bombing missions at transport hubs, military bases, and U.N. headquarters. More than twenty thousand people were killed and two million more displaced. Women and children were routinely kidnapped and killed. Boys were made into soldiers. By 2013, Nigeria, the largest economy in Africa, had declared a state of emergency. Considering the North is still without any real resources or education, it's not all that hard for them to recruit new members.

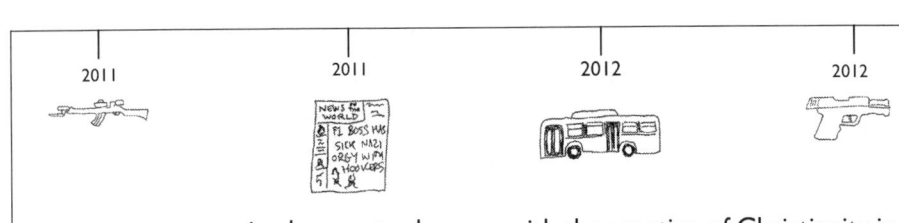

2. BASHAR AL-ASSAD
2013 - East Ghouta, Syria

In 2011, when Bashar al-Assad took over Syria after his father's disastrous forty-year reign, people were hoping for an improvement. They were disappointed. He continued his father's crappy foreign policy tactics of arming a bunch of hateful groups like Hamas, Hezbollah, and jihadists. He's managed to keep poor relations with just about every Middle Eastern country but Iran. Dissenters have been tortured and killed regularly. He banned websites like Facebook and YouTube so people wouldn't be able to share the rampant awfulness. By June of 2012, the ugliness boiled over into an all-out civil war. In 2013, he launched rockets containing sarin gas (or something like it) into anti-Assad suburbs outside of Damascus, killing fourteen hundred, including **426** children. By 2016, nearly half a million people had died in the conflict with seemingly no end in sight.

1. VLADIMIR PUTIN
2014 - Moscow, Russia

After their first meeting in 2001, U.S. President George W. Bush said of Vladimir Putin, "I looked the man in the eye. I was able to get a sense of his soul," then invited him to his ranch in Texas. First of all, someone should tell W. there are more efficient ways to judge character. After all, Rasputin's eyes were downright dreamy. Second of all, Vladimir Putin has no soul. When he first became president, he bombed some apartment buildings in Moscow then blamed it on Chechen rebels so he could launch a devastating attack on Chechnya's capital city. Sure, he had to kill some of his own people but at least it made him look strong (not a surprising concession for a former KGB bagman). Anytime journalists or politicians questioned him, bad things happened to them. Instead of challenging him on bad behavior, the state-run media just broadcasts his judo exhibitions. His human rights record is abysmal—domestic violence has become legal and gay rights are nonexistent. He funded pro-Russian terrorists in eastern Ukraine (including the ones that shot down a Malaysian Air flight in 2014, which killed 298 people). In 2015, he provided Assad with weapons to suppress the people in Syria. He's made a complete mockery of the Russian constitution. And, yes, he has heavily invested resources into global cyber-attacks in attempt to sabotage democracies. To top it off, Vladimir Putin is the kind of guy who posts lots of shirtless vacation pictures of himself online.

Dishonorable Mentions: Hosni Mubarak - 2010 (crooked politician), *Jason Van Dyke*, Darren Wilson - 2014 (murderous cops), Oscar Pistorius - 2013 (murderous paralympian), Joseph Kony - 2012 (evil guerrilla), Floyd Mayweather, War Machine - 2010-2014 (woman beaters), Lance Armstrong - 2012 (bike cheater), Cliven Bundy - 2014 (tax cheat), Jared Loughner, James E. Holmes, Aaron Alexis - 2011-2013 (mass murderers), Megyn Kelly - 2013 ("Jesus and Santa are white"), Andy Coulson - 2011 (News of the World), Lee Joon-seok - 2014 (careless ferry captain), Phil McGraw - 2010 (charlatan), Dzhanet Abdullayeva, Maryam Sharipova - 2010 (suicide bombers), Mel Gibson - 2010 (racist, anti-Semitic, homophobic, misogynist prick), Mehmet Oz - 2014 (miracle pill huckster), Narendra Modi - 2014 (hate-monger)

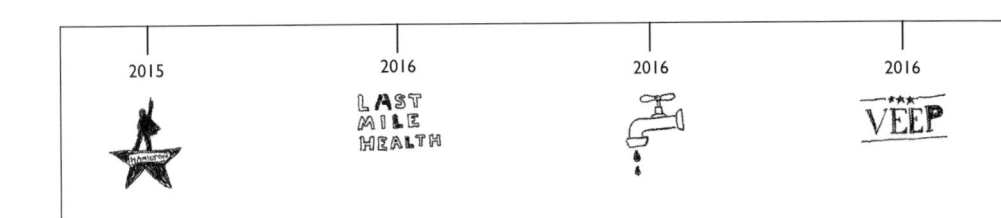

2015-2019

"I want you to act as if the house is on fire, because it is."
-Greta Thunberg

BEST

10. LIN MANUEL MIRANDA
2015 - New York, New York

After reading Ron Chernow's biography on Alexander Hamilton, Lin Manuel Miranda was so inspired by Hamilton's meteoric rise from poor immigrant to Founding Father that he wrote a musical about it. But instead of the standard Broadway Andrew Lloyd Webber-ish cornball lyrics treatment, Miranda told Hamilton's story with rap and cast it with a diverse group that better represented the American population. Much like the man himself, *Hamilton's* rise to the top was quick and monumental (sixteen Tony Award nominations and a chart-topping cast album). Suddenly, school kids were fired up about history. The love for *Hamilton* was so profound that the United States' treasury reversed its plan to dump Hamilton from the ten-dollar bill.

9. LEE GELERNT
2017 - New York, New York

Every person in the United States is afforded certain rights—mainly, the rights to speak your mind, believe in whatever you want to believe, and be treated fairly by the law. Sadly, these rights sometimes get trampled (Scopes monkey trial, *Brown v. Board of Ed*, and many other examples). When that happens, the American Civil Liberties Union steps in to uphold those rights. Just a week into Donald Trump's presidency, he issued an arbitrary, hurtful, and unconstitutional ban on people entering the U.S. from Muslim countries. Right away, the ACLU, led by lawyer Lee Gelernt, jumped in the fight and quickly got a federal judge to block the ban. When news broke of families being separated at the border, Gelernt and the ACLU jumped in the battle to stop this practice. These weren't the first and, certainly, won't be the last times the government loses its way. But, thankfully, heroes like Lee Gelernt and the ACLU will always fight to get it back on track.

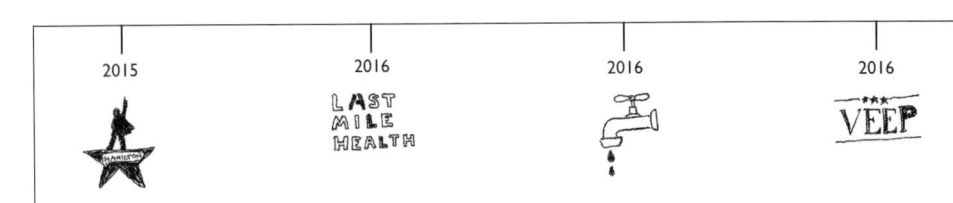

8. ANTHONY ATALA
2016 - Winston-Salem, North Carolina

People are living longer. While longer relationships and more wisdom are great, longevity also leads to organ failure. Lots of organ failure. As the population ages, organ transplant wait-lists swell. People are dying all the time before they can get a new organ. In the 1990s, Dr. Anthony Atala began tackling that problem with a high-tech solution: making fake organs. Through the use of 3D printers and medical tools, Ayala and his team at the Wake Forest Institute for Regenerative Medicine started with a lab-manufactured bladder. Over the years, they've also implanted lab-grown vaginas and urethras. Thanks to Atala's work, someday, doctors might one day be able to print out a new liver or kidney just as easily as they print out that nineteen-page set of forms you have to fill out anytime you sit down in a waiting room.

7. JULIA LOUIS-DREYFUS
2016 - Los Angeles, California

After a promising early start to her acting career (*Saturday Night Live, Christmas Vacation*), Julia Louis-Dreyfus was cast as the sole female lead on the new sitcom, *Seinfeld*. Unlike traditional female sitcom roles that involve lots of disapproving looks and "boys will be boys" head-shaking, Julia Louis-Dreyfus' character Elaine was as much a driver of comedy and plot as anyone else on the cast. If she had never followed that role up with anything else, she'd still be a legend on perhaps the greatest sitcom of all time. But, instead, she racked up Emmy nominations (and one win) for each of her five years starring in *The New Adventures of Old Christine* and won the Best Actress Emmy for each of her first seven seasons starring in *Veep*. Wherever she goes, she is exceptional, adding layers to characters who could otherwise easily come across as cartoonish. Forget comedy-versus-drama and male-versus-female, Julia Louis-Dreyfus is the greatest television actor who ever lived.

6. EMMA GONZÁLEZ, DAVID HOGG, AND ALEX WIND
2018 - Parkland, Florida

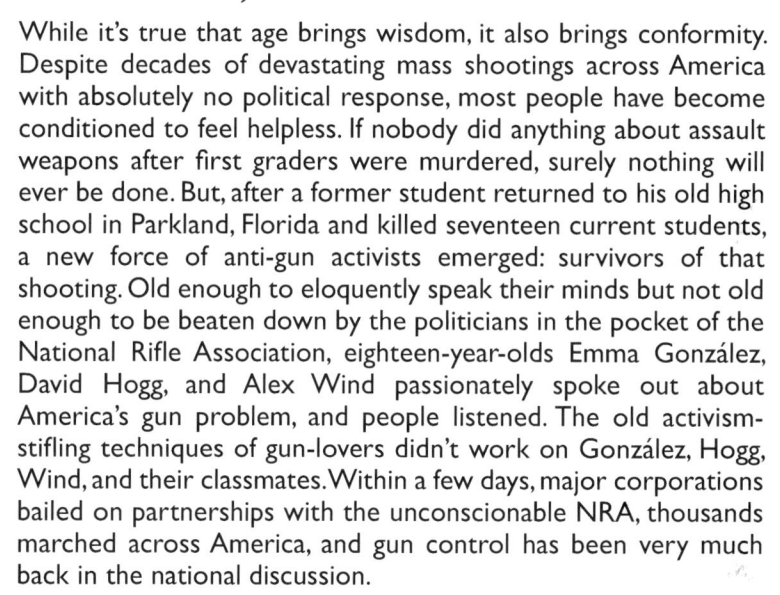

While it's true that age brings wisdom, it also brings conformity. Despite decades of devastating mass shootings across America with absolutely no political response, most people have become conditioned to feel helpless. If nobody did anything about assault weapons after first graders were murdered, surely nothing will ever be done. But, after a former student returned to his old high school in Parkland, Florida and killed seventeen current students, a new force of anti-gun activists emerged: survivors of that shooting. Old enough to eloquently speak their minds but not old enough to be beaten down by the politicians in the pocket of the National Rifle Association, eighteen-year-olds Emma González, David Hogg, and Alex Wind passionately spoke out about America's gun problem, and people listened. The old activism-stifling techniques of gun-lovers didn't work on González, Hogg, Wind, and their classmates. Within a few days, major corporations bailed on partnerships with the unconscionable NRA, thousands marched across America, and gun control has been very much back in the national discussion.

5. PUSHPA BASNET
2016 - Kathmandu, Nepal

More than half the people in Nepal live below the poverty line. Their prisons are, as you'd expect, abysmal. When parents are sent to prison, they have a choice: leave their kids to live on the streets or bring them to stay in prison with them. So, when university student Pushpa Basnet visited a local prison for a social work assignment and saw children behind bars, she was horrified. Right away, the twenty-one-year-old Basnet raised money, rented a building, and opened the Early Childhood Development Center in Kathmandu. For the past dozen years, Pushpa Basnet picks the children up every morning, takes them to her "Butterfly Home," and cares for them until evening. As an alternative to a bleak existence in a prison cell, Pushpa Basnet has been able to give hundreds of children a nurturing, loving childhood and hope for a brighter future.

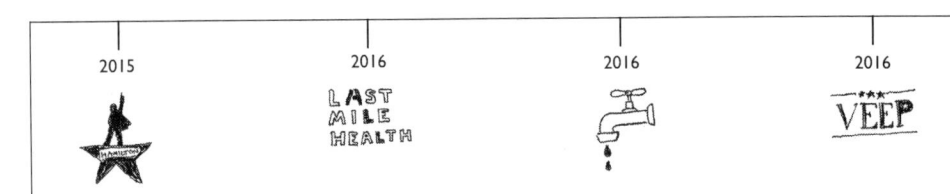

4. GRETA THUNBERG
2018 - Stockholm, Sweden

While the Paris Agreement was a much needed start to fighting the destruction of our planet, the grim reality remains that the world isn't moving fast enough. "Hundred-year storms" and devastating wildfires occur with alarming frequency. Each year becomes the hottest ever recorded. Glaciers disappear. And politicians beholden to monsters like the Koch brothers drag their feet. People worry but feel helpless. Fifteen-year-old Greta Thunberg took it upon herself to take a stand. Starting in October 2018, Thunberg stood in front of Swedish Parliament declaring her refusal to attend school on Fridays until the government showed real efforts in saving the planet ("Fridays For Future"). Over the next year, Thunberg's efforts inspired millions to protest, forced politicians to outline dedicated plans, and even earned her an invite to speak in front of the United Nations. Greta Thunberg is the superhero the world needs right now.

3. MONA HANNA-ATTISHA AND MARC EDWARDS
2016 - Flint, Michigan

In the 1980s, General Motors downsized and the town of Flint, Michigan went from a bustling industrial town of 100,000 people to a struggling town with more than 40 percent of the residents below the poverty line. To cut costs, Flint officials changed the water supply from Lake Huron to the Flint River. Within a month, residents complained about the brown, foul-smelling water that was making them sick. City officials ignored the poor, predominantly black residents. So a woman contacted Virginia Tech civil-engineering professor Marc Edwards (who had a history of fighting the government over poor water quality). Edwards accepted the challenge and, soon, local pediatrician Dr. Mona Hanna-Attisha joined the fight by testing Flint's children for lead poisoning. It turned out that the Flint River's water was nineteen times worse than Lake Huron's. Plus, Flint's pipes were a poisonous mess. Edwards and Hanna-Attisha beat the drum loudly and soon the national media covered the story. Emergency supplies were sent in, Flint was forced to switch back to Lake Huron water, and (while, sadly, it hasn't been done yet) the pressure to replace all the lead pipes is mounting.

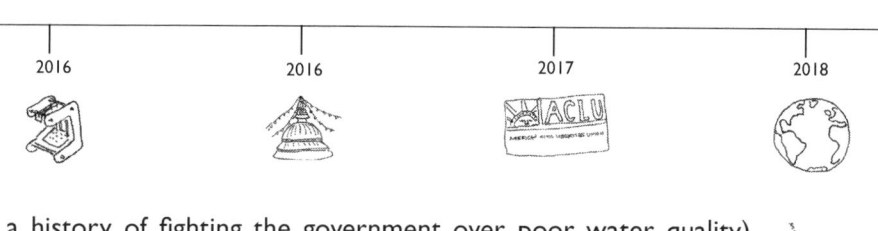

2. RAJ PANJABI
2016 - Monrovia, Liberia

As a boy, Raj Panjabi and his family fled civil war-torn Liberia and moved to America. He grew up to become a doctor. When he returned to his West African homeland in 2005, he found a country no longer at war but in complete shambles. Despite a population of four million, Liberia had only fifty doctors. People with easily treatable diseases were dying needlessly. So Panjabi teamed up with fellow Liberians and scraped together some wedding gift money to form Last Mile Health. It's an organization that recruits, trains, and equips community workers with the tools to help identify and treat the most pressing health threats. In 2016, Last Mile Health workers treated fifty thousand patients for things like pneumonia and malaria. When the Ebola crisis hit, it was Panjabi's group of thirteen hundred workers that treated and eliminated the disease in Liberia. Thanks to Raj Panjabi, millions of lives are no longer ignored.

1. CHRISTIANA FIGUERES
2015 - Paris, France

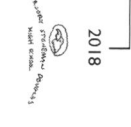

Record high temperatures are reached every year. Oceans are warming up. Polar ice caps are melting. Sea levels are rising. "Hundred-year storms" happen every couple of years. We have messed this planet up. Everyone knows it and yet no one can get on the same page. The 2009 United Nations climate summit in Copenhagen failed miserably. Going forward, the U.N. talk of getting the world to come to some sort of agreement fell into the lap of Costa Rican diplomat Christiana Figueres. This time, instead of bumming everyone out about the negative consequences and strong-arming people into an agreement, she promoted positivity (e.g., how it can lead to more jobs, money, and security for each country). By December 2015, Figueres did the impossible: she got 195 different countries to agree to a global average temperature threshold. The only holdouts were Syria (because Assad is a dick) and Nicaragua (who thought the agreement wasn't tough enough). After nearly two hundred years of assault by machines, humanity actually agreed to make the Earth a priority.

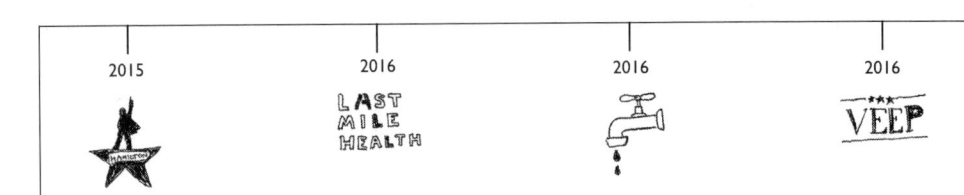

| 2016 | 2016 | 2017 | 2018 |

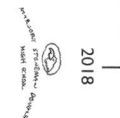

2018

Honorable Mentions: Naeem Rashid - 2019 (Christchurch shooting hero), Phoebe Waller-Bridge - 2016 (*Fleabag*), Elena Milashina - 2016 (investigative reporter), Robert Smigel - 2016 (Triumph the Insult Comic Dog), Thelma Aldana - 2017 (fought corruption in Nicaragua), Simone Biles - 2016 (gymnast), Jennifer Maddox - 2017 (community organizer), Jonathan Smith, Taylor Winston - 2017 (Vegas heroes), Biram Dah Abeid - 2017 (fought slavery in Mauritania), Misty Copeland - 2015 (ballet), Joanne Liu - 2015 (Doctors Without Borders), Joshua Wong - 2017 (Chinese election activist), Anuradha Koirala - 2015 (human trafficking activist), John Cena - 2019 (pro wrestling, Make-A-Wish hero) Colin Kaepernick - 2016 (football, activist), Megan Rapinoe - 2019 (soccer, activist)

WORST

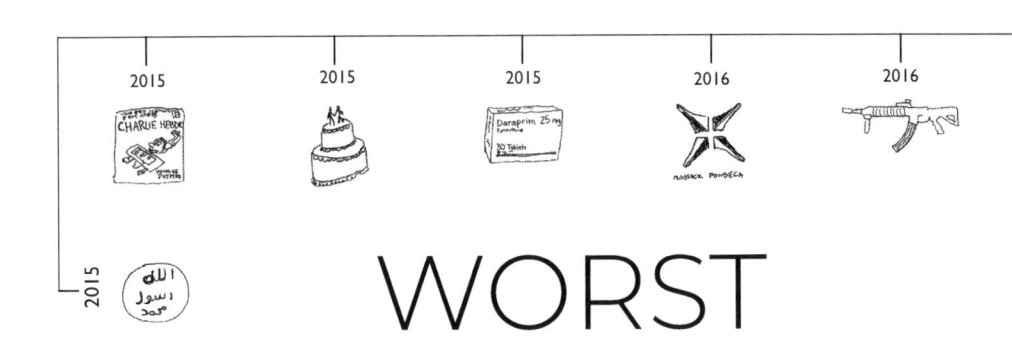

10. (TIE) MARTIN SHKRELI
2015 - New York, New York

Martin Shkreli, a former *Forbes* "30 Under 30" honoree and internet troll, held great power over people with serious medical conditions. In 2015, Shkreli's company, Turing Pharmaceutical, bought an anti-parasite medication called Daraprim and immediately jacked up the price from $13.50 a pill to $750. The heartless move brought the soulless Shkreli the fame he so desperately craved and caused panic for AIDS and chemo patients who were at severe risk if they couldn't afford the drug. After the story made national headlines, the sociopathic turd Shkreli went on TV and social media, flaunting his wealth and disparaging everyone who opposed him. In a heartwarming twist of fate, Shkreli's moral bankruptcy wasn't just confined to Daraprim pricing. Soon after the scandal, he was arrested for and convicted of securities fraud. The jury hated him. The judge hated him. His trolling on Twitter caused his bail to be revoked. Even the Wu Tang Clan trashed him. Everyone hates Martin Shkreli.

10. (TIE) JUERGEN MOSSACK AND RAMON FONSECA
2016 - Panama City, Panama

In 2015, an anonymous source sent the German newspaper *Süddeutsche Zeitung* 11.5 million files from one of the biggest offshore law firms in the world, Mossack Fonseca, dating back to 1977. It wasn't a great surprise that Mossack Fonseca was up to no good (e.g., helping criminals set up shell companies to launder money and helping the rich avoid taxes). The eye-opening part was the seventy-two current or former heads of state who were on Mossack Fonseca's client list. Those foreign leaders could use those untraceable shell companies to avoid paying taxes, finance terrorism, hide bribes, or siphon funds from their own governments. The most notable of those heads of state was Vladimir Putin. The Russian president had one of his buddies (a millionaire cellist?) hide more than two billion dollars from Russian state banks. Russian journalists believe Putin viewed this leak as a personal attack sponsored by Hillary Clinton's camp and vowed revenge—hence, Russian meddling in the 2016 U.S. presidential election. Regardless, Juergen Mossack and Ramon Fonseca had been helping bad guys do bad things for decades.

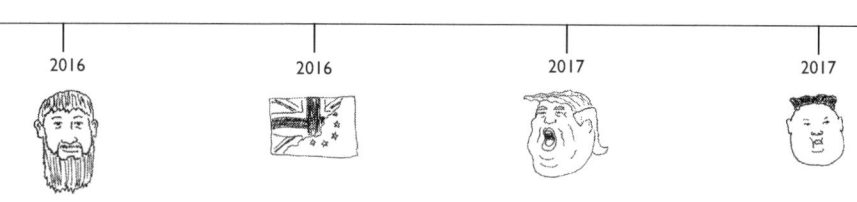

9. MIKE PENCE, PHIL BRYANT, DENNIS DAUGAARD
2015 - Indianapolis, Indiana; Jackson, Mississippi; Pierre, South Dakota

In the twenty-first century, Americans are increasingly realizing love is love, regardless of sexual orientation. Even two-thirds of Catholics got on board with gay marriage. In conjunction with that trend, in 2015, the Supreme Court ruled that same-sex marriage was legal in every state. Unfortunately, hateful pricks like Indiana Governor Mike Pence, Mississippi Governor Phil Bryant, and South Dakota Governor Dennis Daugaard weren't ready to open their hearts to support the lifestyles of all their constituents. So they drafted various "religious freedom" bills which allowed business owners and child service agencies to blatantly discriminate against the LGBTQ community.

8. DANIEL HANNAN, NIGEL FIRAGE, AND BORIS JOHNSON
2016 - United Kingdom

In 1990, Britain agreed to the Maastricht Treaty (which closely bonded the UK and eleven other European countries). Oxford student Daniel Hannan was livid. For the next two and a half decades, the nineteen-going-on-seventy-year-old chipped away at fellow conservatives to repeal it. Along the way, his movement attracted the far right to join him. But, for this withdrawal to become reality, he needed more than just ultraconservative politicians and businessmen. He needed votes. That's where buffoonish former London Mayor Boris Johnson and used car-salesman-operating-out-of-a-pub Nigel Firage got involved. The two played to the masses by stoking fires of nativism and xenophobia. The movement rode a wave of misleading stories and a sluggish economy all the way to victory on June 23, 2016, when the UK trampled on post-World War II diplomacy and voted to leave the EU.

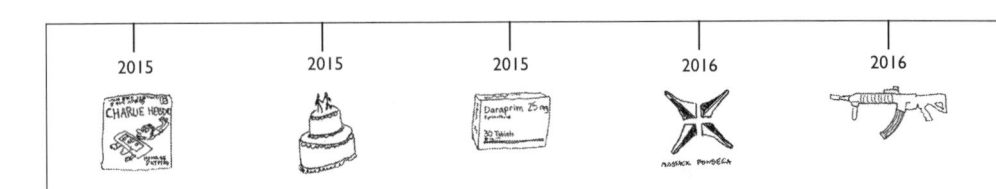

6. (TIE) BRENTON TARRANT
2019 - Christchurch, New Zealand

The most recent decade has seen a spike in far-right conservatism. Thanks to an uncertain, evolving global economy and a more diverse population, this leaves a lot of white guys afraid of their place in the world. These fears have manifested themselves in xenophobic votes for Trump or Brexit. Sadly, they also manifest themselves in unthinkable violence. Inspired by his racist allies on hateful websites like 4Chan, on March 15, 2019, twenty-eight-year-old Brenton Tarrant opened fire on two New Zealand mosques, killing fifty-one and injuring another fifty. His reasons, as listed in his poorly written seventy-four-page screed, were all too familiar. He was "just an ordinary white man" who wanted to "show the invaders that our lands will never be their lands." All racist bullshit coming from a loser trying to allocate blame away from himself for his unremarkable existence. New Zealand Prime Minister Jacinda Ardern and parliament quickly moved to ban military-style semi-automatic weapons in their country. Tarrant will join a growing list of "white power" failures who have only made the world worse.

5. OMAR SADDIQUI MATEEN, STEPHEN PADDOCK
2016, 2017 - Orlando, Florida; Las Vegas, Nevada

| 2016 | 2016 | 2017 | 2017 |

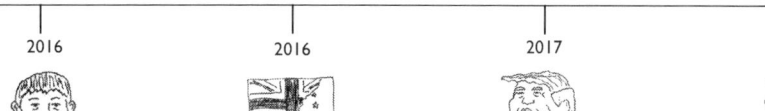

American politicians love gun lobbyist money more than they love their constituents. Consequentially, random Americans like Omar Mateen and Stephen Paddock are allowed to purchase automatic weapons and excessive amounts of ammunition that can ruin hundreds of lives in an instant. Despite being flagged and interviewed by the FBI on numerous occasions for being unstable, pledging his loyalty to ISIS, and leaning toward violence, Omar Mateen went through the legal "security check" and purchased a Glock pistol and AR-15 semiautomatic weapon. A few days later, he walked into a gay nightclub in Orlando and killed forty-nine people, injuring another fifty-three. That was the worst shooting in U.S. history… until the following year. Domestic abuser Stephen Paddock legally purchased thirty-three guns (many of them assault rifles) over a twelve-month span. Then on October 1, 2017, he took some of those weapons, outfitted them with legally purchased bump stocks (things that make semiautomatic weapons automatic), and opened fire on a country music concert in Vegas, killing fifty-eight and injuring another 527 people. Another job well done by the NRA.

6. (TIE) ANWAR AL-AWLAKI AND NASSER BIN ALI AL-ANSI
2015 - Paris, France

Sometimes, the best way to point out ridiculousness or injustice in the world is through satire. In France, publications like *Le Canard Enchaine* and *Charlie Hebdo* have led the satirical charge for years. In 2011, after publishing cartoons featuring Prophet Muhammad, the *Charlie Hebdo* offices were fire-bombed. For years the magazine had poked fun of politicians, the pope, and just about everything else under the sun. But, apparently, Muhammad was off limits. So Anwar al-Awlaki, a radicalized American-born al Qaeda spokesman, put wheels in motion for a grander attack on the cartoonists at the magazine. The plan was then taken up by Nasser bin Ali al-Ansi, another al Qaeda member, and two French-born brothers. On January 7, 2015, the gunmen burst into *Charlie*

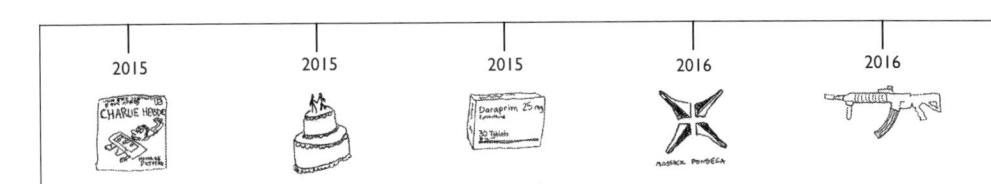

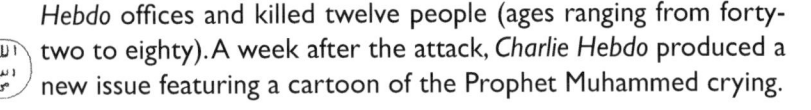

Hebdo offices and killed twelve people (ages ranging from forty-two to eighty). A week after the attack, Charlie Hebdo produced a new issue featuring a cartoon of the Prophet Muhammed crying.

4. KIM JONG UN
2017 - Pyongyang, North Korea

When his dad, Kim Jong Il, took a dirt nap in 2011, Kim Jong Un was given the keys to the kingdom of North Korea. How did a spoiled brat behave after being made a world leader? Not well. Anyone who shared his name or toupee-on-a-watermelon haircut was forced to change. Since he was woefully inexperienced at leading people, his uncle helped him out… until Kim had him executed. If anyone shows anything less than unbridled enthusiasm for Kim's choices and ruling power, they disappear. Fall asleep during a meeting with Kim (like the defense minister in 2015 or an education official in 2016)? You get shot by anti-aircraft guns in front of a crowd of people. After his brother shamed the family by getting arrested for using a fake passport trying to enter Japan, Kim had him poisoned. Like his father and grandfather, Kim Jong Un has been a doughy thorn in the side of the global community.

3. DONALD TRUMP
2017 - Palm Beach, Florida

Donald Trump inherited $40 million (worth $800 million today), gambled on struggling Manhattan real estate in the seventies, dodged taxes, and became insanely wealthy. Ever since, the only thing he's been really good at is promoting his name. Despite bankruptcies, unpaid bills, and endless litigation, Trump shamelessly bragged about being a genius and an arbiter of greatness. Naturally, when reality television came around, the cartoonish Trump got himself cast as a super-successful businessman. Over time, rubes confused reality TV with reality and actually believed he was indeed a great businessman. After the show ended, Trump threw his hat into the political ring (and by "threw his hat," he made outlandish, racist comments questioning the nationality of America's first black president). As we know, in 2016, Trump won the electoral vote and America was stuck with a racist, sexist, selfish, fragile egomaniac as its leader. Predictably, the guy who spent a lifetime only caring about himself has been consistent only in one area as president—helping the rich get richer. Beyond that, the presidency has been a whirlwind of lies, corruption, vindictiveness, incompetence, cruelty, attacks on unfavorable-yet-credible news, and divisive insults to pretty much everyone but the white guys who support him. His stubborn and catastrophic handling of the global pandemic in 2020 led to tens of thousands of preventable deaths. But he did achieve number-one at something—he was the first U.S. president to be impeached in his first term.

2. RAMZAN KADYROV
2017 - Grozny, Chechnya

When the Soviet Union fell apart, Chechnya wanted independence. Russia disagreed and, for the better part of the next two decades, relentlessly bombed the separatists. Then, in 2007, Vladimir Putin gave his blessing for Ramzan Kadyrov to be the Chechen president. Russia would shower Kadyrov's country with money (the Kremlin funds 80 percent of Chechnya's budget) and support as long as he kept separatists in his country at bay. Ever since, Kadyrov has ruled like a monster. He funded a special military called the Kadyrovtsy which carries out every ghoulish strong-arm Kadyrov whim. Journalists and political opponents have been threatened and killed. Women's rights are nonexistent. Kadyrov has led an anti-gay purge in Chechnya, executing or detaining thousands and encouraging parents to kill their gay children.

1. ABU BAKR AL-BAGHDADI
2015 - Mosul, Iraq

When the United States attacked Iraq for Saddam's imaginary weapons of mass destruction, it left a lot of disillusioned and out-of-work soldiers in the region. The Islamic State of Iraq and Syria (ISIS) pounced on the opportunity and recruited those Iraqis to join their turn-back-the-clocks (to the eighth century) club. After conquering vast territories in Iraq, ISIS took advantage of the morally bankrupt Bashar al-Assad in Syria, who let the extremists run amok (just as long as he got to continue his evil regime). The world then stepped in to curb the spread of this rapidly expanding "state" and bombed the hell out of them. Led by Abu Bakr al-Baghdadi, they've responded by carrying out massive deadly attacks abroad—143 attacks in more than twenty-nine countries, which have killed more than two thousand people. Even when they're not directly involved, the work of ISIS has led to inspired attacks as well. They've bombed a plane in the Sinai Peninsula, the Brussels airport, a Beirut suburb, a Paris nightclub, an Istanbul tourist attraction, a Manchester stadium, a peace rally in Ankara, and many other places. ISIS has unleashed hell on the world. On October 26, 2019, al-Baghdadi blew himself up right before being captured by U.S. Special Forces.

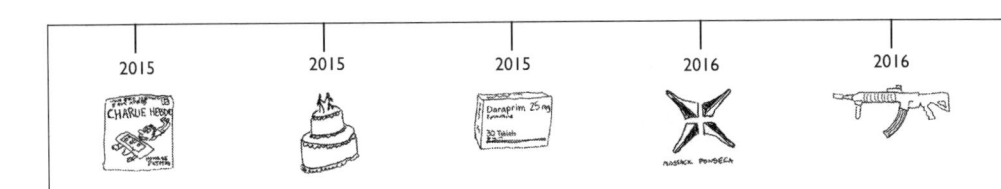

2016

2016

2017

2017

2017

Dishonorable Mentions: Rick Snyder, Dayne Walling, Darnell Earley, Ed Kurtz, Nick Lyon, Eden Wells, Howard Croft, Liane Shekter-Smith, Stephen Busch - 2015 (Flint water monsters), Bill O'Reilly, Kevin Spacey, Louis CK, Charlie Rose, Matt Lauer, Harvey Weinstein, Bryan Singer, John Lasseter, Brett Kavanaugh, Les Moonves, R. Kelly, Mario Batali, Roy Moore - 2017-2019 (#MeToo), Robert Bowers - 2018 (antisemite terrorist), Mark Zuckerberg - 2016 (fraud), John Stumpf - 2016 (fraud), Elizabeth Holmes - 2016 (fraud), Syed Rizwan Farook and Tashfeen Malik - 2015 (San Bernadino office shooters), Brock Turner - 2015 (rapist), Robert Coury - 2017 (jacked Epipen prices), Steve Bannon, Stephen Miller - 2017 (white supremacists), El Chapo - 2015 (drug kingpin), Scott Tucker - 2017 (payday loan jackal), R. Kelly - 2019 (pedo), Victoria Cobb - 2019 (ERA opponent), Sepp Blatter - 2015 (FIFA ghoul), Kim Davis - 2015 (anti-gay crusader), Dylan Roof - 2016 (racist terrorist), Mohammad bin Salman - 2018 (murderous Saudi crown prince), Jared Fogle - 2015 (Subway pederast), Rodrigo Duterte - 2016 (evil Philippines president), Gurmeet Singh - 2017 (rapist cult leader), Antonin Scalia - 2015 (gay marriage = "threat to American democracy")

EPILOGUE

In times of catastrophe, we often consider the words of philosopher George Santayana, "Those who cannot remember the past are doomed to repeat it." And they're right. People rarely take the time to think about history, even though it gives us a decent blueprint about what may happen again. For example, in every era dangerous egomaniacs have risen to power and caused large-scale destruction. Greed, intolerance, and hate are part of everyday life, now as much as thousands of years ago. And yet, the cycle continues.

Even so, the world keeps improving. Well, maybe not the planet itself. Mother Earth could use some serious environmental loving. But after reflecting upon just about every major event in human existence, it's clear that life has improved over time. Don't you think? Ask a black person in South Africa if they'd like to go back to the 1970s. How about women in America in the early twentieth century? Go smell someone's breath before toothpaste was invented in 1826! Today, we walk around with a singular device in our pocket that serves as a phone, computer, music player, and camera. Whenever disaster strikes, the Red Cross lends a hand. Surgery doesn't usually result in death. We can easily travel near and far. We have pizza!

While there have been a whole lot of jerks over the past two million years, nothing was harder than picking just ten heroes per chapter. Sure, selfishness and bigotry will continue. But they don't stand a chance of keeping up with the cascade of kindness, innovation, and joy that is generated every day. Humans are inherently good. Hopefully, we learn some lessons from the past and feel excited about the limitless possibilities of amazing still to come.

ACKNOWLEDGEMENTS

Thanks to the London pubs where most of this book was written: The Elgin, King's Head Theatre Pub, The Alwyne Castle, The Angelic, The Hen & Chickens, The Drapers Arms, and The York.

Thanks to the teachers (well, maybe not my creepy middle school gym teacher who watched us take showers). It's a vital, noble profession that is wildly under appreciated. You deserve a standing ovation at three o'clock every afternoon.

Thanks to my parents, who taught me to be curious about the world… and to have a healthy sense of humor about it.

Thanks to my boys, Lucas and Cameron, who make laugh and well up with pride every single day.

And, finally, thanks to Juan Dixon.

BIBLIOGRAPHY

There were about three thousand resources used for this book. The sites I used the most were britannica.com, smithsonianmag.com, history.com, biography.com, theguardian.com, and washingtonpost.com. A full bibliography would add another few hundred pages to this book. That's not fair to the trees (or anyone's eyes). Instead, a full listing of sources can be found on heroesandjerks.com.

INDEX

Aaron, Hank	411	Aldrin, Buzz	392
Abbott, Bud	345	Alexander II	192
Abdul-Jabbar, Kareem	397	Alexander III	215
Abdulaziz	227	Alexis, Aaron	535
Abdulhamid II	227-228	Ali, Mohamed	132
Abdullayeva, Dzhanet	535	Ali, Muhammad	392, 417
Abeid, Biram Dah	543	Allah, Rakim	452
Abel, Rudolf	368	Allen, Steve	358
Abercrombie, James	99	Allen, Woody	354, 369, 419
Abramoff, Jack	506	Allende, Salvador	416
Achebe, Chinua	515	Amadinejad, Mahmoud	521
Ackroyd, Dan	420	Amenhotep IV	9
Adams, John	92, 96, 368	Ament, Jeff	469
Adams, John Quincy	147-148	Ames, Aldrich	460
Adams, Kenneth	377	Amir, Yigal	491
Adams, Randall Dale	412	Ampatuan, Andal	521
Adams, Samuel	94	Amundson, Roald	259
Addams, Jane	306	Ananenko, Alexei	450-451
Addington, Henry	131-132	Anaya, Ignacio	327
Addis, William	106	Anderson, Hans Christian	151
Adichie, Chimamanda	529	Anderson, Marian	319, 320-321
Adler, Robert	371	Anderson, Mary	232
Admin, Idi	429-430	Anderson, Paul Thomas	485
Agnew, Spiro	342	Andrés, José	525
Ahern, Michael	205	Andu, Momofoku	371
Ahlwardt, Hermann	229	Annan, Charles	205
Aidid, Mohamed Farrah	475	Anne, Queen of England	77
Ailes, Roger	489-490	Anning, Mary	126
Aislabie, John	80	Anthony, Susan B.	182, 186, 282, 435
Aitchison, David	179	Antoinette, Marie	91, 108, 119
Akhenaton	9	Apgar, Virginia	356
Al-Abbas, Abu	457	Apted, Michael	383
Al-Ansi, Nasser Bin Ali	547-548	Arabadjian, Artenik	417
Al-Assad, Bashar	534	Arafat, Yasser	415
Al-Awlaki, Anwar	547-548	Arbuthnot, John	72, 74, 84
Al-Baghdadi, Abu Bakr	549-550	Archer-Landau, Amy	277
Al-Bashir, Omar	504-505	Archer, Lee	331-332
Al-Zomor, Aboud	443	Ardern, Jacinda	546-547
Aldana, Thelma	543	Aristophanes	13

Aristotle	13, 16, 45	Barnett, Ross	382, 389
Arledge, Jimmy	386	Barnum, P.T.	154
Armstrong, Lance	535	Barr, Roseanne	380
Armstrong, Louis	293	Barre, Mohamed Siad	475
Armstrong, Neil	392	Barrier, Eric	452
Arnold, Benedict	110	Barrow, Clyde	286, 313
Asahar, Shoko	487	Barry, James	137
Aschenbrenner, Albert	237	Bartholdi, Frédéric	211
Asclepiades	16	Bartlett, Bob	256-257
Ashcroft, John	501	Barton, Clara	210
Ashe, Arthur	411	Barton, Mark	491
Astley, Philip	100	Barton, William	108
Atahualpa	40	Basil II	31
Atala, Anthony	538	Basnet, Pushpa	539-540
Attila the Hun	12, 20, 309	Batali, Mario	551
Austen, Jane	128	Bates, Norman	373
Austin, Thomas	176	Bathory, Elizabeth	50
Avery, Tex	330	Batista, Fulgencio	375
Axgil, Axel & Eigil	495	Batman, John	142
Babbage, Charles	138, 162	Baum, Dan	402
Bacall, Lauren	347	Baum, L. Frank	235
Bach, Johann Sebastian	73, 75, 116	Bazalgette, Joseph	175
Bacon, Francis	53-54	Beach, Alfred Ely	187
Baez, Joan	383	Beaumont, William	135-136
Bagdasarian, Ross	377	Becquerel, Henri	222
Bagosura, Theoneste	475-476	Bee, Samantha	511
Baha, Abdu'l	255	Beethoven, Ludwig Von	4, 73, 116
Bahá'u'lláh	255	Begin, Menachem	443
Bai, Lakshmi	175	Behram, Thug	110-111
Baird, John Logie	295	Belafonte, Harry	383, 449-450
Baker, Dusty	419	Bell, Alexander Graham	198, 203-204, 207
Baker, Marshal Francis	202	Bell, Joseph	199
Baker, Norman	309	Bellau, Ken	512
Bakker, Jim	460	Bellingham, John	131
Baldwin, James	358	Bellissimo, Dom	379
Ball, Lucille	354-355	Bellissimo, Teressa	379
Bang, George	235	Belushi, John	420
Banks, George	445	Bender, Lawrence	466
Banneker, Benjamin	103-104	Benedict, Lemuel	223
Bannon, Steve	551	Benioff, Marc	485
Banting, Frederick	283	Benna, Ted	433
Baranov, Boris	450-451	Berg, Gertrude	345
Barbie, Klaus	445	Berkley, William	70-71
Barbier, Charles	136	Berkowitz, David	426
Barnett, Horace	386	Berkshire, Jane & George	154

Berlin, Irving	255-256
Berner, Edward	211
Berners-Lee, Tim	437
Bernstein, Carl	408-409
Bernstein, Leonard	447
Berry, Chuck	369-370, 391
Bethune, Mary McLeod	317
Beveridge, Albert	239
Beyoncé	511
Bezpalov, Valeri	450-451
Bhindranwale, Jarnail	440
Bhutto, Benazir	469
Bias, Len	452, 460
Bickerdyke, Mary Ann	187
Biden, Joe	477
Bielski brothers	333
Biko, Steve	425, 429
Biles, Simone	543
Bin Laden, Osama	49, 503, 505
Bin Salman, Mohammad	551
Birdseye, Clarence	279
Bíró, Lászlo & György	305
Blackbeard	79-80
Blackwell, Elizabeth	160
Blair, Henry	214
Blanc, Mel	330
Blanck, Max	262-263
Blatter, Sepp	551
Blay, Ruth	98
Blaylock, Alfred	333
Bligh, William	119
Blink, Kid	223
Bliss, Dave	500
Bliss, Doctor Willard	217
Block, Harlon	344
Blokzijl, Max	350
Blonde, Mr.	90
Blow, Kurtis	436
Blum, Leon	319
Bly, Nelly	211
Bobrikov, Nikolai	236
Bogart, Humphrey	341, 347
Bogle, Jack	420
Bohlin, Nils	371
Bolivar, Simon	124, 128
Bolt, Usain	515
Bonaparte, Napoleon	111, 114, 115, 116, 122, 128
Bonaparte III, Napoleon	184
Bonaparte, Louis	181
Bond, James	368
Bond, Victoria	434
Bonhoffer, Dietrich	345
Bonill, William	154
Bono	449, 499
Booth, Herbert Cecil	235
Booth, John Wilkes	190-191
Borden, Lizzie	229
Borg, Björn	438
Bork, Robert	460
Borlaug, Norman	411
Bose, Jagadish Chandra	220
Botkin, Cordelia	229
Bouboulina, Laskarina	135
Bourdin, Marial	229
Bowers, Robert	551
Bowers, Sam	386
Bowie, David	433, 450
Bowser, Mary	183
Boynton, Amelia	395
Bradman, Don	307
Bragg, Braxton	189
Braille, Louis	136, 275
Brandeis, Louis	266, 269
Brando, Marlon	358, 383
Brearly, Harry	255
Breivik, Anders Behring	532
Bresci, Gaetano	240
Brezhnev, Leonid	403
Brin, Sergey	496-497
Brinkley, John	296
Briseno, Theodore	474
Brod, Max	280
Brooks, Albert	425
Brooks, Jim	465
Brooks, Mel	354, 405
Brooks, Preston	177
Brown, Chris	521
Brown, Helen Gurley	397
Brown, Henry Billings	225-226

Brown, James	367, 397	Butts, John	331-332
Brown, Jim	397, 454-455	Byron, Lord	162
Brown, John	179, 190	Caesar, Sid	353-354, 405
Brown, Michael Martin	381	Cagney, James	341
Browne, Thomas	63	Cai Lun	15
Bruce, Lenny	384-5	Cailliau, Robert	437
Brussel, James	372	Calhoun, John	167-168
Brutalists	400	Caligula	20, 309
Bryan, William Jennings	296-297	Calley, William	399
Bryant, Anita	427-428	Cameron, James	262
Bryant, Carolyn	375	Campbell, Clive	407
Bryant, Martin	488-489	Candy, John	452
Bryant, Phil	545	Canfield, Richard	223
Bryant, Roy	375	Cannon, Martha Hughes	223
Buchanan, James	177	Cao Futian	236-237
Buckner, Jerry	445	Capone, Al	298
Buffet, Warren	420	Capote, Truman	381, 397
Buffett, Jimmy	427	Capra, Frank	341
Bugs Bunny	201	Caracalla	18-19
Bulgakov, Mikhail	295	Cardinal De Rohan	108-109
Bulger, Whitey	491	Cardinal Richelieu	60-61
Bumstead, John	333	Cardini, Caesar	280-281
Bundy, Cliven	535	Carell, Steve	511
Bundy, Ted	414	Carlin, George	392, 404, 405, 481
Burger, Reinhold	237	Carlos the Jackal	413
Burke, Glenn	419	Carlos, John	397
Burke, Jimmy	431	Carlson, Chester	319
Burke, Tarana	515	Carnegie, Andrew	225, 286
Burnell, Jocelyn Bell	411	Carothers, Wallace	317
Burnett, Carol	411	Carrey, Jim	380
Burnett, Peter	167	Carrier, Willis	233-234
Burnett, Tom	497	Carroll, Lewis	176
Burns, Ed	509	Carroll, Matt	499
Burr, Aaron	104, 120-121	Carruth, Rae	491
Burr, John	223	Carson, Johnny	379-380, 420, 436, 470
Burress, Hannibal	441	Carson, Rachel	397
Burrows, Jim	438	Carter, Harlon	431
Burt, John	473	Carter, Jimmy	429, 442, 499
Burton, Mary	89-90	Carter, Shawn	485
Busch, Stephen	551	Cartier, Jacques	38
Bush, George H.W.	475, 503	Cartright, Alexander	159
Bush, George W.	501, 503, 534-535	Caruso, Enrico	231
Bush, Jeb	521	Carvey, Dana	420
Butler, Andrew	177	Casanova	109
Butler, Pierce	177-178	Cassidy, Butch	434

Cassiodorus	24	Chopin, Frederic	155
Cassius, Avidius	18	Christian VII	101
Castro, Fidel	374-375	Chrysler, William	304
Cates, Phoebe	438	Chun Too Huan	457-458
Catherine the Great	94, 111, 118	Church, Francis	223
Catt, Carrie Chapman	282-283	Churchill, John	331-332
Cavell, Edith	271	Churchill, Winston	326, 329-330
Cayley, George	114	Cianciuli, Leonarda	321
Cayne, Jimmy	518	Cincinnatus	14
Cazale, John	425, 524	Clanton, Ike	217
Ceausescu, Nicolae	443-444	Clap, Margaret	89
Cena, John	543	Clapton, Eric	431
Cervantes, Miguel	54-55	Clark, Dick	519
Cezanne, Paul	223	Clark, Jim	395
Chanel, Coco	335	Clark, Marion	229
Chang and Eng	154	Clark, William	113, 119
Chaplin, Charlie	281	Claude, George	259
Chapman, Ben	350	Clay, Henry	142-143
Chapman, Graham	421	Cleese, John	421
Chapman, John	125	Clemenceau, Georges	273
Chapman, Mark David	445	Cleveland, Grover	219
Chapman, Peter	445	Clifton, Nat "Sweetwater"	358
Chappelle, Dave	493	Cline, Patsy	380
Charlemagne	28	Clinton, Bill	475, 477
Charles I	58-59	Clinton, Hillary	545
Charles II	64, 69	Clokey, Art	372
Charles V	40	Cobain, Kirk	469
Charles IX	51	Cobb, Victoria	551
Charles, Les & Glen	438	Cochrane, Jacqueline	328
Charles, Ray	450	Cochrane, Josephine	211
Charriere, Henri	345	Coen, Joel & Ethan	74, 480
Chase, Chevy	420, 477	Coffee, Megan	524
Chastain, Brandi	485	Cohen, Ben	425
Chaucer, Geoffrey	25	Cohen, Sarah	494
Chavez, Cesar	394	Cohen, Sasha Baron	499
Chelmsford, Lord	203	Colbert, Stephen	511
Chen, Steve	509	Cole, Jack	345
Cheney, Dick	503-504	Cole, Nat King	341
Chernow, Ron	469, 537	Cole, Samuel	53
Chesbrough, Ellis	175	Coleman, Bessie	283
Chester, Thomas Morris	187	Coleman, Franklin	179
Cheyne, George	91	Collazo, Oscar	365
Chikatilo, Andrei	426-427	Collins, Michael	392
Chilowsky, M. Constantin	267-268	Colt, Samuel	189
Chippendale, Thomas	94-95	Columbus, Christopher	31

Colvin, Claudette	371	Croft, Howard	551
Comaneci, Nadia	425	Cromartie, Antonio	39
Comiskey	272	Cromwell, Oliver	60, 64
Commodus	19	Crosby, Caresse	254, 258
Comstock, Anthony	201-202, 270	Crowley, Richard	205
Connor, Bull	386-387	Crowther, Welles	497
Conway, Thomas	108	Cruise, Tom	516
Cook, Frederick	247, 249	Crum, George	175
Cooke, Sam	383	Cullors, Patrisse	527
Coolidge, Calvin	289	cummings, e.e.	339
Cooper, Chuck	358	Cunanan, Andrew	491
Cooper, Martin	407-408	Curie, Marie	222
Cooper, Peter	147	Curley, Tim	518
Coover, Harry	333	Curtin, Jane	420
Copeland, Misty	543	Curtis, Charles	247
Copernicus, Nicolaus	32, 35-36, 45	Curtis, Jeremiah	193
Coppola, Francis Ford	369, 406	Custer, George	202
Corddry, Rob	511	Czolgosz, Leon	235
Corman, Roger	406	Da Vinci, Leonardo	22, 25
Coroebus	7	Dahmer, Jeffrey	471-472
Cortes, Hernan	40	Daimler, Gottlieb	209-210
Cosby, Bill	438, 441	Dalai Lama	452
Cosby, William	85, 88	Dalton, Emmett	229
Costanza, George	463	Dangerfield, Rodney	438
Costello, Elvis	450	Dante, Silvio	85
Costello, Lou	345	Darrow, Charles	308
Cotton, Mary Ann	200	Darrow, Clarence	295
Coubertin, Pierre	223	Darwin, Charles	115, 149
Coulson, Andy	535	Daugaard, Dennis	545
Coury, Robert	551	Davenport, Charles	286
Cousteau, Jacques	327	David, Larry	463
Covey, Edward	156	Davies, Chuck	346
Cowlings, Al	470	Davis, Jacob	198
Cox, William	386	Davis, Jefferson	140, 183, 189
Craft, Christine	438	Davis, Kim	551
Craig, Jim	438	Davis, Sammy	341
Crandon, Mina	280	Davison, Emily	259
Crane, Stephen	223	Davy, Humphrey	199
Crazy Horse	202	Day, Thomas	98
Cream, Thomas Neill	224	De Beauterne, Antoine	93
Crick, Francis	355	De Castro, Joao	37
Crick, George	131	De Chaumereys, Hugues	132-133
Cristofori, Bartolomeo	74	De Chiaro, Steve	497
Crocker, Betty	305	De Cordoba, Juan	41
Crockett, David	148	De Forest, Lee	247

De Galvez, Bernardo	107
De Havilland, Olivia	333
De Jesus, Luisa	101
De Klerk, F.W.	467
De La Beckwith, Byron	385-386
De La Cruz, Juana Inés	65
De la Rue, Warren	199
Dé Medici, Catherine	51
De Mestral, George	371
De Montaigne, Michel	43-44
De Oñate, Juan	49
De Rais, Gilles	30
De Rohan, Chevalier	89
De Villalobos, Gregorio	34
Dearborn, Henry	133
Deere, John	148-149
DeFreeze Donald	412-413
DeGeneres, Ellen	380, 482
Delaney, Joe	438
Della Spina, Alessandro	24
Delligatti, Jim	403
Demian, Cyrill	140
DeMille, Cecil B.	374
DeNiro, Robert	425
Denison, Edmund	175
Dennehy, Patrick	500
Dershowitz, Alan	506
DeSalvo, Albert	389
Descartes, René	52, 56
Devi, Sampat Pal	512-513
DeVito, Danny	452
Dewar, James	237
Dewey, John	223
Dewey, Thomas	346
Diagne, Mbaye	467
Diamond, Michael	452
Diamond, Neil	403
Dias, Bartolomeu	24
Diaz, Porfirio	263
DiCaprio, Leonardo	78
Dick, Charlie	380
Dickens, Charles	54, 146, 150, 510
Dickson, Earle	282
Dickson, Josephine	282
Dickson, W.K.L	221
Dies, Martin	336
Diller, Phyllis	371
DiMaggio, Joe	333
Dimitrijevic, Dragutin	264
Dinwiddie, Robert	90
Dippel, Johann	81
Disney, Walt	334-335, 347
Dix, Dorothea	161-162
Dixon, Thomas	251-252
Djemal, Ahmed	275-276
Djerassi, Carl	357
Djoser	9
Domino, Fats	367, 371
Donner Party	166
Donohue, Phil	511
Donovan, James	368
Donovan, Marion	358
Dorgon	60
Dos Reis, Alves	299
Doss, Desmond	345
Doss, Nancy "Nanny"	361
Dostoyevsky, Fyodor	184
Dotson, Carlton	500
Douglas, Stephen	177, 178-179
Douglass, Frederick	156, 170, 172-173
Dow, Charles	179
Dow, Neil	181
Doyle, Arthur Conan	223
Draco	10
Dracula, Vlad	30-31
Drais, Karl	127-128
Drake, Francis	48
Draper, Don	463
Drayton, William	452
Drebbel, Cornelius	53
Drew, Daniel	213
Drew, Richard	303
DuBois W.E.B.	230, 234-235
Dumas, Alexandre	161, 166
Dunant, Henri	174-175
Duncan, David	502-503
Dunford, Col.	203
Dunn, Warrick	485
Durant, Clark	193
Duterte, Rodrigo	551

Duvalier, Baby Doc	376, 417	Evans, Matthew	199
Duvalier, Papa Doc	376	Evans, Oliver	151
Dylan, Bob	383, 397, 450	Evers, Medgar	383, 385-386
Earhart, Amelia	295	Evinrude, Ole	247
Early, Darnell	551	Eyre, Edward John	188
Eastman, George	208	Fahd of Saudi Arabia	477
Edhi, Abdul Sattar	358	Fahrenheit, Daniel	73
Edison, Thomas	198-199, 211, 212-213, 221, 243, 250, 294, 513-514	Fall, Albert	285
		Falloppio, Gabriele	35
Edson, Marcellus	208	Falwell, Jerry	407, 429, 482
Edward I	29	Fandino, Juan	90
Edward VI	38	Farley, Chris	420
Edwards, Marc	540-541	Farnsworth, Philo	294, 297-298
Edwards, Robert	424	Farook, Syed Rizwan	551
Ehrlichman, John	402	Farouk	320
Eichengrun, Arthur	220	Farrinor, Thomas	68
Einstein, Albert	242, 246-247, 292	Fast, Andrew	502-503
Einthoven, Willem	235	Faubus, Orville	374
Eisenhower, Dwight	331-332, 374, 409	Faulkner, William	295
El Chapo	551	Federer, Roger	515
El Greco	44	Feinberg, Louis	304-305
Elbert, Donald	403	Felson, Eddie	434
Eliot, T.S.	271	Felt, Mark	411
Elizabeth I	44, 46	Felton, Rebecca	217
Elkins, Thomas	196	Feodorovna, Alexandra	251
Ellington, Duke	293	Ferdinand	31
Elliot, Bob	345	Ferdinand, Franz	264
Ellison, Ralph	355	Ferrell, Will	420
Ellsburg, Daniel	409-410	Ferris, George W.	223
Emerson, Ralph Waldo	149-150	Fey, Tina	420, 510
Emperor Theodosis	19	Fick, Adolph	211
England, Lyndie	521	Fields, W.C.	280
English, John	205	Figueres, Christiana	541-542
Enrique of Malacca	34	Finnbogadóttir, Vigdis	438
Ensler, Eve	480	Fiorelli, Giuseppe	187
Epperson, Frank	247	Firage, Nigel	546
Epps, Moultrie	229	Fish, Albert	301
Epstein, Jeffrey	506	Fisher, Carrie	409
Eric the Red	31	Fisk, Jim	213
Erricheti, Angelo	445	Fitzgerald, Ella	341, 371
Escobar, Pablo	474-475	Fitzgerald, F. Scott	328
Esposito, Raffaele	209	FitzRoy, Robert	149
Euclid	16	Fleming, Alexander	294-295
Euler, Leohnard	84	Fleming, Ian	358
Evans, Alice Catherine	268	Flockhart, Calista	480

Flood, Curt	397
Florence Griffith-Joyner	452
Florey, Howard	294-295
Flynt, Larry	456
Fogle, Jared	551
Follis, Charles	232
Fonseca, Ramon	544-545
Force, Mrs. William	248
Ford, Henry	263-264
Ford, Robert	413
Forrest, Nathan Bedford	191
Foster, Marcus	413
Fox, George	333
Fox, John	331-332
Fox, Michael J.	448
Fox, William	250-251
Foxx, Red	371
Franco, Francisco	322
Franco, Giuseppe	271
Frank, Anne	331
Frank, Jacob	101
Franklin, Aretha	397
Franklin, Benjamin	82, 85, 108, 151
Franklin, Rosalind	355
Frederick, Prince of Wales	88-89
Freed, Alan	358
Freud, Sigmund	231
Frick, Henry	225
Friedan, Betty	383
Friedman, Albert	377
Fry, Arthur	397
Fuchs, Klaus	361
Fuld, Dick	518
Fulton, Robert	116
Gable, Clark	280, 330, 341
Gable, Dan	411
Gacy, John Wayne	427
Gad, Josh	511
Gadgil, Ashok	466
Gagarin, Yuri	381
Gagnon, Rene	344
Gaisberg, Fred	231
Galilei, Galileo	45, 53, 59
Gallaudet, Thomas	127
Galvani, Luigi	105
Galvin, Frank	434
Gandhi, Indira	440
Gandhi, Mohandas	150, 270-271, 330, 345, 348, 382, 393, 394, 440
Ganz, Joan	393
Garavito, Luis	491
Garcia, Anastasio Somoza	321
Garcia, Gary	445
Garcia, Macario	331-332
Gard, Eddie	360
Gardiner, Julia	164
Garvey, Marcus	387
Garza, Alicia	527
Gates, Bill	225
Gates, Daryl	474
Gaudi, Antoni	231-232
Gaugin, Paul	221
Gaye Sr., Marvin	445
Gaye, Marvin	4, 411
Gayetty, Joseph	172
Gehrig, Lou	319
Gehry, Frank	485
Gein, Ed	373
Gekko, Gordon	83
Gelbart, Larry	354
Geldof, Bob	449-450
Gelernt, Lee	537
Genghis Khan	30
Geoghan, John	504
George II	88
George III	81, 110
George IV	80
George, Lloyd	273
Gerber, Daniel Frank	295
Gerber, Henry	283, 285
Gerry, Elbridge	133
Gershwin, George	283
Gervais, Ricky	499
Gessner, Conrad	43
Gibson, Mel	535
Gies, Miep	330
Giffard, Henri	175
Gilgamesh	8
Gillars, Mildred	334
Gilliam, Terry	421

Gillooly, Jeff	477
Gingrich, Newt	491
Glass, Ira	485
Glass, Louis	223
Glenn, John	381, 456-457
Goddard, Robert	256
Godfrey of Boullion	31
Godse, Nathuram	348
Godwin, Henry	229
Goebbels, Joseph	311
Goering, Herman	311
Goetz, Bernhard	445
Goizueta, Roberto	454
Golding, William	358
Goldman, Emma	271
Goldman, Ronald	470
Goldsmith, Fred	199
Goldwater, Barry	389
Golikov, Yvgeny	250
Gombos, Gulya	313
Gompers, Samuel	209
Gondorff, Henry	434
González, Emma	539
Goode, Alexander	333
Goodyear, Charles	149
Gorbachev, Mikhail	449, 456
Gordon, William	188
Gordy, Berry	423
Gore, Tipper	445
Gossard, Stone	469
Gotti, John	460
Gould, Jay	213
Goulding, Ray	345
Graham, Billy	429
Graham, Gwendolyn	460
Graham, Rev Sylvester	275
Grandmaster Flash	438, 447
Granger, Thomas	61
Grant, Ulysses S.	183, 191
Gray, Elisha	198, 203
Greatbatch, Wilson	370
Green, Harry	308-309
Greene, Robert	48
Greenfield, Jerry	425
Gregory, Dick	383

Gregory, Hanson	159
Greiter, Franz	317-318
Grenville, George	99
Gretzky, Wayne	452
Griffin, Merv	379
Griffin, Michael	473
Griffith, D.W.	274
Griswold, Estelle	383
Groening, Matt	465
Grohl, Dave	469
Gropius, Walter	400
Guest, Christopher	438
Guevara, Che	375
Guinness, Alec	423
Guinness, Arthur	95
Guiteau, Charles	217
Gunmere, William	187
Gunness, Belle	238
Gurdon, John	527-528
Gutenberg, Johannes	25
Guthrie, Woodie	333
Haarmann, Fritz	299
Haas, Earle	293-294
Habyarimana, Juvenal	476
Hader, Bill	420
Hagan, Thomas	403
Haigh, John George	347
Hale, Clara	448-449
Haley, Alex	425
Hall, Daryl	450
Hamburger, Christian	358
Hamilton, Alexander	66, 104, 108, 120, 537
Hamilton, Andrew	85-86
Hamilton, Joseph	347
Hamilton, Laird	291, 485
Hamilton, Thomas	488-489
Hancock, Thomas	136
Handel, George	83
Handwerker, Nathan	271
Hanks, Tom	485
Hanna-Attisha, Mona	540-541
Hannan, Daniel	546
Hansen, Gerhard	199
Hanssen, Robert	506
Harding, Tonya	477

Harding, Warren	284, 285	Henson, Jim	393
Harlan, John Marshall	226	Hepburn, Katherine	397
Harpe, Micajah & Wiley	110	Heron Ho Alexandreus	13
Harriman, E.H.	190	Hersey, John	342-343
Harrington, John	46	Hess, Orvan	333
Harris, Eric	488	Hesse, Herman	345
Harris, Isaac	262	Heth, Joice	154
Harrison, Benjamin	214-215	Hetrick, John	353
Harrison, George	382	Heumann, Judy	411
Harrison, J. Hartwell	358	Higham, Scott	494
Harrison, John	83	Hill, George Roy	411
Harrison, William Henry	169	Hill, Rowland	147
Harry, Deborah	425	Hillenburg, Stephen	485
Hartley, Fred	403	Himmler, Heinrich	311
Hartman, Phil	420, 452	Hindley, Myra	389
Harvey, William	55	Hinkley, John	445
Hasan, Nidal	521	Hirschfeld, Magnus	219
Hasselhoff, David	291	Hitchcock, Alfred	358
Hastert, Dennis	417	Hitchcock, Ethan Allen	140
Hastings, Lansford	166	Hitler, Adolph	201, 212, 264, 281, 286,
Hathorne, John	70	304, 310, 311, 312, 316, 324, 330, 332, 335,	
Hausen, Harald Zur	515	337-338, 343, 385, 405, 430	
Hawk, Tony	485	Hobbes, Thomas	68-69, 93
Hawking, Steven	452	Hobby, Oveta Culp	328
Hayden, Ferdinand	197	Hobhouse, Emily	235, 239
Haydn, Joseph	116	Hoffa, Jimmy	377
Hayes, Ira	344	Hoffman, Felix	220
Haynie, James	205	Hogg, David	539
Haywood, William	248-249	Holiday, Billie	293, 341
Hazelwood, Joseph	460	Holland, John Phillip	223
Hazzard, Linda	261	Hollerith, Herman	223
He Shen	109	Holmes, Elizabeth	551
Hearst, Patty	413	Holmes, H.H.	227
Hearst, William Randolph	224, 315	Holmes, James E.	535
Heimlich, Henry	409	Homer	4-5
Hells Angels	398	Homo Erectus	5, 10
Helms, Ed	511	Homo Habilis	3
Helmsley, Leona	460	Hong Xiuquan	179
Hemingway, Ernest	54, 258, 328	Hook, Theodore	130
Henderson, Russell	491	Hoover, Herbert	298, 310
Hendrix, Jimi	397	Hoover, J. Edgar	281, 387
Hennard, George	472	Hopffer, French	74-75
Henry IV	44-45	Hopper, Dennis	397
Henry VIII	38, 39-40, 44	Hoppocrates	16
Henry, O.	247	Hormel, Jay	325

Horovitz, Adam	436, 452	Iwane, Matsui	323
Horta, Victor	223	Jack the Ripper	217
Horwitz, Jerome	304-305	Jackson, Andrew	134, 143-144, 148, 177
Horwitz, Moses	304-305	Jackson, Bo	452
Horwitz, Sari	494	Jackson, Charles Thomas	137
Hoskinson, John	79	Jackson, James Caleb	200
Hotchner, A.E.	435	Jackson, Michael	231, 367, 434, 438, 450, 477
Houdini, Harry	279-280	Jacob, Polly	258
Howard, Ron	485	Jacuzzi, Candido	275
Howlin' Wolf	391	Jagger, Mick	391, 450
Hubbard, L. Ron	363	James VI	48
Hubble, Edwin	283, 292	James, Jesse	193
Huberty, James	441-442	James, LeBron	529
Hudson, Rock	465	Jannings, Emil	297
Hughes, John	452	Jay-Z	499
Hughes, Langston	282, 355	Jay, John	104
Hugo, Victor	183-184	Jayner, Charles	229
Hull, Cordell	322-323	Jefferson, Thomas	1, 56, 66, 104, 113, 115-116, 119-120, 121, 282
Hull, George	205		
Hulsmeyer, Christian	235	Jeffreys, Alec	438
Hunt, Walter	160	Jeffries, Mark	142
Hunter, Robert	80-81	Jenkins, Robert	90
Hurley, Chad	509	Jenner, Bruce	425
Hurston, Zora Neale	315	Jenner, Edward	106-107
Hussain, Hasib	519	Jenney, William LeBaron	211
Hussein, Saddam	413, 458-459, 503	Jessel, George	295
Hutchinson, Lewis	100	Jessup, Violet	271
Huxley, Aldous	302, 307	Jewell, Richard	485
Huygens, Christiaan	63	Joan of Arc	26
Hypatia	13	Jobs, Steve	481, 513-514
Ibsen, Henrik	199	Joel, Billy	450
Idle, Eric	421	John II (Zápolya)	43
Igataki, Seishiro	311	John, Elton	411
Il-Sung, Kim	363	John, King of England	29
Iovine, Jimmy	425	Johns, Barbara	358
Iqbal, Javed	489	Johnson, Andrew	183, 188
Irving, John	447	Johnson, Ben	457
Irving, Washington	127	Johnson, Boris	546
Isabella	31	Johnson, Henry	270
Ishii, Shirt	337	Johnson, Jack	247, 262
Ishiwara, Kanji	311	Johnson, James	282
Islambouli, Khalid	443	Johnson, Katherine	392
Islamiyah, Jemaah	506	Johnson, Lyndon	356, 395, 401, 409
Ivan IV	50-51	Johnson, Marsha P.	406
Ivins, Bruce	506	Johnson, Michael	485

Johnson, Samuel	78
Johnson, William	93-94
Johnston, Joseph	189
Jones, Bob	415
Jones, Brian	391
Jones, Chuck	330
Jones, Cleve	450
Jones, Eric	497
Jones, Genene	445
Jones, Jim	428
Jones, Mick	425
Jones, R. William	417
Jones, Roy	452
Jones, Terry	421
Jong-rak Lee	515
Jope, John	60
Joplin, Scott	235
Jordan, Michael	258
Joyce, James	258, 267, 328
Joyce, William	334
Joyner-Kersee, Jackie	452
Jung, Carl	283
Kaczynski, Ted	486
Kadyrov, Ramzan	549
Kaepernick, Colin	543
Kafka, Franz	280
Kahanamoku, Duke	291
Kaluza, Robert	531
Kameny, Frank	397
Kant, Immanuel	107
Karadzic, Radovan	490-491
Karim, Jawed	509
Kataktovik	257
Kaufman, Benjamin	471
Kavanaugh, Brett	551
Kazan, Elia	353
Kazantzakis, Nikos	345
Kearney, Andrew	495
Keating, Charles	456-457
Kehoe, Andrew	298
Keitel, Harvey	466
Keller, Hellen	207
Kellogg, John Harvey	200
Kelly, Florence	282
Kelly, Megyn	535
Kelly, Ned	217
Kelly, Oscar	229
Kelly, R.	551
Kemler, William	213
Kennedy, John F.	387, 409
Kennedy, Joseph	389
Kennedy, Robert F.	400-401
Kennedy, Ted	398-399
Keough, Donald	454
Kepler, Johannes	45
Kesey, Ken	383
Kevorkian, Jack	479
Khan, Fazlur Rahman	411
Khan, Mohammad Sidique	519
Khan, Salman	515
Khan, Yahya	416
Khousrau	23
Killen, Edgar Ray	386
Kilminster, Joe	455
Kilpatrick, Scotty	319
Kim Ark	223
Kim Il Sung	477
Kim Jong Il	548
Kim Jong Un	548
King, Billie Jean	411
King, Don	460
King, Martin Luther	150, 235, 293, 346, 349, 372, 378, 382-383, 387-388, 394, 395, 401, 402, 429
King, Philip Gidley	121
King, Rodney	474
King, Stephen	425
King, Steven	161
King, William Rufus	177
Kingsley, Ben	499
Kinsey, Alfred	343
Kipping, Frederick	235
Kiss, Bela	277
Kissinger, Henry	402, 416
Kitchener, Horatio	239
Klebold, Dylan	488
Kleinrock, Leonard	395-396
Klosterman, Chuck	499
Knoxville, Johnny	499
Koch, Ilse	336-337

Koechlin, Maurice	211	LaPierre, Wayne	532-533
Koen, Fanny Blankers	345	Lasseter, John	481, 551
Koenig, Sarah	523	Lassing, Louis	233
Kohl, Helmut	513	Lauer, Matt	551
Koirala, Anuradha	543	Lauper, Cyndi	450
Kolff, Willem	343	Lavallée, Calixa	211
Kony, Joseph	535	Law, Bernard	504
Koon, Stacey	474	Lawrence, D.H.	258
Kopechne, Mary Jo	398-399	Lawrence, Florence	268
Korematsu, Fred	333	Lawrence, Thomas E.	271
Koresh, David	472-473	Lay, Kenneth	502-503
Kranz, Gene	392	Le Corbusier	400
Kriesberg, Daniel	308	Leakey, Mary & Louis	368
Kroft, Sid & Marty	431	Lear, Norman	407
Krok, Ray	362	Led Zeppelin	450
Kroll, Joachim	373	Lee Joon-seok	535
Kuh, Richard	384	Lee, Bruce	411
Kuhn, Fritz Julius	321-322	Lee, Early	229
Kuklinski, Richard	460	Lee, Harper	381
Kurosawa, Akira	369	Leeds, Josiah	217
Kurtz, Ed	551	Leggett, William	187
Kurtzman, Harvey	358	Leibacher, Friedrich	506
Kushnick, Helen	470	Leibniz, Gottfried Wilhelm	65
Kwan Fai Mak	445	Leifer, Carol	510
Kwolek, Stephanie	397	Lemieux, Mario	469
L'Ollinaise, Francois	69-70	Lemmon, Jack	409
L'Ouverture, Toussaint	114	Lennon, John	74, 382, 445, 449
La Quintrala	59	Leno, Jay	470-471
La Rock, Coke	407	Lenoir, Etienne	175
Laemmle, Carl	250-251	Leonard, Elmore	464
Laennec, Rene	126	Leonardi, Francesco	103
Lafayette, Marquis de	104-105	Leopardi, Giacomo	152
LaLanne, Jack	319	Leopold	216
LaLaurie, Delfine	143	Leopold, Nathan	286
Lama, Dalai	371	Letterman, David	380, 421, 436, 470
Lamaitre, Georges	292	Lewis, Carl	438
Lamarr, Hedy	330	Lewis, Daniel Day	515
Lamb, William	304	Lewis, Ida	175
Landis, John	425	Lewis, Jerry	105
Landru, Henri	277	Lewis, John	395
Langevin, Paul	267-268	Lewis, Meriwether	113, 119
Langlade, François	81	Lewis, Sinclair	279, 339
Lantz, Walter	339	Li Hung-Chang	219
Lanza, Adam	532-533	Li Peng	456
LaPierre, Wayne	520-521	Licklider, J.C.L.	395-396

Limbaugh, Rush	506	Maathai, Wangari	492, 495-496
Lincoln,		Mabley, Moms	319
Abraham	174, 183, 186, 188, 189, 190, 195, 264, 442	MacArthur, Douglas	331-332, 365
		MacDonald, Norm	420
Lind, James	84-85	MacLean, Roderick	217
Lindbergh, Charles	295, 339	Maddox, Jennifer	543
Lindsay, Germaine	519	Madison, Dolley	125-126
Lipman, Hymen	175	Madison, James	66, 104, 125
Lister, Joseph	186	Madoff, Bernie	516-517
Liszt, Franz	159-160, 166	Madonna	4, 231, 367, 432, 435, 450
Little, Samuel	445	Magee, Carl	325
Liu Xiaobo	526	Magee, Robert	346-347
Liu, Joanne	543	Magie, Lizzie	308
Liuzzo, Viola	388, 397	Mahmound, David	497
Livingston, Henry	139	Major, Leo	331-332
Lloyd, Earl	358	Malan, Daniel Francois	349
Locke, John	66	Malcolm X	397, 401
Loeb, Richard	286	Malik, Tashfeen	551
Lombardi, Gennaro	247	Mallett, Elizabeth	75-76
Lord Seymour	38-39	Mallon, Mary	272
Loughner, Jared	535	Malone, Sam	53
Louis CK	551	Maloney, Pat	346
Louis XIII	60	Malott, Darius	193
Louis XIV	62, 71	Malvo, Lee Boyd	501-502
Louis XV	89, 93	Mandela, Nelson	428, 451, 462, 467-468
Louis XVI	111, 119	Mann, James Robert	262
Louis-Dreyfus, Julia	538	Manners-Sutton, John	191
Louis, Joe	319	Manning, John	193
Lovejoy, Elijah	154-155	Manson, Charles	399, 426
Lovelace, Ada	162	Mansor, Rosmah	521
Lovitz, Jon	420	Manuel I	40
Low, Jho	521	Maradona, Diego	452
Lubanga, Thomas	506	Marconi, Guglielmo	235, 394
Lucas, Frank	417	Marcos, Ferdinand	445
Lucas, George	369, 406, 423, 481, 491	Marcy, William	134
Luciano, Lucky	313	Marder, Barry	484
Ludwig I	125, 166	Marino, Tony	308
Lumet, Sydney	371	Markbreit, Leopold	248
Lumiere, Auguste & Louis	223	Markoe, Merrill	436, 438, 510
Lund, Robert	455	Markopolos, Harry	516
Lustig, Victor	301	Marlowe, Christopher	47
Luther, Martin	33, 40-41	Marquess of Queensbury	220
Lynde, Paul	482	Marrow, Tracy (Ice T)	452
Lyndesay, David	35	Marsh, Albert	247
Lyon, Nick	551	Marshall, Thurgood	352, 356

Marston, William Moulton	333
Martin, James	229
Martin, Steve	425
Martin, Trayvon	527, 530
Marx, Karl	385
Mary I	44, 49
Mary, Queen of Scots	44
Masaharu, Homma	339
Mason, Jerry	455
Massasoit	54
Masterson, Brian	498
Mateen, Omar Saddiqui	547
Mathews, Bob	445
Matisse, Henri	235
Matthau, Walter	409
Maurer, John	346
Mavrogenous, Manto	135
Maxim, Hiram	214
Maybach, Wilhelm	210
Mayer, Louis B.	347
Mayweather, Floyd	535
McAfee, Mildred	328
McCain, John	456-457
McCall, Jack	205
McCarthy, Joseph	353, 362
McCartney, Paul	382, 431, 450
McClaury, Tom	217
McCormick, Katherine	357
McCoy, Elijah	199
McCready, Mike	469
McCullough, David	499
McDaniels, Darryl	447-448
McDonald, Mac & Dick	362
McEnroe, John	438
McFly, Marty	448
McGinnis, Joe	360
McGraw, Phil	535
McGregor, Gregor	142
McIlhenny, Edmund	187
McKay, Claude	283
McKinley, William	233, 236
McKinney, Aaron	491
McKinnon, Kate	420
McKnight, Ezra	229
McLaughlin, James	226-227
McNamara, Francis X.	354
McRae, John	271
McVeigh, Timothy	490
Mecham, Evan	460
Mechler, Beth	500
Mege-Mouries, Hippolyte	193
Mehserle, Johannes	521
Melville, Herman	175
Mencken, H.L.	303
Mendel, Gregor	286
Mendelssohn, Felix	175
Mendez, Juan	257
Mengele, Josef	337
Merchant, Stephen	499
Mercury, Freddie	425
Meredith, James	381-382
Merkel, Angela	513
Merrett, Christopher	67
Merrill, Alexander	165
Mesopotamians	5-6
Messenger, Peter	69
Metesky, George	372
Michael, George	449
Michaels, Lorne	420, 435
Michelangelo	35, 39
Milam, J.W.	375
Milashina, Elena	543
Milk, Harvey	418, 422, 429
Milken, Michael	460
Mill, Henry	73
Mill, John Stuart	175
Miller, Arthur	353
Miller, Cheryl	452
Miller, Stephen	551
Miller, Steve	417
Miller, William	164
Milne, A.A.	284
Milone, Filippo	223
Milosevic, Slobodan	490-491
Milton, John	64
Miranda, Lin Manuel	537
Miyares, Andy	515
Mizell, Jason	447-448
Mladic, Ratko	490-491
Modi, Narendra	535

Mohtashemipour, Ali	444
Monroe, Marilyn	353
Mons, Wilhelm	79
Montagu, John	95
Montez, Lola	165
Montgomery, Bernard	331-332
Moonves, Les	551
Moore, Clement	139
Moore, Mary Tyler	408
Moore, Roy	551
Moore, Sara Jane	431
Morgan, Garrett	278, 281
Morgan, J.P.	189-190
Morgan, Tracy	420
Morgan, William	141-142
Morissette, Alanis	480
Morosini, Francesco	69
Morris, Errol	412
Morris, Garrett	420
Morrison, Toni	452
Morrissett, Lloyd	393
Morse, Samuel	136-137
Morse, Samuel	319
Mossack, Juergen	544-545
Mott, Lucretia	282
Mozart, Wolfgang	4, 106
Mozilo, Angelo	517-518
Mubarak, Hosni	443, 535
Mückter, Heinrich	364
Mugabe, Robert	521
Muhammad, Ali Mahdi	475
Muhammad, John Allen	501-502
Muir, John	223
Mulloy, Lawrence	455
Munn, Olivia	511
Munoz, Jorge	529
Murad V	227
Murakami, Haruki	438
Murdoch, Rupert	426, 489, 533
Murphy, Audie	331-332
Murphy, Eddie	420, 435, 441
Murphy, Joseph	308
Murray, Annie	259
Murray, Bill	469
Murray, Billy	247
Murray, Conrad	521
Murray, Joseph	358
Murrow, Edward R.	333
Mussolini, Benito	287-288, 309, 322
Muybridge, Eadweard	199
Myers, Mike	420
Nader, Ralph	393-394
Naganori, Asano	78
Naismith, James	223
Nast, Thomas	195, 201
Nation, Carry	237-238
Nebuchadnezzar II	10
Nelson, Earle	297
Nelson, Willie	60, 380, 450
Nestle, Andrew	305
Nettleton, A.B.	197
Newham, Joseph	229
Newhart, Bob	469
Newman, Laraine	420
Newman, Paul	383, 434, 480
Newton, Isaac	65-66
Ng, Benjamin	445
Ng, Tony	445
Ngo Dinh Diem	389
Nicholas I	155
Nicholas II	228
Nicholas II	250, 251
Nicolosi, Joseph	471
Niepce, Claude	137
Niepce, Joseph	137-138
Nieuwoudt, Gideon	428-429
Nightingale, Florence	173
Nijinsky, Vaslav	260
Ninkasi	3
Nixon, Richard	342, 401, 401-402, 409, 416, 430, 442
Nobel, Alfred	184
Nobunga, Oda	51
Nolte, Nick	435
Norgay, Tenzing	358
Noriega, Manuel	460
North, Frederick	101
North, Oliver	460
Northup, Solomon	165-166
Novoselic, Krist	469

Nowell, Alexander	47	Pasteur, Louis	185
Nutcracker Man	10,	Pastorius, Francis D.	63
O'Brien, Conan	85, 420, 421, 469, 471	Paterno, Joe	518
O'Donohue, Michael	411, 420	Paterson, William	70
O'Keefe, Joseph "Specs"	360	Paul I	118
O'Reilly, Bill	551	Paul, Alice	282-283
Oakes, Richard	411	Paul, Les	345
Oakley, Annie	221	Pavelic, Ante	339
Oates, John	450	Peabody, Dr.	138
Obama, Barack	511, 523-524	Pearson, Charles	187
Obote, Milton	430	Pearson, Robert	438
Oliver, John	511	Peary, Robert	249
Oliveri, Pat	333	Peay, Austin	296
Orbinski, James	485	Pedro I	152
Orozco, Pascual	263	Pedro II	152
Oswald, Lee Harvey	385	Peel, Robert	113
Otis, Elisha Graves	171	Pekar, Harvey	436
Owen, Robert	113	Pele	371
Owens, Jesse	318	Pell, Paula	510
Oz, Mehmet	535	Pence, Mike	545
Pacino, Al	406, 425	Peng Chang-Kuei	367
Packer, Thomas	98	Peng, Li	456
Paddock, Stephen	547	Penn, Arthur	397
Page, Hilary Fisher	319	Penn, William	63
Page, Larry	496-497	Perceval, Spencer	131
Pai, Lou	502-503	Percy, Walker	391-392
Paige, Satchel	345	Pericles	16
Palin, Michael	421	Perkins, Benjamin	193
Palmer, Mitchell	273-274	Perkins, Charlotte	283
Panjabi, Raj	541-542	Perkins, Jacob	150-151
Pankhurst	211	Perrault, Charles	68
Panopoulos, Sam	389	Perry, Nick	445
Panzram, Carl	287	Peruggia, Vincenzo	260
Paracelsus	33-34	Pétain, Philippe	348-349
Parche, Gunter	477	Peters, Mildred Vera	370
Park In-Keun	457-458	Peterson, Richard	377
Parker, Bonnie	286, 313	Petty, Tom	450
Parker, Col. Tom	384	Pfeiffer, Sacha	499
Parker, John	226	Phalaris	31
Parker, Trey	485	Phelps, Fred	500-501
Parks, Bernard	491	Phelps, Michael	291
Parks, Rosa	186, 222, 366, 371	Phelps, Michael	515
Pasha, Enver	275-276	Philip II	49
Pasqua, Francis	308	Phillips, Sam	367
Passannante, Giovanni	205	Little Richard	367

Piaget, Jean	283	Posey, Billey Wayne	386
Picasso, Pablo	328	Potter, Beatrix	235
Pichushkin, Alexander	506	Potter, Harry	482, 494
Piennar, D.H.	388	Powell, Colin	506
Pierce, Franklin	181	Powell, Jake	325
Pierce, William	181	Powell, Laurence Michael	474
Pierce, William Luther	431	Pratt, James	154
Pierre, Abbe	358	Pravik, Volodymyr	451
Pincus, Gregory	357	Presley, Elvis	85, 231, 367, 384-385
Pinkerton, Allan	187	Pretenders	450
Pino, Tony	360	Price, Cecil	386
Pinochet, Augusto	402, 416	Price, Victoria	310-311
Pistorius, Oscar	535	Prince	434
Pizarro, Francisco	40	Prince, Erik	506
Plato	13, 15	Prince, Tommy	331-332
Plessy, Homer	221-222, 226	Princess Diana	486-487
Pliny the Elder	13	Princip, Gavrilo	264
Plunkett, Roy	319	Pryor, Richard	421, 481
Poe, Edgar Allan	161	Psalmanazar, George	78
Poehler, Amy	420	Puente, Dorothea	445
Poindexter, John	460	Pulitzer, Joseph	208-209, 224, 229
Poitier, Sydney	383	Putin, Vladimir	513, 534-535, 545, 549
Pol Pot	402, 431	Puyi	257
Poling, Clark	333	Puzo, Mario	406
Politkovskaya, Anna	515	Qadaffi, Muammar	375, 413, 458
Polk, James	166	Qianglong	109
Polzl, Klara	212	Qin Shi Huang	19-20
Pompadour, Madame	85	Quant, Mary	397
Ponzi, Charles	275	Queen	450
Pop, Iggy	397	Queen Beatrix	495
Pope Alexander VI	39	Quevedo, Leonardo	247
Pope Benedict XV	261	Quisling, Vikdun	339
Pope Damasus	21	R. Kelly	551
Pope John XI	28	Rabelais, Francois	34
Pope John XII	28	Rachmaninoff, Sergei	271
Pope Julius II	39	Radner, Gilda	420
Pope Julius III	49	Rafael	37
Pope Paul III	39	Raftery, Bill	452
Pope Pius V	42, 50	Rainey, Lawrence	386
Pope Pius IX	181	Ramirez, Richard	441
Pope Pius XI	309	Ramis, Harold	438
Pope Sergius III	28	Rand, Ayn	373-374, 465
Pope Stephen VI	28	Randall, Lisa	515
Pope Urban VIII	59	Randolph, A. Philip	290, 293
Portis, Charles	397	Rankin, Jeannette	271

Ranking, Andrew	187	Rivera, Giraldo	460
Rapinoe, Megan	543	Rivera, Sylvia	406
Rashid, Naeem	543	Rivers, Joan	380, 448
Raskob, John	304	Roberts, Ed	380
Rasputin, Grigori	251	Roberts, Henry Edwards	425
Rauf, Rashid	519	Roberts, Lawrence	395-396
Ray, Charlotte	196	Roberts, Wayne	386
Ray, James Earl	402	Robespierre, Maximillian	111
Razak, Najib	521	Robin, Christopher	284
Reagan, Ronald	347, 400, 442-443, 465	Robinson, Jackie	232, 343
Reard, Louis	345	Robinson, Walter V.	499
Redding, Otis	397	Rock, Chris	419, 420, 478, 481
Reed, Walter	235	Rock, John	357
Reese, Harry Burnett	291	Rockefeller, John D.	213
Reid, Richard	502	Rockwell, Norman	271
Reiner, Carl	354, 405	Roddenberry, Gene	397
Reiner, Rob	438	Roden, Lois	472
Remarque, Erich Maria	295	Rodin, Auguste	211
Rembrandt	55	Roebling, Emily	207
Renninger, George	212	Roebling, John	207
Rescorla, Rick	497	Roentgen, Wilhelm	223
Resnick, Adam	529	Rogers, Alonzo	229
Reubens, Paul	452	Rogers, Edwin	229
Rezendes, Michael	499	Rogers, Fred	493-494
Rhee, Syngman	363	Rohwedder, Otto	292
Rhodes, Cecil	203-204	Rolfe, John	58
Rice, Thomas Dartmouth	155	Romanov, Pyotr	79
Rich, Richard	38	Romero, George	397
Richard, Little	371	Roof, Dylan	551
Richard I	29	Roosevelt, Eleanor	305-306, 320-321
Richards, Bill	371	Roosevelt, Eleanor	387
Richards, Keith	391, 450	Roosevelt, Franklin	293, 306-307, 310, 317, 321, 322, 335, 357
Richards, Mary	408		
Richie, Lionel	450	Roosevelt, Teddy	210, 226, 233, 246, 305
Richter, Charles	319	Rose, Charlie	551
Rickey, Branch	232, 343	Rosenberg, Julius & Ethel	361
Rickles, Don	371	Rosenthal, Joe	344
Rickman, Alan	452	Ross, Robert	131
Ride, Sallie	438	Roth, Philip	397
Ridenhour, Carlton	452	Rothstein, Arnold	272
Ridgway, Gary	442	Rousseau, Jean-Jacques	93
Riefenstahl, Leni	309-310	Rowe, Dick	389
Righetto, Renato	417	Rowling, Joanne	482
Ripken, Cal	485	Ruben, Mel	354
Ritty, James	199	Rubenstein, Helena	358

Rubin, Rick	435-436, 447
Rudolph, Eric	487-488
Ruef, Abe	249
Rumsfeld, Donald	503-504
Russell, Howard Hyde	229
Russell, Joseph	165
Rustin, Bayard	340, 345
Ruth, Babe	295
Rutherford, Ernest	259
Ryan, Leo	428
Rylands, Dan	211
Sacagawea	113
Sackler, Rich, Mort & Ray	520
Sadat, Anwar	443
Sado	100
Sailors, Kenny	303-304
Salameh, Ali Hassan	415
Salazar, António	298
Saldivar, Yolanda	491
Salieri, Antonio	116
Salk, Jonas	357, 380
Saltykova, Darya	101
Salvi, John	477
Samberg, Andy	420
San Marco, Jennifer	521
Sand, George	163
Sand, Julia	211
Sanders, Bernie	543
Sandler, Adam	420
Sandusky, Jerry	518
Sanger, Margaret	270, 358
Santa Ana, Antonio Lopez	164-165
Santorio, Santorio	55
Sanzo, Tsuda	229
Saperstein, Abe	291-292
Sarkeesian, Anita	529
Sarnoff, David	297-298
Saunders, Clarence	267
Savić, Milunka	269
Savile, Jimmy	519
Sax, Adolphe	163, 275
Scalia, Antonin	551
Schenkman, Jan	181
Schiavo, Terry	521
Schimmel, Bernard	295
Schindler, Oskar	330
Schlafly, Phyllis	414
Schmitz, Eugene	249-250
Schnatter, John	445
Scopes, John	296
Scorsese, Martin	127, 369, 463
Scott, Dred	177, 178, 226
Scott, Tony	466
Sea Peoples	8
Sebastien, Louis	107
Secord, Laura	129
Seeger, Pete	371
Seinfeld, Jerry	380, 463
Selassie, Heile	371
Sendler, Irena	330
Seung-Hui Cho	521
Sewall, Samuel	70
Seward, William	183
Shah of Iran	402
Shakespeare, William	43, 46, 48, 369
Shakur, Tupac	479
Shandling, Garry	380, 485
Shankowitz, Frank	438
Sharington, William	38-39
Sharipova, Maryam	535
Shaw, George Bernard	259
Shekau, Abubakar	533-534
Shekter-Smith, Liane	551
Shelley, Kate	211
Shelley, Mary	65, 118, 129
Shepard, Alan	381
Shepherd-Barron, John	397
Sheppard, Kate	222
Sherman, William	399
Sherrill, Patrick Henry	460
Shields, Brooke	516
Shippen, Peggy	110
Shkreli, Martin	544
Sholes, Christopher	187
Short, Martin	438
Siccard, Abbe	127
Siddhartha Guatama	7
Sidgier, H.	103
Silver, Spencer	397
Simmons, Bill	499

Simmons, Joseph	436, 447-448	Solon	2, 4
Simmons, Russell	436, 438	Sonoy, Diederik	51
Simon, David	508, 509-510	Soprano, Tony	463
Simon, Neil	354	Soulsley, Franklin	344
Simon, Sam	465	Spacey, Kevin	551
Simonon, Paul	425	Spade, David	420
Simpson, Homer	131, 284	Spalding, Albert	199
Simpson, Nicole Brown	470	Speed, Fredric	193
Simpson, O.J.	286, 470	Speight, Johnny	397
Sims, J. Marion	167	Spencer, Richard	342
Sinatra, Frank	207, 341	Spielberg, Steven	406, 422
Singer, Bryan	551	Spielberg, Steven	512
Singh, Gurmeet	551	Spitz, Mark	411
Singh, Mukesh	531-532	Spock, Benjamin	341-342
Sirhan Sirhan	400-401	Springsteen, Bruce	425, 450
Sitting Bull	226-227	Squanto	54
Skilling, Jeffrey	502-503	SquarePants, SpongeBob	284
Skrenta, Rich	440	Squier, George	313
Slater, Kelly	469	St. Martin, Alexis	135-136
Slick, Grace	455-456	St. Nicholas	16
Smalls, Robert	185	Stagg, Amos Alonzo	223
Smigel, Robert	543	Stalin, Josef	299-300, 323
Smith, Adam	83	Stallone, Sylvester	425
Smith, Edward	261-262	Standing Bear	199
Smith, James (LL Cool J)	436	Standish, Miles	54
Smith, John	154	Stanton, Elizabeth	
Smith, Jonathan	543	Cady	158, 162-163, 186, 282
Smith, Joseph	153	Starkweather, Charles	377
Smith, Soapy	229	Starr, Kenneth	491
Smith, Tilly	494-495	Starr, Ringo	382
Smith, Tommy	397	Stein, Joe	354
Smith, William Owen	229	Steinbeck, John	314, 316
Smothers, Dick & Tommy	397	Steinem, Gloria	394, 429, 435
Smuts, Jan	349	Stephens, Alexander	193
Smythe, Reg	377	Steptoe, Patrick	424
Snider, Arthur	409	Stern, Howard	464, 523
Snoop Dogg	60	Steunenberg, Frank	248-249
Snow, John	175	Stevens, Samuel	89
Snowden, Jimmy	386	Stewart, Hyde	115
Snyder, Jimmy	460	Stewart, James	341
Snyder, Julie	523	Stewart, Jimmy	330
Snyder, Rick	551	Stewart, Jon	510-511
Socarides, Charles	471	Sting	449
Socrates	14-15, 18	Stockton, Robert	164
Sollazzo, "Tarto"	360	Stoker, Bram	223

Stokes, Henry	229
Stone, Lucy	175
Stone, Matt	485
Stone, Oliver	463
Stoughton, William	70
Stowe, Harriet Beecher	171-172
Strank, Michael	344
Strauss, Levi	198
Stravinsky, Igor	260
Streep, Meryl	524
Strummer, Joe	425
Stumpf, John	551
Sugihara, Chiune	330
Sullivan, Anne	207
Sullivan, Ed	382-383
Sullivan, James Edward	238
Sumner, Charles	177
Sun Myung Moon	417
Sun Yat-Sen	257
Sundback, Gideon	257-258
Swaggert, Jimmy	460
Swan, Joseph	199
Swift, Jonathan	84
Switzer, Katherine	397
Taibbi, Matt	515
Takami, Koushun	485
Talaat, Mehmet	275-276
Tallchief, Maria	358
Talleyrand, Charles	109-110
Tamerlane (Timur)	30
Taney, Roger	178
Tank Man	452
Tanweer, Shehzad	519
Tarantino, Quentin	369, 466
Tarrant, Brenton	546-547
Tauko, Io	141
Taupin, Bernie	455-456
Taylor, Charles	234
Taylor, Elizabeth	465
Taylor, Liz	409
Taylor, Recy	333
Tchaikovsky, Pyotr Ilyich	223
Tesla, Nicola	190, 211. 212. 294
Thayer, Sylvanus	140
The Who	450
Theresa, Maria	91
Therese of Saxe	125
Thomas, Clarence	477
Thomas, Mickey	455-456
Thomas, Vivien	333
Thompson, Frank	445
Thompson, Hugh	397, 399
Thompson, Hunter S.	411, 447
Thompson, Jack	477
Thompson, Robert	202
Thoreau, Henry David	150
Thorpe, Jim	258, 525
Thumb, Tom	154
Thunberg, Greta	536, 540
Thurmond, Strom	346, 349
Tien-Lcheu	3
Till, Emmett	375
Till, Mamie	371
Tito, Josip Broz	361-362
Tojo, Hideki	336
Tolkin, Mel	354
Tolstoy, Leo	54, 197
Tometi, Opal	527
Tomlinson, Ray	411
Toole, John Kennedy	390, 391-392
Toppan, Jane	229
Torquemada, Tomas	31
Torrescola, Grisello	365
Torricelli, Evangelista	53
Toulouse-Lautrec, Henri	221, 223
Tracy, Spencer	330
Train, George Francis	187
Trevelyan, Charles	179-180
Tribble, Brian Lee	460
Trotsky, Leon	299
Truman, Harry	346, 349, 409
Trumbo, Dalton	347
Trump, Donald	537, 548
Trump, Fred	301
Trung sisters	14
Truth, Sojourner	185-186
Tryon, William	99
Tsarnaev, Dzhokhar	530-531
Tsarnaev, Tamerlan	530-531
Tubman, Harriet	173

Tucker, Scott	551	Wade, Dwyane	529
Tulips	58	Wade, Henry	412
Tupper, Earl	345	Wagner, Richard	201
Turner, Brock	551	Wakefield, Andrew	517
Turner, Ellen	141	Wakefield, Edward	141
Turner, Tina	450	Wakefield, Ruth Graves	305
Turning, Alan	330	Waldheim, Kurt	460
Turpin, Dick	88	Wałęsa, Lech	437
Tussaud, Marie	119	Walken, Christopher	466
Tutu, Desmond	446, 451	Walker, Alice	434
Twain, Mark	1, 64, 194, 196-197, 207	Walker, Arthur James	460
Tweed, Boss	201	Walker, John	139
Tyler, John	164	Walker, Madam C.J.	259
Ullman, Tracey	465	Walker, Maggie	235
Unruh, Howard	350	Walker, William	181
Utzon, Jorn	371	Wallace, George	387, 395
Vacher, Joseph	229	Waller-Bridge, Phoebe	543
Vader, Darth	274	Walling, Dayne	551
Valance, Henry	141-142	Walpole, Robert	80
Valckenier, Adriaan	91	Walton, Bill	411
Valenti, Jack	445	Walton, Frederick	187
Van Buren, Martin	144, 148, 152-153	War Machine	535
Van Dyke, Jason	535	Ward, David	411
Van Gogh, Vincent	221	Ward, Ferdinand	217
Van Hall, Wally	344-345	Ward, Joshua	181
Van Leeuwenhoek, A.	64	Ward, Martin	229
Van Lew, Elizabeth	183	Warner, Pop	258
Vedder, Eddie	469	Washington, Booker T.	206, 210-211
Verne, Jules	199	Washington,	
Victoria (Queen)	147, 157, 251	George	14, 102, 104, 105, 126, 154
Vidrine, Donald	531	Washington, John	333
Villa, Pancho	263	Waters, Muddy	367, 391
Virchow, Rudolph	205	Watkins, Sharon	499
Vitruvius	14	Watson-Watt, Alexander	318
Vivaldi, Antonio	73	Watson, Emma	529
Volta, Alessandro	105	Watson, James	355
Voltaire	75, 89	Watt, James	96
Von Bismark, Otto	215-216	Watts, Charlie	391
Von Braunhut, Harold	385	Wayans, Kenan Ivory	469
Von Humboldt, Alexander	112, 114-115	Weaver, Charles	223
Von Ossietzky, Carl	316	Webber, Andrew Lloyd	537
Von Trotha, Lothar	239-240	Webster, W.A.	229
Von Wallenstein, Albrecht	59	Weinberg, Mel	445
Vreeland, Diana	383	Weinhold, Carl August	118
Vuitton, Gaston Louis	335	Weininger, Al	285-286

Weinstein, Harvey	551
Weir, Harrison	205
Weiss, Sammy	346
Welles, Orson	315-316
Wells, Eden	551
West, Fred	403
West, Mae	315
Westinghouse, George	211, 212
Weyler, Valeriano	225
Wheeler, Wayne	287
Wheelwright, John Tyler	195
White, Dan	422, 431
White, Gerald & Ronnie	423
White, Jack	493
White, Walter	463
Whitehead, Gordon	301
Whitman, Charles Joseph	403
Whitman, Walt	171
Whittinghill, Dick	377
Wigand, Jeffrey	483
Wiggins, Calvin	455
Wiig, Kristen	420
Wilberforce, William	113-114
Wild, Jonathan	78-79
Wilde, Oscar	218, 219-220
Wilhelm II	251
Wilhelm IV	33
Wiliams, Robin	425
Wililams, Hosea	395
Wilkerson, Billy	347-348
Wilkins, Maurice	355
Wilkinson, James	121
Willebrandt, Mabel Walker	285
Williams, Daniel	223
Williams, Harrison	445
Williams, Robin	380
Williams, Serena	525
Williams, Tennessee	345, 371
Williams, Venus	525
Willis, Bruce	466
Wilmot, David	168
Wilson, Brian	397
Wilson, Darren	535
Wilson, Heather	506
Wilson, William Griffith	319
Wilson, Woodrow	252, 273, 274
Wimpie, J. Wellington	233
Wind, Alex	539
Wind, Timothy	474
Winder, William	131
Windsor, Edie	529
Winfrey, Oprah	511-512
Winnfield, Jules	233
Winston, Taylor	543
Winton, Nicholas	330
Wolf, Peter	455-456
Wolfe, Tom	447
Wonder, Stevie	423, 450
Wong, Jiverly	521
Wong, Joshua	543
Wood, Anthony	483
Wood, Catherine May	460
Wooden, John	425
Woodhull, Victoria	199
Woodland, Joseph	345
Woodward, Bob	408-409
Woodward, Henry	199
Woodward, Joanne	480
Woolf, Virginia	295
Workies	135
Worth, Adam	205
Wournos, Aileen	460
Wozniak, Steve	514
Wren, Christopher	67
Wright, Frank Lloyd	339, 368-369, 400
Wright, Seman	190
Wright, Wilbur & Orville	114, 234, 370
Wu Tang Clan	544
Wyman, Bill	391
Yamanaka, Shinya	527-528
Yanyong, Jiang	496
Yasgur, Max	397
Yates, Andrea	506, 516
Yauch, Adam	452
Yeager, Chuck	345
Yeats, William Butler	283
Yi Xing	24-25
Yoshimichi, Hasegawa	275
Yoshinaka, Kira	78
Youmans, Edward	199

Young, Andre	469
Yousafzai, Malala	522, 526-527
Yousef, Ramzi Ahmed	477
Yusuf, Mohammed	534
Yusupov, Prince	251
Zaius, Doctor	299
Zangra, Giuseppe	313
Zaragoza, Ignacio	187
Zedong, Mao	376
Zenger, John Peter	85-86, 88
Zhang Heng	16
Zhu Ge Liang	18
Zimmerman, Arthur	272-273
Zimmerman, George	527, 530
Ziryab	23
Zuckerberg, Mark	551
Zuckor, Adolph	250-251
Zworkyin, Vladimir	297-298

Made in the USA
Middletown, DE
06 June 2020